Promises to Keep

PROMISES TO KEEP

The United States Since World War II

PAUL S. BOYER

University of Wisconsin, Madison

D. C. HEATH AND COMPANY

Lexington, Massachusetts   Toronto

Address editorial correspondence to:

D. C. Heath and Company
125 Spring Street
Lexington, MA 02173

Acquisitions Editor: James Miller
Developmental Editor: Lauren Johnson
Production Editor: Melissa Ray
Photo Researcher: Martha Shethar
Art Editor: Gary Crespo
Production Coordinator: Charles Dutton
Permissions Editor: Margaret Roll

Cover photo: The Bettmann Archive

Photo credits: p. 1, AP/Wide World Photos; p. 30, Wide World Photos; p. 90, © 1994 Roger Ressmeyer/Starlight; p. 141, Movie Still Archives; p. 158, Hazel Carew/© Monkmeyer Press Photo Service; p. 226, © Rene Perez; p. 277, © Roger Malloch/Magnum Photos; p. 322, Yoichi R. Okamoto/LBJ Library Collection; p. 356, AP/Wide World Photos; p. 403, © 1993 John Olson; p. 432, UPI/Bettmann Archive; p. 492, © Jean-Claude Lejeune.

Text credits: p. 9, Excerpt from "Losses" from THE COMPLETE POEMS by Randall Jarrell. Copyright © 1948 by Randall Jarrell, renewed © 1975 by Mrs. Randall Jarrell. Reprinted by permission of Farrar, Straus & Giroux, Inc.

Published simultaneously in Canada.

Printed in the United States of America.

International Standard Book Number: 0–669–20350–5

Library of Congress Catalog Number: 94–70648

10 9 8 7 6 5 4 3 2 1

PREFACE

Promises to Keep seeks to make sense of a cycle of American history whose beginnings are fading from memory but whose totality continues to shape the world in which we live. The initial impetus behind the book was a personal one: I was ten years old when World War II ended, and the post-1945 era thus coincides with a span of U.S. history that I myself experienced. Researching this book helped me to understand more about a period still vividly present in my own consciousness. Indeed, I frequently found that my recollections were imprecise and distorted, and needed to be checked against the historical record and current scholarship. I hope that this effort at self-education will prove useful to others as well, including those whose personal memories stop far short of 1945.

No work of history—and especially none dealing with the recent past—can claim to be definitive and final. *Promises to Keep* is an interim assessment intended to stimulate further interpretive efforts. Yet enough time has now passed that we can see some of the past half-century's major contours and fault lines. Thus although the book includes essential factual coverage, it is also selective and interpretive, interweaving four principal themes.

The first of these is the pervasive impact of the Cold War, the superpower struggle that touched all facets of U.S. history from nuclear strategy and international relations to the domestic economy and culture. A second theme is the sweeping effect of a series of broad social-protest movements—among African-Americans, women, and others—that by the 1990s had given rise to a society radically different from the America of 1945.

Third, *Promises to Keep* pays close attention to an interconnected set of economic, demographic, and cultural changes, including the decline of a once mighty manufacturing system; religion's ever-shifting role in American life; population movements and changes in immigration patterns; and, not least, the new technologies that have transformed the way in which Americans communicate and entertain themselves, from television to personal computers, CDs, and VCRs.

Finally, the book takes politics seriously. The study of traditional political history declined after 1960 as many young scholars rightly found it (as then practiced) sterile and boring. But we are now gaining an enlarged understanding of politics as the arena where vital issues are defined, debated, and (sometimes) resolved. Ongoing political wrangles over budget deficits, health care, education reform, and social-welfare policy, for example, are part of a process by which Americans are deciding what kind of society they wish to live in and want their children to inherit.

The structure and style of *Promises to Keep* reflect my commitment to narrative history. History began in heroic tales and epics, and historians abandon these roots at their peril. Although I offer analysis and interpretation and discuss broad themes and trends, I do so within a narrative framework firmly grounded in human action and in the unfolding of the story over time. Reflecting this approach, the chapters are organized chronologically within four major sections. These sections are not arbitrary but reflect historical turning points.

Part One, "The American Century," focuses on the aftermath of World War II—the years when the optimism of victory dissipated amidst the U.S.-Soviet confrontation; a new political generation defined a post–New Deal public agenda; and citizens spooked by depression, war, and fresh global menaces sought the security of 1950s-style material abundance, mass culture, and suburban living.

Part Two, "Dissent, Terror, and Reform," considers another side of the 1950s and carries the story forward to the mid-1960s. While the Cold War ground on, bringing moments of frightening confrontation and all manner of home-front ramifications, a surge of reform inspired by the southern civil-rights struggle crested in 1964–1965 with a wave of legislation that represented the high-water mark of postwar liberalism.

Part Three, "The Loss of Innocence," explores the breakdown of this liberal consensus. The late sixties and early seventies saw turmoil and white backlash on the racial front, conflicts over the Vietnam War, and a wrenching political crisis summed up in a single word: Watergate.

Part Four, "Uncertain Triumph," brings the narrative to the present. As Americans in the seventies coped with the triple traumas of defeat in Vietnam, presidential malfeasance, and runaway inflation, they struggled to chart new directions in public policy and social action. While this reorientation brought feminism and environmentalism to the fore, it also spawned a conservative reaction that propelled Ronald Reagan to the White House in 1980 and that George Bush perpetuated in 1988. In 1992 voters troubled by the consequences of Reagan-Bush policy turned again to the Democrats. President Bill Clinton, steering a wary course between old-style Democratic liberalism and a strong conservative mood in the nation, must grapple with an array of domestic social problems while confronting a world transformed by the Cold War's sudden end.

But structure and thematic generalizations, while essential if we are to make sense of history, are no substitute for attention to the gritty reality of the past. Through the book's fifteen chapters flow the juices of living history: the quiet heroism of civil-rights marchers; the charisma and shocking deaths of John and Robert Kennedy and Martin Luther King, Jr.; the vitriolic rhetoric of George Wallace; the boldness of feminists who challenged entrenched gender stereotypes; the passionate voices of writers such as Rachel Carson, Ralph Nader, and Michael Harrington who changed the way in which Americans perceived their society; the media wizardry of actor-turned-politician Ronald Reagan; the colorful revival preachers and televangelists; the anxiety of blue-collar workers who faced disruptive economic changes; the courage of marchers and activists who revitalized the American reform tradition. History has been made not only in Washington, D.C., or in corporate boardrooms but at the grass roots all across the land—a fact that I have tried to keep constantly in mind while writing *Promises to Keep*.

This, then, is not an authoritative, predigested, take-it-or-leave-it version of recent U.S. history but one perspective on that history presented in a way that I hope will stimulate discussion and reflection. Not only the text but also the charts and graphs, the "Focus On" essays, and the works listed in the "Selected Readings" that close each chapter are all intended to encourage readers to probe facets of the story more deeply and to reach their own conclusions.

No historian works in a vacuum, and certainly not one who rashly attempts an interpretive overview of five decades of American history. In addition to my own research in the sources, I have profited from the books and essays of scores of historians and journalists who have written about specific movements and events. These works are acknowledged in the chapter bibliographies, but I also wish to thank their authors here. Without the wealth of specialized scholarship now in print on the postwar period, the writing of this book would have been vastly more daunting.

I am also grateful to the scholars who reviewed successive drafts of each chapter. The finished product is much stronger because of their unsparing but constructive criticism. Heartfelt thanks to Wesley Bagby, West Virginia University; Numan Bartley, University of Georgia; Hyman Berman, University of Minnesota; Barton Bernstein, Stanford University; David Bernstein, California State University—Long Beach; William Burton, Western Illinois University; Vincent Capowski, Saint Anselm College; William Deverell, University of California—San Diego; Joseph Dowling, Lehigh University; Anthony Edmunds, Ball State University; John Fairfield, Xavier University; Paul Faler, University of Massachusetts—Boston; Elizabeth Faue, Wayne State University; James Ferreira, Western Michigan University; James Findlay, University of Rhode Island; Steven Gillon, Yale University; Thomas Greene, Villanova University; Theodore Grivas, Sonoma State University; George Herring, University of Kentucky—Lexington; Dean Duncan Jamieson, Ashland University; Glen Jeansonne, University of Wisconsin—Milwaukee; John Jeffries, University of Maryland—Baltimore; Wilbur Johnson, Rock Valley College; Christopher Kimball, Augsburg College; Paul Mertz, University of Wisconsin—Stevens Point; William Moore, University of Wyoming; Otis Pease, University of Washington; David Roller, Bowling Green State University; Carl Ryant, University of Louisville; Steven Schoenherr, University of San Diego; Bruce Schulman, Boston University; Richard Sherman, College of William and Mary; James Sorelle, Baylor University; Marcia Synnott, University of South Carolina; Matthew Taylor, Rice University; Francis Thompson, Western Kentucky University; Samuel Webb, University of Alabama at Birmingham; Robert Westbrook, University of Rochester; and Kathleen Xidis, Johnson County Community College.

I am pleased to express my appreciation to the admirable crew of editors at D. C. Heath who remained unfailingly pleasant as they measured out carefully blended dollops of praise and criticism. Thanks and friendly salutations to James Miller, who was present at the creation; Sylvia Mallory, valued advisor on this and other projects; production editor, Melissa Ray; copy editor, Beverly Miller; and developmental editor Lauren Johnson, not only the book's first reader but among the most acute and perceptive. Bruce Carson researched the visual images that vastly enhance the text.

Finally, I take pleasure in acknowledging the friendship and sustained intellectual stimulation of my colleagues in the University of Wisconsin—Madison history department and at the Institute for Research in the Humanities housed in the Washburn Observatory overlooking Lake Mendota on the Madison campus. This fine structure, built when Rutherford B. Hayes occupied the White House, provided not only an ideal workplace but also a living architectural link with the past as *Promises to Keep* was researched and written.

P. B.

CONTENTS

LIST OF CHARTS AND GRAPHS

LIST OF MAPS

Part One

THE AMERICAN CENTURY

This book is the story of three generations of Americans. The first came of age during the Great Depression, fought in World War II or worked in home-front defense plants, and in 1945 looked forward to a future of peace, security, and prosperity. The second generation—the baby boomers—grew up in the affluent yet anxiety-ridden 1950s and reached maturity in the turbulent 1960s. The baby boomers' children, the third generation, will lead the United States in the early twenty-first century. To tell the story of these three generations is to write the history of the United States over the past half-century.

Part One focuses on the generation shaped by World War II and the early postwar years, an era in which we can see in embryonic form the society that would emerge in the following decades. The events and trends of those years molded the diplomacy, the politics, the economic and social agenda—even the cultural climate—of the next fifty years. The vast upheavals of 1941–1945 also set the stage for the Cold War. This confrontation would split the wartime Grand Alliance into two hostile camps, pitting the Soviet Union (and China, after 1949) against the United States and its Western European allies. World War II had scarcely ended before the new all-consuming confrontation began to influence U.S. foreign policy and military planning. Initially focused on Europe and the Middle East, the Cold War soon spread to Asia and elsewhere, including the United States itself. As fear of communism seized the nation, opportunistic politicians stoked suspicions of domestic subversion and disloyalty. Intellectuals who had criticized capitalism in the depression-ridden 1930s now hailed America as humanity's last best hope against the creeping poison of totalitarianism. These thinkers deplored the vulgarity and conformity of middle-class culture but rarely challenged the postwar order in more fundamental ways.

World War II ended the Great Depression, revived the tarnished reputation of big business, and stimulated a protracted economic boom. Military technological developments and production innovations gave rise to a postwar cornucopia of consumer products that enabled millions of Americans to enjoy unprecedented affluence. Construction techniques devised to house war workers made possible the suburbs that burgeoned in the late 1940s and the 1950s. Television, which would dramatically reshape American politics, marketing, and mass culture, burst on the scene just after the war.

Fought against racist regimes abroad, World War II also revealed the irony of ugly patterns of prejudice at home, most notably in the internment of thousands of Japanese Americans in remote detention camps in the West. Yet the global conflict also stimulated social changes that ultimately would defy entrenched gender, racial, and ethnic hierarchies. Women poured into war plants, thousands of African-Americans migrated to cities, and Mexicans immigrated in great numbers to work in agriculture and in urban jobs. These demographic trends created the conditions for social movements that would transform America in the decades ahead.

Finally, the war and the early Cold War years engendered a cultural mood that would wield influence for decades. The conflict stimulated national unity, as Americans mobilized for the struggle against the Axis foes. The global clash and the sweeping victory in 1945 also encouraged feelings of national omnipotence summed up in the phrase the "American Century," coined in 1941 by magazine mogul Henry Luce. To some extent, this spirit of unity and high resolve spilled over into the immediate postwar years, as Washington mobilized public opinion against the new adversary based in Moscow. The stark rhetorical polarities of the early Cold War—polarities that pitted the "Free World" against the dark menace of a global communist conspiracy—enhanced the sense of destiny and mission that had long undergirded the national self-image. Booming prosperity whipped up further optimism about American capitalism, as well as pride in the American way of life.

But beneath the surface, currents of fear and uneasiness eddied. The nuclear arms race—the war's grimmest legacy—yielded nightmares of global annihilation. And beyond the well-tended suburbs with their ranch houses, picture windows, and two-car garages was a very different America, burdened by rural poverty and sprawling inner-city slums. The political process occasionally addressed the racial discrimination and the deep economic disparities plaguing American society, but this early postwar generation more often swept such matters under the carpet. The Fair Deal, President Harry Truman's domestic reform program of 1948–1949, may have set the political agenda for the next generation, but at the time most of Truman's program languished.

As the Democrats' long hold on the White House loosened in the early 1950s before a resurgent Republicanism led by war hero Dwight Eisenhower, the impetus for reform slackened. Dissenters—most notably African-Americans no longer willing to tolerate second-class citizenship— would challenge the status quo more insistently as the decade wore on. Nevertheless, for a brief postwar moment, all seemed bright in America, and the future shone with promise. To a prospering nation bestriding the world like a colossus, the "American Century" was not journalistic hyperbole but unvarnished truth.

Chapter One

CRUCIBLE OF CHANGE: WORLD WAR II AND THE FORGING OF MODERN AMERICA

Few other American entertainers of the 1940s enjoyed greater popularity than the singer Kate Smith, famous for her soaring rendition of "God Bless America." Thus, when CBS radio executives planned "War Bond Day" for September 21, 1943, they invited Miss Smith to host it. From 8 A.M. until well past midnight, she tirelessly urged listeners to buy bonds. Many thousands responded, pledging nearly $40 million in support of the war. The overwhelming success of "War Bond Day," thanks in part to the promptings of a popular-culture celebrity, symbolizes the national mood during World War II. During these years, the American people, reinforced by official propaganda and media publicity, stood united to a degree rare in the nation's experience, either before or since. Social tensions and partisan conflicts simmered beneath the surface, but the widely shared goal of defeating the United States' enemies mostly overcame these differences.

For those who lived through it, World War II remains etched in memory, one of those events used by people to mark the stages of their lives and define their generation. For historians, the war presents multiple layers of significance that go beyond the conflict itself and the immediate objectives for which it was fought, fundamental as they were. Any serious effort to understand modern America must circle back to World War II.

The Grand Alliance, Globalist Dreams, and Big Power Realities

A tangle of postwar international relations emerged from World War II. This great conflict had brought together an alliance of nations committed to the defeat of Germany, Italy, and Japan, the so-called Axis powers ruled by militaristic, expansionist dictatorships that threatened world peace and stability. The United States, Great Britain, and the Soviet Union led the coalition that ultimately defeated the Axis powers, and some policymakers hoped that this "Grand Alliance" among the "Big

Three" would continue after the war. As early as 1941, President Franklin D. Roosevelt referred to the "Big Three," plus China, as the "Four Policemen" who would ensure peace after the defeat of the Axis powers. But the Grand Alliance, forged in opposition to a common foe rather than from a broad range of common interests, proved highly unstable. Although the U.S.-British coalition held firm and became part of a larger Atlantic alliance after the war, linking the United States with Western Europe, the Soviet Union soon moved from the status of ally to that of deeply mistrusted adversary.

As for the Axis powers, in ironic and unexpected ways, World War II laid the groundwork for the eventual emergence of Germany and Japan as world economic giants and major trading competitors. Their industrial infrastructure shattered by bombs, both nations built new factories and the latest equipment from scratch after the war. This retooling depended, in part, on massive aid supplied by the United States, the nation that had defeated them militarily.

During the war itself, some visionaries hoped that out of the struggle would emerge a harmonious new global system based on internationalist principles transcending old national rivalries. This dream, eloquently articulated by Woodrow Wilson during World War I, had survived the disillusionments of the interwar years and remained alive in the early 1940s. Republican Wendell Willkie's *One World* (1943), a wartime best-seller, fervently preached postwar global cooperation. The United Nations Charter, adopted at a fifty-nation conference in San Francisco in June 1945, seemed a step toward realizing the ideal of a finer world rising from the rubble of the old.

Some opinion molders envisioned the new international order as a beneficent *Pax Americana*, or peace imposed by America. As early as 1941, writing in his *Life* magazine, publisher Henry R. Luce had hailed the advent of the "American Century." U.S. goods and popular culture already dominated the globe, proclaimed Luce; now the nation must devote itself to spreading American technical expertise and American values: democracy, capitalism, philanthropy, and benevolence. "We must undertake now to be the Good Samaritan of the entire world," Luce grandly asserted. By 1945 Luce's American Century appeared a realistic prospect. Physically untouched by the war, its industrial infrastructure intact and powerful, a seemingly omnipotent United States could well contemplate establishing a benign world order—the American way of life writ large. The fact that the war had shattered Western Europe and Japan heightened this deceptive sense of national omnipotence.

But World War II had unleashed forces that would quickly break up the Grand Alliance, overwhelm the fledgling United Nations, and radically challenge Henry Luce's scenario. The conflict left Europe prostrate and intensified nationalist stirrings in one-time colonial regions of Asia and Africa. Moreover, it set the stage for confrontation between the United States and the Soviet Union, whose wartime alliance collapsed with the defeat of their common enemy, Nazi Germany.

Soviet dictator Joseph Stalin held a very different view of the postwar world from the one envisioned by the *Pax Americana* theorists. Certainly Stalin had gone to war against Hitler in the early summer of 1941 thereby joining the Grand Alliance. But earlier, in August 1939, Hitler and Stalin had signed a nonaggression pact dividing Poland between them. (It was Germany's attack on Poland a few days later that brought British and French declarations of war against Germany, triggering World War II.) The Soviets had invaded Poland soon after, leaving the crippled nation split between its two powerful and brutal neighbors. The Nazi-Soviet Pact had collapsed in June 1941 when the German *Wehrmacht* (army), rumbling across a 2,000-mile front, attacked the Soviet Union itself. The U.S.S.R. suffered ghastly losses in repelling Hitler's forces. One campaign alone—the terrible German siege of Stalingrad in 1942–1943—cost a million casualties on both sides. The Soviets' experience in what they called the "Great Patriotic War" profoundly shaped their postwar worldview and deepened an already strong determination to maintain absolute security around the perimeter of their vast but unstable empire.

By the summer of 1945, Soviet armed might stood unrivaled on much of the Eurasian land mass. That stark military fact would soon translate into political realities. Repelling the Nazi invaders, the Soviet army had swept across Eastern Europe and thrust deep into Germany in the war's final months. Stalin was determined to build a buffer zone of Soviet-controlled satellite states in this region. Marxist-Leninist ideology, with its prediction of inevitable world revolution, neatly dovetailed with Russian concerns about border security dating to the days of the tsars and massively strengthened during the war. Stalin also sought a sphere of influence in Eastern Europe to match what he saw as Anglo-American dominance in Western Europe. Even as the war wound down, shrewd observers detected the contours of a new conflict in the diametrically opposed worldviews of the two emerging superpowers.

During the war itself, a series of Big Power conferences and pronouncements had glossed over these differences. At the final meeting of the wartime Big Three leaders, held at the Crimean resort of Yalta early in 1945, Stalin, Roosevelt, and British prime minister Winston Churchill called for Germany's unconditional surrender. They then laid plans for pursuing the war in the Pacific and set the course for the early postwar era. Stalin agreed to join the planned United Nations after extracting a pledge from Roosevelt and Churchill to admit two Soviet republics, Ukraine and Byelorussia, as full UN members. The Soviet leader secretly pledged to declare war on Japan within "two or three months" of Germany's surrender, in return for the Kuril Islands north of Japan, an occupation zone in Korea, and other concessions. The Americans viewed Stalin's promise as highly important, because Japan, although battered in the Pacific island campaign and running low on war matériel and fuel, still had more than 4 million troops amassed in China, Korea, and the Japanese main islands.

Negotiations over Poland occupied many hours at Yalta. Germany's invasion of that nation in 1939 had triggered the war, and the Western powers felt a moral obligation to protect Poland's postwar interests. Furthermore, a large Polish-American community in the United States remained vitally interested in the homeland. Nevertheless, Roosevelt and Churchill were in a weak bargaining position, given the Soviets' physical hold on Poland. On the key question of Poland's postwar boundaries, Stalin demanded a slice of the eastern portion of the country. More important, to weaken hated Germany, he proposed moving Poland's western boundary so as to incorporate all German lands east of the Oder and Neisse rivers, including half of East Prussia and all of Pomerania and Silesia. Roosevelt and Churchill neither accepted nor formally rejected these demands, deferring the Polish-border issue to a postwar "peace conference," which never convened. After the war, Stalin unilaterally rearranged Poland's borders as he had proposed at Yalta. In another Yalta agreement that proved meaningless, Stalin pledged to support a "democratic" government and free elections in postwar Poland and offered vague promises of free elections elsewhere in Eastern Europe. In reality, however, Soviet officials held sham elections in Poland in 1945 after Yalta and expanded the so-called Lublin Committee, a pro-Soviet puppet government, to include a few token representatives of the Free Polish government in wartime exile in London. The promises of democracy in Eastern Europe thus faded as Stalin imposed pro-Soviet regimes throughout the occupied lands where his armies held sway.

Yalta played a key role later in American domestic politics as well. In the 1950s, Republicans would charge that President Roosevelt had "given away" Eastern Europe at Yalta in exchange for trivial concessions by Stalin. In fact, Roosevelt had done his best. The realities of Soviet military control of Eastern Europe, hopes that the United Nations might indeed function as a force for peace and world order, and FDR's eagerness to secure Stalin's entry into the war against Japan—a goal that seemed highly desirable in February 1945—all shaped the terms of the Yalta settlement. But the tenacious myth of a "great betrayal" at Yalta would poison American political discourse for years. Republicans would use Roosevelt's decision to portray Democrats not simply as political rivals but as naive dupes, if not traitors, in their dealings with the Soviet Union.

Popular misconceptions of the U.S.-U.S.S.R. wartime alliance helped shape Americans' postwar attitudes toward the Soviets. Behind the scenes, this coalition of wartime convenience crackled with tension, as Stalin made territorial demands and urgently called on the Allies to open a western front against the Nazis, a move that the Allies delayed until 1944. Despite Stalin's cooperation with the West against Germany, his brutal regime in many ways mirrored Hitler's. Indeed, as we have seen, Stalin and Hitler in 1939 had cynically sliced up Poland between them. In 1940 Soviet forces had massacred twenty thousand Polish officers and subsequently blamed the Nazis for the crime. Too, as the U.S. State Department urged an end to "sphere of influence" diplomacy in the postwar era, Churchill and Stalin, meeting in Moscow in October 1944, had agreed on just such a division of power in the Balkans.

The American public, however, remained largely unaware of these tensions. The media and official Washington pronouncements generally presented the Soviet Union as a heroic ally in a struggle for common ideals. One poster depicted a row of cannons bearing the flags of the United States, the Soviet Union, and the other Allies with the caption: "UNITED We Will Win." Hollywood movies such as *Mission to Moscow* (1943), *North Star* (1943), and *Song of Russia* (1944), produced with the Roosevelt administration's encouragement, offered idealized images of the brave Russian people struggling against the Nazi invaders. In a special wartime issue on the nation's ally against Hitler, *Life* magazine glossed over Stalin's tyranny and portrayed pipe-puffing "Uncle Joe" as a benevolent, beloved leader.

Such propaganda encouraged the popular assumption that Soviet-American cooperation would endure into the postwar era. Yet within months of the war's end, as conflicts and power rivalries took shape, U.S. leaders began publicly to portray the Soviet Union in menacing terms. Americans soon came to view the Soviet Union with a deep hostility that was a mirror image of the simplistic and rose-tinted perceptions fostered during the war. In an unfortunate irony, the war that was to have produced a new world order instead led to further friction. Thus, as the war years' unrealistic expectations eroded under harsh postwar realities, disillusionment set in and a stark, black-and-white worldview emerged that would characterize Cold War America. In this, as in many other ways, World War II continued to influence events long after hostilities had ceased.

High Resolve and National Unity

World War II stirred widespread feelings of patriotism and common purpose, a unity unique among twentieth-century American wars. A vocal minority of socialists and pacifists had fiercely opposed World War I, and many German Americans only grudgingly had accepted U.S. intervention in that conflict. The Korean War won broad support at first, but soon Americans reviled the protracted struggle, calling it "Truman's War." Later still, the Vietnam War provoked bitter divisions at home.

World War II was different, and for good reason. Although the conflict started when Germany invaded Poland on September 1, 1939, for Americans it began on December 7, 1941, with Japan's sneak attack on the U.S. Pacific fleet at Pearl Harbor, which killed 2,400 U.S. servicemen. In his war message, President Roosevelt described December 7 as "a date which will live in infamy," and, indeed, "Remember Pearl Harbor" became a driving slogan of the war. Unlike the murky justifications offered for some other wars, the issues in 1941–1945 seemed crystal clear: to avenge Pearl Harbor and to defeat the tyrants in Germany, Italy, and Japan who threatened the United States and the rest of the world with their racism, totalitarianism, and brute strength. With few exceptions, Americans rallied around the flag. If GIs at the front felt less enthusiasm than propagandists suggested, most nevertheless believed that they were fighting for a just cause and performing a necessary job.

The broad consensus in support of the war contrasted sharply with the late 1930s, when a strong peace movement had spread across the nation, particularly on college campuses. Disillusioned by the failure of World War I to produce the shining new world order that Woodrow Wilson had promised and shocked by charges of wartime profiteering by banks and munitions makers, millions of Americans had vowed "Never Again!" This mood had found expression in a series of neutrality acts (1935–1937) and in the isolationist America First movement of 1940–1941. To placate antiwar sentiment and to soothe jittery voters who rightly feared that war was imminent, FDR pledged in the 1940 presidential campaign never to send American boys into any foreign battle. (He made the mental reservation that any war that the United States joined would, by definition, no longer constitute a "foreign" war.)

After Pearl Harbor, the peace movement collapsed, and reluctance to engage in foreign conflict evaporated in a wave of patriotism. Families who had sent a son or daughter into the service proudly displayed a blue star in their window. Those who received the dreaded War Department telegram that began "I regret to inform you . . ." substituted a gold star. Millions purchased war bonds, contributed to paper drives, and planted victory gardens. War workers shared in the sense of national purpose. As one recalled, Pearl Harbor brought "an immediate change in people's attitude toward their work—their sense of urgency, their dedication, their team work." Children chalked caricatures of Hitler and Japan's wartime military leader

Hideki Tojo on walls and turned in pencil stubs so that the graphite could be re-cycled for war production. Gleefully, they passed along anti-German, anti-Japanese jokes overheard from adults. (The German *Messerschmidt* fighter, they told each other, savoring the naughty word, was a "mess o' shit.") When Japan formally surren-dered on August 14, 1945, the nation erupted in celebration.

To be sure, the war spirit was carefully orchestrated. The government's Office of War Information (OWI), headed by radio newscaster Elmer Davis, ground out mas-sive quantities of propaganda leaflets, news releases, magazine ads, and radio spots and worked with Hollywood studios to ensure that wartime movies promoted patri-otism and the preferred ideas about U.S. war aims. By controlling the flow of photo-graphs from the front and by suppressing or carefully screening photographs of U.S. dead, the OWI further molded popular perceptions of the conflict. The OWI also fostered myths of the American GIs' wisecracking under fire, such as the one about the survivors of one bloody U.S. assault in the Pacific who supposedly radioed the jaunty message: "Send us more Japs." Another government agency, the Office of Civilian Defense (OCD), offered an idealized version of the home-front mood to a public still innocent about propaganda. A 1942 OCD pamphlet reported, "The kids still play baseball in the corner lot—but they knock off early to weed the victory garden, cart scrap paper to the salvage center, carry home the groceries that used to be delivered." These manipulative techniques, which today seem crudely heavy-handed, had their desired effect: a nation already well aware of the stakes of the conflict and committed to victory solidified its support for the war.

Influential mass-culture organs—from movies, ads, cartoons, and popular songs to novels, essays, newspaper editorials, and political speeches—contributed to the martial mood. Even comic-strip characters, including the hero of "Terry and the Pi-rates," marched off to war. Of the major male comic-strip characters, an OWI study found, only Superman and Li'l Abner (Al Capp's stereotypical southern hayseed) failed to don a U.S. military uniform. (Superman, of course, already had a uniform in which to fight for "truth, justice, and the American way.")

An antiwar spirit that had pervaded the literature of the interwar years (epito-mized by two novels of 1929: Ernest Hemingway's *A Farewell to Arms* and the Ger-man novelist Erich Maria Remarque's *All Quiet on the Western Front*) dissolved dur-ing World War II. War reporters such as Ernie Pyle and John Hersey and battle-front cartoonists such as Bill Mauldin might underscore the grimmer aspects of war, but they never questioned the righteousness of the war itself. Only rarely in 1941–1945 did an American writer suggest that even a just war could involve official hypocrisy, routinized slaughter, and the denial of the essential humanity of those labeled "the enemy." Among the few who acknowledged this side of the story was the poet Ran-dall Jarrell, whose 1945 poem "Losses" began:

> In bombers named for girls, we burned
> The cities we had learned about in school—
> Till our lives wore out; our bodies lay among
> The people we had killed and never seen.
> When we lasted long enough they gave us medals.
> When we died they said "Our casualties were low."

A small number of pacifists and religious leaders protested the Allies' terror bombing of cities, a practice that had grown more common as the war ground on. (In fact, the firebombing of Tokyo by an armada of U.S. B-29s on the night of March 10–11, 1945, killed more civilians than later died in the atomic bombing of Hiroshima.) The political writer Dwight Macdonald, anticipating a theme later expanded by opponents of the Vietnam War, warned of the anonymity of mass slaughter by modern technological means. In *Politics*, his one-man journal of opinion, Macdonald wrote in 1944:

> One of the things which makes it possible for a modern civilian to participate in war without more psychological resistance . . . is the fact that the murderous aspect of war is depersonalized. Most of the killing is done at such long range that the killers have no sense of the physical effects of their attack. . . . [I]t is one thing to know that one may be responsible for the death and mutilation of invisible people ten miles away or five miles down, and another to cut a man's throat with one's own hands.

But Macdonald's journal reached a tiny readership. And regardless of the validity of his analysis, such reflections were rare as the nation mobilized for the struggle against totalitarianism.

Americans' overwhelming support for the war was undoubtedly fostered by skillful propaganda campaigns that channeled the patriotism in specific directions, but the mood itself was genuine. At the most elemental level, Americans saw the war as a fight for a perhaps semi-mythic but deeply cherished way of life that the Axis powers threatened. Lumps swelled in throats when Kate Smith sang "God Bless America"; when Humphrey Bogart gave up Ingrid Bergman to Paul Henreid, a courageous French resistance leader, in *Casablanca* (1943); when Bing Crosby crooned "I'm Dreaming of a White Christmas," the hit song of 1942; or when the hero of Nevil Shute's *Pied Piper* (1942) managed to get a group of children out of France ahead of the advancing Nazis. A California girl later reminisced, recalling her family's victory garden, "[W]e all wanted to do our part for the war. You got caught up in the mesmerising spirit of patriotism."

This intense support had important implications. In contrast to the post-Vietnam era, World War II veterans came back as heroes. The Servicemen's Readjustment Act of 1944, popularly known as the GI Bill of Rights, gave veterans hiring preference, tuition and other benefits to pursue their education, and loan guarantees to purchase homes, farms, or small businesses. The measure staved off postwar unemployment and facilitated veterans' quick reentry into the labor force, although often displacing women workers. Driving college enrollments to record highs, the act hastened the growth of a college-trained middle class in postwar America. Finally, the program contributed to a surge of suburban housing construction.

Just as wartime unity and idealism affected Cold War attitudes toward the Soviet Union, so, too, did they influence the postwar domestic political climate. As the sense of common purpose gave way to political dissent and sharp ideological differences—normal ferment in a democracy—some Americans responded by charging dissenters with disloyalty and even subversion. The climate of the war years thus contributed to the drive for conformity in the postwar period, as patriots tried to impose on the nation the consensus and dedication to a common purpose that characterized the war years. As early as 1944, while the war still raged, the Republican vice presidential candidate, Senator John W. Bricker of Ohio, ominously previewed the postwar air of suspicion when he warned that sinister and divisive forces were "worming their way into our national life."

The American Economy Goes to War

The war finally broke the back of the Great Depression and laid the foundation for sustained postwar economic growth. A 15 percent unemployment rate had continued to afflict the nation as late as 1940, despite the New Deal. After Pearl Harbor, surging military spending and war production fueled an economic boom, and by June 1942, more than $100 billion in military contracts had poured out of Washington. By 1943–1944, with war production in full swing, joblessness dwindled and almost vanished. The Works Progress Administration (WPA), the New Deal's principal relief agency, distributed its final checks early in 1943.

The war brought unprecedented affluence for millions of Americans. From 1939 to 1945, average real wages for all employees (adjusted for inflation) increased 44 percent, and the gross national product soared from $90 billion to $212 billion. Agriculture, too, fared very well as crop production rose by 50 percent and farm income by 200 percent in the period. Another gauge of reviving prosperity was an upturn in the birthrate. The 1943 birthrate of 22.7 births per 1,000 women, although below that of the fecund 1950s, was still more than 20 percent higher than the mid-1930s rate. Despite the absence of many males at the front, the postwar baby boom actually began during the war itself.

The heavy government spending of 1941–1945 appeared to validate the theories of British economist John Maynard Keynes, who argued that to fight a depression, a government should stimulate consumer demand and buying power through massive spending, even if large budget deficits resulted in the short run. FDR, who never lost his mistrust of unbalanced budgets, had rejected Keynesianism during the 1930s, but the war-induced spending of the early 1940s produced precisely the economic result that Keynes had predicted, although by means of military spending rather than government-encouraged consumer buying.

With the military absorbing much of the nation's industrial and agricultural production, numerous consumer goods and basic foodstuffs fell in short supply (coffee, sugar, butter, and meat) or disappeared entirely (new cars, household appliances). Many citizens, now benefiting from rising wages, apparently saw no contradiction between patriotic support for the war and turning to the black market to acquire and hoard scarce goods, thereby circumventing wartime rationing.

The war drove industrial production to new levels. Factories ran twenty-four hours a day, pouring out planes, tanks, jeeps, guns, and the vast array of support materials, from shoes to typewriters, needed by the military. The mile-long Ford bomber plant at Willow Run, Michigan, with a main building covering sixty-seven acres, employed more than forty thousand workers. One awed observer called it "a sort of Grand Canyon of the mechanized world." Dam builder Henry J. Kaiser, turning to ship construction during the war, accomplished such feats as cutting the manufacturing time for a cargo carrier from 355 days to 14. Securing large government

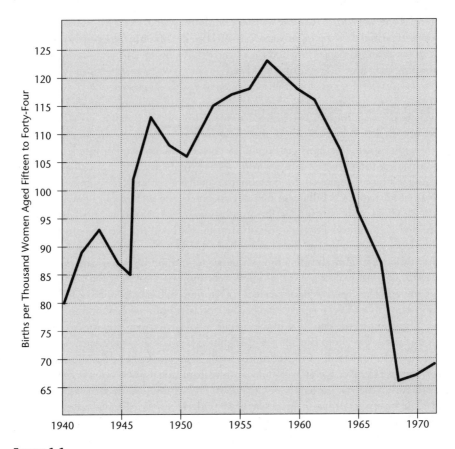

FIGURE 1.1
Birthrate, 1940–1970

loans to cover start-up costs, Kaiser by 1943 held $3 billion in war contracts and controlled 30 percent of U.S. shipbuilding. Even occasional embarrassments such as a ship that sank at the launching dock left intact Kaiser's reputation as a wizard of wartime production.*

Some observers feared that the Depression would come roaring back once the war ended, but in fact the groundwork was being laid for a postwar boom. Mass-production and prefabrication techniques perfected in wartime would soon be converted to peacetime purposes, and the accumulated savings and thwarted purchasing impulses of war workers would provide the initial fuel for a monumental postwar buying binge. Yet wartime productivity feats had ideological as well as economic and military consequences, for the corporate contribution to victory reshaped popular attitudes toward business. After the 1929 stock-market crash, the reputation of busi-

---

* Kaiser also pioneered an employee medical plan that would later provide a model for health-care plans nationwide, another example of World War II's long historical reach.

The Southern Pacific Railroad helps knock out "Japs." Corporate advertising during World War II stressed the patriotic role of American business in furthering the war effort. (*Courtesy of the Dorothea Lange Collection, The Oakland Museum. Gift of Paul S. Taylor.*)

nessmen had plummeted, and in 1936 President Roosevelt had denounced them as "malefactors of great wealth." As war approached, however, Washington now portrayed giant corporations as partners in a common cause. A wartime Senate committee report admiringly noted, "The hand that signs the war contract is the hand that shapes the future." In sharp contrast to the New Deal, Congress granted businesses tax breaks and exemption from antitrust laws in return for their war-production role. Many corporate executives served in Washington as unpaid administrators of wartime agencies, or "dollar-a-year" men, including Donald Nelson of the Sears, Roebuck Company, who headed the War Production Board. Factories proudly flew the "Army and Navy 'E'" banner (a War Department commendation), and a heavy gloss of patriotism overlay corporate advertising. Indeed, some business ads did not mention a product at all but simply featured public-service messages urging conservation, warning against loose talk, or calling on Americans to buy bonds. "War Bonds Mean Bullets in the Bellies of Nazi Hordes," proclaimed one ad sponsored by a New York City banking association.

Businesses showed remarkable ingenuity in linking their products to the war effort. By building bottling plants wherever GIs went, the Coca-Cola Company cultivated a taste for Coke among the troops and developed a worldwide market. The Parker Pen Company boosted sales of its ink 800 percent with an ad campaign reminding Americans of their patriotic duty to write long and frequent letters to lonely GIs overseas. Tobacco companies hooked a new generation of smokers by distributing free cigarettes to soldiers, including those in military hospitals. As John Morton Blum notes in V *Was for Victory* (1976), his absorbing history of the World War II home front, the champion entrepreneur in this marriage of patriotism and profit was Philip K. Wrigley of the Wrigley Chewing Gum Company. Wrigley persuaded the government to include his chewing gum in the "K-Rations" (food packs) distributed to servicemen in combat and urged war plant managers to give each worker five sticks daily. (Lest he be charged with wasting sugar and other scarce commodities, Wrigley sternly added that he would sell his product only to those plants whose managers sent him an official letter "stating the need for chewing gum in that particular plant.") A wartime Wrigley promotional film portrayed chewing gum as a key weapon in the struggle against the Axis powers, claiming that it combated boredom, fatigue, nervous tension, and an insidious condition known as "false thirst."

The war influenced corporate attitudes toward government as well. In the Progressive era and the 1920s, American business had generally made its peace with the regulatory state, particularly when control lay in conservative hands. But in the more adversarial climate of the 1930s, many corporate leaders had vehemently attacked the New Deal and the proliferation of regulatory agencies. Now the mood shifted again. As FDR appointed businessmen to Washington posts and the shower of military contracts demonstrated the profitable possibilities in business-government cooperation, antigovernment hostility faded. In his 1944 book *America Unlimited*, Eric Johnston of the U.S. Chamber of Commerce sought to solidify the heightened prestige of business and to reinforce corporate leaders' newly positive attitude toward government. The wartime rehabilitation of business's image was well justified, declared Johnston, because "credit for the most astounding production job in all human history must go primarily to American capitalism." Calling for a rapprochement between corporate America and the Roosevelt administration, Johnston urged forward-looking capitalists to "end [the] feud . . . between business and government" and to embrace "a middle way . . . of realistic adjustment between old style laissez-faire capitalism and [the] current economy."

The conciliatory views summed up in Johnston's book decisively influenced postwar political thought. President Dwight Eisenhower's espousal of "moderate Republicanism" in the 1950s would rest on the premise of cooperation between government and enlightened leaders from all sectors of society, including business. Thanks in part to memories of the wartime experience, this view won many adherents in the postwar years.

Organized labor, which had thrived in the later New Deal years, experienced further growth but also frustrating setbacks during the war. To head off strikes that could impede war production and to control inflationary wage increases, the Roosevelt administration limited hourly wage raises during the war to no more than the rise in the cost of living. (Thanks to overtime hours at time-and-a-half pay, however, many war workers took home fat paychecks.) To enforce the labor unions' wartime "no-strike" pledge, the National War Labor Board (NWLB), established early in 1942, focused on settling disputes by arbitration. In 1943 conservatives in Congress passed, over Roosevelt's veto, the Smith–Connally Anti-Strike Act. This law forbade political contributions by labor unions, expanded the president's powers to take over war plants threatened by labor disputes, and outlawed strikes in seized plants. When the nation's rail workers threatened a strike late in 1943, the U.S. Army at FDR's direction briefly seized the railroads. In another example of the war's after-effects, these measures anticipated the Taft–Hartley Act of 1947, which would further restrict labor unions.

Despite these constraints, the surge in wartime employment proved a boon to the labor movement. From 1941 to 1945, union membership soared from about 10.5 million to nearly 15 million. By the latter year, nearly 36 percent of the labor force was unionized, an all-time high. Moreover, the NWLB adopted a generally pro-union stance. As one example, the board resisted corporate efforts to impose an open-shop rule, permitting workers in unionized plants to remain outside the union if they wished. The NWLB gave new employees in unionized plants fifteen days to resign from the union if they desired. After that, they were required to pay union dues as long as the plant remained unionized. Overall, the labor movement came of age during World War II, as the principle of collective bargaining gained wide accep-tance. At the same time, the wartime boom and the favorable climate toward unions diluted the militance of the 1930s and led to a bureaucratization of the labor move-ment that would prove costly after the war.

Government and Politics in the War Years

The role of the federal government, already vastly enlarged in the New Deal era, expanded still more over 1941–1945 as a host of wartime agencies mobilized the economy and the American people for total war. The War Production Board over-saw resource allocation and industrial output. The National War Labor Board arbi-trated labor disputes in defense industries. The Office of Price Administration (OPA), initially under director Leon Henderson, touched every American with its rent controls in cities with war plants and its elaborate apparatus of price controls and ration coupons for butter, sugar, coffee, meat, tires, gasoline, and other basic products. Although merchants, landlords, and even many consumers grumbled at the OPA's bureaucracy, it achieved its goal: from mid-1943 to mid-1945, consumer prices rose by less than 2 percent. These and other agencies brought home to Main Street the reality of Washington's expanded regulatory role. As one New Dealer ob-served in 1943, "The most important change wrought by the war has been the greatly increased participation of Government in our economic life."

The war also contributed to substantial growth in the size and functions of the federal government's executive branch. President Roosevelt had broadened the reach of White House control over the economy during the New Deal; under the pressure of war emergency, it increased far more, as a host of regulatory agencies oversaw almost every facet of economic life. In 1942, when Congress balked at FDR's request to set up an agency with the power to freeze prices, the president insisted that he had the constitutional right to take such a step as a war measure, without congres-sional action. Such was the wartime mood that this sweeping claim went largely unchallenged. Even FDR's Republican predecessor, Herbert Hoover, declared, "To win total war, President Roosevelt must have many dictatorial economic powers. There must be no hesitation in giving them to him and upholding him in them."

Overall, the ranks of civilian federal employees more than tripled from 1940 to 1945, growing from a little more than 1 million to nearly 3.4 million. The giant

Pentagon building, erected in 1942 to house the War Department, symbolized the expansion of the executive branch. Celebrated as the world's largest office building, the Pentagon featured 17.5 miles of corridors and an external circumference of 1 mile. Visitors received maps with which to find the office they sought.* This ballooning of the federal bureaucracy, coupled with Washington's enlarged wartime role, accelerated a long-term trend in twentieth-century U.S. history, one that would continue in the decades to come.

Wartime politics cast a long shadow on postwar political history. In 1940 President Roosevelt had won an unprecedented third term with 55 percent of the vote (down from 61 percent in 1936), defeating dark-horse Republican candidate Wendell Willkie. As Roosevelt shifted roles from, as he put it, "Dr. New Deal" to "Dr. Win-the-War," his personal popularity remained high. In 1944, despite undisclosed failing health, he ran for a fourth term against New York governor Thomas E. Dewey and again won, garnering 53.4 percent of the vote. True, voters were frustrated by wartime regulation, and the Republicans made incessant attacks on the administration's alleged radicalism and socialistic tendencies. Yet the Rooseveltian magic and well-coordinated Democratic efforts to retain the Solid South while wooing blacks, union members, and big-city ethnics—all key components of the New Deal coalition—paid off. Roosevelt's wartime role as commander-in-chief, along with favorable news from the battle front, also served him well at the polls.

Nevertheless, the conservative shift already evident in the late 1930s and clearly apparent in the 1940 election was accelerating. In the mid-term election of 1942, Republicans gained nine Senate and forty-four House seats, to pull within thirteen seats of the Democrats. The sharp drop in the 1942 Democratic vote also reflected popular annoyance with wartime controls and the fact that many Democratic voters were either absent in the military or had recently taken war jobs in cities where they were not yet registered to vote. Farmers led the defection from the New Deal coalition. Their goal, however, was not a reduced government role in the economy but an enlargement of it. Specifically, they wanted expanded and increased federal price supports for agricultural commodities. When the administration tried to fight inflation by capping escalating agricultural price supports, the farmers, especially the larger agribusinesses represented by the American Farm Bureau Federation, expressed their resentment at the polls.

Interpreting the 1942 election as a repudiation of the New Deal, a conservative coalition of Republicans and southern Democrats in Congress passed the Smith–Connally Anti-Strike Act in 1943. They also stopped or radically cut the funding of such New Deal agencies as the Civilian Conservation Corps, the National Youth Administration, the Farm Security Administration, and the Rural Electrification Administration, the last a longtime target of private power companies. That same year, the House Un-American Activities Committee, which in the 1950s would stoke the flames of a domestic Red Scare, issued a list of administration officials whom it considered dangerously radical. In 1943, too, Congress killed the National

---

* The construction of the Pentagon was supervised by General Leslie R. Groves, later director of the Manhattan Project, the research effort that developed the atomic bomb.

Resources Planning Board (NRPB), a New Deal agency charged with social and economic planning for the postwar era. For years the NRPB had stirred conservative suspicion; the *Wall Street Journal* called its reports "a halfway house to socialism."

In 1943, one writer observed in the liberal *New Republic*, "The New Deal is being abandoned. . . . A new crowd is preparing to take over. It is a change somewhat slower than the one that took place in 1933, after Roosevelt's first inauguration, but it promises to be almost as sweeping." The conservative coalition that had taken shape in the 1938 mid-term election and solidified in the 1942 election would hold sway in Congress for years thereafter. The shift to the right that would profoundly influence American politics in later decades, in short, had gathered steam in the war years.

The Republican party was united in its desire to unseat Roosevelt, but it otherwise suffered from deep internal divisions. Across a broad swath of states from Ohio to Colorado, conservative GOP members vehemently denounced the New Deal and adopted isolationist stances in foreign policy. Influential legislators such as Representative Charles Halleck of Indiana and Senator Robert A. Taft of Ohio, son of former president William Howard Taft, led this wing of the party. The Republican party's eastern, New York–based wing, by contrast, was more internationalist in outlook and marginally more receptive to the fundamental contours of the welfare state. Thomas E. Dewey, for example, elected governor of New York in 1942 on the strength of his reputation as a racket-busting district attorney, accepted various New Deal programs, including social security. The 1940 Republican presidential candidate, Wendell Willkie, although a native of Indiana and a power-company executive, embodied this internationalist, somewhat more liberal wing of the Republican party. (His 1943 book, *One World*, written after a thirty-one-thousand-mile world tour undertaken with Roosevelt's blessing, underscored his global vision.) Midwestern conservatives viewed the maverick Willkie skeptically, and his campaign for the 1944 Republican presidential nomination had already failed before his death from a heart attack that fall. Yet despite Republican right wingers' strength in the party, they could not control it, and the 1944 presidential nomination went to Dewey. Senator Taft and other arch conservatives mistrusted Dewey, whom Taft called "arrogant and bossy," but the New Yorker's skill at building alliances—he named Ohio's conservative senator John Bricker as his running mate, for example—brought the party a degree of unity.

Dewey's stiff manner cost him votes in 1944 (one critic quipped that he was the only man who could strut sitting down), and in 1948, in one of the great upsets of U.S. political history, he would lose again, this time to Harry S Truman. In the 1950s a more electable candidate, Dwight Eisenhower, would inherit the mantle of moderate, internationalist Republicanism borne by Dewey in 1944 and 1948.

Roosevelt's 1944 decision to change running mates also helped the Democrats to hold the White House until 1952. Vice President Henry Wallace would have continued happily in that post, but his unabashed liberalism had alienated the party's conservative wing, and Roosevelt dropped him. In choosing Senator Truman of Missouri from a large field of prospects, Roosevelt unwittingly bequeathed his final legacy to the American people. A protégé of Kansas City's corrupt Democratic political machine, Truman had won respect as an honest, hard-working senator but enjoyed little national reputation. "Who the hell is Harry Truman?" exploded a top navy official upon learning of the nomination.

The monumental importance of Roosevelt's choice became apparent on April 12, 1945, when the vacationing sixty-three-year-old president died of a massive cerebral stroke. The administration and the media had largely concealed Roosevelt's worsening health, so the news came as a profound shock to all Americans. The radio networks broke into regular programming for the bulletin; newspapers unfurled their blackest headlines; in the Solomon Islands halfway around the world, a U.S. Navy patrol boat received the message in Morse code beamed from a nearby island: "Y-E-S-T-E-R-D-A-Y P-R-E-S-I-D-E-N-T R-O-O-S-E-V-E-L-T D-I-E-D." On the eve of victory, the wartime leader had fallen. As the nation mourned, Truman assumed the presidency. "I'm not big enough for this job," he confessed to a friend. The news of Roosevelt's death, he told reporters, made him feel as if "the moon, the stars, and all the planets had fallen on me." Over the next seven years, however, Truman would prove a far more capable chief executive than most would have predicted in April 1945.

A People in Wartime

World War II generated population movements, social changes, and ethnic tensions that would deeply influence postwar American life. Urbanization, including movement to the outlying suburbs of major cities, gained momentum during the war, continuing a long-term trend. As urban war plants posted "Help Wanted" signs, workers flocked to the cities. Millions of them and their families—perhaps 15 million people in all—moved during the war to take advantage of job opportunities. Indiana farm girls, for example, ventured to Dayton, Ohio, to work as secretaries at Wright-Patterson Air Force Base. Cities in the mid-Atlantic region burgeoned, as did southeastern coastal regions that were home to shipyards and naval bases. The industrial belt around Detroit hummed as auto companies converted to war production. The West Coast, especially California, with its sprawling shipyards and aircraft plants, saw explosive growth. California's population spurted by 3.7 million in the 1940s, much of the increase coming during the war years. Many newcomers would remain in the cities, or more typically move to the suburbs, once the war ended. Indeed, the migration to the suburbs that would reach flood tide in the 1950s was already well under way during the war.

Population movements on such a monumental scale produced severe housing shortages. Municipal officials reported serious overcrowding, with families doubling up in beds or even sleeping in garages. Some landlords devised the "hot bunk" system, renting the same bed to three different tenants working successive eight-hour shifts. In 1942 Roosevelt set up the Federal Housing Agency to respond to this shortage. Through the remaining years of the war, a combination of federal and private construction built more than 1.8 million new housing units. Like shipbuilder Henry Kaiser, construction firms such as Abraham Levitt and Sons of Long Island developed prefabrication techniques that would make possible the boom in suburban housing construction in the postwar period.

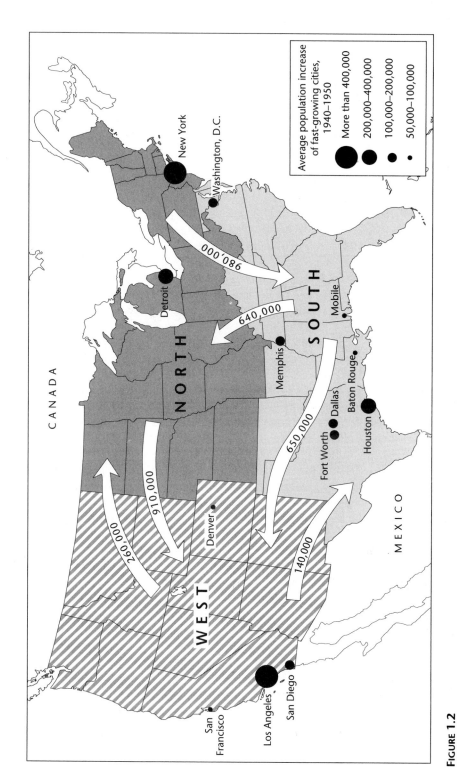

FIGURE 1.2

Internal Migration in the United States During World War II

For the nation's African-American population, the war brought changes heavy with implications for the future. Although the military services remained segregated, for some of the 1 million blacks in uniform,* the experience provided a glimpse of European societies less rigidly racist than the United States. Moreover, military service encouraged broader aspirations among blacks and supplied training in skills transferable to the postwar civilian labor market. Continuing a migration under way for decades, blacks by the thousands joined the trek to the cities, seeking jobs in the booming war plants. By 1945 some 2 million African-Americans worked in the war industry, composing 9 percent of the labor force in war production.

Many of these workers relocated in northern factory centers. Detroit's black population grew from fewer than 150,000 in 1940 to more than 350,000 in 1950. Others moved to the prosperous new industrial cities of the South, such as the shipbuilding center of Mobile on Alabama's Gulf coast. In 1944 black workers in a Mobile shipyard set a yard record for the speed with which they built a merchant ship. Even in the midst of a war emergency, however, some major employers initially confined African-Americans to low-paying job categories or excluded them altogether. The giant Douglas Aircraft plant in Los Angeles, for example, had an overwhelmingly white work force.

The surge in the urban black population generated social tensions that sometimes erupted in violence. Unrest tore at America's cities during World War II, as it would later in the 1960s and again in 1992. Three days of racial conflict in Detroit during the hot summer of 1943, triggered by rumors that whites had pushed a black woman and her baby into a lake in a city park, left twenty-five blacks and nine whites dead before federal troops could quell the violence. Thurgood Marshall, the chief counsel of the National Association for the Advancement of Colored People (NAACP), bitterly criticized the Detroit police for using excessive force against blacks. The police handling of the riot and previous racial incidents, he declared, "reads like the story of the Nazi gestapo." A boiling over of racial unrest in Harlem that same summer, set off by stories of racist abuse of African-American soldiers, caused five deaths, hundreds of injuries, and the looting and burning of white-owned shops and businesses.

But the war years also prepared the way for the civil-rights activism that would sweep America in the 1950s and 1960s. The paradox of a nation's fighting tyranny abroad while tolerating long-entrenched racism at home did not escape African-Americans. Lillian Smith, a white Georgia writer who toured the South in the summer of 1942, commented on "a quiet . . . resentment, running like a deep stream through [young blacks'] minds and hearts." A white Virginia newspaper editor wrote to a friend, "The war and its slogans have roused in the breasts of our colored friends hopes, aspirations and desires which they formerly did not entertain, except in the rarest instances." Membership in the NAACP soared during the war. At its 1942 convention, the NAACP denounced segregation and discrimination against black voters and called for a "double victory": over America's enemies abroad and over

---

* Blacks made up 16 percent of the total armed forces, higher than their proportion (10 percent) of the population as a whole.

racism at home. In *What the Negro Wants* (1944), a group of prominent African-American leaders set forth an uncompromising agenda for the postwar civil-rights struggle.

Anticipating tactics that civil-rights demonstrators of the 1960s would employ, black students at Howard University entered a segregated Washington, D.C., restaurant in 1944 while others marched outside with signs bearing the emotion-laden slogan: "We Die Together. Let's Eat Together." The Congress of Racial Equality (CORE), a biracial organization founded in 1942, organized similar demonstrations at segregated theaters and restaurants in a number of cities.

The Roosevelt administration and the courts responded to this rising discontent. In 1941 FDR issued Executive Order 8802, which barred racial discrimination in defense plants and created the Fair Employment Practices Committee (FEPC) to investigate discrimination in the defense industry and labor unions. The president's immediate goal was to avert a politically embarrassing protest march in Washington, D.C., by a hundred thousand blacks organized by A. Philip Randolph, head of the Brotherhood of Sleeping Car Porters. In a 1944 decision that sent shivers of apprehension through the white South, the U.S. Supreme Court declared the Texas Democratic party's all-white primary unconstitutional. But these few gestures against domestic racism were primarily cosmetic. The FEPC, beset by a minuscule budget, bureaucratic infighting, and hostility from racists, accomplished little. One bigoted southern journalist ridiculed it as "dat cummittee fer de perteckshun of Rastus & Sambo." Because sustaining war production outranked racial justice in Washington's and the nation's priorities, the FEPC could use only moral suasion to combat racial discrimination in war plants. Although the war raised the consciousness of black America and brought a few small steps toward equality, the great struggles for civil rights lay in the future.

For Hispanic Americans, too, the years 1941–1945 brought fresh confrontations with the ugly reality of prejudice. Despite urgent labor needs, war plants discriminated against Mexican Americans and denied them the promotions accorded other workers. Of ten thousand employees at giant Kelley Air Base in Texas in 1944, for example, not one Mexican American held a post above the level of laborer or mechanic's assistant. The vast Los Angeles Shipbuilding and Dry Dock Company employed only three hundred Chicanos among its twelve thousand workers during the war.

Mexican Americans played a key role in western agriculture, however, where labor needs intensified after the internment of Japanese Americans (see p. 22). Many Mexicans entered the United States under the so-called *braceros* ("helping arms") agreement negotiated by the U.S. and Mexican governments in 1942. For the United States, the program met urgent farm needs; for Mexico, it alleviated the desperate poverty of a rapidly growing population.* The *braceros* contracts guaranteed temporary agricultural workers a minimum wage of thirty cents per hour and exemption from the draft. Under the agreement, 220,000 Mexicans entered the United States between 1942 and 1947, laboring in Texas cotton fields, California truck farms, and

---

* From 1940 to 1950, Mexico's population swelled by 16.5 million, some 30 percent.

Northwest sugar-beet fields. Some 67,000 *braceros* worked on U.S. railroads as well. These laborers often endured racism and discrimination, graphically illustrated by signs reading "No Mexicans. White Trade Only," posted in saloons and pool halls in Washington and Oregon. Texas cotton growers, too, unhappy with the protections and wage guarantees of the *braceros* program, pressured Washington to leave the border open, in violation of the 1942 agreement. Thus, many thousands more Mexicans flooded north to work in the agricultural harvest as undocumented laborers.

The Chicano population of West Coast cities grew rapidly amid the wartime employment boom. By 1942 Los Angeles' Mexican population stood at more than three hundred thousand. Anti-Mexican prejudice intensified with this growth and erupted in the so-called Sleepy Lagoon case. In August 1942, after a young Mexican American died in a Los Angeles gang fight, twenty-three male Chicanos were arrested and charged with the murder. Tried before an openly prejudiced judge in a hostile climate fanned by sensational press stories, three of them were convicted of first-degree murder and nine of second-degree murder. A defense committee gained a reversal of the convictions on appeal, but the case exacerbated anti-Mexican feeling. The Los Angeles Police Department, with only 22 Mexican-American officers in a force of 2,547, systematically harassed the Mexican-American community.

Hostility also broke out in the Los Angeles "zoot suit" riots of 1943. During the war, some young men, including Mexican Americans, favored a flamboyant outfit that featured widely draped trousers pegged at the ankle, a broad-rimmed hat, a long double-breasted jacket, and a long gold watch chain. The popularity of this so-called zoot suit with Mexican-American street gangs, or *pachucos*, led the Los Angeles City Council to outlaw the clothes, but with little success. In June 1943, sailors on leave in Los Angeles rampaged against zoot suiters for their alleged lack of patriotism, beating them and pulling off their garb. These flashes of racism and urban ethnic conflict in wartime warned of social tensions that would erupt repeatedly in succeeding decades.

The persistence of racist attitudes in wartime emerged starkly in anti-Japanese propaganda. In ads, political cartoons, and animated cartoons produced by the Disney organization, the "Japs" figured as grotesque, buck-toothed caricatures, subhuman primates, or even insects. "Probably in all our history," wrote historian Allan Nevins in 1946, "no foe has been so detested as were the Japanese." (The Japanese, in equally crude racist propaganda, portrayed Americans as greedy, predatory monsters.) In later years, when Japanese automobiles, TVs, and cassette players flooded the American market, echoes of this wartime anti-Japanese propaganda would reverberate.

Racist attitudes toward the Japanese were echoed in the treatment of the West Coast's Japanese-American population, consisting of some 47,000 Issei (foreign-born aliens) and 80,000 Nisei (Japanese Americans born in the United States and thus U.S. citizens). This minority had long stirred xenophobia and racial prejudice, sometimes rooted in economic rivalry, and after Pearl Harbor, the hostility broke into the open. Powerful groups in California demanded the detention of all Japanese Americans, citizens and aliens alike, for the duration of the war. California's attorney general, Earl Warren (later chief justice of the Supreme Court), told a congressional committee early in 1942 that "something should be done and done immediately" about the threat of sabotage by Japanese Americans. Warren invoked dire images of another Pearl Harbor, this time in California. That no evidence of sabotage or planning for sabotage had been uncovered, he explained, proved the diabolical cleverness of the potential perpetrators. Japanese-American leaders protested. "Is citizenship such a light and transient thing that that which is our inalienable right in normal times can be torn from us in times of war?" asked one.

But their remonstrations were to no avail. In February 1942, President Roosevelt issued Executive Order 9066, authorizing the army to designate any area a military zone from which persons might be excluded. Under this order, the War Relocation Authority (WRA), rounded up 110,000 Japanese Americans in California, Oregon, and Washington and confined them in primitive detention camps hastily built in remote parts of the West. In many cases, the internees' property was confiscated and sold. The WRA gradually released internees who could prove their loyalty (by enlisting in the military, for example) or who were willing to take jobs elsewhere in the country, but as late as 1945 nearly twenty thousand remained in custody. In the 1944 case *Korematsu v. United States*, the U.S. Supreme Court upheld the constitutionality of this action by a six–three vote. Only years later, in the 1980s, would Congress at last partially redress the injustice by compensating surviving internees.

As a side effect of the internment camps, parental authority in Japanese-American families weakened, a phenomenon occurring throughout American society in the war years. One young internee, Ben Yorita, later recalled:

> [In Japanese-American families] the father was the traditional breadwinner and in total command of the family. But after going into the camps, fathers were no longer the breadwinners; the young sons and daughters were. Most of them couldn't even communicate in English, so all the burdens fell on the second generation. And most of us were just kids, nineteen or twenty. Consequently there was a big turnover of responsibility and authority, and the parents were suddenly totally dependent on their children. When we returned to the cities after the war, it was the second generation again that had to make the decisions and do all the negotiating with landlords, attorneys, and the like.

Although racism remained a blot on America's home-front record during World War II, the Nazi foe far more openly pursued a deadly program aimed at wiping out European Jewry. German persecution of the Jews, which during the war became genocide, met with a somewhat ambiguous response in the United States. Americans' humanitarian impulse was strong, but antisemitism and anti-immigrant sentiments also influenced the U.S. reaction to the crisis. While Roosevelt and other national leaders, as well as religious figures and leading media voices, routinely condemned Nazi antisemitism, proposals to admit large numbers of Jewish refugees faced legislative roadblocks, bureaucratic stonewalling, and public opposition as expressed in opinion polls. As word of the magnitude of the Holocaust filtered out of wartime Europe, the story received only muted and fragmentary coverage in the American press, including such leading papers as the *New York Times*. Military planners vetoed proposals to bomb the death camps at Auschwitz and elsewhere, or even the railroads leading to the camps. The best way to help the Jews, they argued, was to win the war.

Only after the war, as accounts and photographs of the death camps, gas chambers, crematory ovens, mountains of corpses, and pathetically emaciated survivors received wide publicity, did the Holocaust's full horror move to the forefront of the American consciousness. In 1940 the American author John Dos Passos had written that the only hope of preserving a sense of humanity as the tide of atrocities mounted lay in "the frail web of understanding of one person for the pain of another." During the years when the Nazis and their collaborators systematically tried to exterminate Europe's Jews, that web of understanding, tragically, failed to develop in America.

Finally, American women experienced profound, if sometimes short-lived, transformations in their lives during the war. Approximately 350,000 women, black and white, became army nurses or went directly into the military, serving in non-combat roles in the female branches of the Army Air Corps (WACS), Navy (WAVES), Coast Guard (SPARS), and Marine Corps Women's Reserve. The number of women government workers, mostly in clerical positions, also increased sharply. After initial reluctance, war-plant managers hired armies of women to replace male workers, now at the front. This development represented a striking change from the Depression of the 1930s, when government policy and popular attitudes had strongly opposed working women because so many men lacked jobs. In wartime, views changed markedly. With the War Department's urging employers to draw upon "the vast resources of womanpower," the female labor force jumped from 14.6 million in 1941 to 19.4 million in 1944. In some plants, including the giant Boeing aircraft factory in Seattle, women composed half the work force. A particularly high rate of married women, many of them servicemen's wives, went to work; by 1945, 25 percent of married women held jobs outside the home. "Almost overnight," wrote one analyst, "women were reclassified from a marginal to a basic labor supply."

Women encountered resentment from male co-workers and the stereotype that they were suited only for simple, repetitive tasks, and few rose to managerial ranks. But in general, a highly favorable public response prevailed. To encourage women to join the work force, the mass magazines featured photos and cover art of strong-armed women assembling warplanes, stitching parachutes, or working in munitions plants. "Rosie the Riveter," a muscular, confident female worker pictured in a Norman Rockwell *Saturday Evening Post* cover in 1943, also became the subject of a popular song of the day. A photo of an eighteen-year-old California airplane-plant employee, Norma Jean Dougherty, adorned a *Yank* magazine article on women war workers. Later she would win fame as Marilyn Monroe.

But one must not exaggerate the change. The increase in women workers reflected a gradual, long-term trend associated with industrialization. The upsurge of female employment in 1942–1945 represented not an awakening of feminism or changing views of gender roles but a response to the war emergency. Government propaganda and the media made clear that traditional notions of women's roles remained intact and treated females' entrance into the work force as strictly temporary. Indeed, wartime concerns about the divorce rate, extramarital sex, child neglect, and juvenile delinquency testify to the uneasiness that the notion of working women aroused. The federal government belatedly funded day-care centers for the children of working mothers in 1943 but appropriated enough to meet a mere 10 percent of the need. In Seattle, for example, only seven publicly funded and three private facilities, accommodating a total of 350 children, served the city's 75,000 working women. In some cases, working mothers themselves opposed government day-care facilities as a form of welfare and left children with friends and relatives instead.

How did these millions of new women workers assess their situation? In various wartime surveys, many described their war jobs as much more interesting than housework, and a majority, especially older women with grown children, consistently expressed a desire to continue working. But when pressed, most admitted that they probably would return to the home when peace came. "My husband wants a wife, not a career woman," said a female naval worker in Washington State. In a poll conducted shortly after the war, about 50 percent of women respondents judged "running a home" as more interesting than holding a full-time job, whereas only 32 percent expressed the opposite view; the rest were undecided or expressed no opinion. But whatever their wish, women workers had little choice about keeping their jobs: they were fired in droves as veterans returned. Day-care centers closed, and the media's celebration of working women abruptly fell silent. But even during the heyday of domesticity in the 1950s, many women who had found employment during the war would remain in the labor force or return to work. Memories of the war years, when barriers to female employment had temporarily fallen, remained vivid, a precedent for the dramatic changes in attitude and practice to come.

On several fronts, then, a war that united the nation against a foreign foe also exposed fissures in American society and darker realities about American attitudes. The racism, prejudice, and mixed messages about the role of women that surfaced during the war—along with the great capacity of millions for self-sacrifice in a common cause—would help to sculpt the nation's social agenda after peace returned.

Technology, Oil, and War

War-spawned technological innovations played their part, too, in shaping postwar America. The Office of Scientific Research and Development (OSRD), set up in 1941 under the directorship of Vannevar Bush, formerly the dean of engineering at the Massachusetts Institute of Technology, sponsored studies on numerous defense-related projects. The computer emerged from wartime research at Harvard, the University of Pennsylvania, and elsewhere, research originally designed to meet the need for precise antiaircraft defense when the German *Luftwaffe* menaced Great Britain. These early calculating machines were massive. The Mark I, completed in 1944 by Harvard physicist Howard Aiken, stretched 50 feet in length, stood 8 feet high, and required 765,299 separate parts. Another prototype computer, the ENIAC, built by John Mauchly and John Eckert, Jr., at the University of Pennsylvania, boasted eighteen thousand vacuum tubes. The acronym stood for Electronic Numerical Integrator and Calculator. One early ENIAC, installed at the Los Alamos laboratory of the federal government late in 1945, was used to run simulations of the as-yet-unbuilt hydrogen bomb. These wartime behemoths laid the groundwork for a revolution that in future years would transform information processing and revolutionize American life.

Numerous advances in aeronautical design and navigation, including radar (developed with OSRD funding), also date from World War II. U.S. pilots tested the first jet planes in 1942. The German V-1 rockets that fell on British cities evolved after the war into intercontinental nuclear missiles and opened the door to space exploration. Synthetic rubber filled in for the scarce real article in automobile tires and other products. Synthetic fabrics such as nylon, introduced by the Du Pont Corporation in 1938, did duty as wartime substitutes for silk and other natural fabrics in short supply. Department stores that advertised "nylons" during the war faced deluges of eager buyers. In the postwar years, a dizzying array of synthetic fabrics would find many and varied uses.

The war, ironically, also produced notable advances in the saving of human lives. Research on blood-plasma technology and on antibacterial sulfa drugs progressed rapidly. Production of penicillin, discovered by Sir Alexander Fleming in 1929, moved from Britain to America when the war began. Funded by the War Production Board, researchers developed new techniques for culturing the penicillin mold and vastly increased the output of this lifesaving antibiotic. Wartime research led to the development of numerous other substances of value to peacetime medicine. Streptomycin, for example, another key antibiotic, was discovered in 1943 by microbiologist Selman A. Waksman of Rutgers University. The insecticide DDT, developed in the 1930s, first received wide use during the war to protect GIs from typhus, malaria, and other insect-borne diseases.

The role of science and technology in ensuring victory over the nation's enemies solidified a protechnology mindset that in later decades would come under heavy challenge. In particular, the government's plunge into large-scale funding of research would generate ambivalence in the future, especially for its environmental implications. DDT, hailed as a lifesaver during the war, later would spark controversy as an ecological menace. During the war, however, the compelling goal of defeating a dangerous foe overrode all other considerations.

Of the war's industrial and technological aspects, none held more portents for the future than the struggle for oil. Like a viscous black stream, oil oozes its way through the history of World War II. Japan's efforts to reduce its dependence on Western oil spurred its aggressive policies in Asia in the 1930s, aggression that led President Roosevelt in July 1941 to freeze all Japanese funds in the United States and in effect to embargo oil exports to Japan. The December 1941 Japanese attack on the U.S. fleet at Pearl Harbor would have been even more catastrophic had the Japanese also destroyed the 4.5 million barrels of oil stored there in surface tanks.

During the initial stages of the war, Japan met its energy needs by seizing British and Dutch refineries in Borneo and Sumatra. But as U.S. forces advanced across the Pacific and sank more and more Japanese tankers en route to the home islands, Japan gradually ran out of the precious commodity. Its oil reserves, nearly 30 million barrels in 1937, had dwindled to 0.8 million by July 1945. The shortage crippled the island's warmaking capacity. Toward the end, Japan resorted to desperate measures to save fuel, sending pilots on *kamikaze* suicide missions against U.S. ships carrying just enough gasoline to crash into their targets.

Hitler frantically sought fuel for his war machine, too. He ordered the invasion of the Soviet Union in part to capture the vast Soviet oil refinery at Baku in the Caucasus and to prevent the Soviets from seizing the rich Ploesti oilfield in Rumania, a German ally. Hitler also channeled enormous resources into developing synthetic fuels. By a process known as hydrogenization, the German chemical giant I. G. Farben, relying in part on slave labor, produced from coal millions of gallons of syn-thetic liquid fuel that supplied 95 percent of Germany's aviation fuel during the war.

But fuel shortages ultimately doomed Germany just as they did Japan. Stalin's counteroffensive denied Hitler the Baku and Ploesti oilfields, and Allied bombing slashed I. G. Farben's synthetic-fuel output from 92,000 to 5,000 barrels a day. The Nazi's North African campaign faltered for want of gasoline, and by the end of the war, the German armies had run dry. In the spring of 1945, military vehicles of the Tenth German Army in Italy were being towed by oxen.

For the Allies, too, oil was critical. U.S. oil shipments to Great Britain under the wartime Lend Lease program helped the British to repel the Nazi *Luftwaffe* during the 1941 Battle of Britain. Once the United States entered the war, Interior Secre-tary Harold Ickes, doubling as petroleum administrator, or "oil tsar," stimulated do-mestic exploration and pushed daily production from 3.7 million barrels in 1940 to 4.7 million barrels in 1945. Two major pipelines, the "Big Inch" and the "Little Inch," built in 1943–1944, carried gasoline and other petroleum products from the Southwest to the East Coast. By such means, the United States met nearly 90 per-cent of the Allies' wartime oil needs. At home, strict rationing coupled with tire shortages, a moratorium on auto production, and a 35-mile-per-hour speed limit cut civilian oil and gasoline consumption by 30 percent.

Meanwhile, the shape of the future emerged on another front when famed oil geologist Everett Lee DeGolyer, on a government mission in 1943, conservatively assessed the oil potential of Saudi Arabia and other Middle East nations at 25 billion barrels. "The oil in this region," reported a member of DeGolyer's team to the State Department, "is the greatest single prize in all history." A major behind-the-scenes struggle unfolded between the United States and Great Britain for control of this find. Early in 1945, following Yalta, President Roosevelt met with King Ibn Saud of Saudi Arabia aboard the *U.S.S. Quincy* in the Suez Canal for a conference that in-cluded intense discussions of oil.* One *New York Times* analyst wrote after the meet-ing, "The immediate oil deposits in Saudi Arabia make that country more important to American diplomacy than almost any other smaller nation."

In August 1944, meanwhile, seeking to resolve their dispute, the United States and Great Britain signed the Anglo-American Petroleum Agreement creating an eight-member International Petroleum Commission (IPC) charged with shaping postwar oil policy, allocating quotas, and recommending production levels. Domes-tic producers in the United States rebelled, however, fearing that the new agency would set oil prices. A 1945 revision of the agreement ensured that the IPC had

---

* The American president and the mideast monarch got along famously. When Ibn Saud, who limped severely from old war injuries, admired Roosevelt's wheelchair, Roosevelt promptly gave him a duplicate, which the Saudi ruler thereafter highly prized.

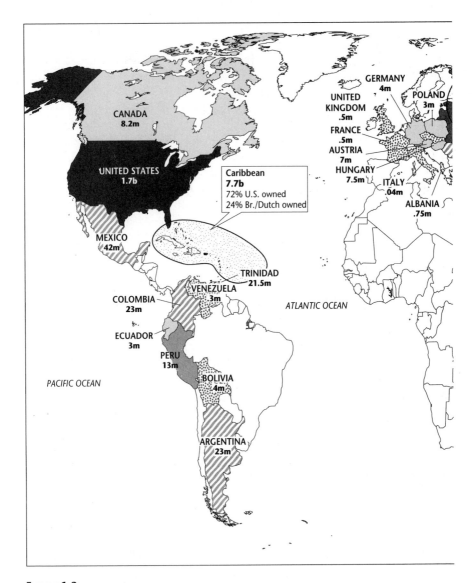

FIGURE 1.3

World Crude Oil Production and Major Petroleum Reserves, 1945

SOURCES: "American Petroleum Interests in Foreign Countries," a report submitted on October 15, 1945, by a group of American oil companies to the Special Senate Committee Investigating Petroleum Resources; and *The Oil Weekly*, compiled by *The Petroleum Almanac*, 1946.

advisory power only and no authority over U.S. production. The postwar American boom would roar forward on a tide of oil, untrammeled by limits or restraints.

Oil, then, was never far from the mind of any world leader during World War II and by 1945 had emerged as a key issue in postwar diplomacy. The war demonstrated the industrialized world's utter dependence on this limited resource and showed

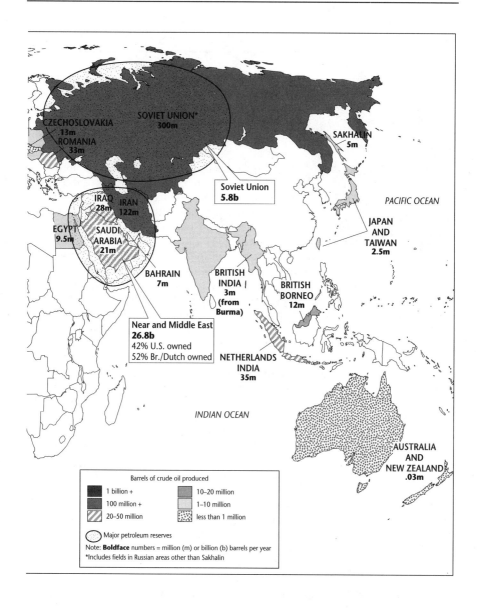

that, in an emergency, America could radically cut its consumption. The conflict also made crystal clear that the Middle East would play a critical role in postwar geopolitics.

Another major scientific breakthrough of World War II—the atomic bomb—had a more immediate impact than oil on the consciousness of ordinary citizens, however. In August 1939, a few weeks before Hitler invaded Poland and plunged Europe into war, Albert Einstein, an emigré German-Jewish physicist who had done seminal work in theoretical physics decades before, sent President Roosevelt a mes-

FOCUS ON: *GOVERNMENT AND SCIENCE: AN UNEASY PARTNERSHIP*

Of all the long-range consequences of World War II, one of the most momentous was the emergence of the federal government as a patron of scientific research and development (R&D). Cooperation between government and science persisted in the decades after the war. The Atomic Energy Act of 1946, for example, set up the Atomic Energy Commission to fund nuclear research, especially in the field of weaponry. The National Science Foundation (1950), the National Institutes of Health, and other federal agencies also funneled taxpayers' dollars into the R&D pipeline.

This partnership, which helped to establish the United States as the world leader in science, also catalyzed criticism and uneasy doubts over the years. As the Cold War deepened in the 1950s, Washington's role in underwriting scientific research grew increasingly politicized. The National Defense Education Act of 1958, passed in a panic after the Soviet Union launched its *Sputnik* satellite in 1957, appropriated an initial $621 million for college student loans and programs to upgrade scientific and foreign-language instruction. In 1961, pushing the Cold War competition with the Soviets into space, President Kennedy called for a race to rocket an American to the moon by 1970. Amid superpower tensions, one historian of science wrote in 1966, "The prospect of peace breaking out, though unlikely, posed a real threat" to federally financed scientific work. During the Vietnam War, protesters often targeted the Pentagon's funding of secret research on the nation's campuses. Indeed, a bombing in 1970 at the University of Wisconsin, which killed a graduate student, aimed to destroy the Army Mathematics Research Center, a federally funded facility on the Madison campus.

The politicization and militarization of science continued into the 1970s and 1980s. President Reagan, emulating President Kennedy, set a new high-tech goal for the nation: a permanent space station staffed by an eight-person crew. The space-shuttle program of the National Aeronautics and Space Administration (NASA), having begun modestly in the early 1970s, was budgeted at over $4 billion in 1987. In 1983 Reagan proposed the Strategic Defense Initiative, a controversial missile-defense shield using futuristic laser and computer technology. As the years passed, the lion's share of federal R&D money ended up in the military's hands. Of a total federal R&D budget of $48.6 billion in 1990, some $36 billion, or 74 percent, found its way to the Pentagon.

By 1990 Washington had become a major player in U.S. science, and American

---

sage sketching the possible implications of current work in his field. Einstein wrote the letter at the initiative of Leo Szilard, a refugee Hungarian physicist fearful that German research in atomic energy was dangerously advanced. Recent research by Szilard and the Italian physicist Enrico Fermi, wrote Einstein,

> leads me to expect that the element uranium may be turned into a new and important source of energy in the immediate future. . . . This new phenomenon would

higher education depended heavily on federal R&D funds. In 1989 Johns Hopkins University received over $400 million in such research support, Stanford nearly $250 million, the Massachusetts Institute of Technology more than $200 million, and on down the list. Yet even as scientists benefited from Washington's largesse, they worried that it compromised their autonomy. The Cold War did more than shake loose billions of dollars in R&D support; it also shaped—and perverted, some argued—that research. The secrecy and destructive purposes of military research, critics charged, mocked the spirit of science. The skeptics worried, as had a physician working for the Army Medical Corps in 1886, lest their torch of knowledge "prove a firebrand and destroy more than it illuminates."

Even the more modest nonmilitary R&D budget has generated controversy. Medical research, for example, funded by Washington to the tune of over $8 billion in 1990, roused passionate debate over such issues as the genetic altering of plants and animals, the experimental use of tissue from aborted fetuses, funding levels for AIDS research, and the speed with which experimental drugs become available.

As the federal deficit mushroomed in the 1970s and 1980s, big-ticket scientific and technological programs such as NASA's space station attracted critical scrutiny. Yet communities that had grown to depend economically on R&D programs bankrolled by Washington fought vigorously for their survival. One disillusioned scientist called the space-station project "an orbiting pork barrel." The Cold War's end at the close of the 1980s brought deep cuts in military spending, including R&D funding, and many communities felt the pinch. As recently as 1989, to cite one example, $2.5 billion in federal R&D money poured into California. Slashes in these funds in the early 1990s contributed to that state's devastating economic tailspin. As the Soviet threat evaporated and governmental red ink spread, expensive research projects faced the ax. The superconductor supercollider, a costly project favored by theoretical physicists and scheduled to be built in Texas, succumbed to congressional budget slashers in 1993.

But although President Clinton would criticize some aspects of federal patronage of science and technology, he did not advocate ending it. Indeed, quite the reverse is true. In the 1992 presidential campaign, Clinton called for a federal "industrial policy" to identify and finance cutting-edge technologies in which the United States could become a world leader.

As the twentieth century closes, the marriage of politics and science faces strains, but neither partner shows any interest in a divorce or even a trial separation. The link forged during World War II, when Washington enlisted scientists in the struggle against fascism, proved not only more enduring but also more complex and problematic than anyone imagined in 1945.

---

also lead to the construction of bombs, and it is conceivable—though much less certain—that extremely powerful bombs of a new type may thus be constructed.

Heeding Einstein's suggestion that the government provide support for further research, Roosevelt approved a modest grant. By 1942, when the army took over the project and code-named it the Manhattan Project, secret work was under way at the University of Chicago; Oak Ridge, Tennessee; and Hanford, Washington. In 1943, bomb construction began at Los Alamos, New Mexico, under the direction of physicist J. Robert Oppenheimer.

Before dawn on July 16, 1945, a group of scientists huddling in the darkness at the Alamogordo Bombing Range in New Mexico detonated the world's first atomic bomb. Physicist Philip Morrison, watching from ten miles away, later wrote, "You felt the morning had come, although it was still night, because there your face felt the glow of this daylight—this desert sun in the midst of night." A few minutes after the blast (code-named Trinity), test director Kenneth Bainbridge approached Oppenheimer, shook his hand, and said, "Oppie, now we're all sons of bitches."

The successful Alamogordo test that propelled humankind into a new era also presented Roosevelt's successor, President Truman, with a fateful decision. Eager to end the war, Truman ordered use of the atomic bomb against Japan as soon as technically possible and without explicit warning. Leo Szilard and other Manhattan Project scientists at the University of Chicago proposed a demonstration, but neither the president nor Secretary of War Henry Stimson appear to have considered this option.

Later, Truman and Stimson would claim that the atomic bomb offered the only sure alternative to a land invasion of Japan that might have extended the war well into 1946 and cost thousands of American lives. Indeed, War Department contingency plans called for an invasion of Japan's southernmost island late in 1945 and of the main island, Honshu, early in 1946 if the war continued. Thousands of GIs serving in the South Pacific in 1945 never doubted that Truman's decision to drop the atomic bomb spared them from death on Japanese soil. But some evidence suggests that other factors may have figured in Truman's decision. Although Japanese warlords were prepared to fight on, a new Japanese government that came to power in April 1945 soon began maneuvering to end the war on the Allied terms, and Washington was aware of this possibility. (U.S. and British cryptologists had broken the Japanese diplomatic code, and all official communications out of Tokyo were monitored.) After postwar research in Japan, the U.S. Strategic Bombing Survey concluded in 1946 that Japan would have surrendered "certainly prior to 31 December 1945, and in all probability prior to 1 November 1945 . . . even if the atomic bombs had not been dropped, even if Russia had not entered the war, and even if no invasion had been planned or contemplated." Moreover, at the Potsdam Conference, when Stalin renewed his pledge to declare war on Japan in mid-August (and before Truman learned of the successful atomic bomb test in New Mexico), Truman noted exultantly in a hasty diary jotting: "[Stalin] will be in Jap War on August 15 . . . Fini Japs when that comes about."

It was not, then, the nightmare of a bloody land invasion months in the future that loomed large in Truman's mind as he made his decision to drop the atomic bomb but rather the precise means by which Japan's imminent surrender would be achieved. If Japan's surrender were perceived to be a response to the Soviet declaration of war (which came on August 8, 1945), Stalin would have won substantial claim to a role in postwar Japan. But if the U.S. atomic bomb appeared to be the major factor in Japan's capitulation, America could claim the upper hand in postwar Japan—indeed, in the entire postwar world. British prime minister Winston Churchill later described U.S. leaders' thinking in late July 1945: "It was now no longer necesary for the Russians to come into the Japanese war; the new explosive alone was sufficient to settle the matter."

The Manhattan Project's enormous cost may have been another influence. How could Truman justify to Congress and to U.S. taxpayers spending $2 billion on a weapon and then not use it? The president himself later insisted that he made up his mind without the slightest qualm: "The final decision of where and when to use the atomic bomb was up to me. Let there be no mistake about it. I regarded the bomb as a military weapon and never had any doubt that it should be used."

Whatever his precise reasoning (and we will never know for sure), Truman issued his order. The first bomb, nicknamed *Little Boy*, utilizing uranium-235, fell on Hiroshima at 8:15 A.M. on August 6, destroying the city and killing upwards of a hundred thousand people. The second, *Fat Man*, a plutonium bomb, dropped on Nagasaki on August 9, leaving more than forty thousand dead. The atomic bomb gave the final push to a Japanese government already on the verge of surrender, but at a terrible cost: a horrendous weapon unleashed on the world, under circumstances that vastly complicated efforts at international control. Within a few years, the United States and the Soviet Union would become locked in a dangerous nuclear-arms race, and nuclear weaponry would spread to other nations as well.

CONCLUSION

The final chapter of World War II, then, also served as the opening chapter of the nuclear age. Americans swiftly realized that their world had changed forever. Dreams of a technological utopia formed one strand of the nation's initial response to the news of the atomic bomb. President Truman hailed atomic energy as "the greatest achievement of organized science in history" and stressed its peacetime promise. Magazine writers and radio commentators conjured up visions of atomic cars that would never need refueling, atomic power too cheap to meter, atomic agriculture that would solve the world's food problems, and atomic medicine that would conquer death itself. But Americans soon recognized that the force that had demolished two Japanese cities could be turned against themselves. Even President Truman, in the privacy of his diary, expressed grave misgivings about the new weapon. After the Alamogordo test, he called the atomic bomb "the most terrible thing ever discovered" and resorted to apocalyptic biblical imagery: "It may be the fire destruction prophesied . . . after Noah and his fabulous Ark." Human beings were like termites boring into the earth, Truman reflected, and someday it might blow up in their faces. Such fears swelled after Hiroshima. Radio newscasters compared Hiroshima with U.S. cities of similar size, such as New Haven and Denver; newspapers printed maps of their own communities overlaid by concentric circles showing the pattern of devastation at Hiroshima. The life expectancy of the human species, commented the *Washington Post* on August 26, 1945, had "dwindled immeasurably in the course of two brief weeks." This initial spasm of terror gradually receded, but fear of nuclear holocaust sank deep into the American consciousness in August 1945, where it would linger for decades, rising and falling with the ebb and flow of Cold War hostilities.

Survival Secrets for Atomic Attacks

ALWAYS PUT FIRST THINGS FIRST

A 1950 book on how to survive a nuclear attack projects naive optimism and simplistic advice. (*From* How to Survive an Atomic Bomb, *by Richard Gerstell, 1950*)

Try to Get Shielded

If you have time, get down in a basement or subway. Should you unexpectedly be caught out-of-doors, seek shelter alongside a building, or jump in any handy ditch or gutter.

Drop Flat on Ground or Floor

To keep from being tossed about and to lessen the chances of being struck by falling and flying objects, flatten out at the base of a wall, or at the bottom of a bank.

Bury Your Face in Your Arms

When you drop flat, hide your eyes in the crook of your elbow. That will protect your face from flash burns, prevent temporary blindness and keep flying objects out of your eyes.

NEVER LOSE YOUR HEAD

Japan surrendered on August 14, 1945, three months after the collapse of Nazi power in Europe. The long-awaited V-J (Victory over Japan) Day had arrived; World War II was over. At a cost of 407,000 dead and 672,000 wounded, the United States had contributed its share to the defeat of powerful foes. The radio news flash set off frantic celebrations. Crowds swarmed the streets, horns honked, whistles blared, screaming headlines confirmed the initial reports. Photographers captured scenes of delirious joy. As the shouting subsided, however, sober thoughts set in. What kind of world would peace bring? What would life be like in the postwar United States? Only time would yield the answers to these questions. With a mixed sense of their nation's vast power and sudden vulnerability, Americans faced the postwar age.

Despite America's heavy losses and sacrifices, the war touched it less heavily than some other nations. Historians conservatively estimate that the conflict cost the lives of some 17 million soldiers and 20 million civilians, plus millions more who were injured or made refugees. Germany lost more than 3 million soldiers, Japan and China around 2 million each. The Soviet Union suffered the heaviest casualties, including the death of more than 6 million soldiers and as many as 20 million civilians; the precise number will never be known. After the war, Stalin would say that Great Britain paid for the war in time, the United States in materials, and the Soviet Union in blood. The war brought massive physical devastation and shattered the industrial infrastructure of Germany, the Soviet Union, Japan, and other nations. By contrast, the United States in 1945—its factories intact, its economy booming, and its occupying armies triumphant in Western Europe and Asia—stood at the pinnacle of world power. What would it do with that power?

One certainty quickly emerged. Despite the soaring rhetoric of some orators, the postwar age would not be a time of entirely new beginnings. In countless ways, the history of the United States since 1945 has its roots in the years 1941–1945. Nearly every important strand of early postwar American history—the booming prosperity, the Cold War, the civil-rights revolution, the nuclear arms race, the cultural conservatism and business-oriented government of the Eisenhower years, the rise of computers, the space program, even social trends such as suburbanization, the growth of the middle class, and the climbing birthrate—can be understood only if one pays careful attention to World War II. When Franklin Roosevelt led the nation into war on December 8, 1941, he little realized how profound would be the long-range consequences of the conflict whose end he did not live to see.

SELECTED READINGS

Wartime Diplomacy

Gar Alperovitz, *Atomic Diplomacy* (1965); Edward M. Bennett, *Franklin D. Roosevelt and the Search for Victory: American-Soviet Relations, 1939–1945* (1990); Russell D. Buhite, *Decision at Yalta* (1986); Diane Shaver Clemens, *Yalta* (1970); Robert Dallek, *Franklin D. Roosevelt and American Foreign Policy, 1932–1945* (1979); Robert A. Divine, *Second Chance: The Triumph of Internationalism in America During World War II* (1971); Herbert Feis, *Churchill, Roosevelt, Stalin: The War They Fought; The Peace They Sought* (1957); John Lewis Gaddis, *The United States and the Origins of the Cold War, 1941–1947* (1972); Patrick Hearndon, *Roosevelt Confronts Hitler: American Entry into World War II* (1987); George C. Herring, Jr., *Aid to Russia: 1941–1946: Strategy, Diplomacy and the Origins of the Cold War* (1973); Walter LaFeber, *America, Russia, and the Cold War* (rev. ed., 1985); Warren Kimball, *The Juggler: Franklin Roosevelt as Wartime Statesman* (1991); Robert James Maddox, *The United States and World War II* (1992); Michael Sherry, *Preparing for the Next War: American Plans for Postwar Defense, 1941–1945* (1977); Martin Sherwin, *A World Destroyed: The Atomic Bomb and the Grand Alliance* (1975); Christopher Thorne, *Allies of a Kind: The United States, Britain and the War Against Japan, 1941–1945* (1978); David Wyman, *The Abandonment of the Jews: America and the Holocaust, 1941–1945* (1984); Daniel Yergin, *The Prize: The Epic Quest for Oil, Money, and Power* (1991).

Domestic Social Trends During World War II

Rodolfo Acuña, *Occupied America: A History of Chicanos* (1981); Karen Anderson, *Wartime Women: Sex Roles, Family Relations, and the Status of Women During World War II* (1981); Allan Berube, *Coming Out Under Fire: The History of Gay Men and Women in World War Two* (1990); Dominic J. Capeci, *The Harlem Riot of 1943* (1977); John Costello, *Virtue Under Fire: How World War II Changed Our Social and Sexual Attitudes* (1985); Richard M. Dalfiume, *Desegregation of the United States Armed Forces: Fighting on Two Fronts, 1939–1953* (1969); Clete Daniel, *Chicano Workers and the Politics of Fairness: The Fair Employment Practices Committee in the Southwest, 1941–1945* (1991); Roger Daniels, *Concentration Camps USA: Japanese Americans and World War II* (1981); Philip J. Funigiello, *The Challenge to Urban Liberalism: Federal-City Relations During World War II* (1978); Mario T. Garcia, *Mexican-Americans: Leadership, Ideology, and Identity, 1930–1960* (1989); Susan M. Hartmann, *The Home Front and Beyond: American Women in the 1940s* (1982); Peter Irons, *Justice at War: The Inside Story of the Japanese-American Internment* (1983); Ruth Milkman, *Gender at Work: The Dynamics of Job Discrimination by Sex During World War II* (1987); Gerald D. Nash, *The American West Transformed:*

The Impact of the Second World War (1985); William L. O'Neill, *A Democracy at War: America's Fight at Home and Abroad in World War II* (1993); Geoffrey Perrett, *Days of Sadness, Years of Triumph: The American People, 1939–1945* (1974); Paula E. Pfeffer, *A. Philip Randolph: Pioneer of the Civil Rights Movement* (1990); Richard Polenberg, *War and Society: The United States, 1941–1945* (1972); Merl E. Reed, *Seedtime for the Modern Civil Rights Movement: The President's Committee on Fair Employment Practices, 1941–1946* (1991); Louis Ruchames, *Race, Jobs and Politics: The Story of FEPC* (1948); Robert Shogan and Tom Craig, *The Detroit Race Riot: A Study in Violence* (1964); William M. Tuttle, *Daddy's Gone to War: The Second World War in the Lives of America's Children* (1993); Allan M. Winkler, *Home Front U.S.A.: America During World War II* (1986); Neil A. Wynn, *The Afro-American and the Second World War* (1976).

Cultural Trends and Wartime Propaganda

Jeanine Basinger, *The World War II Combat Film: Anatomy of a Genre* (1986); John Morton Blum, *V Was for Victory: Politics and American Culture During World War II* (1976); John Dower, *War Without Mercy: Race and Power in the Pacific War* (1986); Lee Finkle, *Forum for Protest: The Black Press During World War II* (1975); Clayton R. Koppes and Gregory D. Black, *Hollywood Goes to War: How Politics, Profits and Propaganda Shaped World War II Movies* (1987); Ralph Levering, *American Opinion and the Russian Alliance* (1976); Richard R. Lingeman, *Don't You Know There's a War On? The American Home Front: 1941–1945* (1970); Robert K. Merton, *Mass Persuasion: The Social Psychology of a War Bond Drive* (1946); George H. Roeder, Jr., *The Censored War: American Visual Experience During World War II* (1993); Leila J. Rupp, *Mobilizing Women for War: German and American Propaganda, 1939–1945* (1978); Holly Cowan Shulman, *The Voice of America: Propaganda and Democracy, 1941–1945* (1990); Studs Terkel, *"The Good War": An Oral History of World War II* (1984); Alan M. Winkler, *The Politics of Propaganda: The Office of War Information, 1942–1945* (1978).

The War's Impact on the Economy, Labor, and Technology

James Phinney Baxter III, *Scientists Against Time* (1947); Joseph C. Boyce, *New Weapons for Air Warfare* (1947); Alice R. Burks and Arthur W. Burks, *The First Electronic Computer* (1988); Bruce Catton, *The War Lords of Washington* (1948); Gerard H. Clarfield and William M. Wiecek, *Nuclear America: Military and Civilian Power in the United States, 1940–1980* (1984); Alan Clive, *State of War: Michigan in World War II* (1979); James W. Cortada, *The Computer in the United States: From Laboratory to Market, 1930–1960* (1993); Donald W. Cox, *America's New Policy Makers: The Scientists' Rise to Power* (1964); Richard G. Hewlett and Oscar E. Anderson, Jr., *The New World, 1939–1946* [atomic-bomb project] (1972); Gregory Michael Hooks, *Forging the Military-Industrial Complex: World War II's Battle of the Potomoc* (1991); Eliot Janeway, *The Struggle for Survival* (1951); Daniel J. Kevles, *The Physicists: The History of a Scientific Community in Modern America* (1979); Paul A. C. Koistenen, *The Military-Industrial Complex: A Historical Perspective* (1980); Nelson Lichtenstein, *Labor's War at Home: The CIO in World War II* (1982); Alan I. Marcus and Howard P. Segal, *Technology in America: A Brief History* (1989); Richard Rhodes, *The Making of the Atomic Bomb* (1986); Irving Stewart, *Organizing Scientific Research for War* (1948); Michael B. Stoff, ed., *The Manhattan Project: A Documentary Introduction* (1991); Walter W. Wilcox, *The Farmer and the Second World War* (1947).

Chapter Two

"Not Since Rome and Carthage": Into the Cold War

As World War II wound down and Germany's defeat was near, staff at the American embassy in Moscow seemed more worried than joyous. Conflict between Washington and Moscow over a number of issues rumbled ominously; one was that Stalin showed no signs of honoring his Yalta pledge to permit free elections in Poland. On March 8, 1945, young Kathleen Harriman, who lived in Moscow, where her father, W. Averell Harriman, served as U.S. ambassador to the Soviet Union, wrote to her sister back in the States, "The war is going wonderfully well again now. But the news is slightly dampened here by our gallant allies who at the moment are being most bastard-like."

The climate in Washington mirrored the dark mood at the embassy in Moscow. Throughout the war, President Roosevelt had sustained the hope of postwar cooperation with the Soviets, but by March 1945, he had grown disillusioned: "Averell is right," he sighed. "We can't do business with Stalin. He has broken every one of the promises he made at Yalta." Worries about the future, rooted in disturbing Soviet actions and amplified by the news media and political writers, soon rippled across America. C. L. Sulzberger of the *New York Times* wrote shortly after Japan's surrender:

> The most important political development during the last ten years of localized and finally global warfare has been the emergence of [the Soviet Union] as the greatest dynamic and diplomatic force on the vast Eurasian land mass which stretches from the Atlantic to the Pacific Oceans.

From some perspectives, of course, America in 1945 had reason for exuberant confidence. Triumphant in war, it stood at the pinnacle of power. The conflict had taken a heavy toll but had damaged the United States less heavily than other belligerents. Indeed, the demands of war had so vastly extended U.S. productive capacity that by 1945 the United States accounted for 60 percent of the world's industrial output. However, America also faced the challenge of converting to a peacetime economy, rancorous domestic politics, and nascent friction with the Soviet Union. Over all loomed the new weapon that the United States had unleashed: the atomic bomb. To complicate matters, a new and untested president, Harry S Truman, sat at the Oval Office desk that Franklin D. Roosevelt had graced for so long. Treasury Secretary Henry Morgenthau, Jr., offered a cautious preliminary assessment: "[Truman] has a lot of nervous energy, and seems to be inclined to make very quick decisions. But, after all, he is a politician, and what is going on in his head only time will tell."

Uncertainty prevailed at home and abroad. The postwar moment that Americans had hoped would usher in a respite from worry instead gave rise to tension and crises. Internationally, a series of confrontations soon brought the United States into conflict with its erstwhile ally, the Soviet Union. From these clashes emerged a powerful and well-grounded conviction, transmitted from Washington and the media to the grass roots, that Moscow's course profoundly threatened U.S. national-security interests. From this firm belief arose the long political, economic, and military struggle that pundits soon would label the Cold War. Indeed, the most appropriate label for the forty years extending from President Truman to President Reagan is the Cold War era.

Roots of the Cold War

The conflict that erupted after World War II between the Soviet Union and the West, most notably the United States, had deep roots in ideology and history. First, a belief in the New World's divine commission to redeem and uplift humanity had influenced thought in America since the days of the Puritans. Gradually secularized, this sense of mission had become, by the nineteenth century, a conviction of the nation's "manifest destiny" to expand and colonize to the Pacific and beyond. By Woodrow Wilson's day, this belief had evolved into a vision of spreading democracy and a liberal capitalist order around the globe.

Russia, too, had steadily gained territory throughout its history. Under a succession of tsars, an elaborate centralized bureaucracy had ruled a growing empire comprising an array of peoples and languages. Only a firm controlling hand, the tsars believed, could hold this vast domain together. As in America, many Russians viewed their nation as specially favored by God. To millions of serfs, the tsar was almost a deity. After the reign of Peter the Great (1689–1725) and his policy of forced "Westernization," educated Russians looked to Europe, borrowed Western technology, and emulated Western culture. At the same time, however, Russian writers and intellectuals warned of the lure of cosmopolitanism. Glorifying the Russian soul, they urged defense of the sacred homeland from intrusion. Memories of Napoleon's failed invasion in 1812, when Russia's armies and its people had heroically thrown back the foreign foe, evoked patriotic pride. Yet while displaying strong expansionist tendencies under such rulers as Catherine the Great (1763–1796), Russia also endured nagging self-doubt, severe internal weaknesses, a backward economy, and chronic feelings of insecurity. These problems worsened in the nineteenth and early twentieth centuries as a series of reactionary tsars subjected the realm to despotic rule.

When Europe plunged into World War I in 1914, Russia under Nicholas II joined the Allies and declared war on Germany. But after the Bolshevik Revolution of 1917, the communist rulers of the new Soviet Union headed by V. I. Lenin denounced the conflict as a struggle among imperialists. Signing a separate peace with Germany, they proclaimed their primary goal: the overthrow of world capitalism. In 1918 President Woodrow Wilson ordered some ten thousand U.S. troops to the Soviet Union as part of a fourteen-nation force charged with protecting Allied war matériel and preventing Germany from occupying the Soviet Union's Baltic ports. The Western troops, however, also aided Russian counterrevolutionary elements seeking to overthrow the Bolsheviks. Not until 1920 did the U.S. troops depart. Later, Soviet propagandists would hark back to the events of 1918–1920 as proof of the encircling capitalist powers' malicious intentions.

Between World Wars I and II, most Americans, including Washington officialdom, viewed the Soviet regime, with its announced goal of overthrowing capitalism, as a clear threat to U.S. security interests. The Red Scare that swept America in 1919–1920, leading to the deportation of several hundred radicals, was a direct byproduct of the Bolshevik Revolution. The United States did not even grant diplomatic recognition to the Soviet Union until 1933, when President Franklin D. Roosevelt took this step toward normalizing relations.

American aversion to Moscow and its program of fomenting world revolution diminished during World War II, when the two nations joined forces against Nazi Germany. President Roosevelt, although cautiously hoping for postwar accord with the Soviets, never forgot that "a dictatorship as absolute as any . . . in the world" ruled in Moscow. He tried to hide from the Soviets the war's supreme secret, the atomic-bomb project, but Stalin learned of the Manhattan Project anyway through espionage and secretly began his own program to develop the bomb. British prime minister Winston Churchill, for his part, never doubted Stalin's duplicity and urged Roosevelt to beware of the Soviet dictator. The cynicism of the Nazi-Soviet Pact, not to mention Stalin's wartime massacre of thousands of Polish officers in Katyn forest and subsequent effort to pin the blame on the Nazis, lent powerful credence to Churchill's suspicions.

The Soviet Union's postwar outlook reflected its ghastly wartime losses: more than 6 million soldiers dead and 14 million injured. The toll in the Battle of Stalingrad alone was greater than U.S. combat casualties for the entire war. Civilian deaths in the Russian, Ukrainian, and Byelorussian republics, invaded by the Nazis, mounted to incalculable levels. Additionally, enormous physical destruction, homelessness, and malnutrition deepened the Soviets' fierce concern with border security and roused a grim determination that their wartime enemies would never again pose a threat. As Ambassador Harriman cabled the State Department early in 1945, "The overriding consideration in Soviet foreign policy is the preoccupation with 'security' as Moscow sees it." Moscow's wartime foes included not only Germany but nearby Finland, Hungary, and Romania, which had joined the Nazis in attacking the Soviet Union. Bulgaria, too, had allied with Hitler. As the war ended, Moscow expressed its determination to establish a buffer zone in the Eastern European territories held by the Red Army. As Soviet forces rolled across Eastern Europe and into Germany, Western allies protested, then watched nervously.

World War II roused other tensions as well. As the Red Army had grappled with the invading Nazis, Stalin had repeatedly called on his Western partners to launch the invasion that would compel Hitler to divert his forces westward; indeed, this call for a second front became Stalin's most insistent wartime theme. The United States and Great Britain kept promising to comply but waited until 1944 to act. The delay became a source of festering resentment and deepened the Soviet dictator's conviction that the Western democracies had violated his trust.

Sources of conflict were thus already in place when World War II ended in August 1945. Yet Americans were investing great faith in the ability of a new international organization. After World War I, the United States had spurned the League of Nations despite Woodrow Wilson's pleas, but now it would remedy that mistake. The Senate quickly ratified the UN Charter adopted at the San Francisco conference of June 1945. "We have learned from experience," Secretary of State James F. Byrnes told the UN in January 1946, and he pledged America's "wholehearted cooperation."

Internationalist dreams withered, however, with a series of confrontations. The first of these focused on Eastern Europe. Americans—many of whom traced their ethnic roots to this region—had long supported the aspirations of Eastern Europeans for independence and freedom from domination by their powerful neighbors. These hopes had briefly flowered after World War I, but the coming of World War II had squelched them. As the war in Europe wound down early in 1945, U.S. leaders as well as those in London and other Western capitals, already seeking to rebuff Soviet expansionism, deemed independence for the nations of Eastern Europe a prime strategic objective. The West viewed Stalin's determination to control Eastern Europe as clear evidence of imperialist intent, reinforced by an ideology of world revolution, that boded ill for world peace. From Moscow's perspective, however, the United States and Great Britain, now possessing the atomic bomb, seemed poised to pursue the quest for raw materials and markets that, according to Marxist doctrine, the capitalist world required. Age-old Russian fears of encirclement helped to shape—and to skew—Moscow's view of postwar realities. Soviet control of Eastern Europe, Stalin insisted, would serve as a counterweight to America's overwhelming economic and military superiority.

The grim chess game that would determine Eastern Europe's fate initially centered on Poland. The Allies had a strong emotional investment in restoring freedom to that country, which Stalin and Hitler had callously divided between them in 1939 and which had suffered first under the Nazis and then under the advancing Red Army. The Soviet army had even deliberately halted on the outskirts of Warsaw in the late summer of 1944, just as an uprising by Polish insurgents engulfed the city, allowing the Nazis to kill the maximum number of Poles before continuing their retreat to Germany. Furthermore, throughout the war, a Polish government-in-exile had functioned in London. When Roosevelt and Churchill insisted at Yalta that Stalin permit free elections in Poland, he retorted, "The Prime Minister has said that for Great Britain the question of Poland is a question of honor. For Russia it is not only a question of honor, but of security. . . . During the last thirty years our German enemy has passed through this corridor twice." Despite Stalin's vague pledge to support democracy in Poland, the Soviets installed a pro-Soviet puppet government in

Warsaw, barred free elections, and barely acknowledged the Polish government-in-exile in London.

Stalin then moved to tighten his grip elsewhere in Eastern Europe. Within weeks of the Yalta Conference, the Soviets pressured King Michael of Romania to appoint a communist-led government, and they reoccupied Latvia, Estonia, and Lithuania, three territories that they had annexed in 1940 and then lost to Hitler's armies. In mid-1945, Prime Minister Churchill, foreshadowing his famous "iron curtain" speech of 1946, complained to Stalin that an "iron fence" was rising across Europe. "All fairy tales," Stalin scoffed. Moscow tolerated a degree of political autonomy in Hungary and Czechoslovakia until 1948, but the prospects for autonomy and freedom in Eastern Europe looked bleak in 1945–1946.

An assessment of the Soviet Union's postwar actions and the West's response must be based on the fact that the U.S.S.R. was a one-party state under the absolute rule of one man, Joseph Stalin. Born Josif Visarionovich Dzhugashvili in 1879, the son of a Georgian shoemaker, he studied for the priesthood but was expelled for insubordination. In his mid-twenties, he joined the communist cause and adopted the name "Stalin" ("Man of Steel"). He rose in the party and entered the cabinet after the 1917 revolution. Stalin joined the triumvirate that ruled after Lenin's death in 1924, and from this position he soon gained sole power. In the Moscow purge trials of the later 1930s, he ruthlessly eliminated former comrades and potential rivals. Marx had prophesied that the state would wither away under communism, but under Stalin the Soviet government grew all-powerful; no tsar ever wielded power more absolutely or more brutally. Millions of peasants died under Stalin's program of forced collectivization. As the symbol of resistance against the German invaders, Stalin achieved almost mythic status during World War II. After 1945 a cult of personality, promoted by a vast propaganda machine, grew up around him. Despite his standing, however, paranoid fears assailed him before his death in 1953. "He saw enemies everywhere," his daughter Svetlana later would write. This, then, was the ruler and the state that Western leaders confronted in the early Cold War years. Soviet foreign policy cannot be separated from Stalin's terrorist rule. As diplomatic historian Robert H. Ferrell has written, "Stalin almost needed a foreign enemy in order to tighten his control upon the Russian people."

Communist ideology, too, played a role in shaping Moscow's postwar strategy. Karl Marx's prediction of communism's inevitable triumph lent a certain rhetorical coherence to Soviet policy. However, balance-of-power calculations, territorial ambitions, and security fears (legitimate or not) took top priority. Stalin's postwar course, although cautiously executed, followed a long tradition of Russian imperialism, but an imperialism whose limits were hard to discern. Shrouded in secrecy and suspicion, Stalin seemed unable to delimit the state's legitimate security concerns precisely. With maddening inconsistency, he clamped down on some countries while leaving others relatively free. The Soviet leader not only imposed absolutist rule on Eastern Europe; he sought to expand Soviet influence in Western Europe and elsewhere. It was this ill-defined expansionist impulse, not Moscow's justifiable security objectives, that alarmed and alienated the West.

In Washington, the challenge of responding to Stalin's postwar probes and

President Truman with Prime Minister Winston Churchill and Premier Joseph Stalin, July 1945. Barely three months after becoming president, Truman traveled to the Berlin suburb of Potsdam for the last of the Allied leaders' wartime conferences. The smiles and handshakes masked deepening differences. (*Imperial War Museum*)

feints fell to President Truman, a novice in foreign policy. After twelve years of FDR's patrician accent and larger-than-life image, Americans were only slowly adjusting to Truman's flat Missouri twang and folksy style. A farm lad whose poor eyesight had excluded him from boyhood games and from West Point, Truman had served in World War I and had failed as owner of a Kansas City men's store before winning election as a county executive in 1922. His political rise—chief county administrator in 1926, U.S. senator in 1934—had been hardly meteoric. "I look just like any other fifty people you meet in the street," he once observed of himself. Nevertheless, the same weak vision that had limited Truman's activities had also turned him into an omnivorous reader with a love of American history. He had won respect, although not fame, as chair of a Senate committee investigating waste in wartime military procurement. Now he was a world leader.

In diplomatic exchanges, Truman tended toward cocky self-assurance and snap judgments, comparing Stalin to Boss Tom Pendergast of Kansas City, his early political mentor, and he concluded early that Stalin understood only force and blunt language. Soviet expansiveness, coupled with Truman's short-fuse temper, led to volatile early encounters. Outraged by Stalin's failure to hold free elections in Poland, Truman in April 1945, only a few days after becoming president, delivered such a tongue-lashing to visiting Soviet foreign minister V. I. Molotov that, according to Truman, Molotov sputtered, "I have never been talked to like that in my life!" Truman allegedly retorted, "Carry out your agreements and you won't get talked to like that."

Stalin responded with equal vehemence, asserting his plan to impose a pro-Soviet communist regime on the Poles despite his earlier promises. "Poland borders ... the Soviet Union," he cabled Truman sarcastically, "[which] cannot be said of Great Britain and the United States." Stalin's stonewalling on Poland convinced Truman that only an equally tough Western response would deter Moscow's aggression.

A few Washington voices, including Secretary of War Henry Stimson and Army Chief of Staff George C. Marshall, urged a patient search for common ground with the Soviets. Stalin's actions were understandable, argued Stimson, in view of Soviet security concerns. Stimson even wrote later that the Soviets were "more realistic than we were in regard to their own security." This minority view, however, largely vanished from Truman's inner circle when the elderly Stimson retired in September 1945 and when Marshall left Washington in November on an extended mission to China.

1946: The Iron Curtain, Iran, Atomic Energy

In 1946 the dispute over Poland widened into a broader conflict that spilled across Eastern Europe, the Middle East, and the United Nations. *Pravda,* the propaganda voice of the Soviet regime, grew virulently anti-American, and from the White House to Main Street, American hostility toward the Soviets deepened. Early in the year, *Time* published a map portraying the "Communist Contagion" as a global epidemic. Iran, Turkey, and China were already "infected," warned *Time,* and Saudi Arabia, Egypt, Afghanistan, and India had been "exposed" and might sicken at any moment.

Two speeches early that year underscored the chasm opening between the wartime allies. The first, on February 9, 1946, was Stalin's belligerent address in the Soviet Union that blamed the capitalist nations for World War II and reaffirmed Moscow's determination to lead the struggle against Western imperialism. The war-weary Soviet people, Stalin announced, must achieve new feats of military production. His exhortation reverberated through Western capitals. Supreme Court justice William O. Douglas, a New Deal liberal, called the address "the Declaration of World War III." The second was delivered one month later, on March 5, 1946, by Great Britain's wartime prime minister, Winston Churchill, who had traveled to Fulton, Missouri—Truman's home state—to speak at tiny Westminster College. Stung by a recent electoral defeat, Churchill basked in his warm reception in America. As Truman sat behind him on the stage, Churchill bluntly warned of Soviet aggression, declaring:

> From Stettin in the Baltic to Trieste in the Adriatic, an iron curtain has descended across the continent. Behind that line lie all the capitals of the ancient states of central and eastern Europe. Warsaw, Berlin, Prague, Vienna, Budapest, Belgrade, Bucharest, and Sofia, all the famous cities and the populations around them lie in the Soviet sphere and all are subject, in one form or another, not only to Soviet influence but to a very high and increasing measure of control from Moscow.

The Soviets did not want war, advised Churchill; "What they desire is the fruits of war and the indefinite expansion of their power and doctrines." The response, he insisted, had to be unflinching resistance: "There is nothing [the Russians] admire so much as strength, and there is nothing for which they have less respect than military weakness." Eager to continue London's wartime alliance with Washington and to ensure the United States' inclusion of Great Britain as a partner in developing nuclear weapons, Churchill called for Anglo-American cooperation to resist this latest threat to Western civilization.

Americans revered Churchill, symbol of Britain's resistance to the Nazis, and his words carried great weight. Moreover, world events lent his claims credence: Stalin had unleashed his blast only a few weeks earlier, Poland and much of Eastern Europe lay prostrate under Moscow's heel, and a mood of crisis hung over Iran, as we shall see. Repeated and amplified by public leaders and the media, the "iron curtain" image and Churchill's larger themes entered the ideological arsenal of the early Cold War.

European leaders also urged Washington to take the lead in rallying the West against Soviet aggression. A British Foreign Office memo of March 1946 echoed in private what Churchill had proclaimed publicly: "If we cannot have a world community with the Russians as a constructive member . . . , the next best hope for peace and stability is that the rest of the world, including the vital North American arsenal, should be united in defense of whatever degree of stability we can attain."

As a response to threatening events and to Churchill's eloquence, a new ideological consensus coalesced across the United States. Republican senator Arthur Vandenberg of Michigan, head of the Senate Foreign Relations Committee and once a well-known isolationist, wrote in May 1946, "I am more than ever convinced that communism is on the march on a world-wide scale which only America can stop."

One prominent dissenter from this view was Truman's secretary of commerce, Henry Wallace. A New Dealer who had served President Roosevelt as secretary of agriculture and then as vice president, Wallace criticized what he saw as the needless stridency of Western leaders' anti-Soviet pronouncements. In a July 1946 memo to Truman, Wallace deplored "the irrational fear of Russia . . . being built up in the American people by certain individuals and publications." That September he went public with his ideas in an address at New York's Madison Square Garden, triggering a behind-the-scenes uproar in the administration. Secretary of State Byrnes, in Paris for a conference, cabled Truman: "You and I spent fifteen months building a bipartisan policy. We did a fine job convincing the world that it was a permanent policy upon which the world could rely. Wallace destroyed it in a day." Truman had approved Wallace's speech (although apparently without reading it carefully), but faced with Byrnes's fury, he demanded Wallace's resignation.

Against this backdrop of belligerent speechmaking and wrangling over the fate of Poland and Eastern Europe, conflict flared in Iran, long a cockpit of Big Power rivalry. For nearly 150 years, Russian and then Soviet leaders had coveted the warm-water ports of the Mediterranean and the Persian Gulf. In 1940 Soviet foreign minister Molotov had told the Nazi leaders candidly that Iran—rich in oil and a gateway to the Persian Gulf—was "the center of the aspiration of the Soviet Union." During

World War II, the British and Soviets had occupied Iran jointly, agreeing to withdraw six months after Germany's defeat. But Soviet troops remained stationed there into 1946, well beyond the six-month deadline, while Stalin sought to force from Tehran an agreement for joint Soviet-Iranian oil exploration in northern Iran. Stalin hoped to supplement the output of the Soviet Union's Baku oil field, where 1945 production, after years of war, stood at only 60 percent of the 1941 output.

The Red Army's failure to leave Iran posed a major security threat to the West and served as further confirmation to Truman of Stalin's perfidy. "I'm tired of babying the Soviets," he complained to Secretary of State Byrnes in January 1946. In March, Byrnes sent Moscow a strongly worded note demanding immediate Soviet withdrawal. The administration also brought the matter before the fledgling UN Security Council. By May, having extracted from Tehran a pledge of a joint oil-exploration treaty, the Soviets had departed. With the U.S.S.R.'s troops safely gone, Iran's parliament rejected the proposed treaty.

The Iranian crisis resolved, Western oil companies moved swiftly to secure Middle Eastern oil. In September 1947, the British-owned Anglo-Iranian Oil Company and two U.S. companies, Socony and Standard Oil of New Jersey, signed a twenty-year agreement to drill and market Iranian oil. The next year, following up on FDR's 1945 meeting with King Ibn Saud of Saudi Arabia, a consortium of four U.S. oil companies organized as Aramco (Arab-American Oil Company) concluded an oil agreement with the Saudis. At the same time, the American-owned Gulf Oil Company formed a partnership with a Netherlands company, Royal Dutch Shell, to refine Kuwaiti oil and market it in Europe. In short, by 1948 the corporate arrangements were in place for a massive flow of oil from the Middle East to Western Europe, the United States, and elsewhere in the noncommunist world. The Iran crisis thus not only helped to define the early Cold War but also figured in the continued jockeying among the industrialized powers for access to the region's precious resource.

A newer form of energy, derived from the splitting of the atom, molded early postwar diplomacy as well. Indeed, the beginnings of the Cold War coincided with the United States' four-year atomic monopoly, from 1945 to 1949. Wartime planners such as Secretary of War Stimson had realized the bomb's profound implications for postwar Soviet-American relations. When Truman learned of the successful Alamogordo test while at the Potsdam Conference in July 1945, he was, noted Stimson, "tremendously pepped up," showing an "entirely new feeling of confidence" in his dealings with Stalin. In meetings late in 1945 among Soviet, American, and British officials in London and Moscow, the Americans attempted to use U.S. atomic supremacy as a lever to influence Soviet behavior in Eastern Europe and elsewhere, but with disappointing results. Stimson, for one, warned against this heavy-handed atomic diplomacy. As early as September 1945, he wrote to Truman:

> I consider the problem of our satisfactory relations with Russia as not merely connected with but as virtually dominated by the problem of the atomic bomb. . . . These relations may be perhaps irretrievably embittered by the way in which we approach the solution of the bomb with Russia. For if we fail to approach them now

and merely continue to negotiate with them, having this weapon rather ostentatiously on our hip, their suspicions and their distrust of our purposes and motives will increase.

Stalin instantly grasped the bomb's importance for balance-of-power politics. Soon after Hiroshima, he directed Soviet scientists, "Provide us with atomic weapons in the shortest possible time. . . . Hiroshima has shaken the whole world. The equilibrium has been destroyed. Provide the bomb. It will remove a great danger from us." The atomic weapon in American hands fed the generalized fear of foreign menace and encirclement that lurked just beneath the surface in Moscow. The bomb, wrote Ambassador Harriman late in 1945, had "revived [the Soviets'] feeling of insecurity. . . . The Russian people have been aroused to feel that they must again face an antagonistic world. American imperialism is included as a threat to Russia." Lending substance to these fears, Secretary of State Byrnes had used veiled atomic threats at a foreign-ministers' conference held in London in September 1945 in an unsuccessful effort to pressure Moscow to ease its grip on Eastern Europe.

A combination of internationalist idealism and suspicion of Soviet intentions drove Washington's first, abortive efforts to devise a system of international control of atomic energy. Early in 1946, a State Department committee chaired by Undersecretary of State Dean Acheson and including David Lilienthal, head of the Tennessee Valley Authority in the New Deal, unveiled a plan for atomic-energy control under UN auspices. The Acheson–Lilienthal plan won wide praise in the American press, although a few critics dismissed it as a formula for a continued U.S. atomic monopoly. Under the proposal's terms, the United States reserved the right to build and stockpile atomic bombs until full implementation of a control plan acceptable to Washington. Doubts about American intentions intensified when Truman named the vain and fiercely anti-Soviet Bernard Baruch to conduct the atomic-energy negotiations at the UN.

Amid much publicity and hope, Baruch presented the U.S. plan, which he had revised and toughened, to the UN in June 1946. It called for creation of an international atomic development authority, free of the veto power of any nation, that would license and supervise the mining of uranium and thorium and the manufacture of fissionable material. Nations would be encouraged to explore the atom's peaceful uses but forbidden to make nuclear weapons. Any nation violating this ban would be subject to "condign [appropriate] punishment" under UN authority.

The Soviet Union's UN delegate, Andrei Gromyko, rejected the Baruch Plan as a scheme to serve U.S. interests. Talks ground on, but hopes for control of atomic energy soon faded. Some U.S. military planners quietly welcomed the failure of the effort, viewing the bomb as America's "winning weapon" in the emerging conflict with the U.S.S.R. General Dwight Eisenhower, writing Baruch in June 1946, cautioned against any plan that limited America's atomic-bomb-building capacity:

> For the present, I am sure you agree that there must be force behind any system for *preventing* aggression. There must exist for deterrent purposes, provisions for *retaliation* in the event other control and prevention devices should fail. . . . To my mind, this means for the present, that to *prevent* the use of atomic weapons there must exist

the capability of employing atomic weapons against the recalcitrant. . . . The existence of the atomic bomb in our hands is a deterrent, in fact, to aggression in the
world. We cannot at this time limit our capability to produce or use this weapon.

In the summer of 1946, during the UN debate, the United States conducted a
series of atomic tests at Bikini Atoll in the Pacific. (A French designer, introducing
a new line of women's swimwear, named one scanty number "the Bikini," adding a
new term to the fashion glossary.) The Bikini tests' timing actually reflected interservice rivalries between the navy and the air force rather than intentional atomic
diplomacy, but the Soviets nevertheless angrily denounced them as proof of
America's lack of seriousness about international control.

Later that year, in a memo to Truman, presidential adviser Clark Clifford
warned against disarmament negotiations "as long as the possibility of Soviet aggression exists" and called for an urgent military build-up, including readiness for
"atomic and biological warfare." Truman heeded this advice, which came from many
other quarters as well. By 1949, before the Soviets had exploded a single nuclear
weapon, the U.S. arsenal included about 150 atomic bombs, together with a growing
number of nuclear-capable bombers.

Thus, with victory celebrations still a vivid memory, the Cold War already dominated U.S. diplomacy by the end of 1946. The first half of the 1940s had witnessed
the bloodiest war in human history; as the second half unfolded, many sober observers feared the breakout of another full-scale conflict.

1947: The Truman Doctrine, Containment, and the Marshall Plan

The year 1947 brought influential statements of America's Cold War purposes as
well as major initiatives aimed at halting the spread of Soviet influence in war-torn
Europe. The first of the major policy pronouncements, the Truman Doctrine,
emerged from a crisis in Greece. An insurgency backed by Marshall Josip Broz Tito,
the communist ruler of neighboring Yugoslavia, and by the pro-Soviet puppet regimes of Albania and Bulgaria was battling Greece's corrupt, right-wing monarchy.
Great Britain, historically a key player in the eastern Mediterranean, had restored
Greece's monarchy in 1944 after expelling German, Bulgarian, and Italian occupation forces. But in February 1947, the economically strapped British informed Washington that they could no longer finance the Greek government's fight. The Soviet
Union, while tacitly backing the Greek insurgents, was also menacing Turkey's vital
Dardanelles strait, the waterway linking the Black Sea and the Mediterranean. Tsar-
ist Russia had long sought access to the Mediterranean for its Black Sea fleet. In
pressuring Turkey to share control of the Dardanelles through a system of joint bases,
Stalin had revived this long-term goal.

Alarmed U.S. and British strategists agreed that keeping Greece and Turkey in
the Western camp and the Soviet fleet out of the Mediterranean merited the highest
priority. President Truman favored military and economic aid to the two nations, but
congressional approval appeared far from certain. Opponents raised various objec-

tions. Leftists such as Henry Wallace, now a private citizen, continued to denounce the administration's bellicose tone toward the Soviet Union. Greece and Turkey, they pointed out, hardly stood as models of freedom and democracy. The strongest opposition, however, came from conservatives. Republican senator Robert A. Taft of Ohio warned against new global involvements. Some fiscal conservatives deplored the cost; others invoked traditional anti-British sentiments or predicted that aid to Greece and Turkey would lead to deeper, as yet unforeseen, foreign entanglements. Senator Walter George of Georgia, a respected Democratic elder statesman, cautioned against starting down a road whose end no one could predict. Democratic congressman Carl Vinson of Georgia, an administration supporter, scornfully dismissed the critics: "They don't like communism, but still they don't want to do anything to stop it. But they are put on the spot now and they all have to come clean."

At this delicate junction, Truman called congressional leaders to a White House meeting. Dean Acheson presented the administration's case in somber and sweeping terms. Greece, he intoned, was merely a bit player in a much larger drama: "Like apples in a barrel infected by the corruption of one rotten one, the corruption of Greece would infect Iran and all to the East . . . , Africa . . . , Italy, and France." "Not since Rome and Carthage," he concluded in clipped, assured accents, had there been "such a polarization of power on this earth." Senator Vandenberg, even more convinced that only America could halt communism's worldwide march, assured Truman that if he followed Acheson's lead and "scare[d] hell out of the country," Congress would surely support the aid request.

Adopting Vandenberg's advice, Truman addressed Congress on March 12, 1947. Requesting $400 million in aid to Greece and Turkey, he couched the issue in breathtakingly global terms that soon came to be called the Truman Doctrine. The world, he pronounced, must choose between two "alternative ways of life": democracy and freedom or totalitarianism, terror, and oppression. The implication was clear: The United States and the Soviet Union exemplified these two opposed philosophies. Wherever this struggle unfolded, the president declared, America must "support free peoples who are resisting attempted subjugation by armed minorities or by outside pressures." Rewarding Truman with a standing ovation, Congress passed the aid bill on a vote of 287–107 in the House, 67–23 in the Senate. Public-opinion polls strongly supported the aid request, and Truman's poll ratings shot up more than ten points. Democratic congressman Sam Rayburn of Texas, the House minority leader, declared:

> People who love liberty and cry for a fair chance want us to . . . lead the world. . . .
> If we do not accept our responsibility, if we do not . . . extend a helping hand to
> people who need and want help, who are democracies or want to be, who do not
> want to be smothered by communism, . . . [then] God help us; God help this world.

The aid program to resist Moscow's probes in the eastern Mediterranean succeeded. Soviet pressure on Turkey eased, and by 1949 the undemocratic Greek government, with U.S. help and the defection of Tito from the Soviet camp, had quashed the insurgents. Equally important, the Truman Doctrine contributed to a process by which legislators and the American people alike came to view specific confrontations with Soviet power as parts of an all-encompassing, primarily ideological global struggle. This process did not happen all at once. Unswayed by Truman's apocalyptic eloquence, more than one-third of both houses of Congress had opposed his request for aid. But the doubters notwithstanding, the ideological consensus forming about the worldview articulated by Churchill, Truman, Acheson, and many other opinion molders was rapidly gaining credence in Washington and the rest of the nation.

The most influential summation of early Cold War thinking was an essay, "The Sources of Soviet Conduct," that appeared in the July 1947 issue of the journal *Foreign Affairs*. The author, identified only as "X," soon became known: George Kennan, director of the State Department's policy-planning staff. The essay had a lengthy history. On February 22, 1946, Kennan, then a foreign-service officer in Moscow, had sent to Washington a secret "Long Telegram" summarizing his views of Soviet foreign policy. Amid a crescendo of ominous developments—the Iran crisis, Moscow's tightening grip on Eastern Europe, Stalin's alarming speech of two weeks earlier insisting on the inevitability of war with the capitalist powers—the scholarly Kennan had placed U.S.-Soviet relations in a broad historical and philosophical perspective. The telegram had deeply impressed Navy Secretary James V. Forrestal, who in 1947 became the nation's first secretary of defense.* One of the most passionate of the early Cold Warriors, the tight-lipped, rigidly self-controlled Forrestal circulated Kennan's telegram widely and became his loyal ally when Kennan moved from Moscow to the State Department.

Kennan's *Foreign Affairs* article, written at Forrestal's urging, expanded the 1946 "Long Telegram." In this more public forum, the essay proved highly influential in swaying opinion about the Soviet Union and the nature of the Cold War struggle. Soviet rhetoric, Kennan suggested, arose from "a traditional and instinctive Russian sense of insecurity." For historical and ideological reasons, Kennan argued, the Soviets were waging "a patient but deadly struggle" to expand their influence worldwide and to crush all rivals. The U.S. objective must be "a long-term, patient, but firm and vigilant containment of Russian expansive tendencies," a waiting game in which negotiation over specific issues would play little role.

Kennan's summation of America's mission distantly echoed nineteenth-century prophecies of the United States' manifest destiny. Americans should be grateful, he maintained, to "a Providence which, by providing [them] with this implacable challenge, has made their entire security as a nation dependent on their pulling themselves together and accepting the responsibilities of moral and political leadership that history plainly intended them to bear."

Kennan's views, summed up under the rubric "containment," crystallized Washington's Soviet policy. He urged the Truman administration to deploy its economic and military resources to prevent the Soviets from expanding beyond Russia's historic Eurasian sphere of influence. (A traditional balance-of-power diplomat, Kennan accepted spheres of influence as legitimate but their undue expansion as dangerous.) In many respects, Kennan's view constituted a prudent response to the

---

* Prior to 1947, the Department of Defense was known as the War Department, and the cabinet officer who ran it bore the title of Secretary of War.

threat posed by a nation ruled by a paranoid and unpredictable dictator. As head of the policy-planning staff until 1949, Kennan attempted to apply his broad strategic vision to specific areas of U.S.-Soviet confrontation. However, as Kennan himself soon recognized, some Cold Warriors, at least in their public pronouncements, ignored his emphasis on the cautious side of Soviet behavior. They also overlooked his call for patience and restraint—along with military strength—in dealings with the Soviets. Instead, they focused on the belligerent, menacing, and aggressive aspect of Moscow's complex approach to the external world. James Forrestal himself went far beyond Kennan in his obsession with the global communist menace. The navy secretary saw revolutionary conspiracies everywhere and offered nightmarish visions of "Russians swarming over Europe."* Forrestal's apocalyptic anticommunism demonstrated that Kennan's limited, cautious doctrine easily could mutate into a far more aggressive formulation of the nation's Cold War mission.

In the 1960s, deploring what he saw as the perversion of containment doctrine, Kennan would look back on his 1947 essay with "horrified amusement." It now reminded him, he wrote, of "one of those primers put out by alarmed congressional committees or by the Daughters of the American Revolution, designed to arouse the citizenry to the dangers of the Communist conspiracy." He also regretted his early failure to emphasize the difficulties that Moscow would face in trying to rule Eastern and Central Europe permanently, attributing this omission to "what I felt to be Mr. Forrestal's needs at the time when I prepared the original paper for him."

As Washington debated containment doctrine, Western Europe's postwar suffering persisted. The Truman administration's response led to the single most important initiative of the early Cold War era: the Marshall Plan. In early 1947, two years after hostilities ended, Europe still struggled in the grip of inflation, crippled industry, and near-famine conditions. A particularly fierce winter in 1946–1947 deepened the suffering. President Truman, recalling the period later in informal conversations with a journalist, spoke in characteristically down-to-earth language:

> The reports from Europe that I got in the winter and spring of 19 and 47.... It's easy to forget, but I doubt if things in Europe had ever been worse, in the Middle Ages maybe, but not in modern times. People were starving, and they were cold because there wasn't enough coal, and tuberculosis was breaking out. There had been food riots in France and Italy, everywhere. And as if that wasn't bad enough, that winter turned out to have been the coldest in history almost.

The political situation looked equally alarming. European Marxist parties seemed poised to exploit the crisis, with the goal of dragging the whole region into the Soviet orbit. The powerful French Communist party, for example, was quite Stalinist and doggedly loyal to Moscow. The grave problems plaguing Europe, wrote a *New York Times* reporter from Paris in February 1947, proved "the difficulty of treating postwar breakdown by democratic means. They reveal how battered and shaken are the old strongholds of democracy in Europe, and how few these strongholds are.

---

* Forrestal's demons eventually mastered him; he committed suicide in May 1949 while a patient at Bethesda Naval Hospital.

. . . [T]hey throw the ball to us, giving notice that if freedom as we understand it is to survive it's up to the United States to save it."

Against this ominous backdrop, the Truman administration offered a program of massive U.S. economic assistance to Western Europe. Drafted in the State Department, the plan was unveiled in a June 1947 commencement address at Harvard University by George C. Marshall, an aloof, self-disciplined, and highly respected former soldier who had replaced Byrnes as secretary of state the preceding January. A graduate of Virginia Military Institute and a career army officer, Marshall had served with distinction as army chief of staff during World War II.

While appealing to U.S. humanitarian impulses, Marshall also stressed the political issues at stake: "It is logical that the United States should do whatever it is able to assist in the return of normal economic health in the world, without which there can be no political stability or secure peace." The aid program, he insisted, was no mere Cold War stratagem: "Our policy is directed not against any country or doctrine but against hunger, poverty, desperation, and chaos. Its purpose should be the revival of a working economy in the world so as to permit the emergence of political and social conditions in which free institutions can exist."

Beyond the immediate goal of economic recovery, the administration harbored a larger political objective for the Marshall Plan: to promote European unity and to mute the ancient national rivalries that had ignited two major wars in the twentieth century. Only a united Europe, Marshall believed, could present a strong front against Soviet expansionism. To further this aim, the plan specified that the Western European nations should collaboratively draft a unified recovery program. In effect, the Marshall Plan's architects envisioned an American-style liberal capitalist order in Europe, where consumer abundance, economic integration, and a federative political system would dilute national conflicts and ideological differences and inoculate the masses against radical appeals from the Right or Left.

Marshall's proposal set off feverish political activity at home and in Europe. In Washington, despite conservative Republican grumbling about "an international WPA" and renewed warnings from the Left about the "Martial Plan's" anti-Soviet subtext, Congress funded a vast assistance program that by 1951 had channeled $13 billion in aid to Europe. On the Continent, the plan stimulated economic cooperation with profound long-term significance. To promote cooperation (and to win acceptance for the inclusion of Germany in the program), the Washington architects of the Marshall Plan insisted that aid not be distributed on a piecemeal, nation-by-nation basis but collectively as part of a general Europe-wide recovery strategy.

In the summer of 1947, sixteen European foreign ministers gathered in Paris to draft the European Recovery Plan (ERP). From these beginnings evolved the European Coal and Steel Community in 1952, the European Economic Community (the Common Market) in 1958, the collaborative atomic-energy program Euratom (also in 1958), and other joint ventures. By the early 1990s, Western Europe would integrate many of its economic and trade policies, and a United States of Europe would seem a distinct possibility. The Marshall Plan played a crucial role in stimulating this development.

Washington initially included the Soviet Union and Eastern Europe in the Marshall Plan, mainly as a public-relations gesture. The Truman administration assumed that the Soviet bloc would remain aloof, but somewhat to its surprise, Poland and Czechoslovakia showed great interest and tried to join the 1947 Paris talks. Stalin ordered them to withdraw, however. American plans for revitalizing Western Europe directly challenged the Soviet ruler's hope of expanded influence in the region, and the prospect of a thriving West Germany touched an always raw nerve. The Soviet embassy in Washington denounced the plan as a U.S. plot to restore Germany and Japan as major powers, only this time "subordinated to [the] interest of American capital." When Stalin personally ordered Czechoslovak prime minister Klement Gottwald to leave the Paris talks, Gottwald obeyed, visibly shaken by Stalin's rage.

In September 1947, Andrei Vyshinsky, the Soviet deputy minister for foreign affairs, blasted the Marshall Plan in a UN address. He complained that the plan bypassed the United Nations; would "split Europe into two camps"; denied European nations "their inalienable right . . . to plan their national economy in their own way"; and would make Western Europe subservient to "the interest of American monopolies, which are striving to avert the approaching depression by an accelerated export of commodities and capital to Europe." Stalin's decision to reject the Marshall Plan and other Western initiatives for postwar reconstruction, however, in fact underscored Europe's division into hostile camps.

Although Vyshinsky's analysis of the Marshall Plan's economic effect reflected his Marxist assumptions, he had a valid point. Along with its humanitarian and strategic purposes, the plan benefited American business. In 1947 U.S. exports to Europe neared $16 billion, whereas European exports to America totaled barely half as much. Europe thus had no dollars to pay for its imports. One immediate goal of the Marshall Plan was to provide the credit that would swell the transatlantic flow of U.S. goods. Indeed, U.S. trade and investment in Western Europe quickened sharply with economic recovery, and millions of dollars in Marshall Plan aid returned to America in the form of orders for industrial machinery, farm equipment, and other goods.

This trade stimulus influenced a larger pattern of rising U.S. exports. From 1946 to 1952, U.S. merchandise exports jumped from $9.5 billion to $15 billion. These years also saw growing corporate investment abroad. Such investments had sagged during World War II but gradually revived as large U.S. corporations developed multinational operations, built factories abroad, pursued foreign markets, and established distribution facilities. By 1950 foreign investment by U.S. corporations approached $12 billion.*

The Marshall Plan formed one component of a larger American effort to rebuild a world financial structure shattered by depression and war and to ease an acute postwar dollar shortage throughout the industrialized world. Planning for the new world economic order had actually begun in 1944, with a twenty-eight-nation monetary conference at an elegant old mountain-resort hotel at Bretton Woods, New Hampshire. From the Bretton Woods Conference emerged two important agencies: the International Bank for Reconstruction and Development, or World Bank,

---

* The major surge in overseas investment by U.S. corporations began in the mid-1950s. By 1960 such investment would total some $32 billion.

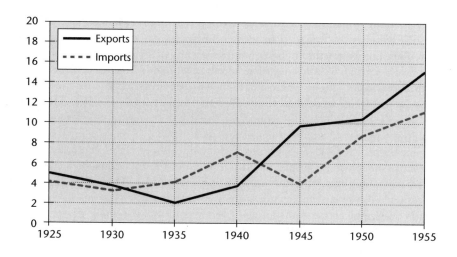

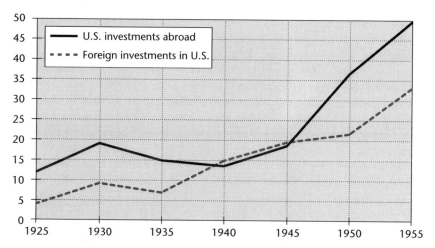

FIGURE 2.1

(a) U.S. Foreign Trade, 1940–1955, (b) Investments, 1925–1955

SOURCE: Adapted from *Historical Statistics of the United States* (Washington, D.C., 1975), pp. 537, 542, 564.

launched in 1945, and the International Monetary Fund (IMF), established in 1946. The World Bank served as a conduit for long-term capital transfers to help poor nations to develop their transportation, health, and education systems. The IMF promoted trade, monetary cooperation, and exchange-rate stability among the non-communist industrialized nations by creating a pool of currency reserves convertible at agreed-upon rates pegged to gold and the U.S. dollar. The IMF started with thirty-nine member nations; the Soviet Union, despite repeated invitations, refused to join. (In 1992, after the Cold War's end, Russia and other former Soviet republics would at last become members.)

The international monetary order that arose in 1944–1946, coupled with the Marshall Plan and U.S. foreign investment, helped to rebuild Europe's economy, create jobs, and better the living conditions of millions of people. It also laid the groundwork for a revival of world trade and the eventual emergence of a network of multinational corporations. These new financial structures strengthened the capitalist system, expanded world markets, and forestalled the economic chaos that would have provided fertile breeding ground for social unrest and communist gains. As such, they represented another front in the Cold War.

The deepening Cold War, besides drawing the United States into military and economic competition overseas, raised the stakes in the traditional budgetary and turf rivalry among the American military services at home. This jockeying for resources and power played a key role in military and strategic planning in the early postwar years. The air force, in particular, felt in danger of becoming, as one Pentagon official put it in May 1947, "a minor addendum to the war department." To address the problem, Congress in July 1947 passed the National Security Act. This measure created a new, high-level strategic planning body, the National Security Council (NSC), and set up the Central Intelligence Agency (CIA) to carry on the espionage operations of the wartime Office of Strategic Services (OSS). The law also combined the old army and navy departments, together with a newly independent air force, into the cabinet-level Department of Defense headed by a civilian secretary of defense and unified the military services under the Joint Chiefs of Staff. Bitter interservice struggles persisted, but under the pressure of the Cold War, the government had introduced greater coordination into the military establishment. The National Security Act also hastened the shift of foreign-policy formation and implementation from the State Department to the White House, a development that by the late 1960s and early 1970s would enable President Richard Nixon and National Security Adviser Henry Kissinger to ignore their secretary of state as they took sweeping foreign-policy initiatives.

By 1947 the fissures that had splintered the Grand Alliance were solidifying. That August, Charles E. Bohlen, a Soviet specialist in the State Department, gloomily assessed the new world order and sketched a scenario for U.S. foreign policy:

> The United States is confronted with a condition in the world which is at direct variance with the assumptions upon which, during and directly after the war, major United States policies were predicated. Instead of unity among the great powers—both political and economic—after the war, there is complete disunity between the Soviet Union and the satellites on one side and the rest of the world on the other. There are, in short, two worlds instead of one. . . . Faced with this disagreeable fact, . . . the United States in the interest of its own well-being and security and those of the free non-Soviet world must re-examine its major policy objectives. . . . [T]he non-Soviet world through such measures as are open to it [should] draw closer together politically, economically, financially, and, in the last analysis, militarily, . . . to deal effectively with the consolidated Soviet area. Only in this way can a free and non-Soviet world hope to survive in the face of the centralized and ruthless direction of the Soviet group.

In the months ahead, the fundamental policy reorientation that Bohlen advised would proceed with breathtaking speed.

1948–1949: The Prague Coup, the Berlin Airlift, and NATO

Moscow's grip on Eastern Europe tightened in February 1948, when Czech and Slovak communists overthrew Prague's fragile coalition government and installed a pro-Soviet communist regime. Soon after, Czechoslovak foreign minister Jan Masaryk, a national hero and friend of the West, died in a plunge from a foreign-ministry window. The country's new rulers rendered a verdict of suicide, but many in the West suspected murder. The Prague coup rang alarm bells in Western Europe and struck Washington as further compelling evidence of Stalin's implacable expansionism.

The sense of gathering crisis deepened that summer, with Germany the focus of attention. At the war's end, the Allies had divided Germany into four occupation zones: the Soviets in the east and the British, French, and Americans in the west. These zones, supposedly temporary, rapidly hardened into long-term political divisions as Moscow clamped down on eastern Germany and the Western powers combined their zones. The introduction of currency reform in early 1948, coupled with U.S. Marshall Plan aid, stimulated a dramatic economic recovery in West Germany. These moves formed part of a larger plan for making West Germany, which contained most of the country's population and industrial muscle, into an independent nation linked to the West.

Stalin, determined to stop this process, took Berlin hostage. Although the former German capital lay deep in the Soviet zone, the four powers governed it jointly and kept it open to access from the west. But on June 24, 1948, as the Western occupiers prepared to extend the currency reform to Berlin, the Soviets abruptly blocked all highway routes to the city. This action posed a major dilemma for President Truman: To smash through the Red Army's highway barricades could bring war, yet to abandon Berlin would make a mockery of the containment doctrine—and weaken Truman's chances in the forthcoming presidential election.

Treading a careful middle path, Truman ordered the U.S. Air Force to maintain a lifeline to Berlin. For the next 321 days, an armada of U.S. and British aircraft flew around the clock into Berlin's Templehof Airport, ferrying food, coal, and other necessities into the beleaguered city. At the airlift's peak, more than a hundred C-54 and C-47 transport planes made several round trips a day, eventually bringing in eight thousand tons of supplies. Grudgingly conceding defeat in May 1949, the Soviets reopened land access to Berlin. Within days, a new constitution launched the Federal Republic of Germany as a parliamentary democracy. In October, Soviet authorities set up the German Democratic Republic in the east.

The communist coup in Czechoslovakia and the Berlin crisis hastened plans for a Western military alliance. In the early postwar years, Washington planners had viewed the contest with the Soviet Union as primarily political and economic; the chances of an actual shooting war had seemed remote. As late as January 1948, George Kennan wrote to George Marshall, "The Soviet effort in Europe is a *political* one, not a *military* one." But in Europe itself, especially Great Britain, fears of a military showdown mounted. Early in 1948, British foreign secretary Ernest Bevin warned Washington of an encroaching "Soviet tide" and urged a military alliance between the United States and Western Europe for "the defense of Western civilization." With twenty-five Soviet divisions in Central Europe facing twelve underequipped divisions in Western Europe, these fears seemed well grounded.

Quietly, behind the scenes, the Truman administration built bipartisan support for an alliance linking the United States and Western Europe while the British pursued the same goal in Europe. In June 1948, Congress adopted, 64–4, a resolution that in principle approved U.S. security alliances with other nations. Talks proceeded, with Dean Acheson taking a leading role. In April 1949, a treaty-signing ceremony in Washington launched the North Atlantic Treaty Organization (NATO) joining the United States, Canada, and ten nations of Western Europe in a mutual defense arrangement: An attack on any member would be treated as an attack on all. The Senate ratified the treaty in July, 82–13. On the day that President Truman signed the treaty, he requested $1.5 billion in military aid for Western Europe. In September—the Soviets having exploded an atomic bomb in the interim—Congress approved Truman's request.

The ancient U.S. policy dating to the 1780s against peacetime foreign alliances had evaporated in the worsening international climate. NATO marked a key step in America's postwar emergence on the world stage and for the next four decades would symbolize Western resolve in the Cold War struggle. Like the Marshall Plan, NATO was intended to prevent a political fragmentation in Europe that would serve Moscow's interests. As Acheson observed, "Unity in Europe requires the continuing association and support of the United States. Without it, free Europe would split apart."

As the NATO pact moved toward approval, President Truman signaled a still greater expansion of America's global commitments. In his 1949 State of the Union message, he announced a new program of U.S. foreign aid to make "the benefits of our scientific advances and industrial progress available for the improvement and growth of undeveloped areas." Like the Marshall Plan, this Point Four program (it was the fourth point of the foreign-policy section of Truman's address) combined humanitarian, anticommunist, and economic objectives. By the early 1970s, the Agency for International Development (AID) had channeled over $100 billion in economic assistance to Latin America, Asia, Africa, and the Middle East to further economic development, to enhance political stability, and to forestall the spread of communism. Point Four assistance, together with other federal agencies such as the Export-Import Bank,* also promoted U.S. exports and foreign investment. Indeed, aid was sometimes tied directly to the recipients' purchase of U.S. manufactured goods or farm commodities.

By the close of 1949, the basic framework of the Cold War was firmly in place. In Moscow, fears of encirclement by "capitalist imperialism" were almost palpable; in some circles in the United States, the conviction that the Soviets harbored a grand design for world conquest had become an article of faith. "There is only one language

---

* The Export-Import Bank, a New Deal agency created in 1934, encouraged U.S. foreign trade by granting loans and credits to U.S. companies seeking to build foreign markets for agricultural commodities and manufactured goods.

FIGURE 2.2

Cold War Europe, 1950

[the Soviets] understand, force," declared Truman to an associate in 1949. George Kennan, leaving the State Department to return to private life, deplored the neglect of diplomacy amid a "general preoccupation with military affairs." Favoring the conduct of foreign affairs by a trained diplomatic elite, Kennan lamented the rhetorical excesses and "flamboyant anti-communism" by which the administration sought congressional and public support for its foreign-policy initiatives. After many years abroad, he was appalled by what he viewed as the vulgarity of American life in the late 1940s, and this broader distaste deepened his revulsion against the clangorous tenor of the Cold War debate.

Kennan's critics insisted that the picture of the world presented in Churchill's iron-curtain address, in the Truman Doctrine, and in countless speeches and editorials accurately reflected postwar realities. The Soviet Union *was* a brutal dictatorship; its military forces *did* prop up pro-Soviet regimes across Eastern Europe. Mao Zedong's triumph in China in 1949 (see p. 59) also seemed to confirm communism's global march. Compared to the Soviet sphere, the United States and many of its allies displayed an incomparably greater adherence to democratic values and individual freedom.

Nevertheless, Kennan had a point. The black-and-white globe portrayed by many early Cold War ideologists obscured the fact that many states of the "Free World"—Greece, Spain, Iran, South Africa, various military dictatorships in Latin America, and authoritarian regimes in the Middle East, for example—fell far short of the democratic ideal. Furthermore, several leading nations of the Western Alliance still held colonies in Africa and Asia. More important, the Truman administration's penchant for highlighting the ideological differences between the two systems, to the neglect of strategic and economic considerations, made it hard for diplomats to isolate specific, limited issues. The hypnotic allusions to the Soviets' alleged master plan of world rule obscured in a fog of verbiage the diplomatic processes by which Washington and Moscow might have reached accommodation on concrete issues in which each side had legitimate and conflicting interests.

In its internal strategic assessments, the White House understood that "the communist world" was not monolithic and that it faced varied stresses and tensions. (This fact had become starkly clear in 1948 when Marshall Tito, the communist ruler of Yugoslavia, broke with Moscow.) As historian Ralph Levering has noted, however, the Truman administration sometimes permitted "its obsession with the evils of communism to cloud its thinking." Some early Cold Warriors proved better at portraying the Soviet menace luridly than at pursuing the demanding, complex art of negotiation. In 1947, amid the crisis over Greece and Turkey, Dean Acheson had written, "[I]t is a mistake to believe that you can, at any time, sit down with the Russians and solve questions. I do not think that is the way that our problems are going to be worked out with the Russians." How would differences be resolved other than by negotiation? Acheson did not provide an answer.

Thus, in these early Cold War years, the nation that had invented pragmatism threatened to succumb to a rigidly ideological mind-set that impeded the practical resolution of specific issues. Some Cold War rhetoric even resembled theological disputation more than diplomatic exchange. The Truman administration's effort to build support for its national-security program by promulgating exaggerated and simplistic representations of world realities succeeded in its immediate purpose but impeded the longer-term goal of finding ways to ease tensions. With Soviet diplomacy proving even more inflexible under a dictator increasingly mired in paranoia, the conflict wore on.

Deeper into the Cold War: China, the H-Bomb, Korea

The rhetorical portrayals of a monolithic communist threat under Moscow's absolute control especially hobbled Washington's ability to understand and respond to developments in Asia. Late in 1949, after years of civil war, a communist government came to power in China. China's long struggle, dating to the late 1920s, had pitted the communist forces of Mao Zedong (Mao Tse-tung) against the proWestern government of Jiang Jieshi (Chiang Kai-shek). The conflict had abated somewhat during World War II as both sides turned their energies to expelling the Japanese invaders, but full-scale civil war had erupted again in 1945.

Jiang's regime was corrupt, massively inefficient, and increasingly unpopular. Rampant inflation further eroded its support. Meanwhile, communist organizers, heeding Mao's advice to move among the people like fish in a stream, built a base among China's peasants, who made up 80 percent of the population. Jiang's position steadily weakened as fighting ground on, and in 1949 the communists claimed victory. Jiang and what remained of his once-large army withdrew to the offshore island of Taiwan and established a regime that for the next quarter-century the United States would insist on recognizing as China's legitimate government.

Mao's triumph sent shockwaves across the United States. America's long and somewhat paternalistic interest in China, a legacy of the eighteenth-century New England China trade, had intensified with the activities of Christian missionaries to China. (Henry Luce, the publisher of *Time* and *Life* magazines, which vigorously espoused the Chinese Nationalist cause, was the son of missionaries to China.) China's role as an early victim of Japanese aggression in the 1930s had strongly appealed to American sympathies.

In the Chinese civil war, the United States had backed Jiang Jieshi, whom Roosevelt had superficially treated as a coequal during wartime meetings of the so-called Big Four. Although FDR had no illusions that China was a superpower, he hoped that a noncommunist China under Jiang Jieshi could replace Japan as a stabilizing force in postwar Asia. At the Yalta Conference, FDR, seeking to deprive the Chinese communists of Soviet aid, had persuaded Stalin to sign a treaty of friendship and alliance with Jiang. In return, Roosevelt supported restoration of the Soviet Union's prewar influence in Manchuria.

As the Nationalists' power crumbled, Washington's ties to Jiang became a growing liability. Unqualified U.S. support for him, the head of the State Department's Far Eastern division shrewdly predicted, would bring "only trouble, trouble, trouble." The victorious Mao Zedong established a new government, the People's Republic of

China, and early in 1950 signed a trade and mutual-assistance treaty with the Soviet Union. Moscow pledged to aid China in the event of an attack by Japan or any other foreign power.

To the casual observer, the Eurasian land mass from the Elbe River in Germany to the China Sea seemed one vast domain of communist power. In reality, as Washington officials well understood, deep differences rooted in history and geography divided Moscow and Beijing. Stalin and Mao distrusted one another profoundly, and the Soviet leader had given Mao virtually no help in the Chinese civil war. Even as he negotiated the 1950 treaty, Stalin had angled behind the scenes to restore Moscow's influence in Manchuria and Mongolia, objects of Russian imperialist attention since tsarist days. But for most Americans, "the world communist conspiracy" so beloved by Cold War orators seemed all too real. U.S. politics blazed with accusations over who had "lost" China.

On September 3, 1949, as climactic events unfolded in China, a U.S. B-29 aircraft patrolling the Pacific detected high levels of atmospheric radiation. Fulfilling Stalin's urgent command, Soviet scientists had developed and tested an atomic bomb. The United States' brief reign as the world's only nuclear power had ended. "This is now a different world," Senator Vandenberg wrote gloomily. The Soviet test triggered an intense debate in the inner circles of the Truman administration. Some advisers advocated a crash program to build the hydrogen bomb, an awesome doomsday weapon a thousand times more powerful than the atomic bomb. Physicist Edward Teller, long an advocate of the "Super," the H-bomb's nickname, urged this course. Opponents included the chairman of the Atomic Energy Commission (AEC), David Lilienthal, and most of the AEC's scientific advisory committee, chaired by physicist J. Robert Oppenheimer, who had headed the wartime Los Alamos project. These critics argued for a new effort at international control of atomic energy. But Truman rejected their advice and in January 1950 ordered full-scale research on the hydrogen bomb. In a public-opinion poll, 78 percent of Americans endorsed the decision. The post-Hiroshima fear of atomic war and support for international control had given way to a grim determination to maintain U.S. nuclear supremacy.*

The ominous developments of 1949 gave rise to NSC-68, an important formulation of Cold War strategy drawn up by the National Security Council. NSC-68 began as a planning document drafted in April 1950 by, among others, Paul Nitze, a hard-liner who had replaced George Kennan in the State Department's policy-planning office. Discerning in postwar events a Soviet master plan for global domination, NSC-68 envisioned "an indefinite period of tension and danger." "The Kremlin is inescapably militant," the document declared,

> because it possesses and is possessed by a worldwide revolutionary movement, because it is the inheritor of Russian imperialism and because it is a totalitarian dictatorship. Persistent crisis, conflict and expansion are the essence of the Kremlin's

---

* The United States exploded its first hydrogen device in November 1952, and the Soviet Union soon followed suit. By the mid-1950s, both sides were testing full-scale hydrogen bombs. For discussion of the nuclear arms race in the 1950s, see Chapter 4.

militancy. . . . [The American people] in the ascendancy of their strength stand in their deepest peril.

A few months later, as the Korean War raged, President Truman approved NSC-68 as official U.S. policy.

NSC-68 set the nation's strategic agenda for the 1950s and summed up a view of the Cold War, which would survive well into the 1960s, as an all-consuming global struggle. Although much evidence buttressed its scenario of a worldwide communist advance directed from Moscow, the document paid little heed to weaknesses or potential sources of division within the communist world, to strategies for reaching accommodation with the Soviets, or to trends in a complex world seething with change that did not fit its bipolar model. Foreseeing indefinite military confrontation between two nuclear-armed superpowers, NSC-68 called for massive increases in military spending to build up America's conventional and nuclear arsenal and to rearm NATO. Short of Soviet capitulation, which would come many dangerous years and many billions of dollars later, the document offered few hints for constructive steps that the United States might take to reduce hostilities.

Mao's victory helped to inspire NSC-68; it also focused U.S. attention on Asia, especially Indochina, where the French were fighting to maintain their colonial power against a nationalist insurgency led by the communist Ho Chi Minh. Ho had courted U.S. support, but the Truman administration, eager to ensure France's entrance into NATO, had rejected his overtures. In May 1950, Dean Acheson, who had replaced George Marshall as secretary of state in 1949, announced a small program of U.S. aid and military assistance to the French in Indochina. This decision initiated an involvement that fifteen years later would suck the United States into the most disastrous war of its history.

It was Korea, however, that soon dominated U.S. newspaper headlines. In 1945, ending forty years of Japanese rule, the United States and the Soviet Union had jointly occupied this country, with the 38th parallel demarking the two occupation zones. Both powers had withdrawn most of their troops by 1949, but, as in Germany, each continued to dominate its respective sector. In 1948, with U.S. support, the autocratic Syngman Rhee, elected South Korea's president that year, proclaimed the Republic of Korea, with its capital in Seoul. In the north, the Soviets set up their own client government in Pyongyang, headed by Kim Il Sung. Each regime was armed by its respective Big Power sponsor, and each claimed sovereignty over all Korea. The stage was set for confrontation.

Late in 1949, according to the memoirs of Nikita Khrushchev, who was a high government official under Stalin and later prime minister of the Soviet Union, Kim Il Sung asked for Stalin's approval to invade South Korea. Stalin at first held back, but when Kim persisted, the Soviet ruler agreed. Although Stalin did not order the attack, he may have hoped that Pyongyang could win control over all Korea, an outcome that, from Moscow's perspective, would have provided a counterweight not only to the United States and Japan but also to China, with which the Soviet Union's deep rivalries had persisted despite Mao's 1949 victory. Statements emanating from Washington that downgraded Korea's importance may also have encouraged Kim and Stalin. In a January 1950 speech, Secretary of State Acheson defined the U.S. defense perimeter in Asia in a way that excluded South Korea.* In May, Texas senator Tom Connally, chair of the Senate Foreign Relations Committee, dismissed Korea as of little importance given the United States' strong line of defense in Asia extending from the Philippines through Okinawa and Japan. America's rapid postwar demobilization and subsequent emphasis on nuclear rather than conventional military strength probably figured in Kim Il Sung's calculations that a move against South Korea was a risk worth taking.

On June 25, 1950, Soviet-armed North Korean troops stormed across the 38th parallel. Capturing Seoul and pushing southward, they soon pinned the South Korean defenders and a few U.S. troops within a small defensive perimeter around the southern port of Pusan. President Truman responded by ordering full-scale U.S. military action to expel the invaders. Korea was the Greece of Asia, he argued—a further test of America's will to contain Soviet-sponsored communist aggression. The United States also rushed the case to the UN Security Council. With the U.S.S.R.'s delegate absent because of a Soviet boycott, the council passed U.S. resolutions demanding North Korea's withdrawal and calling on member nations to aid South Korea. The conflict was thus fought under UN auspices, and the Truman administration dubbed it a "police action" rather than a war. Congress never formally declared war, as required by the Constitution, an additional example of the expansion of executive power in these early Cold War years. Under whatever flag, though, Americans, Koreans, and eventually the Chinese were by far the primary combatants.

General Douglas MacArthur, the World War II hero who had directed the U.S. occupation of postwar Japan, commanded the UN forces in Korea. On September 15, 1950, in a brilliant counter to North Korea's advance, MacArthur led a daring amphibious landing behind the enemy lines at Inchon, near Seoul. Simultaneously breaking out of the Pusan perimeter, MacArthur's forces swept across the 38th parallel and by the end of October had captured Pyongyang and advanced within fifty miles of the Yalu River, the boundary between Korea and the Chinese province of Manchuria. Washington now began to consider not merely repelling the invaders but overthrowing Kim Il Sung and uniting Korea under a noncommunist government. However, China warned that it would not "sit back with folded hands and let the Americans come to the border." MacArthur, dismissing this statement as "hot air," promised to have "the boys home by Christmas" after they had completed their sweep to the Yalu River. He also made the tactical error of dividing his strongest forces, with a weaker South Korean contingent in the middle.

MacArthur and the entire U.S. military command, as well as Acheson and Truman, had failed to anticipate a major Chinese invasion. On November 26, after several weeks of sporadic Chinese troop movements across the border, thirty-three Chinese divisions poured across the Yalu. Once more, the North Koreans, now massively reinforced by the Chinese, drove down the peninsula. Viewing the Korean fighting as a prelude to a larger struggle against communism in Asia, MacArthur urgently asked permission to widen the war by bombing Chinese bases in Manchuria and

---

* The defense of parts of Asia outside this perimeter, asserted Acheson, rested with "the entire civilized world," acting through the United Nations.

Korea, Winter 1950. U.S. marines retreating from North Korea's Changjin Reservoir after Chinese Communist forces entered the war in massive numbers. (*UPI/Bettmann Archive*)

"unleashing" Jiang Jieshi from his base on Taiwan for an invasion of the Chinese mainland.

President Truman and his military advisers rejected the general's request. With the Sino-Soviet alliance still in force, they feared that MacArthur's aggressive plan would trigger a third world war. Further, Washington strategists still saw Europe as the central Cold War arena and feared that a wider war in Asia would weaken the U.S. ability to respond to hostile Soviet moves in Europe. Truman also vetoed using atomic bombs in Korea, a course favored by about half the American people in public-opinion polls. In private jottings, however, which surfaced years later, Truman toyed with the idea of giving the Soviets a nuclear ultimatum. In December 1950, an alarmed British prime minister Clement Atlee flew to Washington, fearful that nuclear weapons in Korea might provoke Moscow to attack Western Europe and even launch an atomic offensive against Great Britain.

General MacArthur, meanwhile, pushing his proposals to the point of insubordination, gave media interviews and wrote a leading Republican congressman, Joseph Martin of Massachusetts, complaining of the restraints imposed on him by the White House. "Here in Asia is where the communist conspirators have elected to make their play for global conquest," MacArthur stormed. "Here we fight Europe's war with arms while the diplomats there fight it with words." In war, he summed up, "there is no substitute for victory." Senator Taft, *Time* magazine, and other influential voices endorsed MacArthur's call for a wider war.

Furious over MacArthur's open defiance of administration policy, Truman relieved him of his command on April 10, 1951. Despite his challenge to the constitutional subordination of the military to civilian authority, the seventy-one-year-old general, erect and imposing, returned to a hero's welcome. His reception reflected not only enthusiasm for a legendary warrior but public frustration with the Korean stalemate and an apparently endless Cold War struggle. Sixty-six percent of Americans initially opposed Truman's firing of MacArthur. On the day that New York City gave the general a ticker-tape parade, fans booed Truman when he threw out the first

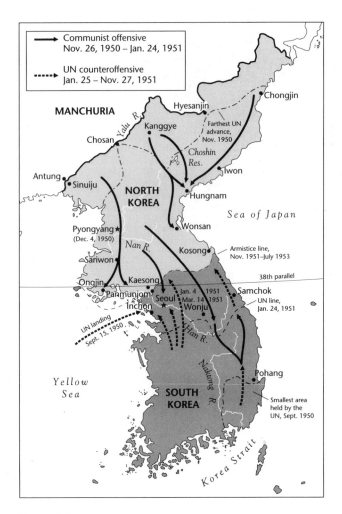

FIGURE 2.3
The Korean War, 1950–1953

ball on opening day of the baseball season at Washington's Griffith Stadium.* Thirty thousand letters, mostly critical of Truman, deluged the White House. A cartoon in the Republican *Chicago Tribune* portrayed Truman as a little boy in short pants, gazing up enviously at the larger-than-life profile of a heroic MacArthur, his trademark corncob pipe clamped firmly between his teeth.

To a joint session of Congress, MacArthur delivered an emotional address that ended with the words of a barracks ballad: "Old soldiers never die, they just fade away." His fans held congressional hearings to air his views, but Truman countered

---

* In 1951 the nation's capital still had a big-league baseball team, the Washington Senators.

Cartoonists had a field day with President Truman's unpopular decision to relieve General MacArthur of his command in Korea. Eventually most historians would endorse Truman's action as wise and courageous. (*Leo Joseph Roche, courtesy* Buffalo Courier Express)

with General Omar Bradley, another war hero and chairman of the Joint Chiefs of Staff. Bradley testified that MacArthur's strategy would "involve us in the wrong war, at the wrong place, at the wrong time, and with the wrong enemy." Public support for MacArthur wilted as Americans had sober second thoughts about the issues at stake, and the general soon faded away, as predicted.

In Korea, armistice talks began in July 1951, but the fighting dragged on for two more years, taking a heavy toll of lives and dogging the Democrats in the 1952 campaign. The U.S. defense budget, fueled by Korean War spending as well as by the military build-up outlined in NSC-68, surged to $44 billion by 1952 and $50 billion in 1953, up sharply from the 1946–1949 levels of about $13 billion annually.

Even as the Korean war raged, Cold War strategists never lost sight of Europe. In April 1950, the administration had begun to plan the rearmament of West Germany within a NATO framework. The aim was less to repel a Soviet invasion, which few expected, than to ensure West Germany's integration into the European community. When Dean Acheson proposed the idea in September, Great Britain, France, and the other NATO powers, with war memories still fresh, angrily protested. To sweeten the proposal, Truman in December appointed General Dwight Eisenhower commander of SHAPE (Supreme Headquarters, Allied Powers in Europe), NATO's new integrated command structure.

Truman also pledged to send four more U.S. divisions to Europe, joining the two already there. Senator Taft and others sharply attacked the plan, but Congress eventually approved it. The NATO ministers in December 1950 agreed in principle to the integration of German forces in a joint defense force. Not until 1955, however, over die-hard French resistance, did West Germany formally join NATO. In March 1952, the Soviet Union called for a Big Power conference to discuss German reunification. Whether this request was a propaganda ploy or a serious proposal aimed at preventing West German rearmament may never be known; Dean Acheson rejected the proposal out of hand.

As additional U.S. divisions flew to Europe, NATO military strategizing proliferated, including plans for a nuclear response if the Soviets attacked. Greece and Turkey entered NATO in 1952. Turkey, on the Soviet Union's border, bristled with an imposing armada of U.S.-supplied air power, including 180 F-47 fighter planes, 30 B-26 bombers, and 81 C-47 cargo planes.

Cold War ideology, somewhat open to debate in the late 1940s, rigidified after Korea. Beset by Republicans who smelled victory in '52, the administration redoubled its efforts to prove itself "tough on communism." A similar intransigence gripped Moscow, where the aging, fear-ridden Stalin still ruled. George Kennan, appointed ambassador to the Soviet Union in 1952, found vitriolic anti-Americanism among Soviet leaders. In his memoirs he would later write, "I began to ask myself whether . . . we had not contributed, and were not continuing to contribute—by the overmilitarization of our policies and statements—to a belief in Moscow that it was war we were after." Kennan understated the degree to which the Soviet Union's own actions bore responsibility for the frigid climate of 1952, but his assessment of the dismal state of relations was on the mark. From their wartime alliance against a common foe, Washington and Moscow had become bitter enemies.

CONCLUSION

For years, diplomatic historians hotly debated the origins of the Cold War, some echoing Washington's version of events and placing the blame entirely on Moscow, others rejecting this position. Some revisionists, glossing over the dark side of Stalin's regime, found the United States almost wholly culpable and the Soviet Union essentially blameless. Viewing history through the reductionist prism of economic determinism, some Marxist historians portrayed American Cold War policies as dictated solely by capitalism's global search for raw materials, markets, and investment opportunities.

Gradually, however, a consensus among historians emerged that reemphasized the serious challenges the United States and Western Europe faced after the war and the merits of the responses devised by statesmen of the era. John Lewis Gaddis's thoughtful *The Long Peace: Inquiries into the History of the Cold War* (1987), although far from uncritical of U.S. Cold War policy, stresses the remarkable stability in U.S.-Soviet relations through their long confrontation. Writing in the mid-1980s, before the Cold War's end, Gaddis observed:

> Given all the conceivable reasons for having had a major war in the past four decades—reasons that in any other age would have provided ample justification for such a war—it seems worthy of comment that there has not in fact been one. . . . The Cold War, with all of its rivalries, anxieties, and unquestionable dangers, has produced the longest period of stability in relations among the great powers that the world has known in this century; it now compares favorably as well with some of the longest periods of great power stability in all of modern history.

Although the "stability" of Gaddis's "long peace" saw bloody conflict in Korea, Vietnam, and elsewhere and a potentially deadly nuclear arms race, his point merits recognition in any assessment of U.S. Cold War policy.

Melvyn Leffler's A Preponderance of Power: National Security, the Truman Administration, and the Cold War (1992) is moderately revisionist but concedes the reality of the Soviet threat. It was not the risk of global war or even of a Soviet invasion of Western Europe that most troubled Cold War strategists but the danger of Moscow's extending its influence by subversion, economic means, or electoral victories by local communist parties. Leffler credits Washington for shaping a diplomacy that ensured Western Europe's recovery and the emergence of Germany and Japan as healthy democracies allied to the West while containing the Soviet threat. Rejecting the caricature of U.S policymakers as warmongering imperialists, Leffler portrays them for the most part as prudent, responsible leaders intent on protecting American security interests as they understood those interests. He concludes that American diplomacy in the Truman years "helped to force a configuration of power in the industrial core of Eurasia that continues to safeguard vital U.S. interests."

But Leffler, like George Kennan, also finds many misjudgments and lost opportunities in the formulation and execution of U.S. postwar policy. For example, he sees a persistent tendency to denigrate the value of diplomacy in resolving Cold War issues, to exaggerate rhetorically the danger of all-out Soviet attack, and to downplay the caution that often characterized Soviet policy. He also documents simplistic, inflated views of Moscow's global power and a consequent inattention to the indigenous sources of social unrest, anticolonialism, and nationalistic fervor seething in many parts of the world. This myopia, he and others suggest, ultimately led to America's disastrous intervention in Vietnam.

Historians continue to analyze the origins of the Cold War and to emphasize the important fact that the two sides avoided global war. Nevertheless, few question the degree to which the conflict became all-consuming for both sides or the risks that it posed for humanity. That the Cold War arose just as nuclear weapons entered the world sharply heightened those risks. Indeed, the convergence of these two developments, one political and the other technological, may not have been mere coincidence. The existence of the ultimate weapon may have encouraged both sides' tendency to identify the Cold War adversary as the ultimate enemy.

Yet the bomb, for all its terrors, may in fact have helped to prevent the Cold War from escalating into world war. The specter of nuclear holocaust and the fear of reprisal pulled the superpowers back from the brink. President Truman had early recognized this paradox. As the Soviets maneuvered menacingly in Iran and Eastern Europe in late 1945, an adviser tried to lift his spirits by commenting, "Mr. President, you have an atomic bomb up your sleeve." Truman replied, "Yes, but I'm not sure it can ever be used." John Lewis Gaddis, exploring the reasons for what he called the long peace, claimed in 1987, "It seems inescapable that what has really made the difference in inducing this unaccustomed caution has been the workings of the nuclear deterrent. . . . [T]he development of nuclear weapons has had, on balance, a stabilizing effect on the postwar international system."

Although the horror of nuclear weapons severely constrained their use, the risk of nuclear war nevertheless terrified many Americans in these years. In 1947, concluding a report on the air-war aspects of World War II, General H. H. ("Hap") Arnold, chief of the U.S. Army Air Force, reflected on the future. The combination of atomic bombs and guided missiles (another legacy of World War II), he cautioned, would make the United States infinitely more vulnerable in any future global war. "Without warning," wrote Arnold, nuclear-armed missiles could "pass over all formerly visualized barriers or 'lines of defense' and . . . deliver devastating blows at our population centers and our industrial, economic, or governmental heart." Reiterated time and again by many others, Arnold's somber warning deeply penetrated the American psyche and held in check any impulse to push the frustrating Cold War impasse beyond the point of no return.

Quite apart from the nuclear arms race, the Cold War by the early 1950s had led to an arms build-up of unprecedented peacetime magnitude. Military historian Walter Millis observed in 1951 that one of the Truman administration's principal legacies was "an enormously expanded military establishment, beyond anything we had ever contemplated in time of peace." This expansion, he continued, had called forth "a huge and apparently permanent armament industry now wholly dependent . . . on government contracts." Yet, Millis reflected, the administration seemed unsure about the long-term objectives of its heavily militarized strategy or how the Cold War might be brought to closure. And every dollar appropriated for military purposes meant one dollar less for domestic social needs.

Nuclear fear and the rise of a vast peacetime military establishment were only two of many ways by which the Cold War seeped from the White House, the State Department, and the Pentagon into the fabric of U.S. society and into the lives of an entire generation of Americans. The Cold War, whose beginnings young Kathleen Harriman had watched during those bleak March days of 1945 in Moscow, had America in its grip.

SELECTED READINGS

The Early Cold War: General Studies

Stephen E. Ambrose, *Rise to Globalism: American Foreign Policy Since 1938* (1991); Terry H. Anderson, *The United States, Great Britain, and the Cold War, 1944–1947* (1981); Barton J. Bernstein, "American Foreign Policy and the Origins of the Cold War," in Bernstein, ed., *Politics and Policies of the Truman Administration* (1970); Thomas H. Etzold and John L. Gaddis, eds., *Containment: Documents on American Policy and Strategy, 1945–1950* (1978); John L. Gaddis, *The United States and the Origins of the Cold War, 1941–1947* (1972), *Strategies of Containment: A Critical Appraisal of Postwar American National Security Policy* (1982), and *The Long Peace: Inquiries into the History of the Cold War* (1987); Lloyd C. Gardner, *Architects of Illusion: Men and Ideas in American Foreign Policy, 1941–1949* (1970); James L. Gormly, *The Collapse of the Grand Alliance, 1945–1948* (1987); Walter Isaacson and Evan Thomas, *The Wise Men: Six Friends and the World They Made* (1986); Michael J. Lacey, ed., *The Truman Presidency*, Part II, "Foreign Policy and National Defense" (1989); Walter LaFeber, *America, Russia, and the Cold War, 1945–1984* (1985); Melvyn Leffler, *A Preponderance of Power: National Security, the Tru-*

man Administration, and the Cold War (1992); Melvyn Leffler and David S. Painter, eds., The Origins of the Cold War: An International History (1994); Robert L. Messer, The End of an Alliance: James F. Byrnes, Roosevelt, Truman, and the Origins of the Cold War (1982); Thomas G. Paterson, On Every Front: The Making of the Cold War (1979); Ronald Steel, Pax Americana (1967); Adam B. Ulam, The Rivals: America and Russia Since World War II (1971) and Expansion and Coexistence: The History of Soviet Foreign Policy, 1917–1973 (1974); Samuel Walker, Henry A. Wallace and American Foreign Policy (1976); Daniel Yergin, Shattered Peace: The Origins of the Cold War and the National Security State (1977).

Nuclear Policy; Postwar Diplomacy in Europe and the Middle East

Barton J. Bernstein, "Truman and the H-Bomb," Bulletin of the Atomic Scientists (March 1984); Michael J. Cohen, Truman and Israel (1990); William C. Cromwell, "The Marshall Plan, Britain, and the Cold War," Review of International Studies (October 1982); Lynn Etheridge Davis, The Cold War Begins: Soviet-American Conflict over Eastern Europe (1974); Lawrence Freedman, The Evolution of Nuclear Strategy (1981); James F. Good, The United States and Iran, 1946–1951 (1989); Fraser J. Harbutt, The Iron Curtain: Churchill, America and the Origins of the Cold War (1986); Gregg Herken, The Winning Weapon: The Atomic Bomb in the Cold War, 1945–1950 (1980); Michael Hogan, The Marshall Plan (1987); Timothy P. Ireland, Creating the Entangling Alliance: The Origins of NATO (1981); Ethan B. Kapstein, Insecure Alliance: Energy Crises and Western Politics Since 1944 (1989); Jon V. Kofas, Intervention and Underdevelopment: Greece During the Cold War (1989); Bruce R. Kuniholm, The Origins of the Cold War in the Near East (1980); Geir Lundestad, America, Scandinavia and the Cold War, 1945–1949 (1980); David S. Painter, Oil and the American Century: The Political Economy of U.S. Foreign Oil Policy, 1941–1954 (1986); Robert A. Pollard, Economic Security and the Origins of the Cold War, 1945–1950 (1985); David Alan Rosenberg, "American Atomic Strategy and the Hydrogen Bomb Decision," Journal of American History (June 1979); Martin J. Sherwin, A World Destroyed: The Atomic Bomb and the Grand Alliance (1975); Avi Shlaim, The United States and the Berlin Blockade (1983); Lawrence L. Wittner, American Intervention in Greece, 1943–1949 (1982); Daniel Yergin, The Prize: The Epic Quest for Oil, Money and Power (1991).

The Korean War and the Cold War in Asia

Barton J. Bernstein, "New Light on the Korean War," International History Review (April 1981); Clay Blair, The Forgotten War: America in Korea, 1950–1953 (1988); Robert M. Blum, Drawing the Line: The Origins of the American Containment Policy in East Asia (1982); Russell D. Buhite, Soviet-American Relations in Asia, 1945–1954 (1982); Ronald J. Caridi, The Korean War and American Politics: The Republican Party as a Case Study (1969); Bruce Cumings, Child of Conflict: The Korean-American Relationship, 1943–1953 (1983); Roger Dingman, "Atomic Diplomacy During the Korean War," International Security (Winter 1988–89); John K. Fairbank, The United States and China (1979); Rosemary Foot, The Wrong War: American Policy and the Dimensions of the Korean Conflict (1985); Lloyd C. Gardner, Approaching Vietnam: From World War II Through Dienbienphu (1988); June Grasso, Harry Truman's Two-China Policy (1987); Jon Halliday and Bruce Cumings, Korea: The Unknown War (1988); Gary Hess, The U.S. Emergence as a Southeast Asian Power (1986); Akira Iriye, The Cold War in Asia (1974); Burton I. Kaufman, The Korean War: Challenges in Crisis, Credibility, and Command (1986); Ernest R. May, The Truman Administration and China, 1945–1949 (1975); Andrew J. Rotter, The Path to Vietnam: Origins of the American Commitment to Southeast Asia (1987); Michael Schaller, The Occupation of Japan: The Origins of the Cold War in Asia (1985); Howard

Schonberger, *After the War: Americans and the Remaking of Japan* (1989); John W. Spanier, *The Truman-MacArthur Controversy and the Korean War* (1965); William W. Stueck, Jr., *The Road to Confrontation: American Policy Toward China and Korea, 1947–1950* (1981); Kathryn Weathersby, "From the Russian Archives: New Findings on the Korean War," *Cold War International History Project Bulletin* [Woodrow Wilson International Center for Scholars], 3 (Fall 1993).

Chapter Three

UNEASINESS AT DAWN: DOMESTIC
TRENDS IN THE EARLY
POSTWAR YEARS

New York City, September 1945. As the writer James Agee watched a victory parade from a window high above the city streets, his pleasure was edged with apprehension: "The whole city has a kind of love-feast warmth of thousands of great and small homecomings," he wrote a friend. "It is lovely." But immediately he added, "God, what most of the homecomers, and those they come home to, are in for!"

Agee had reason to worry. Even as they welcomed the end of World War II, many Americans eyed the future with concern. Would wartime prosperity collapse without the stimulus of military production? Would peace bring a return of hard times? In fact, demobilization proceeded remarkably smoothly. The economy absorbed the returning veterans as industry switched promptly to peacetime production. These years launched an economic boom that with periodic interruptions would last for several decades.

Nevertheless, as peace returned, the political cleavages of the 1930s reappeared. Truman and his liberal supporters sought to expand the New Deal, but conservatives in both parties doggedly hacked away at what they called its "socialistic" excesses, and business groups gained a greater voice in shaping public policy. Although Truman won a come-from-behind electoral victory in 1948, disputes over the nature of the postwar domestic order raged on.

The war had stirred changes that society was not yet ready to confront. Women had donned uniforms or worked in war plants. African-Americans had served in the military or moved northward and cityward to seek work. Mexican workers had immigrated to the United States in great numbers. Poverty and economic inequities pervaded America. Yet the early postwar era generally failed to address the social and political implications of these developments. President Truman's reform program, offered in the 1948 campaign and after, made little headway. Indeed, in contrast to the New Deal years, the late 1940s brought a generally conservative drift in U.S. politics and social thought. In celebrating the good life of suburbia and an idealized domestic ideal for women, mass culture, including television, the newest medium, sought to contain the forces of social change, much as Cold War planners worked to contain communism abroad. In this crucial transitional era, the Cold War shaped U.S. politics and culture. Just as Cold War calculations drove U.S. foreign policy, so, too, did the anticommunist struggle influence, and in some ways poison, the domestic scene.

Demobilization and the Limits of Liberalism at Home

Doubts about America's ability to shift to a peace economy and fears of a new depression as military contracts dried up and veterans reentered the labor market hung heavily in many minds in August 1945. Producer Sam Goldwyn's bleak movie about veterans' problems, sardonically titled *The Best Years of Our Lives*, won the Academy Award for best picture of 1946. In fact, demobilization proceeded smoothly as industries quickly retooled to meet pent-up demands for consumer goods, from automobiles and refrigerators to everyday items. "From tanks to Cadillacs in two months," boasted General Motors. Except for an uptick in 1949–1950, unemployment remained under 4 percent from 1946 to 1952. These figures in part resulted from millions of veterans who, taking advantage of the GI Bill's educational benefits, enrolled in school rather than entering the labor market.* Many women workers unceremoniously fired to make room for veterans chose not to seek other employment. Other women left the workplace voluntarily to resume what the culture presented as the more appropriate roles of wives and mothers. The female labor force fell from 35.8 million in 1945 to 30.8 million in 1946; not until 1956 would it regain its 1945 level.

Demobilization was not entirely painless. Housing shortages and inflation plagued postwar America. Addressing the latter issue, Truman in June 1946 asked Congress to extend the authority of the wartime Office of Price Administration (OPA), which had held prices and rents at artificially low levels. But conservative legislators, ill disposed toward this unhappy reminder of wartime controls, radically cut the OPA's powers. Within two weeks, prices shot up 25 percent. A Tulsa grocer even advised customers not to buy his shrimp, so outrageous was the cost. By the end of 1946, price controls had been lifted on all but a few items, and inflation remained a chronic headache. Coffee prices rose by 54 percent from 1945 to 1947; the cost of meat nearly doubled.

Galloping inflation sparked a rash of strikes for higher wages. During the war, despite some wildcat walkouts, workers had generally honored their unions' "no strike" pledge. In late 1945 and early 1946, by contrast, nearly five thousand walkouts idled some 4.6 million workers. President Truman reacted firmly to stoppages that he believed threatened the national welfare. When railway workers struck early in 1946, he told the union leaders, "If you think I'm going to sit here and let you tie up this whole country, you're crazy as hell." As Truman prepared to ask Congress for

---

* By the time the GI Bill's educational provisions expired in 1956, some 7.8 million veterans had attended college or technical schools with federal support.

Left: Union leaders in 1941 adopted a "No Strike" policy for the duration of the war. Government propaganda such as this 1942 War Production Board poster urged patriotic workers to stay on the job. With the war's end, however, pent-up frustration produced a wave of strikes. (*War Manpower Commission, 1942*) *Right:* Labor unrest, February 1946. Philadelphia police struggle to seize a flag carried by striking electrical workers, many of them World War II veterans. (*Temple University*)

powers to resolve the crisis, the workers returned to the job. When four hundred thousand coal miners belonging to John L. Lewis's United Mineworkers union walked out on April 1, 1946, Truman ordered the army to seize the mines. Lewis finally called off the strike late in 1947, after a long court battle. Truman took these conflicts as personal challenges; when the miners went back to work, he wrote his mother, "Well, John L. had to fold up. He couldn't take the gaff. No bully can."

The Republicans seized the moment, capitalizing on labor unrest and consumer anger over high prices and adopting a simple slogan for the 1946 midterm elections: "Had enough? Vote Republican." The strategy worked: Republicans won control of both houses of Congress for the first time since 1928. Among the newcomers, reported *Time* magazine, were Joseph McCarthy of Wisconsin, elected on the slogan "Washington Needs a Tail-Gunner"; a "dark, lank, Quaker attorney" from California, Richard M. Nixon; and a Democrat, "boyish, raw-boned, Harvard-bred" John Kennedy of Massachusetts.

The strains of demobilization intensified the ongoing debate over America's political course. FDR's Depression-spawned New Deal in effect had sketched the preliminary outlines of a welfare state. The legacy of the 1930s to postwar America was a federal government committed to maintaining prosperity, regulating capitalism, and ensuring at least a minimal level of well-being for all. For liberal ideologists, the reforms of the 1930s offered an admirable long-term blueprint that they wished to make permanent and to extend to include other objectives such as full employment.

Others, in both parties, accepted basic New Deal reforms such as social security and were sympathetic to the goal of full employment but believed that the nation needed breathing space. Consolidation, not more reform, they argued, should be the order of the day. Sometimes Truman himself shared this view. "I don't want any experiments," he told an adviser in 1945. "The American people want a rest . . . from experiments." The president and his administration, steering a course between liberals and moderates, kept their eye on a more mundane goal as well: electoral victory in 1948.

Further right on the political spectrum gathered those who thought that the New Deal had undermined individualism and free enterprise. Down with government regulation and welfare programs, they urged; up with laissez faire. This camp much admired the emigré Austrian economist Friedrich Hayek, whose *The Road to Serfdom* (1944) portrayed the welfare state as a step down the slippery slope to socialism and, eventually, totalitarianism. Widely publicized, Hayek's work propelled a resurgent conservative ideology that a generation later would loom large in American political life.

The reputation of corporate America, tarnished in the 1930s, had taken on fresh lustre during the war, and business groups such as the National Association of Manufacturers, the U.S. Chamber of Commerce, and the Council for Economic Development sought to use this new prestige to influence domestic policy. As one business leader wrote in 1944, corporations in the postwar era should work together to "rid the economy of injurious or unnecessary regulation, as well as administration that is hostile or harmful," and to create a political climate "in which a private enterprise system can flourish."

The Advertising Council, founded during World War II by ad agencies and corporate advertisers to publish public-service ads in support of the war effort, led this campaign. After the war, the council supplemented its ads for driver safety and charitable giving with pitches aimed at "selling" the free-enterprise system and the "economic miracle" of modern capitalism to the American people. In the words of the council's head, the organization strove to counteract popular tendencies to make business "the 'villain' in the American drama."

For a while after the war, advocates of expanding the New Deal appeared to hold the political high ground. In September 1945, President Truman proposed to Congress a sweeping twenty-one-point reform program that included an extension of social security, slum clearance, public housing, and a federal commission to combat racism in employment. Most of these proposals extended New Deal programs or initiatives undertaken by the Roosevelt administration during World War II. But much of Truman's program languished in a Congress veering more and more rightward. One exception, the Employment Act of 1946, enacted with bipartisan support, committed the government to a policy of "maximum employment, production, and purchasing power." To this end, the law required the president to submit an annual economic report to Congress, with recommended programs to promote economic growth. It also set up the Joint Committee on the Economic Report and created a three-person Council of Economic Advisers (CEA) to advise the president on economic policy.

The Employment Act of 1946 reflected the ideas of the British economist John

Maynard Keynes, who advocated using the government's tax, credit, and spending powers to stimulate economic growth. Economist Leon Keyserling, who served on the CEA and became its chairman in 1950, supported Keynesian strategies for promoting growth by federal policy. But the law also illustrated the business community's growing influence in shaping public policy. The initial drafts had a distinctly "New Dealish" tone, calling for government spending on health, education, public works, rural electrification, urban renewal, and so on, to promote full employment. Intense lobbying by business groups blunted this activist thrust, however, and in its final form, the bill called for such measures as tax cuts to stimulate investment and business-government cooperation in achieving economic growth.

The Employment Act of 1946 reveals the growing links between foreign affairs and domestic policy. At the 1944 Bretton Woods Conference, the British had insisted that if the dollar were to become the world's monetary standard, Washington must ensure the dollar's strength and economic stability at home. This pressure from abroad proved a major impetus behind the passage of the 1946 legislation committing the government to an expanded economic role.

The Atomic Energy Act of 1946 further highlights the political crosscurrents of the period. The law mandated public control of atomic energy under the civilian Atomic Energy Commission (AEC) and called for research on peacetime uses of the atom. The appointment of David E. Lilienthal, head of the New Deal's Tennessee Valley Authority (TVA), as the AEC's first chairman strengthened the act's link to the liberal tradition. In reality, the AEC functioned primarily as a supplier of nuclear weapons to the military. Although Lilienthal maintained an optimistic public facade about the peacetime benefits of atomic energy, in the privacy of his diary he deplored his agency's preoccupation with bomb production. When he left in 1950, after losing his battle against development of the hydrogen bomb, he confessed to an aide that the AEC had become "nothing more than a major contractor to the Department of Defense."

Measures that reflected even a watered-down liberalism were rare in the early postwar years. Some conservative legislators ridiculed the Employment Act of 1946 even as they voted for it, assuming that its lofty rhetoric and high-sounding new Council of Economic Advisers meant little. Although basic New Deal reforms such as social security remained firmly in place, Republicans and many southern Democrats expressed strong unhappiness with the reforms of the Franklin Roosevelt era. The Taft-Hartley Act of 1947 evidenced this hostility with particular clarity.* Business leaders and their political allies had long chafed at the expansion of union power in the 1930s. The 1935 Wagner Act, they insisted, with its guarantees of union rights, had gone too far in a prolabor direction. In 1943, over President Roosevelt's veto, conservatives had taken advantage of the war emergency to pass the Smith-Connally Act, which placed various restraints on unions' right to strike.

The Taft-Hartley Act, passed over Truman's veto, reflected a similar impulse to curb organized labor. An amalgam of various labor bills that had been introduced over the years, the legislation outlawed the closed shop, wherein hiring must be done

---

* Named for its sponsors, Senator Robert Taft of Ohio and New Jersey congressman Fred Hartley, the bill's official title was the Labor-Management Relations Act.

through a union hall; permitted states to pass so-called right-to-work laws barring contracts that excluded nonunion workers from unionized plants; permitted employers to sue unions on various grounds; and authorized federal injunctions against strikes that jeopardized the public health or safety. Finally, reflecting the nation's growing antiradical mood, Taft-Hartley required union leaders to swear that they were not communists.

Denounced by union officials as a "slave labor" law, the Taft-Hartley Act symbolized the conservative bent of postwar social thought and the resurgence of corporate interests in late-1940s America. It also helped to undercut union leaders eager to make organized labor a forceful voice in shaping public policy. One bitter Congress of Industrial Orrganizations official complained, "When you think of [the Taft-Hartley Act] as merely a combination of individual provisions, you are losing entirely the full impact of the program, the sinister conspiracy that has been hatched."

For organized labor, then, the postwar era eroded the substantial influence that unions had gained in the 1930s and the war years. For African-Americans, different circumstances prevailed. Largely ignored during the New Deal, millions of blacks emerged from the war aroused by the racism prevalent in democratic America and determined to force the nation to live up to its egalitarian ideals.

African-Americans and the Liberal Agenda

The growing political clout of northern urban blacks, the surge of black activism during World War II, and the court challenges to segregation by the National Association for the Advancement of Colored People (NAACP) gave racial issues high priority in the Truman years. So, too, did the logic of America's wartime struggle against fascism. This point was underscored in *An American Dilemma: The Negro Problem and American Democracy* (1944), a study of race in the United States by the Swedish economist Gunnar Myrdal. In a key section, Myrdal emphasized that World War II had thrown in bold relief the paradox of racism in a nation fighting to preserve human freedom:

> This war is an ideological war fought in defense of democracy. . . . Fascism and nazism are based on a racial superiority dogma. . . . [The fascists and Nazis] came to power by means of racial persecution and oppression. In fighting fascism and nazism, America had to stand before the whole world in favor of racial tolerance and cooperation and of racial equality.

Similarly, Myrdal continued, the United States would confront the issue even more directly in the internationalist climate of the postwar era:

> Probably no other modern people has cared less about what impression it makes on other nations. . . . America has now joined the world and is tremendously dependent upon the support and good-will of other countries. . . . The treatment of the Negro is America's greatest and most conspicuous scandal. It is tremendously publicized, and democratic America will continue to publicize it itself. For the colored

people all over the world, whose rising influence is axiomatic, this scandal is salt in their wounds.

Myrdal proved an accurate prophet. As the Cold War took on global dimensions, American racism became a growing embarrassment. When U.S. hotels and restaurants refused service to dark-skinned diplomats from developing nations, the insults received worldwide publicity. As foreign-policy considerations helped to propel race onto President Truman's agenda, once again the line between domestic and international issues in the Cold War era blurred.

For Truman, civil rights posed a thorny dilemma both personally and politically. The grandchild of slaveowners, he had grown up when blatant racism had pervaded American life and showed little early evidence of sensitivity to the issue. While a senator, he had supported a federal antilynching bill while privately assuring southern colleagues that he did so only because of blacks' voting power in Kansas City and St. Louis. But Truman showed great capacity for growth during his White House years, and his innate sense of decency eventually responded to injustice when it was made plain to him. As a politician, Truman realized that the Democratic coalition depended on northern black and liberal white voters as well as southern white voters—most of the latter dyed-in-the-wool segregationists. As president, he daily faced Democratic southern legislators who wielded enormous power in Congress, but as "leader of the Free World," he realized that racism represented a painful liability in America's ideological war with the Soviet Union.

Amid this welter of contradictory impulses and political calculations, Truman cautiously identified his administration with the black cause. Late in 1946, after heavy Democratic losses in that year's midterm elections, Truman set up the presidential Committee on Civil Rights, with a preponderance of liberal activists. The committee's 1947 report, *To Secure These Rights*, called for vigorous action against racism, including an end to school segregation. That year Truman delivered a strong address to the NAACP, and early in 1948 (by no coincidence, an election year) he sent a civil-rights message to Congress. Truman proposed action on several fronts, including a federal antilynching law and a permanent Fair Employment Practices Commission patterned on FDR's temporary wartime agency. Southern Democrats in Congress, egged on by state politicians such as Governor J. Strom Thurmond of South Carolina, easily buried Truman's proposals.* Nevertheless, the message gave racial issues visibility at the highest political level for the first time.

Truman's major civil-rights achievement, Executive Order 9981 of July 1948, established procedures for ending racial discrimination in the military. Strict segregation had partially eroded during World War II (the army had integrated its officer-training program, for example), but the pattern of military Jim Crow remained firmly in place. Although not fully implemented until the Korean War, Truman's order hastened the long process of breaking down structures of institutionalized racism

---

* Of the entire Democratic congressional delegation from the South, only liberal congressman Claude Pepper of Florida supported Truman's civil-rights program.

built up over many decades. The *Chicago Defender,* a black newspaper, euphorically called it "unprecedented since the time of Lincoln."

In contrast to the tumultuous 1950s and 1960s, America in the late 1940s hesitated painfully to confront its racist history. Despite Truman's civil-rights proposals, the nation could not admit to the urgency of this issue. In the absence of a broad-based movement, attention focused on individual black achievers: diplomat Ralph Bunche, boxer Sugar Ray Robinson, and baseball player Jackie Robinson, who broke the major-league color barrier in 1947. In 1949, playing second base for the Brooklyn Dodgers, Robinson led the National League in batting and was the league's most valuable player. After years of segregation in the separate Negro League, black baseball stars could now compete on the same fields with whites.

But these were isolated achievements; racism held a relentless grip on America. Although Robinson inspired cheers on the diamond, he stayed in segregated hotels when the Dodgers traveled. Jazz was hailed as a great cultural contribution, but black jazz musicians still faced the humiliation of racial segregation. In 1946 a security guard pistol-whipped bandleader Cab Calloway as he tried to enter Kansas City's all-white Pla-Mor Ballroom. Despite gradual economic and educational gains, blacks by every measure lagged far behind the white majority. In 1950, when some 39 percent of white families earned annual incomes under $3,000, the figure for black families was an appalling 77 percent. Black high-school graduates attended college in the early 1950s at less than half the rate of whites.

Postwar antiradical obsessions discouraged racial protest. African-American leaders such as Paul Robeson and W. E. B. Du Bois, because of their ties to the Communist party, encountered ostracism even by black organizations like the NAACP. The absence of grass-roots civil-rights activism also reflected the NAACP's preference for litigation over marches and protests. In 1947, when two small interracial civil-rights organizations, the Fellowship of Reconciliation and the Congress of Racial Equality (CORE), challenged segregation by organizing an interracial "Journey of Reconciliation" on interstate buses operating in the South, the NAACP stayed on the sidelines. The NAACP proved equally cool to A. Philip Randolph's wartime calls for a black march on Washington to focus attention on black grievances.

Yet changes were astir. As President Truman's election-year attention to civil rights made plain, blacks' political clout was growing. Even the South, bastion of white supremacy, saw a new order taking shape. Southern election boards still used various devices to bar blacks, but the number of African-American voters rose from 250,000 to more than 1 million between 1940 and 1950. The NAACP's patient legal approach, too, although undramatic, showed signs of paying off. In three landmark cases of 1950—all argued by NAACP lawyer Thurgood Marshall—the Supreme Court undermined the legal foundation of Jim Crow. The first case outlawed segregated railroad dining cars; the second ruled that if a state did not provide equal schools for black students, it could not segregate them in a white school; and the third stressed the key role of psychological factors in determining whether segregated schools could in fact offer "equal" education to both races. These decisions failed to overturn *Plessy* v. *Ferguson,* the 1896 decision upholding the constitutionality of segregated schools and other public facilities, yet they gnawed at segregation's legal underpinnings. As the NAACP observed, "Some might call these [rulings] mere straws in the wind, but they do indicate the direction in which the wind is blowing."

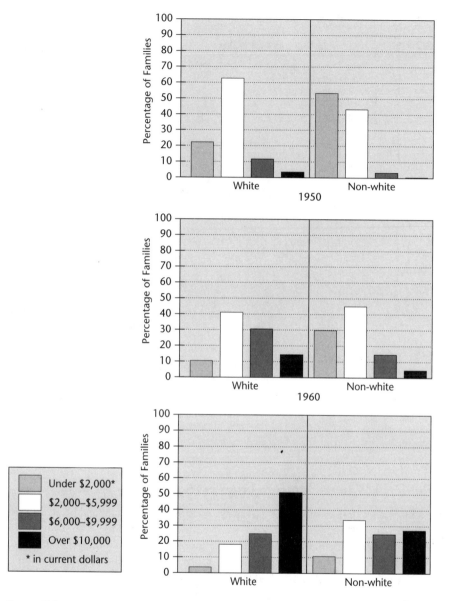

FIGURE 3.1

Family Income by Race, 1950–1970

SOURCE: Adapted from *Statistical Abstract of the United States, 1974* (Washington, D.C., 1973), p. 382.

Despite this progress, substantive civil-rights gains eluded the United States in the early postwar years. While black discontent mounted and pressure for change intensified, white America for the most part overlooked the ugly stain of racism. As journalist John Gunther wrote in 1947, the fact that America was 10 percent black

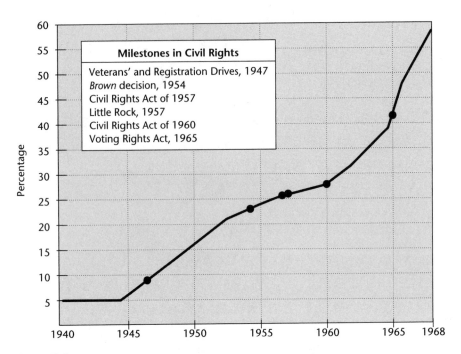

FIGURE 3.2
Percentage of Voting-Age Southern Blacks Registered, 1940–1968

was "known to everybody and ignored by almost everybody—except maybe the ten percent."

The Cold War at Home and the 1948 Election

The ideological fallout of the early Cold War not only silenced radical black leaders; it had a lamentable impact on home-front politics overall. The 1946 dismissal of Commerce Secretary Henry Wallace (see Chapter 2) signaled a more general stifling of dissident opinion in Washington and across the nation. The president's March 1947 Truman Doctrine address had forged an implicit rhetorical link between anti-communism abroad and at home. Politicians and conservative groups eager to further their own goals responded to the drumfire of warnings about the red menace by raising the specter of domestic disloyalty. The democratic-socialist leader Norman Thomas, visiting California in 1947, expressed shock at the "hysterical anticommunism" sweeping the state.

To be sure, fears of subversion at home, like Truman's larger view of the world situation, had a basis in fact. The tiny American Communist party did follow the Moscow line slavishly, and the Soviets, like most other nations, did conduct espionage. In March 1945, when OSS security officials raided the office of a left-wing

Anticommunism in Los Angeles, July 1950. Auto workers attack a fellow employee for refusing to tell them whether he was a communist. (*AP/Wide World Photos*)

journal of Asian affairs, *Amerasia,* they found three hundred secret OSS reports, State Department memos, and other government documents. One file bore the cryptic label "'A' Bomb." In 1946 Canadian authorities uncovered a Soviet spy ring operating in their country. And in 1948, amid newspaper stories about a "Beautiful Blonde Spy Queen," the Republican-controlled House Un-American Activities Committee (HUAC) questioned middle-aged Elizabeth Bentley, a former government employee. Bentley had confessed to the Federal Bureau of Investigation (FBI) that during the war she had transmitted secret documents to a Soviet agent who was then her lover (later he jilted her). Bentley repeated charges against various government officials already investigated and cleared by the FBI. One such hapless bureaucrat was Harry Dexter White, an assistant secretary of the treasury prominent in the wartime Bretton Woods Conference. White died of a heart attack shortly after heatedly denying any treasonable activity.

The spreading hysteria about domestic subversion bore little relation to the actual situation. In fact, such terror was a wholly predictable by-product of the fear of communism that the Truman administration, J. Edgar Hoover's FBI, and media voices such as Henry Luce's *Life* and *Time* magazines fanned to build support for the Cold War. As *Life* put it, "The fellow traveler [communist sympathizer] is everywhere, in Hollywood, on college faculties, in government bureaus, in publishing companies, even on the editorial staffs of eminently capitalist journals." Conservatives who evoked the bogey of "communist subversion" to attack dissidents of all kinds and politicians who hammered at the same theme for partisan purposes exploited an opening that the Democrats in the White House had already provided them.

Attuned to the rising clamor, Truman on March 21, 1947, a few days after enunciating the Truman Doctrine, launched the domestic corollary of his global anticommunist struggle: a federal loyalty-review program. By 1952 the FBI had investigated some twenty thousand government employees, of whom about four hundred were fired and twenty-five hundred resigned "voluntarily." Although Truman warned against "witch hunts," his loyalty program invited abuse. Persons accused of subversive associations or sympathies had the right to counsel and the right of appeal, but they received only summaries of derogatory material in their FBI files and had no opportunity to confront their accusers. The attorney general compiled a list of "subversive" organizations. Some of these had expired years before in the 1930s, but even past membership in such organizations drew suspicion. Employees faced questions about their opinion of Henry Wallace or the Truman Doctrine, or whether they owned recordings by Paul Robeson. Persons active in civil-rights causes endured special scrutiny. Because homosexuals were considered vulnerable to blackmail, they were targeted by the loyalty investigators. Following Washington's lead, local groups and institutions launched their own loyalty-review programs. Although the postwar paranoia about domestic subversion crested in the McCarthyite witch hunts of the early 1950s, the Truman administration's loyalty program nurtured it.

Meanwhile, as the 1948 election approached, Truman's chances looked bleak. The Republicans had gained heavily in 1946 and still seemed on the rise. Inflation and other grievances fed voter discontent. Henry Wallace had announced his candidacy for president on a third-party Progressive ticket and seemed likely to siphon votes from the Democratic ticket. Worse, the Democratic convention in Philadelphia that nominated Truman also saw a major party split. Following a plan adopted by administration strategists and big-city Democratic leaders, the convention featured a ringing civil-rights speech by the young mayor of Minneapolis, Hubert Humphrey. "The time has come," declaimed Humphrey, "to walk out of the shadow of states' rights and into the sunlight of human rights." Prodded by Humphrey and other northern liberals, the convention not only embraced the black cause rhetorically but adopted a strong civil-rights plank—not part of the White House game plan. Southern delegates who tried to protest found their microphones dead. An outraged Mississippi delegation and some Alabama delegates walked out. Soon after, six thousand cheering whites in Birmingham, Alabama, formed the States' Rights Democratic party (known as the Dixiecrats) and nominated Governor Thurmond of South Carolina as president. The Democrats' prospects appeared bleaker still. "Send up a bottle of embalming fluid," a roomful of thirsty Democrats in Philadelphia told room service. "If we're going to hold a wake, we might as well do it right."

By contrast, the Republicans oozed confidence. Their candidate, New York governor Thomas Dewey, was more liberal than his chief rival, Senator Taft, or than most Republicans in Congress. Dewey had run well against Roosevelt in 1944 and appeared certain to beat the lackluster Truman. "How long is Dewey going to tolerate Truman's interference in the government?" mused one reporter as the campaign unfolded. Dewey's running mate, California's popular governor Earl Warren, strengthened the ticket in the rapidly growing West Coast states.

In fact, however, Truman's liberal advisers had devised a potent campaign strategy. The plan, embodied in a 1947 memo by Clark Clifford, "The Politics of 1948," called for appeals to the old Roosevelt coalition, notably blacks and union members, and aimed to deflect anger over inflation and other problems from the White House to Congress. Clifford also urged Truman to stress the anticommunist theme. The "battle with the Kremlin," he noted, offered "considerable political advantage to the Administration." Implementing Clifford's plan, Truman peppered Congress with reform proposals, including repeal of the Taft-Hartley Act, a housing bill, and a civil-rights program. Most of these proposals predictably died, but they projected the image of Truman as a reformer in the FDR tradition and of a reactionary Congress deaf to social issues. Heeding his advisers' call for "bold and dramatic steps" to stop Dewey, Truman called a special session of Congress for late July 1948, supposedly so that the Republicans could pass all the measures that they had promised in their platform. As Truman anticipated, this two-week session accomplished little.

The president undertook a grueling national campaign by rail, traveling 22,000 miles and delivering 271 speeches. He spoke tirelessly, lambasting the "gluttons of privilege," the "economic tapeworms of big business," and, above all, "the do-nothing Eightieth Congress." By this strategy, he shrewdly shifted voter attention from the bland Dewey to the Republican Congress. The drama of the Berlin airlift that summer helped Truman as well. The crowds grew larger and the shouts of "Give 'em hell, Harry" more exuberant. The aloof Dewey, meanwhile, confident of his lead, spoke in vague generalities. ("Your future is still ahead of you," he informed one audience.) With his short height, stiff manner, and trim black mustache, Dewey reminded one commentator of "the little man on top of the wedding cake." But still the polls predicted a Dewey landslide. The vast illusion continued into the early balloting. The *Chicago Tribune*, in an instantly famous election-night headline, proclaimed, "DEWEY DEFEATS TRUMAN!"

The pollsters had stopped their calculations a week or more before the election and missed a crucial last-minute swing to Truman. In a stunning upset, Truman amassed 24.2 million votes to Dewey's 22 million, with coattails broad enough to enable the Democrats to regain control of both houses of Congress. The day after the election, a Kentucky store offered framed portraits of Truman with the sign, "Were $1.98, Now $10.00."

Accounts of the '48 campaign understandably focus on Truman's personality and campaign style, but the Democratic National Committee, tireless speechmaking by Senator Barkley and various cabinet members, and a brilliant campaign strategy played key roles. Truman ran as the leader of the battle against communism abroad and reaction at home. "The issues in this campaign are not hard to define," he told voters in Rock Island, Illinois. "The issue is the people against the special interests." He struck an array of themes that touched millions of Americans, including, historian Donald McCoy writes, "housing, federal aid to education, health care, higher minimum wage and Social Security benefits, flood control, public power, civil rights, labor, conservation, agriculture, and regulation of business, among others."

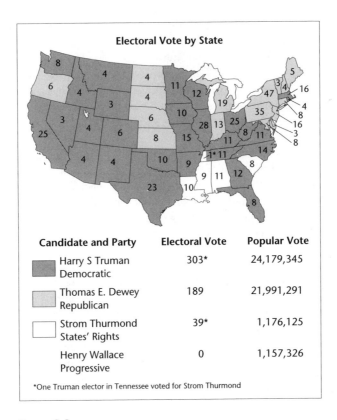

FIGURE 3.3
Presidential Election of 1948

The splinter parties fared less well than expected, bolstering Truman's cause. Most voters rejected Wallace's attacks on the administration's foreign policy and objected to the Communist party's role in his campaign. Wallace, who garnered just over a million votes, may even have helped Truman by validating the president's anticommunist credentials and shielding him from Republican red-baiting. The States' Rights party, criticized in the media for its racism, raised little campaign money. The Democrats' civil-rights plank that triggered the Dixiecrats' defection also produced a tide of northern black votes for Truman. Governor Thurmond, however, with 1.7 million votes, carried four Deep South states, portending long-term problems for the Democrats in a no longer Solid South.

Truman did well among farmers, urban ethnics, and union members angered by the Taft-Hartley Act. The election was hardly a ringing call for "a new era of reform" (as the liberal *New Republic* magazine declared); nevertheless, it signaled that the battered New Deal coalition still held. Although it was eroding and in four years the Republicans would regain the White House, the victorious Democrats celebrated in 1948. Harry Truman had emerged from Roosevelt's giant shadow to win the presidency in his own right and gain respect for his feisty, never-say-die style; he stood at the pinnacle of his career. It is ironic that his final four years in the White House would bring mostly frustration and setbacks.

The Fair Deal and McCarthyism

While fighting a hot war in Korea and the Cold War in Europe, the Truman administration struggled to chart a domestic agenda in an increasingly venomous political climate. In his January 1949 State of the Union address, Truman proposed a far-reaching domestic program soon labeled the Fair Deal. Building on existing programs, the president recommended broader social security coverage, an increase in the minimum wage from forty to seventy-five cents an hour, and development programs for the nation's river systems modeled on the TVA. Truman addressed organized labor's big grievance by urging repeal of the Taft-Hartley Act. He proposed aid to education as well as a cabinet-level department of welfare and an expanded public housing program. Pleas for a national health-insurance system featuring prepaid medical, dental, and hospital care and funded by a combination of federal payments and employer and employee contributions capped Truman's program. To finance all this, and to combat inflation, the president recommended a $4 billion tax increase. On the civil-rights front, Truman once more asked for the Fair Employment Practices Commission (FEPC) and, in later messages, federal laws against lynching and the poll tax, a stratagem used to exclude black voters in the South.

Representing the consensus of advanced liberal thinking on domestic issues, the Fair Deal assumed an expansive capitalist economy and an array of Washington-based programs to promote the public welfare. Beyond these expectations, it counted on measures to combat racial discrimination and the use of federal economic policy to maintain prosperity and to ensure fair play in the marketplace. In the light of these prerequisites, it is not surprising that most of the Fair Deal got nowhere. Lacking the broad public support that FDR had rallied behind the New Deal, Truman's program also faced strong legislative opposition. The president's party nominally controlled Congress, but in practice a coalition of Republicans and conservative Democrats held sway. Furthermore, Truman was unwilling to weaken bipartisan support for the Cold War—especially after the outbreak of the Korean War in June 1950—by pushing too hard for his domestic program. Angered by conservative Democrats who opposed his domestic program, he nevertheless declined to purge them or to strip them of their congressional chairmanships. Finally, Truman's health-insurance plan met a firestorm of opposition from the American Medical Association (AMA), which denounced it as "socialized medicine" and peddled horror stories about Great Britain's health system. Fearful of federal regulation and lower physicians' income, the AMA posted billboards that showed a worried doctor at a patient's bedside and warned, KEEP THE GOVERNMENT OUT OF THIS PICTURE.

Truman's farm program also ran into strong opposition—from farmers. The New Deal's strategy for raising farm income had included buying and storing the "surplus" production of basic commodities. By the late 1940s a glut of wheat, corn, and other products choked government warehouses. To cope with this headache,

Secretary of Agriculture Charles Brannan in 1949 proposed a complicated plan whereby the government would stop buying surpluses of perishable commodities and simply allow the total output to be sold on the open market. Because this strategy would depress farm prices, Brannan proposed cash subsidies to farmers to compensate them for their losses. Labor and consumer groups welcomed the Brannan Plan for its promise of lower food prices, but the Farm Bureau Federation, speaking for the nation's largest farmers, charged that the scheme, even with the subsidy provision, would cut into farm income. When the Marshall Plan and other foreign-aid programs depleted the overflowing farm surpluses, the administration quietly shelved the Brannan Plan. Once again, the Cold War's pervasive influence on domestic politics made itself felt.

The president's civil-rights program fared no better, as southern Democrats, joined by conservative Republicans, blocked his proposals in this area. Even a bill to grant self-government to the heavily black District of Columbia failed in the Senate. The only real progress on the civil-rights front came through executive action. Truman named several African-Americans to midlevel federal posts and in 1951 took steps to deny government contracts to firms practicing racial discrimination.

A few items on Truman's Fair Deal agenda won Congress's approval. The National Housing Act of 1949, supported by the construction industry, authorized federal subsidies for eight hundred thousand low-income housing units. Even so, the postwar housing shortage had eased, and only half the authorized units were built. In 1950, as Truman had urged, Congress raised the minimum wage and expanded the coverage of social security, a program whose retirement benefits appealed to middle-class and working-class Americans.

Overall, Truman's domestic record proved thin. A conservative postwar climate, assertive opposition, the distractions of the campaign against reds and radicals, and the weakened voice of Left-liberal social thinkers amid the intellectually repressive early Cold War climate all contributed to the faltering of postwar reform. An increasingly thwarted Truman lashed out at powerful congressional barons more attentive to special interests than to the public good. In a sarcastic diary entry, he attacked southern lawmaker Richard Russell as "the great Georgia Senator, representative of the National Chamber of Commerce, the Coca Cola Company, etc." In his frustration, he advocated twelve-year term limits on congressional service to "help cure senility and seniority—both terrible legislative diseases." Nevertheless, the Fair Deal remains historically significant. On civil rights, medical insurance, and education, it set the liberal domestic agenda for years to come. Indeed, the issue of national health care, first raised by President Truman at midcentury, continues to dominate the political agenda as the twentieth century closes.

As Truman's second term wore on, charges of corruption beset his administration. Early in the Truman years, journalist I. F. Stone had described the president's cronies as "the kind of men one was accustomed to meet in county courthouses . . . , big-bellied, good natured guys who knew a lot of dirty jokes [and] spent as little time in their office as possible." The seedy aura spread. GOP orators denounced the "mess in Washington," especially corruption in the Internal Revenue Service and the Reconstruction Finance Corporation (RFC), a New Deal agency that lent large sums to banks and corporations. The "mess" also included "five percenters," or administration officials who took payoffs for helping favored corporations to secure government contracts.

The accusations offer a revealing glimpse into postwar consumer society. A Truman military aide allegedly accepted no fewer than seven freezers, which he gave to friends, including Mrs. Truman; a White House secretary received an $8,000 mink coat from a corporation seeking an RFC loan; the Lustron Corporation got $37.8 million in RFC funds, none of it ever repaid, to build pastel-tinted prefabricated houses of a new plasticlike material. Although not personally implicated in wrongdoing, Truman drew severe criticism for his lax judgment in friends and advisers. But while his public-opinion ratings fell and anti-Truman jokes proliferated, the president seemingly remained in good spirits; perhaps he sensed that his historical reputation would outdistance his contemporary standings in the opinion polls.

Rivaling the accusations of government corruption, charges of domestic subversion rooted in the larger anticommunist preoccupations of the era increasingly poisoned national politics. The Truman administration continued to display its toughness on domestic radicals and in January 1949 put on trial eleven Communist party leaders under the 1940 Alien Registration Act (also known as the Smith Act), which made advocating the forcible overthrow of the government illegal. The eleven were convicted in a decision upheld by the Supreme Court in 1951.

Along with the Elizabeth Bentley case, two other highly publicized spy cases surfaced in these years. The first began in August 1948 when ex-communist Whittaker Chambers, an editor at *Time*, told HUAC that as a spy for the Soviets in the 1930s he had received secret government documents from Alger Hiss, a State Department official who had later become head of the Carnegie Foundation for International Peace. With a flair for drama, Chambers led reporters to his Maryland farm, where he showed them a hollowed-out pumpkin containing microfilms of documents allegedly given him by Hiss. The handsome, urbane, and self-assured Hiss denied Chambers's charges. But Congressman Richard Nixon of California doggedly pursued the case. In a major break, HUAC investigators traced a typewriter once owned by Hiss and found that it matched the typing on Chambers's documents. Convicted of perjury in January 1950, the statute of limitation on treason having expired, Hiss served five years in prison.

The second of these sensational espionage cases began in England in 1950 when Klaus Fuchs, an emigré German physicist who had worked in the wartime atomic-bomb project at Los Alamos, was arrested as a Soviet spy. Fuchs fingered David Greenglass, a serviceman who had worked in the Los Alamos machine shop, as one of his channels for smuggling out A-bomb information. Greenglass in turn charged that his sister and brother-in-law, Ethel and Julius Rosenberg, had recruited him for Soviet espionage. The Rosenbergs were arrested, convicted of spying for the Soviets, and sentenced to death. Despite worldwide protests, they went to the electric chair in 1953.

The Hiss and Rosenberg cases have continued to inspire debate. Recent scholarship suggests that all three were guilty but that the Rosenbergs to some extent were victims of Cold War hysteria. Ronald Radosh and Joyce Milton argue in *The Rosenberg File: A Search for the Truth* (1983) that prosecutors sought the death sentence for Ethel Rosenberg, despite her marginal role in the espionage plot, hoping that at the last minute Julius Rosenberg would name other spies to save his wife. If this was the plan, it failed: Both Rosenbergs maintained their innocence and went silently to their deaths. E. L. Doctorow's novel *The Book of Daniel* (1971) explored the psychological and political dimensions of the Rosenberg case. In one insightful passage, Doctorow linked the shrill anticommunism of the early Cold War to the passions of World War II. "Enemies must continue to be found," he reflected. "The mind and heart cannot be demobilized as quickly as the platoon. . . . [L]ike a fiery furnace at white heat, it takes a considerable time to cool."

The Hiss and Rosenberg cases worsened a political climate already heavy with suspicion. From 1945 to 1952, HUAC conducted some eighty probes of atomic scientists, black activists, Hollywood writers, and others. Ten directors and screenwriters who refused to discuss their political beliefs or to implicate others before the committee went to prison for a year. In 1951 the chairman of HUAC, J. Parnell Thomas, himself convicted of fraud, found himself in the same federal prison in Connecticut with Ring Lardner, Jr., one of the "Hollywood Ten." One day, Thomas was assigned to work in the prison chicken yard while Lardner cut grass with a sickle nearby. "Hey Lardner," Thomas called out, "I see you've got part of your old communist emblem. Where's the hammer to go with the sickle?" Lardner replied, "I see you're up to your old tricks, Congressman, shoveling chicken shit."

HUAC's circuslike investigations and unproved accusations left a trail of shattered reputations and broken lives. When a former State Department official committed suicide by leaping from a building, a HUAC committee member announced that HUAC had been investigating him and added jovially, "We will give out the other names as they jump out of windows." Under director J. Edgar Hoover, the FBI maintained bulging files on alleged radicals, including rumor, second-hand gossip, and material gathered by illegal wiretaps.

The anticommunist hysteria found expression in two laws passed over Truman's veto. The Internal Security Act of 1950 required communist and "communist-front" organizations to register with the government. The McCarran-Walter Immigration Act of 1952 set up screening measures to keep out "subversives" and mandated the deportation of immigrants, even those who had become U.S. citizens, who belonged to suspect organizations. In the spirit of the wartime confinement of Japanese Americans, the law provided for the imprisonment of suspected security risks in the event of a national emergency. Of all the politicians to capitalize on the postwar communist scare, none gained greater notoriety than Senator Joseph McCarthy of Wisconsin. In February 1950, McCarthy burst from obscurity with a Lincoln Day speech in West Virginia. Waving a piece of paper, he claimed to have a list of 205 communists harbored by the State Department. In what would become a typical pattern, McCarthy soon reduced the number to fifty-seven, and eventually to one. Refusing to release his "list," he hedged on whether he meant actual communists or more vaguely defined "policy risks." But the public responded avidly, and for five years McCarthy basked in the limelight as the media reported his endless charges, countercharges, and sensational revelations. "McCARTHY WILL ACCUSE STATE DEPT. BIG SHOT" announced one *Washington Post* headline in May 1950. In a rambling four-hour Senate speech punctuated by swigs from a bottle of "cough medicine," McCarthy smeared the reputation of Owen Lattimore, an Asian specialist at Johns Hopkins University and occasional State Department adviser. "Ask almost any schoolchild who the architect of our Far Eastern policy is," McCarthy declared inanely at one point, "and he will say 'Owen Lattimore.'"

Lattimore was one of many Asian specialists who had viewed Mao Zedong's revolution as a complex phenomenon rooted in China's history and politics, not simply a manifestation of a "world communist conspiracy" controlled from the Kremlin. The forty thousand pages of documents in Lattimore's FBI file reveal not a shred of evidence for McCarthy's claims that Lattimore was the villain who had "lost" China and was "the top Russian spy in America." At worst, Lattimore was "guilty" of possessing a prickly personality and of having written naively upbeat assessments of Stalin and the Soviet system in the 1930s and the war years. But Lattimore's challenge to Cold War oversimplifications in his view of Chinese politics made him vulnerable. By their crude demonizing techniques, McCarthy and those who took his charges seriously blighted the careers of a generation of Asian specialists whose wisdom would be sorely missed.

In the summer of 1950, a Senate committee chaired by Millard Tydings of Maryland found McCarthy's charges "a fraud and a hoax," but this evaluation failed to silence the senator. When McCarthy campaigned against several Democratic senators that fall and won credit for defeating four of them, including Tydings, the potency of the "communist issue" became chillingly clear. At first, Republican leaders viewed McCarthy as an asset in their campaign to regain the White House in 1952. Senator Taft advised, "Keep talking and if one case doesn't work out, proceed with another." McCarthy, invariably lugging a briefcase crammed with "documents," became a fixture on the right-wing lecture circuit.

"McCarthyism," however, was not the creation of a lone senator. Many others in Congress and the nation emulated McCarthy, HUAC, and Hoover's FBI in the frantic search for subversives. Crusty Senator Pat McCarran of Nevada, chair of the Senate Internal Security Subcommittee, although less publicity-mad than McCarthy, grimly pursued the quest for security risks. Senators from both parties— Democrat James Eastland of Mississippi and Republican William Jenner of Indiana, for example—joined in. Blacklists circulated by shadowy organizations of superpatriots called for boycotts of suspected actors and performers; one influential list was called *Red Channels*. American Legion Post No. 41 in Syracuse, New York, set up its own Un-American Activities Committee.

Radio and television performers, labor organizers, public-school teachers, college professors, ministers, civil-rights activists, and librarians found their careers blighted by charges of disloyalty. Methodist bishop G. Bromley Oxnam, folksinger Pete Seeger, playwright Arthur Miller, and actors Charlie Chaplin, John Garfield, and Zero Mostel ranked among the victims. Some three hundred New York City school teachers were fired as security risks. University of Michigan mathematician Chandler Davis went to jail for six months for having refused to tell HUAC whether he was a communist. Witnesses before investigative committees who invoked their constitutional right not to testify were smeared as "Fifth Amendment Communists." Soviet spies were not a figment of the Right's imagination, but the peddlers of

FOCUS ON: *THE NATIONAL-SECURITY STATE*

It was in the near-hysterical days of the early Cold War that Congress, fearful of communist subversion at home and abroad, created what came to be called the national-security state. In 1947 Congress transformed the wartime Office of Strategic Services into the Central Intelligence Agency (CIA) and set up the high-level National Security Council to advise the president on security matters. The Internal Security Act of 1950 restricted the civil rights of communists and alleged "fellow-travelers." In these years, too, the Justice Department's Federal Bureau of Investigation, headed since 1924 by J. Edgar Hoover, expanded its national-security role, gathering files on individuals and organizations stigmatized as subversive or disloyal. There were 890 FBI agents in 1940 and 10,000 by 1970.

Initially, the public paid little heed to these agencies' activities. When security operations did impinge on Americans' awareness, the response was generally favorable. "The FBI in Peace and War," a popular radio show of the 1950s, presented Hoover's agency in a heroic light, as did the 1959 movie *The FBI Story.* Visitors to Washington, D.C., flocked to FBI headquarters, where exciting exhibits showed how the G-men had cracked tough cases.

The heyday of the national-security state came in the 1950s and 1960s. The CIA, exceeding its intelligence-gathering mandate and operating largely outside congressional oversight, plotted assassinations, overthrew hostile governments, and conducted clandestine operations all over the world. It promoted anticommunism by secretly funding Radio Free Europe, the Congress of Cultural Freedom, and other front organizations. In addition, CIA money financed activities of the National Student Association, the largest and most significant student organization in the 1960s. At home, the FBI pursued its antiradical activities, even conducting illegal break-ins and tapping telephones to spy on what it considered extremist groups. Reflecting Hoover's hostility to the civil-rights movement, the FBI, with the approval of Attorney General Robert Kennedy, tapped the telephones and hotel rooms of Martin Luther King, Jr., in 1963. America's national-security apparatus, created to protect U.S. freedom, began to threaten that freedom.

The CIA's botched Bay of Pigs invasion of Cuba in 1961 had stimulated some criticism of national-security agencies, but far harsher attacks came in the mid-1970s in the wake of the Watergate scandal. In 1974 the *New York Times* reported that the CIA, although legally banned from domestic activities, had assembled dossiers on thousands of American citizens and organizations. In 1976 President Ford's attorney

hysteria and ideological conformity spread their nets widely and destructively, ruining lives and shattering careers.

Unions, film studios, school boards, professional societies, and even the American Civil Liberties Union purged alleged radicals. Universities imposed loyalty oaths to placate outside investigators. With politicians, patriotic groups, and right-wing general, Edward Levi, revealed that J. Edgar Hoover, who had died in 1972, had secretly assembled derogatory files on presidents and legislators as a way of protecting his vast power. Responding to the shifting mood, by 1974 Congress had already conducted a broad investigation of federal security agencies. It expanded the 1966 Freedom of Information Act ensuring citizens' access to their government files, and it restricted the CIA's power to carry out clandestine operations.

But abuses continued. The National Security Council became the focus of controversy in 1986–1987 with revelations that staffer Oliver North, operating out of the White House, had funneled millions of dollars to a CIA-backed army fighting Nicaragua's leftist government. Congress had explicitly banned such funding. Much evidence linked CIA director William Casey to these illegalities, but Casey died before his role could be fully explored.

In 1986, at last Congress reined in the FBI, requiring that all future FBI directors be approved by Congress and limited to ten-year terms. (Hoover had enjoyed a forty-eight-year tenure.) At the same time, historians and journalists began to chip away at the FBI's carefully burnished image. Books such as Athan Theoharis's and John Stuart Cox's *The Boss* (1988) and Curt Gentry's *J. Edgar Hoover: The Man and the Secrets* (1991) revealed shocking details about the FBI and its director. As Americans requested their FBI files under the Freedom of Information Act, the scope of the agency's snooping emerged. Even Walt Disney was exposed as an FBI informant. (Disney gave FBI agents free admission to Disneyland, while Hoover permitted Disney to film an episode of TV's "Mickey Mouse Club" at FBI headquarters after Disney assured him that the show would portray the FBI as "something which children would look up to.") Among the more bizarre twists in the dismantling of the FBI legend was the revelation that Hoover, the paragon of rectitude, had been a closet homosexual and cross dresser. Questions about the FBI's shadowy relations with a succession of presidential administrations from Roosevelt's to Nixon's remain unanswered.

The end of the Cold War further eroded the national-security state, as the CIA struggled to redefine its role in a political culture no longer obsessed by the Soviet menace. In 1993, fending off calls for deep cuts in the agency's budget, CIA director R. James Woolsey portrayed the post–Cold War world as a jungle in which a dragon had been killed but where deadly snakes still abounded. Reflecting the shift from military to economic issues, the agency turned its sleuthing skills to ferreting out the positions of America's economic rivals in sensitive trade negotiations.

The period from the mid-1970s to the early 1990s, in short, proved trying for the national-security state. Having enjoyed high public esteem in earlier years as leaders in the crusade against communism abroad and subversion at home, these agencies now confronted an uphill battle to reshape their mission and rebuild their tarnished reputations in a new era.

broadcasters such as Fulton Lewis, Jr., fanning the anticommunist flames, it is hardly surprising that many organizations failed to take a courageous stand.

Eventually Congress and the nation would turn against McCarthy (see Chapter 4), but in the early fifties, he reigned as one of the most powerful and feared men in America. For all his apparent zealotry, though, McCarthy was primarily an opportunist, increasingly gripped by alcoholism, who cared about little beyond tomorrow's headlines. Nevertheless, the fears that he rubbed raw in the American psyche represented the Cold War's principal domestic legacy. A climate of suspicion and ideological conformity, exploited by politicians and others for their own purposes, pervaded the nation as the 1952 election approached.

Boom Times

The same years that saw the deepening Cold War, the coming of the Korean War, and a bitterly divisive political climate at home also brought an economic boom that, with periodic setbacks, would endure through the 1970s. By late 1948 unemployment stood at an amazingly low 2 percent. The gross national product, which had risen from $100 billion to $211 billion during the war, dipped briefly afterward but soon resumed its upward climb, hitting $346 billion by 1952. Released at last from the heavy hand of depression and war, their savings accounts bulging with wartime earnings, Americans binged on a buying spree. *Holiday* magazine, founded in 1946 to capitalize on the wanderlust of newly affluent Americans, embodied the new culture of consumption. *Holiday*, proclaimed the editors, borrowing Thomas Jefferson's ringing phrase, was "dedicated to the pursuit of happiness."

As consumer spending jumped 60 percent between 1945 and 1950, businesses expanded, modernized, and retooled to meet the demand. When young Henry Ford II took over Ford Motor Company from his aging grandfather in 1945, the moment seemed to symbolize a new era for American capitalism. The goods that gushed from U.S. factories in 1950 included 6.2 million refrigerators, 14.6 million radios, and 6.2 million automobiles. Nearly 5 million new housing units sprang up between 1945 and 1950. Corporate America prospered as never before. By 1952 the United States boasted fifty-nine companies with more than $1 billion in assets, led by Standard Oil of New Jersey ($4.7 billion), General Motors ($3.7 billion), and U.S. Steel ($3.1 billion).

The military demands of the Korean War did cut civilian output somewhat and contributed to an inflationary uptick in 1951 and 1952 and annual federal budget deficits that hit $9.4 billion by 1953, but overall the conflict stimulated the economy. In addition to its own defense build-up, the United States sold large quantities of military equipment to its Cold War allies. U.S. military exports, about $500 million in 1946, reached $2.1 billion by 1952, translating into jobs and profits for defense industries. As we saw in Chapter 2, nonmilitary foreign aid also drove exports of farm commodities and industrial goods. Farm surpluses shrank as the military's needs for food increased. Unemployment, too, which had crept up to 5 percent in the spring of 1950, fell to less than half that level by autumn. To sustain the economic boom during the Korean War, the government permitted corporations to depreciate capital investment in five years rather than the usual twenty-five, spurring a wave of plant construction, expansion, and modernization.

A baby boom fueled postwar prosperity. From a 1930s low of fewer than twenty births per thousand population, the U.S. birthrate climbed steadily during and after the war to more than twenty-five per thousand in 1947, as young couples looked to the future with hope.* Maternity wards thrived, along with home building, school construction, and sales of baby food, diapers, strollers, children's clothes, and play equipment. The surging birthrate was one more stimulus to the boom. With ample raw materials and energy, pent-up demand, a mature corporate structure, and well-established systems for advertising and distributing goods, the economy took off.

Yet not all Americans enjoyed prosperity. As we shall see in Chapter 4, poverty remained a fact of life for millions, especially the rural poor and minorities in urban ghettos. In 1950 over a third of U.S. families earned annual incomes of under $3,000. Although the buying power of the 1950 dollar was about five times what it would be in the 1990s, these figures suggest the precarious situation of many families. For those at the lower end of the scale, the new cars and appliances that glittered in show-rooms, department stores, and magazine ads remained distant dreams. This grimmer underside of the economic picture, however, attracted little notice as the consumer boom roared on.

Contributing to the boom was a parade of new products that swiftly became part of daily life, from ballpoint pens and televisions to transistor radios and Polaroid cameras. In 1947 a small company in Rochester, New York, bought the rights to a machine that could reproduce print copy by means of "xerography," a technique copyrighted by Chester Carlson in 1940. Soon the company would become the Xerox Corporation. Photocopying machines, spreading from corporate offices, government bureaus, and academia into the larger society, launched a revolution in communications.

Computer technology, spurred by wartime antiaircraft research (see p. 25), also burgeoned after the war. In 1946 University of Pennsylvania engineers John Eckert, Jr., and John Mauchly formed a company to produce and market a computer that they called UNIVAC (Universal Automatic Computer), one of which became the first government computer, delivered to the Census Bureau in 1951. International Business Machines (IBM), already a leader in the office-equipment industry, marketed its first computer, the 701 model, in 1953. In coming years, IBM would emerge as a giant in the information-processing revolution.

The computer age still lay ahead, but its theoretical and technical foundations were in place by the early fifties. Norbert Weiner, a professor of mathematics at the Massachusetts Institute of Technology, speculated on the computer's social and intellectual implications. A child prodigy who had earned his Ph.D. in mathematical logic from Harvard at age nineteen, Weiner in a 1940 memo to the U.S. government's Office of Scientific Research and Development had set forth key theoretical elements of the modern computer. In *Cybernetics* (1947) and *The Human Uses of Human Beings* (1950), Weiner explored the computer's implications for American society. Although conceding the new technology's promise—in medical research, for example—Weiner remained apprehensive. As computers took over routine production functions, he warned, "the average human being . . . [will have] nothing to sell that is worth anyone's money to buy." Weiner also foresaw a time when the computer's ability to process data would vastly extend the power of governments, the

---

* By contrast, the 1990 birthrate would be 16.7 per 1,000 population.

military, and corporate giants. Still only a distant blip on the radar screen, the computer would grow steadily more important in the decades ahead.

Beyond "Rosie the Riveter": Women in Postwar America

For American women, the post-1945 era brought transition and uncertainty as strong cultural and social forces buttressed the status quo in the face of incipient pressures for change. At first glance, postwar employment data suggest major changes in women's lives. The drop in female employment immediately after the war soon reversed itself. By 1950, 29 percent of U.S. women held jobs, higher than in 1940 although still below the wartime peak. As during the war, women who entered the labor force in this period—especially middle-class married women—seemed more interested in contributing to the family income than in pursuing feminist goals or breaking new ground professionally. Discriminatory hiring practices and subtle cultural pressures channeled most of them into traditional "women's jobs" as secretaries, salespersons, or clerks.

A few old-line feminist organizations carried on the fight for women's rights, but efforts to better women's lot through legislation fared badly. When the Senate in 1946 failed to muster the necessary two-thirds vote to pass an equal rights amendment, the *New York Times* intoned approvingly, "Motherhood cannot be amended." That same year, an equal-pay bill for women workers failed in the Senate. The conservative mood, revealing a longing for stability after the traumas of depression and war, recoiled against even moderate challenges to traditional notions of proper gender roles and activities.

Perhaps in delayed reaction to the upsurge of female workers during the war, countless writers in the late 1940s and the 1950s urged women to embrace the domestic role that they said nature intended. Dr. Benjamin Spock's best-selling *Common Sense Book of Baby and Child Care* (1946) assumed the mother's presence at home with children. In a 1950 *Atlantic Monthly* article, "Women Aren't Men," the female author exclaimed, "God protect us from the efficient go-getter business woman whose feminine instincts have been completely stifled." In *Modern Woman: The Lost Sex* (1947), Freudian analyist Marynia Farnham and sociologist Ferdinand Lundberg dismissed feminism as a neurotic response by women to male dominance. Women who resisted the domestic and maternal roles, Farnham and Lundberg warned, would suffer emotional disorders and social difficulties.

The mass culture drove home the message. Lucille Ball, star of the early TV comedy "I Love Lucy," invariably met disaster when she sought a job or pursued interests beyond the home. (She never stopped trying, however, revealing the underlying tension in the cult of domesticity.) In the 1950 film *All About Eve*, Ann Baxter played a coldly ambitious career woman whose charming manner masked a calculating drive to succeed, hardly an admirable role model for young women in postwar America. While Tennessee Williams's play *A Streetcar Named Desire* (1947) and Mickey Spillane's murder mysteries such as *I, the Jury* (1947) featured violent, supermacho protagonists, the mass media increasingly domesticated the American

Left: Government propaganda such as this poster urged women to take jobs in industry. When the war ended, the message suddenly changed. (*War Manpower Commission, 1942*) *Right:* Reinforcing several female stereotypes, this 1952 beer ad portrayed the typical wife as a fashion-conscious consumer devoted to making her husband happy, yet manipulative as well. (*Courtesy The Stroh Brewery Company*)

woman. Predictably, this theme pervaded the *Ladies Home Journal, Women's Home Companion,* and other leading women's magazines.

The day of the WACS, the WAVES, "Rosie the Riveter," and "Wonder Woman," a comic-book character introduced in 1941, seemed remote by the late 1940s. Betty Friedan's *The Feminine Mystique,* the book that would trigger a new wave of feminist activism, still lay fifteen years in the future. The idealized domesticity that loomed so large in the 1950s had roots in a long tradition of American social thought, but it received strong reinforcement from the early postwar reaction to the unsettling changes in women's roles during World War II. Just as the anticommunist crusaders responded to global threats by attempting to enforce political conformity at home, so the celebrators of the domestic ideal coped with the threat of radical changes in gender relations by seeking to reimpose the imagined harmony and clearcut distinctions of an earlier era.

Diversion and Doubt:
Culture in the Early Postwar Years

Popular culture in the Truman years reflected the ambivalence of a nation powerful and prospering yet unnerved by Cold War anxiety and nuclear fears. The movie industry quickly took note of the atomic bomb. *The Beginning or the End?* (1946),

Hollywood's version of the Manhattan Project, offered a cautiously hopeful answer to the question posed in its title. In *The Day the Earth Stood Still* (1951), highly evolved aliens arrived in a spaceship to urge earthlings to stop their foolish quarrels before they self-destructed. Mass magazines—notably *Reader's Digest,* with a circulation of 8.5 million, and *Life,* at 5.3 million—offered dire warnings of the communist menace and occasional lurid scenarios of World War III. A few Hollywood movies presented heavy-handed anticommunist sermons, but the mass culture offered escape more frequently than overt propaganda and in this sense played a crucial role in Cold War America. With the atomic bomb, the Cold War, and domestic economic problems stirring fear and uneasiness, the media often offered a reassuring alternative to the stresses of the early postwar era. A series of Broadway musicals—*Guys and Dolls* (1949), *South Pacific* (1950), *The King and I* (1951)—with their movie and record spinoffs, provided diversion as well.

America's radio stations, whose numbers nearly tripled from 1945 to 1950, remained important mass culture outlets. In the late 1940s, millions of housewives tuned in daily for teary soap operas such as "Stella Dallas" and "When a Girl Marries." World issues rarely intruded into these sagas of romance and domestic crisis. (How could so many listen so long to so little? marveled one critic.) To adolescents, radio offered a series of mostly male role models and stereotypes: "Jack Armstrong, All-American Boy," "Sergeant Preston of the Yukon," and "The Lone Ranger" with his faithful Indian companion, Tonto. The whole family gathered for the evening comedy shows of vaudeville veterans Jack Benny, Bob Hope, and Fred Allen.

Radio's preeminence soon ended, however. The first commercial television broadcast dated from 1939, when NBC televised Franklin Roosevelt's opening the New York World's Fair. Soon after the war's end, TV sets with tiny screens attracted fascinated crowds to store windows. The flickering green images held viewers spellbound even when transmitting only a test pattern. In 1948 a minuscule 0.4 percent of U.S. households had television; by 1952, more than a third did. Indeed, the resulting mass-culture explosion went hand-in-glove with the postwar economic boom. Corporate sponsors had paid liberally to hawk their wares—from toothpaste to breakfast cereal to shampoo to cigarettes—on radio. Then they discovered TV's potential. Spending on TV advertising would surge from $171 million in 1950 to $454 million by 1952; by mid-decade it would surpass $1 billion.

Early TV shows often copied radio programming. "Faraway Hill," the first TV soap opera, debuted in 1946, as did two durable variety shows: Ed Sullivan's "Toast of the Town" and "Arthur Godfrey's Talent Scouts." Some shows such as "The Life of Riley" and "The Lone Ranger" moved directly from radio to TV. Live drama began in 1947 with the "Kraft Television Theater"; that year also launched the popular children's show "Howdy Doody." One mother remarked, "The hours between play and bed used to be the most hectic part of the day. Now I know where the children are. The television set is the best nurse in the world."

At first, many local channels did their own programming with home-grown talent—one Atlanta station spotlighted "Morgus, the Crazy Weatherman"—but television soon went national. NBC, broadcasting forty hours a week by 1947, put together the first television network two years later. CBS, under hard-driving William

Paley, soon passed NBC in the ratings. Paley perfected the concept of "audience flow" programming, luring the audience for one show to stay tuned for the programs that followed.

Although Hollywood and TV eventually formed a profitable alliance, movie moguls initially viewed the new medium as a dire threat, and with good reason: Movie attendance fell by 14 percent between 1946 and 1949. The *New York Times* reported in 1949, "The very mention of television, in many important [movie] industry quarters, evokes only icy silence." Politicians, on the other hand, loved this new medium, trimming their long-winded speeches to fit the demands of TV schedules. Planners of the 1948 Democratic convention warned delegates to behave, for the proceedings would now be seen as well as heard. The cameras had "caught a moment of history just as it happened," exclaimed *Time* magazine when television covered Truman's 1949 inaugural. "Ten million televiewers from the Atlantic coast to the Mississippi felt that they had truly been there with Washington's cheering thousands."

Others held high hopes for the new medium as well. A media executive in 1945 glowingly described TV's promise: "There is something about television that is going to make every city, town, and village in the United States a more democratic, more progressive, more closely knit community." For a time, intelligent, well-written dramatic shows like "Playhouse 90" and "Studio One" and light-classical musical programs such as "The Bell Telephone Hour" and "The Voice of Firestone" seemed to fulfill such hopes.

But advertisers' demands for ever-larger audiences inevitably sounded the death knell for quality fare. Scriptwriters for the popular show "Men Against Crime," for example, which premiered in 1949 under the sponsorship of Camel cigarettes, were instructed, "It has been found that we retain audience interest best when our story is concerned with murder. Therefore, although other crimes may be introduced, somebody must be murdered, preferably early, with the threat of more violence to come." (The cigarette-company sponsor of "Men Against Crime" also insisted that no actor ever cough on the show.) Hand-wringing over the medium's banality replaced the early enthusiasm; Fred Allen called TV "chewing gum for the eyes." Television did sometimes give viewers a window on the world—the UN debates when the Korean War broke out were carried live, for example—but mediocrity and the trivial predominated. By the midfifties, as historian William O'Neill observes, television had become "a great industry but a failed art."

The marketing of goods drove other elements of the mass media besides television and thereby hastened the emergence of a standardized popular culture organized around consumerism. As in the rest of corporate America, large companies dominated. Three networks—CBS, NBC, and ABC—controlled early television. Four periodicals—*Life, Collier's, Saturday Evening Post,* and *Reader's Digest*—ruled the magazine world. Five major studios—MGM, Paramount, Warner Brothers, RKO, and 20th Century Fox—produced nearly all U.S. movies. Through their control of a network of big-city theaters, these five studios also raked in 70 percent of box-office revenues. But these industries proved sensitive to more than just advertisers. Under pressure from powerful institutions and interest groups, the mass culture turned bland. The Catholic Church's Legion of Decency and Hollywood's own Production Code Authority monitored movie morals. (The Legion of Decency condemned the 1953 film "The Moon Is Blue," for example, because the word *virgin* appeared in a dialogue.) The Cold War climate of intellectual conformity intensified what a 1948 critic called the movies' "retreat into apathy" and "ideological fatigue." The mass media thus helped to create a national culture shaped by market calculations and a quest for the lowest-common-denominator level of diversion. Innovation, creativity, or the thoughtful exploration of public issues had little part.

Beneath the popular culture's bland, escapist surface, currents of apprehension vaguely connected with the nuclear threat eddied, symbolized by a rash of "flying saucer" sightings beginning in 1947. (Soviet diplomat Andrei Gromyko, in a rare flash of humor, quipped that they came from his nation's discus throwers practicing for the Olympics.) Postwar movies of the "film noir" genre, such as *He Walked by Night* (1949), featured betrayal, sinister shadows, and menacing dangers lurking in familiar settings. The mystified hero of one such film complained, "I'm backed up in a dark corner and I don't know who's hitting me!" In *Knock on Any Door* (1949), a defense attorney (Humphrey Bogart) defends a young murderer by describing the youth's sordid, poverty-stricken boyhood, but the kid goes to the electric chair anyway.

The nervousness revealed in these movies came to the light in American religion as well. Evangelist Billy Graham rocketed to fame on the strength of a Los Angeles tent revival in September 1949, just as the Soviet Union exploded its first atomic bomb. Graham thundered, "An arms race unprecedented in the history of the world is driving us madly toward destruction! . . . Time is desperately short. . . . [P]repare to meet thy God!" Other religious leaders preached less apocalyptic remedies for nuclear worries. In *A Guide to Confident Living* (1948) and *Faith Is the Answer* (1950), the Reverend Norman Vincent Peale advised anxious Americans to "say confidently to yourself: 'Through God's help and the application of simple techniques, I will be free from fear.' Believe that—practice it, and it will be so." Pharmaceuticals offered a chemical means to the same end; the year that witnessed the advent of hydrogen-bomb research and the outbreak of the Korean War (1950) also brought the first commercially available tranquilizer, called Miltown.

While popular culture offered its mix of diversion, escape, and foreboding, a trio of young writers probed the stresses and fault lines of American culture. (In all three books, interestingly, women are either absent or serve as ineffectual background figures.) Norman Mailer's cynical war novel *The Naked and the Dead* (1948), set in the South Pacific, offered a view of the brutal, coarse, and mechanical behavior of men in combat that differed strikingly from wartime propaganda images of cheerful, idealistic GIs. Arthur Miller's play *Death of Salesman* (1949) searingly portrayed a bewildered loser, sixty-three-year old Willy Loman, caught up in fantasies of success pathetically at odds with the realities of his defeated life. Finally, J. D. Salinger's *The Catcher in the Rye* (1951) sardonically viewed middle-class pretenses through the eyes of seventeen-year-old Holden Caulfield. An atomic-age Huck Finn, Holden clings to his innocence—trying, for example, to erase "Fuck You" graffiti so that his kid sister won't see it—in a grown-up world shadowed by the bomb. A classic coming-of-age novel, *Catcher* captured the historical moment when the moral clarity and national unity of the war dissolved into postwar ambiguities. Salinger uses Holden's youthful naiveté to judge a "phony" society troubled by Cold War obsessions, nuclear angst, and an inconclusive war in Korea, a society that determinedly insists that all is well because the economy is thriving. Huck had headed west at the end of Mark Twain's novel; Holden narrates his story from an institution where he has been confined after a nervous breakdown.

A few postwar writers explored specific social problems that roiled beneath the surface of American life. Nelson Algren's *Man with the Golden Arm* (1949) looked at drug addiction, gambling, and crime in Chicago's inner city, subjects largely ignored in the 1940s. Laura Hobson's *Gentlemen's Agreement* (1946), written in the shadow of the Jewish holocaust, whose full horror emerged in shocking photographs of the Nazi death camps, exposed the many faces of antisemitism in American society. Hobson, whose father had edited New York's *Jewish Daily Forward*, began writing her novel after reading in a 1944 *Time* article that when Mississippi congressman John Rankin called radio newsman Walter Winchell "the little Kike" on the House floor, not a single legislator rebuked him. In Hobson's story, a Gentile journalist explores antisemitism by pretending to be a Jew. Both as a novel and a 1947 movie starring Gregory Peck, *Gentlemen's Agreement* spotlighted a hitherto-neglected social issue.

Ralph Ellison's *Invisible Man* (1952), a novel of enormous imaginative power, explored the theme of race in America from a black perspective. In a succession of often surreal episodes that move from the turn-of-the-century rural South to the urban North of World War II, the nameless narrator seeks his identity ("When I discover who I am, I'll be free") and probes the psychological experience of African-Americans living in a society that is simultaneously racist and blind to their existence. He joins "The Brotherhood," a thinly fictionalized Communist party, but finds that it, too, exploits him. He quits in disillusionment.

Ellison challenged the tendency of white, middle-class culture to distort. "When the white American holding up most twentieth-century fiction says 'This is the American reality,'" he commented in 1946, "the Negro tends to answer . . . 'Perhaps, but you've left this out, and this, and this. And most of all, what you'd have the world accept as *me* is not even human." Despite this challenge, *Invisible Man*, apart from its anticommunist theme, did not take an overtly political stand. This apolitical quality, along with the book's ambiguity, complex symbolism, and hallucinatory states of consciousness, reflect the early Cold War cultural climate. Ellison rejected both the radical politics and the naturalistic style of Richard Wright's *Native Son* (1940), with its stark picture of life in Chicago's black ghetto. "This is not an attack upon white society," Ellison insisted. "[The hero] must assert and achieve his own humanity." *Invisible Man*, a work of stunning psychological clarity, avoided politics in ways that spoke volumes about the times in which it was written.

Postwar social critics, too, employed the neutral vocabulary of psychology and sociology rather than of radical politics. In *The Lonely Crowd* (1950), sociologist David Riesman looked at the psychological effects of mass society and consumer abundance. Exploring changes in "the American character" (that is, the white, middle-class character), Riesman discerned a progression from "inner directedness" to "other directedness." Americans, he claimed, lacked a firm sense of self in the new consumerist age and thus placed a high premium on social acceptance and "fitting in." *The Lonely Crowd*, as we shall see, opened a floodgate of books lamenting the conformism and cultural insipidity of 1950s America.

All Aboard the Freedom Train: Mobilizing Against Communism

Early postwar culture mobilized behind the Cold War in an engagement that took many forms. A red, white, and blue "Freedom Train," its gleaming engine named "The Spirit of 1776," toured America in the late 1940s, bringing replicas of the Declaration of Independence, the Constitution, and other icons of American freedom to hundreds of cities and towns. Hollywood, having idealized the heroic Soviet people during the war, quickly shifted gears after 1945. *Red Danube* (1949) chronicled Eastern Europe's fall to Soviet imperialism. In *My Son John* (1952), an American Legion member finds the communist taint in his own family. *Big Jim McClain* (1952) starred John Wayne as a HUAC investigator tracking communist spies in Hawaii.

The art world, too, reflected Cold War preoccupations. When abstract-expressionist artist Jackson Pollock began to drip paint on canvas to produce his swirling "action paintings" in the late 1940s, Henry Luce's *Life* magazine promoted him as a symbol of New York's rise to artistic supremacy that paralleled America's global dominance in other spheres. *Life* also pointed to the success of avant-garde artists like Pollock—whose work many of *Life*'s readers must have found utterly baffling— as heartening proof of U.S. cultural freedom in contrast to the artistic repression found behind the Iron Curtain.

Intellectuals who wrote about politics in the Truman years usually called for a toughened liberalism purged of the naiveté of the 1930s, more appreciative of American democracy, and more alert to the communist menace. Many had embraced Marxism themselves in the 1930s only to be disillusioned by Stalin's show trials and by the Nazi-Soviet Pact of 1939. The Soviet dictator's postwar actions in Eastern Europe confirmed these chastened intellectuals in their anticommunism. The era brought a stream of confessional literature—the 1950 anthology *The God That Failed* and Whittaker Chambers's *Witness* (1952) are the best-known examples—in which intellectuals and writers repented of their flirtation with communism.

The critic Lionel Trilling, professor of English literature at Columbia University, was one star in a constellation of New York intellectuals who influenced early Cold War political thought. In his 1947 novel *The Middle of the Journey* and 1950 collection of essays entitled *The Liberal Imagination*, Trilling repudiated Marxism and criticized liberals' naive faith in reform and their optimism about human nature. Although he insisted on the morally ambiguous nature of all political systems, Trilling argued passionately that a democratic, culturally diverse society was far preferable to an absolutist one (such as Stalinist Russia), whatever its ideological pretensions.

In *The Vital Center* (1949), Arthur Schlesinger, Jr., who taught American history at Harvard, offered a chastened liberalism—sternly anticommunist yet committed to the New Deal's social-welfare agenda—as the fighting faith that could fortify America against totalitarianism. Schlesinger carefully distinguished his anticommunism from HUAC's red-baiting, yet his own discussion of communism was fairly monolithic. Graphically describing Stalin's dictatorship, Schlesinger went on to imply that the Soviet Union could never be negotiated with, only defeated, if not in war then through the West's superior "technological dynamism." Like NSC-68, *The Vital Center* largely ignored legitimate Soviet security interests and world realities that did not fit the book's starkly bipolar analytical framework.

The Protestant theologian Reinhold Niebuhr profoundly influenced Trilling, Schlesinger, and many other Cold War intellectuals. A Missourian of German immigrant stock, Niebuhr attended Yale Divinity School, held a parish in Detroit, and after 1928 taught at New York's Union Theological Seminary. Initially drawn to the reform-minded Social Gospel, Niebuhr had embraced Marxism in the early 1930s. But disillusionment soon set in, and in a stream of books and essays, he deplored all absolutist ideologies. Outgrow your sentimental optimism, Niebuhr exhorted Americans, and recognize the power calculations that underlie international relations and the sinfulness inherent in the behavior of all nations and social groups.

Communists were especially fearsome, Niebuhr warned in *The Irony of American History* (1952), because in their absolutist zeal they tried to achieve by force the social ideal that Western liberals only fitfully pursued. As such, they translated their utopian vision into "noxious forms of tyranny." Indeed, Niebuhr found communism in its "fanatical fury" more sinister than nazism, because its gloss of idealism made its evil less obvious. At the barricades stood the West and its leader, the United States. Although highly skeptical of American political thought, Niebuhr, like Trilling, argued that the United States, with its pragmatism, freedom of expression, and relatively open politics, offered far greater promise of a reasonably just social order than did the communist world.

Niebuhr held highly precise strategic views and translated these generalities into avid support for the Cold War. The Soviets would not stop with swallowing Eastern Europe, he predicted in 1946, but would try to "extend their power over the whole of Europe." To avoid war, he advised, do not be too afraid of it. He praised the apocalyptic tone of the Truman Doctrine. That the governments of Greece and Turkey were undemocratic was irrelevant, he insisted. "What is at stake is not the internal structure of these nations, but the peace of Europe, which cannot be preserved if the communist tide inundates it."

Niebuhr exerted enormous influence in the early Cold War era. One journalist called him "the official Establishment theologian." Opinion molders cited his authority, and George Kennan called him "the father of us all." Popularized versions of his message appeared in *Time, Life,* and *Reader's Digest.* His somber, world-weary visage on the March 8, 1948, cover of *Time* seemed to personify the desperate nature of the Cold War struggle. (*Time* did publish a photograph of the theologian playing with his dog. "Sometimes he relaxes," the caption assured readers.) Under Niebuhr's influence, anticommunism became the one absolute for Cold War liberals otherwise wary of absolutist thinking.

In 1947 Niebuhr, Schlesinger, and others founded Americans for Democratic Action (ADA) to rally New Deal liberals who were also staunchly anticommunist. In 1948, after toying with the idea of an Eisenhower candidacy, the ADA endorsed Truman and, with reason, denounced Henry Wallace's Progressive party as a communist front. These Truman-era liberals wrote from their own experience, which for many included an interval when they themselves had succumbed to Marxism's lure. They wrote, too, at a time when Joseph Stalin ruled the Soviet Union as absolute dictator. (Introducing a new edition of *The Vital Center* in 1970, Schlesinger would advise his critics, "Perhaps it would help if, every time they see the word 'communism' in this book, they would read 'Stalinism.'") They also formulated their anticommunist dogma as the Soviet grip on Eastern Europe tightened and as Mao Zedong's communists triumphed in China. The changes triggered by Stalin's death in 1953, the break-up of the Sino-Soviet alliance, Moscow's more moderate stance in the era of détente, and the collapse of communism and of the Soviet Union itself in the 1990s all lay ahead in the late 1940s and early 1950s.

These liberal intellectuals' worldview is understandable and merits respect, yet such thinkers served as cheerleaders for the Cold War in its period of maximum rhetorical excess. Their broad generalizations about the essential nature of communist ideology tended to ignore the Soviet Union's actual history and legitimate interests and to blur the complexity of specific issues. Despite their caveats, the logic of their position led to an unquestioning embrace of "the West" and of the Truman administration's version of Cold War issues. The oversimplification became even cruder as the media packaged the intellectuals' ideas for mass consumption. When the *New York Times Magazine* in April 1948 published an article by Schlesinger entitled "Not Left, Not Right, But a Vital Center," the magazine's cover illustration, reminiscent of the propaganda posters of the 1930s, showed the armies of "the Left" and "the Right" frantically retreating as a giant Statue of Liberty hand bearing the Torch of Freedom smashes a wedge between them.

As liberals enlisted for the Cold War, the other end of the ideological spectrum, conservatism, found few intellectual champions. Indeed, in *The Liberal Imagination*, Lionel Trilling insisted that the Right had no ideas, only "irritable mental gestures which seek to resemble ideas." Even as he wrote, however, the stirrings of a conservative ideological resurgence could be discerned, not only in the popularity of Hayek's *Road to Serfdom* but elsewhere. In 1951, for example, young William F. Buckley, Jr., entered the polemical wars with *God and Man at Yale*, a caustic attack on the secular rot eating away at the soul of his alma mater. Soon Buckley's magazine, the *National Review*, would arise as a witty and vigorous conservative voice challenging the assumptions of Marxists, democratic socialists, and liberals.

Whereas liberals like Trilling, Schlesinger, and Niebuhr contributed to a Cold War consensus on international issues, the Left-liberal, social-welfare themes of their domestic program stirred far less enthusiasm. Postwar Americans, including key spokespersons for the business community, may have come to terms with the New Deal, but they were in no mood for further reforms such as those espoused by intellectuals and embodied in Truman's Fair Deal. Advocating an aggressive, confrontational foreign policy, they sought a politics of stability, continuity, and maintenance of the status quo on the domestic front.

CONCLUSION

What underlying themes emerge from the welter of events, foreign and domestic, chronicled in the last two chapters? First, of course, these years gave rise to the Cold War, with all its ramifications. President Truman's handling of the early postwar differences with the Soviets and his presentation of the issues to the American people set a course that would influence U.S. history for decades. But many voices contributed to the molding of Cold War ideology, from Washington politicians to theologians, historians, literary critics, magazine editors, and moviemakers. In their sweeping rhetorical portrayals of the communist menace, the ideologists of 1945–1952 fashioned a more "tough-minded" liberalism, tried to pinpoint the "vital center" of U.S. political thought, and introduced powerful and enduring themes into American public discourse. Despite the quest for consensus on the domestic front as well as on international issues, the comparative unity of World War II soon gave way to heated political controversies and dark suspicions that pitted American against American. The nuclear-arms race dates from these years as well. Truman's fateful decision of August 1945, the failure of the postwar international-control effort, and critical actions in Washington and Moscow in the late 1940s and early 1950s launched a struggle for nuclear supremacy that for four decades would shadow the world with fears of thermonuclear annihilation.

Together with the Cold War and the nuclear-arms race, the postwar boom dramatically molded American history. Building on the production feats of the war years, the U.S. economy in the late 1940s and early 1950s achieved new levels of consumer abundance. Corporate America, taking credit for this cornucopia of consumer goods, moved to translate economic achievement into political influence. Although not directly attacking the New Deal, business organizations redefined some of its basic premises on their own terms. The rhetoric of "business-government partnership" that would pervade the politics of the 1950s took shape in this period. Organized labor, which had been so influential in the 1930s, found itself increasingly marginalized in debates over public policy.

The paradoxically upbeat and escapist, yet occasionally ominous, tone of postwar mass culture and the bleak outlook of some writers and social critics also held important implications for the future. During the war, most Americans had stood together in support of the common cause. This unity continued after 1945 in the foreign-policy arena, as the nation's political, intellectual, and media leaders promulgated a broadly supported Cold War consensus. But the story differed on the domestic front. Despite the postwar boom, millions remained outside the banquet hall looking in. Regardless of the social changes transforming the lives of African-Americans, institutionalized racism persisted. And in contrast to the culture's celebration of domesticity, the constraints that early postwar society imposed on women in its quest for stability would prove infirm and ultimately unsustainable. The elements of future conflict and unrest, in short, were already evident in the early 1950s to anyone observant enough to see them.

While red-baiters flung their charges of "subversion" and "disloyalty," novelists, playwrights, and social thinkers criticized the hypocrisies and evasions of postwar America. The America of Hobson, Salinger, Mailer, Ellison, and Riesman was not the America of the TV shows, the mass magazines, and the glossy ads. The alienation of an articulate minority of intellectuals would intensify as the 1950s wore on and would reach crisis proportions in the later 1960s.

The Truman years thus marked an uneasy transition from an era of depression and global war to one of economic abundance tempered by Cold War fears, nuclear

menace, divisions in the body politic, and only fitful attention to a variety of troubling social issues. The apprehensions that James Agee had felt as he watched the
victory celebrators in August 1945 were all too well founded.

By 1952 war memories were fading; Americans no longer self-consciously perceived themselves as living in a "postwar" era. In that year, Harry Truman, the residual legatee of a reform movement that had started twenty years before under Franklin Roosevelt, neared the end of a remarkable political career. In electing a new
president, Americans turned not to Truman's annointed successor, Adlai Stevenson,
but to a war hero known more for his generalship than for his political views. The
Eisenhower era was about to dawn.

SELECTED READINGS

Demobilization and Early Postwar Politics

Jack S. Ballard, *The Shock of Peace: Military and Economic Demobilization After World War II*
(1983); William C. Berman, *The Politics of Civil Rights in the Truman Administration* (1970);
Gerard H. Clarfield and William M. Wiecek, *Nuclear America: Military and Civilian Nuclear
Power in the United States, 1940–1980* (1984); Richard O. Davies, *Housing Reform During the
Truman Administration* (1966); Robert Donovan's two-volume history of the Truman presidency, *Conflict and Crisis* (1977) and *Tumultuous Years* (1982); Sidney D. Drell, *In the Shadow
of the Bomb: Physics and Arms Control* (1993); Andrew Dunar, *The Truman Scandals and the
Politics of Morality* (1984); Robert H. Ferrell, *Harry S. Truman and the Modern American Presi-
dency* (1983); Alonzo L. Hamby, *Beyond the New Deal: Harry S. Truman and American Liberalism* (1973); Richard G. Hewlett and Oscar E. Anderson, Jr., *Atomic Shield, 1947–1952*
[Atomic Energy Commission] (1989); Michael J. Lacey, ed., *The Truman Presidency* (1989),
Part I, "Domestic Politics and Issues"; Stephen Lawson, *Running for Freedom: Civil Rights and
Black Politics in America Since 1941* (1977); Donald McCoy, *The Presidency of Harry S. Truman*
(1984); Donald McCoy and Richard Ruetten, *Quest and Response: Minority Rights and the Tru-
man Administration* (1973); David McCullough, *Truman* (1992); Norman Markowitz, *The Rise
and Fall of the People's Century: Henry A. Wallace and American Liberalism, 1941–1948* (1973);
George T. Mazuzan and J. Samuel Walker, *Controlling the Atom: The Beginnings of Nuclear
Regulation, 1946–1962* (1984); William L. O'Neill, *A Better World: The Great Schism: Stalinism
and the Intellectuals* (1982); Herbert Parmet, *The Democrats: The Years After FDR* (1976);
Monte S. Poen, *Harry S. Truman Versus the Medical Lobby: The Genesis of Medicare* (1979);
Gary W. Reichard, *Politics as Usual: The Age of Truman and Eisenhower* (1988); Irwin Ross,
The Loneliest Campaign: The Truman Victory of 1948 (1968); Alice Kimball Smith, *A Peril and
a Hope: The Scientists' Movement in America* (1965); Athan Theoharis, *The Truman Presidency:
The Origins of the Imperial Presidency and the National Security State* (1979); Allen Yarnell, *Dem-
ocrats and Progressives: The 1948 Presidential Election as a Test of Postwar Liberalism* (1974).

Postwar Society, Economy, and Culture

Erik Barnouw, *Tube of Plenty* [television] (1982); Paul Boyer, *By the Bomb's Early Light: American Thought and Culture at the Dawn of the Atomic Age* (1985); Andrew Cherlin, *Marriage,
Divorce, Remarriage* (1981); John Patrick Diggins, *The Proud Decades: America in War and in
Peace, 1941–1960* (1988); Mary Ann Doane, *The Desire to Desire: The Woman's Film of the
1940s* (1987); Chester E. Eisinger, *Fiction of the Forties* (1963); David Goldfield, *Black, White,*

and Southern: Race Relations and Southern Culture (1990); Joseph C. Goulden, *The Best Years: 1945–1950* (1976); William S. Graebner, *The Age of Doubt: American Thought and Culture in the 1940s* (1991); Alvin H. Hansen, *The Postwar American Economy: Performances and Problems* (1964); Susan Hartman, *The Homefront and Beyond* [women in the war and early postwar era] (1984); Kenneth T. Jackson, *Crabgrass Frontier: The Suburbanization of the United States* (1985); Nelson Lichtenstein, "From Corporatism to Collective Bargaining: Organized Labor and the Eclipse of Social Democracy in the Postwar Era," in Steve Fraser and Gary Gerstle, eds., *The Rise and Fall of the New Deal Order, 1930–1980* (1989); Lary May, ed., *Recasting America: Culture and Politics in the Age of the Cold War* (1989); William H. Moore, *The Kefauver Committee and the Politics of Crime, 1950–1952* (1974); Geoffrey Perrett, *A Dream of Greatness: The American People, 1945–1963* (1979); Ron Rosenbaum, "The House That Levitt Built," *Esquire* (December 1983); Leila J. Rupp and Verta Taylor, *Survival in the Doldrums: The American Women's Rights Movement, 1945 to the 1960s* (1987); Herbert Stein, *Presidential Economics: The Making of Economic Policy from Roosevelt to Reagan and Beyond* (1984); Allan M. Winkler, *Life Under a Cloud: American Anxiety About the Atom* (1993).

Anticommunism and the Early Cold War at Home

Michael Belknap, *Cold War Political Justice: The Smith Act, the Communist Party, and American Civil Liberties* (1977); H. W. Brands, *The Devil We Knew: Americans and the Cold War* (1993); Virginia Carmichael, *Framing History: The Rosenberg Story and the Cold War* (1993); David Caute, *The Great Fear: The Anti-Communist Purges Under Truman and Eisenhower* (1978); James K. Davis, *Spying on America: The FBI's Domestic Counterintelligence Program* (1992); Sigmund Diamond, *Compromised Campus: The Collaboration of Universities with the Intelligence Community, 1945–1955* (1988); Bernard F. Dick, *Radical Innocence: A Critical Study of the Hollywood Ten* (1988); Richard Freeland, *The Truman Doctrine and the Origins of McCarthyism* (1972); Richard M. Fried, *Nightmare in Red: The McCarthy Era in Perspective* (1990); Robert Griffith and Athan Theoharis, eds., *The Specter: Original Essays on the Cold War and the Origins of McCarthyism* (1974); Alan Harper, *The Politics of Loyalty: The White House and the Communist Issue, 1946–1952* (1969); Earl Latham, *The Communist Controversy in Washington* (1966); Mary McAuliffe, *Crisis of the Left: Cold-War Politics and American Liberals, 1947–1954* (1978); David M. Oshinsky, *A Conspiracy So Immense: The World of Joe McCarthy* (1983); Ronald Radosh and Joyce Milton, *The Rosenberg File* (1983); Thomas C. Reeves, *The Life and Times of Joe McCarthy* (1982); Natalie Robins, *Alien Ink: The FBI's War on Freedom of Expression* (1992); Richard Rovere, *Senator Joe McCarthy* (1960); Ellen W. Schrecker, *No Ivory Tower: McCarthyism and the Universities* (1986); Athan Theoharis, *Seeds of Repression: Harry S. Truman and the Origins of McCarthyism* (1971); Allen Weinstein, *Perjury: The Hiss-Chambers Case* (1978); Stephen J. Whitfield, *The Culture of the Cold War* (1991).

Chapter Four

MODERN REPUBLICANISM & SUBURBAN TOGETHERNESS IN THE 1950s

In the 1955 movie *Strategic Air Command*, World War II Air Force veteran Dutch Holland, playing third base for the St. Louis Cardinals, is recalled to active duty. Dutch (James Stewart) grumbles at first; he and his pregnant wife, Sally (June Allyson), have just redecorated their home and are settling into cozy domesticity. But when a giant bomber flies overhead, Dutch recalls the lure of the skies and gladly joins the new Strategic Air Command (SAC). Sally gamely supports Dutch as he defends the nation. "Anything you do is fine with me," she assures him, "just as long as you don't leave me behind."

The movie reflected several key realities of the 1950s: SAC revealed the new emphasis on air power, including nuclear bombers, in U.S. defense policy; SAC's complex organizational hierarchy, into which Dutch smoothly fit, paralleled that of the decade's large business corporations; and Sally's loyal support of her husband echoed the idealization of domesticity at a time of rising birthrates and migration to the suburbs. Indeed, the movie repeatedly equates real-life families with the SAC "family" of pilots and crews carefully tending their B-47s and "the new family of nuclear weapons" that the bombers are designed to deliver.

As the public flocked to view *Strategic Air Command* with its blend of menacing and upbeat themes, the Cold War and the postwar economic boom surged on. Americans, prosperous yet worried about communist subversion at home and abroad, had little patience with social critics or political dissidents. Ready enough to endorse Washington's vigorous pursuit of the Cold War overseas, most people turned away from public concerns at home. Also, as middle-class white families abandoned the cities, the media presented the burgeoning suburbs as a microcosm of an affluent America, downplaying such social problems as poverty and ignoring the citizens excluded from the charmed circle of economic abundance.

In the White House, a new president, Dwight D. Eisenhower, mirrored the nation's cautious, conservative, inward-turning mood. To understand the national experience of the 1950s, we first turn to the political context.

The Politics of Moderation

Dwight Eisenhower, in Paris as supreme commander of NATO forces, faced a stream of visitors in 1951 and early 1952 as top Republicans flew in from the States to implore him to run for president. He seemed a sure winner, although few knew anything about his politics. Indeed, Harry Truman, who had decided not to be a candidate in 1952, had earlier urged him to run as a Democrat.

Born in Texas in 1890, Eisenhower had graduated from West Point and served for years in obscure army posts before winning fame during World War II as commander of the North African invasion in 1943 and the Normandy landing in 1944. After postwar tours as army chief of staff and president of Columbia University, he had returned to Europe to head NATO's military forces. Americans weary of the Korean War and of Truman administration scandals saw in Ike a refreshing political outsider and delighted in his sterling war reputation, easy smile, and avuncular manner.

To compete in the election, Eisenhower would have to grapple with the split in the Republican party, which, rooted in the politics of the 1940s and earlier, persisted into the 1950s. Republicans from the party's eastern, moderate, internationalist wing who now wooed him mistrusted what they perceived as the reactionary and isolationist midwestern wing, headed by Ohio's senator Robert Taft. Taft's three-piece suits, gold watch-chain, and droning, professorial voice embodied the stodgy image that progressive Republicans wanted to shed. Eastern leaders feared that if Taft won the 1952 party nomination, he would either lose the election (the more likely prospect) or win and turn the party sharply to the right. Behind Taft, too, loomed Senator Joseph McCarthy. For the moment, McCarthy served GOP interests by attacking Democrats, but a strong Republican was needed in the White House to curb his excesses. All of these reasons—plus the overriding desire to regain the White House—led moderate Republicans to view Eisenhower as their great hope. As Thomas Dewey put it, "We must look around for someone of great popularity and who has not frittered away his political assets by taking positive stands against national planning, etc., etc. Elect such a man to the Presidency, *after which* he must lead us back to safe channels and paths."

Ending the suspense early in 1952, Eisenhower proclaimed himself a Republican and threw his hat in the ring. He won several state primaries, but Taft loyalists controlled other states' delegations. The situation recalled 1912, when Taft's father, President William Howard Taft, had manipulated the party machinery to fight off challenger Theodore Roosevelt. However, 1952 brought a different outcome: Eisenhower's floor managers at the GOP convention in Chicago won a battle over disputed delegates, and the general was nominated on the first ballot. As his running mate, Eisenhower tapped Senator Richard Nixon of California, famed for his dogged pursuit of Whittaker Chambers's treason charges against Alger Hiss. After twenty years in the political wilderness, Republicans scented victory.

The Democrats nominated Harry Truman's choice: Illinois governor Adlai Stevenson. Stevenson's witty speeches charmed liberals, but he was no match for Eisenhower, the popular war hero. Given Eisenhower's appeal, plus the potent themes hammered at tirelessly by the Republicans—Korea, China, communism, and corruption (summed up in the formula K_1C_3)—few oddsmakers bet on a Democratic upset.

Yet two incidents during the campaign illuminated McCarthy's power and Richard Nixon's political style, both of which would pose dilemmas for Eisenhower. Americans who loathed McCarthy bridled when Eisenhower dropped from a prepared speech in McCarthy's home state of Wisconsin a passage implicitly criticizing the senator for his attacks on General George Marshall. Marshall had served as Eisenhower's superior in World War II, and Ike deeply admired him. Yet the candidate, refusing to discuss "personalities," dared not challenge McCarthy's smear even of his old comrade-in-arms and benefactor.

When the press revealed a secret Nixon fund to advance his political interests set up by rich California businessmen, Eisenhower declined to defend his running mate, the first of many indications over the years that Ike neither trusted nor much liked Nixon. Nixon fought back with a cloying television speech, potently demonstrating the political clout of this new medium, that included a reference to his daughters' little dog, Checkers, another campaign gift. An outpouring of popular support ensured Nixon's place on the ticket and a long run in U.S. politics. For decades, connoisseurs of political demagoguery would cherish videotapes of the "Checkers speech."

That November, Eisenhower garnered 55 percent of the popular vote and a lopsided electoral-college victory. Foreshadowing later Republican successes, he even did well in the once solidly Democratic South, winning 49 percent of the vote and carrying Virginia, Florida, Tennessee, Texas, and Oklahoma. He would score another firm victory in 1956 and extend his presidency to two terms.

Hardly a sophisticated political thinker, Eisenhower was on firmer ground on foreign affairs than on domestic issues. Nevertheless, he possessed a well-formulated and fairly coherent set of political views. He deplored, for example, the politicization of class conflict. All Americans had "areas of common interest," he believed, and the political process should identify and further these shared concerns. In this cooperative process, he hoped that enlightened, public-spirited business leaders would play a key role.

The "drift toward statism" troubled him as well. Like many conservatives, he chafed at the growing concentration of power in Washington and the consequent weakening of both the private sphere and the constitutionally mandated balance of power between the federal government and the states. On the other hand, he was no knee-jerk enemy of "big government" or mindless cheerleader for laissez faire. Like Herbert Hoover in the 1920s, he thought that government should promote economic growth, productivity, and foreign trade.

As had Theodore Roosevelt, Eisenhower espoused a capitalism moderated by regulatory laws and a concern for social welfare, and he advocated a government strictly limited yet strong enough to attend to the national interest. His outlook reflected that of the more sophisticated and liberal corporate leaders of these years. Rejecting the rhetoric of laissez faire and the backward-looking politics of people like Taft who still fought the New Deal, this corporate elite accepted the main outlines of FDR's reforms, including Social Security, the rights of organized labor, and a central role for government in the economy. A partnership of government, business, and "responsible" labor leaders, they argued, could lead the country in progressive paths.

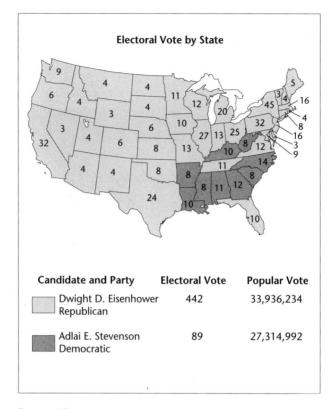

FIGURE 4.1
Presidential Election of 1952

Eisenhower Republicans thus endorsed the basic reforms of the New Deal, yet they also believed that the New Dealers had created a bloated federal bureaucracy and had pushed America in a "socialistic" direction. One task of moderate Republicans, then, was to rectify the "excesses" of the 1930s while preserving New Deal gains. Accordingly, Eisenhower always balanced his calls for governmental and fiscal restraint with a concern for the general welfare. The Republican party must be "progressive," he insisted, "or it is sunk." The party should avoid the "ruts and ditches" of the political extremes, he advised, and hew to the center of the road "where the traction is best and where you can bring the most people along with you." This was "the middle way," and he adhered to it devoutly. Eisenhower's admirers argued that his moderation provided a needed respite after the traumas of depression and war. His liberal critics, a small band in the 1950s, charged that his cautious approach to politics offered no vision of a larger national purpose and muffled important social issues and conflicts in the bland rhetoric of cooperation and shared interests.

Eisenhower's personal popularity only briefly propelled his party to majority status. The Republicans narrowly controlled both houses of Congress in 1953 and 1954. But in the 1954 midterm election, despite general prosperity, the end of the Korean War, and McCarthyite attacks on Democrats' disloyalty, the Democrats regained

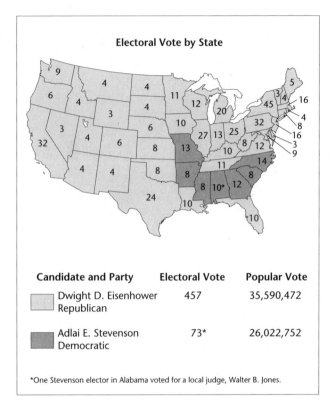

FIGURE 4.2
Presidential Election of 1956

control of both houses of Congress. For the rest of the decade, the party ruled Congress. To Eisenhower, the setback proved that the GOP must purge its reactionary elements and broaden its base.

In Congress, Ike thus faced not only a hard core of reactionary Republicans but also a powerful Democratic delegation led by Sam Rayburn and Lyndon Johnson, two wily Texans who through most of Eisenhower's term served, respectively, as speaker of the house and Senate majority leader. The decade's legislation thus emerged from a complex three-way process of negotiation among the White House, various stripes of congressional Republicans, and congressional Democrats.

Several crucial measures reflected the Republican belief that twenty years of Democratic rule had concentrated too much power in Washington. In 1953, reversing the policy of the Truman administration, Eisenhower transferred control of offshore oil rights, and the lucrative tax revenues from such rights, from the federal government to the states. This change opened the door to private drilling and fulfilled a long-sought objective of U.S. oil companies. One firm, Oklahoma's Kerr-McGee Company, the pioneer in offshore drilling, had brought in its first offshore well in 1947 from a rig in the Gulf of Mexico more than ten miles off the Louisiana coast. In 1954 the administration also supported a private power company's challenge to the Tennessee Valley Authority, a New Deal showpiece.* Finally, in 1955 the Federal Power Commission rejected congressional calls for a TVA-like public-power project on Idaho's Snake River and instead authorized privately financed hydroelectric dams on the river. All of these measures testified to Eisenhower's suspicions of statism and his wish to encourage private entrepreneurial energies.

Further venting their hostility to FDR and the New Deal, conservative Republicans in Congress killed the Reconstruction Finance Corporation (RFC), a once-powerful New Deal agency. (Ironically, the RFC actually arose in 1932, when the Republican Herbert Hoover was still in the White House.) They changed the name of Boulder Dam to Hoover Dam and nearly passed the Bricker Amendment. Introduced by Senator John Bricker of Ohio, this constitutional amendment would have (1) prevented the executive branch from signing any treaty that violated the Constitution, (2) granted a treaty the force of law only if supported by legislation that "would be valid in the absence of a treaty," and (3) subjected presidential "executive agreements" with foreign powers to the same Senate ratification requirement established by the Constitution for treaties. The amendment, a belated attack on Roosevelt's alleged giveaway of Eastern Europe to Stalin at the 1945 Yalta Conference, fell one vote short of the necessary two-thirds majority in the Senate in 1954.

In other respects, the Eisenhower administration lived up to its progressive claims. To build his record in this area, Eisenhower relied on the Democratic leadership in Congress, especially Lyndon Johnson. The wheeling-dealing Texan dominated the Senate (from 1955 to 1961 he served as majority leader), and no piece of legislation came close to passing without his approval. Eisenhower was a political novice and much admired Johnson, whom he privately called "the best Democrat of them all." By Johnson's count, Democratic votes passed no fewer than fifty-eight bills favored by Eisenhower over 1953–1955 alone. Most notably, Johnson would play a critical role in passage of the landmark Civil Rights Act of 1957 (see pp. 173–174).

Of course, Johnson never lost sight of his party's interest in building its own liberal record. Frequently, as on housing and school construction bills, for example, the Democrats voted more money than Eisenhower requested. However, except for election time, Johnson, with his House counterpart Sam Rayburn, cooperated so closely with the White House that more partisan Democrats often criticized them. To a later generation who would forever identify Johnson with the disastrous Vietnam War, his outstanding legislative record in the 1950s sank into undeserved obscurity.

This close working relationship between the White House and Congress in the Eisenhower years led to the creation of the Department of Health, Education and Welfare; an increase in the minimum wage from seventy-five cents to a dollar an hour; and the extension of social security to more than 7 million workers, most of

---

* Eisenhower later reversed himself on this issue when evidence surfaced of legal improprieties by the private-power interests.

them farmers. In 1954, with White House support, Congress approved construction, in collaboration with Canada, of the Saint Lawrence Seaway, which gave oceangoing freighters access to Great Lakes ports. That year Eisenhower signed a housing act that expanded the Truman housing program. This and later measures provided large sums for slum clearance and urban renewal and guaranteed housing loans and low-cost mortages to Korean War veterans.

Eisenhower's belief that government should promote economic growth also sustained the prosperity of the 1950s. As government spending rose both in absolute terms and as a percentage of the GNP (from 7 percent in 1950 to 9.4 percent in 1960), federal outlays for housing, highways, and, above all, defense yielded many thousands of jobs. The Saint Lawrence Seaway Project alone revitalized the economies of the Northeast and the Great Lakes.

The Eisenhower era's most enduring monument was a vast highway program, and it rivaled the New Deal's public-works projects. The Federal Highway Act (1956) allocated more than $30 billion for a 41,000-mile interstate-highway system. Soon ribbons of concrete and asphalt were winding through prairies, cornfields, and urban districts. The program created jobs, stimulated the economy, and eventually allowed Americans to drive cross-country without encountering a single stop sign or traffic light. One major rationale for building the interstate system illustrated again the Cold War's effect on domestic policy: Highways would provide easy escape from cities in the event of nuclear war.

What historian Kenneth Jackson calls the 1950s "drive-in culture" arose in the wake of this vast highway program. Motels proliferated, and fast-food franchises mushroomed along the new interstates, offering identical fare to travelers nationwide. In 1954 a visionary salesman named Ray Kroc bought a locally popular hamburger restaurant from the McDonald brothers of San Bernardino, California. Soon McDonald's golden arches would rise across America. The negative effects of this orgy of highway building emerged only gradually: a decayed rail system, profligate gasoline consumption, air pollution, and a degraded landscape. Countless city neighborhoods, usually the poorest and most vulnerable, were shattered by the tangle of overpasses, concrete pylons, and access ramps.

The highway program proved a gold mine for the construction industry, merely one example of the many ways in which Eisenhower's policies and the ideology of modern Republicanism, in this case with strong bipartisan support, nurtured a pro-business climate in Washington. Ike's cabinet, drawn mainly from the upper reaches of corporate America, revealed this orientation as well. A much-quoted comment by Secretary of Defense Charles E. Wilson summed up the prevalent view. Asked about possible conflict of interest between his public duties and his former role as head of GM, Wilson replied, "I have always assumed that what was good for the United States was good for General Motors, and vice versa."

Meanwhile, Senator Joseph McCarthy, little interested in such mundane topics as housing, highways, or heads of corporations, continued to exploit the obsession with communism that the Truman administration had aroused. Eisenhower himself was blind to the red danger, McCarthy hinted. In 1953 McCarthy warned of communist infiltration of the U.S. Army, focusing on an obscure left-wing army dentist. "Who promoted Major Peress?" he rumbled. During the so-called Army-McCarthy

They liked Ike. Although he was no silver-tongued orator, Dwight Eisenhower's infectious grin and status as a World War II military hero drew adoring throngs during the 1952 presidential campaign. (*Joe Scherschel* Life Magazine, © *Time-Warner*)

hearings, televised live in the spring of 1954, a riveted nation watched as McCarthy badgered witnesses, including a timid secretary of the army.

Still on a rampage, McCarthy and other witch-hunters ruined reputations and trampled constitutional rights in the early Eisenhower years as they had in the Truman era. Citizens who fell into their clutches were pressured not only to "confess" their own radical pasts but to implicate others. Filmmaker Elia Kazan, hauled before the House Un-American Activities Committee in 1952, agreed to "name names." In his next movie, *On the Waterfront* (1954), Kazan justified his action by making a hero of a dockworker (Marlon Brando) who informs on the mobsters who control his union. "I'm glad what I done—you hear me?—glad what I done!" Brando stridently insists.

McCarthy, a Roman Catholic, won strong support from influential parts of the Catholic community. The magazine *Columbia*, voice of the Knights of Columbus, a 920,000-member Catholic fraternal organization, strongly backed the crusading senator. Francis Cardinal Spellman of New York, America's most influential Catholic, warmly endorsed him, asserting, "[McCarthy] is against communism and he . . . is doing something about it. He is making America aware of the dangers."

Under McCarthyite pressure, the State Department in 1953 ordered books or art works by "Communists, fellow travelers, etc." removed from United States Information Agency libraries abroad. Eisenhower condemned "bookburners," but when asked whether he meant McCarthy, he characteristically backed off, again declining to discuss personalities. Indeed, the president consistently avoided challenging McCarthy. In 1953 he even agreed to Senator Taft's demand that McCarthy, in effect, be given a veto over all diplomatic nominations. This concession came after a bruising Senate battle over the White House's nomination of a career diplomat, Charles Bohlen, as ambassador to the Soviet Union. McCarthy, typically, had found Bohlen soft on communism. In a 1953 diary entry, Eisenhower rationalized his policy of silence: "Nothing will be so effective in combatting [McCarthy's] particular kind of troublemaking as to ignore him. This he cannot stand."

The McCarthyite taint infected the administration itself. In 1953 Eisenhower issued an executive order revoking the safeguards built into President Truman's internal-security program. Now it became easier to fire government workers suspected of being security risks or of harboring radical views. Indeed, both parties played the politics of anticommunism. In 1954 congressional Democrats initiated the Communist Control Act. Toughening the 1950 McCarran Act, this law limited the legal rights of "Communist-infiltrated" organizations and required them to register with the government. All the same, in that fall's elections, Vice President Nixon accused Democrats of being "blind to the Communist conspiracy."

Fame offered little protection against the spreading miasma of suspicion. In 1954 Eisenhower approved the Atomic Energy Commission's decision to cancel the security clearance of physicist J. Robert Oppenheimer. This action, ostensibly based on old charges that Oppenheimer had had communist friends in the 1930s, in reality grew out of the scientist's opposition to the H-bomb in 1950. Acknowledging the "growing paranoia," political journalist I. F. Stone wrote of the Oppenheimer case, "The impossible search for 'absolute security' is incompatible with a free and healthy society. If this is to be national policy, why should anyone be trusted?"

Stone was right. The climate of fear prevented the vigorous debate over the precise nature of the Soviet threat that might have moderated the rhetorical excess and tendency to oversimplify. As politicians endorsed the ideal of a "bipartisan foreign policy," the Cold War assumptions that had solidified in the late 1940s and early 1950s went largely unexamined. Leading Democrats, terrified of the "soft on communism" label, outdid each other in denouncing the Soviet Union to prove their patriotism. Even prominent liberal senator Hubert Humphrey endorsed the Communist Control Act. Young Robert Kennedy, brother of the future Democratic president John F. Kennedy, served on Senator McCarthy's staff.

But the four-year McCarthy melodrama was wearing thin. To most television viewers, the Wisconsin senator came across as little better than a barroom bully. Joseph Welch, a Boston lawyer representing witnesses in the Army-McCarthy hearings, shrewdly heightened this impression. When McCarthy attacked one of Welch's young assistants, Welch burst out, "At long last, Senator, have you no decency?" A damning TV documentary on McCarthy by CBS newsman Edward R. Murrow in 1954 hastened the senator's decline while underscoring TV's growing influence.

Gradually, key Republican senators concluded that McCarthy had become a liability. A motion to censure him, introduced by GOP senator Ralph Flanders of Vermont in June 1954, passed in December by a 67–22 vote. McCarthy responded predictably, accusing his foes of abetting world communism, but he was finished. Drinking more and more heavily, he died in 1957.

By the end of the fifties, the McCarthyite fever would fade, and Americans could assess Eisenhower's overall domestic record. Although he sought to curb federal power, Eisenhower also endorsed measures that buttressed and even extended the basic reforms of the New Deal. Some of his measures benefited corporate interests, but others responded to the needs of a broader spectrum of the population. Farmers and other self-employed persons, for example, were helped by the extension of Social Security. Construction workers prospered thanks to large-scale public housing and road-construction projects. The pitfalls of urban renewal would later loom large, but the administration's support for aid to cities at the time impressed many as socially enlightened public policy.

Two major failures counterbalanced the positive side of the domestic record. Eisenhower remained nearly mute as the McCarthyites assaulted the fundamental values of an open society, and he failed to exert strong leadership on the most profound moral issue to emerge in the 1950s: racism and civil rights. As we shall see in Chapter 8, the politics of moderation proved ill-adapted to cope with this volatile, divisive issue that stirred the strongest of passions and challenged deep-rooted beliefs.

Ike's reputation has shifted radically over the years. At first, historians echoed 1950s critics such as I. F. Stone, who saw him as an amiable cipher. In 1953 Stone wrote, "Eisenhower . . . seems to be a rather simple man who enjoys his bridge and his golf and doesn't like to be too much bothered; . . . [leaving] a sort of political vacuum in the White House which other men will struggle among themselves to fill." Part of Eisenhower's image problem lay in his formal manner. Ike's naturally reserved personality was reinforced by years in the military and by his desire to reassert the dignity of the presidency after Truman's highly publicized outbursts and garish wardrobe. Too, he often struck observers as maladroit and unsure of himself when thrust from the military planning room into the political arena. Ike's rambling answers to reporters' questions confirmed skeptics' doubts. When he produced statements like, "Great Britain has a hard row to hoe to keep its economic head above water," the knowing chuckled patronizingly. His press conferences, observed humorist Jules Feiffer, were "headlong leaps into verbal gridlock." Eisenhower also slowed down noticeably during his two terms, partly as a result of a heart attack in 1955 and intestinal surgery in 1956. An aide noted privately in 1958, "He can sprint a few yards, but he tires quickly. . . . [H]e can become momentarily fascinated by individual pieces of the international jigsaw puzzle, [but] he does not seem to be able to see what the picture would look like when all the pieces were put together."

In recent years, however, a more nuanced picture of Ike has emerged. Eisenhower's letters and diaries and his associates' memoirs reveal a man of high intelligence who actively, if unobtrusively, pursued his political goals. One historian has described his administration as "the hidden hand presidency." Ike's talent for coordinating his staff and hammering out compromises served him in good stead as both general and as president. In his own words, he was "pragmatic . . . by inclination." But he was no bloodless manager. Behind the easy smile lay a hot temper capable of explosive rages and barracks-room language. And the puzzling verbal gridlock was often deliberate. He once told his press secretary, James Hagerty, who worried about how his boss would handle a complex issue in a news conference, "Don't worry, Jim, I'll just confuse them."

1953–1956: Nuclear Strategy
and Global Containment

On the international front, Eisenhower's first task was to fulfill his campaign pledge to end the Korean War. As promised, he flew to Korea soon after the election to prod the cease-fire talks. He also dropped hints to China, through various diplomatic channels, of his readiness to use nuclear weapons in Korea. In July 1953, negotiators signed a cease-fire that restored the line between North and South Korea more or less at the 38th parallel, where it had stood when hostilities began in 1950.

In shaping its overall strategic policy, the Eisenhower administration faced a dilemma. The primary planning document of the Truman years, NSC-68, had called for an across-the-board military build-up to prepare the nation for everything from local conflict to nuclear war. The resulting expansion, coupled with the costs of the Korean War, drove up military spending from $13 billion in 1950 to more than $50 billion in 1953 and produced a budget deficit of $9.5 billion in fiscal 1952–1953.

Eisenhower was firmly committed to waging the Cold War, but he also believed in limited government and balanced budgets. Whereas the military services called for ever-greater defense spending, the budget balancers—led by Treasury Secretary George Humphrey, Arthur Burns of the Council of Economic Advisers, and Eisenhower himself—warned that uncontrolled defense outlays could undermine the United States from within as surely as communist expansion abroad. Eisenhower cautioned, "We must not create a nation mighty in arms that is . . . bankrupt in resources." The tension between these conflicting perspectives exerted a significant impact on military policy in the Eisenhower years.

The deterrent threat of nuclear weapons offered one path of compromise. Far cheaper than large armies and a full panoply of conventional weaponry, nuclear armaments promised to maintain U.S. military might at less cost, or, in the blunt phrase of Defense Secretary Wilson, to give "more bang for the buck." Such reasoning underlay what became the Eisenhower administration's rhetoric of "massive retaliation." John Foster Dulles, who soon would become secretary of state, coined a variant of the phrase—"the deterrent of massive retaliatory power"—in a 1952 *Life* article, in which he referred to the full range of weapons, including nuclear arms. In the event of war, declared an NSC document that Eisenhower approved in October 1953, "the United States will consider nuclear weapons to be as available for use as other munitions." In the future, warned Dulles in January 1954, U.S. defenses would "depend primarily upon a great capacity to retaliate, instantly, by means and at places of our own choosing."

To be effective, the massive-retaliation doctrine had to be believable. Dulles observed in a 1953 NSC meeting, "Somehow or other we must manage to remove the taboo from the use of these [nuclear] weapons." To increase the credibility of its threat, the United States stepped up construction of hydrogen bombs and planes capable of dropping them on the Soviet Union. By 1956, SAC possessed an armada of 1,400 such aircraft and had begun deploying 600 B-52s. The Soviets, in contrast, had no more than 150 strategic bombers.

This so-called New Look defense policy (a term borrowed from the Paris fashion world), coupled with the end of the Korean War, enabled Eisenhower to slash defense spending by some 20 percent in his first two years in office (over vocal protests from the Pentagon and military contractors) and to produce a budget surplus in 1956. The cuts were imposed selectively, however; army appropriations fell sharply, but the air force budget soared.

Massive-retaliation strategy came under fire from analysts at think tanks such as California's RAND Corporation who charged that it lacked credibility. Did anyone truly believe that the United States would respond with nuclear weapons to a localized Soviet move in Asia, Africa, or the Middle East? Some ethicists and religious leaders attacked the doctrine on moral grounds: Would it be right to respond to a local confrontation with behavior that risked a global thermonuclear war? Furthermore, the strategy assumed decisive U.S. nuclear superiority, but Moscow was steadily balancing the scales. The Soviets tested a small hydrogen device in 1953, and May Day air shows in Moscow in 1954 and 1955 featured overflights by strategic bombers capable of delivering nuclear bombs to North America. (The Soviets apparently flew the same ten planes repeatedly over Red Square, convincing U.S. observers that they possessed hundreds of nuclear bombers.) In Eisenhower's second term, as we shall see in Chapter 6, the nuclear balance of terror would grow more precarious still.

In placing its nuclear strategy in a global context, the Eisenhower administration adhered to the Cold War dogma laid down in the Truman years. Administration leaders continued in their public pronouncements to focus on the ideological sources of Soviet behavior and the all-or-nothing nature of the conflict. As Eisenhower warned in his first inaugural address, "We sense with all our faculties that forces of good and evil are massed and armed and opposed as rarely before in history."

Although Eisenhower played the central role in shaping U.S. foreign policy, that outlook also bore the imprint of Secretary of State Dulles. "We felt that Dulles was the United States, and the United States was Dulles," recalled one foreign diplomat. Under Dulles, U.S. Cold War policy, essentially continuous with that of the Truman years, became more ideologically charged. A Presbyterian lay leader and top Wall Street lawyer, Dulles brought to the conduct of diplomacy a rigid moralism; a single-minded preoccupation with "world communism," which he portrayed as "a vast, monolithic system"; and a passion for encircling the Soviet Union with a network of treaties and military alliances. By the end of the 1950s, the United States was treaty-bound to defend no fewer than forty-three different nations against "communist aggression." The secretary of state delivered boring, sanctimonious harangues that even his supporters found tedious. "Dull, duller, Dulles," went one Washington joke. Eisenhower himself occasionally lost patience with Dulles, calling him in a 1958 diary entry "a sort of international prosecuting attorney."

A shrewd negotiator behind closed doors, Dulles also had a penchant for scary public rhetoric. In 1956 he boasted of his readiness to go to "the brink of war" to defeat communism. Rejecting George Kennan's containment doctrine as insufficiently militant, he insisted that the United States not only contain communism but aggressively challenge its influence everywhere. To this end, he asserted America's readiness to help the "captive peoples" of Eastern Europe to "liberate" themselves from the Soviet shackles. "You can count on us," he assured them early in 1953 on a Radio Free Europe broadcast.

Such talk was largely intended to stir unrest behind the Iron Curtain and to win ethnic East European voters to the Republican camp. In practice, U.S. policy toward

Eastern Europe proved cautious. When Soviet and East German troops in 1953 put down uprisings in East Berlin and elsewhere in East Germany, the United States did nothing. Similarly, when Russian tanks brutally crushed an anti-Soviet revolt in Hungary in October 1956, the United States expressed verbal support for the insurgents but refrained from intervention. Dulles's militant rhetoric gradually grew more muted, particularly with reference to Eastern Europe. The terrible logic of nuclear stalemate, plus the realities of Soviet conventional military might, significantly limited U.S. options in this part of the world. After the Hungarian incident, President Eisenhower explicitly disavowed any interest in stirring rebellion in Russia's European satellites.

The death of Joseph Stalin in 1953 and the rise of Nikita Khrushchev to power in Moscow contributed to the moderation of U.S. posturing. Khrushchev was no democrat, but neither was he another Stalin. He not only softened some brutal features of Stalinist rule but in 1956, at a Communist party congress, emotionally denounced the "crimes of the Stalin era." These signs of change in the Soviet Union encouraged a more temperate U.S. stance, particularly as McCarthyite hysteria faded.

Eisenhower even saw potential value in a Big Power "summit"—a term coined by Winston Churchill in 1953—despite Dulles's doubts. In July 1955, Eisenhower and Khrushchev, with their British and French counterparts, met in Geneva for the first top-level conference of the wartime allies since the 1945 meeting at Potsdam. The gathering failed to settle such thorny issues as European disarmament and German reunification, and Khrushchev refused to buy Eisenhower's "Open Skies" proposal that the two sides permit aerial surveillance of their territories. (When the Soviets rejected this idea, Eisenhower authorized a plan by the Central Intelligence Agency [CIA] for secret photographic spying on the Soviet Union by high-altitude U-2 spy planes, a decision that would return to plague him.) But the somewhat nebulous "Spirit of Geneva" suggested an easing of Cold War tensions. Ignoring advice by the grim-faced Dulles that he maintain an "austere countenance" in all photographs taken at Geneva, Ike flashed his famous grin throughout the proceedings. In 1956 the Soviets contributed to the thaw by proclaiming a policy of "peaceful coexistence" with the capitalist world.

Although the power balance in Europe somewhat stabilized, a series of regional conflicts kept Cold War antagonisms raw. These situations had complex origins, but Washington viewed them as aspects of the U.S.-Soviet struggle. This tendency is evident, for example, in U.S. policy toward the oil-rich Middle East. The formation of the new nation of Israel with U.S. backing in 1948 had created a serious problem of Palestinian Arab refugees and had generated bitter opposition among the Arab countries, whose animosity toward Jews had ancient roots. The Arab nations vowed to destroy the hated Jewish state and launched a war against the fledgling nation.

The Eisenhower administration, like its predecessor, backed Israel diplomatically and economically, in part because the Jewish state represented a bastion against Soviet penetration in the Middle East. At the same time, Washington worked to weld the divided Arab nations into an anticommunist alliance. In 1955, pursuing his strategy of encircling the Soviet Union with military treaties, Dulles masterminded the Baghdad Pact, a mutual-defense treaty linking Turkey, Pakistan, Iran, and Iraq.

Although Washington declined officially to join the pact, in a futile effort to avoid antagonizing Iraq's rival Egypt, it cooperated closely with the members on security matters. Furious over U.S.-Iraqi military cooperation, Egyptian leader Gamal Abdel Nasser late in 1955 allied Egypt with Moscow and began to stockpile Soviet arms for the stance against Israel. The crisis worsened in the summer of 1956, when Dulles, angered by Nasser's flirtation with Moscow, abruptly withdrew promised U.S. aid for the construction of the Aswan Dam on the Nile, a major Egyptian development project. In retaliation, Nasser nationalized the Anglo-French-owned Suez Canal.

Nasser's actions sparked another war in the Middle East. In late October 1956, as Soviet tanks rumbled through Budapest, Israel, France, and Great Britain attacked Egypt. The Israeli army rolled across the Sinai Peninsula, advancing to within ten miles of the Suez Canal, and the British and French bombed Egyptian military targets and seized the canal in a paratroop assault. But the days of imperialistic ventures by European nations had ended, as the new giants on the world stage quickly made clear. The Soviet Union threatened to come to Egypt's defense and, appropriating Dulles's "massive retaliation" threat, hinted at nuclear offensives on Paris and London. The Eisenhower administration, unwilling to be sucked into war by its allies and concerned about the flow of oil, refused to support the British-French-Israeli action. A cease-fire soon followed, and the invading forces pulled back. The episode left a residue of bad feeling among the NATO allies, but the larger threat of war had been avoided.

Rather than resorting to direct military intervention, as the British and French had done so clumsily in the Suez crisis, the Eisenhower administration more often pursued its goals through alliances, foreign aid, and clandestine action. The CIA under Allen Dulles, brother of the secretary of state, expanded its role beyond intelligence gathering to a wide range of political activities, including the overthrow of foreign governments. CIA activities in Iran and Guatemala illustrate the pattern.

After the Soviets withdrew from Iran in 1946 (see page 45), the British-owned Anglo-Iranian Oil Company gained monopolistic control over the country's vast oil resources. But by 1951 Mohammed Mossadegh, a wily and intensely nationalistic premier given to fits of histrionic weeping, dominated Iranian politics. As part of his program, Mossadegh nationalized the Anglo-Iranian Oil Company. When the United States rejected his requests for aid, Mossadegh turned to the Soviet Union. The hint of Soviet involvement galvanized Washington. A 1953 coup, planned, financed, and orchestrated by the CIA, overthrew Mossadegh and consolidated power in the hands of Iran's pro-Western monarch, Shah Reza Pahlavi.* Ruling with an iron hand, the shah kept his nation firmly in the anti-Soviet camp for more than a quarter of a century.

The Iran coup illustrates how anticommunism could mesh with less ideological concerns, in this case, the need to preserve the flow of oil. President Eisenhower noted in his diary, "Unless the areas in which these materials [such as oil] are found are under the control of people who are friendly to us and want to trade with

---

* CIA agent Kermit Roosevelt, a grandson of President Theodore Roosevelt, was a key figure in this coup.

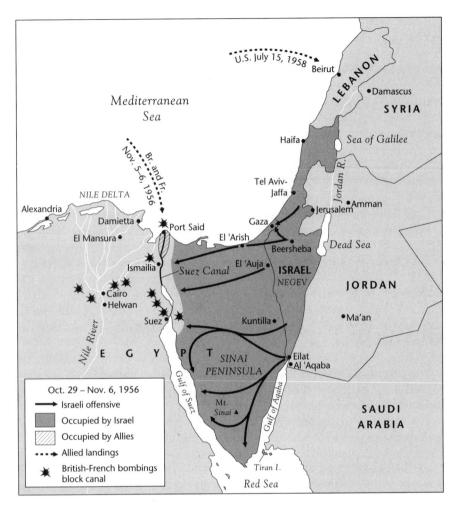

FIGURE 4.3
The Suez Crisis, 1956

us, then . . . we are bound in the long run to suffer the most disastrous and doleful consequences."

A similar mix of economic and ideological considerations shaped U.S. policy toward Guatemala, a nation long dominated by the United Fruit Company, a U.S. corporation with close links to the Eisenhower administration. John Foster Dulles's former law firm represented United Fruit, the assistant secretary of state for Latin American affairs held a large block of stock in the company, and the husband of Eisenhower's personal secretary headed the firm's public-relations department. In the early 1950s, United Fruit found itself less concerned with bananas and avocados than with Guatemala's leftist president, Jacob Arbenz Guzmán, elected in 1950. Launching a land-reform program, in a country where 2 percent of the people owned

70 percent of the land, the Arbenz government appropriated more than 200,000 undeveloped acres controlled by United Fruit, at a price that the corporation considered unfair.

When a small shipment of arms from Czechoslovakia reached Guatemala in May 1954, John Foster Dulles warned that the country could become an outpost of communist power in Latin America. Thoroughly alarmed, the Senate passed, 69–1, a resolution introduced by Lyndon Johnson denouncing "Soviet interference" in Guatemala. The CIA, meanwhile, in collaboration with United Fruit, organized and financed an anti-Arbenz coup. In June, right-wing conspirators overthrew Arbenz and installed a military government headed by the CIA's handpicked man, Carlos Castillo Armas, who promptly restored the appropriated lands to United Fruit and abandoned efforts to tax the corporation's profits. Millions in U.S. aid poured into Guatemala, and in 1956 the two nations signed a military pact.

These clandestine operations proceeded with minimal congressional supervision. In 1956, when the Senate rejected a proposal to tighten oversight of the CIA, Senator Richard Russell of Georgia declared, "If there is one agency of the Government in which we must take some matters on faith without a constant examination of its methods and sources, I believe this agency is the Central Intelligence Agency." This see-no-evil, hear-no-evil attitude would haunt the nation in future years, particularly during the Watergate and Iran-Contra scandals.

Deepening Entanglements in Asia

The Cold War unfolded in a world also torn by resistance to European colonialism. The ambiguities to which this combination could lead emerged starkly in Vietnam, where the Vietnamese Communist party under Ho Chi Minh led the fight against the French colonial power and its puppet government in Saigon. Confronted with an apparent choice between anticommunism and anticolonialism, the United States supported the colonial power against nationalists who were also communists. By 1954 Washington was paying 80 percent of the cost of France's war against the Vietminh, the military arm of the Vietnamese Communist party.

The war reached a crisis early in 1954 when the Vietminh besieged an eleven-thousand-man French garrison at Dienbienphu in northern Vietnam. Facing defeat, the French urgently requested direct U.S. military intervention. Some top administration officials favored this course. The chairman of the Joint Chiefs of Staff proposed Operation Vulture, an air strike by sixty B-29s including the dropping of three atomic bombs. Air Force chief Nathan Twining backed this strategy, he later recalled, as a way to "clean those Commies out of there. The band could play the 'Marseillaise' and the French would come marching out of Dienbienphu in fine shape." Eisenhower vetoed Operation Vulture as too risky, however, and the French garrison surrendered on May 7, 1954.

That July, the French and the Vietminh signed an armistice in Geneva that temporarily divided Vietnam at the 17th parallel, gave Ho Chi Minh control of the north, and provided for elections throughout Vietnam in 1956. Ho's negotiators left Geneva confident that all of Vietnam would soon be theirs. Eisenhower announced that the United States would abide by the Geneva Accords, but the United States kept its distance from the agreement and did not sign it. In fact, Washington had already decided on a major effort to foil Ho Chi Minh's plans. Drawing an analogy that would enjoy a long life in justifying U.S. intervention in Vietnam, Eisenhower observed, "You have a row of dominoes set up, and you knock over the first one, and . . . the last one . . . [will] go over quickly." The implication was clear: If Vietnam fell to communism, the rest of Southeast Asia would inevitably follow.

The administration realized, as Eisenhower conceded in his memoirs, that the popular Ho Chi Minh would win in a free election. The challenge was to find an alternative leader. Pushing aside the French-backed puppet emperor, Bao Dai, Washington installed as head of state in Saigon Ngo Dinh Diem, a Vietnamese nationalist and devout Catholic living a monklike existence in a New Jersey seminary. The CIA's top agent in Vietnam, Edward Lansdale; Senator John Kennedy; and Francis Cardinal Spellman were among the leaders convinced that Diem could rally Vietnam against communism. In a phrase that would soon gain currency, Washington had decided to "sink or swim with Ngo Dinh Diem." U.S. aid flowed to Diem, and the first U.S. military advisers arrived in South Vietnam in February 1955. Energetic, idealistic Americans, the White House thought, could certainly succeed where the jaded, world-weary French had failed.

As he pursued the Cold War in Asia, Dulles in 1954 set up yet another anticommunist military alliance, the Southeast Asia Treaty Organization (SEATO). Under the terms of this agreement, the United States pledged to defend Australia, New Zealand, Thailand, Pakistan, and the Philippines against communist aggression. Vietnam, Laos, and Cambodia did not formally join SEATO, but the treaty nevertheless extended U.S. military protection to them. SEATO, an extension of Dulles's strategy of hemming in the Soviet Union and communist China with military alliances, would later provide a legalistic basis for U.S. intervention in Vietnam.

Elsewhere in Asia, relations with the People's Republic of China (PRC) remained frigid. When China's foreign minister, Zhou Enlai (Chou En-lai), offered to shake hands with John Foster Dulles at the 1954 Geneva Conference on Vietnam, Dulles rebuffed him. Refusing to recognize the PRC or even to permit travel between China and the United States, Washington continued to recognize the nationalist regime of Jiang Jieshi on Taiwan as China's legitimate government. Egged on by a powerful pro-Jiang "China Lobby," including the magazine publisher Henry Luce, Eisenhower in 1953 ordered the U.S. 7th fleet out of the straits of Taiwan, supposedly unleashing Jiang to renew the war against the PRC. Eisenhower and Dulles hoped for an eventual Sino-Soviet split, and the administration considered strategies for promoting such a break. But with congressional opinion strongly pro-Jiang, Eisenhower publicly remained unbendingly hostile toward Mao Zedong's communist government.

Washington also supported Jiang in a long-simmering territorial dispute with the PRC. In late 1954, when the PRC began shelling two nationalist-held islands and the nationalists responded by shelling a PRC-held island, Washington signed a treaty with Jiang pledging to resist any PRC attack on Taiwan or the nearby Pescadores Islands. (How the United States would respond to a PRC attack on other islands was left deliberately vague.) By overwhelming majorities, and with Lyndon

Johnson again providing crucial support, both houses of Congress passed resolutions authorizing Eisenhower to defend Taiwan and the Pescadores by any means necessary. For a time, war between the United States and China—perhaps even the "massive retaliation" invoked by Dulles—over a few tiny specks of real estate seemed likely. In a March 1955 memo to Eisenhower, Dulles saw "at least an even chance that the United States will have to go to war." When the PRC made conciliatory gestures, announcing its shelling schedule in advance, for example, the crisis eased. But the deep freeze in U.S.-Chinese relations continued.

Overall, Eisenhower's first-term foreign-policy record was mixed. He ended the Korean War and showed restraint in dealing with crises in Suez and Dienbienphu; additionally, U.S.-Soviet relations improved somewhat. Yet the administration's public inflexibility toward China set a pattern that would continue into the early 1970s, and decisions made in the early Eisenhower years laid the groundwork for Washington's later decision to defend South Vietnam at almost any cost.

The administration lavished attention on global issues that fit its Cold War preoccupations but paid scant attention to the upsurge of nationalism, as well as the poverty, illiteracy, disease, and overpopulation that plagued much of Asia, Africa, the Middle East, and Latin America. The moralistic image of a globe divided between good and evil that Eisenhower evoked in his first inaugural address limited his administration's ability to respond to complex global realities. As John Lewis Gaddis has observed, this ideological rigidity represented "a fundamental failure of strategic vision . . . , probably the administration's single most significant one."

Moreover, although Eisenhower's New Look defense policy held down military spending, it was at the cost of an accelerated nuclear-arms race and a disconcerting willingness to consider a nuclear response in a variety of Cold War confrontations. Some of these conflicts, in retrospect, were quite minor. These years also saw the expansion of what some called Washington's "secret government" of shadowy Cold War agencies epitomized by the CIA, with its far-flung clandestine operations. Thus, despite Eisenhower's loathing of statism, the Cold War's home-front ramifications included a significant extension of government power.

Indeed, Congress's abdication of legislative responsibility under Cold War pressures emerged not only in its failure to rein in the CIA but also in a readiness to grant the White House broad powers to pursue almost any action that could be construed as advancing the struggle against communism. This de facto surrender of Congress's constitutional warmaking powers established a dangerous precedent. The 1955 resolution granting Eisenhower a free military hand against the Chinese in the offshore-islands dispute, in which Senator Johnson played a central role, uncannily anticipated the 1964 Gulf of Tonkin resolution (see p. 306) that would give Johnson as president a virtual blank check to escalate the Vietnam War.

While embracing the anti-Soviet policy inherited from Truman, the Eisenhower-Dulles team infused it with a quasi-religious rhetorical fervor and extended it globally. For many who lived during these years, the apocalyptic rhetoric, the nuclear build-up, and particular crises, such as the sparring over China's offshore islands, remain fixed in memory. Yet at crucial junctures, Eisenhower refrained from the military response that some urged—and from any nuclear response. This restraint averted an irrevocable turn to open hostilities and gave the world a chance to work toward an eventual end to the Cold War. In Eisenhower's second term, discussed in Chapter 6, a series of crises would wither the hopeful spirit of the midfifties and propel the Cold War to new levels of intensity as the sixties began.

Presidents must handle specific crises, but they also shape the national discourse on issues of war and peace, and here, too, Eisenhower compiled a mixed record. Following the logic of the massive-retaliation strategy, he occasionally spoke of nuclear weapons as simply another arrow in the quiver. Asked in 1955 whether he would use atomic bombs if the crisis with China escalated to war, he replied, "I see no reason why they shouldn't be used just exactly as you would use a bullet or anything."

On the other hand, Eisenhower revealed a profound insight into war's tragic toll and the social cost of excessive military spending. A career military man, he had been reared in a small Mennonite-related pacifist denomination, the Brethren in Christ, whose values remained close to him. Addressing a group of newspaper editors in 1953, the president pointed out that for the cost of one modern bomber, the nation could build thirty schools or two hospitals. "Every gun made, every warship that is launched, every rocket fired," he asserted, "signifies, in the final sense, a theft from those who hunger and are not fed, those who are cold and are not clothed."

The best remembered of Eisenhower's presidential pronouncements would come in his 1960 farewell address to the nation, in which he reflected on the wastefulness of the arms race and warned of the growing influence, "economic, political, and even spiritual," of the "military-industrial complex" in Cold War America. This phrase referred to the large and politically influential sector of the U.S. economy, including labor unions and entire regions, that relied heavily on Pentagon contracts for research, development, and production of military weaponry. Eisenhower found troubling the extent to which the demands for military preparedness influenced many facets of American life.

One must not exaggerate the importance of rhetorical calls for peace, however. Eisenhower presided over a major build-up of the nuclear-arms competition, authorized CIA operations hardly in keeping with the peaceful world that he evoked, and enjoyed only limited success in curbing the military-industrial complex that he so deplored. Indeed, he contributed to its expansion even as he sought to curb its political and social ramifications. The irony in this complex picture is that Eisenhower, one of the great military leaders of the twentieth century, would leave as his principal legacy somber warnings of an increasingly militarized American society.

The Economic Boom Rolls On

As the administration pursued the Cold War abroad, the nation's economy continued to flourish. President Eisenhower saw a close link between these two realities. "[There is] a direct connection," he observed to Dulles in 1953, "between a prosperous and happy America and the execution of an intelligent foreign policy." A thriving United States, he believed, offered a powerful testimonial to the superiority of the free-enterprise system over the Soviet Union's state-run economy. The president thus had several reasons to take pleasure in the economic abundance. The business cycle underwent periodic downturns, and many Americans still lived in want, but a booming economy overall provided an upbeat accompaniment to 1950s politics and culture. In *People of Plenty* (1954), historian David Potter even argued that America's material well-being explained much of U.S. history and "the American character." Whatever the validity of Potter's thesis, it held true for the fifties. Economist Walt Rostow's 1960 study, *The Stages of Economic Growth,* argued that the United States had reached the ultimate stage: "high mass consumption." With 75 percent of adult Americans owning automobiles and 87 percent of households containing television sets, Rostow's analysis seemed justified.

Not all was rosy, however. Mild recessions slowed growth in 1953–1954, 1957–1958, and 1960–1961. The first dip stemmed in part from defense-spending cuts after the Korean War. The 1957–1958 slowdown, triggered by plant overexpansion and a drop in exports, stirred uneasy memories of depression. As unemployment rose to 7.5 percent, one Democratic wag wrote, "Eisenhower is my shepherd, I am in want. . . . He leadeth me through still factories. He restoreth my doubt in the Republican Party." Ike's popularity fell below 60 percent for the first and only time, and the Democrats won big in the 1958 midterm elections. Still, joblessness in the 1950s averaged a modest 4.6 percent, and when Ike left office, a record 73 million Americans held jobs, in contrast to 66.5 million when he took office. Per-capita income, in constant dollars, grew by about 10 percent in the 1952–1960 period.*

Another blight on 1950s prosperity was the persistence of poverty. As in the Truman years, many Americans—including older citizens, inner-city blacks, small farmers, displaced New England millworkers, female-headed households, and rural southerners both white and black—did not share in the decade's abundance. A 1957 study by Robert Lampman of the University of Wisconsin found that more than 32 million Americans, nearly one person in four, fell below the government's poverty line. Furthermore, although overall wealth increased, its distribution remained dramatically unequal. In 1950 the bottom one-fifth of American families received only 4 percent of the total national income, whereas the top fifth garnered 43 percent. Ten years later, these figures remained practically unchanged. Historian Gabriel Kolko wrote in 1962, "The basic distribution of income and wealth is essentially the same now as it was in 1939, or even 1910."

But despite recession, chronic poverty, and uneven income distribution, prosperity in the 1950s was real and widespread. Encouraged by federal spending and by Eisenhower administration policies promoting economic growth, the GNP increased 25 percent between 1953 and 1961, inspiring investors to a decidedly bullish mood. Stock prices in 1954 roared past the level that they had reached before the 1929 crash. General Motors shattered another record in 1955 by posting a profit of $1 billion, the first time that a U.S. corporation had reached that mark. By 1960, on the basis of income levels, demographers defined 60 percent of Americans as "middle class." And unlike other boom times, runaway prices did not eat up rising income: inflation averaged only 1.5 percent annually in the 1950s.

Home construction provided a major economic stimulus, as millions of Americans bought tract houses in the suburbs. Many such buyers, newcomers to the middle

---

* In constant (1958) dollars, per-capita income in 1953 was $1,969; in 1961, $2,184.

Its rakish tailfins poised for take-off, the 1959 Buick epitomized the era's love affair with big, chrome-laden cars. One critic called them "Insolent Chariots." (*Archive Photos*)

class, spent freely on a dizzying variety of household goods, from bedroom sets and automatic dishwashers to television sets, power mowers, and lawn furniture. The rising birthrate stimulated sales of products for infants and children, as well as school construction. Suburban families needed transportation, and auto sales soared. Car models changed yearly amid great hoopla, and two-car households became common. To entice buyers further, the typical 1950s auto flashed some 180 separate pieces of chrome or stainless steel "brightwork."

New products poured into the marketplace. TV had the highest visibility, as the number of sets in U.S. living rooms zoomed from 1 million in 1950 to 50 million in 1960. Other industries contributed as well, with goods ranging from freezers to 45-RPM record players to electric knives to ballpoint pens. Westinghouse introduced all-color refrigerators in 1956. Du Pont and other chemical companies offered a rainbow of new synthetic fabrics with such futuristic names as Orlon, Dacron, and Acrilan. Advertising, a $12-billion-a-year industry by 1960, fueled the boom. TV screens and the pages of *Life, Collier's,* and *Saturday Evening Post* glittered with ads. "Home Means More with a Carpet on the Floor," proclaimed the Carpet Institute. "Drive More . . . It Gets Cheaper by the Mile," advised the Ethyl Corporation. "Be Happy, Go Lucky," urged the makers of Lucky Strike cigarettes.

Credit sales spurred the economy even more. The first credit card, Diner's Club, made its debut in 1950; American Express cards appeared in mid-decade. When Sears Roebuck offered its own credit card, 10 million Americans snapped them up. By 1960 consumer indebtedness neared $200 billion. Setting a trend that would intensify in future years, Americans plunged into debt to acquire the consumer products that the system made so abundantly available.

The glorification of American business, rooted in the war years, continued unabated in the 1950s. "The $9 billion-a-year chemical industry has transformed American life," gushed *Life* in 1953. "It has scrubbed the modern world with detergents, doctored it with synthetic drugs, dressed it in synthetic textiles, cushioned it with synthetic rubber and adorned it from head to toe with gaudy plastic." What the media trumpeted, scholars confirmed. Economist John Kenneth Galbraith, in titling his 1957 book *The Affluent Society,* also named the era. Although critical of the way in which Americans expended their abundance, Galbraith did not question its reality. For him, as for many other social scientists in the 1950s, poverty scarcely existed.

The typical modern American, Galbraith wrote, "has access to amenities—foods, entertainment, personal transportation, and plumbing—in which not even the rich rejoiced a century ago."

America's global economic situation looked bright as well. U.S. exports—mainly machinery, cars and trucks, grain, metals, and manufactured goods—nearly doubled during the decade, reaching just under $20 billion by 1960. Imports rose also, but most of the goods that Americans bought still bore the "Made in the USA" label. In 1960 the United States enjoyed a trade surplus of nearly $5 billion. To a later generation staggering under massive trade deficits, such statistics make the 1950s seem almost a golden age.

The rise of the multinational corporations that would soon dominate the global economy accelerated in the 1950s, as U.S. companies increasingly built plants and distribution centers near their foreign markets. As early as 1951, twenty-three General Motors plants in seven foreign countries were manufacturing 176,000 cars and trucks annually. By 1960 the value of such corporate investment abroad stood at nearly three times the 1950 level. This trend meshed neatly with the ideology of the Cold War, for Washington viewed corporate America's global operations as a key bulwark against communism. As U.S. capital and productive skills brought jobs and consumer goods to a waiting world, U.S. leaders thought, the lure of Marxism would surely evaporate. The State Department, the Commerce Department, and the Agency for International Development, which bankrolled some corporate investment in developing nations, all promoted U.S. business expansion abroad.

The globalization of American capital emerged with particular clarity in the Middle East. Before World War II, this region had played only a minor role in world oil markets; in the 1930s, the United States produced and consumed 60 percent of the world's oil. But the postwar boom demanded more and more of the precious commodity. In a little-noted turning point, the United States in 1953 imported more oil than it exported for the first time. As access to oil fields in the Middle East grew more vital, U.S. companies muscled aside the British firms that dominated the region. In 1950 a U.S. consortium led by Texaco, Socony (now Mobil), and Standard Oil of New Jersey (now Exxon) built a thousand-mile pipeline from Saudi Arabia to Lebanon, from which tankers shipped oil to European refineries. U.S. corporations led the Western oil companies that regained access to Iranian oil after the overthrow of Mohammed Mossadegh in 1953. These developments required vast investments, not only in the Middle East but also in European production and distribution facilities. By 1960, thanks to favorable U.S. tax laws and other government policies, five of the world's seven largest oil companies (quaintly nicknamed the Seven Sisters) were American owned. Ironically, the centralized, tightly controlled structure of oil production and distribution developed by U.S. and other Western oil companies in the 1950s would later prove serviceable to the oil-producing nations themselves when they set up their own cartel, the Organization of Petroleum Exporting Countries (OPEC), in 1960.

While the flow of consumer goods most obviously characterized the postwar economy, deeper structural changes were coming to the light as well. Business consolidation, a long-term trend, continued. In 1960 the top 5 percent of U.S. corporations earned nearly 90 percent of all corporate income. The ranks of the self-employed continued to dwindle, falling from 26 percent of the work force in 1940 to

11 percent in 1960. The American economy was losing individual entrepreneurs and small-scale businesses and increasingly featuring giant conglomerates that controlled an ever larger share of the market.

Other economic changes hinted at trouble ahead. As one example, the German-made Volkswagen, nicknamed the Bug or the Beetle for its rounded body, became a familiar sight on U.S. highways. Although Detroit still dominated domestic sales, the popularity of the cheap and fuel-efficient VW foretold the day when the American car-buying public would increasingly turn to foreign imports. In another portentous development, the number of industrial workers dropped from 39 to 36 percent of the labor force in the fifties, and the ranks of professional and service workers crept up from 40 to 46 percent. The long decline in the farm population continued as well, as mechanization and the rise of agribusinesses rendered the family farm an endangered species. GM alone employed about one hundred thousand salaried white-collar workers by the mid-1950s. Some analysts saw this shift as an inevitable result of automation and the rise of a consumer-oriented economy, but others worried about the decline of a labor force once celebrated for its feats of productivity. Home to only 6 percent of the world's population, the United States in the 1950s produced about half the globe's manufactured goods, yet the trend of labor statistics suggested that this imbalance might not last. Few foresaw the industrial decline ahead, but the caution lights were blinking.

The growth of the "professional and service workers" census category attracted the notice of social observers. As early as 1951, in his study *White Collar*, sociologist C. Wright Mills speculated that the rise of a new class that shuffled paper rather than tilled the soil or ran machines would transform the very "tang and feel of the American experience." A society shaped by the farm, frontier, and factory, wrote Mills, had to rethink its fundamental identity. "What must be grasped," he wrote, struggling to define that new identity, "is the picture of society as a great salesroom, an enormous file, an incorporated brain, a new universe of management and manipulation." To Americans nurtured on an image of America as a land of free enterprise and individual opportunity, Mills offered a much darker vision in which repetitive labor performed for large bureaucracies would become the lot of millions.

Even the feats of productivity and consumption that 1950s publicists so proudly hailed look different from a later perspective. The statistics on energy use and raw-materials consumption cited at the time as proof of a thriving economy suggest incredible heedlessness to a later generation worried about energy costs, the environment, and dwindling resources. When *Life* boasted in the 1950s that U.S factories could supply every American woman with ten pairs of nylon stockings a year, gloated over foreign visitors' awe at the shelves of pet food in U.S. supermarkets, or photographed housewives posed on suburban front lawns flanked by mountains of foodstuffs, detergents, and other goods representing the typical middle-class family's annual consumption, it all seemed wonderfully reassuring. In retrospect, these images evoke other reflections: of a society wallowing in material bounty, oblivious to poverty at home; the limits of the earth's resources; the chasm separating the world's rich and poor societies; and the ecological costs of unchecked consumption.

A few observers criticized the consumerist binge on aesthetic grounds—one journalist complained that "the loudest sound in the land has been the oink-and-

Welcome to suburbia! Hundreds of would-be buyers turned out in 1951 to view the model homes planned for Levittown in Bucks County, Pennsylvania. By 1958, this development boasted more than 17,000 nearly identical houses. (*Temple University*)

grunt of private hoggishness"—but more typically praise for capitalism replaced the criticism of the 1930s. Columbia University law professor Adolph A. Berle, who in the 1930s had warned against the concentration of corporate power, now exulted that American business had "left every other system in recorded history far behind" as a mechanism for supplying consumer goods to the maximum number of people. *Life* summed up the prevailing mood by quoting a steelworker: "In the 1930s I worried about how I could eat. Now I'm worrying about where to park." Such cheery assessments resonated powerfully with the millions for whom the 1950s brought unprecedented prosperity.

The determinedly upbeat tone of many 1950s commentators on America's economic and social health was clearly linked to Cold War fears and anxieties about subversion that pervaded the political culture of the decade. At a time when Americans longed for a respite to enjoy the good life that the publicists of consumer capitalism so tantalizingly promised, the menace of communism seemed especially intolerable. In the face of the free-enterprise system's obvious beneficence, many believed, only traitors or foreigners blinded by ideology could doubt the United States' superiority. The conviction that America, having survived depression and war, at last stood on the threshold of a millennium of material well-being reinforced the Cold War image, shared by Democrats and Republicans alike, of a world in which the forces of good and evil grappled in deadly combat.

The prosperity of the fifties forms the essential context of the cultural and social conflicts explored in Chapter 5. As millions of middle-class citizens—or aspirants to middle-class status—pursued their versions of the American dream, they grew puzzled and angry at those who challenged Eisenhower's America, whether Beat poets, antinuclear activists, or alienated youths. As for the most significant social movement of the decade, the civil-rights struggle, most upwardly mobile white suburbanites with little direct awareness of racism viewed the problem as confined to the South and thus mainly a regional concern. Cultural criticism, youthful rebelliousness, and racial protest seemed so out of step with the abundance and optimism suffusing the consumer culture of the 1950s that, to many citizens, these disruptions appeared to emanate from some altogether alien realm. When Michael Harrington in 1962 published *The Other America*, a study of poverty in the United States, his title could have described the reality of a deeply divided nation as well as the economic fact of want amid plenty.

Suburban Living and Family Togetherness

The family loomed large throughout 1950s American culture. After two decades of depression, war, and postwar deconversion, America longed for social stability and traditional values, and no other institution embodied these virtues more than the nuclear family.

The focus on the family was rooted in demography. Along with economic data, the statistics that compelled the most attention in the early postwar era were those tracking marriages and births. Young people had delayed marriage in the Depression-ridden 1930s and the war-torn 1940s; now they rushed to the altar. The median age at first marriage for both men and women dropped nearly a full year between 1947 and 1957, and these young couples had children in record numbers. The birthrate, which had hovered at around eighteen per thousand population during the 1930s, stood at more than twenty-five per thousand through most of the 1950s, a spurt of nearly 40 percent. Awesome in their numbers, the baby boomers would influence U.S. social history throughout their lives. In the 1950s, they fueled the economic boom. In the 1960s, they would protest racism and the Vietnam War. In the seventies and eighties, many would become Yuppies, or young urban professionals entranced by the trendy trappings of affluence. In the 1990s, female baby boomers would snap up books about menopause. In the twenty-first century, social planners warn, the toddlers of the 1950s could swamp the nation's health-care facilities and retirement homes.

As the most immediate consequence of soaring marriage and birthrates, suburban growth exploded. Of course, throughout recorded history, people have abandoned crowded cities to settle on the outskirts. One cuneiform letter written to the ruler of Persia in 539 B.C. boasted, "Our property . . . is so close to Babylon that we enjoy all the advantages of the city, and yet when we come home we are away from all the noise and dust." Suburban growth, a major U.S. social trend throughout the early twentieth century, proceeded at a sizzling pace in the 1950s. Aided in many cases by low-cost government loans for veterans, young couples and many older families flocked in record numbers to the single-family housing developments that sprang up around America's cities. From 1950 to 1960, the suburban population surged from 21 million to 37 million.

The wave of suburban construction had come in response to the severe postwar housing shortage. New housing starts had fallen by more than 90 percent during the Depression, and the wartime migrations of workers seeking jobs in defense plants had exacerbated the problem. One firm sold scrapbooks during the war for people to collect ideas for their postwar dream house. The 2 million young married couples forced to crowd in with relatives in the early postwar years found the housing shortage especially galling.

The postwar builders who eased the shortage used mass-production techniques pioneered by Abraham Levitt and Sons. In the late 1940s, the Levitts had transformed four thousand acres of Long Island potato farms into Levittown, a community of seventeen thousand houses. Similar projects followed in Pennsylvania and New Jersey. The Levitts standardized every stage of the process, from grading the land, laying out streets, and hooking up utilities to pouring concrete-slab foundations and erecting as many as thirty houses a day from components assembled elsewhere. Thanks to mass-production wizardry and nonunion labor, the Levitts sold their standard two-bedroom house for less than $8,000. The average new house elsewhere cost more—about $14,500—but low-cost FHA and VA loans made these dwellings accessible to millions. The year 1955 alone saw 1.65 million new housing starts, most of them one-family residences. Farmland and rolling hills on the outskirts of the nation's cities sprouted rows of identical tract houses. If the gaunt-eyed sharecropper represented the quintessential visual image of 1930s, the sprawling suburban housing development became the central symbol of the 1950s.

The more capacious of the new suburban residences were called "ranch houses," but despite the evocation of the Old West, the design, as historian Clifford Clark has pointed out, actually reflected architectural styles originating in postwar California. Many of them, in fact, had sprung up in California, the fastest-growing state in these years. "Picture windows" showcased the material goods within and opened the family to neighbors' scrutiny. The interior design expressed the occupants' aspirations to affluence, offering, for example, not one but two bathrooms, the second attached to the "master bedroom." Roomy two-car garages sheltered what one writer called the "insolent chariots" that became another icon of the decade. Family togetherness found expression in designs that combined kitchen, dining room, and living room into one large space, plunging occupants and visitors alike into a swirl of family activity. In larger houses, a separate "den" or "rumpus room," soon to become the "family room," provided space for TV, pool table, and board games and testified to the proliferation of leisure time.

As we shall see, these suburban communities attracted the attention of critics who deplored their alleged uniformity, cultural aridity, and lockstep conformity. The naysayers often overstated their case, but the suburban migration did produce communities that were relatively homogeneous economically and demographically. The Levittowners' newsletter noted: "Our lives are held closely together because most of us are within the same age bracket, in similar income groups, live in almost identical houses, and have common problems." The suburbs were racially homogeneous as well. As whites abandoned the decaying inner cities, low income or discriminatory real-estate policies forced most blacks to remain behind, a development that exacerbated the nation's racial stratification and laid the groundwork for future problems.

The new suburbanites came from small-town America or once-vibrant urban immigrant neighborhoods. Cut off from extended networks of kinfolk and ethnic compatriots, they turned for emotional support to their immediate families and sometimes to their new neighbors, uprooted like themselves and thrown together by chance. The conformity and cloying family togetherness that some social observers lamented in the 1950s stemmed in part from the isolation and disorientation that suburbanites felt.

While the critics carped, the suburbs soared. Levittown, nicknamed Fertility Valley, epitomized a process that was transforming America. For millions, suburban life was a dream come true. "Houses are for people, not critics," declared Abraham Levitt's son William. "We who produce lots of houses do what is possible—no more—and the people for whom we do it think it's pretty good." When asked, suburbanites vehemently denied that they were mindless conformists. One of them objected, "We're not peas in a pod. I thought it would be like that, especially because incomes are nearly the same. But it's amazing how different and varied people are."

Suburbia played an important metaphorical role in the cultural discourse of the fifties. For some, it proved the vitality of the U.S. free-enterprise system; for a vocal minority, it summed up all that they disliked about Eisenhower's America. (As recently as 1986, a historian of postwar America dismissed the suburbs of the fifties as "the faceless dormitories of the middle class.") The truth lay somewhere in between. Suburbia was not utopia, but neither was it the wasteland of conformity and cultural aridity conjured up by some. The rise of the suburbs and their accompanying network of highways unquestionably promoted middle-class homogeneity (a category that included many blue-collar workers) and cut off millions of whites from the poor and minorities of the inner cities. Yet it also provided affordable, safe, and pleasant housing and a crucial boost up the ladder for these same millions. For them, as cultural historian Warren Susman has put it, a house in the suburbs symbolized "the world of new possibilities" that the postwar era seemed to promise.

Advertisers zeroed in on the suburban market of young marrieds, children, and teenagers. *Life* pointed out in 1959 that the typical teenager, possessing phonograph, camera, sports gear, and bulging clothes closet, was a "big-time consumer." In the process, the ads shaped the decade's cultural discourse. Images of young parents and excited children hovering worshipfully around the new Chevrolet automobile, Zenith television set, or Kelvinator refrigerator conveyed a potent unspoken message: consumption itself was a sufficient goal and gave meaning to life. Sages such as Benjamin Franklin had once urged frugality: "A penny saved is a penny earned." Now advertisers struck a different note: In an era of abundance, everyone had a right to share the bounty. One cultural observer commented at mid-decade, "Thrift now is un-American."

Targeting consumers, advertisers offered endless variations on a single image: the clean-cut nuclear family—young, white, and middle class—in a sunlit suburban

Icon of the Eisenhower era. The ubiquitous jukeboxes of the 1950s initially featured syrupy love ballads, but the rock 'n' roll revolution soon changed that. (*Library of Congress*)

house, puttering about the weed-free lawn, or gliding along in a shiny new car. Blacks and other minorities, manual laborers, city-apartment dwellers, and single-parent or multigenerational families rarely intruded. To people who vaguely fit the image, the ads confirmed their vision of America. Those outside the scenario also hungered for the good life portrayed in the ads, but they knew first hand about the vast national diversity, as well as the patterns of discrimination and deprivation, that the ads ignored.

The visual media reinforced this fantasy of the United States as one big suburb. Many movies, despite undercurrents of unease and menace, offered upbeat family entertainment. Five of the ten movies that captured the best-picture Oscars of the 1950s were lighthearted musicals or escapist epics, including *An American in Paris* (1951), *Around the World in Eighty Days* (1956), and *Ben Hur* (1959). *Bedtime for Bonzo* (1951), featuring Ronald Reagan and Diana Lynn as the long-suffering "parents" of a chimpanzee, typified the 1950s frothy domestic comedy.

TV producers loved suburbia. The few dramatic shows of the early 1950s that realistically addressed contemporary social issues soon vanished under the sponsors' relentless quest for larger audiences. TV turned into what a later chairman of the Federal Communications Commission would call a "vast wasteland" of game shows, formulaic westerns, and vapid comedies. Shows like "Ozzie and Harriet," "Father Knows Best," and "Leave It to Beaver" peddled a standard image of middle-class family life and gender roles: supportive wives and mothers who never leave home or remove their aprons, benign fathers who materialize at dinnertime to resolve the petty crises of the day, wisecracking kids who get into amusing scrapes and indulge in innocuous protest gestures but who ultimately recognize their parents' authority.

In "I Love Lucy," which remained immensely popular from its debut in 1951 through 1960,* Lucille Ball's bandleader husband, played by Desi Arnaz, her real-life spouse, treated her like a lovable but irresponsible child. Reality and make-believe blended when the producers incorporated Ball's pregnancy and the birth of her child into the show. Ball and Arnaz later divorced, but off camera. Only a few shows—such as "Our Miss Brooks," with Eve Arden as a tart-tongued, unmarried schoolteacher, and "The Honeymooners," with Jackie Gleason and Audrey Meadows as a childless working-class couple living in a bleak apartment—broke free of gender stereotypes or hinted at the world beyond suburbia.

The homogeneous society portrayed in 1950s mass culture masked the full American reality: The nation was not all white, few teenagers fit the bland and doc-ile stereotype of the TV sitcoms, white-collar workers did not dominate the labor force as completely as they did the media, and not all women spent their days happily as aproned housewives. Nevertheless, the idealized image captured part of fifties social reality and affected the way Americans at the time and since perceived the decade.

Suburbs also influenced 1950s religious life. Church membership soared from 64 million in 1940 to 114 million in 1960. When Dwight Eisenhower joined a Wash-ington church in 1953 and Congress added "under God" to the Pledge of Allegiance and "In God We Trust" to the nation's coinage in 1954, religion gained an official imprimatur. Many of the newly devout were no doubt sincere in their faith, but other factors played a part as well. Church membership represented a way to overcome isolation and to embrace community norms. Indeed, as churchgoing increased, spe-cific theological belief seemed to fade for some. As a vogue for ecumenical mergers swept liberal Protestantism, the media celebrated the virtue of "belief" for its own sake, regardless of substantive content. A series of Religion in American Life public-service messages sponsored by the Advertising Council ignored theological details and instead stressed the family closeness and sense of belonging that church at-tendance provided. One church advertised in 1955, "Lots of acquaintances, not many friends? Is this increasingly true for you? . . . Meet future friends in church next Sunday."

Religion's social utility emerged in *The Organization Man* (1956), William H. Whyte's study of the white-collar suburb of Park Forest, Illinois. Most Park Forest residents, Whyte found, considered a church's ability to provide a sense of commu-nity more important than its creed. "This is the basic need—the need to belong to a group," one minister told him. "In a community like Park Forest, when young people see how many other people are going to church regularly, they feel they ought to."

Churchgoing also highlighted the contrast between America and the officially atheistic Soviet Union. *Life* observed that the United States might seem "secular and often impious," but "religion plays a vital role in community life. Against the force of Communism, we still have faith that the force of Christendom, arrayed with the other great religions of the world, will prevail." The staunchly anticommunist Cath-olic bishop Fulton J. Sheen became a TV celebrity of the 1950s. (Accepting an

---

* From 1957 to 1960, the show was called "The Lucy-Desi Comedy Hour."

award for his show "Life Is Worth Living," Sheen modestly thanked his writers, "Matthew, Mark, Luke and John.") Evangelist Billy Graham, his popularity growing throughout the decade, endlessly wove the latest alarming escalation of the nuclear-arms race into his sermons. Theologian Reinhold Niebuhr remained enormously influential among intellectuals as he defined the issues of the Cold War in a series of incisive books and essays.

Like much else about the 1950s, the religious reality of the 1950s was complex. Despite the bland ecumenicity and suburban "social religion" of mainstream Protestantism, traditional evangelicalism remained strong. Staunchly evangelical bodies such as the Assemblies of God and the Southern Baptist Convention attracted many new members. The ranks of Southern Baptists alone grew from 7 million to 9.7 million in the decade. The National Association of Evangelicals provided an organizational haven for conservative Protestant denominations. Billy Graham might hobnob with presidents and use sophisticated electronic technology and organizational techniques in his "crusades," but the message that he sent forth in his riveting voice, Bible in hand, was the age-old one of human sinfulness and God's grace. Underestimated at the time, evangelicalism would surge to prominence in the 1970s.

Suburban culture and the rites of family togetherness had obvious implications for women, as 1950s mass media celebrated domesticity. In *A Man Called Peter* (1953), Catherine Marshall eulogized her recently deceased husband, the popular minister Peter Marshall, and regretted the wifely rebelliousness that she had felt living in his shadow. Adlai Stevenson told the 1955 graduates of Smith College that "the humble role of housewife" was vital to the Cold War. Wives, he advised, refurbishing an argument mossy with age, must help their career-minded husbands to remain sensitive to the finer things of life. "Keeping your man straight on the difference between Botticelli and Chianti," he suggested, was surely challenge enough for any woman.

Movies and television programs preached the same message. In *The French Line* (1954), a feisty, buxom Jane Russell was literally carried away in the final scene by a Frenchman with whom she had a shipboard romance. In 1950s ads, women invariably played subordinate roles. Ads for one household cleanser, Mr. Clean, featured a brawny superman performing tough chores for pitifully grateful housewives.

The pressure on women to conform to the dominant culture's expectations extended to the highest reaches of business. In a 1951 study of corporate executives, William H. Whyte found that most businessmen viewed the ideal wife as one who devoted herself to her husband's career, scintillated at parties while never saying anything controversial, accepted his work transfers cheerfully, soothed and satisfied her man at night, and ran the household so that domestic worries need not intrude on his professional concerns. As one corporate leader put it, the business wife should maintain a "constructive attitude . . . that will liberate her husband's total energies for the job." Most corporate wives happily accepted this role, Whyte insisted, having concluded that "nurturing the male ego . . . is not only a pretty good fulfillment of their own ego, but a form of therapy [for the husband] made increasingly necessary by the corporation way of life."

These stereotypes and the prescriptive literature distorted the actual situation of many women. The late 1940s rise in female employment continued in the 1950s, and by 1960, some 22 million American women—40 percent of the total adult female population—held jobs. Even in this heyday of culturally promoted domesticity, millions of these working women were also wives and mothers. By mid-decade, one-quarter of all mothers with young children were wage earners as well.

Largely confined to jobs as domestics, waitresses, secretaries, clerks, nurses, and school teachers and paid less than men performing the same or comparable tasks, working women continued to face discrimination. Few held high political office*, rose to the executive ranks in business, or became doctors, lawyers, or professors. Even a strong-willed and independent woman such as playwright Clare Booth Luce, who served as U.S. ambassador to Italy in the 1950s, owed her influence mainly to her marriage to the powerful publisher Henry Luce. African-American, Hispanic, and other minority women faced dual discrimination on gender and racial grounds.

The rise in female employment was not accompanied by an organized women's movement, and social observers of the time missed its long-term significance. Frederick Lewis Allen, for example, compared "the strident suffragettes" of earlier days with the working women of the 1950s who, he insisted, did not work as a result of feminist impulses or dissatisfaction with domesticity but only "for the double paycheck that makes it possible to buy a TV set, a car, or in many cases simply to make ends meet." As soon as the family's economic needs were satisfied, Allen implied, women would return to the kitchen, and the natural order would return.

Indeed, many housewives professed to find their lives fulfilling. As one woman told a University of Michigan psychologist in 1955, "[Marriage has given me] my place in life. I feel I am doing exactly as I am fitted—with an occasional spurt of independence growing less all the time." And Allen was doubtless correct that most women worked not from ideological conviction but for practical economic reasons. The cultural climate of the 1950s did not encourage feminist theorizing or challenges to gender stereotypes. But change lay ahead, and the working women of the 1950s laid the groundwork. If they did not themselves become feminists, their daughters, social researchers found, looked to their working mothers as role models and came to question the status quo.

CONCLUSION

Working women represented only one of many groups that did not fit the 1950s picture of America as a society of placid, prosperous, lily-white suburbs populated by happy nuclear families led by hard-working dads and contented, homebody moms. The stereotype never offered more than a blurred approximation of one slice of 1950s social reality, and forces astir in America would soon undermine it further. Nevertheless it wielded enormous power. Historian Elaine Tyler May argues in *Homeward Bound*, a study of 1950s culture, that this image intersected in complex

---

* Most prominent of the very few women active in national politics in the 1950s was Senator Margaret Chase Smith, a Maine Republican who served from 1949 to 1973. Smith was first elected to the House of Representatives in 1940, replacing her congressman husband who had died.

ways with the ideology of the Cold War. Policymakers' obsession with containing communism abroad paralleled a strong compulsion to contain threatening social pressures at home with a rhetoric of domesticity, consumption, and firmly drawn gender boundaries. As homebuilder William Levitt put it, "No man who owns his own house and lot can be a Communist. He has too much to do." The conviction that "the American way of life" faced heavy ideological assault from abroad intensified pressures to defend the status quo at home.

Richard Nixon's famed 1959 "kitchen debate" with Nikita Khrushchev at the U.S. exhibit in Moscow, conducted as the two leaders gazed earnestly at automatic dishwashers, scouring pads, and boxes of laundry detergent, epitomized the interconnectedness of global anticommunism and the home-front ideology of domesticity. It was as though the essential meaning of America could be deduced from the suburban kitchen and its panoply of consumer products. One of capitalism's finest achievements, boasted Nixon, was to ease the domestic labor of women. Khrushchev, by contrast, insisted that Soviet women were valued as workers, not just as housewives. Ridiculing the brave new world of U.S. kitchen technology, the Soviet leader jeered, "Don't you have a machine that puts food into the mouth and pushes it down?"

Like Nixon in Moscow, many powerful cultural voices insisted throughout the 1950s that the postwar American social order approached perfection, and they predicted a glorious future. "Looking ahead 10 years, 25 years, there is nothing to hold us back," exulted *Life* in 1954. Ike's resounding reelection victory in 1956 attested to the upbeat mood at mid-decade.* But the picture-book image of the 1950s told only part of the story; *Life*'s crystal ball was clouded. The twenty-five-year time frame that the magazine evoked in 1954 in fact would bring fierce struggles against racism, ghetto riots, bitter divisions over an unpopular war, a resurgent women's movement, and deep worries about economic decline and limited resources. Indeed, the decade of the fifties itself offered many evidences that beneath the deceptively placid surface of American life roiled powerful currents of anxiety, unease, and protest.

SELECTED READINGS

Politics in the Eisenhower Era

Charles C. Alexander, *Holding the Line: The Eisenhower Era, 1952–1961* (1975); Craig Allen, *Eisenhower and the Mass Media: Peace, Prosperity and Prime-Time TV* (1993); Stephen E. Ambrose, *Eisenhower: The President* (2 vols., 1983–1984); Jeff Broadwater, *Eisenhower and the Anti-Communist Crusade* (1992); Robert F. Burk, *Dwight D. Eisenhower* (1986); Blance Wiesen Cook, *The Declassified Eisenhower: A Divided Legacy* (1981); Robert Gilbert, *Television and Presidential Politics* (1972); Fred L. Greenstein, *The Hidden-Hand Presidency: Eisenhower as Leader* (1982); Robert Griffith, *The Politics of Fear: Joseph McCarthy and the Senate* (1970) and "Dwight D. Eisenhower and the Corporate Commonwealth," *American Historical Review* (Feb-

---

* Again running against Adlai Stevenson, Eisenhower piled up 35.6 million votes to Stevenson's 26 million. The electoral tally was a lopsided 457–73.

ruary 1982); Robert P. Newan, *Owen Lattimore and the "Loss" of China* (1992); Herbert Parmet, *Eisenhower and the American Crusades* (1972); Gary W. Reichard, *Politics as Usual: The Age of Truman and Eisenhower* (1988); David W. Reinhard, *The Republican Right Since 1945* (1983); Elmo Richardson, *The Presidency of Dwight D. Eisenhower* (1979) and *Dams, Parks and Politics: Resource Development and Preservation in the Truman-Eisenhower Era* (1973); Mark H. Rose, *Interstate Express Highway Politics, 1939–1989* (1991).

Foreign Policy and Nuclear Strategy in the 1950s

Stephen E. Ambrose with Richard H. Immerman, *Ike's Spies: Eisenhower and the Espionage Establishment* (1981); James R. Arnold, *The First Domino: Eisenhower, the Military, and America's Intervention in Vietnam* (1991); Howard Ball, *Justice Downwind: America's Nuclear Testing Program in the 1950s* (1986); Scott D. Breckinridge, *The CIA and the Cold War: A Memoir* (1993); Robert Divine, *Eisenhower and the Cold War* (1981); Robert Gilpin, *American Scientists and Nuclear Weapons Policy* (1962); Norman Graebner, ed., *The National Security: Its Theory and Practice, 1945–1960* (1986); George C. Herring and Richard H. Immerman, "Eisenhower, Dulles, and Dienbienphu," *Journal of American History* (September 1984); Richard G. Hewlett and Jack M. Holl, *Atoms for Peace and War, 1953–1962: Eisenhower and the Atomic Energy Commission* (1989); Richard H. Immerman, *The CIA in Guatemala: The Foreign Policy of Intervention* (1982); Loch K. Johnson, *America's Secret Power: The CIA in a Free Society* (1989); Fred Kaplan, *The Wizards of Armageddon* (1963); Burton Kaufman, *Trade and Aid: Eisenhower's Foreign Economic Policy* (1982); Douglas Kinnard, *President Eisenhower and Strategy Management: A Study in Defense Politics* (1977); Michael Mandelbaum, *The Nuclear Question: The United States and Nuclear Weapons, 1946–1976* (1979); Richard A. Melanson and David Mayers, eds., *Reevaluating Eisenhower: American Foreign Policy in the 1950s* (1987); Donald Neff, *Warriors at Suez: Eisenhower Takes America into the Middle East* (1981); Ronald E. Powaski, *March to Armageddon: The United States and the Nuclear Arms Race, 1939 to the Present* (1987); John Ranelagh, *The Agency: The Rise and Decline of the CIA* (1986); Andrew Rotter, *The Path to Vietnam: Origins of the American Commitment to South East Asia* (1987).

Economic and Social Trends in the 1950s

Richard J. Barber, *The American Corporation: Its Power, Its Money, Its Politics* (1970); John F. Bauman, *Public Housing, Race, and Renewal: Urban Planning in Philadelphia, 1920–1974* (1987); Robert H. Bremner and Gary W. Reichard, eds., *Reshaping America: Society and Institutions, 1945–1960* (1982); David P. Calleo, *The Imperious Economy* (1982); Clifford E. Clark, Jr., "Ranch-House Suburbia: Ideals and Realities," in Lary May, ed., *Recasting America: Culture and Politics in the Age of the Cold War* (1989); John Patrick Diggins, *The Proud Decades: America in War and Peace, 1941–1960* (1988); John Kenneth Galbraith, *The New Industrial State* (1971); Mark I. Gelfand, *A Nation of Cities* (1975); Claudia Dale Goldin, *The Great Compression: The Wage Structure in the United States at Mid-Century* (1991); Jeffrey Hart, *When the Going Was Good: American Life in the Fifties* (1982); Delores Hayden, *Redesigning the American Dream* (1984); Kenneth T. Jackson, *Crabgrass Frontier: The Suburbanization of the United States* (1985); Howard B. Jacobson and Joseph S. Soucek, *Automation and Society* (1959); Landon Y. Jones, *Great Expectations: America and the Baby Boom Generation* (1980); Elaine Tyler May, *Homeward Bound: American Families in the Cold War Era* (1988); Douglas T. Miller and Marion Nowak, *The Fifties: The Way We Really Were* (1977); Zane I. Miller, *Suburb: Neighborhood and Community in Forest Park, Ohio, 1935–1976* (1981); William L. O'Neill, *American High: The Years of Confidence, 1945–1960* (1986); Geoffrey Perrett, *A Dream of Greatness: The American People, 1945–1963* (1979); Richard Polenberg, *One Nation Divisible: Class, Race,* and Ethnicity in the United States Since 1938 (1981); Herbert Stein, Presidential Economics: The Making of Economic Policy from Roosevelt to Reagan and Beyond (1984); Gwendolyn Wright, Building the Dream: A Social History of Housing in America (1981).

Women in the Fifties

Wini Breines, Young, White and Miserable: Growing Up Female in the Fifties (1992); William H. Chafe, The Paradox of Change: American Women in the Twentieth Century (1991); Ruth Schwartz Cowan, More Work for Mother: The Ironies of Household Technology from the Open Hearth to the Microwave (1983); Benita Eisler, Private Lives: Men and Women of the Fifties (1986); Cynthia Harrison, On Account of Sex: The Politics of Women's Issues, 1945–1968 (1988); Brett Harvey, ed., The Fifties: A Women's Oral History (1993); Eugenia Kaledin, Mothers and More: American Women in the 1950s (1984); Susan Estabrook Kennedy, If All We Did Was to Weep at Home: A History of White Working-Class Women in America (1979); Leila Rupp and Verta Taylor, Survival in the Doldrums: The American Women's Rights Movement, 1945 to the 1960s (1990); Rickie Solinger, Wake Up Little Susie: Pregnancy and Race Before Roe v. Wade (1992).

Mass Culture and Popular Religion

Hollis Alpert, The Dreams and the Dreamers [movies] (1962); Glenn T. Altschuler and David I. Grossvogel, Changing Channels: America in T.V. Guide (1992); Erik Barnouw, Tube of Plenty: The Evolution of American Television (1975); James L. Baughman, The Republic of Mass Culture: Journalism, Filmmaking and Broadcasting in America Since 1941 (1992); Peter Biskind, Seeing Is Believing: How Hollywood Taught Us to Stop Worrying and Love the Fifties (1983); William Boddy, Fifties Television: The Industry and Its Critics (1990); Stephanie Coontz, The Way We Never Were: American Families and the Nostalgia Trap (1992); Carol George, God's Salesman: Norman Vincent Peale and the Power of Positive Thinking (1993); George Lipsitz, Class and Culture in Cold War America (1981) and Time Passages: Collective Memory and American Popular Culture (1990); David Marc, Democratic Vistas: Television in American Culture (1984) and Prime Time/Prime Movers: From I Love Lucy to L.A. Law: America's Greatest T.V. Shows and the People Who Created Them (1992); William Martin, A Prophet with Honor: The Billy Graham Story (1991); Donald Meyer, The Positive Thinkers: Religion as Pop Psychology from Mary Baker Eddy to Oral Roberts (1980); Nora Sayre, Running Time: Films of the Cold War (1982); Lynn Spiegel, Make Room for TV: Television and the Family Ideal in Postwar America (1992); Max Wilk, The Golden Age of Television (1976); Robert Wuthnow, The Restructuring of American Religion: Society and Faith Since World War II (1988).

Part Two

DISSENT, TERROR, REFORM

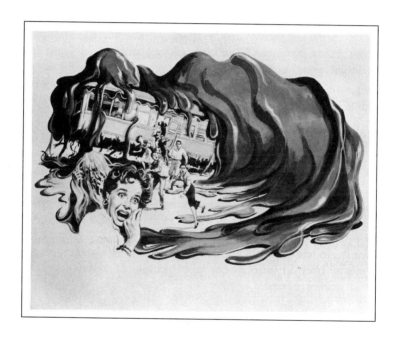

Looked at from some perspectives, the United States in the mid-1950s radiated confidence and self-assurance. Ike presided benignly in the White House, the Cold War consensus enjoyed broad support, and the media offered reassuring images of an affluent society typified by TV sitcoms' smiling, middle-class, white suburban families.

But no society, and certainly not Eisenhower's America, is wholly homogeneous or uncomplicated. America in the 1950s concealed more turbulence and tension than a casual foreign observer might have guessed. This darker, more ambiguous side of the picture emerged with growing starkness as the decade wore on, coming to the light most graphically in the popular culture. Anxieties about nuclear war, alien menace, and social-conformist pressures all surfaced intriguingly in the Hollywood films of the fifties. As the baby-boom generation reached adolescence, the bland world of pop music found itself shaken and rattled by rock-and-roll. Indeed, the gyrating Elvis Presley and other new rock-and-roll icons won a fanatically loyal following among the young. The Beats sounded a jarring, assertive new note in the decade's literature. And social critics, although they stepped gingerly around fundamental issues of social injustice and class inequities in capitalist America, offered sharp-edged critiques of middle-class conformity and mass-culture insipidity.

Regarding race, the Supreme Court in 1954 thrust a profoundly important issue onto the national agenda by outlawing segregation in public schools. This ruling, reflecting years of painstaking legal effort by the National Association for the Advancement of Colored People (NAACP) and other groups, launched a civil-rights movement that would transform America. In 1955–1956, African-Americans in Montgomery, Alabama, organized a successful, year-long boycott of the city's segregated buses that radically challenged the political passivity of the decade. From the Montgomery movement emerged Martin Luther King, Jr., a young black minister who raised a powerful moral voice against racism and on behalf of Americans' common humanity.

As the nation confronted the ugly reality of racism, a new menace materialized: radioactive fallout from U.S. and Soviet nuclear tests in the Pacific that posed alarming environmental and health hazards. Further roiling the political waters, citizens organized campaigns to ban nuclear testing and to bring the nuclear-arms race under control. Moviemakers, television producers, and science-fiction writers explored the not-so-hidden terror of nuclear holocaust underlying the surface optimism of the fifties.

A further shock came in 1957 when the Soviet Union launched its space satellite, *Sputnik*. Sharply eroding the sense of global invincibility in which Americans had gloried since World War II, *Sputnik* unleashed an orgy of self-doubt and self-scrutiny. Continued Cold War jousting only worsened the national attack of the jitters. Despite a partial thaw in East-West relations after the death of Soviet dictator Joseph Stalin in 1953, tensions remained high as the fifties drew to a close.

This intensifying sense of unease contributed to the Democratic victory of 1960 that put a charismatic young Massachusetts senator, John F. Kennedy, into the White House. The "Eisenhower generation" that had led the nation during World War II now yielded power to the generation that had been only in their twenties during the war. JFK, however, pursued the Cold War as relentlessly as had his predecessors. Championing an activist, liberal foreign policy, he espoused economic development, social programs, and nation building as strategies for winning over the Third World. Kennedy was also determined to prove his toughness to the Kremlin leaders. As he saw it, the United States must stand firm militarily against the Soviets. In this spirit he presided over an expanded defense budget, a nuclear-weapons build-up, an abortive invasion of Castro's Cuba, and a missile crisis that brought the world perilously close to the nuclear abyss. Moreover, the new president moved cautiously toward a deeper engagement in Vietnam. In contrast to these aggressive strategies, Kennedy's foreign-policy legacy also included the Peace Corps and the 1963 limited nuclear-test ban treaty, the product of a joint recognition in Moscow, Washington, and other capitals of the urgent need to bring the nuclear demon under control.

At home, Kennedy brought the cool, pragmatic, and liberal outlook of his generation to domestic policy. The result was a surge of reform matched in the twentieth century only in the Progressive era and in Franklin D. Roosevelt's New Deal. In the later 1950s, congressional Democrats led by liberals such as Senator Hubert Humphrey and the wily Senate majority leader Lyndon Johnson had helped the Eisenhower administration to pass a landmark civil-rights bill over conservative opposition. In the early sixties, with the Democrats now in control of both the White House and the Congress, the momentum for reform gained strength. President Kennedy proposed various measures but did not live to see many of them enacted. His successor, Lyndon Johnson, used the nation's grief over Kennedy's assassination and his own political genius to push through Congress a remarkable array of reforms, from civil-rights legislation to anti-poverty, education, and urban measures to environmental-protection laws. In 1964, facing opponent Barry Goldwater, whom many voters found frighteningly militaristic, Johnson won one of the great landslide victories of U.S. political history.

The years 1964–1965 represented both the pinnacle of Johnson's career and the high-water mark of postwar liberalism. The civil-rights campaign lay at the heart of the reformist wave that crested in the mid-1960s. Since its beginnings in the 1950s, the movement had broadened and deepened into a full-scale and remarkably successful assault on the South's deeply entrenched racial caste system. The moment of liberal ascendancy would prove brief. The electorate veered rightward as early as the 1966 midterm election, and by the later 1960s a troubled economy, racial divisions, and civil turmoil over the war in Vietnam had shattered the fragile consensus over which Johnson had presided in the bright noonday of his presidency.

Chapter Five

THE OTHER SIDE OF THE PICTURE WINDOW: OUTSIDERS, DISSIDENTS, AND CRITICS IN THE 1950s

The year is 1954, and in movie houses and drive-ins across the United States, wide-eyed Americans are watching *Them!* an early entrant in what would soon become a deluge of "mutant" movies. The film depicts a storybook American family—father, mother, and daughter—vacationing in New Mexico. But even before the action begins, disaster has struck: Unknown monstrous creatures have ripped apart the family's camper and brutally murdered the parents. Only the daughter survives, so traumatized that she cannot speak except to scream, "*THEM!!!*" Soon we learn that the killers are giant ants, hatched from the radioactive soil of the atomic-bomb test site at Alamogordo, who spread death and destruction in their insatiable search for sugar. The army is called in and finally exterminates the last of the loathsome mutants in the storm sewers beneath Los Angeles.

In its bizarre fashion, *Them!* and its terrified young vacationer epitomized a central paradox of the 1950s. Americans should have been happy and confident. They had won a terrible war, and a booming economy, cheap suburban housing, and a cornucopia of consumer products placed the good life within reach of millions. Hollywood, television, and mass magazines provided diversion. But an undercurrent of anxiety reflected in movies, youthful rebelliousness, introspection by troubled intellectuals, fear of nuclear tests, and rising waves of protest against racial segregation all belied the decade's upbeat mood. The United States in the 1950s clearly was not as trouble-free as a quick visit to suburbia or a glance at television might have suggested. Yet the ill-defined social issues of that decade made their presence felt only sporadically and indirectly.

Domestically, the quality of American life in these affluent years struck cultural critics as deplorable. The by-products of prosperity—rampant materialism, the rise of a homogenized mass culture, and the enormous growth of a desk-bound white-collar class—roused dissident artists, writers, and intellectuals. Was a nation long proud of its individualism becoming timid and conformist? Alexis de Tocqueville had raised the question more than a century before, and it resurfaced with fresh urgency in the 1950s. Furthermore, although John Kenneth Galbraith's 1958 book, *The Affluent Society*, focused on the persistence of want amid abundance, many people misunderstood its ironic title as a celebration of U.S. prosperity. In 1959 economist Robert Lampman of the University of Wisconsin estimated the size of the American underclass at a whopping 32 million. Journalist Michael Harrington published several articles in small-circulation magazines between 1950 and 1960 with titles such as "Our Fifty Million Poor." At the time, these reports attracted little notice. Untold numbers of poor Americans struggled in rural regions and inner cities, but the realities of poverty and wide economic inequities remained relegated to the periphery of the nation's consciousness.

Globally, the nuclear-arms race, the spread of communism, and Moscow's alleged drive for world domination loomed menacingly on the horizon. Such Cold War anxieties constantly undercut efforts to sustain a positive cultural tone. Nevertheless, in this arena, too, tensions rarely found political voice except in McCarthyite hysteria about domestic subversives.

With two notable exceptions—the movement to halt nuclear testing and an emerging civil-rights campaign—protest impulses stood little chance against the stand-pat outlook expressed in Eisenhower's two electoral victories; suburban complacency and Cold War clichés were too powerful. And despite the increasing tempo of civil-rights activism in the South, awareness of racism as a national shame penetrated white America only slowly and fitfully.

In contrast to the 1930s or the 1960s, the current of reform flowed sluggishly in Eisenhower's America. Discontent with the status quo found a variety of outlets rather than coalescing into a single movement. To trace the patterns of cultural alienation and social activism in the fifties, we will range widely, from the writings of critics and novelists to the world of jazz and folk-music clubs, drive-in theaters, coffee houses, rock-and-roll concerts, antinuclear marches, the Supreme Court, and southern black churches. The churches are especially important. The civil-rights movement, whose 1950s beginnings we examine in this chapter, ultimately would unravel the patterns of racism woven through American history and embedded in the structure of American society.

Films of the Fifties:
Undercurrents of Menace

The Hollywood dream factory has always both molded and reflected American hopes and fears, and the films of the fifties are no exception. They mirrored the decade's ambiguities, with some offering escapist fare and optimistic images of suburban life and endorsing the Cold War and conventional social values but others revealing often indirectly the anxieties of the era and laying bare more about the fifties than moviemakers may have intended.

The messages of these films were rarely obvious. Producers, their eye on box-office receipts, crafted movies that appealed to the largest possible audiences. Many films of the decade therefore can be interpreted in a variety of ways. In Howard

Hawks's *The Thing* (1951), for example, the alien blob buried in the Arctic ice may represent communist subversion, repressed sexuality, modern science—or simply an alien blob. The popular western *High Noon* (1952) invites a similar array of interpretations. As the movie opens, badman Frank Miller rides into town to kill former marshal Will Kane (Gary Cooper), who had sent him to prison years before. Kane expects the townspeople to rally to his aid, but they are a cowardly lot and abandon Will to confront Miller and his two equally unsavory brothers alone. Once the Miller boys lie dead in the street, the townspeople rush out to congratulate Kane, but in disgust he throws his badge in the dust and rides out of town.

High Noon's director and scriptwriter, fierce opponents of McCarthyism, intended the film as a critique of those who displayed moral cowardice in the face of McCarthy's demagoguery. Did the moviegoers who flocked to *High Noon* catch this subtle political message, or did they view it as a traditional western extolling individualism, a classic American theme? Kane's Quaker bride (Grace Kelly) is portrayed as naive in her efforts to persuade him to walk away from the violence. Thus, the film could also be interpreted as a Cold War tract preaching the inevitability of an H-bomb "shootout" with the Russians.

Despite the thematic ambiguity in many 1950s movies, an underlying pattern also emerges. Typically, a menace lurks just beneath a tranquil surface. The films begin with cheerful, everyday scenes in an ordinary community, followed by mounting tension as horrible, inexplicable events shatter the routine. The giant ants of *Them!* spawned a frightening progeny of shrinking men, towering women, prehistoric monsters jolted from their long slumber, and unclassifiable creatures from black lagoons.

The Invasion of the Body Snatchers (1956) is particularly terrifying because the monsters appear in human guise. As the movie opens, Dr. Miles Bennell (Kevin McCarthy) gradually realizes that something has gone terribly awry in the community of Santa Mira, California. People look the same, but they are different. As Miles's girlfriend Becky (Dana Wynter) says of her Uncle Ira, "There's something missing. Always when he talked to me there was a certain look in his eyes. Now it's gone. There's no emotion." Uncle Ira is actually a robotlike clone, hatched from a pod brought from outer space by aliens. The pod people are zombies, carrying out the malevolent wishes of their alien masters.

Like many other 1950s movies, *Invasion of the Body Snatchers* played on different anxieties. Most obvious is the Cold War obsession with subversion, the suspicion that alien ideologies menaced America, and that people were not what they seemed. One's best friend or neighbor could be a traitor. Unlike earlier stereotypical enemies such as the "redskins" of countless westerns or the "Japs" of World War II propaganda, the communists were physically indistinguishable in a crowd, yet threatened everything Americans held dear.

As pod people gain control of the town, Becky and Miles flee for their lives. Finally Becky herself falls victim to the pods, and only Miles is left. In the film's original ending, he stares wild-eyed at the camera and screams, "You're next!" In the more upbeat ending actually released, a police official telephones Washington and shouts, "Get me the FBI!" Even so paranoid a film as *The Invasion of the Body Snatchers* had to offer assurance of some center of stability and authority.

Other movies exposed the fragility of the middle-class family ideal. In William Wyler's *The Desperate Hours* (1955), an escaped convict terrorizes a storybook suburban family. In the 1958 potboiler *I Married a Monster from Outer Space*—a knock-off of *Invasion of the Body Snatchers*—a housewife discovers that her model husband is not what he seems. Whatever the specific danger in these films, the pervasive mood was one of impalpable menace lurking just beyond the campfire. In *The Thing*, the scientist who wants to communicate with the mysterious entity rather than destroy it is portrayed as dangerously naive. Sure enough, as he approaches the blob, calling out, "I am your friend," the malicious creature zaps him. This sense of encroaching horror—of amorphous but nevertheless deadly forces that cannot be understood, only destroyed—captured a powerful undercurrent in the national mood.

Rebellious Youth

Movies of the fifties often featured alienated or ominous teenagers very different from the cheery juveniles of the TV sit-coms. In *Rebel Without a Cause* (1955), a film freely adapted from a 1944 psychological case study of maladjusted adolescents, James Dean, Natalie Wood, and Sal Mineo play a trio of disturbed youths from affluent homes who are frustrated with their privileged lives and hell-bent on trouble. Dean's character races hot rods and pretends to be tough. Actually, he is unsure of his masculinity because his father is a poor role model; Dad wears aprons and helps with the housework. Natalie Wood's character, troubled by her puritanical father's inability to deal with her budding sexuality, has turned to promiscuity.

Sentimentalizing its teenage delinquents, *Rebel Without a Cause* pictured a suburbia awash in psychopathology. Society as a whole is presented favorably, however, and by the end, Dean and Wood have fallen in love (with Mineo as a kind of surrogate child) and have begun to accept middle-class values. *Rebel Without a Cause* was thus a fundamentally conservative film, idealizing Dean's juvenile-court officer and other therapeutic experts. In the 1930s, experts had blamed delinquency on poverty. In the 1950s, film portrayals of the affluent middle class faulted psychosexual problems instead.

Far more sinister were *The Wild One* (1953) and *Blackboard Jungle* (1955), both filmed in black and white. In *The Wild One*, based on an actual incident, Marlon Brando and Lee Marvin play the leaders of rival motorcycle gangs that invade a sleepy California town. When an intrigued young woman asks Brando what he's rebelling against, Brando sneers, "What have you got?" A message that followed the opening credits made the movie's point frighteningly clear: "This is a shocking story. It could never take place in most American towns—but it did in this one. It is a public challenge not to let it happen again."

Blackboard Jungle offered a sanitized look at inner-city schools, a subject rarely examined in the 1950s. After various scenes of violence and mayhem at North Manual High, accompanied by a raucous rock-and-roll soundtrack, the idealistic teacher (Glenn Ford) finally wins the respect of his tough class and even persuades one bright black student (Sidney Poitier) to apply to college. Like *The Wild One*, *Blackboard Jungle* treats its unsettling subject matter cautiously. Not only is the ending optimistic, but the movie insists that schools like North Manual are rare. When Ford visits an orderly suburban high school, a teacher assures him, "For every school like [North Manual] there are thousands like this one." To prove it, he takes Ford to an assembly where rows of well-groomed youth are fervently singing the national anthem.

The free-floating discontent with mainstream culture of many 1950s youth found expression above all in music. The early-fifties pop-music scene was numbingly bland, with singers such as Perry Como, Bing Crosby, and Pat Boone crooning insipid love ballads devoid of sexuality and authentic emotion. Rock-and-roll and its first superstar, Elvis Presley, defied all that. Born in 1935 in Tupelo, Mississippi, Elvis was a nineteen-year-old truck driver when he recorded demonstration tapes for Sun Records, a small Memphis label, in 1954. The young entertainer crafted his singing style from rhythm and blues. Indebted to legendary black singers such as Robert Johnson of Mississippi, R&B, with its powerful rhythms and raw sexual energy, was popular with African-Americans but largely unknown in white America. Elvis blended R&B with the cadences of country music and the gospel songs of his boyhood Assemblies of God church, concocting a potent formula that scored an instant hit. Midway through Eisenhower's first term, teenagers thrilled deliriously to his version of such R&B standards as "That's All Right Mama."

The new star enthralled screaming audiences, his records sold phenomenally, and radio stations catering to the young programmed hours of rock-and-roll. Elvis's "Heartbreak Hotel" topped the charts in 1956 in three separate categories: pop, country, and R&B. Songs such as "I'm All Shook Up" and "Don't Be Cruel" sustained his popularity. Ultimately, he would be credited with twenty-one million-record sellers. His male fans even adopted his glistening pompadour hairstyle and his sequined black jackets. As rock-and-roll caught on, the dulcet tones of the crooners gave way to the shouts, moans, percussive beat, and open eroticism of rock. Teenagers' record hops became loud, rocking affairs, the antithesis of the sedate and well-chaperoned high-school dances of a few years earlier.

Elvis was king, but other rock stars drew youthful fans as well. Bill Haley and the Comets won fame with "Rock Around the Clock," heard on the soundtrack of *Blackboard Jungle*. Out of Georgia burst the black R&B singer Little Richard (born Richard Wayne Penniman in 1935) with such hits as "Tutti Frutti" (1955) and "Long Tall Sally" (1956). Chuck Berry, the product of a lower-middle-class black neighborhood in St. Louis, had spent three years in reform school and was an auto worker when he formed an R&B band in 1953. He enjoyed his first big hit, "Maybelline," in 1955. In Texas, teenager Charles "Buddy" Holly assembled a band and achieved stardom before his death in a plane crash in 1959. In the Mexican barrio of East Los Angeles, Ritchie Valens (his surname shortened from Valenzuela) headed a popular Chicano rock-and-roll group until he perished in the same plane crash in 1959.

The mainstream culture recoiled from this multiethnic explosion of raucous music-making. Church leaders denounced rock-and-roll as indecent and attacked Elvis's lyrics and his suggestive hip thrusting that earned him the nickname Elvis the Pelvis. In a 1955 Florida concert, police insisted that Presley sing without moving his midsection. "Elvis is a symbol, of course, but a dangerous one," wrote one worried parent. "The gangster of tomorrow is the Elvis Presley type of today."

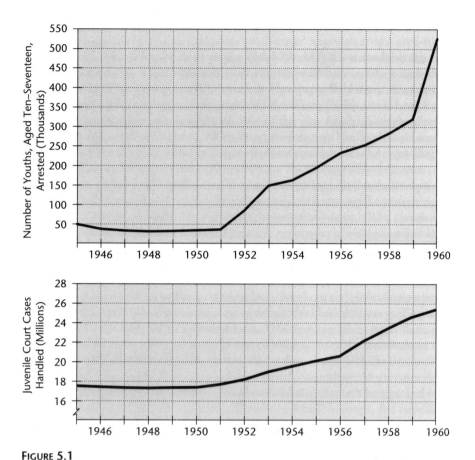

FIGURE 5.1

(a) Number of Youths, Aged Ten to Seventeen, Arrested, 1945–1960
(b) Juvenile Court Cases Handled, 1945–1960

SOURCE: *Historical Statistics of the United States: Colonial Times to 1970*, U.S. Department of Commerce, Bureau of the Census.

Indeed, fears of "juvenile delinquency," comparable to a later generation's concern about drugs, swept America. Now-forgotten movies like *Rock All Night* (1957), *Dragstrip Girl* (1957), and *High School Hellcats* (1958) fed the fantasy of an entire generation sliding into anarchy. Stories of rebellious youth filled the newspapers. In 1953 the U.S. Senate set up a special subcommittee to investigate the problem. Under Senator Estes Kefauver of Tennessee, who became chairman in 1955, the group called a parade of expert witnesses and received a flood of mail from concerned parents.

Leonard Bernstein elevated gang warfare to the status of Shakespearean tragedy in his 1957 hit musical, *West Side Story*, but adults' anxieties about the younger generation continued. These fears had a basis in fact: The number of young people who ran afoul of the law, on charges from petty vandalism to murder, rose sharply in the fifties. In New York City, historian James Gilbert notes, arrests of youths under the age of sixteen more than tripled in the decade, rising from 3,424 in 1950 to 11,365 in 1959. But the "juvenile-delinquency" hysteria also expressed more intangible concerns about the youthful subculture emerging in 1950s America. For one thing, worried pronouncements on the younger generation often had links with broader Cold War fears. Moral rot from within and the communist menace from without, many believed, represented two facets of the same danger. As the head of the Chicago Crime Prevention Bureau put it, "The obscene material that is flooding the Nation today is another cunning device of our enemies, deliberately calculated to destroy the decency and morality which are the bulwarks of society." The communists' alleged skill at "brainwashing" the innocent into accepting their doctrines thus dovetailed psychologically with fears about the power of the mass media to mesmerize impressionable youth.

The older generation's handwringing about wayward youth revealed as well adults' rising uneasiness about the mass media's ability to sabotage parental authority and to peddle alternative cultural values to the young. In *Seduction of the Innocent* (1954), psychiatrist Frederic Wertham pointed with alarm to comic books that glorified crime and violence. Senator Kefauver's hearings heavily emphasized this menace. Exchanges such as this 1954 colloquy between Kefauver and the publisher of *Horror* comic book, William Gaines, shocked many Americans:

> *Kefauver:* Here is your May 22 issue. This seems to be a man with a bloody ax holding a woman's head up which has been severed from her body. Do you think that is in good taste?
>
> *Gaines:* Yes, sir, I do, for the cover of a horror comic. A cover in bad taste, for example, might be defined as holding the head a little higher so that the neck could be seen dripping blood from it and moving the body over a little further so that the neck of the body could be seen to be bloody.

Most of the pretended experts on teenage rebelliousness indicted not just the comics but the mass media in general. Harvard sociologist Pitirim Sorokin warned in *The American Sexual Revolution* (1956) of a "sexualized" youth culture and exhorted parents to protect their children from rock-and-roll, suggestive movies, and violent, crime-ridden radio shows.

As if to confirm Sorokin's assessment, radio disc jockeys adored by the young struck frightened elders as demonic Pied Pipers luring children away from their parents' influence. DJ Alan Freed, using the name Moondog, popularized rock-and-roll on his radio shows, first in Cleveland and then, after 1954, in New York City. In 1955 twenty-five-year-old Buffalo DJ Guy King caused a massive traffic jam by broadcasting his show from atop a large billboard in the heart of the city. He urged youthful drivers in the cars below to blow their horns if they liked "Rock Around the Clock," the song that he was playing. Hundreds obeyed, creating a deafening cacophony. King spent six hours in jail.

Generational conflict that in the sixties would erupt in campus protests and street marches took the form in the fifties of angry quarrels over music, dress, and hairstyles. The school board in San Antonio, reported *Cosmopolitan* magazine in 1957, had banned from high schools "tight blue jeans worn low, or ducktail haircuts, on the grounds that there is a connection between undisciplined dress and undisciplined behavior." This tough dress code, the magazine continued, had reduced "school disciplinary problems to almost nothing." The rock revolution offered its response to such pronouncements in the title of one hit song: "Yakkety Yak."

The forces that gave rise to this distinct youth culture had their roots in larger social changes of the postwar period. With young people remaining in school through their teens, the American high school became a cultural bazaar where youth of diverse backgrounds shared tastes and fads. As early as 1950, the White House Conference on Children noted with alarm that "the standards of the lowest class" of youth threatened to infect "the boys and girls of other social groups." Furthermore, the economic boom gave young people new discretionary income, reducing their dependence on parents. Many high school students held part-time jobs, boosting their buying power even more. The automobile, too, played a role. Increasingly, teenagers had access to a family car or owned one of their own. Hot rods, congregated at drive-in hamburger shops or other oases, became an instantly recognizable symbol of teenage autonomy.

The rock-and-roll revolution gave youth a way to protest the blandness and superficiality of 1950s mass culture. Although the decade's artists and their fans did not evolve into a politically conscious counterculture, they laid the groundwork for a distinctive style among the baby-boom generation's advance guard. In the 1960s, that style would take an overtly political turn.

Ironically, the youth subculture rested on the same affluence that underlay the middle-class suburban culture that it challenged. The phenomenon would have been unthinkable, for example, without the radios and 45-RPM record players in countless teenagers' bedrooms. Indeed, corporate America profited hugely as it supplied the records, movies, fashions, foods, automobile accessories, and reading matter by which the younger generation defined itself. In a further irony, the dominant culture displayed a powerful capacity to absorb and tame the challenge of rock-and-roll and youthful unrest. Presley's own career illustrates the point. As early as 1956, Elvis signed a movie contract and appeared, from the waist up, on Ed Sullivan's TV variety show. The Presley movies and soundtrack albums released in the late fifties and early sixties proved bland and forgettable. The corporate mass-entertainment industry neutralized Presley's iconoclastic energy and turned him, with his full cooperation, into a conventional romantic idol and pop star. Ceasing to produce innovative music, he became merely a celebrity. Toward the end of his life (he died in 1977), even a sympathetic admirer observed, "Elvis transcends his talent to the point of dispensing with it altogether." Moreover, although a hero of the musical and cultural revolution of the sixties, the older Presley kept his distance from the movement that he had spawned. He even volunteered his services as an informant to FBI director J. Edgar Hoover, who tactfully declined the offer.

As the mainstream culture absorbed and co-opted the youthful discontent of the rock-and-roll revolution, the public's obsession with juvenile delinquency faded. By 1959 a movie such as *Teenagers from Outer Space* could celebrate the virtues of suburban togetherness as perceived by a familyless visitor from a futuristic society. The alien mourns, "I have learned how it once was: families, brothers, and sisters. There was happiness; there was love." *Blue Denim* (1959), starring Brandon De Wilde as the new James Dean (Dean had died in an auto accident in 1955), offered a similarly reassuring message. At the film's end, teenage rebel De Wilde sees his error and joins the family for dinner as his father says grace. Nevertheless, the waning of generational conflict would prove short-lived. Both the strength of youthful dissent, and society's ability to absorb that dissent, would be tested again in the late 1960s, with the stakes incomparably higher.

Cultural Resistance:
The Arts and Social Criticism
in Cold War America

Some artists and social critics also expressed doubts about Eisenhower's America. But in contrast to the Depression-ridden 1930s and the politicized 1960s, the dissidents of the 1950s rarely took political stands. They focused instead on the psychological and cultural toll of affluence, not on the ravages of poverty, gaping economic inequities, and wildly unequal diffusion of power across the lines of class, race, and gender in modern America. Rather than proposing structural changes in society, they looked for ways whereby the individual could achieve a more authentic existence in a materialistic, conformist age. The existentialist credo of French intellectuals Jean-Paul Sartre and Albert Camus, with its focus on the dilemma of individuals' seeking meaning in a meaningless universe, enjoyed considerable vogue on U.S. college campuses in these years.

In the realm of jazz, the postwar cultural crosscurrents encouraged the decline of swing and the rise of bebop. Swing, the most popular jazz form of the 1930s and the war years, had evolved from its African-American roots to reach a mass audience through the big bands of Benny Goodman, Tommy Dorsey, and others. The more challenging and innovative bebop, featuring long, introspective solos, found favor with small jazz ensembles instead. Whereas swing offered jazz adaptations of familiar melodies, bebop involved complex improvisation. Highly cerebral and demanding close concentration by the listener, bebop arose outside a profit-driven music industry that, in the view of bebop artists, had compromised the authentic jazz tradition. Tense and edgy, bebop expressed the anxious underside of the fifties. Bebop musicians, turning their backs on the suburban middle-class, shared their highly personal vision with small audiences of rapt fans in smoky jazz clubs.

White bandleaders and musicians had dominated swing; bebop returned jazz to its African-American roots. Its high priests included trumpeter Dizzy Gillespie, drummer Max Roach, pianist Thelonious Monk, and saxophonists Charlie Parker and Lester Young. Although bebop musicians avoided direct political engagement, they saw their music as an expression of black consciousness and as an art form containing political implications. Bebop stood "in the vanguard of social change," Gillespie would later write, adding, "We didn't go out and make speeches or say 'Let's play eight bars of protest.' We just played our music and let it go at that. The music proclaimed our identity."

In the visual arts, abstract expressionism remained the most vital movement of the 1950s. Like bebop, this trend represented an intensely individual art form rather than overt social or political commentary. Jackson Pollock's career illustrates the shift. Pollack began in the late 1930s as a student of Thomas Hart Benton, who had portrayed workers, farmers, and cowboys in realistic canvases and murals. After World War II, however, Pollack began to drip and swirl paints directly onto large canvases stretched on the floor. Initially, the new style aroused much ridicule. Norman Rockwell, a magazine illustrator famous for his sentimental view of American life, produced a drip painting in imitation of Pollack (as if to say: "Anybody can do it") but as part of a larger realistic painting of a gallery scene. In Rockwell's tableau, a middle-aged, business-suited museum-goer scratches his head in bemused wonderment at the abstract style.

Like the beboppers, leading abstract expressionists such as Pollack, Robert Motherwell, and Mark Rothko viewed their radical stylistic innovations as a response to the postwar world. "Modern art to me is nothing more than the expression of . . . the age that we're living in," Pollack commented in 1950. "The modern painter cannot express this age, the airplane, the atom bomb, the radio, in the old forms of the Renaissance or of any other past culture. Each age finds its own technique." But what was the nature of that response? Abstract expressionism's relationship to the larger world of 1950s political culture remains complex. Unquestionably, these artists abandoned the realism and overt social engagement that had characterized U.S. art in the 1930s. Indeed, they rejected an entire tradition of literal representation in Western art. Whether this abrupt break with the past and turn to pure self-expression represented a reaction to the atomic bomb and the nuclear arms race as Pollack implied, it did suggest skepticism about the political relevance of art. To this extent, abstract expressionism mirrored the decade's larger movement away from political engagement. Yet that same turning inward to the realm of feeling and sensation also implicitly mocked those who were summoning the nation to mobilize for the Cold War struggle. To this extent, abstract expressionism could be seen as a mode of resistance against the forces of intellectual conformity.

But like rock-and-roll, the history of both bebop and abstract expressionism demonstrates the dominant culture's capacity to adapt even incipiently subversive cultural manifestations to its own purposes. Indeed, the line between "mainstream" and "dissident" in 1950s culture is hazy, for the processes of absorption and co-option never ceased. Musicians such as Gillespie and artists like Pollack may have felt alienated from the postwar consensus, but the government and powerful media voices promoted their art as weapons in the ideological Cold War. Gillespie, for example, gave concerts in Europe for the State Department in the late 1950s, implicitly countering allegations of racism in America. His performances underscored Western cultural freedom at a time when the Soviet Union forbade jazz and kept innovative classical composers like Dmitri Shostakovitch on a tight rein. Similarly, an abstract expressionist exhibit toured Europe in the 1950s with a State Department subsidy, offering pointed contrast to the heavy-handed "socialist realism" enforced behind the Iron Curtain. *Life* magazine heavily promoted Pollack and abstract expressionism as proof not only of New York's postwar artistic dominance but also of the Free World's cultural openness and respect for individual freedom.

To the degree that musicians and abstract expressionists acquiesced or collaborated in such interpretation of the meaning of their careers, they provided cultural support for the Cold War consensus. Yet the Cold War's cultural ramifications could cut both ways. While Washington patronized some artists and writers, those having radical pasts or leftist leanings suffered. Folksinger Pete Seeger, for example, an unabashed leftist and Cold War critic, found his career stymied in the conservative 1950s.

On the literary front, a group of younger writers struggled to come to terms with suburbs and material abundance. John Cheever's *The Wapshot Chronicle* (1957) dissected the lives of contemporary New Englanders cut off from their ancestral roots. Cheever's short stories in the *New Yorker*, peopled with white-collar characters who commute from bland jobs in New York City to bland Connecticut suburbs, commented even more pointedly on alienation in the midst of prosperity.

If Cheever offered a depressing picture of life in the upper middle class, John Updike presented a mordant view of existence on its lower fringes. Updike's *Rabbit Run* (1960) tells the story of Harry "Rabbit" Angstrom, a high-school basketball hero who as a young family man in the fifties senses that his best years are already behind him and that his life lacks meaning. "He feels underwater," Updike wrote, "caught in chains of transparent slime." Imagining himself back on the basketball court, he experiences the nightmarish sensation of "an abyss he will fall into when the ball leaves his hands." Bored by his job as a vacuum-cleaner salesman and lacking inner resources, Harry finds illicit sex his only anodyne to despair. Things get worse: His alcoholic wife, Janice, accidentally lets their baby drown in its bath. In typical 1950s fashion, Angstrom has no real understanding of his malaise, its larger social context, or steps that he might take to alleviate his troubles.

A few writers commented more directly on the political and cultural realities of the 1950s. Arthur Miller's *The Crucible* (1953), a play ostensibly about Salem witchcraft, was widely and correctly read as an exploration of the morally corrupting effects of McCarthyism. Ray Bradbury's science-fiction story *Fahrenheit 451* (1953) projected the Cold War, McCarthyism, and mass culture into the future. In Bradbury's nightmarish fantasy, the state has outlawed books entirely; any volumes discovered are systematically burned by the authorities. (Four hundred fifty-one degrees Fahrenheit is the temperature at which paper ignites.) The masses are narcotized by a state-run television network whose propaganda and mindless entertainment dominate giant wall screens that surround the living room. Only a handful of dissidents, who have memorized the classics and recite them to each other in remote hideaways, preserve humanity's cultural heritage. Bradbury's novel powerfully evoked the sense of a radical minority's struggle to preserve both their own independence of thought and a vanishing cultural tradition.

Expressing the cultural coming of age of immigrants who had arrived several decades earlier, young Jewish writers produced notable novels in the fifties, two of which won the prestigious National Book Award. Philip Roth's *Goodbye Columbus* (1959), a collection of stories about urban middle-class Jewish life, conveyed the same claustrophobia that pervades the stories of Cheever and Updike. Saul Bellow's *The Adventures of Augie March* (1953) told of a young Chicago Jew's quest for personal authenticity and meaning, the classic theme of the fifties. (Augie's search eventually brings him to Mexico on a bizarre but perhaps symbolic project: He trains American eagles to capture iguanas.) Bellow's *Henderson the Rain King* (1959) takes its hero even farther afield, as he abandons wife, family, and stifling daily routine to immerse himself in African tribal culture.

Some novelists criticized 1950s culture obliquely and ironically; the Beats challenged it frontally.* The Beat movement began soon after World War II when Allen Ginsberg, a Columbia University undergraduate, befriended Jack Kerouac, a Columbia dropout of Massachusetts working-class origins. Both men were influenced by William Burroughs, whose account of his heroin addiction appeared in the pseudonymous 1953 novel *Junkie* and continued in *The Naked Lunch* (1959). The Beat movement coalesced in 1955 at a San Francisco poetry gathering where Ginsberg read *Howl*, a hallucinatory, drug-influenced work of considerable artistic power excoriating America as a ravenous beast sacrificing its young on the altars of commerce and technology. Ginsberg's poem reached a larger audience with its publication in 1956 by Lawrence Ferlinghetti, owner of San Francisco's City Lights Bookstore.

Kerouac's *On the Road* (1957), a sprawling, quasiautobiographical novel, arrived at the publisher's office in a single 250-foot roll of paper. It recounts the adventures of two central characters, one based on Kerouac himself and the other on Neil Cassady, a figure on the fringes of the Beat movement, as they crisscross the country by car and bus. *On the Road*, together with *Howl*, published two years earlier, launched the Beats' brief celebrity and notoriety.

The Beat movement streaked like a garish Fourth of July rocket across the grey skies of Eisenhower's America. Thousands of Americans, especially college students, young people, and the minority dissatisfied with the blandness of mass-media pap, welcomed the outrageous assertiveness of this new literary movement. *On the Road* sold half a million copies, and *Howl* became a campus favorite, its cachet heightened by the efforts of San Francisco authorities to suppress it. Like the satirical songs of Tom Lehrer and the mordant humor of coffeehouse comics Lenny Bruce and Mort Sahl, the Beats appealed to those seeking alternatives to banality. In common with Elvis and other luminaries of rock-and-roll, Ginsberg, Kerouac, and lesser Beats became cultural heroes and models for the disaffected, their literary iconoclasm underscored by their readiness to flout middle-class taboos. Asked at a poetry reading what his work meant, Ginsberg responded, "Nakedness," and proceeded to remove all his clothes.

Repudiating the America of Levittown and *Life*, the Beats embraced an antithetical cultural style. For middle-class restraint and propriety, they substituted a cult of spontaneity, immediate sensation, and "transcendent" perceptions induced by alcohol, marijuana, benzedrine, and other mind-altering substances. In a decade that idolized family life and domesticity, they cultivated frenetic movement, fleeting relationships, and casual sex. *On the Road*, which begins with the breakup of the narrator's marriage, is a classic tale of footloose males seeking freedom and friendship outside the constricting bonds of familial obligation. In the male-centered and often homoerotic world of the Beats, women provided diversion but otherwise played little role.

---

* The origin of the term *Beat* is unclear. Jack Kerouac, asserting the movement's fundamentally religious impetus, claimed that it was short for "beatitude."

The Beats idealized outsiders and the marginalized—criminals, addicts, deviants, jazz aficionados, inner-city blacks, the truckers whose sixteen-wheelers rumble through the night—as more vibrant and stimulating than the washed-out middle class. In the famous opening of *Howl*, Ginsberg wrote:

> *I saw the best minds of my generation destroyed by madness,*
> *starving hysterical naked,*
> *dragging themselves through the negro streets at dawn*
> *looking for an angry fix*

Novelist Norman Mailer, although not part of the movement, shared the Beats' fascination with the underclass. In his essay "The White Negro" (1957), Mailer romanticized the intense and dangerous world of "hipsters"—criminals, juvenile delinquents, and streetwise blacks—as an alternative to that of white middle-class America.

Anticipating a vogue for Eastern religions that would gain prominence in the 1960s and 1970s, the Beats sprinkled their writings with knowing references to *Satori*, *Dharma*, *Karma*, Hinduism, and Zen Buddhism. But for all their cultural exoticism, the Beats were solidly in the American tradition. Their quest for inner awareness recalled Ralph Waldo Emerson and the transcendentalists. Ginsberg's summons to "return to nature and . . . revolt against the machine" echoed early-nineteenth-century Romantic poets and painters. Kerouac's *On the Road* evoked Mark Twain's *Huckleberry Finn* in its preference for freedom over civilization and Walt Whitman in its exuberant patriotism. Looking eastward from San Francisco Bay, the narrator exults in "the great raw bulge and bulk of my American continent."

Furthermore, the Beats' view of blacks and other outsiders as a source of vitality echoed late-nineteenth and early-twentieth-century writers who saw the immigrant masses as energizing. Their sentimentalizing of outside groups, however, was tainted not only by misogyny but also on occasion by ethnic prejudice. Describing the efforts of his fictional alter ego to persuade a young Hispanic woman to have sex with him in a Los Angeles hotel room, Kerouac writes, "How I moaned and pleaded, and then I got mad and realized I was pleading with a dumb little Mexican wench, and I told her so."

In a pattern typical of the fifties, the mass media soon took up and exploited the Beats. *Life* ran a feature on the movement in 1957, and Kerouac, looking remarkably like James Dean, read from his work on a network television talk show. The stereotyped "Beatnik" or "Hipster"—bearded, lascivious, and unkempt—became a menacing symbol for the middle class, at once fascinating and scary. A paperback 1950s potboiler, *Pads Are for Passion,* bore the alarming caption, "Anita Was a Virgin— Till the Hipsters Got Hold of Her."

The Beat movement, like rock-and-roll, paved the way for the more politicized counterculture of the 1960s. Indeed, Ginsberg would become a campus guru in the Vietnam War era. Kerouac, however, followed a different course. The gushy patriotism of *On the Road* soon turned rancid, and he, like Presley, would end up denouncing the young radicals of the 1960s. But however they viewed their progeny, the Beats' role as fomenters of cultural change ensures their place in the history of the Eisenhower era.

On the whole, the literature of the 1950s, like the art, was more introspective and individualistic than political or socially engaged. Yet this work had political implications, for in focusing on the individual search for authenticity, authors challenged the conformism and standardization of thought that they saw as dangerous consequences of the Cold War, mass culture, and the all-pervasive capitalist system.

Amid this cultural ferment, social and cultural critics offered their own dissections of postwar America. William H. Whyte's *The Organization Man*, for example, whose comments on suburban religion and on the role of wives in corporate America we have already noted, offered a wide-ranging exploration, rich in anecdotal detail, of middle-management business culture. Whyte was no radical; in fact, as an editor of the business magazine *Fortune*, he saw much to praise in postwar U.S. capitalism. But he found the system's psychological effects generally deplorable. The modern corporation, he argued, bred cautious conformity while discouraging originality, risk taking, and any behavior that might be labeled eccentric or offbeat.

Dwight Macdonald examined middle-class life in a series of essays reprinted in his 1962 book, *Against the American Grain*. Macdonald acerbically criticized both mass culture and what he called midcult, or the watering down of high culture to expand its commercial appeal. Skewering a whole herd of sacred cows, Macdonald lambasted the Book-of-the-Month Club, the *Encyclopedia Britannica*'s "Great Books" program, and the Revised Standard Version of the Bible (1952), which, he charged, reduced the King James Bible's majestic seventeenth-century English to the level of prose produced by a committee.

Historian Daniel Boorstin in *The Image* (1961) criticized the mass-produced culture made possible by modern technology. Americans, he argued, were settling for derivative, second-hand experience. They listened to Muzak instead of going to concerts, bought Van Gogh prints instead of visiting museums, took vacations prepackaged by travel agents, skimmed *Reader's Digest* condensed books instead of reading the original works, and accepted television's ersatz version of reality. Anticipating later criticism of TV's effects on politics, Boorstin attacked the "news conference" that generated no news and the "pseudo-event" staged for the media by public-relations flacks. Like Bradbury, Boorstin feared a world drained of individuality and devoid of vigorous political discourse. Such a world, he fretted, would be populated by brain-dead men and women wholly dependent on the version of reality spoon-fed to them by the state or by the mass media.

Vance Packard, meanwhile, exposed the machinations of advertisers and vote-hungry election-campaign managers in his 1957 best-seller *The Hidden Persuaders*, while John Keats lambasted suburbia in *The Crack in the Picture Window* (1956). The jacket blurb of Keats's book reads like a caricature of 1950s cultural criticism:

> Even while you read this, whole square miles of identical boxes are spreading like gangrene. . . . In any one of these new neighborhoods you can be sure all other houses will be precisely like yours, inhabited by people whose age, income, number of children, problems, habits, conversation, dress, possessions, and perhaps even blood types are precisely like yours.

To understand the complexities of 1950s social thought, one must place it in historical context. Many of these critics had come of age in the intensely political

FOCUS ON: *THE MASS-CULTURE DEBATE*

The culture critics of the 1950s drew on a long tradition in American thought. A century earlier, writer Nathaniel Hawthorne had attacked the fickle, novel-devouring public for slighting him in favor of a "damn'd mob of scribbling women." In the twentieth century, movies, radio, and television gave the critics a succession of new targets.

Postwar mass-culture critics fell into three broad camps. Conservatives such as Dwight Macdonald dismissed popular culture as *kitsch*—German for "rubbish." Its worthlessness, and the avidity with which the vulgar hordes consumed it, they declared, proved the low state of American culture and the need to defend elite standards. This dismissive view often, although not always, reflected a deeper bias against democracy itself.

Marxists treated mass culture as another form of capitalist exploitation, a view most fully articulated at the University of Frankfurt's Institute for Social Research, founded in 1923. With Hitler's rise in the 1930s, the leaders of the Frankfurt school fled to America, where, traumatized by European fascism, they cast a critical eye on U.S. mass culture. In *The Eclipse of Reason* (1947), the emigré Frankfurt scholar Max Horkheimer probed the mass media's totalitarian potential. In "Television and Patterns of Mass Culture" (1954), refugee scholar Theodor Adorno portrayed television as a weapon of class manipulation, numbing the masses to their own alienation. Horkheimer and Adorno charged in a coauthored essay that radio and the movies left "no room for imagination or reflection on the part of the audience. . . . [T]hey react automatically [and] fall helpless victims to what is offered them."* The Italian Marxist Antonio Gramsci, who died in a fascist prison in 1937, elaborated his theory of cultural hegemony in a series of influential essays in the 1920s and 1930s. Elites employ mass culture, Gramsci argued, to achieve hegemonic control, thereby persuading the rest of society willingly to embrace the existing social order, with all its inequities, as wholly desirable and "natural."

Others viewed mass culture more positively. They found an unlikely guru in Canadian medievalist Marshall McLuhan. In *Understanding Media* (1964) and other works, McLuhan hailed the new electronic media, especially television, as a quantum leap in human communications as profound as that introduced by Gutenberg. McLuhan's aphorism, "The medium is the message," summed up his belief that the

---

* The ideas of another emigré Frankfurt School social theorist, Herbert Marcuse, are discussed briefly in Chapter 9.

1930s. FDR's New Deal had won the passionate allegiance of numerous intellectuals; others had embraced Marxism in response to the Great Depression and looked to the Soviet Union as a model. By the 1950s, however, the New Deal was history, Depression-era misery had given way to prosperity, and Stalin's brutalities had shattered communism's appeal, turning the youthful radicalism of many intellectuals into a matter of embarrassment rather than pride. Sociologist Daniel Bell, having bidden

technology of television itself, apart from program content, would transform the world by transforming human perception of reality. In place of the static, linear medium of print, television's ceaseless flow of images would bring the world into the living room with compelling immediacy.

As the mass-culture debate wore on into the 1980s and 1990s, all three viewpoints found adherents. In *The Closing of the American Mind* (1987), the elitist Alan Bloom railed against rock music as "junk food for the soul" that softens the brain and ruins the young for serious intellectual pursuits. Giving up on the masses, Bloom placed his hope in an elite who would carry on the great traditions of Western civilization. The religious Right, meanwhile, like earlier generations of moral reformers, attacked the media for promulgating sex and violence. The American Family Asssociation of Tupelo, Mississippi, for example, founded by the Reverend Donald Wildmon, organized boycotts of the sponsors of television programs that it considered indecent or immoral. The radical critique of mass culture continued to find champions as well. Historian T. J. Jackson Lears, in "The Concept of Cultural Hegemony" (*American Historical Review*, June 1985), restated the Gramscian view of mass culture as a means by which capitalist elites market goods, mute class tensions, set the cultural agenda, and in general legitimate the status quo.

Other mass-culture observers persisted in the more upbeat view. In *The Global Village* (1989), Marshall McLuhan envisioned a world united electronically—an image that would resurface in President Bill Clinton's dream of America linked by an "electronic highway." A more positive outlook emerged, too, in historian Lawrence Levine's studies of popular culture. Rejecting the view that moviegoers, radio listeners, and TV viewers constitute an inert mass that can be manipulated at will, Levine in *The Unpredictable Past: Explorations in American Cultural History* (1993) emphasized the active role of mass-culture consumers. They not only choose which movies and television shows to watch, but they imaginatively adapt and reinterpret these products to their own purposes. Indeed, in a 1992 *American Historical Review* essay, Levine portrayed mass culture as an arena of dynamic interaction between producers and consumers that creates a kind of TV-age folk culture. He cited research documenting how listeners and viewers continually criticize and comment on radio and TV programs rather than passively absorbing them. In a sharp rebuttal, Jackson Lears rejected this view as romantic sentimentality. As early as the 1930s, Lears insisted, America's "culture industry . . . had reached an advanced stage of oligopolistic concentration."

This was hardly the last word. The mass-culture debate that flared so vigorously in the 1950s shows no signs of abating four decades later. And as the controversy rolls on, so does the output of the mass-culture industry, playing an ever larger role in American life.

---

farewell to his own prewar radicalism, applied the definitive label to the 1950s in the title of his 1960 book about postwar America: *The End of Ideology*.

Postwar capitalism's feats of productivity, the declining influence of organized labor, the lure of suburbia, the stifling effects of McCarthyism—all these factors served to mute the vigorous political debates that had characterized prewar America. So, too, did the Cold War consensus that had evolved as the domestic corollary of the U.S.-Soviet confrontation. Promulgated by politicians, public intellectuals, and the mass media, the central motif of this consensus was an endorsement of America's political, economic, and social systems as bulwarks against the red menace. American democracy might be characterized by media manipulation and the jostling of powerful interest groups, but it was clearly superior to totalitarianism. The capitalist system might be dominated by vast corporations and faceless managers, but it was obviously preferable to the lumbering state-run economies behind the Iron Curtain. The ethic of consumption, abundance, and endless growth could be faulted for encouraging materialistic excess, but it moderated the class conflict that Marxists saw as inevitable. This pattern of simplistic, defensive thinking narrowed the range of public debate and discouraged incisive critical social or political analysis. Historian Christopher Lasch, who grew up in the 1950s, later complained that his generation "lacked a political education."

In this climate, many intellectuals concluded that the safe course lay in remaining at the margins, criticizing cultural and psychological aspects of American society but not challenging its basic structure or ideological premises. Radical politics seemed at best naive; at worst, subversive. One observer wrote in 1957, "Almost all the problems that were once called 'political' now belong to a different context, psychological, sociological, and cultural."

Perceptive as they sometimes were, critics such as Whyte, Macdonald, and Boorstin focused on a narrow sector of 1950s America, the middle class, and largely ignored minorities and the poor. Anyone reading the social criticism of the decade might well conclude that all Americans were corporate executives or comfortable suburbanites. Sharing the prevailing view that U.S. capitalism had ensured unlimited abundance for all and that the remaining pockets of poverty would quickly vanish, these intellectuals concentrated on the cultural and emotional lives of the newly affluent.

Because they wrote in an era of political lassitude and flagging reform energies, critics paid scant attention to the economic system that underlay the mass culture that they deplored. William Whyte offered no structural analysis of modern U.S. capitalism even as he criticized its social effects. Macdonald and Boorstin wrote hundreds of pages deploring mass culture and midcult while ignoring questions of social class, social power, or the nature of postwar consumer capitalism. Nor did these critics suggest how the problems they identified might be solved. Like 1950s novelists, they aimed not to mobilize collective action but to heighten individual awareness. Through books such as *The Lonely Crowd*, *The Organization Man*, *The Image*, and *The Hidden Persuaders*, readers could become more conscious of and perhaps somewhat resistant to the cultural pressures that victimized the less knowing. These thinkers emphasized consciousness and sensibility, not society or politics. The jacket blurb for *The Crack in the Picture Window* ended by breathlessly exclaiming, "The shaken reader puts down the book, stares for a moment, and then screams, 'Somebody do something! Quick!'" Such a response, however, would have been alien to the mood of the 1950s, when criticism rarely led to action. One might gain insight and heightened awareness from these works, but they were not summonses to the streets, or even to the ballot box.

American historians of the 1950s, similarly influenced by the apparent placidity of the decade's early years, downplayed social and economic conflict as factors in U.S. history and instead stressed consensus and continuity as the central themes of the nation's past. Repudiating historians such as Charles A. Beard who earlier in the century had focused on the reform crusades, class conflicts, and economic struggles that had shaped America, historians now emphasized the ideas and values on which all Americans agreed. In *The Genius of American Politics* (1953), Daniel Boorstin, another 1930s radical turned conservative, praised Americans' freedom from ideological debate and the pragmatic way in which they had fashioned their social and political institutions. Historian Arthur Schlesinger, Jr., published admiring studies of presidents Andrew Jackson and Franklin D. Roosevelt as pragmatic leaders who advanced the liberal cause while remaining firmly antiradical.

Other scholars, while agreeing that U.S. history featured a lack of ideological conflict, felt less convinced than Boorstin that this trait was good. Historian Richard Hofstadter in *The Age of Reform* (1955) viewed with a skeptical eye the anti-intellectualism and self-serving individualism that he found at the core of the American political tradition. Political scientist Louis Hartz argued in *The Liberal Tradition in America* (1955) that Americans' lack of exposure to class conflict and their ideological naiveté made it hard for them to understand the power that Marxism exerted in large parts of the world.

An important exception to the prevailing emphasis on consensus and to the lack of a strong political component in 1950s intellectual life was Columbia sociologist C. Wright Mills. A product of Depression-era Texas and the University of Wisconsin, where a tradition of radical social thought remained alive, Mills produced two books in the 1950s that challenged the dominant tenor of social thought. In *White Collar* (1951), as we have seen, he offered a dismaying picture of middle-class futility and discontent. But he surpassed other critics who were making similar points by linking his insights to a structural analysis of the political and economic order. The impotence felt by low- and midlevel functionaries in the new technocratic order was well founded, he insisted; these people had little voice in the political or corporate decisions that shaped their lives. In a memorable phrase evocative of the 1930s, Mills called them "sharecroppers in the dustbowl of business."

Mills extended his argument in *The Power Elite* (1956). Rejecting the orthodox Marxist view of power as something exercised solely by those controlling the instruments of production, Mills argued that the reins of power in contemporary America lay in the hands of a shifting but basically stable group, concentrated at the upper levels of the corporate, political, and military elites. The heads of top corporations, the Joint Chiefs of Staff, and the National Security Council were "the Ones Who Decide." Mills went on to explore the social and cultural apparatus—family, schools, clubs—by which this elite perpetuated itself and recruited new members.

Liberal democratic theorists who celebrated the power of the ballot box, argued Mills, ignored the many techniques by which voters could be bamboozled and the electoral process perverted. Similarly, Mills rejected the theory advanced by economist John Kenneth Galbraith in *American Capitalism* (1951) that various competing and countervailing interest groups divided power among them. This argument, he protested, obscured the enormous concentration of power at the top and ignored the way in which weaker groups and interests limited their demands in response to these fundamental power realities.

Mills's radicalism drew much criticism, even though his analysis anticipated President Eisenhower's 1961 farewell address, with its warning about the military-industrial complex. His polemical style, his casual methodology, the imprecision of his "power elite" model, and even his unconventional ways (he built his own house and rode a motorcycle to work) heightened his vulnerability to criticism. But in a decade when intellectuals studiously avoided radical analysis of the basic structure of American society and systematically separated the personal from the political, Mills's impassioned, highly readable books expressed what most Americans knew in their bones: that some groups and individuals wielded enormous power and influence, while most did not. To understand the culture and psyche of the middle class, Mills insisted, one must look at the economic and political framework within which that class functioned.

Perhaps for these reasons, Mills is one of the few cultural critics of the Eisenhower era whose work has outlived the historical moment that produced it. In the 1960s, young radicals who were seeking intellectual tools for understanding and changing American society rediscovered Mills and claimed him as their own. Mills's period of greatest influence came posthumously, however; he died of a heart attack in 1962 at the age of forty-five.

Mills's was a lonely voice in the 1950s, when dissidence was widespread but ill focused and lacked a sharp critical edge. The dominant trend of thought favored culture over politics and stressed continuity over conflict in American history and society. Yet this line of thinking carried an implicit political message: It tended to dismiss New Deal–style reformist surges as historical anomalies and to uphold cautious middle-of-the road conservativism as the political norm. When reformist energies and even radical attacks on American society revived in the 1960s under the New Left rubric, the movement's leaders lost little time repudiating what they saw as the tepid, ennervating liberalism of 1950s intellectuals. Those intellectuals, 1960s critics justifiably would charge, had offered the bark of cultural criticism without the bite of tough action.

Despite the political lassitude and diminished social activism of the Eisenhower years, two issues of profound importance stirred organized protest: the nuclear threat and racial discrimination. Each would continue to arouse passionate attention long after the fifties had become a memory.

Fallout Fears and Test-Ban Activism

With the onset of the Cold War and the nuclear-arms race, the fear of atomic war that had gripped America after Hiroshima subsided. President Truman's 1950 decision to build the hydrogen bomb won overwhelming public approval. By the early 1950s, under a steady barrage of Cold War propaganda, the dreaded destroyer of 1945 had become the cornerstone of the nation's security.

But public acquiescence in the stockpiling of nuclear weapons represented a fragile consensus that proved highly vulnerable to the unsettling news that began to seep into the popular consciousness in the mid-1950s as scientists reported measurable increases in radioactive fallout from hydrogen-bomb tests conducted in the South Pacific. The U.S. test series of 1954 set off the first alarm, spreading radioactive ash over a vast area and causing illness and death to a Japanese fishing crew that had sailed unwittingly into the test zone. In 1955 radioactive rain fell on Chicago, and meteorologists began to plot the diffusion of high-level radioactive clouds over North America. Geneticists, medical researchers, and radiation specialists warned of the health hazards of fallout: leukemia, bone cancer, and long-term genetic damage, among others. Strontium-90, a deadly by-product of thermonuclear tests, especially horrified Americans. An element featuring calciumlike properties, strontium-90 accumulated in human bone marrow and teeth, particularly in infants and children. Despite efforts by the Eisenhower administration to downplay the danger, a full-blown fallout scare gripped the nation. Even so staid an organ of mainstream culture as the *Saturday Evening Post* ran a two-part feature called "Fallout: The Silent Killer."

Fallout fear permeated the popular culture. The monster and mutant movies that poured out of Hollywood in these years usually blamed the scary creatures on nuclear tests that dislodged and reanimated prehistoric monsters or that gave rise to genetically altered creatures. A 1954 rock-and-roll song by Bill Haley and the Comets, "Thirteen Women (and Only One Man in Town)," offered a male fantasy of endless sex and female subservience in the aftermath of an H-bomb attack. Tom Lehrer won a following on college campuses by extracting black humor from the prospect of nuclear annihilation with such songs as "We'll All Go Together When We Go." In another Lehrer song, a nuclear-age cowboy roams the test sites of the Southwest safe in his lead underwear. *Mad* magazine, a favorite with teenage cognoscenti, some of whom would become sixties rebels, fantasized a postnuclear war Hit Parade of songs that young lovers would sing as they "walk down moonlit lanes arm in arm in arm."

Novels like Nevil Shute's *On the Beach* (1957) and Walter Miller's *A Canticle for Leibowitz* (1959) imagined apocalyptic scenarios of human extinction. Science-fiction writers, too, had a field day with images of nuclear war. In Mordecai Roshwald's *Level 7* (1959), the inhabitants of a vast underground shelter die, level by level, as radiation seeps deeper into the earth. As the last survivors await their end, they create a new religion in which strontium-90 substitutes for Satan as the ultimate embodiment of evil. Even television, rarely a bearer of bad news in the fifties, occasionally reflected the spreading miasma of fear. The science-fiction series "Outer Limits" and Rod Serling's "Twilight Zone" frequently explored nuclear war, radioactivity, and the psychological effect of atomic terror.

In one "Twilight Zone" episode, warning sirens go off, and the residents of a typical suburban neighborhood rush to the home of the one man who has built a shelter. He barricades himself and his family inside, refusing their pleas. As panic mounts, the neighbors turn on each other, and this once-tranquil community disintegrates into a screaming mob. Eventually the all-clear signal sounds—it has only been a test—but the shaken neighbors realize that their facade of togetherness has shattered as surely as if the bomb actually had fallen.

In an "Outer Limits" program, bees that have been genetically altered by radio-active fallout decide to take over the world. They transmute their queen into a sexually alluring young female humanoid who takes employment in the home of a cozy suburban couple and sets out to seduce the weak-willed husband. But the wife grows suspicious when she sees the newcomer in the yard one night pollinating flowers. As a swarm of bees stings the wife to death, the bee-woman offers herself seductively to the distraught husband. In his revulsion he kills her, foiling, for the moment, insect-world challenges to middle-class propriety. Laden with multiple cultural messages, this episode reflected not only fallout fears but also uneasiness about threats to sub-urban domesticity posed by the youth culture's brazen sexuality.

The resurgence of nuclear fear brought a spate of conferences and symposia at which theologians, psychiatrists, psychologists, and other experts pondered the larger implications of living with the bomb and nuclear war. A sense of personal helplessness in the face of the global nuclear threat, some writers speculated, contributed significantly to the political passivity of the decade.

The federal government, ironically, intensified nuclear anxiety with a civil-defense program of school drills, propaganda films, and a fallout-shelter campaign. Few home owners actually built shelters, but the subject received much publicity, and manufacturers of shelters prospered. In a civil-defense test in Washington in 1956, ten thousand federal workers scattered to secret relocation centers, and President Eisenhower was helicoptered to an underground command post in Maryland. In 1959, *Life* persuaded a newlywed couple to honeymoon in a cramped underground shelter, publishing photographs of them kissing as they descended for their two weeks of subterranean marital bliss. "Fallout can be fun," quipped *Life*. School-children of the 1950s would carry into adulthood indelible memories of crouching under desks as the test sirens wailed, or of watching government films such as *Duck and Cover*, in which Burt the Turtle explained what to do when the nuclear flash came.

The fallout scare eventually spawned a national movement to stop nuclear tests. When Adlai Stevenson called for a test ban in the 1956 presidential campaign, the Republicans accused him of aiding the enemy, but the issue would not fade. Soon it was taken up by action groups with names like the Council for a Livable World, Physicians for Social Responsibility, and SANE, the National Committee for a Sane Nuclear Policy. One memorable SANE ad featured the famous baby doctor Benjamin Spock gazing with furrowed brow at a little girl under the caption, DR. SPOCK IS WORRIED. In New York, antinuclear activists went to jail for refusing to take shelter during a civil-defense drill.

In the early 1960s, the test-ban movement became a major focus of protest activity on college and university campuses. An antinuclear group called Women's Strike for Peace drew thousands of supporters and organized marches in several big cities. Often led by religious pacifists, long-time political activists, or well-known public figures, these movements nevertheless attracted thousands of ordinary citizens terrified by the nuclear threat.

Responding to scientific warnings and world opinion, the superpowers halted nuclear testing in 1958. This voluntary moratorium broke down in 1961, however, as first the Soviet Union and then the United States resumed atmospheric assays.

Nuclear war, anyone? In this posed *Life* magazine photo of 1961, family members embody gender stereotypes as they await the end: Dad ready to dig through the rubble, Mom with kitchen gear, son in charge of flashlight and radio, and daughters with blankets and board games. (*Dmitri Kessel*/Life Magazine, © *Time Warner*)

But in 1963, after the Cuban missile crisis (see Chapter 6), the United States, the Soviet Union, and Great Britain signed a treaty banning such tests. The 1950s test-ban movement thus at least partially achieved its objective; it also provided one avenue of political engagement for many thousands of Americans during a mostly passive decade.

Brown and Beyond: The Civil-Rights Movement in Eisenhower's America

The movement to ban nuclear testing provided refreshing evidence of political activism in an otherwise lethargic decade, but it was the drive for racial justice that gathered momentum as the decade wore on. Focused initially on segregation in the South, this movement gradually broadened in scope, building the foundation for a revolution in race relations whose full implications would continue to unfold a generation later. The civil-rights campaign radically undermined the stereotyped image of 1950s America as one big, happy suburb. In this chapter we look at the early stages of the modern drive for racial justice in America; in Chapter 8, we explore the explosive changes that overtook this effort in the late 1950s and beyond, propelling it in new and far more radical directions.

Institutionalized racism pervaded American life as the fifties began. Although some of its cruder and more brutal manifestations had faded since the early years of the century, prejudice and discrimination infected every national institution from schools and churches to the media and the workplace. Throughout the South, and, informally, in parts of the North as well, blacks attended racially segregated schools, a practice ruled constitutional in 1896 by the U.S. Supreme Court in the famous case of *Plessy* v. *Ferguson*. This decision upheld the constitutionality of a Louisiana law requiring racially segregated railroad accommodations.

The high court in *Plessy* had specified that the facilities provided for blacks must be equal to those available to whites, a stipulation that formed the legal underpinnings of the so-called separate but equal public-school system found across the South. In reality, schooling was separate and unequal; funding for black education fell far below that for whites, and the facilities provided for black students proved appallingly inferior. But segregated schools formed only one piece in a vast mosaic of institutionalized racism. Wherever one looked in early postwar America, blacks were treated as second-class citizens.

A convergence of social and ideological trends began to challenge this pervasive reality. World War II had dramatically changed the lives of many blacks. Thousands served in the military, and thousands more flocked to the North and West where they took jobs in war plants, joined labor unions, and swelled the voting ranks. The narrator of *Invisible Man* (1952), Ralph Ellison's brilliant novel exploring the modern African-American experience, comes North during the war to find work. (Ellison, writing on the symbolic as well as the realistic plane, gives his narrator a job at the Liberty Paint Company, a factory that specializes in an eye-dazzling paint called Optic White. The few drops of black added to each batch totally disappear.) In the postwar period, leaders of both political parties recognized the growing importance of the black vote, a fact that inspired President Truman's flurry of civil-rights activism before the 1948 election.

At the same time, industrialization and urbanization were straining the racial caste system of the old Cotton South. As blacks poured into the cities and factories of the New South and as the urban black middle class grew, segregation proved increasingly difficult to enforce. In the civil-rights activism that would soon sweep the South, white corporate and financial leaders, worried that protests would threaten the region's economic health, often worked behind the scenes to moderate the more extreme forms of racial segregation. The affluence of the 1950s, although unevenly distributed, played a role as well, increasing the urban black work force, adding to the ranks of middle-class black churches and colleges, and fattening contributions to civil-rights organizations. The mass media, meanwhile—including, increasingly, television—spotlighted civil-rights activism and violent white resistance in southern communities that might otherwise have gone largely unnoticed.

At the ideological level, long-held racial attitudes no longer commanded unthinking assent in these years. Hitler's rabid antisemitism and the Holocaust to which it led discredited a once quasirespectable body of racial thought that had long

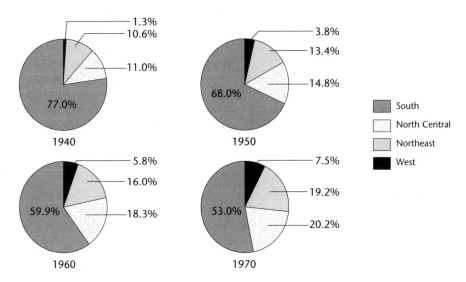

FIGURE 5.2

Regional Distribution of the Black Population, 1940–1970

NOTE: The Northeast consists of New England and the Middle Atlantic states of New York, Pennsylvania, and New Jersey. The North Central region consists of the Great Lakes states along with Missouri, Kansas, Iowa, Nebraska, and the Dakotas. The South is made up of all states south of the Mason-Dixon line (including the border states of Delaware, West Virginia, and Kentucky) and extends as far west as Texas and Oklahoma. The remaining states are in the West.

SOURCE: *The Negro Almanac: A Reference Work on the African American* (5th Edition, Detroit, Gale Research Inc., 1989).

undergirded the southern caste system and American racism in general. Indeed, Gunnar Myrdal in *An American Dilemma* viewed this changed intellectual climate as the most important factor propelling the United States toward racial reform. Indeed, Myrdal's 1944 study helped to accelerate the shift in attitudes.

Cold War realities further undermined engrained patterns of racism. As Washington denounced the Soviets for their betrayal of human rights and courted allies among newly independent nations in Asia and Africa, the reality of racism at home became highly embarrassing. President Truman emphasized such considerations in his civil-rights messages. The worldwide revolutionary upsurge against colonialism stirred U.S. blacks as well. Thus economic, demographic, ideological, and strategic trends converged in the early postwar years to erode the cultural foundations of racial segregation.

The immediate impetus for change came from the National Association for the Advancement of Colored People (NAACP), which for years had mounted court challenges to racism, including segregated schools. As early as 1938, the Supreme Court had ordered the University of Missouri Law School to admit a black applicant on the grounds that because Missouri had no law school for blacks, the separate-but-equal standard obviously could not be met. A trio of Supreme Court decisions in 1950, in cases brought by the NAACP (see p. 78), had made further inroads into *Plessy* v. *Ferguson*. Particularly important of these three cases were *McLaurin* v. *Okla-*

homa State Regents and *Sweatt* v. *Painter*, in which the high court outlawed segregated educational institutions at the advanced and professional levels that were not fully equal to the comparable facilities available to whites.

The years of painstaking legal activity paid off with dramatic suddenness on May 17, 1954, when a unanimous Supreme Court under Chief Justice Earl Warren, in the case of *Brown* v. *Board of Education of Topeka*, ruled that racially segregated public schools violated the constitutional principle of equal treatment for all citizens. The NAACP brief, presented by Thurgood Marshall, who later would become the first black Supreme Court justice, relied heavily on psychological and sociological studies showing the effects of segregation on children. Particularly influential was the work of the black psychologist Kenneth Clark. Clark found, for example, that black children as young as three years old, when presented with otherwise identical brown-skinned and white-skinned dolls, usually chose the white doll. Clark attributed this behavior to pervasive patterns of cultural conditioning: "The fact that young Negro children would prefer to be white," he wrote, "reflects their knowledge that society prefers white people."

Citing the work of Clark, Myrdal, and others, the Supreme Court justices posed and answered a crucial question:

> Does segregation of children in public schools solely on the basis of race, even though the physical facilities and other "tangible" factors may be equal, deprive the children of the minority group of equal educational opportunities? We believe that it does. . . . To separate them from others of similar age and qualifications solely because of their race generates a feeling of inferiority as to their status in the community that may affect their hearts and minds in a way unlikely ever to be undone. . . . We conclude that in the field of public education the doctrine of "separate but equal" has no place. Separate educational facilities are inherently unequal.

With the stroke of a pen, the Court repudiated sixty years of legally sanctioned racial segregation.

At first, it seemed that opponents might thwart the Supreme Court's intent. Representative John Bell Williams of Mississippi, in a congressional diatribe against the *Brown* decision, described May 17, 1954, in a none-too-subtle pun as "Black Monday." A Jackson, Mississippi, newspaper editorialized:

> Members of the Nation's highest tribunal may be learned in the law, but they were utterly lacking in common sense when they rendered Monday's decision, common sense of the kind that should have told them about the tragedy that will inevitably follow. . . . Human blood may stain Southern soil in many places because of this decision, but the dark red stains of that blood will be on the marble steps of the United States Supreme Court building.

Although the Court declared in a follow-up ruling of 1955 that school segregation should end "with all deliberate speed" and instructed the federal courts to ensure that local school districts made "a prompt and reasonable start toward full compliance," southern white segregationists organized a campaign of massive resistance. White "Citizens' Councils"—more "respectable" versions of the Ku Klux Klan—sprang up across the region to fight integration. Early in 1956, echoing the states-rights battles of the pre–Civil War era, the Virginia legislature proclaimed the right of a state to "interpose its sovereignty" to stop enforcement of the *Brown* ruling. In March 1956, one hundred southern senators and congressmen announced their intent to use "all lawful means" to overthrow the *Brown* decision. When the Clinton, Tennessee, school board integrated the high school, segregationist mobs shouted "Kill the niggers!" at the black students. Soon after, a dynamite blast demolished the school.

President Eisenhower played a muted role in the deepening controversy. Criticizing the Supreme Court's ruling in private, he would later describe his choice of Earl Warren as chief justice as "the biggest damnfool mistake I ever made." Citing Prohibition as an example, Eisenhower insisted to friends that deep-seated social mores could not be changed by legal fiat or by force. The *Brown* decision, he grumbled, had "*set back* progress in the South *at least fifteen years.*" Political calculations reinforced Ike's personal distaste for the *Brown* decision. He had won four southern states in 1952 and five in 1956, and the Republican party's long-term southern strategy, which presidents Nixon, Reagan, and Bush would continue to pursue decades later, assumed growing white support in the once solidly Democratic stronghold.

Eisenhower's grudging response to the profound moral issue of racial equality constitutes his greatest failure as president. Instead of using his enormous prestige to help white America to confront the reality of racial injustice, he held back, tacitly encouraging those fighting to preserve white supremacy. The cabinet rarely discussed civil-rights issues, and White House meetings with black leaders were rare and tense. When the one black in the Eisenhower White House, a special assistant in foreign affairs named E. Frederick Morrow, alerted Eisenhower to rising racial tensions, Ike replied, "Oh Fred, you're an alarmist." When pressed, Eisenhower claimed that his was the path of moderation, as though racism and a determination to fight racism were equally deplorable extremist positions.

Eisenhower conceded, however, that the law must be obeyed, whatever one's personal feelings. In a press conference after the *Brown* decision, he insisted, "The Supreme Court has spoken, and I am sworn to uphold the constitutional processes in this country; and I will obey." Eisenhower's anxiety over southern resistance to the rule of law, not any enthusiasm for the substance of the *Brown* decision, finally forced him to take a decisive stand.

The flashpoint came in Little Rock, Arkansas, a moderate city whose school board, in cooperation with local black leaders, had worked out a plan for gradual integration. But the politics of race had spread across the South. When Alabama's George Wallace lost a gubernatorial primary campaign to an outspoken segregationist in 1958, he commented, "They out-segged me that time, but they'll never do it again." Arkansas governor Orval Faubus, hitherto something of a moderate on racial issues among southern governors, took the same demagogic low road as he sought an unprecedented third term in 1956. As school opening approached that September, Faubus called out the National Guard to prevent nine black students from enrolling at Little Rock's all-white Central High School. In a radio address the night before the fall term began, Faubus peddled alarmist rumors about caravans of white racists converging on Little Rock from all over the South. "Blood will flow in the streets" if the integration of Central High went forward, he intoned, announcing the deployment of the Arkansas National Guard.

After Faubus's speech, black leaders handling the enrollment of the nine students decided to delay the teenagers' appearance at the school, fearful for their safety. However, one of the nine, Elizabeth Eckford, did not get the word. Showing up at the school the next morning, she encountered ranks of stony-faced Arkansas national guardsmen and a screaming, spitting mob. "Lynch her! Lynch her!" they shouted. "No nigger bitch is going to get into our school. Get out of here!" Befriended by two sympathetic whites, she barely managed to escape.

A meeting between Faubus and President Eisenhower failed to heal the impasse; Eisenhower and his staff had treated him like a child, fumed the governor. Faubus withdrew the national guardsmen in the face of a federal court order, but when the black students tried to enroll at Central High, mobs of segregationists again blocked their way.

At long last, Eisenhower acted. In a national television address on September 24, he denounced the Little Rock mob as "disgraceful" and demanded that the law be obeyed. Responding to a telegraphed call for help from Little Rock's mayor, he ordered a thousand paratroopers from the 101st Airborne Division to the city and federalized the Arkansas National Guard. Under the protection of federal troops, the black students enrolled. When white racists bombed the home of one student, Carlotta Walls, she went to school as usual. "Nothing has changed," she told reporters. Although local school boards raised interminable roadblocks to integration and the white Citizens' Councils opened private schools for whites only across the South to circumvent the desegregation rule, school segregation in the South would slowly erode in the later 1950s and the 1960s under the steady pressure of demonstrations, court challenges, and the glare of media publicity.

Meanwhile, the revolution that middle-class blacks and liberal whites had pursued in the courts spread to the streets and churches as years of suppressed anger and aspirations for equality burst forth. Attention focused early on Montgomery, Alabama, the self-proclaimed "cradle of the Confederacy." As was customary throughout the South, Montgomery had a segregated public transportation system: blacks sat in the back of the bus, whites in the front. When a bus filled, blacks had to yield their seats to whites on demand. On December 1, 1955, Mrs. Rosa Parks, secretary of the state NAACP and a longtime active resister of segregation, riding home after a day's work as a department-store seamstress, refused the driver's order to give up her seat to a white man. "I felt it was just something I had to do," Parks would later recall of a simple act of defiance that challenged an entire structure of racial injustice. With Parks's arrest, the state NAACP led by E. D. Nixon, a railroad porter, proposed that Montgomery's blacks organize a bus boycott, a technique that had been briefly tried in 1953 in Baton Rouge, Louisiana. Jo Ann Robinson, a college English teacher and president of a political council of African-American women in Montgomery, stayed up all night mimeographing fifty thousand leaflets announcing the boycott. "The next time it may be you, or your daughter, or your mother," the leaflets declared.

The boycott planners recruited as their leader the Reverend Martin Luther King, Jr., the newly appointed twenty-six-year-old pastor of a middle-class black Baptist church in Montgomery. Thus began the civil-rights career of a man who over the next eleven years would emerge as the premier American moral leader. King, the son and namesake of a prominent Atlanta Baptist minister, had just received his

Ph.D. in theology from Boston University. King gained inspiration not only from Christian thought but also from Henry David Thoreau, who had gone to jail rather than pay taxes to support the Mexican War, and from Mohandas Gandhi, whose nonviolent tactics had helped to end British rule in India.

Sensing that appeals to conscience would further the black cause in America, King underscored the ethical issues at stake and drew on the nation's religious heritage. Although he preached nonviolence, he never advocated passive acquiescence in oppression. Rather, he promoted strategies that would dramatize patterns of racism and generate a "creative tension" between the principle of equality and the fact of injustice. Charismatic and eloquent, heir to a rich tradition of black pulpit oratory, King would ultimately win a vast following of blacks and whites. A skillful tactician, he knew how to translate principles into actions.

King and his associates set three goals for the bus boycott: more courteous treatment of blacks, additional black drivers, and seating on a first-come, first-served basis. (Attesting to the cautious approach in this early stage of the civil-rights movement, the boycott leaders did not initially challenge the custom that relegated blacks to the rear of the bus.) For nearly a year, by walking or sharing rides, blacks stayed off the buses. "I'm not walking for myself," reflected one boycotter, "I'm walking for my children and my grandchildren." A bomb shattered the front of King's house in January 1956, and in February he and the other boycott leaders briefly went to jail, but they held firm. In weekly mass meetings at his church, King and the other leaders not only provided inspiration and guidance but placed the boycott in a broader context. King promised his followers in December 1955:

> When the history books are written in the future, somebody will have to say, "There lived a race of people . . . who had the marvelous courage to stand up for their rights and thereby they injected a new meaning into the being of history and of civilization. And we are going to do that.

At last, in November 1956, a federal court ruled unconstitutional all state and local laws upholding segregated buses in Alabama. Montgomery's leaders capitulated; the lawsuit and the long boycott that lay behind it had succeeded. Beyond its immediate results, the boycott had energized the black community and replaced resignation with hope. When an auto caravan of Ku Klux Klan members prowled through Montgomery's black neighborhood the night after the court ruling, expecting to inspire terror, a crowd of blacks trailed it fearlessly through the streets. And rather than huddling in the dark behind lowered shades, as in the past, the residents flung their shades up and left their lights blazing.

For Martin Luther King, Jr., the Montgomery bus boycott launched a career that would propel him to world fame, bring him the Nobel Peace Prize in 1964, and end with an assassin's bullet in 1968. But in 1956, with the drive for civil rights still in its infancy, all that lay ahead. Moving back to Atlanta to become copastor of his father's church, King with other black ministers in 1957 started the Southern Christian Leadership Conference (SCLC) to guide the burgeoning movement. In *Stride Toward Freedom* (1958), he told the story of the bus boycott and provided a blueprint for similar actions elsewhere. His experience in Montgomery proved crucial in helping him to refine and elaborate his philosophy of nonviolent resistance.

Montgomery, 1956. In "Walking Together," a charcoal drawing sketched from life, New York City artist Harvey Dinnerstein captured the unity and quiet determination that propelled the Montgomery bus boycott to success. (*"Walking Together, Montgomery", by Harvey Dinnerstein, 1956. Charcoal on paper. Gift of the Artist, The Parrish Art Museum, Southampton, NY. Photo by Studio Nine, NY.*)

Black writers also shaped the new consciousness spreading among African-Americans. Ralph Ellison's *Invisible Man*, mentioned above, exerted an important influence through the 1950s and beyond. Like other writers of the decade, Ellison concerned himself less with immediate political action than with heightened individual consciousness. His "invisible" hero lives in an underground room blazing with more than a thousand light bulbs. Some reviewers criticized the withdrawal and apparent passivity of the narrator's furtive subterranean existence. But like jazz artist Dizzy Gillespie, Ellison viewed his work as a valuable step on the path to organized action. Any work by a black writer or artist, he insisted, inevitably represented a political act. "The consciousness of a race is the gift of its individuals who see, evaluate, record. . . ," observes his narrator. "We create the race by creating ourselves." No less than the Montgomery bus boycott, *Invisible Man* heralded a growing resistance to decades of subordination and humiliation, a resistance that had internal psychological and external activist manifestations.

Writer James Baldwin, born in Harlem in 1924, drew even more direct influence from the spirit of the civil-rights movement. Baldwin's first novel, *Go Tell It on the Mountain* (1953), incorporated his own experience as the eldest of nine children of an embittered, self-hating, and often abusive black preacher in a Harlem mission. In a series of penetrating essays in the 1950s and early 1960s—collected in *Notes of a Native Son* (1955), *Nobody Knows My Name* (1961), and other books—Baldwin explored race relations in America and the role of black intellectuals and writers with unsparing clarity. In these often bleak essays, Baldwin explained how racism penetrated both the nation's institutions and the consciousness of whites and blacks alike. Elaborating the point documented earlier by psychologist Kenneth Clark,

Baldwin emphasized that this attitude tainted even the self-image of black children, "taught from the moment their eyes open on the world that their color was a badge of inferiority."

Far from arising in a historical vacuum, the Montgomery bus boycott drew upon a long tradition of African-American protest. In the 1930s, black activists in Harlem had organized boycotts of white-owned businesses that refused to hire black salespersons. Tuskegee, Alabama; St. Augustine, Florida; Greensboro, North Carolina; and other southern communities had witnessed black activism against segregated institutions well before World War II. But Montgomery was unique in scope and visibility, and it propelled black protest to unprecedented new levels.

The surge of civil-rights activism posed ticklish problems for both major political parties. Republicans sought to enlarge their traditional appeal to black voters while retaining their base in the white South.* The Democratic party was torn between its northern and southern wings. The northern wing included a significant black and white-liberal component but also many conservative white ethnics. The southern wing was lily white and overwhelmingly segregationist, although with a small but influential contingent of liberals on racial and other issues, mostly concentrated in university centers.

Out of this political minefield emerged the historic Civil Rights Act of 1957, the first such federal legislation since the 1870s. Attorney General Herbert Brownell, a top Eisenhower political adviser, had argued that by introducing a civil-rights bill, Republicans could deepen the split in the Democratic party and win back northern black voters who had been voting Democratic since the New Deal. Blacks, Brownell calculated, held the balance of power in seven states and sixty congressional districts. After initial resistance, Eisenhower acquiesced in Brownell's proposal. (Strengthening Brownell's case, black congressman Adam Clayton Powell, Jr., of Harlem bolted the Democratic party and supported Eisenhower in 1956.) The administration's civil-rights bill, first introduced in the election year 1956, passed the House but died in the Senate Judiciary Committee, where it was bottled up by Chairman James Eastland of Mississippi, a dyed-in-the-wool segregationist.

Senate majority leader Lyndon Johnson at first opposed the 1956 bill, aware of the risks that it posed for the Democrats. But when Eisenhower again sent Congress a civil-rights bill in 1957, Johnson, eager for the 1960 Democratic presidential nomination and seeking to shed his image as a purely regional politician, cautiously supported it. Meeting with Martin Luther King, Jr., Roy Wilkins of the NAACP, and other black leaders, Johnson cajoled his fellow southern Democrats to accept such a bill.

The compromise bill that emerged from this complex political manuevering was much watered down by southern legislators yet established certain important precedents. Bypassing other forms of racial discrimination, the measure focused entirely on voting rights. Although only part of the larger struggle, this issue was vital, for the disfranchisement of southern blacks by a variety of subterfuges posed a massive roadblock to the civil-rights cause. The 1957 Civil Rights Act authorized the attorney general to seek court injunctions to stop local electoral officials from interfering with

---

* Martin Luther King, Sr., a prominent and well-to-do Atlanta clergyman, was a staunch Republican.

any citizen's voting rights. It created a civil-rights division within the Justice Department and a new federal agency, the U.S. Civil Rights Commission, to monitor racial issues. A follow-up measure, the Civil Rights Act of 1960, authorized federal courts to appoint referees to ensure compliance with the voting-rights laws in local electoral districts.

This early phase of the civil-rights movement stood in sharp contrast to 1950s complacency. Nevertheless, it also illustrated the limits of the nation's understanding of racism's grip on American life. Liberal whites and even the middle-class leaders of the NAACP saw the problem as primarily a legal one involving racial segregation in the South. If Congress and the Supreme Court outlawed the more blatant and obvious forms of legalized racism, they believed, the problem would ease. Once Americans of goodwill united against southern segregation and condemned outspoken racists like Orval Faubus and George Wallace, the stain of racism would fade.

Considerable evidence encouraged this reassuring view, including the Supreme Court's unanimity in the *Brown* decision, the enactment of the Civil Rights Act of 1957 with bipartisan support, the eloquence of Martin Luther King's appeals to Americans' better selves, and the drama of the Montgomery bus boycott. In short, in the 1950s the liberal consensus seemed able to accommodate the racial grievances of African-Americans by a series of moderate actions, without radical upheaval or undue social turmoil. In the next decade, this comfortable assumption would shatter as the inexorable logic of the struggle drove the civil-rights movement in unexpected and, for many Americans, frightening directions. New strategies, new leaders, and new issues were radically transforming the fight for racial equality in America as the 1950s closed.

CONCLUSION

The baby boomers who were children and teenagers in the 1950s later displayed a strong tendency to bathe the decade of their youth in a warm glow of nostalgia. A 1989 TV promotion for a collection of fifties pop hits called these "warm, wonderful years, filled with magical memories." A 1980s television comedy series about teenage life in the 1950s revealed its point of view in its title: "Happy Days." In some ways, this nostalgia is justified. Compared to later decades that brought urban riots, campus turmoil, environmental hazards, industrial decline, trade deficits, inner-city crises, drugs, and AIDS, the prosperous, comparatively tranquil decade of the 1950s does seem almost idyllic. In these years, the economy hummed, joblessness remained low, Americans by the millions bought new homes in the suburbs, and many young couples looked confidently to the future after fifteen years of depression and war. The period holds profound appeal for Americans of a later generation beset by a pervasive sense of malaise and of national decline and disarray.

Historians, however, tend to be chary of easy nostalgia. Too often, rose-tinted memories rely on a highly selective version of the past. Viewed more comprehensively, the "warm, wonderful" Eisenhower years take on a complex and more foreboding aura, shadowed by the nuclear-arms race. As the Cold War became institutionalized, touching peoples across the globe, it corroded home-front life as well, narrowing the range of political debate and cultural expression and forcing dissidents to the periphery.

Politically, the Eisenhower years produced a turn to the right and the rehabilitation of American business, a process that had begun during World War II. These shifts, however, remained within the basic framework of welfare liberalism that was the New Deal's continuing legacy. Nineteen-fifties conservatism stemmed from a reaction against the turbulence and upheavals of the recent past. Yet it also reflected a somewhat smug self-satisfaction in capitalism's capacity to produce unrivaled levels of material well-being for unprecedented numbers of people.

On the cultural front, the decade witnessed the emergence of television as the dominant new medium. A potent instrument for marketing and entertaining, TV nevertheless rarely offered a critical perspective on the consumerist culture to which it contributed. Only intermittently did it acknowledge the America that lay outside the affluent suburbs. Television occasionally riveted the nation's attention on the issues of public significance and would do so increasingly as the civil-rights movement gained momentum. In the 1950s, however, it served mainly to further the political apathy and privatization of American life so deplored by critics of the decade, as families gathered around the bulky sets in darkened living rooms. Sometimes, it seemed, Americans related more intensely to the black-and-white images on the screen than to each other or to the flesh-and-blood world beyond.

But this decade, so disparaged for its passivity, also spawned a passionate campaign against nuclear testing, a historic Supreme Court school-desegregation ruling, an important if limited civil-rights bill, and the moral drama of the Montgomery bus boycott. The rise of television, the civil-rights movement, and the deepening U.S. involvement in Vietnam—perhaps the three most important enduring legacies of the decade—all would mold the 1960s and beyond. What finally impresses one most about the fifties is less its bland uniformity than its vibrant diversity. The decade of Dwight Eisenhower, Norman Vincent Peale, Milton Berle, Lucille Ball, and Ed Sullivan also gave rise to James Dean, C. Wright Mills, Allan Ginsberg, Jack Kerouac, Little Richard, Elvis Presley, Martin Luther King, Jr., Ralph Ellison, and James Baldwin. Any ten-year period that can accommodate such a range of voices, viewpoints, and causes clearly defies easy categorization.

Amid cultural ferment and rising waves of social protest, politicians again geared up for the quadrennial race for the White House. Vice President Richard Nixon, after serving two terms in Eisenhower's shadow, announced his own candidacy for the presidency. But Nixon would have to wait eight more years to sit in the Oval Office. The streaking meteor on the political horizon in 1960 was not the Republican Nixon but a handsome, boyish Democratic senator from Massachusetts, John Fitzgerald Kennedy.

The election that brought Kennedy to the White House highlighted what many feared was a dangerous erosion of America's position in the Cold War. This anxiety, which the Democratic campaigners harped on, arose from a series of events in Eisenhower's second term that suggested alarming Soviet gains, from Cuba to outer space. Although the United States still possessed the strongest military, the later fifties and early sixties brought an ominous deterioration in superpower relations. Cold War tensions, which had briefly thawed in the mid-1950s, abruptly froze again as the decade closed.

SELECTED READINGS

Outsiders and Innovators

Rodolfo Acuna, *Occupied America: A History of Chicanos* (1981); Carl Belz, *The Story of Rock* (1969); Paul A. Carter, *Another Part of the 1950s* (1983); Eva Cockcroft, "Abstract Expressionism: Weapon of the Cold War," *Artforum* (June 1974); Bruce Cook, *The Beat Generation* (1971); Annette Cox, *Art-as-Politics: The Abstract Expressionist Avant-Garde and Society* (1982); Erika Doss, "The Art of Cultural Politics: From Regionalism to Abstract Expressionism," in Lary May, ed, *Recasting America: Culture and Politics in the Age of the Cold War* (1989); Colin Escott, *Good Rockin' Tonight: Sun Records and the Birth of Rock 'n' Roll* (1991); Francis Frascina, ed., *Pollock and After: The Critical Debate* (1985); Simon Frith, *Sound Effects; Youth, Leisure, and the Politics of Rock and Roll* (1981); Mario T. Garcia, *Mexican Americans: Leadership, Ideology, and Identity, 1930–1960* (1989); James Gilbert, *A Cycle of Outrage: America's Reaction to the Juvenile Delinquent in the 1950s* (1986); Albert Goldman, *Elvis* (1981); William Graebner, *Coming of Age in Buffalo: Youth and Authority in the Postwar Era* (1990); Clement Greenberg, *Art and Culture: Critical Essays* (1961); Serge Guilbaut, *How New York Stole the Idea of Modern Art: Abstract Expressionism, Freedom, and the Cold War* (1983); John A. Jackson, *Big Beat Heat: Alan Freed and the Early Years of Rock and Roll* (1991); Jacqueline Jones, *The Dispossessed: America's Underclasses from the Civil War to the Present* (1992); Kenneth Keniston, *The Uncommitted: Alienated Youth in American Society* (1965); W. T. Lhamon, Jr., *Deliberate Speed: The Origins of a Cultural Style in the American 1950s* (1990); Mark Thomas McGee and R. J. Robertson, *The J.D. Films: Juvenile Delinquency in the Movies* (1982); Greil Marcus, *Mystery Train: Images of America in Rock 'n' Roll Music* (1982); Douglas S. Massey, *American Apartheid: Segregation and the Making of the Underclass* (1993); Jane deHart Mathews, "Art and Politics in Cold War America," *American Historical Review* (October 1976); Mark Crispin Miller, "The King" [Elvis], *New York Review of Books*, December 8, 1977; Maria Reidelbach, *Completely Mad: A History of the Comic Book and Magazine* (1991); Ross Russell, "Bebop," in Martin T. Williams, ed., *The Art of Jazz* (1959); Irving Sandler, *The New York School: The Painters and Sculptors of the Fifties* (1978); David P. Szatmary, *Rockin' in Time: A Social History of Rock and Roll* (1991); Mick Tosches, *Unsung Heroes of Rock 'n' Roll: The Birth of Rock in the Wild Years Before Elvis* (1991).

Fiction and Social Thought in Eisenhower's America

William Barrett, *The Truants: Adventures Among the Intellectuals* (1983); Bernard Bell, *The Afro-American Novel and Its Tradition* (1987); Alexander Bloom, *Prodigal Sons: The New York Intellectuals and Their World* (1986); William Chace, *Lionel Trilling: Criticism and Politics* (1980); John P. Diggins, *The Proud Decades* (1989) and "Consciousness and Ideology in American History: The Burden of Daniel J. Boorstin," *American Historical Review* (February 1971); Robert Booth Fowler, *Believing Skeptics: American Political Intellectuals, 1945–1964* (1978); Warren French, ed., *The Fifties: Fiction, Poetry, Drama* (1970); Richard Gillam, ed., *Power in Postwar America* [C. Wright Mills and his critics] (1971); Sam B. Girgus, *The New Covenant: Jewish Writers and the American Idea* (1984); Irving Louis Horowitz, *C. Wright Mills: American Utopian* (1983); Neil Jumonville, *Critical Crossings: The New York Intellectuals in Postwar*

America (1991); Nathan Liebowitz, *Daniel Bell and the Agony of Modern Liberalism* (1985); George Lipsitz, *Class and Culture in Cold War America* (1981); Richard H. Pells, *The Liberal Mind in a Conservative Age: American Intellectuals in the 1940s and 1950s* (1984); Sanford Pinkser, *Jewish-American Fiction, 1917–1987* (1992); Thomas Hill Schaub, *American Fiction in the Cold War* (1991); John Tytell, *Naked Angels: The Lives and Literature of the Beat Generation* (1976); Alan M. Wald, *The New York Intellectuals* (1987); Chaim I. Waxman, ed., *The End of Ideology Debate* (1968); Stephen Whitfield, *The Culture of the Cold War* (1991); Kingsley Widmer, "The Beat in the Rise of of the Populist Culture," in French, ed., *The Fifties*.

1950s Protest: Nuclear Testing and Racial Segregation

Taylor Branch, *Parting the Waters: America in the King Years, 1954–63* (1988); Robert Frederick Burk, *The Eisenhower Administration and Black Civil Rights* (1984); Clayborne Carson et al., eds., *The Eyes on the Prize Civil Rights Reader* (1991); Robert Divine, *Blowing on the Wind: The Nuclear Test Ban Debate, 1954–1960* (1978); Charles W. Eagles, ed., *The Civil Rights Movement in America* (1986); David Garrow, *Bearing the Cross: Martin Luther King, Jr., and the Southern Christian Leadership Conference* (1986); Elizabeth Huckaby, *Crisis at Central High: Little Rock, 1957–1958* (1980); Ralph E. Lapp, *The Voyage of the Lucky Dragon* (1958); David Lewis, *King: A Critical Biography* (1970); Susan Lyan, *Progressive Women in Conservative Times: Racial Justice, Peace and Feminism, 1945 to the 1960s* (1992); Stephen B. Oates, *Let the Trumpet Sound: The Life of Martin Luther King, Jr.* (1982); Howard L. Rosenberg, *Atomic Soldiers: American Victims of Nuclear Experiments* (1980); Bernard Schwartz, *Super Chief: Early Warren and His Supreme Court* (1983); Bernard Schwartz and Stephen Lesker, *Inside the Warren Court, 1953–1959* (1983); Jack G. Shaheen, ed., *Nuclear War Films* (1978); Harvard Sitkoff, *The Struggle for Black Equality, 1954–1992* (1992); Mark Tushnet, ed., *The Warren Court in Historical Perspective* (1993); Arthur I. Waskow and Stanley L. Newman, *America in Hiding* [effects of the civil-defense campaign] (1962); Robert Weisbrot, *Freedom Bound: A History of America's Civil Rights Movement* (1990); J. H. Wilkinson, *From Brown to Bakke: The Supreme Court and School Integration, 1954–1978* (1979).

Chapter Six

THE COLD WAR HEATS UP:
FROM SPUTNIK TO VIETNAM

An eight-inch snowfall hit Washington, D.C., on January 19, 1961. January 20, Inauguration Day, remained cold and blustery, but the newly elected president, buoyant John Fitzgerald Kennedy, stood coatless and hatless, tousled hair blowing in the breeze, as he took the oath of office from Chief Justice Earl Warren. An aged, frail Dwight Eisenhower huddled behind him. For a brief moment, the flow of history seemed to pause, suspended between past and future. JFK's short inaugural address, delivered in the high-pitched, staccato bursts that would become his oratorical trademark, offered a series of confident, ringing assertions. The most memorable passage came near the end: "And so, my fellow Americans, ask not what your country can do for you; ask what you can do for your country."

The speech, declared Senator Hubert Humphrey of Minnesota, was "the American message to the world—a true picture of our country." Rose Kennedy, the president's mother, later described her emotions at the moment: "I felt that Joe [her husband, Joseph P. Kennedy] and I had given our country a young President whose words, manner, ideas, character, everything about him bespoke future greatness."

Kennedy took office at a time of deepening global tension. The late 1950s had seen a deterioration in Cold War relations, and as the struggle with the Soviet Union entered its second decade, disturbing developments stirred fears that the United States was lagging militarily. Kennedy had struck an alarmist note in the 1960 campaign, and as president he displayed a tough aggressiveness in the Caribbean, Europe, Africa, and Southeast Asia, where he edged inexorably toward fuller U.S. engagement in Vietnam. In the Cuban missile crisis of October 1962, twenty-two months into JFK's term, the world came closer to nuclear war than at any other time in the Cold War's forty-five years.

Nevertheless, the 1960s opened on a note of fresh beginnings and new possibilities, a mood embodied in Kennedy's youthful confidence. In March 1961, in one of his most popular actions, Kennedy created the Peace Corps. Young people by the thousands signed up to volunteer two years of service in educational, agricultural, and technical assistance projects in developing countries around the globe. In 1963

Kennedy took the lead in securing a treaty halting atmospheric nuclear tests. The Peace Corps and the Test Ban Treaty would represent the best of the Kennedy legacy and define the elusive quality of the early sixties that at times seemed capable of inspiring the finest in the American spirit. Despite dramatic peaks and moments of high drama, however, Kennedy's brief record in international affairs remains sketchy and inconclusive.

On the domestic front, as we shall see in Chapter 7, Kennedy offered a flurry of proposals and moved aggressively to stimulate the economy through Keynesian fiscal and tax policies, but much of his program remained bogged down in Congress. As for the most important social movement of the era, the civil-rights revolution, the administration played primarily a behind-the-scenes role, urging caution and restraint. The Kennedy era ended prematurely in violence on November 22, 1963, leaving as its major legacy an idealized image of the fallen leader and bleak speculation about what might have been.

From the Heavens to Havana: Cold War Alarms in the Late Fifties

Americans awoke to alarming news on October 4, 1957: The Soviet Union had launched a 184-pound space satellite, called *Sputnik*, or "Little Traveler." One month later, a second satellite joined *Sputnik*, this one carrying a dog, the first living creature to leave Earth's atmosphere. The next May came *Sputnik III*, weighing nearly three thousand pounds. More Soviet satellites and space probes followed in 1959–1960. On October 4, 1959, two years after the *Sputnik* launch, the Soviets released a photograph of the hidden side of the moon, never before seen by human eyes.

Initially, the Eisenhower administration had pooh-poohed the Soviet Union's achievement as a mere stunt. Secretary of Defense Charles Wilson ridiculed *Sputnik* as a basketball in space. But in reality, Moscow's breakthrough deeply disturbed the United States. *Sputnik* and its successors jolted Americans' smug assumptions about U.S. scientific and technological superiority and stimulated a fierce debate over American public education. In *The American High School Today* (1959), former Harvard president James B. Conant called U.S. schools woefully deficient in contrast to those in the Soviet Union, with their emphasis on science, math, and foreign languages.

In direct response to *Sputnik*, Congress in 1958 passed the National Defense Education Act, appropriating $800 million for loans to college and university students and to the states to beef up science and foreign-language instruction. Federal aid to education had been considered—and rejected—by every Congress since 1938. That this piece of the liberal agenda finally fell into place in a post-*Sputnik* climate illustrates both the persistence of welfare liberalism in the Eisenhower era and the degree to which it was skewed by Cold War calculations. But whatever the act's origins, colleges and universities welcomed federal help in serving a crush of students. From 1952 to 1960, enrollment in America's institutions of higher learning surged from 2.1 million to 3.6 million, and their operating budgets rose from $529 billion to a whopping $1.3 trillion.

Sputnik sent the United States a still more chilling message that quickly sank into the public consciousness: The Soviets now had the technology to deploy intercontinental ballistic missiles (ICBMs) that could whisk nuclear warheads to U.S. targets in a matter of minutes. Late in 1957, spooked by *Sputnik* and radioactive fallout, 64 percent of Americans cited the nuclear threat as the nation's top problem. For strategists, the possibility of war carried less weight than the prospect that the Soviets would use their edge in rocketry to advance their broader foreign-policy goals. Policy analyst Herbert Dinerstein developed this point in a January 1958 article in *Foreign Affairs*:

> If the Soviet Union should continue to gain technologically . . . [and] acquire . . . preponderant military strength, they would have policy alternatives even more attractive than the initiation of nuclear war. By flaunting presumably invincible strength, the Soviet Union could compel piecemeal capitulation of the democracies. This prospect must indeed seem glittering to the Soviet leaders.

As the Russians flexed their nuclear muscle, John Foster Dulles's doctrine of influencing Soviet behavior by the threat of massive retaliation lost credibility. Dulles himself, speaking at the Pentagon in 1958, acknowledged that events had overtaken strategy. Although the United States clung to massive-retaliation doctrine, the policy's underlying assumptions began to crumble.

At the time, U.S. intelligence reported no evidence of an operational Soviet ICBM system, yet Soviet advances in rocketry spurred warnings of a "missile gap" and demands from Congress, columnists, and Pentagon officials for the United States to deploy its own ICBM force quickly. A physically weakened Eisenhower resisted this panicky response on several grounds. Uncontrolled military spending, he cautioned, would bring inflation and the government controls that he so abhorred. Strategically, he adhered to the doctrine of "sufficiency": the idea that beyond a certain point, ever-larger nuclear arsenals made no sense.

Eisenhower only partially succeeded in slowing the nuclear-arms race. The first U.S. ICBM, the Atlas, became operational in 1959, and by the end of his term, despite his reservations, the president had authorized some eleven hundred nuclear missiles for deployment in the United States, intermediate-range missiles to be based in Europe, and nineteen nuclear-powered Polaris submarines, each carrying sixteen nuclear missiles. This proliferation of high-tech delivery systems vaulted the nuclear-arms race to new levels of sophistication and menace. Ike battled with similarly mixed results to control overall military spending. As his term ended, defense spending rebounded to Korean War levels, contributing (along with a short-lived recession) to the 1959 budget deficit of $12.5 billion, the largest peacetime deficit up to that time. But the emphasis on cost control had some effect: Defense spending represented a smaller percentage of the GNP in 1960 than it had in 1957.

Given the bipartisan support for the Cold War, the lingering effects of McCarthyism, and the economic benefits of Pentagon contracts, the Democrats rarely challenged military spending levels in these years; indeed, some urged still higher appropriations. In 1957 the liberal Americans for Democratic Action argued for more defense spending, especially on conventional forces. Only a few mavericks criticized wasteful Pentagon procurement practices such as the "cost-plus" contracts that guaranteed a fixed profit regardless of cost overruns. The radical journalist I. F. Stone wrote in 1957, "How can there possibly be wise and adequate expenditure in the field of social welfare if the military are allowed a blank check . . . [that] they fill in every year with ever larger amounts?" Stone underrated Eisenhower's efforts to control defense spending, yet his question cried out for an answer.

Although Stalin's death and the 1955 Paris Summit conference temporarily had eased U.S.-Soviet relations—the two sides voluntarily suspended nuclear testing in 1958 in a moratorium that held until 1961—the Cold War was far from over. Indeed, a string of crises around the globe during the last years of Eisenhower's second term brought the tension to new heights. First, in the aftermath of *Sputnik,* the Soviet Union agreed to assist the Chinese in building an atomic bomb. Chinese Communist leader Mao Zedong declared on a visit to Moscow in November 1957, "The East wind is prevailing over the West wind. . . . The forces of socialism are overwhelmingly superior to the forces of imperialism."

A year later, in November 1958, tempers flared over Berlin when Khrushchev, seeking to force recognition of communist East Germany, set a six-month deadline after which, he insisted, the Western powers would have to deal directly with East Germany, not with Moscow, on matters relating to Berlin. Thoughts of another Berlin blockade haunted many minds when NATO rejected Khrushchev's ultimatum and when a foreign-ministers' meeting in Paris failed to ease the standoff. Fortunately for the White House, the mercurial Soviet leader, unwilling to jeopardize a U.S. trip scheduled for 1959, allowed his deadline to pass. Racing through his American tour, Khrushchev plied his heavy-handed folksiness on visits to Hollywood and an Iowa farm and met with Eisenhower at Camp David, the presidential retreat in Maryland, to discuss Berlin and other issues. The two leaders scheduled another summit meeting for Paris in 1960. Soon Vice President Nixon visited Moscow and engaged in his impromptu "kitchen debate" with Khrushchev. Who won this celebrated colloquy over the respective merits of communism and capitalism remained in dispute, but Nixon's trip implied another small step toward warmer relations.

The promise of a further thaw in U.S.-Soviet relations proved illusory, however. On the eve of the Paris Summit, the Soviets shot down a U.S. U-2 spy plane and captured the pilot, Francis Gary Powers.* Washington initially called the flight a weather-data-gathering mission that had wandered off course, but when the Soviets produced Powers, Eisenhower admitted responsibility for the U-2 flight, citing U.S. security needs. Khrushchev stormed back to Moscow. Although a setback for détente, the incident solidified Eisenhower's popularity at home. Two hundred thousand people turned out to welcome his return to Washington after the failed summit.

In the Middle East, the United States had managed to avoid full-scale war in the 1956 Suez crisis, but Washington remained highly concerned about Soviet influence in the region. In 1957, following a speech by Eisenhower before a joint session of Congress, both houses passed by strong majorities a resolution that came to be called the Eisenhower Doctrine. The new plan authorized the administration to provide economic and military aid and even to intervene militarily, to defend any Middle East nation from "international communism." In the background loomed a funda-

---

* Powers was tried in the Soviet Union and convicted of espionage but eventually was released. Ironically, he later died in a helicopter crash while employed as a radio traffic reporter.

mental objective: protecting the oil vital to the economies of the industrialized West and Japan. From 1948 to 1972, Middle East oil production gushed from 1.1 million to 18.2 million barrels per day, and the region's proved reserves grew from 28 billion to 367 billion barrels. Largely because of this rapid expansion, America's share of world oil production fell from 64 percent to 22 percent in the same twenty-four-year period. As petroleum from the Middle East gained importance in the world market, keeping the region securely in the Western camp became a foundation stone of U.S. foreign policy.

A major test of the Eisenhower Doctrine came in 1958 when Iraq, after a leftist coup engineered by Egyptian leader Gamal Abdal Nasser, left the Baghdad Pact (see p. 118). Dreading similar coups elsewhere, Eisenhower ordered fifteen thousand U.S. Marines to nearby Lebanon, a nation torn by internal conflict. British troops, meanwhile, landed in Jordan, whose pro-Western government faced threats by Nasser supporters. The troops soon withdrew as the immediate danger faded, but Washington's broad and somewhat contradictory goals in the Middle East—to quarantine the area against Soviet influence, to protect the flow of Arab oil to the West, and to maintain a close alliance with Israel—guaranteed that the United States would remain deeply enmeshed in the struggles and intrigues of this region long torn by deep-seated hatreds and rivalries.

In Cuba, guerrilla leader Fidel Castro overthrew pro-U.S. dictator Fulgencio Batista in 1959. Castro's insurgency, under way for several years, initially received favorable U.S. press coverage, but as he allied Cuba with the Soviet Union, Castro mounted a Marxist revolution, imprisoned his opponents, expelled U.S. businesses, including gambling casinos operated by organized-crime figures, and seized U.S.-owned oil refineries. Relations with Washington soured. After persuading the Organization of American States to pass anti-Castro resolutions, the administration halted U.S. imports of Cuban sugar, vital to the island's economy. In this context, the CIA planned and Eisenhower approved an anti-Castro invasion of Cuba that would take place in 1961, after Eisenhower left office.

In Vietnam, an increasingly autocratic Ngo Dinh Diem, a Catholic in a largely Buddhist country, ignored the political and economic reforms urged on him by Washington (see p. 122). Declaring South Vietnam independent, he canceled the elections promised by the Geneva Accords. As his regime lost support, communist military action intensified. So, too, did American involvement; by 1960, the United States had sent some seven hundred military advisers to South Vietnam.

These disturbing events formed the dark backdrop to the 1960 presidential campaign. Each candidate focused his campaign not on domestic issues but on foreign policy. The efforts of each to portray himself as the stronger Cold Warrior set the tone of the electoral rhetoric that summer and fall.

Campaign 1960: Variations on the Cold War Theme

The 1960 presidential race pitted John F. Kennedy, a senator from Massachusetts, against Vice President Richard Nixon, two men from opposite coasts and vastly different backgrounds. Kennedy, born in the Boston suburb of Brookline, was shaped from boyhood by his family's great wealth, Irish-Catholic roots, and tradition of immersion in politics going back to his maternal grandfather, John "Honey Fitz" Fitzgerald, a Boston saloonkeeper who became mayor. Young Kennedy graduated from Harvard College in 1940. Nixon was born in Whittier, California, to lower-middleclass Quaker parents who operated a small grocery store. He attended tiny Whittier College during the depths of the Depression, graduating in 1934.

These two very different men had followed curiously parallel paths to the political summit. Both had served as naval officers in World War II, and both had won election to Congress in 1946. Whereas Kennedy's congressional years proved relatively undistinguished, Nixon had achieved visibility, if not universal admiration, for his dogged service on the House Un-American Activities Committee and had been tapped to run with Eisenhower in 1952. His eight years as vice president had brought more than the usual frustrations associated with that office. In various subtle ways, Eisenhower had conveyed his lack of enthusiasm for his vice president. Prodded at a press conference in 1960 to name a major policy decision that Nixon had participated in, Ike laughed and asked the reporter to give him a week to think about it. Eventually, late in the campaign, the revered Ike gave Nixon at least a pro forma endorsement.

The most important force in John Kennedy's life was his father, Joseph P. Kennedy, who had made a fortune in the stock market and in the movie business. An ambitious Democrat, the elder Kennedy was appointed U.S. ambassador to Great Britain by President Roosevelt in 1938. His isolationism and belief in the inevitability of a Nazi victory thwarted his political plans, however, and he turned to his sons instead, grooming them for high office. Until a stroke felled him in December 1961, Jospeh Kennedy played a powerful and persistent role in his sons' political careers.

When his eldest son, Joseph, Jr., was killed in World War II, Joseph, Sr., turned his attention to the next son, John, a handsome navy veteran who had received a medal for rescuing some of his crew when a Japanese destroyer struck the PT boat that he was commanding in 1943 off the Solomon Islands in the South Pacific. Pressured by his father, John Kennedy ran for Congress in 1946. He won, and in 1952, only thirty-four years old, he moved up to the Senate. In 1953 he married Jacqueline Bouvier, a Rhode Island socialite twelve years his junior.

Kennedy made little mark on the Senate; he and his father had set their sights higher. After testing the waters with a bid for the vice-presidential nomination in 1956 (and losing to Estes Kefauver), in 1960 he joined a crowded field seeking the Democratic presidential nomination.* Senator Hubert Humphrey dropped out after Kennedy, aided by his father's heavy spending, won primary victories in Wisconsin and West Virginia. His most formidable opponent, Senate majority leader Lyndon Johnson, avoided the primaries and entered the race only five days before the party convention. By then, Kennedy had the votes and won a first-ballot nomination. Despite a high level of animosity between the two ambitious men, he offered the vice-presidential slot to Johnson, who accepted.

---

* Among the Democratic also-rans in 1960 were Adlai Stevenson, Senator Stuart Symington of Missouri, and Senator Wayne Morse of Oregon.

The campaign demonstrated the growing political clout of television. Launching what would become a tradition in presidential races, the two candidates participated in four national television debates. In the first, on September 26, the awkward, defensive, and sweaty Nixon, his makeup failing to mask his heavy five o'clock shadow, struggled to make a good impression. Kennedy, handsome, smiling, and spewing facts like a machine-gun, dominated the event. The Massachusetts senator's charisma won over millions of Americans. His promises to bring fresh ideas and vigorous leadership to the White House and to "get America moving again" after eight years of stodgy Eisenhower Republicanism captured the public's attention. A recession that pushed joblessness to a postwar high in 1960 also increased voters' readiness for change.

Taking nothing for granted, however, Democratic strategists turned to securing the critical African-American vote. The 1960 Democratic platform included a vigorous civil-rights plank and promised "strong, active, persuasive, and inventive" presidential leadership on this front. In an interview with a black newspaper, candidate Kennedy assured blacks that he would never sacrifice civil rights for political expediency. On October 26, Kennedy phoned Coretta Scott King to express support for her husband Martin Luther King, Jr., in jail on trumped-up charges involving a minor traffic violation. Through the intervention of the candidate's younger brother, Robert F. Kennedy, the judge in the case released King. Although he stopped short of an actual endorsement, King praised Kennedy extravagantly after his release. King's father, who had planned to endorse Nixon, switch his support to the Democratic candidate.

Foreign-policy issues loomed large as the campaign unfolded. Playing on Cold War fears, Kennedy warned of a dangerous missile gap separating the United States and the Soviet Union, a gap that after the election would prove illusory. In the TV debate on foreign policy, the two candidates vied in portraying themselves as staunch Cold Warriors. Kennedy, however, argued that Eisenhower should have apologized for the U-2 flight to keep the Paris Summit on track. He also took the position that two islands lying between Taiwan and the Chinese mainland, Quemoy and Matsu, claimed by both the Chinese nationalists and the Chinese communists, were not worth the risk of war with China despite America's support for the nationalists.

Only Kennedy's Catholicism seemed to threaten his otherwise textbook campaign. No Catholic had ever been elected president, and the only other one ever nominated, Governor Al Smith of New York in 1928, had suffered resounding defeat at the hands of Herbert Hoover. When queried about the religion issue in the primary campaigns, Kennedy shot back, "Nobody asked if I was a Catholic when I joined the United States Navy. . . . Nobody asked my brother if he was a Catholic or a Protestant before he climbed into an American bomber to fly his last mission." Kennedy's primary victory in overwhelmingly Protestant West Virginia helped to rebut the claim that a Catholic could not win, but concerns persisted. In September, 150 prominent Protestants led by Reverend Norman Vincent Peale warned that a Catholic president inevitably would be influenced by the church hierarchy. Confronting the matter head-on, Kennedy flew to Houston and assured a group of Protestant ministers that, although proud of his religion, as president he would not allow Catholic doctrine or official pronouncements to dictate his decisions.

In the strikingly close election, Nixon carried every state west of the Mississippi except Texas, New Mexico, Nevada, and Alaska. In the South, he won Tennessee, Kentucky, Virginia, and Florida. Kennedy did well in the industrial belt and the big cities, and black support proved decisive for him in several key states. Seventy percent of black voters pulled the Democratic lever, providing the decisive margin of victory in Pennsylvania, Michigan, Texas, and South Carolina. Black voters' preference for the Democratic party, solid since New Deal days, continued.

Kennedy's razor-thin successes in Illinois and Texas edged him to victory with a 120,000-vote margin. Even so, because of a scattering of votes for minor-party candidates, Kennedy received only 49.7 percent of the total vote to Nixon's 49.6 percent. Native-son Johnson helped the ticket in Texas, and in Illinois the powerful and notoriously corrupt Cook County Democratic machine run by Chicago mayor Richard J. Daley threw its formidable resources behind Kennedy. When Kennedy phoned Daley on election night, as Illinois teetered in the balance, the mayor promised him, "Mr. President, with a bit of luck and the help of a few close friends, you're going to carry Illinois." Kennedy's charisma, effective Democratic organizing, a strong showing among black voters, and widespread worries about the economy and Cold War setbacks combined to turn the tide for the Democrats. Kennedy's coattails were short, however. Although the Democrats retained control of both houses of Congress, the Republicans gained twenty-one seats in the House.

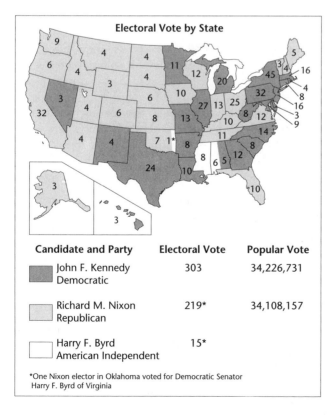

FIGURE 6.1

Presidential Election of 1960

The first family of Camelot. John F. Kennedy, Jacqueline Bouvier Kennedy, and daughter Caroline. The president's dashing good looks and his wife's cool sophistication underlay a carefully cultivated image that helped Kennedy win the presidency. (*AP/Wide World Photos*)

For Richard Nixon, the defeat seemed the end of the road. A loss in a California gubernatorial race two years later pounded another nail in his political coffin. "You won't have Nixon to kick around anymore," he bitterly told reporters in a valedictory after the 1962 defeat. His self-pitying prediction proved decidedly premature.

Kennedy launched his presidency on a tide of popular support verging on adulation. In his inaugural address, the new president, remarkably boyish looking at forty-three, invoked a "new frontier" of social progress and underscored the theme of generational change:

> Let the word go forth from this time and place, to friend and foe alike, that the torch has been passed to a new generation of Americans—born in this century, tempered by war, disciplined by a hard and bitter peace, proud of our ancient heritage—and unwilling to witness or permit the slow undoing of those human rights to which this nation has always been committed, and to which we are committed today at home and around the world.

The Cold War, Kennedy-Style

For both partisan and personal reasons, John Kennedy's approach to Cold War leadership differed markedly from Eisenhower's. Kennedy brought to the contest with Moscow the drive and assertiveness that formed the core of his personality. Shaped by an intensely competitive family and a hard-driving father whom he both admired and feared, he eagerly sought to prove his toughness to the Soviet adversary. America, he declared in a particularly strident passage of his inaugural address, would "pay any price, bear any burden, meet any hardship, support any friend, oppose any foes, in order to assure the survival and success of liberty." Few expected that the nation would soon be asked to fulfill that grandiose pledge in the jungles and rice paddies of Vietnam.

In addition to his personal character traits, the new president brought the outlook of Democratic liberals to the Cold War. While supporting the basic strategy of containment that had undergirded U.S. strategy since the late 1940s, liberals had placed a distinctive ideological stamp on Cold War policy. Rooted in New Deal activism, the liberal tradition had been toughened and chastened in the early years of the Cold War when Democrats such as Harry Truman, Dean Acheson, George Kennan, Averell Harriman, and James Forrestal had first committed the nation to the anticommunist cause.

Cold War liberalism sprang from the idealistic belief, grounded in years of domestic reform effort, that through intelligent, planned effort, the federal government could serve as an instrument of social betterment. Kennedy-style liberals such as White House special assistant and speechwriter Arthur Schlesinger, Jr., a well-known New Deal historian, applied this commitment globally. Priding themselves on their clear-eyed anticommunism, they believed that the United States under liberal leadership could pursue the Cold War more effectively than the Republicans could by working for social and democratic change worldwide as an alternative to the siren song of Marxist revolutionaries. They did not wish to remake the world on the American model, but neither did they want to see it remade on the Soviet model. President Kennedy in 1963 described his goal as "a world of diversity in which no one power, or no one combination of powers, can threaten the security of the United States." Above all, Cold War liberals repudiated what they caricatured as Eisenhower's policy of drift and called for energetic, aggressive tackling of foreign as well as domestic challenges. In the 1930s, Franklin Roosevelt had portrayed the fight against the Depression as a great national crusade, and liberal Cold Warriors infused the anticommunist cause with the same high rhetoric. As Undersecretary of Defense John McNaughton put it in a 1961 memo to the White House, "The United States needs a *Grand Objective*. . . . [W]e behave as if . . . our real objective is to sit by our pools and contemplate the spare tires around our middles."

The Kennedy administration's sense of new possibilities in foreign policy intensified through growing awareness of the split between Moscow and Beijing as ancient rivalries and border conflicts reasserted themselves. The CIA reported in 1963, "The U.S.S.R. and China are now two separate powers whose interests conflict on almost every issue." Not until the 1970s, under President Nixon, would Washington fully exploit this division, but awareness of its possibilities hovered in the background of American Cold War strategy from the early 1960s onward.

Kennedy's choice as secretary of state, Dean Rusk, a soft-spoken, moon-faced Georgian, epitomized Cold War liberalism. As a liberal southerner, Rusk had worked for civil rights. As a political scientist specializing in Asian affairs, he had served in the Truman years as assistant secretary of state for UN affairs and then as assistant secretary for Far Eastern affairs. In the 1950s, as president of the Rockefeller Foundation he had initiated health-care programs and other social reforms in the vast and diverse region of the globe that was coming to be called the Third World. But Rusk also proved a tough-minded Cold Warrior who had long urged a hard line toward communist China.

Rusk's influence in the Kennedy administration was muted, however. Quiet and self-effacing, he lacked the drive and ambition of other top administration officials. In high-level meetings, he often maintained a Buddha-like silence, allowing others to control the debate. On foreign-policy issues, Kennedy relied less on Rusk than on a team of advisers, recruited from academia and corporate America, who prided themselves on being "hard-nosed realists." Secretary of Defense Robert McNamara, formerly president of Ford Motor Company, specialized in systems analysis and statistical studies of policy options. McNamara's tightly brushed-back and slicked-down hair, rimless glasses, no-nonsense manner, and fondness for charts and graphs epitomized the Kennedy team's approach to foreign policy. Barry Goldwater called him a computer with legs. National security adviser McGeorge Bundy had served as dean of Harvard College. Kennedy's deputy, Walt Whitman Rostow, later head of the State Department's Policy Planning Staff, had taught government at the Massachusetts Institute of Technology.

The grand strategist was Rostow, a facile synthesizer of big ideas. "Walt can write faster than I can read," Kennedy joked. His *Stages of Economic Growth: A Non-Communist Manifesto* (1960) had argued that the United States could win the Cold War by supplying aid and technical assistance to speed the evolution of Third World nations into modern industrial democracies. Don't rely on entrenched elites in Asia, Africa, and Latin America, Rostow advised, but seek out and encourage noncommunist groups that can resist Marxism's lure while serving as agents of economic modernization within a framework of political democracy. Too often, he warned, communists in these countries, backed by Moscow, presented themselves as the only force willing to rescue the masses from grinding poverty. In Rostow's view, an intelligently crafted U.S. foreign policy could change all this by strengthening democratic alternatives.

Rostow summed up his ideas in a 284-page document, "Basic National Security Policy," presented to Kennedy in mid-1961. In this treatise, he advocated an activist foreign policy that would support progressive, noncommunist forces in the developing world. Rather than continuing the Eisenhower-Dulles habit of backing entrenched conservative regimes as long as they opposed communism, Rostow argued, "our interests are likely to be better served by accepting the risks of leaning forward towards more modern groups." Such action-oriented liberalism led Rostow to support the idea of a highly interventionist U.S. role in these nations threatened by leftist uprisings. American interests demanded, he insisted, that such nations "develop along lines broadly consistent with our own concepts of individual liberty and government based on consent."

The administration's emphasis on social and economic development as a Cold War strategy had the added advantage of downplaying direct nuclear confrontation with the Soviet Union. Indeed, one way in which Kennedy liberals distinguished themselves from Republican Cold Warriors was in repudiating the latter's overreliance on nuclear weapons in military planning. Kennedy's favorite general, Maxwell Taylor, who became chairman of the Joint Chiefs of Staff in 1962, in his 1959 book

The Uncertain Trumpet had called for supplementing nuclear weapons with a wide range of conventional armaments and strategies capable of meeting all kinds of foreign challenges. Taylor's "flexible-response" doctrine exerted great influence in the Kennedy years. As the president himself summed up the goal of flexible response in 1961, "We intend to have a wider choice than humiliation or all-out nuclear war."

Focusing initially on Latin America with its reactionary elites and yawning social inequities, Kennedy in March 1961 announced the Alliance for Progress, which pledged $20 billion in new foreign aid for the region over the decade. This aid, however, hinged on the recipients' committing themselves to radical social change, including reforms in their land-tenure and tax policies. The Alliance for Progress gave practical expression to the Rostow doctrine of encouraging fundamental social changes in societies threatened by communist insurgency. As Roger Hilsman of the State Department put it, "A revolution is inevitable in Latin America. If you don't do it peacefully, you'll end up with blood." Soon, however, the idealism of the Alliance for Progress was mocked by a debacle that, although not of Kennedy's doing, had consequences that fell at his doorstep.

Disaster at Bahia de Cochinos

Upon taking office, Kennedy learned from central intelligence director Allen Dulles* of the CIA's plan to invade Cuba. The plan, hatched early in 1960 by a team led by CIA staffer Richard Bissell, came after the successful coups in Iran and Guatemala. The plot ignored the vast differences between the Cuban situation and that in other countries where CIA coups had succeeded, but it was far advanced when the new administration took office. Anti-Castro Cuban refugees being trained in Guatemala as guerrilla warriors to carry out the attack joked that "CIA" stood for Cuban Invasion Authority. With misgivings, Kennedy gave the green light for the invasion to proceed.

The plan assumed that the Cuban masses would rise up and overthrow Castro. But when the sixteen hundred invaders landed on April 17, 1961, at the Bahia de Cochinos (Bay of Pigs), the local populace showed no interest in joining them. Castro, who often vacationed at Bahia de Chocinos, enjoyed great popularity in the region. Furthermore, as Arthur Schlesinger ruefully noted in a post-mortem on the invasion, the Escambray Mountains that the CIA planners had envisioned as a hiding place for the invaders "lay *eighty miles* from the Bay of Pigs, across a hopeless tangle of swamps and jungles." In short, the invasion was bungled from inception to execution.

In a disaster that delivered a sobering dash of reality to both the CIA and Kennedy, Castro's forces killed more than 100 invaders and captured 1,189. Eventually the administration ransomed them for $10 million in medical supplies. One U.S. diplomat commented that the only thing that could have been worse than the failure was success; had the plan worked, the United States might have been saddled with a protracted military occupation of Cuba amid a hostile population, evocative of the imperialistic days of the Spanish-American War.

---

* The younger brother of John Foster Dulles, who had died in 1959.

The Bay of Pigs fiasco injected "new urgency" into the planning for counter-insurgency warfare, according to a top Kennedy military aide. It also may have increased Kennedy's receptiveness to creative strategies for fighting communism in Vietnam. More immediately, it intensified the administration's vendetta against Castro. Furious at his humiliation, Kennedy ordered the CIA to disrupt Cuba's economy and discredit its government. The intelligence agency responded with Project Mongoose, under which CIA operatives burned cane fields, blew up factories and power plants, and persuaded European industries to ship Castro defective equipment such as off-center ball bearings. CIA planners also devised numerous schemes for embarrassing or even killing Castro, including lacing his cigars with poison, exploding giant clamshells near where he snorkeled, and even trying to make his trademark beard fall out by sprinkling depilatory powder into his shoes. In this campaign for revenge, the CIA recruited various organized crime figures eager to regain control of their Havana operations. All of this scheming built the foundation for the far graver missile crisis that would erupt in Cuba in October 1962.

Meanwhile, the administration watched carefully as Moscow and Beijing feuded and as China's nuclear-weapons program forged ahead. China would not test its first atomic bomb until October 1964, but Kennedy knew from intelligence sources that a Chinese bomb was imminent. The president hoped to exploit these circumstances to improve U.S.-Soviet relations, but for the first two years of his administration, this hope went unfulfilled. Kennedy's and Khrushchev's first opportunity to size each other up came at a meeting in Vienna in June 1961. The discussion, as so often in the past, centered on Germany. The Berlin Airlift of 1948 had only temporarily thwarted Soviet efforts to pressure the NATO powers to acknowledge the East German communist state. In defusing the Berlin crisis of 1959, Khrushchev had only postponed, not abandoned, this goal. In 1961, testing the new administration in Washington, Khrushchev again made a pawn of Berlin as part of his larger strategy of forcing the West to accept the Soviet-backed East German regime. The continual flow of East German refugees seeking asylum in the West by way of Berlin posed another thorny problem for Moscow.

The Vienna meeting, convened amid this atmosphere of crisis, fared badly. The sixty-seven-year-old Soviet leader, who had a son older than Kennedy, treated the new president like an immature youth whom he could intimidate through bullying and bluster. Kennedy left Vienna convinced that danger lay ahead. He called for $3.25 billion more in defense spending, tripled the draft call, and activated thousands of reserves. With little planning, Kennedy delivered a frightening television address warning the nation that nuclear war could break out at any time. Echoing John Foster Dulles's language of brinksmanship, Kennedy cautioned the Soviets not to make the "dangerous mistake of assuming that the West [is] too selfish and too soft and too divided to resist invasions of freedom in other lands." Once again, he declared, evoking the crisis of 1948, Berlin had become "the great testing place of Western courage and will."

As part of his war of nerves with Moscow, Kennedy urged a crash program of fallout-shelter construction. Civil-defense planning included a program called NEAR (National Emergency Alarm Repeater) in which alarms would have been installed in every home and apartment. Nuclear fear, muted since 1958 when the

The Berlin Wall, erected in 1961, not only bisected a city but also symbolized a world divided by Cold War hostilities. (*U.S. Army Photograph*)

superpowers had temporarily halted atmospheric nuclear testing, reawakened with new intensity.

Khrushchev chose an unexpected route out of the impasse. On the night of August 13, 1961, the Soviets erected a barrier across divided Berlin to stop the embarrassing East German exodus westward. The Berlin Wall blocked all movement between the two halves of the city, and would-be East German refugees challenged it at peril of their lives. Traveling to the divided city in June 1963, Kennedy denounced the barricade as proof of communism's failure and crowed to the cheering throng, "*Ich bin ein Berliner*" ("I am a Berliner").* Although the wall caused much anguish for divided families and hardened the division of Europe, it ended the cycle of confrontation over Berlin. It in fact represented a retreat by Khrushchev disguised as a bold initiative. As Kennedy told an adviser, "This is his way out of his predicament. It's not a very nice solution, but a wall is a hell of a lot better than war."

The Cold War erupted also in Central Africa, where the former Belgian Congo (present-day Zaire), now independent, was led by a nationalist premier, Patrice Lumumba. Lumumba had received training in Moscow, and Western leaders feared that he would halt the export to the West of copper, uranium, and other minerals from the southern province of Katanga. When Katangan leader Moise Tshombe announced the province's independence, the United States supported the move. Lumumba's assassination in January 1961 aroused persistent rumors of CIA involvement. As civil war in the Congo continued, the Kennedy administration gave aid and air support to Lumumba's right-wing successor, Joseph Kasavubu, whom it viewed as a bulwark against Soviet expansion in Africa. This policy of orchestrating the downfall and possibly the assassination of a nationalist leader who tilted toward

---

* Directly translated, Kennedy's phrase meant "I am a jelly doughnut," causing some initial confusion in his German-speaking audience. What the president should have said was, "Ich bin Berliner."

Moscow planted seeds of ill will against the United States in Third World states struggling to throw off colonial shackles.

October 1962: To the Brink

Heightened Cold War tension turned to terror during the Cuban missile crisis of October 1962, the most dangerous episode of the Cold War era. The incident began when the CIA informed President Kennedy that high-altitude photos by U-2 spy planes had confirmed reports earlier provided by a spy operating in Cuba: The Soviet Union had deployed in Cuba SS-4 intermediate-range ballistic missiles (IRBMs) designed to carry one- to three-megaton nuclear warheads.* With a range of 1,020 nautical miles, the SS-4s could reach targets in the eastern United States, including New York City and Washington, D.C., in eight minutes. The U-2 photos revealed even more disturbing news: Some Soviet missile sites in Cuba were designed to house SS-5 missiles, which carried even larger warheads and had a range of more than two thousand nautical miles—enough to destroy most big cities in the continental United States. Washington's precise knowledge of the capacity of the SS-4s and SS-5s rested on information provided by a spy high in Soviet military intelligence, Colonel Oleg Penkovsky, who had microfilmed and transmitted to the CIA a key Soviet missile manual. Soviet authorities arrested Penkovsky in October 1962 and executed him in 1963. Whether the missiles had actually been armed with nuclear warheads remained uncertain. Years later, in 1992, when the Cold War was over, Russian military men would reveal that the U.S.S.R. had installed nuclear weapons in Cuba and that the local Soviet commander had the authority to use them in the event of a U.S. invasion. Thus, the crisis was even graver, and the risks of nuclear war even higher, than Washington realized at the time.

Why did Khrushchev take this dangerous step? There is no evidence that he planned an actual nuclear attack, but he surely sought to increase Moscow's bargaining power on a range of Cold War issues by achieving nuclear parity. Overall, despite Kennedy's loose talk in the 1960 campaign about a missile gap, the United States possessed many more nuclear missiles than the Soviets. As the Soviet ambassador to Cuba in 1962 later recalled, "[Khrushchev] was looking for any way to talk to the Americans equally." Furthermore, in July 1962, following a 1959 U.S. agreement with Turkey, the Kennedy administration had deployed fifteen U.S. Jupiter missiles in Turkey, placing much of the Soviet Union within a few minutes' striking time. Finally, Fidel Castro, justifiably alarmed by the Bay of Pigs attack and by subsequent CIA plots against his regime and against him personally, had begged the Soviet Union to beef up its military presence in Cuba.

From Khrushchev's perspective, putting SS-4s and SS-5s in Cuba seemed a quick and easy way to please Castro, counter the Jupiter missiles in Turkey, and redress the larger strategic imbalance. The Bay of Pigs fiasco, and the poor impres-

---

* A megaton, the standard unit for measuring nuclear bombs, is the explosive force of one million tons of TNT. The bomb that destroyed Hiroshima in August 1945 had the explosive force of twenty thousand tons of TNT.

sion that Kennedy had made on Khrushchev in Vienna, also may have encouraged the Soviet leader to believe that the young American president would not dare challenge this provocation, especially in the midst of the 1962 midterm electoral campaign.

Whatever the underlying motives, the Soviet move sparked an urgent, top-secret policy debate within the Kennedy administration. Defense Secretary McNamara acknowledged that the Cuban missiles did not actually change the balance of power, which remained overwhelmingly in America's favor, but they gave the impression of a dramatic Soviet gain, and this Kennedy could not tolerate. The Cuban missile deployment, he complained to his advisers, "makes [the Soviets] look like they're co-equal with us." In short, as historian Stephen Ambrose has observed, "The most serious crisis in the history of mankind . . . turned on a question of appearances. The world came close to total destruction over a matter of prestige."

Kennedy secretly assembled a team of top advisers soon labeled the Executive Committee, or EXCOM. Some members—former Secretary of State Dean Acheson; General Maxwell Taylor, chairman of the Joint Chiefs of Staff; and air force general Curtis LeMay—favored a preemptive air strike, followed by an invasion if necessary. Several top congressional Democrats also urged this course when they learned of the Soviet move. Others, notably Undersecretary of State George Ball, advocated a blockade of Cuba, with the option of a military strike later. Kennedy, rejecting a surprise attack as too risky and too reminiscent of Japan's attack on Pearl Harbor in 1941, chose the blockade.

In a TV address on Monday evening, October 22, the president revealed the existence of the missiles in Cuba and demanded their withdrawal. He also announced a naval blockade of Cuba to begin at 10 A.M. Tuesday. The next morning, when several Soviet ships approached the blockade line and then turned back, tensions eased somewhat. Dean Rusk commented, "We're eyeball to eyeball and I think the other fellow just blinked." But the crisis was far from over. Fear ran high over the next few days as EXCOM—and the world—awaited the Soviet response. The Strategic Air Command moved to DEFCON 2, a high state of readiness. Presidential speechwriter Theodore Sorensen recalled, "Our little group seated around the Cabinet table in continuous session . . . felt nuclear war to be closer . . . than at any time in the nuclear age." Kennedy called his wife and children, who were traveling, back to the White House so that they could escape to a presidential nuclear shelter if necessary.

Millions of Americans watched with mounting fear and helplessness as their fate hung in the balance. Office workers and students in classrooms nervously eyed the clock as it crept toward the hour of Kennedy's deadline on October 22. Others tried to carry on with daily routines that suddenly seemed devoid of meaning. People somberly debated whether they would rather die in the first moments of a nuclear war or survive to face a devastated world. Through much of the Cold War, the nuclear threat loomed as a disturbing but somewhat abstract menace; in October 1962 it suddenly became starkly immediate, and chronic anxiety spiked into heart-throbbing terror. Journalist Tom Morgenthau, looking back on the Cuban missile crisis thirty years later, wrote, "Few who lived through that period . . . will ever forget the drama that unfolded day by day."

Unknown to the American people, urgent communications were passing between Washington and Moscow by various channels. On Friday, Khrushchev sent a long, rambling, but essentially conciliatory message that expressed his own dread of nuclear war and offered to remove the IRBMs in exchange for a U.S. pledge not to invade Cuba. A second message the next morning took a harder line: The United States must also remove its missiles from Turkey. Again the Joint Chiefs and some EXCOM members clamored for an invasion. Still the president held back. At the suggestion of his brother, Attorney General Robert Kennedy, JFK answered Khrushchev's more accommodating first message, pledging not to invade Cuba if the missiles were withdrawn. That night, Robert Kennedy met privately with Soviet ambassador Anatoly Dobrynin and assured him that once the Cuban crisis was resolved, the administration would soon remove the Turkish missiles, although a public pledge to that effect could not be made part of the deal. With these promises, Khrushchev agreed to remove the IRBMs. On Sunday, October 28, Kennedy announced the news, and the world heaved a sigh of relief. The Soviets dismantled and removed the missiles, and Kennedy lifted the blockade. In April 1963, the U.S. Jupiter missiles quietly disappeared from Turkey, as well as from Great Britain and Italy, to be replaced by seaborne missiles aboard Polaris submarines.

How close the world came to thermonuclear war that autumn, we can never know for certain. But as years passed and more information emerged, many of those most intimately involved in the crisis, on both sides, became convinced that the risk had run dangerously high. John Foster Dulles had talked of going to the nuclear brink; Kennedy and Khrushchev had peered into the abyss.

Viewed at the time as a victory for U.S. firmness and a personal triumph for Kennedy on the eve of the 1962 elections, the Cuban missile crisis held several unexpected ramifications. It undermined Khrushchev's position with his Kremlin colleagues, who perceived him as having buckled under U.S. pressure, and within two years he had fallen from power. The crisis also affected the Atlantic alliance. French leader Charles de Gaulle, convinced that when the chips were down the United States would pursue its own interests without consulting NATO, accelerated France's nuclear-weapons research, ordered NATO's headquarters out of Paris, and eventually withdrew altogether from NATO's military command structure.

Over the years, more information about the crisis surfaced. Dean Rusk revealed in 1987 that Kennedy, using UN Secretary General U Thant as an intermediary, would have publicly pledged to withdraw U.S. missiles from Turkey, had that seemed the only alternative to war. Although he was obsessed with the need to prove himself, Kennedy nevertheless showed restraint and recognized the imperative of avoiding nuclear war. Even for fiercely competitive Cold Warriors such as Kennedy and Khrushchev, the deadly logic of nuclear stalement served as a powerful constraint.

Most important, the crisis compellingly underscored the risk of global war. As economist John Kenneth Galbraith commented, "We were in luck. But success in lotteries is no argument for lotteries." After the heart-stopping crisis, Kennedy moderated his Cold War rhetoric and stepped up efforts to bring the nuclear-arms race under some control. In August 1961, confronted with a major U.S. nuclear-weapons build-up, the Soviets had resumed nuclear testing, including the detonation of a blockbuster fifty-eight-megaton bomb, far larger than anything in the U.S. arsenal and the equivalent of three thousand Hiroshima-type bombs. Kennedy reluctantly ordered another round of U.S. tests, but he acknowledged the fallout danger and genuinely desired a test ban. In addition, China's well-advanced nuclear-weapons program raised the specter of nuclear proliferation. Indeed, the prospect of a Chinese bomb so worried Kennedy that he proposed a joint U.S.-Soviet military strike against China's nuclear facilities, an idea to which Khrushchev proved unresponsive.

In an address at the American University in Washington, D.C., on June 10, 1963, Kennedy spoke of the "nuclear sword of Damocles" hanging over the earth and exhorted world leaders to diminish the danger. The president eloquently declared, "In the final analysis, our most basic common link is the fact that we all inhabit this planet. We all breathe the same air. We all cherish our children's future. And we are all mortal." As Kennedy spoke, test-ban talks in Geneva and Moscow moved forward. From the Soviet perspective, the talks had the advantage of suggesting nuclear parity between the two sides. In August 1963, the United States, the Soviet Union, and Great Britain signed a treaty banning nuclear testing in the atmosphere or underwater. Kennedy shrewdly shepherded the treaty through the Senate. To allay the suspicions of conservative legislators, he persuaded Senator Everett Dirksen of Illinois, a leading Republican, to announce his support. On September 24, the Senate ratified the treaty by an overwhelming margin, 80–19. Important as an environmental and public-health measure and as a gesture of goodwill, the test-ban treaty nevertheless did not halt the nuclear-arms race. Underground testing continued, and France and China, which became nuclear powers in 1963 and 1964, respectively, carried on their atmospheric testing.

In a step to reduce the risk of nuclear war through miscalculation in times of crisis, the United States and the Soviet Union also set up a direct telecommunications system, or hot line, between the White House and the Kremlin. One cartoonist pictured a frustrated Khrushchev reaching Kennedy's daughter, Caroline, on the hot line and sputtering in exasperation, "No, I don't want your *dolly*, I want your *daddy*!" In still another effort toward improved relations, Kennedy in October 1963 authorized U.S. wheat sales to the Soviet Union.

Despite these measures, the Kennedy years saw a major escalation of the arms race, including nuclear competition. The president increased the defense budget from $40 billion to $56 billion by 1962 and initiated a nuclear build-up that by 1967 gave the United States 41 Polaris subs armed with more than 650 missiles; 600 strategic bombers; and 1,000 intercontinental ballistic missiles (ICBMs)—a fivefold increase over the 200 inherited from the Eisenhower administration. The Soviet Union strove to keep pace. By 1967 even Defense Secretary McNamara conceded that the nuclear escalation had been a mistake; it had increased tensions and risks without strengthening U.S security.

Why did Kennedy authorize this expansion when strategists were downplaying nuclear missiles in favor of a flexible-response approach stressing nonnuclear weaponry? Essentially, nuclear weapons had become the symbol of world power. Kennedy had no intention of launching a nuclear war, and apart from the nerve-wracking days of the Cuban missile crisis, he little expected that the Soviets would start one. But in the post-Hiroshima world, status required nuclear power. Paul Nitze, assistant secretary of defense, noted in a December 1961 speech, "We believe this [nuclear] superiority, particularly when viewed from the Soviet side, to be strategically important in the equation of deterrence and strategy." The Soviets naturally held the same view, and the nuclear-arms race proceeded at full tilt, propelled by the dynamics of Cold War diplomatic maneuvering.

Southeast Asia and Vietnam: Deeper into the Tunnel

Although the nuclear competition continued to spiral upward, more conventional patterns of conflict increasingly preoccupied Washington strategists, especially when they turned to Southeast Asia. The map of this region presented a complex mosaic of poor and developing nations, many emerging from a colonial past, in which rival and often shadowy groups vied for dominance. Viewing this confusing reality through a Cold War lens, Kennedy-era policymakers tended to see each region as an arena of East-West confrontation that their predecessors had dangerously neglected. Asian specialist Dean Rusk warned in a May 1961 press conference, "If you don't pay attention to the periphery . . . the first thing you know the periphery is the center. . . . [W]hat happens in one place cannot help but affect what happens in another."

This shift in focus came in response to changes in Soviet policy, which in the Kennedy years oscillated between conciliation and belligerence. When in their belligerent mode, the Soviets revealed a readiness to foment revolution throughout the Third World. In a January 1961 speech, just as Kennedy took office, Nikita Khrushchev made clear that Moscow, despite still seeking peaceful coexistence with the West, would happily sponsor "wars of national liberation" in Africa, Latin America, and Southeast Asia. Washington planners in turn focused on strategies for containing this new threat. Walt Rostow, as we have seen, emphasized social and economic development. The Alliance for Progress applied this approach in Latin America. In September 1961, Congress created the Agency for International Development (AID) to coordinate all U.S. foreign-aid programs. Throughout the 1960s, AID funneled an average of $4.7 billion annually to development programs throughout the world. The Food for Peace program, another Kennedy initiative, had the dual function of easing hunger in poor nations while reducing U.S. farm surpluses. Chester Bowles, a prominent liberal appointed undersecretary of state by Kennedy, became a particularly eloquent advocate for social and economic development.

But the liberal Cold Warriors of the Kennedy era saw the Third World struggle in military as well as economic terms. Maxwell Taylor's flexible-response strategy included new techniques of counterinsurgency warfare designed to respond to local military threats in Asia, Africa, and Latin America. A strong U.S. counterinsurgency capability, Taylor argued, could show Moscow that its fomenting "wars of national liberation" would not be "cheap, safe, and disavowable" but "costly, dangerous, and doomed to failure." President Kennedy, an admirer of Ian Fleming's debonair fictional hero James Bond, found counterinsurgency planning particularly intriguing. Even Walt Rostow had no qualms about supplementing economic development with military measures against insurgents who looked to Moscow rather than to Washington. Arthur Schlesinger called Rostow "Chester Bowles with a machine gun."

The shift of focus from Europe to the Third World did not diminish the tendency of Washington Cold Warriors to portray the conflict in black-and-white terms. In an April 1961 speech to the American Newspaper Publishers' Association, Kennedy described the struggle in phrases that John Foster Dulles would have found wholly familiar, updating the analysis to convey the new emphasis on developing regions. As the president declared, "We are opposed around the world by a monolithic and ruthless conspiracy that relies primarily on covert means for expanding its sphere of influence."

These principles found application in specific situations. In Southeast Asia, attention initially focused on Laos, where a three-way civil war raged among a right-wing general supported by the United States, a neutralist prince, and a communist prince backed by the Soviet Union. This small, poverty-stricken nation had little strategic significance, but it possessed symbolic importance for Kennedy. He told columnist Walter Lippmann early in 1961, "We cannot and will not accept any visible humiliation over Laos." Victory was not worth a war, however. While some advised Kennedy to take a military stand in Laos, he chose the path of negotiation instead. At the 1962 Geneva Conference, in which the United States participated, the warring factions agreed to a neutral Laos. This decision encouraged Kennedy; negotiations had staved off a communist takeover in an Asian nation. At least one small region of the world had been withdrawn from the arena of U.S.-Soviet conflict.

In neighboring South Vietnam, conditions were deteriorating. As a senator, John Kennedy had vigorously supported the Eisenhower administration's handpicked ruler in South Vietnam, Ngo Dinh Diem. But Diem's autocratic, corrupt, and nepotistic regime never won popular support. The Vietminh, the procommunist force that remained in South Vietnam after the 1956 Geneva Accords, worsened the situation by systematically killing village leaders and local officials. In 1960 an anti-Diem coalition of communists and Buddhists, the latter of whom made up 80 percent of the population, established the National Liberation Front (NLF) in South Vietnam, which, with its military arm, the Vietcong, began operations against Diem's forces.

Kennedy determined to stand firm in South Vietnam. In May 1961 he warned that the United States would not tolerate the military overthrow of the Saigon government. After the Vienna meeting with Khrushchev, Kennedy told James Reston of the *New York Times* that the United States must prove its resolve to the Soviets and that the place to do so was Vietnam. The logic of containment doctrine required U.S. resistance to the expansion of either Chinese or Soviet power in Vietnam. In addition, the United States had pledged in the 1954 SEATO pact to defend South Vietnam against external aggression.

This interview revealed a series of key assumptions guiding Kennedy's thought: that the Vietnam conflict was simply one front in a larger Cold War struggle; that the Vietnamese communist leader, Ho Chi Minh, was little more than a pliant tool of Moscow or Beijing; that South Vietnam was a distinct nation subject to aggression from abroad (that is, from North Vietnam). Though simplistic and misguided, these assumptions would underlie U.S. policy in Vietnam for the next five years and beyond.

Moreover, South Vietnam seemed the ideal laboratory to test antiguerrilla strat-

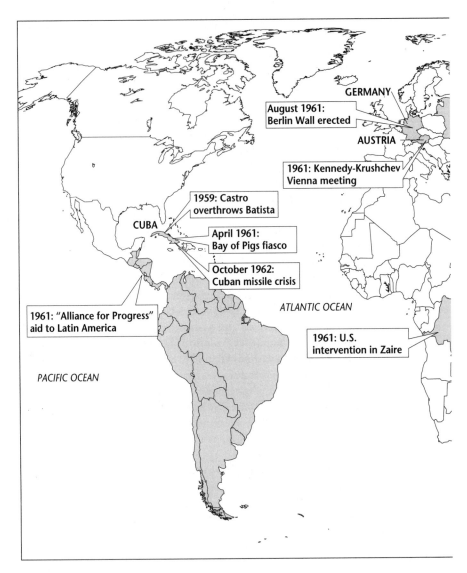

FIGURE 6.2
The Cold War Heats Up

egies. While U.S. Green Berets, a counterinsurgency unit, advised the South Vietnamese army, U.S. civilian specialists introduced medical programs, technical aid, and economic and political reforms designed to win "the hearts and minds" of Vietnamese peasants. One reform measure, the Strategic Hamlet program, uprooted peasants from lands that their ancestors had occupied for generations and concentrated them in settlements supposedly secure from communist infiltration. The program only deepened the peasants' hatred of the Diem regime.

Administration leaders nearly unanimously viewed Vietnam as a vital Cold War

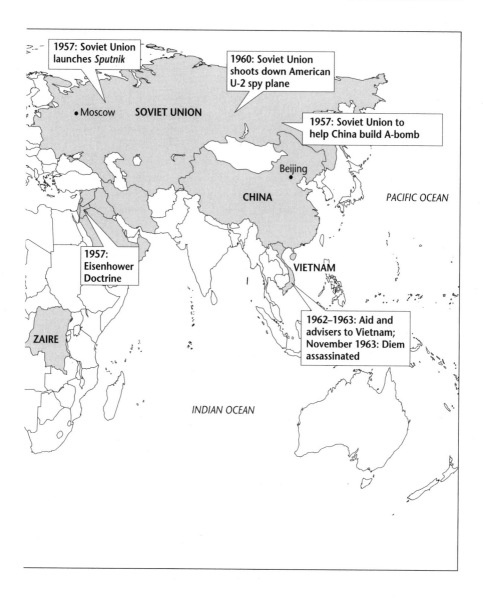

1957: Soviet Union launches *Sputnik*

1960: Soviet Union shoots down American U-2 spy plane

•Moscow   **SOVIET UNION**

1957: Soviet Union to help China build A-bomb

Beijing•

CHINA

PACIFIC OCEAN

1957: Eisenhower Doctrine

VIETNAM

1962–1963: Aid and advisers to Vietnam; November 1963: Diem assassinated

ZAIRE

INDIAN OCEAN

battlefield. After touring South Vietnam early in 1961, Vice President Johnson advised, "The basic decision in Southeast Asia is here. We must decide whether to help these countries to the best of our ability or throw in the towel in the area and pull back our defense to San Francisco and a 'fortress America' concept." After visiting Saigon that fall, General Maxwell Taylor, who soon would become chairman of the Joint Chiefs of Staff, called for eight thousand U.S. combat troops, plus heavy U.S. air support. He warned that such a build-up should not be undertaken "unless we are prepared to deal with any escalation by the Communists," but added, "As an area for the operations of US troops, [South Vietnam] is not . . . excessively difficult or unpleasant." Secretary of Defense McNamara, visiting in 1962, concluded that "every quantitative measurement we have shows we're winning this war."

A rare cautionary note came from Undersecretary of State George Ball, who warned Kennedy in November 1961, "Within five years we'll have three hundred thousand men in the paddies and jungles and never find them again. That was the French experience. Vietnam is the worst possible terrain both from a physical and political point of view." Kennedy replied, "George, I always thought you were one of the brightest guys in town, but you're just crazier than hell." In fact, within five years, U.S. troop strength in Vietnam would reach nearly four hundred thousand.

Against the drumfire of calls for escalation from influential figures in his administration, Kennedy proceeded cautiously, as he had in the Cuban missile crisis. Privately skeptical of the military's clamor for more troops, he rejected General Taylor's recommendation for a major infusion of combat units in 1961, presciently sensing that the ante would inevitably rise. "It's like taking a drink," he reflected. "The effect wears off and you have to take another." Nevertheless, Kennedy continued to sip. In his public statements, he echoed Eisenhower's domino theory and insisted on America's determination to prevent a communist victory in Vietnam. He dreaded a 1964 presidential race dominated by Republican cries of "Who lost Vietnam?" as Democrats of the 1950s had faced the accusatory question, "Who lost China?" American abandonment of Vietnam, he feared, could unleash a new wave of McCarthyism. By mid-1962 Kennedy had increased the number of U.S. military "advisers" in Vietnam from seven hundred to twelve thousand. He added another five thousand in 1963 and gave the Saigon government $500 million in aid. As more American blood spilled in Vietnam—U.S. casualties rose from fourteen in 1961 to more than four hundred in 1963—withdrawing became progressively more difficult.

In May 1963, a Buddhist monk in the ancient religious city of Hué burned himself to death to protest the Diem regime; Diem's sister-in-law, the powerful Madame Nhu, joked that she would "supply the mustard for the monks' next barbecue." But Buddhist resistance spread and Diem's position eroded, and Kennedy gave the green light for an anti-Diem coup. On November 1, South Vietnamese military officers working in coordination with the U.S. embassy in Saigon arrested and shot Diem and his brother and set up a new military government.*

Had Kennedy's own death not followed within three weeks of Diem's, what further course might he have taken in Vietnam? Some argue that he planned to withdraw, but the evidence for such speculation is slim. A dedicated Cold Warrior, Kennedy had little doubt that U.S. toughness and military might, coupled with the techniques of counterinsurgency and nation building, could contain communism anywhere in the world. Had he lived, he surely would have received the same advice, from the same advisers, that determined Lyndon Johnson's course.

In one of his last comments on the war, Kennedy acknowledged that the United States could not control the outcome of a civil struggle in a small, distant country.

---

* Ambassador Henry Cabot Lodge and other U.S. officials who set the coup in motion apparently did not anticipate Diem's assassination; they had advised that he and his family be flown into exile. On the other hand, neither the U.S. embassy nor the coup leaders had made any plans for such an evacuation.

"In the final analysis," he mused, "it is their war." But he quickly added, "For the United States to withdraw . . . would mean a collapse not only of South Vietnam but [of] Southeast Asia. So we are going to stay there." The *New York Times*, a powerful voice of the eastern liberal establishment, heartily agreed. Chiding Kennedy for his "it is their war" comment, the *Times* editorialized that Vietnam was America's war, "a war from which we cannot retreat and which we dare not lose." The fundamental dilemma summed up in Kennedy's ambivalent comments would continue to haunt American policymakers, liberal and conservative alike, for another decade.

The Kennedy Cold War: A Summary

The six years from *Sputnik* in 1957 to the assassination of Diem in 1963 saw the management of the Cold War pass from moderate Republicans to liberal Democrats, who defined the Cold War in terms that reflected John Kennedy's temperament as well as the idealism and activism of the FDR/New Deal tradition. The blend of anti-communist militance and social-reform zeal, combined with a drive to systematize and rationalize the policy-formation process, that one finds in New Frontiersmen such as Walt Rostow and Robert McNamara epitomizes the distinctive quality of Kennedy-style liberalism applied to world affairs.

This approach to the Cold War would come in for sharp attack in later years. In *The Kennedy Promise* (1973), British journalist Henry Fairlie deplored JFK's craving for empty displays of energy and his compulsive competitiveness. The Kennedy-era shift of focus from Western Europe to the murkier terrain of Third World struggles led by nationalistic and anticolonial forces, Fairlie suggested, robbed Washington's Cold War leadership of some of its legitimacy and moral clarity and led directly to the debacle in Vietnam that finally would shatter the liberal consensus. Garry Wills in *The Kennedy Imprisonment* (1982) dissected even more mercilessly Kennedy's fascination with power and with displays of machismo in the international arena. JFK's attraction to tests of will and to power struggles for their own sake, rooted in his father's strong influence, Wills contends, found expression in his campaign to destroy Castro, in his alarmist response to Khrushchev's maneuvering over Berlin, in the unrelenting build-up of nuclear weapons, and in the deepening engagement in Vietnam. Overall, Wills argued, these traits, and the appeal that they held for liberals determined to move beyond Eisenhower's alleged inertia, exerted a dangerous impact on the conduct of foreign policy.

But Kennedy's approach to the Cold War, flawed though it may have been, had legitimate roots in the Progressive and liberal tradition dating back to Theodore Roosevelt and Woodrow Wilson. The continuities in that tradition from the 1930s to the 1960s symbolically emerge in the ideological odyssey of the writer John Steinbeck. In his 1939 novel *The Grapes of Wrath*, Steinbeck produced the classic New Deal–era paean to ordinary people battered by the Depression but enduring with the help of a socially engaged government. Three decades later, in the years before his death in 1968, Steinbeck gave qualified support to the U.S. cause in Vietnam as enunciated by John Kennedy and his successor, Lyndon Johnson.

The Kennedy years solidified an uneasy nuclear stalemate as the United States and the Soviet Union piled up ever more destructive panoplies of missiles and warheads. Nuclear fears eased after the Cuban missile crisis of October 1962, although the inherently unstable balance of terror sustained by two bristling arsenals capable of destroying civilization many times over hardly inspired long-term confidence. Still, with a rough nuclear balance in place and the Big Power confrontation in Europe stabilized, Cold War attention shifted to the Third World. From the days of President Truman's Point Four program, Washington strategists, with their counterparts in Moscow and later in Beijing, had recognized that developing nations represented an important, perhaps decisive arena of ideological, economic, and potentially military competition. In the later 1950s and early 1960s, this arena moved from the periphery to the center of strategists' thinking.

When applied to a specific region, Southeast Asia and South Vietnam in particular, this shift of emphasis set the stage for a war that would leave its stamp on American history more than any other event from the end of World War II to the end of the Cold War forty-five years later. In Chapter 9, after further exploring domestic politics and social movements in the 1950s and 1960s, we return to the grim Vietnam story as it unfolded following the shocking end of the Kennedy presidency.

Tragedy in Dallas

On November 21, 1963, President Kennedy flew to Texas, a state that he barely had carried in 1960, to patch up a bitter quarrel among Texas Democrats that threatened his reelection hopes for 1964. Jackie Kennedy accompanied her husband, something that she rarely did. At 12:30 P.M. on Friday, November 22, the presidential motorcade wound through Dallas. The Kennedys rode in the back of an open car, with Texas governor John Connally and his wife seated in front. Three shots rang out. The first bullet struck the president in the neck; the second tore a gaping hole in his head, killing him almost instantly. Nine minutes later a bulletin raced over the newswires: "FLASH. Kennedy wounded. Perhaps seriously. Perhaps fatally by assassin's bullet."

The presidential car sped to Parkland Hospital, where two Roman Catholic priests administered last rites, and Kennedy was pronounced dead at 1 P.M. For the rest of their lives, Americans would remember where they heard the news. One young historian, working in the reading room of the Enoch Pratt Free Library in Baltimore, received word from a trembling librarian that the library was closing: President Kennedy had been shot.

Lyndon Johnson took the oath of office aboard Air Force One as the white-and-red jet waited at Dallas's Love Field, ready to carry the dead and living presidents back to Washington. An anguished Jacqueline Kennedy, a coat covering her blood-spattered dress, looked on hollowly.

The nation mourned as a horse-drawn caisson, the same that had borne Abraham Lincoln's body in 1865, carried Kennedy's remains from the White House to the Capitol. The young historian, down from Baltimore for the day, watched as the cortege wended its slow way along Pennsylvania Avenue, followed by the closed black limousines carrying the bereaved family and the Johnsons. Secret Service

November 1963. In a solemn ceremony shaped by tradition, President Kennedy's body was transported from the White House to the Capitol on the same caisson that had carried the remains of Abraham Lincoln in 1865. (*UPI/Bettmann Archive*)

agents scanned the crowd from the rooftops of nearby government buildings. The burial took place in Arlington National Cemetery, the grave marked by a perpetual flame. An administration launched with such élan and promise had ended suddenly and brutally, the vibrant young president struck down.

Within hours of the assassination, Dallas police arrested Lee Harvey Oswald, a twenty-four-year-old ex-marine. Two days later, as police transferred Oswald to another prison, Dallas nightclub owner Jack Ruby shot and killed him. The circumstances surrounding these events aroused much speculation. Oswald, with a record of mental instability and threats against other public figures, had moved to the U.S.S.R., married a Russian woman, and belonged to a pro-Castro group, Fair Play for Cuba Committee. To many, these circumstances hinted at a larger conspiracy.

To quell rising rumors, President Johnson appointed a blue-ribbon commission of seven prominent public figures chaired by Chief Justice Earl Warren. After exhaustive research by legal and forensic experts and interviews with 552 witnesses, the Warren Commission issued its report in September 1964. It concluded that Oswald had acted alone in shooting the president. There was no conspiracy, foreign or domestic, the report pronounced categorically. But rumors of a conspiracy—by Cubans, by the Mafia, by Lyndon Johnson, by a right-wing cabal within the government—persisted, echoing the speculation that had grown up around Abraham Lincoln's assassination ninety-eight years earlier. Despite the Warren Commission's insistence on the fullness of its research, some critics at the time and in later years charged the investigation with slipshod research and insisted that the commission had failed to pursue all leads thoroughly. The political motive of reassuring the public, rather than the larger task of sifting all the evidence, these critics argued, had led the commission to assert an overly confident lone-assassin conclusion.

Although no credible evidence ever surfaced to disprove the Warren Commission report, the guesswork and theorizing continued, fed by a rash of books by freelance writers and amateur sleuths such as Mark Lane's *Rush to Judgment* (1966). Later revelations of actual high-level conspiracies—from the Watergate cover-up to the Iran-contra affair, further encouraged those convinced that more than met the eye lay behind Kennedy's death. Such suspicions would gain a new lease on life in 1992 with the release of the Hollywood film *JFK*, directed by Oliver Stone and starring Kevin Costner. Cleverly interspersing invented dialogue, fictional "witnesses," and imagined scenes with actual newsreel footage, *JFK* portrayed an elaborate web of conspiracy involving Vice President Johnson, the FBI, the CIA, the Pentagon, defense contractors, and assorted other officials and agencies.

Why have these conspiracy theories endured in the absence of any hard evidence to support them? When the Warren Commission report appeared in 1964, Harrison Salisbury of the *New York Times* offered an explanation:

> The evidence of Oswald's single-handed guilt is overwhelming. Yet, few Americans will feel that this is the final word. Not, I submit, because the evidence is not toweringly clear. But rather because there is in each of our hearts some feeling, however small, of responsibility; some feeling that each of us had some share in the crime because we had a role in a society which made it possible; which gave birth to a young man who by a long, dreary, painful path became distorted into an assassin. Thus, there remains in each of us some communal share of guilt in the senseless loss of a man so young and brilliant as John F. Kennedy; some feeling of a step not taken; an act not completed; a word not spoken; a thought not carried into life which would have spared us so great a tragedy.
>
> And it is this secret gnawing at our conscience that not all the efforts, not all the millions of words in the many volumes of the Warren findings, will ever still. It is this, in the end, that will keep the spark of the Kennedy legend aglow.

CONCLUSION

As president, Kennedy had enjoyed increasing popularity; in death, he assumed mythic proportions. Journalists referred to the Kennedy White House as Camelot, the imaginary kingdom of King Arthur and his knights. Later, a reaction would set in. Historians would point out that for all Kennedy's glitz and hype, his achievements proved modest. On the international front, they would praise the Peace Corps and the Test Ban Treaty but deplore the strident Cold War rhetoric, the nuclear build-up, and the escalation in Vietnam. On the personal side, the Kennedy myth would be tarnished by revelations of his ruthless behavior, his use of amphetamines, and his compulsive promiscuity both before and during the White House years, including affairs with the actress Marilyn Monroe, whom he shared with his brother Robert, and with the mistress of Chicago mobster Sam Giancana. Critics also questioned his concealment of serious physical ills, including agonizing back pain and Addison's disease, a failure of adrenal function that required constant and heavy cortisone medication.

Three decades after Kennedy's death, the Camelot myth had lost its magic for some Americans but remained potent for millions of others. It had always revealed more about the needs and hopes of the American people than about Kennedy himself. A flawed man, Kennedy's surface charm brought him such easy success that he had little need to develop the more complex qualities that make for character. George Ball, who knew Kennedy well, would write in 1992, "His major political assets were his good looks and the glamor of a golden boy." For historian Thomas Reeves, the author of a critical biography of Kennedy, A *Question of Character* (1991), the lesson of his presidency was sobering:

> In the early 1960s, we became involved in a sort of mindless worship of celebrity; it was a love affair largely with images. That could happen again. . . . In our longing to find heroes in a greedy, anonymous, and insensitive age, we might once more be swayed by someone who is wonderfully attractive, has a glib tongue, a bottomless wallet, and a conscience that asks little and demands even less. And the target of our affection might be much worse than Jack Kennedy.

Nevertheless, long after the mystique had faded, and in full awareness of Kennedy's flaws, many still remembered the promise and the finer moments of his presidency. For a fleeting instant, the New Frontier—not as it was, perhaps, but as Americans longed for it to be—offered another chance to bring the American reality closer to the imagined ideal.

The violent shattering of the Kennedy presidency was only one of a series of events that fragmented the liberal consensus. Rooted in the 1930s and the chastening experiences of World War II and the early Cold War, this consensus underlay the Democratic party's activist, reform-minded approach to domestic problems and to global challenges in the 1950s and early 1960s. As we shall see in Chapter 7, Lyndon Johnson would sustain that consensus briefly during a remarkable season of reform legislation in 1964–1965, much of it assisted by Johnson's shrewd political use of Kennedy's memory. But the shining liberal hour that Kennedy had personified would ultimately lose its lustre, darken, and pass into history.

SELECTED READINGS

Foreign Affairs and Defense Policy in the Later 1950s

Richard Aliano, *American Defense Policy from Eisenhower to Kennedy* (1975); Michael R. Beschloss, *Mayday: Eisenhower, Khrushchev, and the U-2 Affair* (1986); H. W. Brands, "The Age of Vulnerability: Eisenhower and the National Security State," *American Historical Review* (October 1989); Bernard Brodie, *Strategy in the Missile Age* (1959); Michael E. Brown, *Flying Blind: The Politics of the U.S. Strategic Bomber Program* (1992); Barbara B. Clowse, *Brainpower for the Cold War: The Sputnik Crisis and the National Defense Education Act of 1958* (1981); Theodore Draper, *Castro's Revolution: Myth and Realities* (1961); Lawerence Freedman, *The Evolution of Nuclear Strategy* (1985); Lloyd C. Gardner, *Approaching Vietnam: From World War*

II Through Dienbienphu (1988); James R. Killian, Jr., *Sputnik, Scientists, and Eisenhower* (1977); Douglas Kinnard, *President Eisenhower and Strategic Management* (1977); Walter A. McDougall, . . . *The Heavens and the Earth: A Political History of the Space Age* (1985); Donald Neff, *Warriors at Suez* (1981); Carroll Pursell, Jr., ed., *The Military-Industrial Complex* (1972); Stephen G. Rabe, *Eisenhower and Latin America* (1988); Jack M. Schick, *The Berlin Crisis, 1958–1962* (1971); Jean Edward Smith, *The Defense of Berlin* (1963); Tad Szulc, *Fidel: A Critical Portrait* (1986); Richard E. Welch, Jr., *Responses to Revolution: The United States and the Cuban Revolution, 1959–1961* (1985); David Wise and Thomas B. Ross, *The U-2 Affair* (1962). See also the Selected Readings for Chapter 4.

Kennedy, Nixon, and the 1960 Election

Edgar M. Bottome, *The Missile Gap* (1971); Doris Kearns Goodwin, *The Fitzgeralds and the Kennedys: An American Saga* (1986); Donald Lord, *John F. Kennedy: The Politics of Confrontation and Conciliation* (1977); Allen J. Matusow, *The Unraveling of America: A History of Liberalism in the 1960s* (1984), Chap. 1, "The Liberals, the Candidate, and the Election of 1960"; Richard M. Nixon, *Six Crises* (1962); Thomas Reeves, *A Question of Character: The Life of John F. Kennedy in Image and Reality* (1991); Theodore Sorensen, *Kennedy* (1965); Theodore White, *The Making of the President 1960* (1961); Garry Wills, *Nixon Agonistes* (1969) and *The Kennedy Imprisonment* (1983).

Kennedy and the Cold War

Elie Abell, *The Missile Crisis* (1966); Graham T. Allison, *Essence of Decision: Explaining the Cuban Missile Crisis* (1971); Desmond Ball, *Politics and Force Levels* (1981); Barton Bernstein, "The Week We Almost Went to War" [Cuban missile crisis], *Bulletin of the Atomic Scientists* (February 1976); Michael Beschloss, *The Crisis Years: Kennedy and Khrushchev, 1960–1963* (1990); H. W. Brands, *The Devil We Knew: Americans and the Cold War* (1994); David Burner and Thomas R. West, *The Torch Is Passed: The Kennedy Brothers and American Liberalism* (1984); Herbert Dinerstein, *The Making of a Missile Crisis: October 1962* (1976); Henry Fairlie, *The Kennedy Promise* (1973); Bernard Firestone, *The Quest for Nuclear Stability* (1982); John Girling, *America and the Third World* (1980); David Halberstam, *The Best and the Brightest* (1972); George Herring, *America's Longest War: the United States and Vietnam* (rev. ed., 1985); Trumbull Higgins, *The Perfect Failure: Kennedy, Eisenhower, and the Bay of Pigs* (1987); Haynes Johnson, *The Bay of Pigs* (1964); George McT. Kahin, *Intervention: How America Became Involved in Vietnam* (1986); Stanley Karnow, *Vietnam: A History* (1983); Robert Kennedy, *Thirteen Days* [Cuban missile crisis] (1969); Walter LaFeber, *Inevitable Revolutions: The United States in Central America* (1985); Sir Bernard Lovell, "The Great Competition in Space," *Foreign Affairs* (October 1971); Richard D. Mahoney, *JFK: Ordeal in Africa* (1983); Bruce Miroff, *Pragmatic Illusions: The Presidential Politics of John F. Kennedy* (1976); John M. Newman, *JFK and Vietnam: Deception, Intrigue and the Struggle for Power* (1992); Herbert S. Parmet, *JFK* (1981); Thomas G. Paterson, ed., *Kennedy's Quest for Victory: American Foreign Policy, 1961–1963* (1989) and "Bearing the Burden: A Critical Look at JFK's Foreign Policy," *Virginia Quarterly Review* (Spring 1978); Thomas G. Paterson and William J. Brophy, "October Missiles and November Elections: The Cuban Missile Crisis and American Politics, 1962," *Journal of American History* (June 1986); Arthur M. Schlesinger, Jr., *A Thousand Days* (1966); Glenn T. Seaborg, *Kennedy, Khrushchev, and the Test Ban* (1981); Robert M. Slusser, *The Berlin Crisis of 1961* (1973); Richard J. Walton, *Cold War and Counter-Revolution: The Foreign Policy of John F. Kennedy* (1972); Peter Wyden, *Bay of Pigs* (1980).

Chapter Seven

THE LIBERAL HOUR

In October 1967, Lady Bird Johnson, the wife of President Lyndon Johnson and a powerful Washington figure in her own right, received an honorary degree from Williams College in Williamstown, Massachusetts, and spoke on her favorite subject: the need to preserve and enhance America's natural beauty. Amid the autumn foliage of western Massachusetts, in a picture-book New England college town, the setting and the theme meshed perfectly. But the sylvan tranquility shattered when hecklers protested not Mrs. Johnson's environmental message but a war raging in distant Vietnam. The scene was repeated the next day at Yale University in New Haven, Connecticut. While an audience of eight hundred listened attentively to Mrs. Johnson's speech inside the hall, an equal number of antiwar protesters milled outside, shouting and waving placards.

Her New England visit, wrote an aide, left the First Lady "very disheartened." During the preceding four years, she had emerged as a strong environmental advocate. Yet her audience seemed to be drifting away as the Vietnam War muscled its way into the public discourse. Soon, she feared, she would be unable to travel freely to promote the cause that she cared about so deeply.

The dilemma confronting Lady Bird Johnson that autumn reflected a deep tension within the administration and indeed in the nation. The Johnson years had begun on a note of high resolve, as the new president moved quickly to bring an ambitious reform agenda to fruition. Four years later, the mood had soured. The protests that greeted Lady Bird Johnson at Williamstown and New Haven soon would mushroom, forcing President Johnson to abandon any hope of reelection in 1968.

Johnson's downfall proved especially shocking because it followed a period of apparent political invincibility. Thrust into the presidency by an assassin's bullets, Johnson seized the reins adroitly. After pushing Kennedy's stalled program through Congress, he went on to win passage of a reform agenda more far-reaching than any other since the New Deal. Johnson's domestic achievements surely would place him among the greatest of reform presidents. His overall record, as we shall see, presents a far more muddied picture.

Having examined how the liberal political tradition shaped U.S. foreign policy in the Kennedy years, in this chapter we trace liberalism's influence on domestic policy: the revival of liberals' confidence in the late 1950s, the domestic initiatives of John Kennedy's truncated presidency, and the flood of reform legislation in 1964–1965—the high-noon of postwar liberalism. Chapter 8 picks up the story with a close look at the civil-rights movement in the 1960s, from the confident days of the early sixties and President Johnson's monumental legislative achievements to the fragmenting of the civil-rights consensus at mid-decade. By the end of Johnson's term, the liberal consensus would collapse under the battering of domestic turmoil, urban unrest, and the divisive war in Vietnam.

Shaping a Liberal Agenda: The 1950s

Through much of the 1950s, the once-powerful trumpet of New Deal liberalism sounded only feebly. As liberal intellectuals rallied behind the Cold War, criticism of the United States' domestic social and economic order gave way to handwringing over the devalued state of American mass culture. Economic issues that had preoccupied reformers in the 1930s attracted little notice. "[T]he jobless, distracted, and bewildered men of 1933," wrote historian Richard Hofstadter reassuringly in 1955, "have in the course of the years . . . become homeowners, suburbanites, and solid citizens." In this climate, party politics held scant interest for intellectuals. To them, the provocative issues lay in the cultural arena. It is small wonder, then, that liberal ideological discourse, so vigorous in the 1930s, grew tepid. In 1957 historian Arthur Schlesinger, Jr., lamented, "[L]iberalism in America has not for thirty years been so homeless, baffled, irrelevant, and impotent as it is today."

Toward the end of the prosperous fifties, this climate changed. Even if poverty, economic inequity, and corporate wrongdoing no longer posed severe problems, some liberals concluded, the nation's squandering of its vast wealth merited criticism. Inspired by John Kenneth Galbraith's *The Affluent Society* (1958), liberals called for restraints on private consumption and increased investment in the public sector—schools, hospitals, roads, civic services, and so on. Schlesinger contrasted this "qualitative liberalism" with the "quantitative liberalism" of FDR's era and proposed the former as the liberal agenda for the 1960s. Schlesinger's three-volume eulogy to the New Deal, *The Age of Roosevelt* (1957–1960), presented Roosevelt's first term in glowing language calculated to inspire a new generation of liberals.*

Other liberals argued that the issues of the 1930s still lived. In a biting review of *The Affluent Society*, Leon Keyserling, chair of the Council of Economic Advisers under President Truman, rejected Galbraith's assumption that modern America enjoyed near-universal affluence. Despite the spread of middle-class suburbs, he insisted, the postwar boom had left many millions of Americans behind. To fight poverty and want, Keyserling argued, liberals should work for government policies designed to promote economic growth. Further to the left, socialists criticized Cold War liberals who turned a blind eye to domestic economic injustice while attacking the nation's cultural flaws. Amid all the cultural criticism, wondered Irving Howe in

---

* Significantly, perhaps, Schlesinger never continued his history into the years after 1936, when the New Deal stalled and ultimately failed to end the Great Depression.

the journal *Dissent* in 1955, why did liberals ignore the plight of southern sharecroppers, displaced New England textile workers, or Puerto Rican immigrants in New York City? As a sign of rising ferment on the Left, the socialists' elder statesman, Norman Thomas, became increasingly popular on the college lecture circuit.

Although the liberal agenda that took shape by the end of the 1950s did not include the radical restructuring advocated by socialists, it did incorporate elements of both the Galbraith and Keyserling programs. Liberal academics and journals of opinion stressed greater investment in the public sector, as Galbraith urged, and government stimuli to promote economic growth, as Keyserling advocated. Indeed, the decade's end found the public increasingly receptive to liberals' calls for renewed governmental activism. Domestically, the civil-rights movement spotlighted an urgent social issue in which government could play an important role. Globally, *Sputnik* and other events fed the growing conviction that America had lost ground. When anti-American riots forced President Eisenhower to cancel a visit to Japan in 1960, the gnawing sense of national impotence deepened. As anxious discussions of "the national purpose" broke out in the media, liberals' spirits rose. The election of a group of young, reform-minded Democrats to the Senate in 1956 and 1958, including Edmund Muskie of Maine, Eugene McCarthy of Minnesota, Frank Church of Idaho, William Proxmire of Wisconsin, and Phil Hart of Michigan, further roused the liberals' sense of anticipation.

These proponents of reform did not automatically rally to John Kennedy's candidacy for president. Many remained loyal to Adlai Stevenson or supported Senator Hubert Humphrey of Minnesota, whose liberal credentials outshone Kennedy's. In addition, Kennedy's father had favored appeasement of Hitler, and the Kennedy family had openly admired Senator Joseph McCarthy. Kennedy's choice of the Texan Lyndon Johnson as his running mate further alienated liberals, for Johnson had a reputation as a conservative from a conservative state. As late as August that year, Arthur Schlesinger, Jr., warned Kennedy that the liberal Americans for Democratic Action had backed his nomination only with the "utmost tepidity."

Kennedy avidly courted reformist intellectuals, and his campaign speeches stressed the liberal themes of economic growth and renewal of the public sector, summed up by the slogan, "It's time for a change." As he asserted in one speech, "My campaign . . . is founded on . . . the assumption that the American people are tired of the drift in our national course . . . and that they are ready to move again."

Richard Nixon, of course, pointed proudly to the 1950s economic boom and denied that the country had stagnated in the Eisenhower years. At an Oregon shopping mall, Nixon declared, "If you think the United States has stood still, who built the largest shopping center in the world, the Lloyd Shopping Center right here?" But Nixon's gloating over the flood of consumer goods inundating America simply confirmed another liberal complaint about the Eisenhower era: that the public sector had atrophied amid a self-indulgent consumerist orgy.

Despite Kennedy's razor-thin victory margin, liberals felt a thrill of expectancy as he took office. Political scientist Michael Walzer wrote in a postelection assessment, "There is an openness to new ideas probably unlike anything since the 1930s." Still, Walzer noted, Kennedy's vision of change remained hazy. A vote for Kennedy, Walzer observed, was more an act of faith than an endorsement of a fully formed liberal agenda. Liberals thus watched nervously to see whether events would justify their faith.

Implementing a Liberal Agenda: The Kennedy Years

Although civil-rights marches, confrontations, and Freedom Rides during the early sixties captured the nation's attention, President Kennedy turned his energies to other domestic economic and social issues. His approach, reflecting a liberal, social-activist orientation, yielded at best mixed results. In the economic sphere, JFK's advisers, more vigorously than the Eisenhower Republicans, embraced the interventionist New Deal model of federal activism. The most powerful figure in shaping economic policy was Walter Heller, chairman of the Council of Economic Advisers (CEA). A University of Minnesota economist, Heller had advised Hubert Humphrey. Heller and the CEA argued that the government should use its full fiscal powers to fight recessions, control inflation, and stimulate economic growth—in short, to fulfill Kennedy's campaign pledge to "get the country moving again." Heller endorsed the activist model of government intervention first formulated by John Maynard Keynes, and even more than most Keynesians he was prepared to accept federal budget deficits as a price of economic growth.

As a senator, Kennedy had been an economic conservative, suspicious of governmental intervention in the economy. Heller converted him to Keynesian thinking: the promotion of economic growth through federal tax and spending policies. The Roosevelt administration, despite FDR's lack of sympathy for Keynes's ideas, had adopted a de facto Keynesian approach with its heavy spending during World War II. In the Truman era, Leon Keyserling, CEA head, had tried to push Keynesian strategies. But it was in 1961–1963, when Kennedy made economic growth a top priority, that Keynesianism won broad acceptance in the White House. Guided by Heller and the CEA, Kennedy fought the recession of 1960–1961 with increased federal spending. At his request, Congress extended eligibility for unemployment compensation, raised the minimum wage, broadened Social Security benefits, increased the defense budget by almost 20 percent, and approved over $4 billion in long-term spending on federally financed housing. The Area Redevelopment Act authorized the secretary of labor to identify economically "distressed areas," which would become eligible for federal aid. By the end of 1961, Labor Secretary Arthur Goldberg had designated nearly seven hundred such regions. As these programs kicked in, the recovery that had started in early 1961 gained momentum.

Three measures of 1962 further stimulated the economy. The Trade Expansion Act, which the president proposed as a way of increasing commerce with Europe, granted the White House broad powers to cut tariffs on imported goods. The Manpower Retraining Act provided some $435 million in matching grants to the states for programs to retrain workers who had lost their jobs to automation. Finally, the administration-sponsored Revenue Act of 1962 granted $1 billion in tax breaks to business, in the form of investment credits and broadened depreciation allowances, to stimulate corporate spending on new machinery, factories, and equipment.

Kennedy's stimulus measures, including the vast increase in defense spending, gave the economy a jolt. From 1961 to 1964, the GNP grew by an annual average of 5.3 percent, a rise in productivity significantly above the 3.2 annual average of the 1950s. The unemployment rate, which stood at 6.7 percent in 1961, began a steady

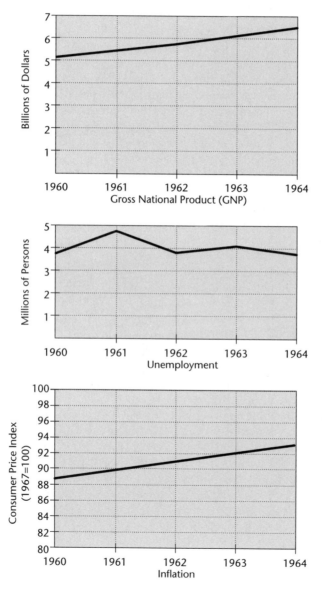

FIGURE 7.1

The Economy During the Kennedy Years

SOURCE: Statistical Abstract of the United States (1987).

decline that by 1964 had reached 5.2 percent. But with recovery came rising prices, and by 1962 inflation loomed. For the CEA, the power of large labor unions and giant corporations over wages and prices posed a major inflationary threat, which a face-off between the administration and the steel industry in 1962 dramatically underscored. That March, Kennedy and Labor Secretary Goldberg managed to avert a steel strike and encouraged the steelworkers and management to negotiate a noninflationary contract. A few weeks later, however, Roger Blough, the head of United States Steel, called at the White House and coolly informed Kennedy of a $6-a-ton price increase. The other big steel companies quickly followed suit. This inflationary action, which Kennedy found especially galling after persuading the steelworkers not to strike for higher wages, infuriated the president. "My father always told me that all businessmen were sons-of-bitches," he fumed, "but I never believed it until now." When the Defense Department announced that no contracts would go to steel companies that raised their prices, the industry giants backed down.

The showdown with the steel industry, together with lawsuits against the General Electric Company for price fixing, turned most business leaders against Kennedy. In a 1962 survey of six thousand business executives, 52 percent rated the administration "strongly anti-business," and 36 percent deemed it "moderately anti-business." In fact, the administration had compiled a probusiness record, with its tax-credit plan to promote investment, its trade-reform bill, and its support for a private communications-satellite corporation, a plan strongly backed by the American Telephone and Telegraph Company.

Despite a number of important initiatives, Kennedy's domestic record reflected more promise than achievement. Democrats controlled both houses of Congress, but a working alliance of Republicans and conservative southern Democrats still fighting the New Deal stymied many of JFK's proposals. The Democratic congressional leadership, weakened by Lyndon Johnson's elevation to the vice presidency, eroded further in 1961 with the death of the near-legendary Sam Rayburn, who with two brief interruptions had served as Speaker of the House since 1940.

All these obstacles impeded Kennedy's domestic program: Of twenty-three bills that he submitted in his early months in office, only seven were enacted. The administration's health-care plan for the elderly, for example, roused the ire of the American Medical Association (AMA). Having battled Truman over this issue, the AMA now fought Kennedy's proposals. As key Democrats in the House and Senate also opposed the bill, it languished.

A White House proposal for federal aid to education, introduced in 1961 and again in 1962, met the same fate after being whiplashed by complex political crosscurrents. Catholic leaders argued that such aid should go to parochial schools as well as to public schools, but Kennedy, unwilling to appear as yielding to church pressure, refused to concede this point. Southern legislators, meanwhile, saw the education bill as a tactic to force integration, and some civil-rights leaders, including New York congressman Adam Clayton Powell, refused to support any bill that did not explicitly exclude segregated schools.

Other administration proposals, including ideas for medical-education assistance, immigration reform, help for migrant workers, federal aid to mass transit, and a department of urban and housing affairs, received an equally cool reception. Like

President Truman, Kennedy placed many reform ideas on the national agenda but saw few of them translated into law.

In a rare domestic success, JFK managed to stimulate the space program. The technological race with the Soviets stirred the president's competitive juices, particularly when Moscow capped a series of triumphs by orbiting cosmonaut Yuri Gagarin around the earth in 1961. In answer, the United States had produced only a short suborbital flight from Cape Canaveral, Florida. Prodded by Kennedy, Congress doubled the budget of the National Aeronautics and Space Administration (NASA) and approved a plan to put an American on the moon by 1970. The program, Project Apollo, received a boost in February 1962 when astronaut John Glenn became the first American to orbit the earth. On July 20, 1969, beating Kennedy's deadline by five months, Neil Armstrong would become the first human being to set foot on the moon. In a related 1962 program, Congress at Kennedy's initiative passed the Communications Satellite Act, which set up a private corporation to develop, finance, and operate a system of telecommunications satellites. The first Telstar satellite, orbited by the American Telephone and Telegraph Company in 1962 using a government-furnished rocket, proved the forerunner of a global system of instantaneous telephone and television transmissions. Along with promoting world communications, the space program rebuilt confidence in U.S. technological know-how and opened a new arena for the arms race. As roving satellites sent back breathtaking images of Earth, they also dramatized humanity's common fate. Some critics charged, however, that the billions spent on space research would be better channeled to urgent social needs.

The space program, the economic recovery, the successful outcome of the Cuban

The romance of space. Astronaut John Glenn, the first American to orbit the globe, gives a thumbs-up before liftoff on February 20, 1962. Reflected in his suit is back-up astronaut Scott Carpenter. (*NASA*)

missile crisis, and Kennedy's general aura of activism all aided the Democrats in the 1962 midterm elections. Kennedy campaigned vigorously, with gratifying results. Reversing the usual midterm pattern, the Democrats increased their Senate margin by four seats and held their House losses to a minimum. In 1963, looking ahead to 1964, Kennedy pushed his domestic program enthusiastically but again with scant results. Introducing a theme that his successor would pick up and amplify, Kennedy urged an "unconditional war on poverty," yet his efforts failed to produce legislation.

Kennedy's most innovative fiscal-policy initiative, which he would not live to see enacted, came early in 1963. Troubled by a dip in the annual growth rate to only 3.6 percent in the summer of 1962, well behind Western Europe's progress, and by hints of another recession, Walter Heller and the CEA urged a major tax cut to stimulate business investment and productivity. In August JFK announced on television that in January 1963 he would ask the new Congress for a $10 billion, two-year cut without a corresponding slash in spending. Openly embracing Keynesianism, Kennedy used charts and anecdotes to show how a tax cut would promote economic growth. The resulting boom would increase tax revenues despite lower rates, he insisted, thereby avoiding the drastic budget deficit that a cut would normally cause. In 1980, when President Ronald Reagan argued for a substantial tax reduction, and minimized its effects on the federal deficit, on precisely the same grounds, Democrats ridiculed "Reaganomics." Yet it was a liberal Democrat, John Kennedy, who first proposed to jump-start the economy by this means.

The president soon got cold feet, however. Powerful Democrats in Congress proved skeptical, and influential figures in the administration favored higher government spending rather than reduced revenues. Even some liberal economists who praised Kennedy's conversion to Keynesianism did not share Heller's enthusiasm. Leon Keyserling criticized the proposed cut as unfairly tilted toward the well-to-do. The wealthiest 12 percent of taxpayers, he calculated, would get 45 percent of the cut.* Worse, the CEA soon projected deficits far higher than those that Kennedy had anticipated in his August 1962 speech. The president nevertheless introduced the bill as promised in January 1963, although he spread the cut over three years rather than two. The measure finally passed the House in September 1963 but stalled in the Senate. The speech that JFK was scheduled to deliver on November 22, 1963, to a Dallas business group was intended to argue again for deficit financing.

Kennedy's domestic program stood largely unrealized at the time of his death in November 1963. He had offered the sketchy outlines of a new liberal agenda but never brought it to fruition. His major achievement centered on economic policy, especially his open embrace of Keynesian principles. Thanks in part to JFK's initiatives, even a conservative president such as Richard Nixon later could assert, "We are all Keynesians now."

Kennedy's failure to cultivate close relations with Congress, even during his years on Capitol Hill, had hampered his efforts to enact his programs. In this respect, his successor, a master of manipulating the springs and levers of congressional power, would prove far more effective.

---

* In the 1980s and 1990s, with the shoe on the other foot, Democrats would lambast a similar strategy of the Reagan and Bush administrations as "trickle-down economics."

LBJ: The Making of a President

Lyndon Baines Johnson was born in 1908 in Stonewall, Texas, the eldest child of Sam and Rebecca Baines Johnson. Sam worked at various pursuits, from ranching to real estate to school teaching, with little success, and served several terms in the Texas state legislature. Rebecca, whose grandfather had founded Baylor University, harbored great hopes for Lyndon; through her encouragement he graduated from Southwest Texas State Teachers' College in nearby San Marcos. As a campus debater and student politician, he already exhibited the skills that he would later hone to a fine art. After a brief stint of schoolteaching, he took a job in Washington, D.C., in 1931 as clerk to a Texas congressman. Except for brief intervals, he would remain in Washington for the next thirty-eight years.

In 1935 Johnson's political contacts with Sam Rayburn and other powerful legislators gained him appointment as Texas director of the National Youth Administration, a New Deal agency. Two years later, he won a special election to Congress when the incumbent died in office. Johnson enormously admired Franklin Roosevelt, whom he described as "like a daddy to me." For Johnson, the New Deal became the model of activist, reform government at its best. He styled himself "LBJ," in imitation of Roosevelt's "FDR." He lost a Senate race in 1941, served as a lieutenant commander in the navy, and in 1948 went to the Senate in an election so close that it earned him the derisive nickname "Landslide Lyndon." Ballot-box stuffing by Johnson operatives in the tiny town of Alice, Texas, had put him over the top by eighty-seven votes.

Johnson quickly mastered the mechanisms of power in the Senate. In 1953 his Democratic colleagues chose him as minority leader; two year later he became majority leader. He worked closely with the Eisenhower administration, playing a key role in the passage of the Civil Rights Act of 1957, for example, while remaining a highly partisan Democrat. Indeed, as a central figure in shaping the Highway Act of 1956, the 1958 National Defense Education Act, and other measures, he helped to set the liberal agenda in the era of the Cold War. He once summed up the art of political bargaining this way: "Before you do anything, your last thought ought to be 'I've got to live with the son-of-a-bitch.'" Surviving a near-fatal heart attack in 1955, Johnson sought the Democratic nomination in 1960 and grudgingly took second place on the ticket when Kennedy offered it.

A tall, physically imposing man characterized by a large nose and ears, earthy language, a vast capacity for scotch whisky, and calculated crudity, Johnson overwhelmed those from whom he wanted a favor; no one subjected to the famous "Johnson treatment" ever forgot it. He made promises, turned on the charm, called in old debts, scratched backs and rolled logs with a master's touch, bullied and blustered where necessary, and in general wore down opposition by the sheer force of his personality. Images of tornados and volcanos came to mind when associates tried to describe his style. He often met with aides in his bedroom, while seated on the toilet, or even while swimming naked in the White House pool.

A man of enormous ambition, LBJ often resorted to crass manipulation. In 1965, eager to put his friend Abe Fortas on the Supreme Court, he persuaded the talented Arthur Goldberg, a Kennedy appointee, to leave the Court, offering vague promises of future preferment that went largely unfulfilled. The nation's loss of Goldberg's service as a Supreme Court justice was serious. Johnson's many petty slights toward Hubert Humphrey, his vice president from 1965 on, left Humphrey deeply embittered. After LBJ's death in 1973, journalist Robert Caro launched a massive, multivolume biography portraying him as virtually a monster of ego. Johnson, Caro concluded, "displayed a genius for discerning a path to power, an utter ruthlessness in destroying obstacles in that path, and a seemingly bottomless capacity for deceit, deception and betrayal in moving along it." Johnson's press secretary, George Reedy, similarly minced no words in portraying LBJ as brutally selfish, insensitive, and exploitive. "There was no sense in which he could be described as a pleasant man," Reedy wrote. "His manners were atrocious—not just slovenly but frequently *calculated* to give offense."

These accounts capture part of the truth of this larger-than-life character but fail to explain how Johnson managed, over the course of a long career, to inspire loyalty in scores of people who willingly overlooked his faults. A comment by George Reedy provides one clue. Conceding all of Johnson's flaws, Reedy also noted that LBJ at times would "do something so magnificent that all of his nasty characteristics would fade. . . . He was a tremendous figure—a combination of complexities and simplicities that bewildered all observers."

Johnson's wife, Claudia, known from childhood as Lady Bird, played a vital role in his career. An accomplished, strong-willed woman with a journalism degree from the University of Texas, Mrs. Johnson promoted her husband's efforts while pursuing her own interests. With piercing eyes, jet black hair, and a wide Texas smile, Lady Bird Johnson possessed a razor-sharp mind, political instincts equal to her husband's, and a commitment to public service that outmatched his. She managed his congressional office during his navy service and oversaw the family's financial interests in Texas, which eventually included real estate, ranch lands, and an Austin radio station and television channel. During the White House years, she exerted strong influence behind the scenes, especially on environmental issues.

This, then, was the man who ascended to the presidency on November 22, 1963. A somber and shaken Johnson exhibited a quiet dignity in the traumatic days following Kennedy's assassination. Addressing Congress on November 26, he pledged to carry on the slain president's agenda. Echoing JFK's clipped inaugural exhortation "Let us begin," Johnson intoned in his Texas twang, "Let us contin-yah."

The Apex of a Liberal Agenda: The War on Poverty

As Johnson took office, he stressed continuity, asking the Kennedy cabinet and top advisers to stay on. Most did, although many resented him as a usurper in Camelot. Johnson channeled the nation's grief into support for the slain president's legislative program and for major proposals of his own. He pushed through a number of key measures on the Kennedy agenda, including the civil-rights bill that JFK had introduced in 1963 (see Chapter 8). Early in 1964, Congress at Johnson's initiative also enacted the Kennedy tax-cut plan. A steady economic boom seemed to validate the wisdom of this pump-priming measure. Indeed, the nation's GNP rose from $591 billion in 1963 to $977 billion in 1970. Not content merely to be the president who completed the Kennedy agenda, however, Johnson sought a program that would bear his personal brand. He found it initially in the War on Poverty.

Even liberal social thinkers of the 1950s had downplayed poverty as a social issue. Galbraith in *The Affluent Society* admitted that it still existed but "more nearly as an afterthought" than as a "massive affliction." Michael Harrington's *The Other America: Poverty in the United States* (1963) radically challenged such perceptions. Seething with passion, Harrington documented the extent of hardship in inner cities and rural backwaters and among the neglected elderly, minorities, migrant laborers, and unskilled workers. Estimating the ranks of the poor at 40 to 50 million, Harrington argued that the problem was not simply isolated pockets of poverty but long-term, structural destitution—a vast subculture of poverty—that government must address. Introducing his study, Harrington wrote, "I would ask the reader to respond critically to every assertion, but not allow statistical quibbling to obscure the huge, enormous, and intolerable fact of poverty in America. For, when all is said and done, that fact is unmistakable, whatever its exact dimensions, and the truly human reaction can only be outrage."

Prodded by Harrington's work and by Walter Heller, John Kennedy had moved toward making this issue a major theme of his legislative program in the campaign year 1964. At a meeting on November 19, 1963, Kennedy had authorized Heller to draw up a detailed set of legislative proposals to fight poverty. President Johnson, meeting with Heller on November 23, enthusiastically endorsed this initiative. He

Haggard Hollow, Kentucky. Michael Harrington's *The Other America* (1962) explored the many faces of poverty in the United States, including that of isolated Appalachian families such as this one. (©*Charles Harbutt/Actuality, Inc.*)

knew poverty well from his Texas boyhood, and he responded instinctively to the program. Furthermore, civil-rights activists were increasingly focusing on economic issues. Indeed, one civil-rights group, the Student Non-Violent Coordinating Committee saw the economic plight of lower-class blacks, not integration, as the real issue. With more than 40 percent of African-American families earning under $3,000 a year, a program to fight poverty clearly would have major implications for black America. An antipoverty initiative, Johnson realized, provided a way to address the racial unrest stirring in the inner cities, but as part of a larger program. Legislators who might hesitate to appropriate massive funds to aid urban minorities might more readily support a broadly focused "war on poverty." Americans were accustomed to uniting in wartime, and Johnson, as he would recall in his memoirs, hoped to use the rhetoric of war "to rally the nation, to sound a call to arms which would stir people."

Cold War considerations also may have shaped Johnson's calculations. The contest with the Soviet Union increasingly had taken on economic as well as military tones. Improving the skills and employment rate of the inner-city jobless offered one way to stimulate the nation's overall economic health and thereby tout the virtues of the capitalist system. Johnson's embrace of the antipoverty cause arose, too, from his exuberant, can-do personality. America was rich enough and resourceful enough, he believed, to uplift the poor without seriously inconveniencing the well-to-do. As a British journalist commented, the antipoverty campaign was "the archetypal liberal program . . . , inspired by a characteristic blend of benevolence, optimism, innocence and chauvinism." Americans were problem solvers, and this problem, too, could be solved. As LBJ grandly put it, "We know what must be done, and this nation of abundance can surely afford it."

On January 8, 1964, Johnson called on Congress to declare an "unconditional war on poverty. . . . [W]e shall not rest until that war is won. The richest Nation on earth can afford to win it. We cannot afford to lose it." In this election year, he proposed a battery of programs and approaches to attack poverty head-on. For Kennedy's lofty rhetoric, he vowed, he would substitute action and achievement. And in the remarkable political climate of 1964–1965, he chalked up a striking string of successes.

The antipoverty package had taken shape at Johnson's Texas ranch over the 1963 Christmas vacation in the hands of a team including Walter Heller; budget director Kermit Gordon; and Jesse Kellam, a Johnson aide since the 1930s. The program that emerged incorporated poverty-fighting ideas dating from the Truman and Eisenhower eras, Kennedy-era proposals, and programs initiated by private philanthropies such as the Rockefeller Brothers Fund and the Ford Foundation. Wilbur Cohen, secretary of the Department of Health, Education and Welfare, and Francis Keppel, the U.S. commissioner of education, played key roles as well.

Johnson's omnibus antipoverty bill, the Economic Opportunity Act, passed in August 1964 after extensive hearings but with a minimum of critical scrutiny. As one Republican complained, to criticize the program was to put oneself "under the suspicion of being in favor of poverty." In a shrewd move, Johnson had chosen a southern conservative, Phil Landrum of Georgia, as the bill's House floor manager, thereby blunting southern opposition. Nevertheless, many conservative Republicans

and southern Democrats remained unconvinced. The final vote on the measure—
226–185 in the House, 61–34 in the Senate—reflected this uncertainty.

The Economic Opportunity Act comprised ten major components. A key section expanded the 1962 Manpower Development and Training Act and focused it on job training of the poor. The new law created the Job Corps to teach marketable skills to unemployed inner-city youth. Volunteers in Service to America (VISTA), a domestic parallel of the Peace Corps, recruited middle-class volunteers to work on programs in inner cities, rural communities, and other low-income areas. The most innovative of the antipoverty measures, Head Start, offered basic-skills training to preschool youngsters. The Upward Bound program helped gifted students from poor families to go to college. Other antipoverty measures funded public-works projects in poor areas and loans for small businesses and needy small farmers. The law also created the Office of Economic Opportunity (OEO) as command center of the antipoverty battle. To head OEO, Johnson chose Peace Corps director R. Sargent Shriver, the husband of John Kennedy's sister Eunice. Shriver had absorbed the Kennedy clan's drive, competitiveness, and zest for politics, and he brought these traits to his new post.

Despite the ambitious scope of the antipoverty war and the fanfare that accompanied its launching, the first-year funding proved modest: $500 million in new money and $462 million from funds already budgeted. Opponents had managed to keep a tight lid on the money. Later appropriations would increase somewhat but never really match the sweeping goals that Johnson had laid out. Furthermore, the funds were divided among numerous programs, diminishing their effect even more.

The program's basic approach proved far from radical. Its framers never proposed to challenge the nation's basic socioeconomic structure by redistributing wealth and power on a massive scale. As a member of the CEA wrote to Walter Heller, "Probably a politically acceptable program must avoid completely the use of the term . . . 'redistribution' of income or wealth." Nor did the architects of the War on Poverty propose direct income transfers—payments to bring all Americans up to a minimal income level. Instead, they chose a different strategy. Their approach, implicit in the title Economic *Opportunity* Act, aimed to provide education, skills training, employment opportunities, and an aura of hope and motivation, so that everyone who wished a decent job could get one. In the phrase of the day, they favored "a 'hand up,' not a 'hand-out.'" Despite later criticism to the contrary, the aim was not welfare but helping the poor to become self-sufficient. As Johnson asserted on signing the bill, "The days of the dole in this country are numbered." This basic objective gave an underlying coherence to the War on Poverty's diverse programs.

The Economic Opportunity Act's most controversial section was the Community Action Program (CAP), a plan based on a Ford Foundation project of the 1950s. It authorized local antipoverty programs involving the "maximum feasible participation" of local community members and allocated $300 million for the purpose. The CAP initiative reflected the view of some analysts that social-policy formulation had become top-heavy with experts and bureaucrats and needed grass-roots input. As a 1965 *Community Action Workbook* issued by Shriver's office stated, the CAP program sought to empower the poor so they could challenge the more "politically effective sectors of society."

Advocates of the CAP approach hoped that community groups in poor districts would arise to coordinate OEO programs and develop local antipoverty initiatives. Their goal was to stimulate political activism and collective effort among the poor themselves. And indeed, by 1966 more than a thousand CAPs were functioning in cities across the country. The program led to unexpected consequences. In Chicago, for example, Mayor Daley's lieutenants simply commandeered it and operated it as an adjunct of the Daley machine. In some big-city ghettos, radical black activists dominated the CAPs. More typically, however, local CAPs were led neither by the poor nor by machine politicians but by local middle-class, college-trained advocates skilled at the politics of poverty. These CAP activists typically decried the local power structure—city government, welfare agencies, school boards, the police, private charities—which they dismissed as more interested in keeping the poor pacified than in real reform. Local CAP activists formed tenant unions, used public funds to bail out demonstrators arrested in protest actions, and organized voter-registration campaigns aimed at throwing out elected city officials.

The OEO's apparent call to class conflict alarmed the establishment. Democratic officials groused that a Democratic-sponsored program was muscling them aside. Baltimore mayor Theodore Roosevelt McKeldin, a liberal Republican, complained to the president about CAP hotheads "who do not understand the problems and operations of local governments." When Johnson learned that a CAP group in Washington, D.C., was attacking local Democratic leaders, he dashed off a note to his aide Bill Moyers: "For God's sake get on top of this and put a stop to it at once." But the turmoil persisted. At a 1966 Washington conference of the Citizens Crusade Against Poverty, a major advocacy group, Sargent Shriver was shouted off the stage, and a succession of militants took the platform to denounce one aspect or another of the antipoverty program.

CAP became a prime target of critics of the War on Poverty. In 1969, when the political climate had turned chilly toward reform, President Nixon's urban affairs adviser, Daniel Moynihan, attacked LBJ's plan in a book called *Maximum Feasible Misunderstanding*. Singling out the CAP initiative for special scorn, Moynihan dismissed it as the brainchild of befuddled liberals who little understood the real world of politics and power. CAPs, he charged, had functioned mainly as a welfare program for the middle-class activists who ran them. Given American political realities in the 1960s, Moynihan had a point. The ideology of the War on Poverty, emphasizing expanded individual opportunity through job training and education, had been carefully devised to appeal to moderates. The Community Action Programs, in encouraging collective action by the poor themselves, ultimately would rouse warning bells and bring discredit to the entire effort. As the 1964 election neared, however, few anticipated the intensity of these controversies.

Election 1964: Liberalism Triumphant

Riding a wave of liberal support for the War on Poverty and bathed in JFK's lingering aura, Johnson seemed a shoo-in for the 1964 Democratic nomination. At the party's Atlantic City convention, after a bitter dispute over the make-up of the Mississippi delegation (see Chapter 8), Johnson won the nomination by acclamation. As his running mate, he chose Hubert Humphrey, the party's most outspoken champion of civil rights and of old-fashioned, New Deal liberalism.

LBJ's giant presence dominated the proceedings. Journalist Loudon Wainwright, who covered the event for *Life*, marveled:

> I had the feeling . . . that this was not a convention at all, [but] rather a party being thrown by the President in celebration of himself. The delegates, the visitors in the hall, the press, the television audience—we were all *his* guests. The convention wasn't giving him anything; he was giving the delegates the opportunity to share his wholehearted enthusiasm for his leadership and his vision. Like a good host, or perhaps more correctly a good emperor, he thanked his subjects for coming, praised their little acts of fealty, and then said how things were going to be.

The Republicans, meanwhile, had lurched sharply rightward. The party's moderate eastern wing, in control since 1940 when it ran Wendell Willkie against FDR, failed to produce a candidate who had the appeal of an Eisenhower. With Richard Nixon biding his time after defeats in 1960 and 1962, the party's right wing reasserted its power. Abetted by William Buckley's conservative journal, *National Review*, conservative radio commentators, and Far-Right organizations such as the John Birch Society, the Republican Right had steadily gained strength among conservatives disturbed by the welfare state and by the civil-rights movement and intent on escalating the global crusade against communism.

Right-wing activists rallied around Senator Barry Goldwater of Arizona, an air-force reservist and heir to a department-store fortune. Goldwater's 1960 book, *The Conscience of a Conservative*, ghostwritten like Kennedy's *Profiles in Courage*, accurately summed up his creed: aggressive pursuit of the Cold War, untrammeled free enterprise, and a dismantling of character-sapping welfare programs such as Social Security. As a senator, Goldwater had praised Joe McCarthy's crusade against the reds, and now in 1964, emulating McCarthy, he again hurled the tired "soft on communism" charge at the Democrats.

Defeating New York governor Nelson Rockefeller, the moderates' hope, in the crucial California primary, Goldwater handily won the nomination at the party convention in San Francisco. He even welcomed the "extremist" label slapped on him by critics. "Extremism in the defense of liberty is no vice," he orated. "Moderation in the pursuit of justice is no virtue." GOP campaign posters offered voters "A Choice, Not an Echo" and asserted of Goldwater, "In Your Heart You Know He's Right." (Democrats retorted, "In Your Guts You Know He's Nuts.") Many citizens who backed Johnson as the "peace candidate" in 1964 would soon regret their choice. But at the time, most voters preferred him to Goldwater, who openly advocated a wider war in Vietnam and who cavalierly spoke of "lobbing one [a nuclear bomb] into the men's room of the Kremlin."

Capitalizing on Goldwater's narrow appeal, LBJ cast his campaign as a big tent and invited all Americans to gather inside. Downplaying divisive issues, he sought votes from business and labor, farmers and city dwellers, and all racial and ethnic constituencies. "The farmer in Iowa, the fisherman in Massachusetts, the worker in Seattle, the rancher in Texas," the president asserted, "have the same hopes and

President Johnson presses the flesh. LBJ's War on Poverty and Great Society programs, together with his strong support for civil rights, seemed to assure him a stunningly successful presidency. Unfortunately, the Vietnam War would soon intervene. (*Frank V. Voire/LBJ LIbrary Collection*)

harbor the same fears. . . . This is the real voice of America. It is one of the great tasks of political leadership to make people aware of this voice, aware that they share a fundamental unity of interest, purpose and belief." The unity theme of Johnson's 1964 campaign takes on special poignancy as one reflects on the conflict and polarization that would plague the end of his term.

The 1964 presidential race, far more than in 1960, highlighted domestic issues. Nevertheless, America's deepening military engagement in Vietnam colored the contest. Whereas Goldwater advocated bombing North Vietnam and using tactical nuclear weapons on the battlefield, LBJ held himself up as the peace candidate. He would not send American boys into any foreign war, he pledged, echoing Franklin Roosevelt in 1940. A *Time* cover story focused on "The Nuclear Issue," and a frightening Democratic TV commercial came close to predicting nuclear holocaust if Goldwater prevailed.

Johnson scored a landslide victory. His role as Kennedy's heir and his advocacy of civil rights and domestic reform, together with fear of Goldwater, brought him an overwhelming 61.1 percent of the vote, more than even Franklin Roosevelt's lopsided victory in 1936. The electoral tally stood at 486 to 52. No longer the accidental president, LBJ had won a tremendous personal endorsement. The Democrats' margin in the House widened by thirty-eight seats and in the Senate by two seats. The southern political realignment launched by Dwight Eisenhower continued, however: Of the six states that Goldwater carried, all except for Arizona lay in the Deep South. He might have made even greater southern inroads had not Mrs. Johnson, evoking memories of Harry Truman in 1948, toured the region by rail on the

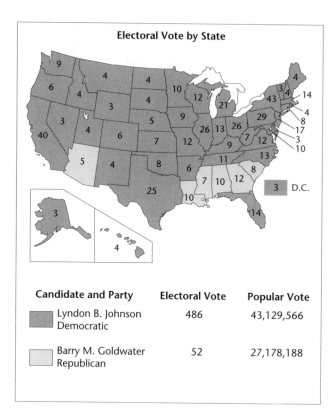

Electoral Vote by State

FIGURE 7.2

Presidential Election of 1964

Candidate and Party	Electoral Vote	Popular Vote
Lyndon B. Johnson Democratic	486	43,129,566
Barry M. Goldwater Republican	52	27,178,188

"Lady Bird Special." But if some southern white voters abandoned LBJ because of his identification with civil rights, black votes more than balanced the defections. Six million African-Americans cast ballots in 1964—a third more than in 1960—and an astounding 94 percent of them voted for the Johnson-Humphrey ticket. Blacks provided the victory margin in Arkansas, Florida, Tennessee, and Virginia.

The Politics of Hope: Johnson's Great Society

While pursuing Kennedy's legislative program, promoting the War on Poverty, and shepherding a major civil-rights bill through Congress, President Johnson had also laid out a still more grandiose reform agenda. As early as May 1964, in a commencement address at the University of Michigan, LBJ had limned an inspiring picture of America as a "Great Society." To intoxicating waves of applause, he had poured out a cornucopia of social goals. Better schools, better health, better cities, safer highways, a more beautiful nation, support for the arts—Johnson's dream for America knew few bounds.

After his 1964 electoral triumph, the president fleshed out his Great Society vision. In his State of the Union message on January 4, 1965, and again in his inaugural address on January 20, he proposed a list of reforms drawn from Truman's Fair Deal, earlier Kennedy proposals, and ideas current among social reformers. "Hurry, boys, hurry," he urged his aides. "Get that legislation up to the Hill and out. Eighteen months from now, Ol' Landslide Lyndon will be lame-duck Lyndon." The heavily Democratic Congress hastily passed a dizzying array of laws intended to improve the lives of millions of Americans. Congress doubled the funding for the antipoverty program and in the Appalachian Regional Development Act appropriated $1.1 billion for public-works projects, rural health centers, and other programs in this chronically depressed region.

Yet the heart of the Great Society program lay in measures to improve cities, education, and health care. In his "Message on the Cities," Johnson informed Congress and the nation:

> Within the borders of our urban centers can be found the most impressive examples of man's skill . . . as well as the worst examples of degradation and cruelty and misery. . . . Our task must be to put the highest concerns of our people at the center of urban growth and activity. . . . The modern city can be the most ruthless enemy of the good life, or it can be its servant.

Congress rose to the challenge. The Housing and Urban Development Act of 1965 offered reduced interest rates to builders of housing for the poor and elderly. It also allocated funds for urban beautification, health programs, recreation centers, repairs on inner-city housing, and a rent-supplement program for the poor. In an important innovation, this law mandated that all applications for federal aid to cities be approved by citywide or regional planning agencies, to bypass competition among various and perhaps overlapping programs. Enacting a proposal first advanced by JFK, Congress in 1965 also created a new cabinet-level agency, the Department of Housing and Urban Development, to administer the new urban programs.

Attention to cities required attention to transportation. The 1950s highway program, for all its benefits, had hastened the decline of public-transit systems, thereby worsening urban traffic congestion and destroying inner-city neighborhoods. In 1964, conceding these problems, Congress granted some $375 million for urban mass-transit planning. The Urban Mass Transportation Act of 1966 allocated more funds for this purpose and created a new agency, the Department of Transportation, to administer them.

Another important urban-development measure, the Model Cities Act of 1966, granted $1.2 billion for slum clearance and renewal. The aim was no less than to revitalize all aspects of inner-city life, from housing and schools to health care, job training, and recreation. The law provided funds for new model communities, reflecting the deep-rooted utopian strand in American social thought. This sweeping approach to the problems of the city represented the Great Society vision at its loftiest.

Convening the White House Conference on Education in 1965, LBJ proclaimed that every child in America "must have the best education our nation can provide." In this spirit, the 1965 Elementary and Secondary Education Act (ESEA) directed over $1 billion for programs to aid "educationally deprived children." Much of this money went to public and private schools in urban slums, but the bill also targeted bilingual education in Hispanic districts and education of the mentally and physically disabled. With this infusion of federal dollars, inner-city and rural schools and institutions serving children with special needs expanded, hired more teachers and aides, and developed new programs. Demonstrating his flair for the dramatic, Johnson in 1966 flew to Cotulla, Texas, to deliver, under the adoring gaze of an aged former teacher, an education speech in the schoolhouse that he had attended as a lad.

Although billed as part of the War on Poverty, ESEA also channeled vast federal sums to support general public-education programs and facilities. In securing its passage, LBJ, again demonstrating his political genius, overcame the divisive issues of race, region, religion, and constitutional scruples that had long blocked federal support for public education.

The Higher Education Act, also passed in that *annus mirabilis* 1965, created a federal scholarship and low-interest-loan program for needy college students and provided library grants to colleges and universities. Public-education funding, as well as policymaking, once exclusively a state and local matter, grew increasingly dependent on Washington. In 1965 federal spending on all levels of education topped $4 billion; it would rise higher still in future years. Liberals hailed this trend as a national investment in the younger generation; conservatives worried that with expanded federal funding would come growing federal control.

The capacious "big tent" motif of LBJ's 1964 electoral campaign found legislative expression in the Immigration Act of 1965, which Johnson warmly supported. This measure eliminated the discriminatory quotas against certain national groups that had been written into the nation's immigration law in 1924 and reaffirmed in the McCarran-Walter Act of 1952. The new law opened the door to an increased flow of immigrants from Asia and Latin America that would profoundly affect American life in the decades ahead.

Johnson scored his most historic achievement in health care when Congress in 1965 enacted his Medicare bill providing health insurance for all Americans over age sixty-five. Initially funded with a $6.5 billion appropriation, Medicare's long-range funding came from increased Social Security payroll deductions. The plan covered most hospital expenses, diagnostic tests, home visits, and some nursing-home costs. A voluntary supplemental program, financed jointly by the government and by contributions from individual participants, covered other medical expenses, such as visits to physicians' offices. To supply the additional medical personnel needed for this expanded health-care program, Congress voted funds for nursing schools, medical schools, and medical-student scholarships. Medicaid, a key section of the law little noticed at the time, provided grants to the states to cover medical care for the poor of all ages. The American Medical Association's dire warnings against "socialized medicine," potent in the conservative 1950s, proved less effective in the reform climate of 1965. LBJ signed the Medicare bill in Independence, Missouri, as a beaming eighty-one-year-old Harry Truman, who had proposed such a measure twenty years earlier, looked on.*

---

* Ironically, Johnson as a freshman senator from conservative Texas had not supported the national health-insurance component of Truman's 1949 Fair Deal program.

FOCUS ON: *THE HEALTH-CARE HEADACHE*

The Medicare law of 1965 was a major step—but only a step—in a long and acrimonious process of defining Washington's role in the U.S. health-care system. This process began after the Civil War, when Congress authorized a network of hospitals for disabled Union veterans. The system of federally funded medical facilities steadily expanded in the twentieth century to serve veterans of World War I, World War II, and later conflicts.

Efforts to extend the government's health-care role further met bitter opposition from the medical profession. The Sheppard-Towner Act of 1921 appropriated $1.2 million for rural prenatal and infant-care centers run by public-health nurses. However, the male-dominated American Medical Association (AMA) objected to this infringement on its monopoly, and Congress killed the program in 1929. Efforts to include health insurance in the Social Security Act of 1935 failed in the face of opposition from the AMA and private insurers. President Truman proposed a comprehensive medical-insurance plan to Congress in 1945, but the AMA again fought back, stigmatizing the plan as an encroaching wedge of "socialized medicine."

Medicare and Medicaid, which provide health insurance for the elderly, disabled, and poor, broke this logjam. Nevertheless, lobbyists for the AMA, hospitals, and private insurance companies succeeded in limiting Washington's function to that of bill-payer, with no role in shaping the health-care system or, most important, in containing costs. The new programs assured millions of Americans better health care, but they proved very expensive. From 1970 to 1990, Medicare costs ballooned from $7.6 billion to $111 billion, and Medicaid from $6.3 billion to $79 billion. As the population aged, long-term care for the elderly became an especially pricey component of Medicare.

Rising costs made up only part of a larger tangle of problems. While America boasted the world's best health care, its benefits were unevenly distributed. Inner-city minorities and rural communities often lacked adequate care. Life expectancy, infant mortality, and other health indexes varied significantly along racial, regional, and income lines. The 1989 infant-mortality rate, for example, stood at 8.2 per 1,000 live births for whites and 17.7 for blacks. Although many workers belonged to prepaid health systems, millions of Americans lacked health insurance.

Despite such inequities, soaring costs remained at the center of the debate. The proportion of the GNP spent on health care jumped from 5.3 percent in 1960 to 14 percent in 1993. In the 1980s, health costs rose twice as fast as the general price index. A resentful public blamed "greedy doctors," but the problem had complex sources. Breakthrough scientific discoveries; exotic new drugs such as tacrine, which improves cognition in some Alzheimer's patients; and new procedures such as an-

The influx of federal dollars stimulated by this legislation generated explosive growth in the health-care and nursing-home industries. By the 1990s, soaring Medicare and Medicaid costs would contribute mightily to a staggering burden of public debt. In the optimistic summer of 1965, however, questions of long-range cost rarely shadowed liberal reformers' triumphant mood.

gioplasty, kidney dialysis, hip replacement, organ transplants, coronary bypass, and magnetic resonance imaging scanners could work medical wonders but at a staggering cost. Indeed, some analysts saw the alleged "cost crisis" in U.S. medicine as stemming from a rational choice by a rich society to absorb the massive expense of new technologies and basic research. The AIDS epidemic, further straining an already floundering health-care system, exacerbated the sense of crisis.

While technology advanced, the human side of health care seemed to wither. Patient dissatisfaction contributed to an epidemic of malpractice suits, which pushed medical costs still higher. The modern physician, observed a medical sociologist in 1991, is no longer typically perceived as a dedicated healer but as "uncaring, uncommunicative, self-interested, and ambitious."

Bill Clinton highlighted this complex "health crisis" in his 1992 campaign, stressing cost containment as crucial to reducing the federal deficit. Once elected, Clinton named his wife, Hillary Rodham Clinton, to head a task force on health policy. As in the past, sharp differences divided the key players: the AMA, hospitals, drug firms, nursing homes, insurance companies, consumer advocates, retirees, spokespersons for the poor, and private prepaid systems. Whereas some participants in the debate favored allowing market forces broad latitude under a system of "managed competition," others advocated strict cost controls and a closely regulated system. Still others warned that regulating costs would inhibit research. Physicians in private practice balked at the income loss that they foresaw if they joined a prepaid plan. Oregon health officials proposed to "prioritize" (that is, ration) expensive medical procedures for Medicaid recipients, but many recoiled from such a concept. Still others favored less emphasis on technology and eleventh-hour heroics and more on preventive measures such as exercise, diet, and regular check-ups and on factors such as tobacco, alcohol, pollution, and poverty that clearly impinge on health.

The health-care debate swirls around fundamental issues of ethics and public policy. Modern medicine achieves results unthinkable a few decades ago, curing oncelethal illnesses and granting men and women vigorous life into their eighties and even their nineties. In coming years, the number and effectiveness of such tests, procedures, and technologies will surely multiply. Yet at what cost? Is everyone to have access to all available treatment, regardless of the expense or the odds of success? Clearly one doesn't weigh the life of one's child or aged parent by the same cost-benefit calculations that one uses to decide whether to repair an old car. Yet as health care becomes an entitlement, funded by resources allocated by the political process, some system for making heart-wrenching decisions will have to be devised.

In short, the launching of Medicare and Medicaid in 1965, important as they were, represented only a breathing space in an ongoing national debate. As Americans focus on domestic issues in the 1990s, health care promises to remain high on the agenda.

While President Johnson rallied the forces of liberalism from the Oval Office, the Supreme Court contributed to the renewal and reassertion of liberalism by maintaining the activist course set by Earl Warren, appointed chief justice by President Eisenhower in 1953. Having spurred the modern civil-rights movement in 1954 with *Brown* v. *Board of Education*, the Court in a series of landmark rulings in the 1960s

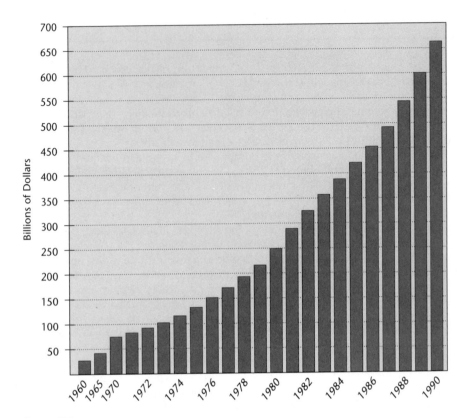

FIGURE 7.3

Total Spending on Health Care, 1960–1990

SOURCE: Department of Health and Human Services.

broke new ground in the areas of individual rights, electoral reform, and equal protection under the law, despite some warnings that the Court was moving into areas more properly left to the legislative process. Warren's closest allies in these endeavors were two FDR appointees, Hugo Black and William O. Douglas, and William J. Brennan, Jr., appointed by Dwight Eisenhower in 1956.

Seeking to give all citizens an equal voice at the polls, a Court majority in *Baker* v. *Carr* (1962) held that states must, "as nearly as practicable," maintain population balance in setting the bounds of congressional and state-legislature electoral districts. Turning to a particularly vulnerable group, the Supreme Court in *Gideon* v. *Wainwright* (1963) extended to the state courts the right of indigent persons to court-appointed counsel. In *Miranda* v. *Arizona* (1966), the justices mandated that all prisoners must be informed of their legal rights at the time of their arrest.

Expanding the First Amendment right of freedom of the press, the court in *New York Times* v. *Sullivan* (1964) protected newspapers from libel suits by public officials except when actual malice could be proved. In a 1966 censorship case, the court reversed a Massachusetts ban on John Cleland's erotic classic *Fanny Hill*, reaffirming a 1957 ruling (*Roth* v. *United States*) that only works "utterly without redeeming social value" could be denied First Amendment protection. In other personal-freedom cases, the Court banned school prayer as a violation of the constitutional prohibition against an establishment of religion (*Engel* v. *Vitale,* 1962) and struck down as an unwarranted invasion of privacy a Connecticut law prohibiting the use of contraceptives or the providing of contraceptive information (*Griswold* v. *Connecticut,* 1964).

These decisions reflected the outlook of an activist Court majority committed to democratic principles and to upholding individual rights against state encroachments. The same commonsense notions of fairness and equity that had underlain the *Brown* decision led the Court in new activist directions in the 1960s. When Warren retired in 1969, he left a harvest of decisions that for decades would make the Warren Court a target of both praise and denunciation. The same activism that liberals applauded dismayed conservatives, who warned of the Court's growing power and its penchant for plunging into highly controversial social issues.

The New Environmentalism

Of all the components of Johnson's domestic program, none seemed more timely a generation later than its environmentalist thrust. Environmental issues lay close to the heart of Johnson's Great Society vision. "Once our national splendor is destroyed," the president cautioned in his May 1964 Ann Arbor speech, "it can never be recaptured." Indeed, he proclaimed, "The desire for beauty and the hunger for community" were the twin impulses driving the campaign to upgrade all facets of American life.

Most at home on his ranch along the Pedernales River in the rolling Texas hill country, Johnson loved the land. Lady Bird Johnson and Interior Secretary Stewart Udall helped to translate that emotion into policy. The environmentalism that emerged in the 1960s, however, reflected not merely a few individuals' efforts but a growing national awareness that a century of industrialization had taken a dire toll: shrinking wilderness areas, vanishing wildlife species, and pollution that threatened human health and well-being.

The roots of modern environmentalism extended far into the past. As early as the Progressive era, when some reformers had campaigned to conserve natural resources to maximize their economic benefit, others had gone further and worked to preserve scenic beauty in national parks and wilderness areas. John Muir's Sierra Club (1889), for example, lobbied to save California's spectacular Yosemite Valley and other areas of great natural beauty from exploitation. Still other Progressive-era reformers had battled the environmental hazards of factory smoke, tainted milk, and filthy slaughterhouses and worked for urban beautification by establishing city parks, boulevards, flower gardens, and civic statuary.

After fading during the probusiness climate of the 1920s, environmental concerns had revived during the New Deal, only to diminish in the booming, expansionist postwar years. Aldo Leopold's *Sand County Almanac* (1948), with its ecological focus and its call for "a new land ethic," later hailed as a classic, at the time attracted little notice. In the late fifties, the mood changed once more. Galbraith in *The Afflu-*

ent *Society* wrote scathingly of environmental degradation amid the orgy of private consumption.

With the resurgence of liberalism in the 1960s, ecological concerns found a voice.* President Kennedy sent a message to Congress in February 1961 addressing environmental issues and in May 1962 convened a White House conference on the subject. Kennedy and Udall pushed for more parks, especially along the crowded eastern seaboard. The Cape Cod National Seashore was one result. But once again, although Kennedy raised the issue, Johnson scored the major achievements. From 1963 to 1968, spurred by Rachel Carson's 1963 environmentalist manifesto *Silent Spring* (see p. 231), Congress at LBJ's initiative passed nearly three hundred measures relating to conservation, beautification, and pollution and appropriated some $12 billion for these purposes.

The decade's reformers combined and modified certain traditional themes of the movement in ways that anticipated the "new environmentalism" of the seventies and beyond. Downplaying conservation, the great cause of many Progressive-era reformers, they emphasized the aesthetic and social benefits of natural beauty and the public-health hazards posed by pollution. More broadly, they insisted that environmentalism was not a fringe issue but central to the quality of human life and social well-being. Stewart Udall summed it up in 1968:

> Presidential leadership has changed the outlook of the nation with regard to conservation and has added vital "new dimensions." No longer is peripheral action—the "saving" of a forest, a park, a refuge for wildlife—isolated from the mainstream. The total environment is now the concern, and the new conservation makes man, himself, its subject. The quality of life is now the perspective and purpose of the new conservation.

Udall praised "presidential leadership," yet he himself did much to foster this new environmental awareness. After practicing law in Tucson, Udall went to Congress in 1954. He became friends with Senator Kennedy in the late 1950s when the two worked together on a labor bill, and Udall played a central role in delivering Arizona to Kennedy at the 1960 Democratic convention. Appointed secretary of the interior in 1961, Udall crafted Kennedy's conservation message of 1961 and planned the 1962 White House conference. He set forth his environmental views in an influential 1963 book, *The Quiet Crisis:*

> America today stands poised on a pinnacle of wealth and power, yet we live in a land of vanishing beauty, of increasing ugliness, of shrinking open space, and of an overall environment that is diminishing daily by pollution and noise and blight. This, in brief, is the quiet conservation crisis of the 1960s.

Continuing to serve in the cabinet until the close of Johnson's term in 1969, Udall remained an important voice on policy issues relating to conservation and the environment.

---

* The science of ecology, central to the modern environmental movement, views all life-forms of a given region, plants and animals alike, including human beings, as part of a single, complex, interdependent biological unit, or ecosystem.

From the intersection of these personal and historical factors emerged a body of law that gives Johnson an environmental record unmatched by any other president, before or since. Observers at the time correctly viewed these measures as expressions of the same Great Society impulse that produced so much landmark social legislation in other areas. Such laws reflected the authentic Johnson compulsion to seize the great issues of the day and to formulate sweeping mandates by which federal policy could address those issues.

The Wilderness Act of 1964 echoed Udall's warning that the American wilderness, once so seemingly boundless, was at risk from the advance of cities, suburbs, highways, and tourism. The culmination of a campaign launched in the 1950s by the Sierra Club and the Wilderness Society, this law set aside over 9 million acres of national forest to be preserved in their unspoiled state. A companion measure, the Wild and Scenic Rivers Act of 1968, similarly protected sections of eight rivers from developers. Other legislation responded to the threat to wildlife posed by the vanishing wilderness. The Endangered Species Act of 1966 for the first time set biodiversity as a national goal. The law did not clearly define endangered species or the procedures for protecting them, but it set an important precedent. A second measure enacted seven years later, the Endangered Species Act of 1974, proved considerably stricter and more precise.

The 1960s also focused attention on an environmental issue that would grow ever more urgent: the pollution of water, air, and land by the toxic by-products of an urban-industrial society. This concern, first voiced by Progressive-era reformers, had faded in the intervening years, but it revived strongly in the 1960s. Much of the credit goes to Rachel Carson's *Silent Spring*, published in 1963. Just as Harrington's *The Other America* had focused attention on poverty, so Carson's work dramatically thrust environmental pollution onto the national agenda.

A marine biologist with the U.S. Fish and Wildlife Service, Carson had written a best-selling collection of nature essays in 1951 called *The Sea Around Us*. She had grown increasingly alarmed by the environmental impact of DDT, the postwar wonder chemical, and other pesticides and herbicides that were draining into the nation's water system. Rather than compiling another book of nature essays, she undertook a very different and more explosive project: a carefully researched article on the dangers of pesticides. Several magazines rejected it because their food advertisers, particularly baby-food manufacturers, worried that it would cause "unwarranted fear" among consumers. The *New Yorker* eventually serialized the work, and it appeared as a book soon after. Citing the mounting evidence of the ecological dangers of DDT and other chemicals, Carson concluded somberly:

> It is not my contention that chemical insecticides must never be used. I do contend that we have put poisonous and biologically potent chemicals indiscriminately into the hands of persons largely or wholly ignorant of their potentials for harm. We have subjected enormous numbers of people to contact with these poisons, without their consent and often without their knowledge. If the Bill of Rights contains no guarantee that a citizen shall be secure against lethal poisons distributed either by private individuals or by public officials, it is surely only because our forefathers despite their considerable wisdom and foresight, could conceive of no such problem.

Carson also offered broader reflections that would make *Silent Spring* a key text of the emerging ecology movement. The vogue for DDT and similar products, she warned, was only one manifestation of a larger heedlessness regarding the environmental consequences of modern technology:

> The "control of nature" is a phrase conceived in arrogance, born of the . . . age . . . when it was supposed that nature exists for the convenience of man. The concepts and practices of applied entomology [the chemical eradication of unwanted insects] for the most part date from the Stone Age of science. It is our alarming misfortune that so primitive a science has armed itelf with the most modern and terrible weapons, and that in turning them against the insects it has also turned them against the earth.

Pesticide manufacturers mounted a massive campaign to discredit Carson as an ignorant, hysterical woman, but her scientific credentials and elaborate scholarly documentation (*Silent Spring* has fifty-five pages of citations to scientific research) gave her work impressive credibility.

Like Upton Sinclair's *The Jungle,* a 1906 exposé of filthy, rat-infested Chicago packinghouses, *Silent Spring* exerted a dramatic impact. Carson's sobering account of the effects of polluted water on marine life and of the way that pesticides and herbicides entered the food chain roused national calls for regulation. Secretary of the Interior Udall avowed, "A great woman has awakened the Nation by her forceful account of the dangers around us. We owe much to Rachel Carson." The *Chicago Daily News* reviewer reflected:

> Miss Carson is a scientist and is not given to tossing serious charges around carelessly. When she warns us, as she does with such a profound sense of urgency, we ought to take heed. *Silent Spring* may well be one of the great and towering books of our time. This book is *must* reading for every responsible citizen.

Responding to the furor, President Kennedy had appointed a scientific advisory committee on pesticides. Under President Johnson's prodding, Congress accelerated the pace of action. The Water Quality Act of 1965 toughened a water-pollution control act dating from 1948 and strengthened in later years. This 1965 measure required all states to enforce water-quality standards for interstate waters within their borders; if they failed to do so, the federal government would step in. The Clean Waters Restoration Act of 1966, pushed by Senator Edmund Muskie of Maine, expanded water-quality regulations and authorized over $3.5 billion to clean up the nation's waterways and to halt further pollution of them by sewage or industrial waste.

The concerns about water pollution roused by Rachel Carson's work heightened public sensitivity to more general environmental hazards. Nearly a decade of intense publicity about radioactive fallout from nuclear tests also contributed to a larger awareness of environmental risks. The Task Force on Environmental Pollution, established by President Johnson in 1964, addressed not only pesticides but also emissions from coal-burning factories and auto exhaust systems. In a 1965 press release, the president described pollution as "one of the most pervasive problems of our society" and placed the issue in a more ample context:

Ours is a nation of affluence. But the technology that has permitted our affluence spews out vast quantities of wastes and spent products that pollute our air, poison our waters, and even impair our ability to feed ourselves. At the same time, we have crowded together into dense metropolitan areas where concentration of wastes intensifies the problem.

A 1958 federal conference on air pollution had attracted little notice, but a series of gatherings in the 1960s drew increasing attention. The Third National Conference on Air Pollution in 1966 was particularly well attended and heavily publicized. Along with media publicity, the conference also set off jitters in corporate America, notably the coal and automobile industries, which recognized the urgency with which the public now viewed atmospheric pollution.

A series of clean-air laws culminating in the Air Quality Act of 1967 set progressively stricter standards, covered a broader spectrum of pollution sources, including automobile exhaust emissions, and appropriated ever-larger sums for air-pollution abatement programs. Reflecting the lobbying influence of the coal industry, the law called for industry-government cooperation in the shaping of air-pollution standards. These and similar laws dealing with water pollution clearly identified environmental protection as a national issue requiring national action. Two major environmental disasters—the 1967 sinking of the giant oil tanker *Torrey Canyon* at the entrance to the English Channel that spilled 30,000 tons of crude oil and damaged 175 miles of British and French coastline, and a 1969 oil drilling accident off Santa Barbara, California, that befouled beaches and devastated marine life—accelerated concern about pollution.

This opening phase of the modern environmental movement culminated in a major law the year Johnson left office: the National Environmental Policy Act of 1969. Among other provisions, the law required federal agencies to file environmental-impact statements for all major activities or proposed legislation. The following year, Congress created the Environmental Protection Agency to enforce the growing body of federal environmental law. Environmental issues would garner still more attention in the 1970s, but the surge of legislation, conferences, and publicity in the Johnson years laid the groundwork for later growth.

Lady Bird Johnson inspired another major component of LBJ's environmental program: the campaign for national beautification. Although some ridiculed its advocates as "the daffodil and dogwood set," the beautification campaign of the 1960s, in its holistic outlook and emphasis on the aesthetic and cultural aspects of environmental issues, provided an important bridge to the ecological concerns of the 1970s and beyond. The beautification and preservation movements had roots in American history. As early as 1791, Pierre L'Enfant had drafted a visionary plan for Washington, D.C., featuring a broad avenue connecting the presidential mansion with the yet-to-be built Capitol. Beginning in the 1820s, landscape artists such as Asher B. Durand and Thomas Cole had gloried in the sublimity of the American wilderness as the New World's answer to the antiquities of Europe. The turn-of-the-century City Beautiful movement had focused on urban beautification projects, including the completion of L'Enfant's plan for the nation's capital.

Lady Bird Johnson herself had always cherished natural beauty and had managed to preserve this sensitivity—perhaps as a defense—during her marriage to Lyndon Johnson, for whom aesthetic sensibility was painfully acquired. While Johnson had headed the National Youth Administration in Texas, Lady Bird had become an advocate of the movement to create roadside parks. During the White House years, Mrs. Johnson devoted her time and considerable talents to the beautification cause. In the process she redefined the First Lady's role and became the most influential presidential spouse since Eleanor Roosevelt. She worked behind the scenes, lobbied the media, and gave dozens of speeches encouraging support of her efforts. In a February 1965 interview in *U.S. News and World Report*, she declared, "[T]his Administration has accepted the commitment to make our cities and country more beautiful for all the people. The time is ripe—the time is now—to take advantage of this yeasty, bubbling desire to beautify our cities and our countryside."

Through Lady Bird's influence, LBJ in 1964 set up the Task Force on the Preservation of Natural Beauty. Early in 1965 he sent Congress a message on "Conservation and the Restoration of Natural Beauty" and laid out a legislative agenda. That May, opening the White House Conference on Natural Beauty, Mrs. Johnson challenged the delegates: "Can a great democratic society generate . . . and execute great projects of beauty?" With LBJ's domestic reform program at flood tide, that rhetorical question could have but one answer.

Much of Lady Bird Johnson's campaign focused on Washington, D.C., itself. In part, she desired simply to make the capital more attractive for the city's residents, government workers, and visitors. But she had a larger goal: to offer Washington as a model for other communities to emulate. In 1965 she invited a select group of wealthy, socially prominent, and civic-minded citizens to a White House conference on beautifying Washington. From this meeting emerged the First Lady's Committee for a More Beautiful National Capital. Stressing the pilot-project aspect of the effort, Mrs. Johnson pronounced effusively, "It is in our own communities that we can best participate in creating an environment which has beauty, joyousness, and loveliness, as well as dignity."

Utilizing resources of the National Park Service, Mrs. Johnson's committee transformed the city's appearance by planting trees and flowers, establishing parks, sprucing up Pennsylvania Avenue, and other measures. Secretary of the Interior Udall enthusiastically backed the First Lady's interest in Washington, recognizing its value in contributing to a larger environmental awareness. (Once, when LBJ came upon Udall and Lady Bird crouched over a large set of plans for the renewal of Pennsylvania Avenue, he burst out in mock rage: "Udall, what in hell are you doing down there on the floor with my wife?")

Another of Mrs. Johnson's interests—and hence another item on LBJ's environmental agenda—was highway beautification. During many auto trips between Texas and Washington in the 1930s and 1940s, Mrs. Johnson had had ample opportunity to observe the highway billboards, commercial clutter, and other eyesores lining the nation's roadways. The Billboard Bonus Act of 1955 had offered increased federal highway funds to states that regulated billboards, but the advertising industry had mobilized its opposition and the offer had found few takers. As First Lady, Mrs. Johnson attacked the problem, and her efforts yielded the Highway Beautification Act of 1965. President Johnson introduced the bill to coincide with the White House Conference on Natural Beauty, but it faced tough sledding. The influential Outdoor Advertising Association mounted powerful opposition. The bill, as finally passed, banned or strictly regulated highway billboards outside commercial and industrial districts and required that unsightly roadside junkyards be concealed by fences. Although a disappointment to environmental purists, who wanted to ban billboards altogether, the law went a long way toward reclaiming the nation's highways from hucksters and visual polluters. Proponents and opponents alike recognized Mrs. Johnson's key role. In parts of the West, billboards appeared demanding: "IMPEACH LADY BIRD JOHNSON."

The beautification campaign reflected Mrs. Johnson's particular concerns, but it also served the interests of the administration at a time of growing divisiveness. In all her speeches, Mrs. Johnson invariably stressed that beautification was an issue upon which everyone could agree. Beautification built consensus, and Mrs. Johnson emphasized this theme to the end. At Yale in the fall of 1967, as protesters marched outside, she insisted almost plaintively that a concern for the environment was "one thing that we all share." Nevertheless, the divisions tearing at America's social fabric intruded even here. Advocates for Washington, D.C.'s large black community, for example, attacked the elitist tinge of the First Lady's Committee for a More Beautiful National Capital. "How many rats can you kill with a tulip?" sneered one critic. Mrs. Johnson, demonstrating both social sensitivity and political savvy, vigorously rejected the notion that her efforts solely concerned rich do-gooders. Maintaining that "beauty cannot be reserved 'for nice neighborhoods only,'" she set up the Neighborhoods and Special Projects Committee as part of the capital beautification drive. Directed by Walter Washington, a black leader who headed the city's housing authority and who later would be elected mayor, this group focused on projects in the city's black districts, including vest-pocket parks and Project Pride, which encouraged neighborhood clean-up and beautification efforts geared to schoolchildren and local residents. Mrs. Johnson took an avid interest in the committee's efforts and frequently visited neighborhoods in the nation's capital that most government leaders rarely saw.

Lady Bird Johnson's efforts, like the War on Poverty and the Great Society reforms, ultimately faded in the face of rising controversy over Vietnam. At the 1966 National Youth Conference on Natural Beauty and Conservation, the First Lady urged the five hundred delegates to "consider making America's beauty a full-time vocation." By then, however, the younger generation had less interest in Lady Bird's home-front beautification campaign than in the war that her husband was waging abroad. She continued to champion the beautification effort to the end of her stay in the White House, and indeed long after, but by 1966 she had largely lost her audience.

The War on Poverty and the Great Society: A Postmortem

With an awesome roster of domestic reforms to his credit and more in the pipeline during 1964–1965, LBJ bestrode the political landscape like a colossus. His approval ratings hovered close to 70 percent. Indeed, a history of the domestic side of the

Johnson presidency written as 1965 ended, and including the commitment to racial justice explored in the next chapter, would have told of soaring aspirations virtually matched by impressive achievement.

Yet by 1968 the spirit of reform would evaporate. In that year, presidential candidate Richard Nixon declared, "For the past five years we have been deluged by government programs for the unemployed, programs for cities, programs for the poor, and we have reaped from these programs an ugly harvest of frustration, violence and failure across the land." The political constituency for the War on Poverty had already collapsed by the time Nixon took office, and as president he would cut back on the program with impunity; in 1974 he shut down OEO altogether. With amazing speed, the U.S. political landscape would alter so rapidly that Americans would find it difficult to recall the reformist zeal that momentarily had seized the nation in 1964–1965.

What forces launched this short-lived wave of reform, and what significance did it ultimately hold for American society? Why did it decline so rapidly? The causes are easiest to analyze. The aftershocks of *Sputnik*, Kennedy's death, and the idealism and unrest roused by the civil-rights movement encouraged a revival of liberalism. Lyndon Johnson, with his New Deal background, legendary political skills, and determination to leave a memorable presidential legacy, translated that mood into tangible achievement.

The long-term ramifications of LBJ's domestic record are more difficult to evaluate. Certainly the Civil Rights Act of 1964 and the Voting Rights Act of 1965, discussed in Chapter 8, left lasting legacies. If their implementation fell short of the ideal, they at least blunted the more blatant manifestations of institutional racism in American society. Similarly, the major Great Society measures—Medicare, aid to education, urban development and mass transit, environmental legislation—had long-term positive significance, especially for the middle class. Yet, as often in politics, efforts to grapple with one set of issues only exacerbated others—including, as we have seen, soaring federal deficits related to the Medicare and Medicaid programs—that three decades later would loom as monumental problems.

Assessing the War on Poverty is still more challenging. By some measures, the program succeeded. The proportion of Americans below the federal poverty line fell from 20 percent in 1963 to 13 percent in 1968.* For African-Americans, who faced the most desperate conditions, the statistics are even more impressive. In 1960 some 40 percent of blacks lived in poverty. By 1968 this figure had been halved. Millions of blacks edged into the middle class in these years. In 1960 only 13 percent of black families had annual incomes of more than $10,000; by the end of the decade, the figure approached one-third. However, a booming economy contributed to these statistics as much as did the antipoverty program. The years of maximum antipoverty expenditures also saw a massive increase in federal spending related to the Vietnam War. The 1968–1969 unemployment rate of about 3.4 percent, the lowest since the Korean War, reflected the increased draft calls, job opportunities, and military spending of the Vietnam era as much as it did domestic economic policies. Similarly,

---

* In 1964 the Council of Economic Advisers had set the poverty line at $3,000 annual income for a family of four—about one-half the median family income in America at the time.

another war-related phenomenon, surging inflation, soon eroded many of the apparent economic gains of the Johnson era. These developments further complicate the task of isolating the effects of the War on Poverty.

The larger goal that LBJ at least rhetorically embraced—poverty's eradication—remained a dream, in part because poverty is always relative. As America's overall wealth and living standard rose, the bottom one-quarter or so of citizens still lived in "poverty" relative to the national norm, although conditions for them may have ranked above those of the poor in earlier times or in other societies. But the problem went beyond simply defining poverty. The tangle of social ills that the antipoverty warriors set out to cure, especially in the inner cities, proved more intractable than they had imagined. Despite the billions spent on social programs in 1964–1967, inner-city joblessness, housing decay, educational problems, and social disorganization stubbornly persisted. The unemployment rate among black males aged sixteen to twenty-four actually rose in the late 1960s, just as various federal job-training programs peaked. The assumption that the cycle of poverty would break given educational opportunities, job training, and a climate of hope was naive. In later years, President Ronald Reagan would joke cynically, "We fought a war on poverty, and poverty won." Reagan had his own political ax to grind, of course, but his criticism would hit home.

Furthermore, the same upbeat enthusiasm that made Sargent Shriver an effective head of OEO inhibited objective assessment of the antipoverty program. A mood of boosterism, not critical self-scrutiny, prevailed. Like the reports from Vietnam that would soon tout "body counts" and other statistical data to prove that America was "winning" the war, the well-intentioned cheerleading for the War on Poverty tended to dwell on its good intentions, overstate its successes, and sweep its failures under the rug.

As the high hopes faded, a conservative backlash set in. Early evidence of the shift came in the midterm election of 1966, when Republicans gained three Senate seats and forty-seven House seats, making Johnson's programs more vulnerable to attack. On the ideological plane, the backlash revitalized the old view that blamed the poor themselves, not society, for their plight. In *The Unheavenly City* (1970), Edward Banfield argued that poverty stemmed from poor people's inability to grasp the concept of delayed gratification.* The backlash was also intimately connected with the racial politics of the 1960s. As white America increasingly identified poverty as a problem of blacks and Hispanics in the inner cities, it viewed the antipoverty program simply as a means of shoveling federal dollars to minorities. The racial backlash that would splinter support for the civil-rights cause in the later 1960s thus also hastened the collapse of the liberal consensus in general and in particular eroded backing for the War on Poverty.

The most sustained and telling assault on Johnson's social agenda and on the ideology that undergirded it came in Theodore Lowi's *The End of Liberalism* (1969). A Cornell University political scientist, Lowi granted the need for government welfare policies to moderate capitalism's social effects. But 1960s-style liberalism, he

---

* In the very different political climate of 1981, George Gilder would reiterate this point in *Wealth and Poverty*, contending that only changed behavior and values by the poor would end the cycle of want.

contended, differed sharply from New Deal liberalism as embodied in the Social Security Act of 1935. Whereas Social Security precisely specified its rules of operation and its criteria for eligibility, Lowi charged, the War on Poverty had a far looser structure, a "grab bag" of programs, and vaguely identified target groups. Rather than encouraging a sense of the common good, the government merely threw money at the inner cities, delegating to local bodies the task of refereeing the resulting free-for-all among clashing interest groups. Lowi also accused the antipoverty crusade of defining social injustices and inequities, especially racial ones, as economic problems when, instead, these problems had cultural and social roots. The War on Poverty, he believed, drained the civil-rights movement of its momentum and moral authority. Lowi minced no words about his purpose: "[This book's] principal target is the modern liberal state itself, its outmoded ideology, and its self-defeating policies." Johnson-style liberalism, he charged, was "sincere humanitarianism gone cockeyed."

The debate would continue into the 1980s. Critics on the Left dismissed the War on Poverty as a typical halfway liberal palliative that offered superficial remedies without addressing underlying power realities, and conservatives blamed the campaign's ideology for encouraging welfare dependency. Two books published in 1984 illustrate these divergent lines of criticism. In *The Unraveling of America*, Allan J. Matusow attacked the War on Poverty as a timid and misdirected effort by a liberal political establishment unwilling to challenge the status quo in any fundamental way. Only a radical redistribution of income and power, argued Matusow, offered hope of eradicating want in capitalist America. The War on Poverty's epitaph, he concluded, should be, "Declared But Never Fought." Although convincing as an ideologically driven critique from the Left, Matusow's work gave little attention to the actual political realities of America in the 1960s. In those years, the electorate's moderate to conservative tendencies put severe constraints on radical reform.

Charles Murray took a different tack in *Losing Ground: American Social Policy, 1950–1980*. By portraying the poor as victims, Murray declared, and by blaming poverty on social maladjustments that the government must correct, Johnson-era policymakers contributed to a breakdown of the stigma associated with welfare. Despite LBJ's announced goal of ending welfare dependence, he suggested, 1960s social policy actually encouraged the poor to accept the dole as a way of life. New York City's welfare rolls did double between 1965 and 1975, with similar trends in other cities. By extending benefits and payments to all whose income fell below a specified cutoff point, Murray contended, the War on Poverty and other well-intentioned programs reduced incentives to self-help. Reformers thereby slowed and eventually reversed what Murray claims was a long-term decline in poverty rates under way since World War II.

Murray's argument is ultimately unverifiable, for it rested on the alleged psychological effects of social programs, factors difficult to measure or document. Moreover, he paid scant attention to programs such as Head Start, the Job Corps, and Upward Bound that encouraged individual initiative and that inculcated "middle-class" values of hard work and personal responsibility. Furthermore, if the problem was a growing dependence on federal largess, the poor were hardly alone. Defense industries boomed as Pentagon dollars showered down after 1965. Under Medicare and Medicaid, physicians and nursing homes set their own fees, and many profited vastly as Uncle Sam picked up the tab. Indeed, total health-care spending exploded from $40 billion to $140 billion in the decade 1965–1975. Too, countless academics, lawyers, administrators, planners, builders, and advocates for the poor prospered from their participation in various War on Poverty programs. The funds designated for community action programs, urban betterment, and job training often landed in the hands of the middle-class staffers who ran the agencies, programs, and centers.

Liberals generally praised the War on Poverty, although they, too, criticized its scattershot approach, inflated rhetoric, and close identification with Johnson and Shriver. They argued as well that the antipoverty campaign, for all the money spent, still suffered from underfunding. One writer called it "a classic instance of the American habit of substituting good intentions for cold hard cash." Finally, liberals and conservatives alike generally agreed that by raising expectations in the inner cities and then failing to follow through, the War on Poverty left a legacy of bitterness and frustration.

Why did support for reform fade so rapidly after 1965? Urban riots offer one reason. Initially, observers cited inner-city unrest such as hit Birmingham in 1963 and the Watts district of Los Angeles in 1965 (see p. 280) as evidence of the urgency of antipoverty efforts. But as city after city erupted in the later sixties, skepticism about Johnson's programs intensified. As urban turmoil worsened and the rhetoric of black activists grew more radical, the white middle class turned hostile. Not poverty but the poor now seemed the enemy. Johnson's hyperbole in 1964–1965 only heightened this reaction, as fierce disillusionment set in.

CONCLUSION

LBJ launched his domestic reforms amid an economic boom, encouraging his advisers' assumption that the nation could afford to divert large sums to social problems without suffering deficit problems, raising taxes, or jeopardizing middle-class living standards. Little sense of bounds or limits inhibited the architects of reform. As Johnson burst out to his speechwriter Richard Goodwin, "I'm sick of all the people who talk about the things we can't do. Hell, we're the richest country in the world, the most powerful. We can do it all, if we're not too greedy; that's our job: to persuade people to give a little so everyone can be better off." In the 1970s, as the boom faded and inflation eroded confidence even as spending on various entitlement programs soared,* expansiveness gave way to resentment. Richard Nixon anticipated the shift in the 1968 campaign when he championed the "Forgotten Americans": an uneasy middle class that saw itself as unjustly put upon.

In terms of economic theory, the Kennedy-Johnson years saw only a partial application of Keynesian principles of fiscal management. Kennedy had adopted the stimulus component of Keynesianism, using popular tax cuts, investment credits, and federal spending increases to spur economic growth. But Johnson resisted the less

---

* An entitlement benefit is one that the recipient is entitled to receive simply by virtue of being in a designated class of people: over age sixty-five or under a certain income level, for example.

popular and more politically risky side of Keynesianism, which called for tax increases and spending cuts to cool an overheated economy. As inflation raged, Johnson did little. The resulting economic slowdown and erosion of consumer buying
power ate away at the liberal consensus.

Above all, the Great Society succumbed to the Vietnam War, a cause that
Johnson pursued with his left hand while championing domestic reform with his
right. From 1965 to 1973, when Washington spent about $15 billion combating pov-
erty, funding for the war reached $120 billion. Vietnam diverted attention from
home-front issues and undermined LBJ's moral authority as a reform leader at home.
In the summer of 1966, a Johnson aide, Joseph Califano, traveled to New York City
to discuss new domestic-policy initiatives with a group of liberal academics. Afterward, one of the participants, historian William Leuchtenberg, wrote Califano a
postmortem of the event. "Like Banquo's ghost," Leuchtenberg observed, "Vietnam
was the unwelcome guest at the feast." As long as the war continued, he concluded
somberly, "there is no hope at all for expanding the Great Society." The domestic
challenge that Johnson set for the nation would have been daunting under the best
of circumstances; after 1965 it proved hopeless, and the reform consensus evaporated
amid turmoil.

Yet much remains admirable in Johnson's domestic record. All the major issues
that he tackled—racism, poverty, the cities, education, health care, the environment—stayed on the nation's agenda long after his presidency had ended. Thanks to
him, the nation not only confronted these problems but for a time granted them
priority. Like FDR, Johnson on domestic issues may not have had all the right answers, but he asked the right questions. The mid-1960s remains the most productive
era in U.S. domestic reform since the New Deal, and the credit largely goes to Lyndon Baines Johnson. The tragedy is not that the War on Poverty and the Great
Society fell short but that the impulse that inspired them faded so quickly.

Americans are still coming to terms with the hulking, grinning, arm-twisting
Texan who figured so prominently in all the events that defined the 1960s—the
civil-rights cause, the War on Poverty, the Great Society, the environmental movement, and the Vietnam War. As we begin to grasp how Lyndon Johnson could with
equal fervor espouse the rights of African-Americans, the cause of the poor, educational and health reform, environmental protection and beautification, and a brutal
and divisive war in Asia, we will begin to understand Johnson and post–World War
II American liberalism.

SELECTED READINGS

The Liberal Agenda in the 1950s and Early 1960s

Irving Bernstein, *Promises Kept: John F. Kennedy's New Frontier* (1991); John Brooks, *The
Great Leap* (1966); Richard Volney Chase, *The Democratic Vista* (1958); Aida DePace Donald,
ed., *John F. Kennedy and the New Frontier* (1966); Wayne Flynt, *Dixie's Forgotten People: The
South's Poor Whites* (1979); Robert Booth Fowler, *Believing Skeptics: American Political Intellectuals, 1945–1964* (1978); Patrick M. Garry, *Liberalism and American Identity* (1992); Alonzo L.

Hamby, *Liberalism and Its Challengers: From F.D.R. to Bush* (2d ed., 1992); Michael Harrington, *The Other America* (1962); Jim F. Heath, *John F. Kennedy and the Business Community* (1969); Walter Heller, *Fiscal Policy for a Balanced Economy: Experience, Problems and Prospects* (1968); Hubert H. Humphrey, *The Education of a Public Man* (1976); Daniel Knapp and Kenneth Polk, *Scouting the War on Poverty: Social Reform Politics in the Kennedy Administration* (1971); Arthur Larson, *A Republican Looks at His Party* (1956); Robert Lekachman, *The Age of Keynes* (1968); Richard H. Pells, *The Liberal Mind in a Conservative Age: American Intellectuals in the 1940s and 1950s* (1985); Edward Purcell, *The Crisis of Democratic Theory* (1973); Hobart Rowan, *The Free Enterprisers: Kennedy, Johnson and the Business Establishment* (1964); Arthur M. Schlesinger, Jr., *A Thousand Days* (1965) and "Where Does the Liberal Go from Here?" *New York Times Magazine*, August 4, 1957; Alan Shank, *Presidential Policy Leadership: Kennedy and Social Welfare* (1980); Barbie Zelizer, *Covering the Body: The Kennedy Assassination, the Media and the Shaping of Collective Memory* (1992).

Johnson, the War on Poverty, and the Great Society

Henry J. Aaron, *Politics and the Professors: The Great Society in Perspective* (1978); Patrick Anderson, *The President's Men* (1968); Vaughn Davis Bornet, *The Presidency of Lyndon B. Johnson* (1983); Robert Caro, *The Years of Lyndon Johnson: The Path to Power* (1982) and *Means of Ascent* (1990); Richard Cloward and Frances Fox Piven, *Poor People's Movements* (1978); Robert Dallek, *Lone Star Rising: Lyndon Johnson and His Times, 1908–1960* (1991); John C. Donovan, *The Politics of Poverty* (1967); Rowland Evans and Robert Novak, *Lyndon B. Johnson: The Exercise of Power* (1968); Chester E. Finn, Jr., *Education and the Presidency* (1977); Mark I. Gelfand, "The War on Poverty," in Robert A. Divine, ed., *The Johnson Years*, Vol. 1 (1987); Hugh Davis Graham, *The Uncertain Trumpet: Federal Education Policy in the Kennedy and Johnson Years* (1984); Robert H. Haveman, ed., *A Decade of Federal Antipoverty Programs* (1977); Lyndon Johnson, *The Vantage Point: Perspectives of the Presidency 1963–1969* (1971); Doris Kearns, *Lyndon Johnson and the American Dream* (1977); Sar A. Levitan, *The Great Society's Poor Law* (1969); Theodore Marmor, *The Politics of Medicare* (1973); Peter Marris and Martin Rein, *Dilemmas of Social Reform: Poverty and Community Action in the United States* (1973); Alan Matusow, *The Unraveling of America: A History of Liberalism in the 1960s* (1984); Philip Meranto, *The Politics of Federal Aid to Education* (1967); Charles Morris, *A Time of Passion* (1984); Daniel Patrick Moynihan, *Maximum Feasible Misunderstanding* (1969); Charles Murray, *Losing Ground: American Social Policy, 1950–1980* (1984); James T. Patterson, *America's Struggle Against Poverty, 1900–1980* (1981); Frances Fox Piven and Richard A. Cloward, *Regulating the Poor: The Functions of Public Welfare* (1971); Diane Ravitch, *The Troubled Crusade: American Education, 1945–1980* (1983); Stephen M. Rose, *The Betrayal of the Poor: The Transformation of Community Action* (1972); Joel Spring, *The Sorting Machine: National Education Policy Since 1945* (1976); Francis E. Rourke, *Bureaucracy, Politics, and Public Policy* (1969); James L. Sundquist, ed., *On Fighting Poverty* (1969); David Zarefsky, *President Johnson's War on Poverty: Rhetoric and History* (1986).

Environmentalism

Craig W. Allin, *The Politics of Wilderness Preservation* (1982); Thomas R. Dunlap, *DDT: Scientists, Citizens, and Public Policy* (1981); Lewis L. Gould, "Lady Bird Johnson and Beautification," in Robert A. Divine, ed., *The Johnson Years*, Vol. 1 (1987); Samuel P. Hays and Barbara D. Hays, *Beauty, Health, and Permanence: Environmental Politics in the United States, 1955–1985* (1987); Lady Bird Johnson, *A White House Diary* (1970); Martin V. Melosi, "Lyndon Johnson and Environmental Policy," in Divine, ed., *The Johnson Years*, Vol. 2; Vera L. Norwood, "The Nature of Knowing: Rachel Carson and the American Environment," *Signs* (Summer 1987); Carroll W. Pursell, Jr., ed., *From Conservation to Ecology: The Development of Environmental Concern* (1973); Elmo Richardson, *Dams, Parks and Politics: Resource Development and Preservation in the Truman-Eisenhower Era* (1973); Walter A. Rosenbaum, *The Politics of Environmental Concern* (1973); Victor B. Scheffer, *The Shaping of Environmentalism in America* (1991); Stewart Udall, *The Quiet Crisis* (1963) and *The Promise and the Performance* (1975); Cynthia Wilson, "Lyndon Johnson: Conservationist," *Audubon Magazine* (March 1973).

Chapter Eight

THE CIVIL-RIGHTS MOVEMENT AT FLOOD TIDE

On Monday, February 1, 1960, four black freshmen from the North Carolina Agricultural and Technical College in Greensboro, Joseph McNeill, Ezell Blair, Jr., Franklin McCain, and David Richmond, entered the local Woolworth's store, bought school supplies, and then sat down at the lunch counter and ordered coffee. This seemingly innocuous moment would reverberate across the nation. When the white waitress uttered the familiar formula, "We don't serve Negroes here," they gave an unfamiliar response:

> We just beg to disagree with you. We've in fact already been served. . . . We wonder why you'd invite us in to serve us at one counter and deny service at another. If this is a private club or private concern, then we believe you ought to sell membership cards.

The four remained seated and waited—all day. Years later, Franklin McCain would look back on that Monday:

> If it's possible to know what it means to have your soul cleansed—I felt pretty clean at that time. . . . Seems like a lot of feelings of guilt or what-have-you suddenly left me, and I felt as though I had gained my manhood. . . . Not Franklin McCain only as an individual, but I felt as though the manhood of a number of other black persons had been restored.

On the next day, twenty-seven black students occupied the Woolworth's lunch counter; on Wednesday, sixty-three. By Friday, more than three hundred protesters jammed the store and the nearby Kress's five-and-dime. That Saturday night, sixteen hundred students attended a mass rally supporting the sit-ins. The movement rapidly spread to Fisk University in Nashville, Atlanta University, and other black colleges and universities across the South.

The sit-ins signaled fundamental changes in the leadership, tactics, and goals of the civil-rights movement. From the early twentieth century to the 1950s, two organizations had spearheaded the African-American cause: the National Association for the Advancement of Colored People (NAACP) and the National Urban League. Led by educated, middle-class blacks, both groups worked quietly through established channels. The NAACP fought discrimination in the courts; the Urban League sought to improve black employment opportunities by negotiations with corporate leaders. Neither encouraged mass demonstrations. These older organizations had significant achievements to their credit. The Supreme Court's 1954 *Brown* v. *Board of Education* decision outlawing school segregation, for example, culminated years of legal effort by the NAACP.

After the *Brown* decision, fresh currents of activism had energized black America, especially in the South. The Montgomery bus boycott of 1955–1956 was an initial challenge to the region's racial caste system and coupled the familiar strategy of litigation with new tactics of nonviolent mass action. Harking back to strategies urged during World War II by labor leader and longtime activist A. Philip Randolph, the Montgomery boycotters won national attention by taking the freedom struggle to the streets. From the Montgomery campaign had emerged a new leader, Dr. Martin Luther King, Jr.; a new organization, the Southern Christian Leadership Conference (SCLC); and the first civil-rights law since Reconstruction, the Civil Rights Act of 1957, with its focus on voting rights.

The NAACP, Urban League, and SCLC remained active in the 1960s, but after the sit-ins, a vigorous new organization, the Student Nonviolent Coordinating Committee (SNCC), won support from both white backers of the black cause and young African-Americans. This proliferation of organizations produced tensions and personal rivalries, but it also yielded a creative array of complementary strategies that on occasion won results that no single organization could have achieved. The long-range goal of ending racial segregation and discrimination remained central, but tactically the 1960s saw a broadening of direct-action approaches that attracted wide public notice and sometimes sparked violent confrontation.

The civil-rights movement that arose in the later 1950s and crested in the 1960s profoundly threatened many white southerners, for whom a racially segregated society seemed the natural order. Rooted in slavery, the South's racial caste system had been reestablished following the end of Reconstruction in 1877. The system was buttressed by custom, law, black exclusion from the political process, and, ultimately, violence or the threat of violence. Through the first half of the twentieth century, two separate and unequal societies, white and black, coexisted in the South. Strict segregation prevailed in schools, churches, courthouses, factories, residences, theaters, parks, even public restrooms. This caste system rested on ingrained white notions of racial superiority and a horror of the "mongrelization" and "race mixing" that supposedly would result from a crumbling of the barriers dividing the races. The guardians of this wall of separation could lash out against those who might challenge it. In one brutal example, local white Mississippi vigilantes lynched a fourteen-year-old black visitor from the North, Emmett Till, in 1955, and threw his body in the Tallahatchie River. The boy allegedly had whistled at a white woman.

Racism was not unique to the South. Northern blacks also faced barriers and prejudice because of their skin color, and de facto segregation existed throughout the nation. But the white South, for reasons embedded in its history, had translated racist thinking into an elaborate, legally based racial caste system that relegated African-Americans to second-class status. Accordingly, it was in the South that the civil-rights movement took shape from the mid-1950s to the mid-1960s.

The "White South" was not a monolith. Differences in region, education, social class, and religious belief influenced white southerners' responses to the civil-rights movement. The Deep South clung to segregation more rigidly than did the border states. Upper-class white southerners, better educated and more cosmopolitan, were more likely to recognize the inevitability of change. As we have seen, the region's business and professional elite often worked behind the scenes to ease racial tensions. Newspaper editors such as Ralph McGill of the *Atlanta Constitution* and Virginius Dabney of the *Richmond Times-Dispatch*, although hardly radical integrationists, spoke for this professional class by denouncing violence and by calling for enlightened responses to the civil-rights campaign. Southern academic centers such as the University of North Carolina at Chapel Hill harbored eloquent critics of segregation. The biracial Southern Regional Council had cautiously raised its voice against racism in the early postwar years, and Georgia novelist Lillian Smith had explored southern racial taboos and the horror of lynching in her 1944 novel, *Strange Fruit*. On the legal front, some southern judges backed segregation, but others, especially at the federal level, supported the black struggle for justice. Federal district judge Frank M. Johnson, Jr., of Alabama, for example, despite vilification by white racists, consistently upheld African-Americans' constitutional rights and exposed the subterfuges by which local election officials kept blacks from voting. The civil-rights movement called out to the conscience and humanity of the white South, and at all levels some responded admirably. One white women told the first sit-in students in Greensboro, "You should have done this ten years ago." The revivalist Billy Graham, one of the nation's best-known white southerners, integrated his crusades and called racism "the most burning issue of modern times."

Nevertheless, the white South had an enormous investment in the prevailing caste system and in general saw any attacks on that system, whether from local blacks or from northern liberals, as a threat to the region's social order. Preserving the status quo seemed especially urgent to poorer, uneducated southern whites. Such folk ranked low on the white social hierarchy, but as long as the racial caste system survived, they knew that they stood at least above blacks in the pecking order. In the ferocious opposition stirred by the civil-rights campaign, poorer, socially marginal whites—and politicians and police officials who pandered to them—typically took the lead. Only a handful of white southerners resorted to actual physical violence to express their hatred of integration, but that tiny minority received a lion's share of media attention. Their actions reinforced the image of a white South united in murderous opposition to racial equality.

The intensity and scope of this new civil-rights activism caught Washington off guard. Both parties recognized the dangerous potential of racial discord, the negative impact of segregation on America's global standing, and the growing political clout of northern black voters. But official Washington was accustomed to working with established race leaders such as Roy Wilkins of the NAACP; the Urban League's Whitney Young; and, more recently, Martin Luther King, Jr. Administration and congressional leaders waffled uneasily as grass-roots activism sprang up across the South. John F. Kennedy courted the black vote in 1960, although he responded only hesitantly to the rising demands for racial justice. But as the pace of demonstrations and the level of violence intensified, the federal courts, the White House, and Congress did extend decisive support to the civil-rights cause at crucial junctures. In 1964, spurred by President Johnson, Congress enacted a major civil-rights law. A second measure, again targeting voting rights, came in 1965.

The civil-rights movement of the early 1960s did not unfold in an orderly fashion, one event at a time. Activists across the South simultaneously sought a variety of goals, from desegregating public facilities to winning voting rights to gaining entry in all-white universities. And although Martin Luther King, Jr., and the SCLC played an important role, no one person or organization dominated the campaign. The maturing movement spawned new leaders. As black college students pushed beyond the tactics that had worked in Montgomery in 1955, King and the churchmen of the SCLC, not to mention the NAACP and the Urban League, struggled to redefine their goals and tactics. Whereas generational friction in white America arose over cultural issues, in black America it took the form of tense debates over how to conduct the struggle against racism.

Grasping the full meaning of the civil-rights struggle requires a multifocal approach that simultaneously keeps in view the strategies of sometimes fractious national organizations and leaders, the grass-roots campaigns often led by obscure men and women seeking specific local objectives, the fears and anxieties of white southerners who saw their way of life under siege, and the national political stage where all these pressures and counterpressures coalesced into a reform movement of enormous magnitude and lasting importance. The civil-rights campaigns of 1960–1965 saw a variety of demonstrations across the South, yet they shared one goal: shattering a racial caste system that denied blacks full freedom and equal opportunity. From the movement that historian C. Vann Woodward has dubbed the "second Reconstruction," nothing less than a new society was painfully emerging.

1960–1962: Tactical Innovation, Political Hesitation

The sit-ins that began at Greensboro captured the imagination of a generation of young blacks. At an April 1960 conference at Shaw University in Raleigh, North Carolina, some three hundred student leaders from more than fifty southern black schools and colleges, as well as delegates from nineteen northern schools, founded the Student Nonviolent Coordinating Committee (SNCC, pronounced "Snick"). White representatives from the American Friends Service Committee, the National Student Association, and other groups attended, but the movement was overwhelmingly black led. Although Martin Luther King, Jr., addressed the conference, the students applauded their own leaders most loudly. James M. Lawson, Jr., a divinity student at Vanderbilt University, drafted the new organization's statement of purpose. In a rousing address, Lawson criticized the NAACP and all "middle class conventional halfway efforts to deal with radical social evil." Cheering delegates dubbed Lawson "the young people's Martin Luther King." The key figure was not a student at all but fifty-seven-year-old Ella Baker. A graduate of Shaw University and SCLC's executive director, Baker planned SNCC's founding conference, provided a modest grant from SCLC to cover expenses, and tirelessly recruited delegates. Years later,

SNCC veterans would honor Baker as the person who more than any other brought definition to the organization.

The emergence of SNCC exacerbated tensions that already divided the leading civil-rights organizations. Despite generational disagreement and tactical disputes, however, SCLC and SNCC, as well as the NAACP and the Urban League, still shared a common goal and usually worked in complementary ways. The key figures still came mainly from the educated middle-class and professional ranks of black America, the group that historically had provided race leadership. Moreover, the movement remained primarily southern in membership and focus, although this characteristic was rapidly changing. Thus, after initial hesitation, both the NAACP and the SCLC threw their prestige and support behind the new student organization.

As the tempo of the sit-ins increased, white resistance kept pace. Governor Ernest Hollings of South Carolina, although not an extreme segregationist, warned that the prominence of protesting black ministers and religious leaders would not spare them from legal reprisals. "Our law enforcement officers have their Bibles, too," Hollings observed. Sit-in participants were assaulted, jailed, burned with lighted cigarettes, and scalded with hot coffee. Even some conservative black college administrators tried to stop the protests. But the demonstrators persisted, winning recruits and honing the strategy of nonresistance that so infuriated their opponents. From the sit-ins emerged the song that would become the civil-rights movement's anthem: "We Shall Overcome," an adaptation of an old slave melody.

The Congress of Racial Equality (CORE), meanwhile, resumed the Freedom Rides that it had initiated shortly after World War II. In 1946 the Supreme Court had barred racial segregation in public vehicles engaged in interstate commerce. The following year, CORE had tested this ruling with an integrated "Journey of Reconciliation" by bus through the South. In the 1960 case *Boynton v. Virginia*, the Supreme Court had extended its previous action by outlawing segregated bus and train stations, airport terminals, and other facilities related to interstate transit. But the South widely ignored these decisions, and early in 1961, CORE director James Farmer announced another Freedom Ride to integrate bus-station facilities. A one-time divinity student who had helped to found CORE in 1942, the eloquent Farmer was among those who had kept the civil-rights cause alive during the difficult years before *Brown*.

On May 4, 1961, biracial teams of CORE volunteers headed south from Washington, D.C., on Trailways and Greyhound buses. They integrated station facilities in Virginia without incident, but as the vehicles lumbered into the Deep South, white racists mobilized. In Rock Hill, South Carolina, young toughs clubbed twenty-one-year-old John Lewis, a Nashville, Tennessee, divinity student, as he entered the white waiting room. In Anniston, Alabama, a mob armed with clubs and metal bars beat the Freedom Riders, inflicting permanent brain damage on one, a retired white schoolteacher. When the bus's slashed tires deflated a few miles out of Anniston, whites following in cars smashed the windows, threw a smoke bomb inside, and assaulted the terrified occupants as they escaped. An armed state trooper traveling on the bus in plain clothes at the order of the Alabama governor held the crowd off with a pistol, preventing worse violence.

The mayhem intensified when the bus reached Birmingham, Alabama, a thriving industrial city that was also a hotbed of anti-integrationist sentiment. The town's most vocal politician, police commissioner T. Eugene "Bull" Connor, spewed bigotry. A high-school dropout and former radio sports announcer, Connor looms large among the demagogic southern politicians who rode the race issue to brief notoriety. Over the next few years, he would become the epitome of the rabble-rousing segregationist and provide the civil-rights movement with a symbol of racism at its rawest. Indeed, according to a paid FBI informant, Connor had promised the Ku Klux Klan a quarter of an hour to assault the Freedom Riders before the police arrived. In Birmingham, the riders endured attacks from about thirty men brandishing baseball bats and bicycle chains, with no police protection in sight.

Opposition to the Freedom Rides and sit-ins only accelerated the overall campaign's momentum, broadened its goals, and sharpened its ideological sophistication. The movement was rapidly expanding beyond schools, bus stations, and lunch counters. As Ella Baker wrote in June 1960, "The current sit-ins are concerned with something much bigger than a hamburger or even a giant-sized Coke." James Lawson in a 1961 essay* offered a more radical analysis of American racism and of the movement's objectives than anything articulated up to that time:

> [W]hile we recognize segregation as harmful to the whole nation and the South, we rarely blame this on . . . the structure of our institutions. Most of us work simply for concessions from the system, not for transforming the system.
>
> But if after over 300 years, segregation (slavery) is still a basic pattern rather than a peripheral custom, should we not question the American way of life which allows segregation so much structural support? . . .
>
> The sit-ins won concessions, not structural changes; the Freedom Rides won concessions, but not real changes.
>
> There will be no revolution until we see Negro faces in all positions that help to mold public opinion, help to shape policy for America.

As the movement unfolded, awareness of racism as a national issue spread. Combating it would involve more than simply dismantling the South's caste system. Gradually, some white Americans recognized a painful truth: Deep-rooted patterns of racism contributed to the joblessness, poverty, and social disruption of the North's sprawling black ghettos. But before the nation could confront these larger realities, officially sanctioned segregation had to be extirpated from its southern bastion. This was the work of middle-class and working-class blacks of the 1950s and early 1960s who, with white supporters, marched; filed lawsuits; organized Freedom Rides, sit-ins, and boycotts; and in some cases suffered physical abuse, imprisonment, even death.

This broadening and deepening of the civil-rights movement coincided with the changing of the guard in Washington. The 1960 Democratic platform had boasted a vigorous civil-rights plank. Candidate Kennedy praised the sit-in movement ("It is in the American tradition to stand up for one's rights—even if the new way is to sit down") and cemented his support among African-Americans with his telephone call to Coretta Scott King and his successful effort to secure the release of

---

* "Eve of Nonviolent Revolution?" *Southern Patriot* (November 1961).

Dr. King from jail. The outpouring of black votes for Kennedy proved crucial in his tight race with Richard Nixon.

Once in office, Kennedy took several positive steps. In 1961 he set up the Equal Employment Opportunity Committee, headed by Vice President Johnson, to combat discrimination in the federal government and in the hiring practices of firms with government contracts. At a time when blacks accounted for only 15 of 3,600 foreign-service officers and only 10 of 950 Justice Department lawyers, this effort paid off. In the administration's early days, joked Roy Wilkins of the NAACP, "everyone was scrambling around trying to find himself a Negro in order to keep the President off his neck."

Attorney General Robert Kennedy beefed up the Justice Department's anemic civil-rights division. Proceeding under the Civil Rights Act of 1957, the department sued thirty-two southern electoral boards for denying voting rights to blacks, in contrast to the Eisenhower administration's six such suits. When some Mississippi whites mounted an economic boycott against blacks who registered to vote, the Department of Agriculture, on JFK's orders, distributed surplus food to the needy blacks. In 1962, in a fairly noncontroversial action, Congress passed an administration-backed constitutional amendment banning poll taxes, long used in some southern states to bar black voters. The amendment was ratified in 1964.

President Kennedy nevertheless kept his distance from the freedom struggle, and his overall civil-rights record proved decidedly mixed. Kennedy, who addressed the issue only episodically, with long intervals of inaction and temporizing, was above all a practical politician interested in securing and holding power, not an idealist. He viewed the civil-rights movement not as an occasion for moral leadership but as a political problem to be managed. His narrow 1960 electoral victory made him extremely sensitive to the lily-white Southern Democratic party and its powerful sachems in Congess. Despite urging by black leaders, Kennedy delayed introducing a civil-rights bill until mid-1963. Such a bill would have no chance, advised Harris Wofford, White House assistant for civil-rights matters, and might even jeopardize the rest of the administration's program.

Until late 1962, JFK also held back from outlawing racial discrimination in federally funded public housing. As a candidate, he had pointed out that a president could effect this change "with the stroke of a pen." (Frustrated civil-rights advocates deluged the White House with pens.) Under pressure from Mississippi's James Eastland, a notorious racist and chair of the Senate Judiciary Committee, Kennedy appointed to a Mississippi federal judgeship a segregationist, William Harold Cox, who used every possible stratagem to thwart the civil-rights cause. On one occasion, Cox, speaking from the bench, referred to litigants seeking voting rights as "a bunch of niggers . . . acting like a bunch of chimpanzees." Bowing to the tradition of senatorial privilege, Kennedy named other segregationists to the federal bench as well. For the most part, the White House moved decisively on civil rights only when forced by events.

The administration's response to the 1961 Freedom Rides illustrates this pattern. Initially, as the media spotlighted the violence in Alabama, Kennedy's anger flared against the victims of racist attacks. Preoccupied with the Berlin crisis and his upcoming Vienna meeting with Nikita Khrushchev, the president viewed the escalating drama as a frustrating distraction. "Tell them to call it off. Stop them," he told Wofford. Kennedy's response was shaped also by limited information. FBI director J. Edgar Hoover knew of Sheriff Bull Connor's conspiracy to allow physical attacks on the Freedom Riders in Birmingham but failed to pass along the information to the president or to the Department of Justice.

Kennedy did telephone Alabama governor John Patterson, who promised to protect the Freedom Riders, a pledge that he promptly broke. Because Greyhound drivers were refusing the dangerous assignment, the president also persuaded Greyhound officials to provide buses to transport the Freedom Riders out of Birmingham. But Kennedy failed to send federal marshals or to speak out publicly except to issue a general call for law and order. Deprived of protection from the local police or from Washington, frightened CORE volunteers flew from Birmingham to New Orleans on May 17, ending the first phase of the Freedom Rides.

This apparent capitulation might have ended the matter in earlier times, but not in 1961. John Lewis, working with SNCC leaders, at once organized a team of volunteers who rushed to Birmingham to continue the Freedom Ride. Police arrested them at the bus terminal, drove them to the Tennessee state line, and dropped them off beside the highway. Friends immediately drove them back to Birmingham, where they conducted a sit-in at the bus station.

On May 20, twenty-one SNCC volunteers set out from Birmingham on a Greyhound bus bound for Montgomery, Alabama's capital and scene of the successful bus boycott five years earlier. Here, more violence broke out. With the local police nowhere in sight, a mob of more than a thousand whites poured from nearby buildings. Screaming "Get those niggers!" the crowd attacked the Freedom Riders as they entered the bus station. John Lewis suffered a brain concussion. James Zwerg of the University of Wisconsin, spending a term at Fisk University, was brutally beaten. When John Siegenthaler, an observer from the Department of Justice, tried to protect two young female Freedom Riders, he was beaten unconscious and kicked as he lay on the pavement. Prodded by the publicity, JFK finally took decisive action, ordering some four hundred U.S. marshals to the beleaguered city.

For decades, the terror that served as the ultimate enforcer of the South's caste system had drawn only casual attention from the white North. But the assaults on the Freedom Riders received front-page newspaper coverage. *Life* and other popular magazines published vivid photographs and stories. Television, above all, captured the story; many Americans watched in dismay as rampaging whites brutalized citizens whose only offense was to exercise their court-guaranteed rights. The media did not create the civil-rights movement, but in publicizing outrages that in earlier days would have gone unnoticed, the press helped to push civil rights high on the national agenda.

On the evening of May 20, more than a thousand Montgomery blacks jammed into Reverend Ralph Abernathy's First Baptist Church. Dr. King and others exhorted them to remain strong and insisted that the Freedom Rides continue. Outside, a howling mob attacked blacks and hurled torches and stink bombs inside the sanctuary. As the terror ratcheted upward, the marshals moved in. For the first time since Little Rock in 1957, a president had drawn on federal power to protect black citizens exercising their civil rights.

In Montgomery and elsewhere during these early years, the administration worked desperately behind the scenes to manage a social revolution whose intensity it barely grasped. James Farmer later recalled his fury when Attorney General Robert Kennedy advised a cooling-off period in the civil-rights struggle. "We had been cooling off for a hundred years," wrote Farmer. "If we got any cooler we'd be in a deep freeze." The movement's uncompromising new slogan, "Freedom Now," evolved in reaction to the calls for restraint by white liberals and some conservative black leaders. When Robert Kennedy, trying another tack, warned that civil-rights demonstrations would embarrass the president in his forthcoming meeting with Khrushchev, the activists grew incensed. Even Dr. King's initial enthusiasm for the Kennedy administration turned into cold-eyed skepticism. "They don't understand the social revolution going on in the world," King concluded.

On May 24, the Freedom Ride resumed as volunteers set out from Montgomery bound for Jackson, Mississippi. Representing all the major civil-rights groups, the participants came from Atlanta, New York, Washington, and other cities, a turnout that symbolized national interest in the crisis. Reading about these events decades later, one can easily forget the courage of these young African-Americans, joined by sympathetic whites, as they moved from city to city through a hostile region. Freedom Rider William Mahoney of Howard University later recalled, "As we rolled toward Jackson, every blocked-off street, every back road taken, every change in speed caused our hearts to leap."

Robert Kennedy, still juggling divergent political interests, struck a deal with governors Ross Barnett of Mississippi and Patterson of Alabama: The administration would not challenge the arrest and jailing of the Freedom Riders, provided that the governors held off the white mobs. The arrangement left Freedom Riders, male and female, to face harsh treatment far from the television cameras in obscure jails and in Mississippi's notorious Parchman state penitentiary. By the end of the summer, more than 1,000 volunteers had participated in Freedom Ride activities, and over 350 had gone to jail, most of them in Jackson. James Farmer himself spent thirty-nine days behind bars. In late September, the attorney general, worn down by the turmoil, finally secured an order from the Interstate Commerce Commission (ICC) barring racial segregation in all facilities serving interstate travelers. Adding its weight to the Supreme Court's rulings, the ICC in this landmark ruling further ordered that signs announcing the new nondiscriminatory policy be prominently posted in all such facilities by November 1. During the next year, segregation in interstate travel gradually ended.

Events again spurred the administration to action in 1962, when Governor Barnett, a demagogic segregationist, denounced the University of Mississippi for obeying a court order to admit black air-force veteran James Meredith. When Barnett personally blocked Meredith's attempt to register on September 20, Attorney General Robert Kennedy sent five hundred federal marshals to the university campus. "The eyes of the nation and all the world are upon you and upon all of us," President Kennedy reminded Mississippians. Nevertheless, on September 30, a mob incited by a Barnett radio address attacked the federal marshals, in a spasm of violence that left 2 dead and 375 injured. JFK, mobilizing a show of federal force as Eisenhower had done in Little Rock, ordered some thirty thousand regular army troops and federalized national guardsmen to Oxford to restore order and ensure Meredith's safety. Barnett backed down, and Meredith enrolled.

On another front in Washington that year, FBI director J. Edgar Hoover, alarmed by the black freedom struggle, undertook a variety of clandestine activities to discredit it. The FBI's shadowy war against the civil-rights movement, little known at the time, eventually emerged in seedy detail. Pandering to Cold War fears, Hoover portrayed movement leaders as communist dupes or worse. Early in 1962, after repeated charges by Hoover that SCLC had links to the Communist party, Attorney General Kennedy authorized an FBI wiretap on the telephone of Stanley Levison of New York City, a King adviser. In his book *The FBI and Martin Luther King, Jr.* (1981), political scientist David Garrow concludes that although Levison did have connections with the Communist party in the early 1950s, no evidence links him to the party after he became associated with King in 1956. As for King's alleged direct ties to the party, these existed entirely in J. Edgar Hoover's imagination.

In September 1963, Hoover's assistant for domestic intelligence, William Sullivan, drafted a memo describing King as "the most dangerous and effective Negro leader in the country." Warning of the "social revolution" sweeping the nation, Sullivan called for "stepped-up [FBI] activities" to document the Communist party's supposed role in this upheaval. Again with Robert Kennedy's approval, the FBI wiretapped King's home and the SCLC headquarters in Atlanta. By this means, Hoover compiled a damaging file on King's private life, including evidence of extramarital affairs, that he used to besmirch the entire movement. A 1963 FBI document, "Communism and the Negro Movement," full of baseless innuendo, circulated through the government, provided ammunition for enemies of the African-American freedom campaign.

But the civil-rights movement involved more than high-level maneuverings and heavily publicized events. As Hoover pursued his vendetta and as the media highlighted the Freedom Ride drama, an obscure but significant grass-roots effort had arisen in rural Mississippi. In the summer of 1961, Robert Moses, a New York high-school teacher who had come south to work for SNCC, launched a voter-registration drive in Mississippi, where only 5 percent of eligible blacks were registered to vote. In many rural areas, not a single black voted. The campaign centered on the town of McComb in southwestern Mississippi, a Ku Klux Klan stronghold. One of the volunteers, twenty-two-year-old Charles Sherrod, later described the SNCC workers' informal conversations with local blacks in lunch rooms, nightclubs, and pool halls: "We would tell them of how it feels to be in prison, . . . in jail for the cause. . . . We referred to the system that imprisons men's minds and robs them of creativity. We mocked the system that teaches men to be good Negroes instead of good men."

As the SNCC volunteers tried to register black voters, hostile whites struck back with beatings and threats. When Herbert Lee, a black farmer who had endorsed the voter-registration drive, was shot and killed by a local white, a jury acquitted the perpetrator, accepting his claim of "self defense." When SNCC worker Lawrence Guyot asked a local sheriff about jailed SNCC volunteers, the sheriff assaulted him brutally and then arrested him on a charge of attempted murder. One SNCC worker recalled, "[Fear] was always there, stretched like a tight steel wire between the pit of the stomach and the center of the brain."

Unlike the Freedom Rides, this lonely struggle in a remote corner of the Deep South drew little national attention. Some Justice Department observers briefly visited McComb, but the Kennedy administration declined to intervene despite blatant evidence of civil-rights violations. Many local blacks also fearfully stood aside, but others responded to SNCC's challenge. Sixteen-year-old Brenda Travis spent September in jail after joining a sit-in at a local Woolworth's. Released in October shortly after Herbert Lee's murder, Travis led 115 black high-school students in a march on the McComb city hall.

As the McComb volunteers struggled on, a series of setbacks elsewhere forced a reappraisal of civil-rights strategy. Frustrating at the time, these setbacks demonstrated the movement's underlying strength and resilience. A campaign in Albany, Georgia, proved particularly trying. In the fall of 1961, SNCC, backed by King and SCLC, targeted Albany for a major desegregation campaign that organizers hoped would prod the attorney general to intervene as he had on behalf of the Freedom Riders. Month after month, Albany black residents marched for voting rights and a dismantling of Albany's elaborate structure of segregated schools, libraries, parks, and lunch counters. Hundreds were imprisoned. In contrast to other cities, however, the local white establishment handled the demonstrations shrewdly. The police treated the arrestees reasonably well, avoiding the brutality that could rivet television viewers and galvanize the White House. Police Chief Laurie Pritchett even prayed with the demonstrators prior to arresting them.

Divisions within the black community further weakened the Albany action. Some local black leaders viewed the outside organizations as interlopers, and relations among SNCC, SCLC, and the NAACP remained tense, with SNCC's youthful leaders ridiculing the NAACP as stodgy and timid and the older organization resenting SNCC's lack of appreciation for its efforts. NAACP head Roy Wilkins complained, "We paid some of the expenses of the Albany movement, only to be insulted for being on the wrong side of the generation gap." Privately, Wilkins also attacked Martin Luther King, Jr., whose growing prominence rankled him. Papered over at the time, these feuds hampered the movement's effectiveness at crucial junctures.

Late that year, when white leaders in Albany orally accepted the demonstrators' demands, King proclaimed victory and left town. The white establishment quickly reneged on its agreement, however, and the campaign dragged on. With minimal media attention and no federal intervention, it petered out by August 1962, leaving Albany's walls of segregation still firmly in place. This failure undermined the credibility of the civil-rights leadership and heightened blacks' frustration with the Kennedy administration. Attorney General Kennedy, eager not to offend powerful southern Democrats, insisted that the Constitution permitted federal action only when local officials disobeyed a specific court order or when law and order totally collapsed.

Thus, despite isolated successes, the movement seemed to flounder by the end of 1962. Eight years after the *Brown* decision, 92 percent of southern black children still attended segregated schools, most southern blacks could not vote, and segregation, although weakened, remained firmly in place across much of the South. In a strategy session that fall, SCLC leaders reached two sobering conclusions. First, the Albany disappointment made plain that moral suasion alone would not break down the South's caste system; tough new federal laws were needed. Second, the Kennedy administration would not push such legislation except in the face of dramatic, media-grabbing confrontations. These conclusions led directly to a showdown in Birmingham, Alabama—a clash between determined demonstrators and a rampaging police force that riveted the nation's attention for four dramatic days in May 1963.

1963: Victory in Birmingham, Rising Black Anger, Action in Washington

Birmingham displayed the full spectrum of southern views on race. The city's white elite in their gracious, tree-shaded homes deprecated poor whites' crude racism and violent assaults on civil-rights activists. Yet while some worked cautiously for racial change, others tacitly supported segregation. Birmingham also had the Klan and Bull Connor's violence-prone police. Indeed, civil-rights leaders ranked Birmingham as America's most segregated big city, calling it the "Johannesburg of North America," in reference to South Africa's notorious apartheid system.

The SCLC targeted Birmingham as the focus of its spring 1963 campaign at the urging of Reverend Fred Lee Shuttlesworth, pastor of the city's Sixteenth Street Baptist Church and an SCLC founder. To avoid the Albany mistakes, SCLC recruited 250 local black leaders to coordinate the drive. Determined to provoke encounters that would dramatize the city's institutionalized racism and prod Washington to action, SCLC set forth its strategy in a planning document tellingly labeled Project C—for confrontation. Along with marches, Project C included a boycott of Birmingham's department stores, which relied on African-Americans' patronage while denying them equal employment opportunities. Department-store sales plummeted as blacks stayed away on principle and whites hung back in fear.

On April 6, Reverend Shuttlesworth led a march on city hall and was arrested. Martin Luther King's brother, A. D. King, suffered the same treatment the next day. Dr. King himself, with consciously planned symbolism, led a march on Good Friday and spent three days behind bars, where he composed the memorable "Letter from Birmingham Jail." Widely reprinted, the letter became a central manifesto of the civil-rights movement. In the document, King explained the strategy of nonviolent civil disobedience and its religious and philosophical underpinnings. He made the telling point that disfranchised blacks jailed for disobeying local statutes had had no voice in framing those statutes, and he insisted on the necessity of unremitting pressure to force change on resistant, privileged groups. To those who criticized the timing of Project C, he commented wryly, "Frankly, I have never yet engaged in a direct action movement that was 'well timed.'"

In the missive's most powerful passage, King articulated the anger spawned by policies that denied blacks citizenship and even their full humanity. He described his daughter's disappointment when he explained that she could not go to an amusement park advertised on television, and his sorrow on seeing "the depressing clouds of inferiority begin to form in her little mental sky, and [to] see her begin to distort her little personality by unconsciously developing a bitterness toward white people." Introducing an economic theme that would loom larger in the years ahead, he mentioned the "air-tight cage of poverty in the midst of an affluent society" that intensified black rage. If the moderate, religiously based movement that he represented failed, King concluded somberly, upheavals of incalculable ferocity could ensue. A bitter and alienated segment of the black community had already "lost faith in America," he warned, and was "perilously close" to violence.

Although "Letter from Birmingham Jail" won worldwide support, circumstances in Birmingham deteriorated. A series of marches, some comprising schoolchildren and students, provoked an ever fiercer reaction by Bull Connor's police, who attacked the singing, chanting demonstrators with clubs, cattle prods, snarling police dogs, and high-pressure fire hoses. Many protesters suffered injuries, and waves were sent to jail. Other signs confirmed King's warnings about the unrest simmering in black America. While the KKK lashed out in rage, bombing SCLC's Birmingham headquarters, some blacks struck back against weeks of brutality. In a frightening four-day outbreak beginning on May 3, gangs of young black men from the city's poorest neighborhoods roamed the streets, assaulting police, throwing rocks, bricks, and bottles, and burning white-owned businesses. The riot involved far fewer blacks than the thousands who had peacefully demonstrated, but only urgent pleas by King and Shuttlesworth brought it under control.

The climax came on Tuesday, May 7, as fire hoses ripped into four thousand

Birmingham, Alabama, 1963. Firehoses batter young black marchers as the city's white power structure fights in vain to preserve racial segregation. (©*Charles Moore/Black Star*)

black marchers assembled in a local park. The water tore clothing from bruised bodies and knocked adults and children to the ground as though they had been struck by bullets. Reverend Shuttlesworth was hospitalized. Bull Connor, by now a parody of the die-hard segregationist, chortled when he heard the news, regretting only that the black leader had not been carried away in a hearse. Unlike McComb and Albany in 1962, the Birmingham violence attracted intense media coverage, and national outrage mounted. As the city's jails overflowed with thirteen hundred arrestees, marchers continued to pour from the Sixteenth Street Baptist Church, command center for the demonstrations.

At last the white elite had enough. Dismayed by the boycott's economic toll and the barbaric image of their city being projected to the world and facing intense behind-the-scenes pressure from the Justice Department, the authorities muzzled Connor's police dogs and turned off the fire hoses. On May 10, a group of Birmingham political and business leaders granted the SCLC's demands: an end to discriminatory hiring practices and the formation of a biracial council to supervise the dismantling of the city's elaborate structure of segregated facilities according to an agreed-upon timetable.

This triumph, hailed by Martin Luther King, Jr., as "the most magnificent victory for justice we've ever seen in the Deep South," reverberated across the region. Eager to avoid a repeat of Birmingham's ordeal, some fifty southern cities desegregated in the summer of 1963. Nevertheless, change did not come painlessly. Bombings of homes and churches, police brutality, and even murders continued as white supremacists, sensing the crumbling of an age-old social order, struck out in impotent fury. Moreover, even as Birmingham riveted the nation's attention, the locus of activism was shifting northward geographically and downward socially, into the ranks of the urban poor. The civil-rights struggle, originating in the black middle class, now energized a seething urban underclass trapped in poverty. SCLC's ministers, SNCC's college students, and CORE's Freedom Riders had conducted carefully planned actions in pursuit of specific civil-rights goals, but young ghetto blacks felt little patience with such planning or with King's doctrine of nonresistance. As the uprising of Birmingham's black slum made clear, rage was surging from the urban black poor.

As militancy rose, the mainstream civil-rights organizations—CORE, SCLC, SNCC, even the sedate NAACP—scrambled to keep up. "The [NAACP's] arena of combat," warned Herbert Hill, the organization's national labor secretary, in May 1963, "has shifted from the courtroom to direct mass action." Martin Luther King, Jr., speaking in Chicago that June, vowed to a cheering throng of five thousand, "We're through with tokenism and gradualism and see-how-far-you've-comeism. . . . We can't wait any longer. Now is the time." After mid-decade, King largely shifted his focus from integration—a goal of the black middle class—to the economic plight of the urban black poor.

A leader no less charismatic than King most powerfully articulated the new note of militancy and the new focus on the plight of the urban black poor. Malcolm X, born Malcolm Little in 1925 in Omaha, was the son of a freelance Baptist preacher and a follower of black nationalist leader Marcus Garvey. In 1941 Little moved to Boston to live with a half-sister and soon drifted into the urban underworld of nar-

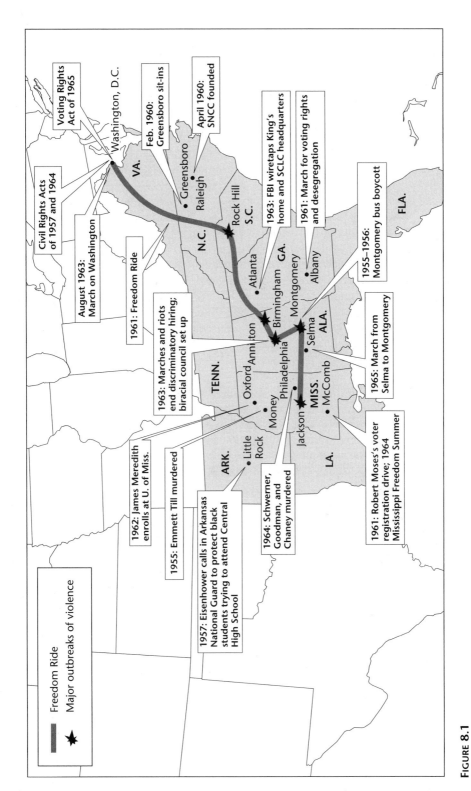

FIGURE 8.1
The Civil-Rights Movement at Flood Tide

cotics, prostitution, and burglary. Imprisoned for robbery in 1946, he converted to the Nation of Islam, or Black Muslims, an ascetic sect that brought discipline into the lives of its members, especially those in prison. Upon joining the Nation of Islam, Little abandoned his "slave name" in favor of Malcolm X; the X stood for his lost African name.

Malcolm X was released from jail in 1952 and traveled to Detroit to meet Black Muslim leader Elijah Muhammad. Assigned to a Nation of Islam temple in Harlem, he soon emerged as the sect's most dynamic minister. His charisma helped to boost the national membership to an estimated forty thousand by 1960. Sixty-nine Black Muslim temples, mostly in large northern cities, and several dozen radio stations carried the word to the black masses. The Nation of Islam preached strict moral purity and the superiority of the black race. Like Garvey's followers in the 1920s, Black Muslims denounced whites as "blue-eyed devils," rejected integration, and called for black pride, black institutions, and, ultimately, a separate black nation. Not until blacks themselves were united, Malcolm X insisted, should they contemplate integration with whites.

Whereas Martin Luther King, Jr., preached nonviolence, integration, and racial harmony, the fiery Malcolm X proclaimed a very different and—to whites—frightening message. Confronted by a violent oppressor, he insisted, the oppressed must use "any means necessary" to break their bonds. "Afro-Americans should [not] be victims any longer. . . ," he declared. "[B]loodshed is a two-way street, . . . dying is a two-way street, . . . killing is a two-way street." By 1963 it was Malcolm, not Martin, who appeared most often on TV screens, in newspaper interviews, and in public forums. Surrounded by stony-faced bodyguards, speaking with absolute confidence, and jabbing his finger to drive home his points, he made an unforgettable impression. Civil-rights leaders committed to the ideal of racial integration and harmony deplored his separatist message. At a 1962 debate in Harlem, James Farmer challenged Malcolm X: "[D]on't tell us any more about the disease—that is clear in our minds. Now, tell us, physician, what is thy cure?" In answer, Malcolm X could only reiterate the utopian dream of a separate black homeland.

Malcolm X's success roused jealousies within the Nation of Islam, and Elijah Muhammad expelled him from the organization in 1963. After a 1964 African tour and pilgrimage to Mecca, Malcolm X's ethical stance shifted. He rejected racism of all kinds, spoke of the common bond linking humanity, and conceded that some American whites did want to end racism. Again he took a new name, one denoting his Mecca pilgrimage: El-Hajj Malik el-Shabazz. But his time was running out. On February 21, 1965, as he addressed supporters in a Harlem ballroom, three Black Muslim loyalists gunned him down.

Despite radical changes during his final months, many Americans still saw Malcolm X at the time of his death as a fomenter of violence. Editorial writers contrasted King, the apostle of peace, and Malcolm X, the preacher of hatred. In fact, as theologian James H. Cone argues in *Martin and Malcolm and America* (1991), the two leaders' views were converging in 1964–1965, with King growing more radical and Malcolm tentatively exploring the possibilities of interracial cooperation.

By the 1990s, Malcolm X would become a folk hero in the inner cities. Rap singers chanted his words, and murals portraying his piercing gaze adorned building walls in black communities. Black filmmaker Spike Lee memorialized him in a 1992 movie. Malcolm X's enduring grip on the American imagination stemmed from the kaleidoscopic nature of his career: the early years as a street hustler; the uncompromising rhetoric of his Black Muslim days; the final, tentative message of racial understanding. Underlying every stage was his fierce intelligence, his powers of language, and his capacity to grow and evolve. His widow, Betty Shabazz, looking back in 1992, offered her own interpretation of her husband's message:

> He said freedom by whatever means necessary to bring about a situation where members of the African diaspora were respected and treated as human beings. . . . A lot of people . . . said "freedom by whatever means necessary" means violence. No, it's not violence. It's a comprehensive statement that says use more than one option. It could be political, social, education, or it could be self-defense.

Malcolm X was far from alone in his rage. In May 1963, James Martin, prominent black Democrat and deputy chairman of the Democratic National Committee, warned Robert Kennedy that the nation faced "the most critical state of race relations since the Civil War." Soon after, the president's brother asked the writer James Baldwin, whose militant manifesto *The Fire Next Time* had just appeared in print, to arrange a meeting of black scholars, writers, and entertainers. Baldwin's assembly included playwright Lorraine Hansberry, singers Lena Horne and Harry Belafonte, and psychologist Kenneth Clark, together with Jerome Smith, a SNCC activist who had survived a severe beating by white racists. The meeting produced a bitter outpouring of black fury against white America that shocked Kennedy. Jerome Smith burst out that he felt physically ill to be in the same room with the attorney general; other participants echoed his rage. Kennedy sat frozen as the anger poured out. Later, he complained, "You couldn't talk to them as you can to Roy Wilkins or Martin Luther King. . . . It was all emotion, hysteria." Kenneth Clark reflected, "There were no villains in that room—only the past of our society."

The rise of Malcolm X and other voices of black militancy stimulated contributions to the NAACP, the SCLC, and other organizations now perceived as bastions of moderation. At a June 1963 meeting in New York, corporate leaders and foundation heads quickly raised a fund of more than one million dollars for the major civil-rights groups. As the strategists of the Birmingham demonstrations had hoped, civil rights again dominated the national agenda. Fear of social upheaval, if not a sudden moral epiphany, rallied white public opinion in support of decisive action. The Kennedy administration, for its part, had watched anxiously as Birmingham had exploded, as Malcolm X had drawn increasing attention, and as even moderates like King had grown more militant. The accelerating pace of black activism, the explosive build-up of racial tensions, and sober warnings of worse to come spurred the president to move from behind-the-scenes manipulation to forthright leadership on civil rights. At Kennedy's direction, the White House prepared a tough new civil-rights bill to submit to Congress.

Another showdown in Alabama provided the occasion for Kennedy's long-delayed action. On June 11, 1963, fulfilling a campaign pledge to "stand in the schoolhouse door" to prevent integration, Governor George C. Wallace physically blocked access to two black students seeking to enroll at the University of Alabama. But under threat of a jail sentence and with the president clearly prepared to step in, the governor nimbly stepped aside when a Justice Department official read a federal court order mandating the students' admission. In contrast to the violence at the University of Mississippi the year before, integration at the University of Alabama proceeded peacefully.

On national television that night, JFK offered a plea for racial justice unprecedented from a U.S. president. The issue confronting the nation, Kennedy announced, was "as old as the scriptures and . . . as clear as the American Constitution." Paraphrasing the Golden Rule, he declared, "Every American ought to have the right to be treated as he would wish to be treated, as one would wish his children to be treated." A century after the Emancipation Proclamation, he went on, African-Americans "are not yet freed from social and economic oppression. And this nation . . . will not be fully free until all its citizens are free." Kennedy offered a stark choice of supporting civil-rights reform or facing disaster: "The fires of frustration and discord are burning in every city, North and South," he proclaimed. "Where legal remedies are not at hand, redress is sought in the streets." A bloody coda to Kennedy's speech came that very night, when a hidden stalker shot and killed Medgar Evers, the president of the Mississippi NAACP.

On June 19, at long last, Kennedy sent his civil-rights bill to Congress. In sweeping language, it outlawed discrimination in all public places and empowered the Justice Department to sue school districts that dragged their feet on integration. To show their support for the bill, two hundred thousand black and white civil-rights advocates from an array of organizations gathered in Washington on August 28. A. Philip Randolph, head of the Brotherhood of Sleeping Car Porters and a veteran civil-rights activist, had proposed the march. (Randolph's call for a similar event in 1941 had prodded President Franklin Roosevelt to ban racial discrimination in federal hiring and in defense industries.) The Kennedy administration initially opposed the march, fearing a backlash. But when the organizers held firm, the White House capitulated and worked closely with its planners.

Under a late-summer sun, a sea of marchers assembled at the Lincoln Memorial. Joan Baez sang "We Shall Overcome," Bob Dylan performed a tribute to Medgar Evers, and black singers Odetta and Mahalia Jackson added their voices. A. Philip Randolph and others urged passage of the civil-rights bill. But it was Martin Luther King's address that transformed a lobbying event into the symbolic capstone of an entire cycle of civil-rights activism. A master orator at his peak, King used vivid, concrete images and biblical language familiar to millions of Americans: "Now is the time to rise from the dark and desolate valley of segregation to the sunlit path of racial justice. . . . Now is the time to lift our nation from the quicksands of racial injustice to the solid rock of brotherhood. . . . We are not satisfied and we will not be satisfied until justice rolls down like the waters, and righteousness like a mighty stream."

In his now-famous extemporized conclusion, King in a few compelling phrases etched a vision of a society in which race did not matter:

Washington, D.C., August 1963. Expressing idealism and unity of purpose, thousands of black and white civil-rights marchers rallied at the Lincoln Memorial. Soon the movement would splinter as the focus moved northward and the demands grew more radical. (*UPI Newsphotos/Bettmann Archive*)

I have a dream that one day on the red hills of Georgia the sons of former slaves and the sons of former slaveowners will be able to sit down together at the table of brotherhood.

I have a dream that one day even the State of Mississippi, a state sweltering with the heat of injustice, sweltering with the heat of oppression, will be transformed into an oasis of freedom and justice. I have a dream that my four little children will one day live in a nation where they will not be judged by the color of their skin but by the content of their character. I have a dream today.

I have a dream that one day down in Alabama with its vicious racists, with its Governor having his lips dripping with the words of interposition and nullification—one day right there in Alabama, little black boys and black girls will be able to join hands with little white boys and white girls as sisters and brothers. . . .

When we let freedom ring, when we let it ring from every village and every hamlet, from every state and every city, we will be able to speed up that day when all God's children, black men and white men, Jews and Gentiles, Protestants and Catholics, will be able to join hands and sing in the words of that old Negro spiritual, "Free at last! Free at last! Thank God almighty, we are free at last."

But moments of moral exaltation are always fleeting. Within two weeks, as if to mock King's eloquence, a bomb blast at Birmingham's Sixteenth Street Baptist Church killed four black girls as they donned choir robes. Furthermore, the movement's apparent unity in August 1963 masked widening rifts. Malcolm X, still in his separatist phase, ridiculed King's plea for unity and the march itself as the "Farce on Washington." A. Philip Randolph originally had wanted to focus the march on the crisis of the urban black poor, but this theme remained muted in favor of the more familiar message of racial integration and harmony. Even as King focused his oratory on the Deep South, attention was shifting northward, where the issues would prove more complex and the modes of protest more divisive. The most prophetic words that August day in Washington were those that the audience did not hear. In the original version of his speech, John Lewis of SNCC had written:

> In good conscience we cannot support the administration's civil rights bill, for it is too little and too late. . . . The revolution is at hand, and we must free ourselves of the chains of political and economic slavery. . . . Mr. Kennedy is trying to take the revolution out of the street and put it in the courts. Listen, Mr. Kennedy. Listen, Mr. Congressman. Listen, fellow citizens. The black masses are on the march for jobs and freedom, and we must say to the politicians that there won't be a "cooling off" period.

Lewis's militancy had alarmed more moderate leaders of the march, not to mention administration officials, and under intense pressure he had deleted the offending passage.

Despite the Washington march and rising black militancy, the administration's civil-rights bill languished in the Judiciary Committee through the rest of 1963 owing to Senator Eastland's stalling tactics. Although Kennedy's June 1963 speech and eventual support of the March on Washington had conveyed a new level of moral commitment, the president's lobbying skills with Congress were notoriously weak. He failed to translate his late embrace of the cause into decisive legislative action. That task would remain for his successor.

1964: Breaking the Legislative Logjam

When JFK was killed in November 1963, President Lyndon Johnson took advantage of the nation's grief to give top priority to Kennedy's stalled civil-rights bill. The midsixties brought a brief moment of near consensus in support of the black cause, and Johnson seized the opportunity.

As a Texas congressman, Johnson had pursued a cautious path on civil rights. In 1948–1949 he opposed President Truman's civil-rights proposals, convinced that to do otherwise would end his political career. At the same time, he attacked racism and deplored political race baiting. In a March 1949 address, he criticized "the unreasoning prejudice against men because of their birth, the color of their skin, or their ancestral background." In 1957, now Senate majority leader and harboring presidential ambitions, Johnson not only supported the Eisenhower administration's civil-rights bill but shepherded it through Congress, protecting his regional base by engineering some compromises favored by southern legislators.

As president, LBJ counted on his regional roots to overcome southern opposition to the Kennedy bill. To speechwriter Richard Goodwin, he confided, "Those Harvards [his term for the Kennedy team] think that a politician from Texas doesn't care about Negroes. . . . But I . . . always vowed that if I ever had the power I'd make sure every Negro had the same chance as every white man. Now I have it. And I'm going to use it." Within days of Kennedy's assassination, LBJ met with Martin Luther King, Jr., James Farmer, A. Philip Randolph, and other civil-rights leaders and pledged to move quickly on this front.

A coalition of civil-rights organizations, liberal labor unions, civic and women's groups, and Christian and Jewish religious bodies rallied support. Churches had involved themselves especially heavily in civil rights in the early sixties. The United Presbyterian church, for example, had budgeted $500,000 to support the cause. Such activism peaked in 1964–1965. Indeed, Senator Hubert Humphrey praised religious groups as "the most important force" in pushing for a civil-rights law. The National Council of Churches (NCC), an association of large Protestant denominations, lobbied, organized marches and letter-writing campaigns, and arranged grass-roots speaking tours by civil-rights advocates. During the 1964 civil-rights debate, the NCC held daily services at a church near the Capitol.

These organizations emphasized the ethical dimension of the civil-rights cause. As James Reston of the *New York Times* wrote, "If there is no effective moral reaction out in the country, there will be no effective political reaction." A woman in Cedar Rapids, Iowa, stressed this theme in a letter to her congressman:

> I have a feeling of sickness inside of me that comes from a realization of the suffering of Negroes and the guilt of whites. I share in the suffering and in the guilt. I write you, as my representative . . . , to help me rid myself and my country of this suffering and this guilt. I feel that passage of the civil rights legislation . . . will make it possible for healing to begin.

The civil-rights bill easily passed the House early in 1964. In the Senate, floor-leader Humphrey labored mightily to overcome stubborn opposition. President Johnson sat on the phone, cajoling opponents and waverers, working his wiles especially on Everett Dirksen of Illinois, a key Republican. For seventy-five days, opponents filibustered against the bill. At last on June 10, 1964, in a dramatic moment, the Senate voted to end the filibuster. Senator Clair Engle of California, unable to speak because of recent brain surgery, nodded his head "yes" from a wheelchair on the cloture vote. The next day, by a 73–27 tally, the Civil Rights Act of 1964 passed the Senate.

This omnibus measure, hailed by the *New York Times* as "the most far-reaching civil-rights bill since Reconstruction days," targeted numerous expressions of racism in American life. The law made it easier for the attorney general to participate in private civil-rights cases and to prosecute segregated school districts and election officials who denied voting rights to blacks. Other sections forbade discrimination in hiring, in federally funded programs, and in public facilities such as restaurants, motels, theaters, and amusement parks.* Finally, the law made permanent the Equal Employment Opportunity Commission, which would monitor compliance with laws against workplace discrimination. The act did not end racism—no law could—but it represented a big step toward eradicating racism's institutional manifestations.†

Out of the limelight, grass-roots civil-rights activists in the meantime focused on the difficult task of local political organizing. After the March on Washington, Rob-

---

* The Supreme Court quickly upheld the public-facilities provision in *Heart of Atlanta Motel, Inc.* v. *United States* (1964).

† In an action little noticed at the time, Title VII of the Civil Rights Act of 1964 barred discrimination on the basis of sex as well as of race. Although introduced by a southern legislator in an unsuccessful effort to discredit the bill, Title VII would play an important role in feminists' efforts against job discrimination.

ert Moses and other SNCC leaders had resumed their dangerous voter-registration campaign in rural Mississippi. Through Moses's efforts, SNCC and CORE formed the Council of Federated Organizations (COFO) to coordinate the effort. Late in 1963, COFO organizers had laid plans for a major voter-registration drive in 1964, to be called Mississippi Freedom Summer. The question of whether to recruit northern white students proved divisive. Some argued that the presence of white volunteers would reduce the threat of violence and heighten media attention, especially if a white volunteer were killed or injured. Opponents warned that an influx of white volunteers would inhibit local blacks from developing their own leadership skills. Advocates of a biracial campaign won, and the call went out to northern colleges and universities. In June 1964, after a brief training period, nearly a thousand white northern student volunteers streamed into Mississippi.

The COFO campaign roused murderous opposition. In mid-June, three young men investigating an arson attack on a black church disappeared. They were Michael Schwerner, a white CORE staff member in Mississippi; Andrew Goodman, a white summer volunteer from the North; and James Chaney, a local black active in the voter-registration campaign. The FBI soon arrested twenty-one Ku Klux Klan members, plus the local sheriff and deputy sheriff, in the kidnapping plot. Six weeks later, the bodies were discovered in shallow graves at a dam construction site near Philadelphia, Mississippi.

The triple murder was the most shocking instance of racist violence, but the summer also brought repeated bombings, arson, gunfire, and attacks on COFO volunteers. Despite a beefed-up FBI presence in Mississippi, J. Edgar Hoover, characteristically deploring the "overemphasis" on civil rights, declined to protect Freedom Summer volunteers. One COFO leader, alluding to the escalating war in Vietnam, noted the irony of Washington's readiness to protect the South Vietnamese from communism while refusing to protect blacks and civil-rights workers in Mississippi.

The violence further radicalized young black activists, hastening their turn from integration to economic and political demands and deepening their skepticism of King's message of nonresistance. For white volunteers, the experience stirred distrust of Johnson-era liberalism. Many would soon emerge as outspoken critics of the Vietnam War. The summer also drove a wedge between white and black civil-rights workers, as some southern blacks criticized the white volunteers as liberal do-gooders who after a few months in Mississippi would return to their safe, affluent world.

In the end, Mississippi Freedom Summer yielded mixed results. Some projects laid the groundwork for future changes. At COFO-run "Freedom Schools," for example, black children and some adults studied not only academic subjects but also African-American history and strategies for community organizing. Yet the goal of increasing blacks' political clout proved elusive: confronted by intransigent election officials, Freedom Summer volunteers registered only about twelve hundred new black voters.

Despite the numerically scant results, the Mississippi Freedom Summer reverberated through the 1964 Democratic convention and ultimately helped to transform southern politics. As part of the project, COFO had formed the Mississippi Freedom Democratic party (MFDP) as an alternative to the lily-white regular Democratic party. Following party rules, the MFDP named forty-two delegates and twenty-two alternates, including maids, carpenters, farmers, ministers, and teachers of both races, to the party's August convention in Atlantic City. Initially the MFDP project was mainly symbolic, but when influential Democratic liberals such as New York lawyer Joseph Rauh endorsed it, COFO began to work to seat MFDP's alternative delegation.

Before the party's credentials committee, a parade of witnesses urged certification of the MFDP. The advocates included Rauh; Martin Luther King, Jr.; Roy Wilkins; Michael Schwerner's widow, Rita; and Fannie Lou Hamer, a forceful forty-seven-year-old sharecropper and MFDP delegate who recounted the persecution that she had suffered, from jail beatings to explusion from her farm, for trying to register to vote.

President Johnson opposed seating the MFDP, fearful of alienating the white South, jeopardizing his election chances, and angering the southern congressional delegation on whose support his Great Society reforms depended. Johnson worried, too, about a primary challenge mounted by Alabama governor George Wallace whose appeal to white, working-class discontent had won him more than a third of the vote in Democratic primaries in Wisconsin, Indiana, and Maryland. Ever the compromiser, however, LBJ proposed that the MFDP delegates be designated "honored guests" of the convention—with no voting rights—and he assigned Hubert Humphrey to sell this plan to the MFDP. The delegates refused to yield, but after heavy negotiations most civil-rights leaders accepted a compromise: Two MFDP delegates would be seated as at-large delegates with voting rights. In addition, the regular Mississippi delegation would be required to pledge support for the party ticket, and in future conventions no delegations would be seated from states that disfranchised blacks. Having settled, or swept under the carpet, this divisive issue, the convention adopted a strong civil-rights plank, nominated Johnson by acclamation, ratified his choice of Hubert Humphrey for vice president, and geared up for the campaign.

But the deal exacted a high price. A disillusioned Fannie Lou Hamer later recalled, "We learned the hard way that even though we had all the law and all the righteousness on our side—that white man is not going to give up his power to us." What many SNCC and CORE volunteers viewed as the sellout of the MFDP, coming after the frustrations and violence of the Mississippi Freedom Summer, contributed to the radicalization of U.S. politics in the later 1960s. The events of 1964 deepened young black activists' distrust of interracial cooperation and eroded their faith in "working within the system." SNCC leader Cleveland Sellers later recalled, "Never again were we lulled into believing that our task was exposing injustices so that the 'good' people of America could eliminate them. . . . After Atlantic City, our struggle was not for civil rights, but for liberation."

For SNCC, the turn toward militancy and "black liberation" intensified when eleven leaders, including James Forman, John Lewis, Robert Moses, and Fannie Lou Hamer, visited Africa in September 1964 as guests of the Marxist government of Guinea. Lewis and another SNCC leader then traveled to Kenya, where they by chance encountered Malcolm X on his own pilgrimage to the African homeland. For two days Malcolm lectured the two on the need for black solidarity and for closer links between U.S. blacks and Africa. Although SNCC did not embrace Malcolm

X's ideology, his views would influence the movement in the later 1960s. Lewis, as president of SNCC from 1963 to 1966, would steer the organization toward increasingly radical goals.*

1965: Selma and the Voting Rights Act

Having partially finessed the politics of race in the 1964 campaign, Johnson hoped to avoid another civil-rights battle. Instead, he sought to pursue his larger reform agenda and to give the South time to digest the Civil Rights Act of 1964. But as with President Kennedy, events forced his hand. Civil-rights leaders, smarting from the MFDP dispute and from the disappointing Mississippi Freedom Summer, refused to take a back seat. Demanding action on a stronger voting-rights law, they took steps to gain their objective.

The SCLC, relatively quiescent since the Birmingham campaign, again took the lead in 1965. Although still committed to nonviolence, King and other SCLC strategists increasingly saw peaceful resistance less in ethical than in tactical terms, as one means of bringing pressure to bear on Washington. Repeating the Birmingham strategy of deliberately courting confrontation, SCLC formulated Project Alabama to force new battles that would draw national attention and bring federal action on voting rights.

The target this time was Selma, some fifty miles west of Montgomery, a bastion of segregation and white supremacy largely untouched by five years of civil-rights activism. The city had moved at a snail's pace to register the fifteen thousand eligible black voters. Selma also had its own version of Bull Connor—Sheriff James Clark, Jr.—who announced his sentiments with a large button asserting: "NEVER!" Asked by a reporter whether a female black demonstrator whom he had arrested was married, Clark sneered, "She's a nigger woman and she hasn't got a Miss or a Mrs. in front of her name."

Selma housed a small but resourceful group of local black activists led by Amelia and Samuel Boynton. When a SNCC voter-registration drive faltered, Amelia Boynton invited in SCLC, and the organization eagerly accepted. The new militance in Dr. King's message emerged as he kicked off the Selma campaign in early January 1965: "We are not asking, we are demanding the ballot." Marchers besieged the courthouse daily, and soon more than two thousand blacks sat in prison. But Sheriff Clark, taking a tip from the 1962 white strategy in Albany, at first avoided the kind of brutality that had attracted media attention. On February 17, however, a state trooper shot and killed civil-rights demonstrator Jimmy Lee Jackson. King at once announced a march from Selma to Montgomery to present a petition to Governor Wallace protesting Jackson's murder and demanding action on voting rights. Nonetheless, when LBJ privately pressured King to call off the march, King and his SCLC lieutenants shelved the idea and returned to Atlanta.

---

* His faith in the system somewhat restored, Lewis would head the federal domestic-service program VISTA during the Carter administration, sit on the Atlanta city council from 1981 to 1986, and in the latter year win election to Congress.

Selma, Alabama, 1965. This haunting photograph evokes the diversity of the civil-rights coalition that had coalesced by 1965, and emphasizes the way the movement employed patriotic and religious symbolism to further its goals. (*Bruce Davidson/©1970 Magnum Photos*)

Other activists in Selma were not so easily diverted. On March 7, soon dubbed "Bloody Sunday," the Reverend Hosea Williams of the SCLC field staff, together with SNCC chairman John Lewis and local supporters, proceeded with the march. As the six hundred protesters approached the Edmund Pettus Bridge over the Alabama River, they met Sheriff Clark with a hundred deputies and state police major John Cloud with a similar number of troopers. Cloud gave the marchers two minutes to turn back. When they refused, troopers and police deputies, some on horseback, plowed into the peaceful demonstrators, throwing tear gas, flailing nightsticks, and jabbing with electric cattle prods. Frightened and bloody, the marchers fell back from the brutal assault. Fifty required hospital treatment.

Television once again carried the images to the nation and the world. Demands for protection of the Selma activists and for a federal voting-rights law rained down on Washington. A group of students attempted a sit-in at the White House as more demonstrated outside. Ministers, priests, nuns, and rabbis poured into Selma in solidarity with the beleaguered marchers.

As King and other top civil-rights leaders hastened to Selma, pressure mounted to complete the march. SNCC's Sellers, one of the most radical of a quickly radicalizing movement, recalled, "We were angry. And we wanted to show Governor Wallace, the Alabama State Highway Patrol, Sheriff Clark, Selma's whites, the federal government and poor Southern blacks in other Selmas that we didn't intend to take any more shit. We would ram the march down the throat of anyone who tried to stop us." Nevertheless, a federal judge banned the march, Wallace and Selma authorities adamantly opposed it, and President Johnson warned King that further violence would hurt the chances for a voting-rights bill, which he had now decided to introduce.

King found himself trapped in the middle. He had just won the Nobel Peace Prize and had been named *Time's* Man of the Year, but in the volatile and rapidly evolving civil-rights movement, his leadership had come under challenge. Juggling conflicting pressures, he agreed to a symbolic gesture: The marchers would proceed to the Pettus Bridge, hold a prayer service, and return to Selma. But King failed to inform the other leaders or the marchers of the plan. With everyone primed for a trek to Montgomery, his instructions to return to Selma produced confusion and anger. Bitter criticism of King's "Tuesday turnaround" deepened the rift in the movement. As in late 1962, the movement again seemed to flounder.

Rabid segregationists, however, once more displayed their ability to reenergize the civil-rights campaign whenever it flagged. Shortly after the "Tuesday turnaround," several whites attacked three Unitarian ministers on the streets of Selma. Chanting "Nigger lover," they assaulted James Reeb so badly that he died a few days later of massive brain injuries. Protesters continued to pour into Selma, now the focus of international attention, and outraged protests deluged the White House. On March 15, 1965, LBJ appeared before a joint session of Congress to propose a voting-rights bill. The president's address, televised live, matched John Kennedy's speech of June 1963 in the eloquence of its call for decisive action on civil rights.

Moving beyond details, Johnson defined racism as "a challenge . . . to the values and purposes and the meaning" of America. "Should we defeat every enemy, and should we double our wealth and conquer the stars, and still be unequal to this issue, then we will have failed as a people and a nation." Praising the Selma demonstrators who had stirred the nation's conscience, Johnson defined Congress's immediate task unambiguously: "Every American citizen must have an equal right to vote." He ended by repeating the refrain of the civil-rights anthem: "We *shall* overcome." With a unanimity that was becoming increasingly rare, black leaders across the ideological spectrum hailed the president's message. Martin Luther King, who watched the broadcast with the family of the murdered Jimmy Lee Jackson, telephoned the president to offer his praise.

The speech transformed the deadlock in Alabama. President Johnson pressured the local federal judge to issue a march permit and warned Governor Wallace that police brutality would not be tolerated. After a send-off sermon by King, eight thousand marchers set out from Selma. A core group of about three hundred continued all the way along Route 80, often in heavy rain but protected by a solicitous Alabama National Guard federalized by LBJ. As they approached Montgomery, three thousand supporters joined them for a triumphant entry into the city. Speaking to the throng near the state house where the Confederacy was born in 1861, King lauded Johnson's speech and demanded passage of the voting-rights bill. He also defined the movement's broadening agenda, calling for action on such issues as de facto housing segregation and joblessness in the black slums of urban America.

As so often in these years, a stab of violence followed the moment of triumph. That evening, night-riding Klansmen shot and killed Viola Liuzzo, a volunteer from Detroit, as she drove marchers back to Selma.

The momentum behind Johnson's voting-rights bill had grown unstoppable.

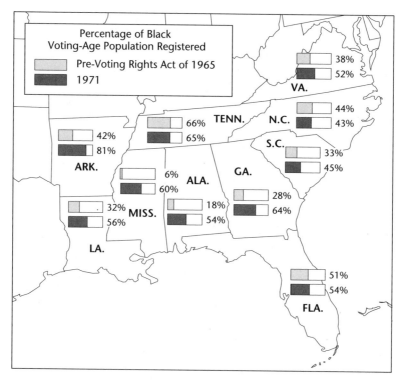

FIGURE 8.2

Voter Registration of African-Americans in the South, 1964–1971

The Voting Rights Act of 1965, passed in August, authorized federal officials to register voters and to supervise elections in electoral districts with a clear record of racial bias.* It outlawed the various devices long used in the South to exclude black voters. Together with the voting-rights acts of 1957 and 1960 and the 1964 constitutional amendment outlawing the poll tax, this law at last opened the door of real political power to southern blacks. By mid-1966, half a million blacks had joined the South's voting rolls; by 1968, nearly four hundred blacks would hold elective office in the region. While southern whites defected to the Republican banner, African-Americans transformed the South's once all-white Democratic party. Even in die-hard Mississippi, black voter registration rose from the single digits in the early 1960s to an astounding 59 percent by 1968. As blacks streamed to the polls, race-baiting politicians changed their tune. George Wallace, always a politician first and a racist second, would successfully court black voters in an Alabama gubernatorial campaign in 1982. President Johnson acknowledged the altered climate in 1965 by naming the first black cabinet member, Robert C. Weaver, to head the new Department of

---

* The law provided that elections could be supervised in any electoral district where fewer than half the eligible voters were registered or where fewer than half the eligible voters had actually cast ballots in the 1964 election.

Housing and Urban Development. In 1967 Johnson appointed NAACP lawyer Thurgood Marshall as the first black Supreme Court justice.

The year 1968 would bring a final civil-rights measure: the Open Housing Act outlawing racial discrimination in the sale or rental of most housing units.* By this time, one long cycle of civil-rights activism would be over; new voices and new issues would hold center stage. Before we turn to this phase, however, the great events that convulsed and transformed the nation from the mid-1950s to the mid-1960s merit a few parting observations.

Reflections on the Civil-Rights Struggle, 1960–1965

Just as historians of the 1930s speak of a "First New Deal" and a "Second New Deal," so students of the African-American freedom struggle have come to divide it into two distinct phases, with the demarcation line in 1965. The first stage, whose beginnings we examined in Chapter 5 and whose culmination we have just explored, focused primarily on the Jim Crow system of the South that denied most blacks the vote, excluded them from equal educational and job opportunities, and subjected them to a rigidly segregated and discriminatory social system.

This movement had deep roots in American history, including the long legacy of religion-based reform and African-American protest. Its immediate catalysts were the Supreme Court's school-integration decision of 1954, the Montgomery bus boycott, and the charismatic leadership of Martin Luther King, Jr. But with the sit-ins and Freedom Rides of 1960–1961, the movement gained fresh energy and emerged from the shadow of any one individual, even one as gifted as Dr. King.

At this stage the movement's leaders succeeded in building a broad consensus behind their goals because they spoke a vocabulary of individual rights and equality of opportunity enshrined in the American political tradition. With the desegregation of Birmingham and other cities across the South, along with the enactment of the Civil Rights Act of 1964 and the Voting Rights Act of 1965, this phase of the struggle essentially closed. Pockets of resistance remained, but as historian J. Mills Thornton III has observed, the first stage of the civil rights campaign ended "for the same reason that World War II ended: the enemies had been defeated."

Yet like a mountain-climbing expedition in which the conquering of one summit reveals higher and even more difficult peaks in the distance, the successes of the early 1960s exposed the next challenge: the social problems, political impotence, and economic marginality of the black masses in the inner-city slums, especially those living in the largest metropolitan centers of New York, Chicago, Detroit, and Los Angeles—the alienated outsiders to whom Malcolm X had appealed. After 1965, the focus shifted from voting rights and legally imposed segregation to the grievances of this disinherited black underclass. The struggle thus entered a new, more controversial phase. The rhetoric, often luridly embellished by fiery young rad-

---

* Only private houses sold without the services of a real-estate agent were excluded from the provisions of the law.

icals, centered not on constitutional rights and equal opportunity but on collective action to advance the interests of a specific portion of the African-American community. As Thornton notes, the ideological shift from equality of opportunity to equality of outcome would prove deeply divisive. Hints of the disagreements that would bedevil the movement in future years came in a little-noted clause of the Civil Rights Act of 1964 that went beyond outlawing racial discrimination in hiring to call for action to rectify the effects of past discrimination. This notion of officially mandated "affirmative action" for the benefit of a designated category of citizens eventually would stir intense controversy.

To concede that this first phase of the civil-rights movement did not address every dimension of racism in America is not to diminish what it did achieve. The thousands of volunteers who joined in this stage of the struggle successfully challenged a caste system embedded in the culture, ideology, legal system, and social structure of the South. In the process they brought about a profound social transformation and became part of the most important social movement of postwar American history. Demolishing a system of segregation and discrimination dating ultimately to the slave codes of the antebellum period was a giant and essential first step before activists could address more complex issues of racial inequity.

This early phase of the civil-rights movement cannot be understood without close attention to its decentralized, grass-roots quality. If one views the local campaigns as only ancillary to the maneuverings of presidents, senators, governors, or mayors, or if one looks only at national leaders such as Martin Luther King, Jr., one misses a key element of the story. Indeed, David Garrow has argued that an understanding of the dynamic of the movement requires redefining the concept of leadership to encompass not only the well-known national figures but also those who worked at the local level—men and women like Robert Moses and Fannie Lou Hamer in Mississippi, Amelia Boynton in Selma, Fred Shuttlesworth in Birmingham, and SNCC's Charles Sherrod, who labored in relative obscurity in southwest Georgia. Individuals such as these, Garrow contends, "equally merit the designation as civil rights 'leaders' if that label is to be applied in its most substantively meaningful way." Such persons, no less than the better-known celebrities, he argues, made possible "the real emergence of a sustained and widespread movement in the South."

The civil-rights movement of the early sixties unfolded in places like Greensboro, Anniston, McComb, Albany, Montgomery, Birmingham, and Selma. Its true heroes were not government officials or civil-rights bureaucrats but ordinary Americans who found within themselves extraordinary reserves of determination and courage. Local figures identified issues of immediate concern and devised creative strategies for addressing them. Sometimes they made use of national organizations like SCLC, yet they were more than bit players in a drama directed from afar that followed a single script. From this perspective, the civil-rights movement dissolves into countless minidramas of personal empowerment and local community action.

Nor was the movement merely a melodrama pitting "good guys" versus "bad guys" or plaster saints against stage villains. The civil-rights leaders from Martin Luther King, Jr., on down were all too human, with their full share of flaws and foibles. The various organizations competed fiercely for contributions and media coverage, and some leaders made unseemly efforts to demean their rivals. Although this competition sometimes proved creative and offered activists a broad pallet of strategies and leadership styles, it also took its toll in effectiveness.

Within white America, too, including the white South, a full spectrum of responses emerged to the radical social changes presaged by the civil-rights struggle. These responses ranged from grim, even murderous resistance to thoughtful acceptance of the inevitability of change. By a leap of imagination, one can even begin to understand the fears of social displacement and of a jeopardized way of life that motivated those who defied the drive for civil rights. The movement, after all, threatened a hierarchical social order that had endured for more than three centuries. Whites who had assumed that all blacks "knew their place" suddenly confronted a mass uprising of the oppressed. In fear and fury, some lashed out in violence. The irony for them is that the more the civil-rights demonstrators suffered, the more supporters rallied to their cause.

Yet when all the complexity, ambiguity, and shades of gray are recognized, the profound historical and moral significance of the civil-rights movement shines through with startling clarity. No longer willing to tolerate a status quo rooted in racial exploitation and injustice, many thousands of black Americans, supported by large numbers of white Americans, took their fate into their own hands and transformed a society. This phase of the civil-rights movement is noteworthy, too, for its influence on the later course of the black freedom struggle. Despite the post-1965 changes in direction and emphasis, the events of 1960–1965 decisively shaped the movement's future. As Harvard Sitkoff and other historians emphasize, the sit-ins, Freedom Rides, voter-registration drives, and community-organizing campaigns of the early sixties provided strategic blueprints for later activists. And the bitter resistance that the escalating movement encountered helped to radicalize a younger generation of blacks and soured them on tactics of moral suasion and working within the system. The ferocity of white opposition inflamed the anger of ordinary blacks North and South, toughening their will to resist. Even the most frightening explosions of ghetto rioting and arson in the later 1960s had as their model the white outlaws who earlier in the decade had greeted civil-rights demonstrators with beatings, bullets, bombs, and fire.

For the civil-rights establishment, the unfolding events of the early sixties revealed the depth of African-American frustration and the explosive potential beneath the surface in urban black slums. These years spurred the movement's leadership to devise new strategies and formulate more ambitious goals. They taught black-liberation activists another important lesson as well: Violent confrontation—even the threat of violence—was one sure way to gain attention in Washington, state capitals, city halls, and the centers of media power. This realization would give rise to more militant tactics consciously designed to elicit the kind of dramatic and visceral confrontations that brought results in 1960–1965. Such a climate was hardly congenial to strategies that preached restraint, patient negotiation, and turning the other cheek.

The civil-rights movement also influenced political and social reforms not directly related to black America. Lyndon Johnson's War on Poverty, for example, gained urgency from the heightened awareness of the economic condition of inner-city blacks that emerged from the civil-rights movement. On another front, the antiwar movement of the later 1960s drew ideological and tactical inspiration from the civil-rights campaign. Indeed, many campus antiwar leaders had gained their first taste of political mobilization as volunteers in the Mississippi Freedom Summer or other civil-rights actions.

Similarly, the feminists who would reanimate the U.S. women's movement in the 1970s (see Chapter 12) owed an enormous debt to the civil-rights cause. The earlier campaign had drawn on the talents of countless strong and resourceful women—not only the relatively well known, such as Rosa Parks, Ella Baker, Fannie Lou Hamer, and Amelia Boynton, but thousands more, black and white, who marched, organized, joined sit-ins, and taught in Freedom Schools. College student Diane Nash, for example, a Nashville sit-in leader, played a key role in reviving the Freedom Ride campaign in May 1961 when repeated violence left it near collapse. Telephoning CORE's James Farmer to insist that the Freedom Rides continue, Nash helped John Lewis to assemble the cadre of volunteers who resumed the rides after the original riders abandoned the campaign in Birmingham. The civil-rights campaign offered later feminists models of strong, committed women as well as a vocabulary for understanding oppression and strategies for confronting that oppression. Of course, the struggles against racism and against sexism differed in many ways, but the links between the two are apparent. Still later, other activists, from disabled citizens to gays and lesbians to environmental crusaders, would draw on the ideology and strategy of the civil-rights pioneers. Few other social movements in American history have had such a protean and broad-ranging impact.

CONCLUSION

For all its transforming power, this phase of the civil-rights movement clearly had lost momentum by the time the last major civil-rights measure, the 1968 open-housing law, was enacted. Indeed, even at the movement's zenith in 1965, the consensus that had taken shape over the preceding decade was splintering. As the focus shifted from South to North, from individual rights to collective goals, from nationally known leaders to fiery young radicals, and from carefully planned demonstrations to seemingly nihilistic explosions of violence, middle America moved from sympathetic support to fearful uneasiness.

Deepening conflict over the escalating Vietnam War further undermined the civil-rights cause. Martin Luther King's rapport with Lyndon Johnson turned to hostility and resentment as the black leader harshly criticized the president's war policies. Thousands of others who had cheered Johnson's stand on civil rights bitterly opposed his actions in Vietnam. White House speechwriter Richard Goodwin, looking back on LBJ's finest hour, the voting-rights speech of March 15, 1965, would reminisce years later, "God, how I loved Lyndon Johnson at that moment; how unimaginable it would have been to think that in two years' time I would—like many others who listened that night—go into the streets against him."

SELECTED READINGS

The Law and Politics of Civil Rights

Numan V. Bartley and Hugh D. Graham, *Southern Politics and the Second Reconstruction* (1975); Monroe Billington, "Lyndon B. Johnson and Blacks: The Early Years," *Journal of Negro History* (January 1977); Jack Bloom, *Class, Race, and the Civil Rights Movement* (1987); Carl M. Brauer, *John F. Kennedy and the Second Reconstruction* (1977); Charles E. Fager, *Selma 1965* (1974); David Garrow, *Protest at Selma: Martin Luther King, Jr. and the Voting Rights Act of 1965* (1978) and *The FBI and Martin Luther King, Jr.* (1981); Richard Goodwin, *Remembering America: A Voice from the Sixties* (1988); Hugh Davis Graham, *The Civil Rights Era: Origins and Development of National Policy* (1990); James C. Harvey, *Black Civil Rights During the Johnson Administration* (1973); Elizabeth Jacoway and David Colburn, eds., *Southern Businessmen and Desegregation* (1982); Steven F. Lawson, *Black Ballots: Voting Rights in the South, 1944–1969* (1976) and *In Pursuit of Power: Southern Blacks and Electoral Politics, 1965–1982* (1985); Neil MacNeil, *Dirksen: Portrait of a Public Man* (1970); Burke Marshall, *Federalism and Civil Rights* (1964); Kenneth O'Reilly, *"Racial Matters": The FBI's Secret File on Black America, 1960–1972* (1989); Gary Orfield, *The Reconstruction of Southern Education: The Schools and the 1964 Civil Rights Act* (1969); J. W. Peltason, *Fifty-eight Lonely Men: Southern Federal Judges and School Desegregation* (rev. ed., 1971); Mark Stern, *Calculating Visions: Kennedy, Johnson and Civil Rights* (1992); James Sundquist, *Politics and Policy: The Eisenhower, Kennedy, and Johnson Years* (1968); Pat Watters and Reese Cleghorn, *Climbing Jacob's Ladder: The Arrival of Negroes in Southern Politics* (1967); Charles Whalen and Barbara Whalen, *The Longest Debate: A Legislative History of the 1964 Civil Rights Act* (1985); Harris Wofford, *Of Kennedys and Kings: Making Sense of the Sixties* (1980); Allan Wolk, *The Presidency and Black Civil Rights: Eisenhower to Nixon* (1971)

Civil-Rights Leaders, Organizations, and Campaigns

Catherine Barnes, *Journey from Jim Crow: The Desegregation of Southern Transit* (1983); Numen V. Bartley, *The Rise of Massive Resistance: Race and Politics in the South During the 1950s* (1969); Sally Belfrage, *Freedom Summer* (1965); Taylor Branch, *Parting the Waters: America in the King Years, 1954–63* (1988); Seth Cagin and Philip Dray, *We Are Not Afraid: The Story of Goodman, Schwerner, and Chaney and the Civil Rights Campaign for Mississippi* (1988); Claybourne Carson, *In Struggle: SNCC and the Black Awakening of the 1960s* (1981); Clayborne Carson et al., *The Eyes on the Prize Civil Rights Reader* (1991); Sean Dennis Cashman, *African Americans and the Quest for Civil Rights, 1900–1990* (1991); William H. Chafe, *Civilities and Civil Rights: Greensboro, North Carolina, and the Black Struggle for Freedom* (1980) and *Never Stop Running: Allard Lowenstein and the Struggle to Save American Liberalism* (1993); David Chalmers, *And the Crooked Places Made Straight: The Struggle for Social Changes in the 1960s* (1991); James H. Cone, *Martin and Malcolm and America: A Dream or a Nightmare* (1991); Charles W. Eagles, ed., *The Civil Rights Movement in America* (1986); Sara M. Evans, *Personal Politics: The Roots of Women's Liberation in the Civil Rights Movement and the New Left* (1980); Adam Fairclough, *To Redeem the Soul of America: The Southern Christian Leadership Conference and Martin Luther King, Jr.* (1987); James Farmer, *Lay Bare the Heart: An Autobiography of the Civil Rights Movement* (1985); James F. Findlay, *Church People in the Struggle: The National Council of Churches and the Black Freedom Movement, 1950–1970* (1993); James Forman, *The Making of Black Revolutionaries* (1972); John Hope Franklin, *From Slavery to Freedom: A History of Negro Americans* (5th ed., 1980); David J. Garrow, *Protest at Selma: Martin Luther King, Jr., and the Voting Rights Act of 1965* (1978) and *Bearing the Cross: Martin Luther*

King, Jr., and the Southern Christian Leadership Conference, 1955–1968 (1986); Peter Goldman, The Death and Life of Malcolm X (2d ed., 1979); Herbert H. Haines, Black Radicals and the Civil Rights Mainstream, 1954–1970 (1988); Richard H. King, Civil Rights and the Idea of Freedom (1992); David L. Lewis, King: A Biography (2d ed., 1978); Doug McAdam, Political Process and the Development of Black Insurgency, 1930–1970 (1982) and Freedom Summer (1988); Neil R. McMillen, The Citizens' Councils: Organized Resistance to the Second Reconstruction, 1954–64 (1971); Malcolm X, with Alex Haley, The Autobiography of Malcolm X (1965); Aldon D. Morris, The Origins of the Civil Rights Movement: Black Communities Organizing for Change (1984); Bruce Perry, Malcolm: The Life of a Man Who Changed Black America (1991); Fred Powledge, Free at Last? The Civil Rights Movement and the People Who Made It (1991); Howell Raines, My Soul Is Rested: Movement Days in the Deep South Remembered (1977); Mary Aickin Rothschild, A Case of Black and White: Northern Volunteers and the Southern Freedom Summers, 1964–1965 (1982); Cleveland Sellers, The River of No Return: The Autobiography of a Black Militant and the Life and Death of SNCC (1973); Harvard Sitkoff, The Struggle for Black Equality, 1954–1992 (1993); Robert Weisbrot, Freedom Bound: A History of America's Civil Rights Movement (1991); Stephen J. Whitfield, A Death in the Delta: The Story of Emmett Till (1989); Miles Wolff, Lunch at the 5 & 10 (1990).

Part Three

THE LOSS OF INNOCENCE

Between 1965 and 1974, American society reeled under a series of crises that pitted generation against generation, black against white, ethnic group against ethnic group, and female against male. The traumatic events of this period redirected and partially derailed the momentum for liberal reform that had taken shape in the late fifties and early sixties.

As this liberal momentum crested in 1964–1965, Congress had enacted a remarkable body of legislation that attacked poverty and addressed such basic social issues as health care, environmental protection, racial segregation, and voting rights. Moreover, a broad national consensus had formed around the twin goals of ending racial segregation and transforming Lyndon Johnson's shimmering Great Society vision into reality. Johnson's stunning electoral victory in November 1964 seemed a mandate to pursue this ambitious domestic agenda.

But the liberal consensus, always fragile, proved ephemeral. On the domestic front, growing cultural, social, and racial tensions foreshadowed conflict. Young black activists, rejecting the moderate leadership of Martin Luther King, Jr., espoused goals and strategies that alarmed white America. King himself adopted increasingly controversial positions, and northern cities erupted in racial violence. Simultaneously, as the affluent baby-boom generation reached college age, campus unrest and cultural rebellion began to intensify. Youthful radicals challenged their politically and now economically dominant parents, as well as the Old Left ideology of the 1930s and the Cold War liberalism personified by Kennedy and Johnson.

The liberal consensus might have survived had not President Johnson escalated the Vietnam War early in 1965. Just as the Berlin Wall once cut a city in half, the Vietnam experience bisects postwar American history. Johnson's decision to expand the conflict, rooted in twenty years of Cold War thinking and strategic calculations that seemed persuasive at the time, not only shattered a small Asian nation but exacerbated divisions at home. Although only a minority of Americans joined the antiwar movement, the drumfire of protest, heavily reported in the media, hastened the unraveling of the liberal dream. In the *annus horribilis* 1968, with its street violence, political upheaval, and shocking assassinations, of Martin Luther King, Jr., and then Robert F. Kennedy, a torn nation reached its nadir of despair.

The chaos of 1965–1968 pushed Americans powerfully to the right as citizens groped for stability and reassurance. The chief beneficiary of this shift was the most durable politician of the postwar age, Richard Milhous Nixon. Capitalizing on the conservative surge and building on the southern strategy that had become central to Republican planning, Nixon won the presidency in 1968 and laid the groundwork for a new political alignment that would wield influence for decades.

Nixon's most pressing task was to grapple with the war in Vietnam that had destroyed his Democratic predecessor. While escalating the air war and maneuvering to avoid a humiliating defeat in Southeast Asia, Nixon and his national security adviser, Henry Kissinger, plotted to muffle antiwar protest at home. They succeeded; after a final outburst in the spring of 1970, the movement quietly expired. Nixon and Kissinger also initiated a sweeping reorientation of a U.S. foreign policy that seemed trapped in the straitjacket of Cold War platitudes. Following a realpolitik strategy guided more by balance-of-power calculations than by anti-communist ideology, they pursued a policy of détente—lessening tensions—with the Soviet Union and a diplomatic opening to the People's Republic of China. Riding the crest of his diplomatic successes, Nixon handily won reelection in 1972.

Meanwhile, new social and cultural trends growing directly from the drama of the 1960s caught the nation's attention in the early 1970s. A heightened ethnic awareness clearly owed a debt to the black-pride movement. Movements as diverse as environmentalism, feminism, gay rights, and so-called New Age self-awareness fads all had their roots in the 1960s. Just as Nixon transformed the political landscape, so the social and cultural trends of the Nixon years would shape American life for years to come.

Yet despite Nixon's larger-than-life role on the global stage, his presidency ended in dismal failure. If the social crisis of the late 1960s played itself out on city streets and college campuses, the political crisis of 1973–1974 began in secrecy and unfolded in the press, the courts, and the halls of Congress. Seeking to destroy his political enemies and to discredit critics of his Vietnam policies, Nixon, with the complicity of his top advisers, conducted illegal activities that violated Americans' constitutional rights. He committed further crimes as he and his aides tried to cover up their wrongdoing. In August 1974, amid a grave constitutional crisis, Nixon resigned to escape almost certain impeachment.

The interlinked traumas of urban upheaval, generational conflict, political violence, searing divisions over Vietnam, and two failed presidencies shattered the self-assurance engendered by the Eisenhower era and the confident liberalism of the early Kennedy-Johnson years. An oil crisis in the mid-seventies worsened matters by triggering inflation and stirring anxieties about what had once seemed a limitless supply of energy. Domestically and internationally, American prospects in 1975 seemed far more clouded than they had in 1955 or even in 1965. The malaise that would shadow American life had its foundation in the years to which we now turn.

Chapter Nine

RADICALIZATION: BLACK POWER, THE NEW LEFT, AND THE COUNTERCULTURE

On August 11, 1965, as civil-rights activists applauded the new voting-rights act, Los Angeles policeman Lee Minikus made a routine speeding arrest of Marquette Frye, an intoxicated young motorist. But Minikus was white and Frye was black, and race soon injected itself into what became a confrontation. As a crowd of 150 blacks gathered, the mood turned ugly, and more patrolmen materialized. As Frye and his brother resisted, they were felled by a policeman's billy club. A young black woman, Joyce Ann Gaines, accused of spitting at the police, was arrested and taken away in a squad car. One onlooker screamed: "We've got no rights at all! It's just like Selma!"

The police soon left, but the crowd remained angry, inflamed by false rumors that Gaines was pregnant and had been brutally beaten. Soon people began lobbing rocks at passing cars, attacking white drivers, and overturning and torching vehicles. As a sweltering heat wave blanketed the city, street violence, looting, and arson swept through Watts, a crowded, run-down section of Los Angeles housing 250,000 black residents. Thousands of blacks, many of them teenagers, roamed the streets, venting their pent-up frustration and rage. Despite the eventual presence of fifteen hundred police and fourteen thousand national guardsmen and four thousand arrests, the uprising raged for thirty-six hours, leaving thirty-four dead, nine hundred injured, and $30 million in property damage that turned the Watts business district into a charred ruin. Over the next three years, each summer brought new waves of riots in the black ghettos of urban America.

As the sixties waned, young black radicals, some inspired by Black Muslim leader Malcolm X, spoke a vocabulary of resistance and separatism strikingly different from the rhetoric of Martin Luther King, Jr. Activists shouted the slogans of Black Power, and city after city erupted in violence. A white backlash formed, splintering the already strained civil-rights coalition. The end of the 1960s would find black America's anger—and white America's resentment—mounting. The unity and moral clarity of the early 1960s, and the era's genuine achievements in combating segregation, would seem remote indeed.

As generational and ideological conflict divided the African-American community, young white radicals, mostly on the nation's college campuses, challenged their parents' political and cultural values. New Leftists dissected Kennedy-Johnson liberalism, and a growing counterculture expressed the mood of rebellion and alienation in dress, music, personal behavior, and even hair style. By the end of 1967, divisions over the Vietnam War exacerbated these conflicts, and American society floundered amid hostility and divisiveness. The passage of time would allow a more balanced assessment of these years. Indeed, for both blacks and whites, the upsurge of youthful radicalism that began in the midsixties would set enduring trends in motion and leave its stamp on the generation that experienced it. However, many Americans who lived through the sixties recoiled from the drama. Their revulsion would ultimately trigger a conservative resurgence that would remain influential for decades.

Ghetto Upheavals and Black Power

A few days after the Watts riot, violence erupted in Chicago's black neighborhoods. The following summer, riots hit Chicago again, then Cleveland, Dayton, Milwaukee, and other midwestern cities. The cycle of inner-city turmoil climaxed in 1967, with outbreaks tearing apart more than twenty cities.

The most serious violence of 1967 struck Newark, New Jersey, and Detroit. Newark's black ghetto, beset by chronic poverty and unemployment, exploded on July 12. As in Watts, reports of police beating black motorist John Smith triggered the outburst. By nightfall, an angry, cursing mob surrounded the police station where Smith was being held. Over the next few days, the rioting spread. The city government clamped down on the mobs, and New Jersey's governor called in the National Guard. Some police and inexperienced national guardsmen shot at each other, suspecting mythic snipers. When the rioting and arson finally ebbed, twenty-five blacks had been killed.

That Detroit's city government was more responsive and numerous antipoverty programs served its residents made it seem a less likely candidate for violence, but on July 23, 1967, the mass arrest of patrons at an after-hours nightclub for liquor-law violations triggered six days of street fighting and burning that left the downtown in ashes. In one incident, an arsonist tossed a Molotov cocktail through the window of a small business. Fanned by hot summer winds, the flames soon engulfed the entire block while residents tried in vain to quench the fire with garden hoses. Oddly, an almost festive mood prevailed. A contemporary account reported, "A spirit of carefree nihilism was taking hold. To riot and destroy appeared more and more to become ends in themselves. . . . [I]t appeared to one observer that the young people were 'dancing in the streets.'" Other ghetto residents, by contrast, toured the riot-torn neighborhoods urging calm.

In retrospect, the 1965–1968 riots should have come as no surprise. For decades northern cities had lured southern blacks seeking a better life. From 1940 to 1960, the net migration of blacks from South to North totaled more than 3 million, and the vast majority of these newcomers settled in metropolitan areas. Yet instead of finding improved lives, they more often were met, once again, with overcrowding,

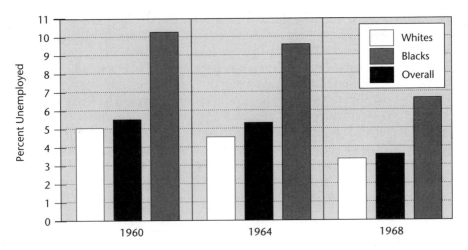

FIGURE 9.1

Unemployment Rates, 1960–1968

SOURCE: *Historical Statistics of the United States, Colonial Times to 1970* (1975).

discrimination, and exclusionary employment patterns that closed opportunities for upward advancement. In 1966, when 32 percent of white workers held blue-collar or unskilled jobs, the comparable figure for blacks was 63 percent; many black men and women found no work at all. That year, more than 1 million nonwhite workers in the nation's central cities were unemployed or held only part-time jobs.

These urban black communities had their stable middle class and professional elite, and boasted numerous strong families, churches, and other supportive institutions. But social disruption and fragmentation were more often the rule. In the black ghettos, high rates of infant mortality, alcoholism, crime, drug abuse, teenage pregnancy, and single-parent households spawned instability and despair. The grim fact of poverty dominated all the statistics. In 1966, 41.7 percent of nonwhites living in urban America fell below the federal poverty line.

The civil-rights movement had roused hopes in the ghettos, but even the most sweeping federal laws could not meet them; analysts spoke of a "crisis of rising expectations." Some black leaders tried to direct the rising anger into organized political action, but the pressure-cooker mood in many cities discouraged reasoned long-term strategies of the kind that had brought results in Montgomery and Birmingham. Too, the issues and the solutions in the South had been considerably more clear-cut: the end of legally enforced racial segregation. Nevertheless, everyone understood that the economic and social problems of the urban ghettos were inextricably entangled with the issue of skin color. Racism may have had a less blatant form in the North, which did not enforce segregation by law, but bigotry pervaded the region, affecting not just the labor market but every other facet of life. By a variety of informal techniques, and sometimes by restrictive clauses in property deeds, de facto residential segregation characterized all northern cities. Blacks who moved into white neighborhoods generally faced hostility and sometimes met with scrawled obscenities or a brick thrown through their window late at night. By the midsixties,

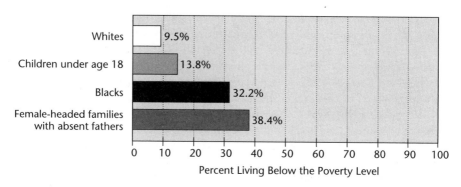

FIGURE 9.2

Poverty, 1969

SOURCE: U.S. Bureau of the Census, *Current Population Reports*, series P-60, No. 149, and unpublished data.

with the burgeoning suburbs 95 percent white, poverty and discriminatory real-estate practices left blacks (and growing numbers of Hispanics) jammed in the inner city.

White political elites had paid scant attention as fast-growing black slums had sunk deeper into poverty and decay. With an eroding tax base owing to the flight of businesses and middle-class taxpayers to the suburbs, cities provided inadequate public services to their sprawling ghettos, from schools to parks to garbage collection. Worse still, the highway and urban-renewal programs of the 1950s had left many once-viable city neighborhoods crisscrossed by freeways and access ramps, with the residents warehoused in ugly high-rise housing projects that had deteriorated into slums. These conditions provided an ample supply of fodder for the riots that erupted in the later 1960s.

Lower-class rioting as an expression of frustration and social tension was hardly new. In antebellum America, poor Irish immigrants had periodically exploded in protest against their economic plight and against the anti-Catholic prejudice of the Protestant majority. Particularly violent Irish riots had struck New York City in 1841, 1863, 1870, and 1871. The 1863 crisis was the worst, as rampaging mobs vented their resentment of labor competition by free blacks and their anger over a Civil War draft law that allowed the wealthy to pay a fee to escape military service. During and after World War I, race riots broke out in East St. Louis and Chicago, where a rapid influx of southern black workers had heightened social tensions and housing pressures. A 1943 outburst in Detroit took the lives of twenty-five blacks and nine whites and caused $2 million in property damage. That same year, pent-up black anger in Harlem ignited in several days of looting, burning, and property damage that left six dead and five hundred injured. Across the continent, in Los Angeles, Mexican Americans bore the brunt of another incident of wartime urban violence.

But despite the obvious catalysts and the many historical precedents, the riots of 1965–1968 stunned white America and official Washington. That they came after a decade of apparent progress in race relations made them all the more puzzling. Already grappling with his Vietnam War critics, President Johnson now also confronted threats to law and order in city after city. In July 1967, he created the eleven-member National Advisory Commission on Civil Disorders, chaired by Governor Otto Kerner of Illinois. The Kerner Report, issued in 1968, rejected the charge that "outside agitators" or criminal elements had caused the upheavals. Moving beyond the immediate circumstances of specific riots, the study explored the larger pattern of engrained white racism and rising black militance—combined with inner-city despair—that provided the fertile breeding ground for violence. Noting that charges of police brutality had triggered many of the riots, the commission documented that most police forces remained overwhelmingly white, even in cities housing large black populations. The report also observed that although the riots had broken out spontaneously, they followed a certain logic: participants often singled out white-owned businesses for arson and spared black-owned enterprises.

Concluding that "white racism is essentially responsible for the explosive mixture which has been accumulating in our cities since the end of World War II," the Kerner Commission warned, "Our nation is moving toward two societies, one black, one white—separate and unequal. . . . To pursue our present course will involve the continuing polarization of the American community and, ultimately, the destruction of basic democratic values." The panel held out hope that this downward spiral could be reversed if white America summoned "new attitudes, new understanding, and, above all, new will" to end racism, but the hope was muted. Similar studies after earlier riots, the commission pointed out, had produced little action. Ironically, just as the report appeared in print, a fresh wave of rioting struck.

While the urban black underclass seethed, some young blacks moved beyond Martin Luther King's integrationist agenda and nonviolent strategies to call for an ill-defined but militant Black Power. As the mainstream civil-rights movement lost steam, its original goals largely achieved, younger black radicals stepped in to fill the vacuum. SNCC led the way by electing as its head the firebrand Stokely Carmichael over the pacifist John Lewis. The abrasive, militant Floyd McKissick replaced the more moderate James Farmer as director of CORE. Carmichael and McKissick turned up the rhetorical voltage sharply. On a march in Greenwood, Mississippi, in June 1966, Carmichael exhorted activists to "stop begging and take power—black power." When he hypnotically shouted "BLACK POWER! BLACK POWER! BLACK POWER!" and the crowd rhythmically responded, the media paid attention.

Carmichael's rhetoric grew stronger. Black Power, he asserted, meant "smash[ing] everything Western civilization has created." At the 1966 CORE convention in Baltimore, he struck a separatist note: "We don't need white liberals. . . . We have to make integration irrelevant!" Early in 1967 he declared, "To hell with the laws of the United States. . . . If we don't get justice, we're going to tear this country apart."

Carmichael's successor as head of SNCC, young H. Rap Brown of Louisiana, outdid even Carmichael in rhetorical overkill. Violence, he announced in a much-quoted aphorism, "is as American as cherry pie." Speaking in Cambridge, Maryland, in July 1967 as flames engulfed Detroit, Brown harangued his volatile young audience:

You better get you some guns. The man's moving to kill you. The only thing the honky respects is force. . . . I mean, don't be trying to love that honky to death. Shoot him to death. . . . Don't you see what your brothers in Detroit are doing? It's time for Cambridge to explode.

Cambridge did explode, and arson destroyed the heart of the city's black district. Soon after, Brown was arrested for inciting a riot. The moral idealism of the early civil-rights movement, and the apparent interracial unity among whites and blacks of goodwill displayed at the 1963 March on Washington, were little in evidence by 1967.

A West Coast manifestation of Black Power came in October 1966 when Huey Newton and Bobby Seale, young black college students in Oakland, California, founded the Black Panther party. Their manifesto demanded self-determination for the black community, full employment, decent housing, better education, and an end to police brutality. There were more radical goals too: exemption from military service for black males, all-black juries for blacks on trial, and "an end to the robbery by the capitalists of our Black Community." The new organization symbolized the angry mood among young urban blacks. In their paramilitary uniforms of black leather jackets and black berets, the Panthers won local celebrity and national media attention. Newton became "Minister of Defense" and Eldridge Cleaver, recently re-leased from prison, "Minister of Information." In May 1967, as the California legisla-ture debated a bill banning the carrying of loaded guns, Black Panther party mem-

Black Power. Bobby Seale (left) and Huey Newton of the Black Panther party pose with as-sorted firearms and paramilitary gear. (*AP/Wide World Photos*)

bers defiantly brought weapons into the capital building. When the Panthers became the targets of FBI surveillance and of raids by local police that sometimes resulted in fatalities, their fearsome aura increased.

Cleaver's autobiographical *Soul on Ice* (1968) expressed the smoldering rage and rising self-awareness in urban black America. The nation's 20 million blacks, he declared, were awakening to the "vast power latent in their mass" and now "must harness their number and hone it into a sword with a sharp cutting edge." *Soul on Ice* became a best-seller and was widely viewed as a no-holds-barred guide to the new spirit sweeping black America. Critic Richard Gilman hailed it in the *New Republic* as "a spiritual and intellectual autobiography that stands at the exact resonant center of the new Negro writing." Cleaver's manifesto, he claimed, was "a book for which we have to make room—but not on the shelves we have already built."

Lacking a clear-cut program, Black Power primarily was a riveting slogan, expressing the mood of heightened militance among some younger blacks; impatience with the middle-class, church-based movement of Martin Luther King; frustration at building coalitions with patronizing white liberals; and, above all, pride in blackness. Beneath their incendiary rhetoric, Black Power advocates also offered a perceptive analysis of the racial power imbalance in America and its role in the marginalization and exploitation of blacks. Martin Luther King had recognized this imbalance as well and had strived to strengthen black power by winning whites to the black cause through appeals to a shared moral tradition. The young radicals dismissed King's strategy as craven and ineffectual and instead sought to weld black America into a powerful, disciplined cadre that would achieve its goals through group solidarity. Collective effort and intense racial consciousness, they believed, would save them.

The movement's long-range political objectives remained unclear, however. What, precisely, did "black power" mean? And once it had been achieved, how would it be used, particularly in a society in which blacks made up only a small minority of the population? The mainstream civil-rights organizations' strategy of building coalitions and working within the political process to combat institutional racism and promote measures to aid the urban black poor held little appeal for Black Power devotees. The oppressed should not collaborate with the oppressor, they insisted, or go hat in hand asking favors of the white enemy. Rather, some Black Power advocates espoused black political organizing, black business enterprises, black cultural institutions, and local control of schools and other institutions in black neighborhoods. This separatist vision had precedents not only in the mobilization of urban blacks by Marcus Garvey in the 1920s, but also in certain strands of antebellum African-American thought, but Black Power enthusiasts pushed the theme much further. These advocates laced their prescriptions with apocalyptic visions of revolution and retaliation against a demonized white oppressor. White and black critics alike dismissed this approach as a dangerous fantasy reflecting political naiveté and a deplorable failure of moral imagination.

But if the political aims of Black Power remained muddled, the movement's psychological meaning was clear. Indeed, it was in the realm of culture and consciousness, not politics, that the movement exerted its greatest long-range impact.

Historian William L. Van Deburg, in his 1992 history of the movement, *New Day in Babylon*, sees Black Power as essentially a ritual of cultural empowerment and racial assertiveness. Van Deburg cites, for example, the playful fantasy of the black poet LeRoi Jones (who adopted the African name Amiri Baraka) of creatures arriving from outer space on a galactic quest for recordings by Art Blakey and other black jazz greats. In this sense, despite their repudiation of the civil-rights movement's goals and strategy, Black Power champions displayed significant continuities with the earlier campaign. From the beginning, as Richard H. King underscores in *Civil Rights and the Idea of Freedom* (1992), the civil-rights movement had centered on empowerment as well as on segregation and voting rights. The word *freedom* meant more than gaining the franchise and eliminating legal restraints based on race; it encompassed as well cultivating racial pride through collective action and breaking what historian David Chalmers has called "the white stranglehold on the black psyche." The call to Black Power intensified this concept of empowerment and in the process altered the course of African-American history.

The Black Power movement, then, involved not just incendiary oratory but a new spirit of pride and assertiveness that swept the African-American community, especially the younger generation, in the late sixties. The black aesthetic summed up in the term *Soul* became the test of racial authenticity. Artists and writers concentrated on creating work rooted in the black experience that spoke to a black audience. Young blacks abandoned elaborate hair-processing techniques and adopted the natural "Afro" look. Some donned colorful African dashikis. Well-educated blacks inspired by the new outlook deliberately flouted white America's linguistic rules and consciously employed black dialect, slang, and nonstandard grammar. *Black* or *Afro-American* replaced *Negro* as the preferred racial designation. Black history courses sprang up on college campuses to explore and redefine the African-American experience in terms of oppression and resistance. Black theologians wrote of a black Christ. In Detroit, the Reverend Albert Cleage opened his Shrine of the Black Madonna featuring a thirty-foot mural of a black Mary and baby Jesus. Cleage also wrote a controversial confessional liturgy for black Christians that concluded, "I have failed to realize that nothing is more sacred in God's sight than black liberation. I now pledge total commitment to that cause, recognizing that there is no other way to be saved."

Carrying the new racial consciousness to the world of sports, black sociologist Harry Edwards of California's San Jose State University urged black athletes to boycott the 1968 Summer Olympics in Mexico City as a protest against racism in the United States and in the International Olympic Committee. Some black athletes joined the boycott; others participated in the games but protested in dramatic ways. When sprinters Tommie Smith and John Carlos mounted the victory stand to accept their gold and bronze medals, they lowered their heads and raised black-gloved fists as the "Star Spangled Banner" was played. Like Rosa Parks's refusal to give up her bus seat in Montgomery in 1955 or the 1960 Greensboro sit-ins, their gesture was a defining moment in the rapidly evolving black-liberation movement.

Soul music captured the new mood. Aretha Franklin's "Natural Woman" (1967), Nina Simone's "Revolution" (1969), and the vastly popular songs of James

In a gesture that stirred both admiration and anger across America, track stars Tommie Smith and John Carlos raise black-gloved fists and bow their heads during the playing of the National Anthem at the 1968 Summer Olympics in Mexico City. (*AP/Wide World Photos*)

Brown, the Godfather of Soul, epitomized the awakening black consciousness. Tony Clarke's "Ghetto Man" (1969) conveyed the devastating reality and psychological toll of slum life:

> *I never knew my papa's name*
> *My ma scrubbed floors to keep me clad*
> *And me and three brothers had to share one bed*
> *When I was young I felt ashamed.*

In one sense, the Black Power movement proved ephemeral. Even at its peak, canny entrepreneurs cashed in on the vogue with such products as "politically correct" Afro wigs and "Soul Brother" T-shirts and automobile plates. By the mid-1970s, the movement would crest, and its erstwhile leaders would scatter, from expatriation in Africa (Stokely Carmichael) to evangelical Christianity and Republican politics (Eldridge Cleaver) to marketing barbecue sauce (Bobby Seale). Yet the cultural ferment summed up in the catch phrase "Black Power" would exert a profound long-range impact. Some participants eventually joined the mainstream. Cleveland Sellers, for example, who spent seven months in prison after a 1968 conviction for inciting a riot in Orangeburg, South Carolina, later earned graduate degrees at Harvard and the University of North Carolina and became a professor of African-American studies at the University of South Carolina. For many thousands of African-Americans, the movement both enhanced racial pride and heightened skepticism toward white America. Sinking deep roots into the black community, the assertive new outlook would be transmitted as a legacy to a younger generation of African-Americans.

Although it launched an exciting era of cultural change and psychological awakening, the Black Power movement had its negative side as well. Its swaggering macho rhetoric contained a strong undercurrent of misogyny that dismayed many black women. When Ruby Doris Smith Robinson presented a paper on the position of women in SNCC in 1964, Stokely Carmichael sneered, "The only position for women in SNCC is prone." Beyond crude insults, the complex gender implications of Black Power rhetoric in the mouths of posturing young males helped to raise the consciousness of a younger generation of African-American women and would lead to the formation of the National Black Feminist Organization in 1972. Black feminists noted the irony of Black Power advocates' ostentatiously rejecting everything white while retaining the most reactionary gender attitudes of 1950s America. Soon a talented group of black women writers, including Toni Morrison, Alice Walker, and Terry McMillan, would explore the hidden world of gender relations in the African-American community. The issue would remain touchy a generation later, as black women protested the coarse antiwoman messages in the lyrics of black male Rap groups in the early 1990s.

The Black Power movement also deepened the rift among the various civil-rights organizations. As the likes of Carmichael and McKissick took over SNCC and CORE, whites as well as more moderate blacks bowed out. Martin Luther King, Jr., and the SCLC tried for a time to maintain links to the newly radicalized SNCC and CORE, but with little success. The young iconoclasts now running those organizations ridiculed King as "Reverend Dr. Chickenwing." The more conservative NAACP and Urban League nervously rejected the Black Power theme entirely. Black Power radicals, in turn, jeered the NAACP's Roy Wilkins as "a white man who somehow came out the wrong color."

If Black Power pronouncements unsettled middle-class blacks, they terrified white America. The language of racial assertiveness came from individuals who in fact wielded pathetically little power and spoke for a historically downtrodden people, but few noted this irony at the time as erstwhile white supporters recoiled from the movement's new emphasis. After Martin Luther King's biblical cadences and uplifting vision of interracial cooperation, this rage-filled talk alarmed white America. The resulting white backlash would soon feed into a larger rightward turn in U.S. politics and culture.

Amid ghetto riots and young militants' calls for revolution, the efforts of mainstream civil-rights organizations to address the problems of the urban black poor faltered. In 1966 the SCLC tried in vain to mobilize Chicago's 800,000 blacks. Moving into a poor black district of the city, called North Lawndale but known locally as "Slumdale," King announced a campaign for better housing and an end to discrimination in the real-estate market. After the Watts disaster and violence in Chicago itself, King aides met with black gang leaders and exhorted them to use planned action, not rioting, to effect change. But Chicago mayor Richard J. Daley, while praising King's goals, shrewdly maneuvered to undercut King by mobilizing the resources of his powerful political machine, including a number of local black politicians. The mayor also made such superficial but popular gestures as bringing ten portable swimming pools into the black slums that hot summer. As the SCLC campaign stumbled, Chicago blacks grew disillusioned. A drive to persuade slum dwellers to withhold their rent sputtered. A black "Freedom Sunday" rally and march on city hall on July 10 drew far fewer participants than expected, and some black youths even heckled King as he spoke. Laws against discrimination in the sale or rental of housing meant little to slum dwellers too poor to move to middle-class white suburbs, and the SCLC campaign struck many Chicago blacks as irrelevant. As one complained, "We're sick and tired of middle-class people telling us what we want."

A rally in a Chicago park in early August turned ugly as local whites, mostly second-generation European immigrants, threw bricks and shouted racial epithets. For a time, King threatened a march on Cicero, a suburban white bastion, but local supporters, fearing more violence, dissuaded him. Late that month, Daley gave King a face-saving out: at a heavily publicized "summit conference," city officials and the Chicago Real Estate Board made vague gestures toward open housing. Hailing the agreement as "the most significant program ever conceived to make open housing a reality" in Chicago, King and his lieutenants left for Atlanta. In fact, little changed in the city. The intractable realities of urban black poverty and white resistance had proved impervious to techniques honed in battles against segregation in the Old Confederacy. In contrast to the South of the 1950s and early 1960, writes historian Robert Weisbrot, "racism moved through Northern cities like Chicago in so many faceless, impersonal forms as to escape detection by a society inclined to ignore it."

In the volatile climate of the late 1960s, then, the consensus on civil-rights goals that had coalesced in 1964–1965 evaporated. By the end of the decade, the movement as it had taken shape over the preceding fifteen years lay in disarray. In retrospect, the cultural and psychological contributions of the Black Power campaign would become apparent, but many at the time deemed it nihilistic and divisive. In addition, the militance of alienated black radicals only further roused conservative anxiety levels when it found an echo among the younger generation of affluent white Americans.

The Personal Is Political:
The New Left and the Counterculture

In the mid-1960s, complex currents converged to stimulate political activism and cultural protest on college campuses. As Black Power ideologues mocked the civil-rights establishment and proclaimed the virtues of Soul, some white youths were making their own break with the politics and values of their elders. The unrest of the 1960s was bimodal. It arose among blacks marginalized by racism and poverty and took root among privileged, middle-class white students at elite colleges and universities who repudiated Cold War liberalism and the older generation's cultural style. Yet the two movements were linked. Many white students who emerged as radical activists in the mid-1960s had earlier rallied to the civil-rights cause, supporting the sit-ins and joining the 1963 March on Washington or the 1964 Mississippi Freedom

Summer. John Lewis, Robert Moses, Ella Baker, Fannie Lou Hamer, and other black-movement leaders became role models and cultural heroes for young white activists.

President Kennedy's summons to social engagement and public service had provided a spur to youthful idealism. The Peace Corps, the nuclear test ban, civil-rights leadership, and rhetorical gestures to issues such as poverty and environmental protection had gathered the allegiance of the younger generation and channeled its reformist impulses into mainstream politics. But after Kennedy's assassination, many youthful activists renounced establishment politics. "The system" was now the enemy. Kennedy had been a hero; Johnson, the old-style politician, became the villain. The overbearing Texan lacked the charisma of the dashing Kennedy, and although his domestic reform program won praise on campuses, the Vietnam War rapidly eclipsed that support. College-age demonstrators would soon vilify him as a war criminal.

The rise of radical politics and campus unrest in the 1960s had demographic sources as well. The early postwar baby boom had left a bulge in the population that by 1960 had created a teenaged "nation within a nation" totaling more than 20 million youngsters.* With some 3 million baby boomers reaching college age each year and a greater ratio of high-school graduates going on to college than in the past, the proportion of those 18 to 24 years old enrolled in colleges or universities surged, from 12.5 percent in 1946 to 32 percent by 1970. Higher-education enrollment soared from 3.6 million in 1960 to almost 8 million in 1970.

The institutions that greeted these eager young people—particularly the large public universities—were ill equipped to handle their vast numbers. Forced to fill out innumerable forms, wait in lines, sit in jammed lecture halls, and endure crowded dorms, students protested the remote and uncaring bureaucracy. In *The Uses of the University* (1963), University of California chancellor Clark Kerr praised the modern "multiversity" for its intellectual diversity, but his characterization of universities as "service stations" and "knowledge factories" hinted at what students found so alienating. Indeed, Kerr himself, celebrating the university as "a city of infinite variety," conceded that "some get lost in the city."

Unrest first erupted in the fall of 1964 at Kerr's flagship campus, the sprawling University of California–Berkeley. When Berkeley administrators tried to ban recruitment tables for civil-rights organizations from a campus area traditionally open to political activity, a coalition of groups organized the Free Speech Movement (FSM). Police arrested a student who challenged the ban, and masses of young men and women mobbed the police car. Later, FSM backers occupied Berkeley's administration building.

Mario Savio, a philosophy graduate student who had just returned from the Mississippi Freedom Summer, emerged as the voice of the FSM—the first of a succession of 1960s leaders who articulated the escalating disgust with university life and with what became known as "the establishment." At one rally, Savio cried, "After a long period of apathy during the fifties, students have begun . . . to act. . . . There is a time

---

* The 1960 federal census reported 35.7 million persons in the 5–14 age cohort and 24.6 million aged 15–24, suggesting a teenaged population (aged 13–19) of approximately 21 million. *Historical Statistics of the United States* (1975), 1:10.

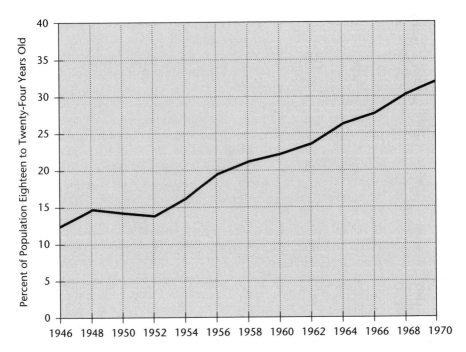

FIGURE 9.3

Rate of Higher-Education Enrollment, 1946–1970

SOURCE: *Historical Statistics of the United States, Colonial Times to 1970* (1975).

when the operation of the machine becomes so odious . . . that . . . you've got to put your bodies upon the gears and upon the wheels, upon the levers, upon all the apparatus, and you've got to make it stop."

Through the fall of 1964 and on into 1965, strikes, marches, and demonstrations involving nearly three-quarters of Berkeley's students paralyzed the campus, until school officials eventually yielded on the specific point at issue. The FSM proved the prelude to a nationwide wave of campus protest; soon, activists from coast to coast were portraying universities as cogs in a vast machine that was grinding up the people of Vietnam as it dehumanized college students at home.

The most politically sophisticated expression of the new mood emerged in Students for a Democratic Society (SDS), an organization whose founders derived from an earlier radical tradition that had faded in the 1950s. In the 1960s, children of leftists who had supported radical causes in the 1930s—the so-called red-diaper babies—launched a fresh critical assault on capitalist America. Trying to revive a moribund New York socialist group, the League for Industrial Democracy, Michael Harrington and others had formed a youth branch, the Students' League for Industrial Democracy (SLID), in 1960. In 1961 University of Michigan students led by Al Haber and Sharon Jeffrey took over SLID and renamed it Students for a Democratic Society. At a 1962 summer retreat at a United Auto Workers (UAW) center in Port Huron, Michigan, some sixty SDS students from the University of Michigan and other colleges and universities set forth SDS's ideology in *The Port Huron Statement,* a founding text of the so-called New Left. The manifesto's principal author, Tom Hayden, of Detroit working-class origins, had just graduated from Michigan, where he had edited the student newspaper. That summer, Hayden had been roughed up by local whites while visiting Robert Moses's voter-registration project in McComb, Mississippi.

Drawing on ideas already in the air in Left-liberal circles, *The Port Huron Statement* recounted the experiences that had shaped its authors' political outlook—nuclear fear, the civil-rights movement, and consciousness of the disparity between America's wealth and power and conditions in much of the rest of the world. "Although mankind desperately needs revolutionary leadership," the manifesto announced, "America rests in national stalemate, its goals ambiguous and tradition-bound instead of informed and clear, its democratic system apathetic and manipulated." The document called for a campaign aimed at "breaking the crust of apathy and overcoming the inner alienation that remain the defining characteristics of American college life." Two years before the Berkeley Free Speech Movement, the statement had challenged universities' "cumbersome academic bureaucracy" and faculty links to "the corporate economy" and defense contractors.

Despite its critique of corporate America, *The Port Huron Statement* reflected Kennedy-era confidence and a belief in liberal ideals and the promise of democracy. Rejecting doctrinaire ideology—"We have no sure formulas, no closed theories"—it proposed a strategy of "participatory democracy." In practice, this slogan meant that cadres of activists, without resorting to a power hierarchy, would work for radical social and political change through grass-roots political organizing aimed at breaking down the "structural separation of people from power." As ordinary citizens discovered their collective strength within the framework of American democracy, manipulative, business-dominated politics would give way to more authentic political processes that promoted community rather than profits.

SDS and *The Port Huron Statement* were largely ignored by the mainstream media, but they attracted notice in leftist circles and among college students already politicized by the nuclear test-ban campaign and the civil-rights movement. By 1964 SDS boasted some fifteen hundred members on a score or more campuses. One early recruit, Harvard senior and student activist Todd Gitlin, later recalled:

> [E]verything these people did was charged with intensity. They moved and attracted me as people in the same spirit that *The Port Huron Statement* first moved and attracted me as a manifesto. . . . They were at once analytically keen and politically committed, but also, with a thousand gestures of affection, these unabashed moralists cared about one another.

Full of hope, young men and women of SDS, as Robert Moses and his SNCC coworkers had earlier done in rural Mississippi, set out to promote grass-roots political action in America's industrial cities. Funded by a small grant from the UAW, they moved into working-class communities to organize the masses. Their aim was to challenge society's power structure by encouraging residents to identify immediate grievances and to devise collective strategies for forcing change.

But SDS evolved rapidly, and in 1963 came a far more radical manifesto, *America and the New Era*, drafted by another young Ann Arbor SDSer, Richard Flacks.

This tract denounced the dead-end "corporate liberalism" of the Kennedy adminis-tration and called for direct resistance to it, domestically and in the Third World. With the 1964 Gulf of Tonkin Resolution and Johnson's 1965 escalation (see pp. 306–307), SDS would shift from organizing the poor to organizing college stu-dents, among whom SDS leaders sensed a responsive mood. If not the working class, then the learning class, would serve as the spark plug of radical change, they decided. In changing its focus, the group would emerge as a leader of antiwar activism in the later 1960s.

The New Left was more than manifestos, however; as Gitlin's recollection sug-gests, it blended the personal and the political. In contrast to 1930s radicals, 1960s activists sought to change consciousness and attitudes as well as the political system. As Tom Hayden has put it, "[M]ost of the sixties generation was not narrowly polit-ical. Most were not interested in attaining office but in changing life-styles. They were not so interested in being opinion makers as in changing the climate of opin-ion." Depression-era radicals had identified with workers, as in Clifford Odets's 1935 play, *Waiting for Lefty*. New Left radicals, historians Maurice Isserman and Michael Kazin have observed, allied themselves more often with social outcasts, even those stigmatized as insane. Some admired British psychiatrist R. D. Laing, who in *The Divided Self: An Existential Study in Sanity and Madness* (1965) romantically argued that psychosis could offer a liberating breakthrough to a deeper level of awareness and could be a rational response to an insane social order. Peter Weiss's gripping 1964 play, *The Persecution and Assassination of Jean Paul Marat as Performed by the Inmates of the Asylum of Charenton Under the Direction of the Marquis de Sade* (usually abbreviated *Marat/Sade*), turned revolutionary politics into lunatic-asylum drama. Ken Kesey's *One Flew over the Cuckoo's Nest* (1962), later made into a movie starring Jack Nicholson, portrayed the "insane" as victims of a repressive society who possess more humanity than their keepers. New Left theorists did not literally view mental illness as simply a response to political repression, but on a metaphorical level the perspectives of Laing, Brook, and Kesey epitomized their understanding of the links between the personal and the political.

In their efforts to forge connections between the public and private realms, the New Left found certain social thinkers particularly relevant. Paul Goodman in *Growing Up Absurd* (1960) urged the young to move beyond conventional politics and to recover America's lost social cohesion. Goodman deplored the fifties as a decade of unparalleled apathy, yet he also discerned stirrings of change: "Deep in the organized system itself there has been an important new effort toward community." To New Left intellectuals, the key to radical change lay in revitalizing—and politi-cizing—the notion of community.

Norman O. Brown, professor of classics at Wesleyan University, urged rejection of external authority, including "the tyranny of books," in favor of inner sources of awareness. In *Life Against Death: The Psychoanalytic Meaning of History* (1959), Brown argued for intuition rather than rationality as the truest source of knowledge and celebrated the erotic potential of human bodies freed from socially imposed in-hibitions. Hailing "polymorphous perversity," he argued that both academia and so-ciety at large needed "more Eros and less strife." Delivering the 1960 Phi Beta Kappa address at Columbia University, Brown suggested that life's deepest mysteries are inexpressible in conventional intellectual discourse. "They cannot be put into words," he intoned, "at least not the kind of words which earn you your Phi Beta Kappa keys."

Herbert Marcuse (born 1898), a German philosopher who had come to America in 1934 as a refugee from Nazism, also attracted New Left disciples. In *Eros and Civilization* (1954), Marcuse drew on both Marx and Freud to explore how elites manipulate sexual energy to maintain their power. Extending Freud's theory of repression, Marcuse argued that modern capitalist societies impose far more repression than is necessary to maintain order. This "surplus repression" is then manipulated by corporations and advertisers to promote consumption. Sexual repression, in short, fuels consumer capitalism. Marcuse, like Brown, offered a utopian vision of instinctual liberation.

In *One-Dimensional Man* (1965), Marcuse examined the "benign" social control by which advanced capitalist states alienate men and women from their true consciousness and thwart their human potential. The manipulation of material wants is so ubiquitous and so skillfully managed, he argued, that most people settle for the illusion of happiness and have lost the capacity for political resistance, critical thought, or true sensual pleasure. Marcuse's apparent message—that breaking free of society's sexual taboos and "surplus repression" is not only an avenue to erotic fulfillment but a revolutionary political act as well—readily appealed to campus radicals. They encapsulated his thesis in an electric slogan: "Make love, not war."

The quest for the true self beneath the false, socially imposed self, a quest deeply rooted in the Romantic tradition, lent a distinctive flavor to 1960s radicalism. An intense, almost obsessive subjectivity saturates *The Port Huron Statement*, with its minute probing of its authors' shifting psychic states—complacency, alienation, disillusionment, estrangement, apathy, and so forth—and its longing for a return to emotional wholeness through "self cultivation, self direction, self understanding, and creativity." All of this introspection reflected a central New Left tenet: the inner world of consciousness and the outer world of politics are inextricably connected, and the outer world must be brought into harmony with the true or natural self.

Soon the media detected the emergence of a youthful "counterculture" that not only challenged the liberal establishment intellectually but repudiated and mocked conventional middle-class mores. The New Left and the counterculture were partially distinct entities; not all radical activists adopted alternative life-styles, and not all members of the amorphous counterculture espoused radical politics. But the dual movements converged at many points. Both fiercely rejected what they considered the repressive, illegitimate authority of the established order, political and cultural. New Left leaders celebrated and often shared in the cultural rebellion of middle-class youth. As thousands of young men and women spurned the life-styles and outlook of their parents' generation, SDS theorists predicted, a broader transformation in U.S. society would inevitably follow. And even the most politically naive counterculture youths sensed that their preferences in music, dress, and hair style were somehow linked to an unfolding process of political change.

Counterculture recruits found their earliest inspiration in dissident voices from the 1950s. They admired Salinger, Ginsberg, and Kerouac. They devoured the mordant humor of Lenny Bruce, Mort Sahl, Tom Lehrer, and other iconoclastic comics.

They gyrated to rock-and-roll and identified with movie rebels like Brando and Dean. But 1960s cultural rebels tended to politicize their rebellion in ways that gave the decade its unique flavor. Joseph Heller's *Catch-22* (1960) perhaps best anticipated the counterculture outlook. Set in World War II, Heller's novel captured the casual inhumanity, bizarre irrationality, and hilarious confusion of officialdom engaged in vast and supposedly noble enterprises such as the conduct of war. At the end, the antihero Yossarian paddles off on a raft bound for neutral Sweden, a forerunner of thousands of young Americans who soon headed for Canada, Scandinavia, and elsewhere to escape the draft.

The young men and women of the counterculture displayed lively imagination in expressing their freedom from bourgeois convention. To the dismay of many older Americans, they let their hair grow and eschewed makeup; they burned candles and incense and decorated their rooms with Eastern symbols; they bought clothes from the Salvation Army or from military-surplus stores. Tie-dyed T-shirts, army fatigue jackets, jeans and long cotton dresses, sandals, beads, and peace symbols became their uniform. They engaged in premarital or extramarital sex more openly than their elders had. The introduction of the oral contraceptive ("the Pill") in 1960 and the intrauterine device (IUD) later in the decade facilitated this sexual revolution. So did sex studies, such as William Masters's and Virginia Johnson's *Human Sexual Response* (1966) and even Helen Gurley Brown's slickly popularized *Sex and the Single Girl* (1962). In 1968 *Life* magazine offered middle America a prurient look at unmarried undergraduates who were sharing bed and board in off-campus apartments. Counterculture youth were hardly the first to discover sex outside the bonds of matrimony, but they invested their erotic adventures with portentous ideological meaning. To flout the dominant culture's sexual repressiveness was also to reject its

Protest in the 1960s took many forms. Here, two young counterculture recruits, complete with sandals, beads, long hair, and technicolor clothes, celebrate the summer solstice. (© *Lisa Law Productions*)

political ideology, its fetishistic consumerism, and, eventually, its war in Southeast Asia.

As the sixties wore on, drugs—mostly marijuana but also stronger substances such as lysergic acid diethylamide (LSD)—pervaded the youth culture as well as parts of the "straight" world. Marijuana and cocaine had been familiar in jazz circles for years, and peyote, a cactus-bud hallucinogen used in Native American religious rites, had appeared on the Beat scene in the late 1950s. Mescaline, a synthetic hallucinogen, soon followed. LSD, first synthesized in England, reached Greenwich Village in the early sixties and hit the West Coast soon after.

Looking back from a time when heroin and crack addiction in inner-city slums and even "recreational" cocaine use among white-collar professionals exact a tragic human toll, it takes an imaginative leap to recapture the casual and benign view of drugs held by many young people in the early days of the counterculture. For a time, marijuana and even LSD appeared as relatively harmless substances that could help users to penetrate deeper levels of consciousness and overcome societal repressions. Together with rock, long hair, and psychedelic posters, drugs became part of a counterculture *Gestalt* that promoted a sense of community and demonstrated youthful alienation from the oppressive, up-tight adult world.

The high priest of LSD was Timothy Leary, a Harvard psychologist who discovered the thrill of hallucinogenic mushrooms in Mexico. Fired from Harvard in 1963, Leary became a full-time missionary for LSD through his *Psychedelic Review*, League for Spiritual Discovery, and International Foundation for Internal Freedom (IF-IF). "Tune in, turn on, drop out," he counseled the young. Something of a huckster and an opportunist, Leary cheerfully combined the sexual and the pharmacological revolutions, describing LSD in a 1966 *Playboy* magazine interview as "the most powerful aphrodisiac known to man."

Another drug-culture guru, novelist Ken Kesey, founded a commune near San Francisco in 1964 with a group of hangers-on called the Merry Pranksters. That spring Kesey and the Pranksters drove east in a psychedelically painted 1939 school bus, wired for sound. The group visited Leary at an estate in Millbrook, New York, provided by a well-heeled patron of the IF-IF foundation. They also conducted "acid [LSD] tests": at multimedia concerts and light shows, they dropped acid into foods or drinks, sometimes without recipients' knowledge.

Above all, the counterculture defined itself through music—first folk, then rock. Joan Baez, Bob Dylan, Judy Collins, and the Beatles rank among the movement's troubadors. Baez, a classically trained Boston folk singer active in the civil-rights movement, became the balladeer of social engagement. Dylan, born Robert Zimmerman in Hibbing, Minnesota, joined the Greenwich Village folk scene in 1961, where his rasping, nasal voice attracted a following. His hugely successful second album, *The Freewheelin' Bob Dylan* (1963), included political songs such as "A Hard Rain's Gonna Fall," "The Times They Are A-Changin'," and "Blowin' in the Wind." The last, with its call to political commitment—"How many times can a man turn his head / Pretending he just doesn't see?"—sold more than a million copies in a version recorded by another (more mellifluous) group, Peter, Paul, and Mary. In "The Times They Are A-Changin'," Dylan prophesied:

There's a battle
Outside and it's ragin'.
It'll soon shake your windows
And rattle your walls
For the times they are a-changin'.

With President Kennedy's violent death, the urban riots, the Black Power phenomenon, and the Vietnam escalation as a backdrop, Dylan's songs caught the edgy new mood on campus. In the early sixties, his politics had reflected the civil-rights movement and Kennedy liberalism, and his music remained in the folk vein. By 1965, as his lyrics grew more radical, his style evolved as well. At the Newport Folk Festival that summer, he dismayed purists by playing "folk rock" on an electric guitar. Songs like "Maggie's Farm" and "Desolation Row" sneered at the establishment and limned an apocalyptic vision of looming cataclysm.

Early in 1964, the Beatles jetted in from Liverpool sporting long hair and boyish smiles. After a seminal TV appearance on the Ed Sullivan show, Beatlemania swept teenage America. Thanks largely to John Lennon, the Beatles soon outgrew their rather insipid early repertoire ("I Want to Hold Your Hand") and became more original musically and more radical politically. They found a new audience on college campuses. Originally inspired in the late 1950s by U.S. rock-and-roll performers and by African-American rhythm-and-blues artists, the Beatles in turn shaped American popular music of the 1960s and beyond. Moreover, as an English import, the group exemplified the cultural cross-fertilization made possible by the new technologies of LP records and transatlantic air travel.

As drug use swept the counterculture, groups such as San Francisco's Jefferson Airplane and The Grateful Dead incorporated LSD-inspired lyrics and encouraged the use of marijuana and other controlled substances at their concerts. Dylan's "Mr. Tambourine Man" and the Beatles's "Lucy in the Sky with Diamonds" (a thinly disguised hymn to LSD) testified to the role of drugs in the music scene. The "Human Be-In" held at San Francisco's Golden Gate Park on January 14, 1967, became a day-long counterculture love feast featuring Day-Glo banners, psychedelic costumes, nonstop musicmaking by bands and blissed-out participants—and the ubiquitous ingestion of mind-altering substances. A flower-bedecked Timothy Leary wandered about in white, proselytizing for LSD.

New Left celebrity Jerry Rubin tried to promote radical politics at the Be-In, but by this time the New Left and the counterculture were on diverging trajectories. As the leftists pursued arcane theoretical disputations and threw themselves into accelerating protests against U.S. imperialism, a large portion of the counterculture, propelled by the logic of consumerism, succumbed to the lure of drugs, new varieties of rock, and the increasingly elaborate accoutrements of their alternative life-style. Leary spoke of his LSD crusade as the "Politics of the Nervous System," but his own career was orbiting into outer space. As historian William O'Neill has observed, "To 'turn on and drop out' did not weaken the state. Quite the contrary, it drained off potentially subversive energies. . . . Pharmacology and nervous strain had already combined to make many adult Americans dependent on drugs like alcohol and tranquilizers. Now the young were doing the same thing."

For all its criticism of consumer capitalism, the counterculture flourished among college-age children of the well-to-do and in fact depended on affluence. And for all the talk of linking the personal and the political, many young people, especially those seduced by mind-altering substances, turned from action to sensation. "We've become obsessed with experience," mourned critic Benjamin Mott in 1969. A narcissistic preoccupation with the self and its potential for gratification would prove to be one of the sixties' more enduring—and questionable—legacies.

The media loved the counterculture. San Francisco's "Human Be-In," gushed *Newsweek*, was "a psychedelic picnic, a hippie happening." *Time* pronounced San Francisco's Haight-Ashbury district the counterculture's "vibrant epicenter" as "flower children" converged there in 1967 for the "Summer of Love." At first, the media overlooked the drug culture's darker side: its passivity, the "bad trips" (drug overdoses), the exploiters and psychotics lurking on the fringes. By the early 1970s, however, this underside would loom large, giving the entire counterculture phenomenon the aura of a pleasant idyll turned sinister.

But just as one should avoid facile and hostile caricatures of the Black Power movement on the basis of the flamboyant rhetoric of a few, one should be wary of reducing the counterculture to its more bizarre manifestations and drug-induced excesses. The counterculture challenged the tepid and conformist features of 1950s and early 1960s suburban culture. In this respect its influence proved longlasting. Long after the "Summer of Love," the "Human Be-In," and the "Kool-Aid Acid Tests" had become quaint exhibits in the museum of 1960s nostalgia, the underlying impulses of the counterculture, and of its more politicized twin, the New Left, would continue to shape American life as the youth of the 1960s moved into adulthood.

This point is dramatically illustrated in the area of gender relations. The women's movement that transformed America in the 1970s and after (see Chapter 12) drew influence not only from the civil-rights campaign but also from the rise of the New Left and the counterculture. Indeed, SDS's community-organizing efforts, like the antisegregation campaigns in the South, gave many young women invaluable political experience. The bible of modern feminism, Betty Friedan's best-selling *The Feminine Mystique*, appeared in 1963, the same year as SDS's *America and the New Era*. In 1966 the National Organization for Women (NOW) was founded by twenty-eight women attending a national conference of state commissions on the status of women. At its second national conference in 1967, NOW demanded an end to legal restraints on abortion and addressed other issues that would dominate the feminist agenda in the years ahead. Neither Friedan nor most of the early NOW activists were themselves New Leftists or counterculture devotees, but those movements created a climate that encouraged women to question gender stereotypes along with other cultural and ideological baggage.

The New Left, like the Black Power movement, also stimulated the rise of feminism in a negative sense. SDS and other radical movements of the period remained male dominated, as young men provided the leadership, established the agenda, and set the tone of "movement" culture. As angry female activists coined the word *sexism* (a direct analogue to *racism*), their charges of gender discrimination initially met a dismissive response. When female SDS members raised gender issues at SDS's 1965 conference, the organization's male leaders shouted them down. But women persisted, laying the groundwork for a powerful reform movement in the 1970s. At an antiwar rally in Washington, D.C., in January 1968, five thousand women from a coalition of feminist groups marched separately as the Jeanette Rankin Brigade, honoring a congresswoman who in 1917 had voted against America's entry into World War I.

CONCLUSION

The early and mid-1960s stands as a crucial transitional era in postwar U.S. social history, as currents of protest and discontent gathered strength across the nation. Far from the power centers of Washington or Wall Street, ferment stirred among young urban blacks, radical students, educated middle-class women, and growing numbers of the younger generation. Although they pursued different goals and adopted different strategies, these groups collectively challenged the social, political, and cultural status quo. Building on the civil-rights movement and the promise of change that suffused politics in the Kennedy and early Johnson years, these movements unleashed activist energies that would continue to flourish long after the sixties had ended.

Behind all the converging social trends—the ghetto riots, Black Power, the rise of the New Left and the counterculture, the reawakening of feminist consciousness—lay the inescapable reality of Vietnam. Richard Goodwin's sad reflections on his evolution from an enthusiastic supporter of President Johnson on civil rights to LBJ's bitter critic over Vietnam point directly to the stain that gradually spread through the Johnson presidency after his 1964 electoral triumph. This scourge blotted out LBJ's domestic achievements and exacerbated the hydra of other conflicts—political, social, and cultural—confronting the nation in the 1960s. As the turbulent decade wore on, the war that began as a troubling distraction burgeoned into an all-consuming obsession.

SELECTED READINGS

Inner-City Riots and the Black Power Movement

Alan I. Altschuler, *Community Control: The Black Demand for Participation in Large American Cities* (1970); Michal R. Belknap, ed., *Urban Race Riots* (1991); James Burton, *Black Violence: Political Impact of the 1960s Riots* (1978); Clayborne Carson, *In Struggle: SNCC and the Black Awakening of the 1960s* (1981); Robert Conont, *Rivers of Blood, Years of Darkness* [Watts riot] (1968); Theodore Draper, *The Rediscovery of Black Nationalism* (1970); Sidney Fine, *Violence in the Model City* [Detroit riot] (1967); Robert M. Fogelson, *Violence as Protest* (1971); James Forman, *The Making of Black Revolutionaries* (1985); Sylvia R. Frey, *Water from the Rock: Black Resistance in a Revolutionary Age* (1991); Peter Goldman, *Report from Black America* (1971); Herbert H. Haines, *Black Radicals and the Civil Rights Mainstream, 1954–1970* (1988); John T. McCartney, *Black Power Ideologies* (1992); Allen J. Matusow, "From Civil Rights to Black Power," in Barton J. Bernstein and Allen J. Matusow, eds., *Twentieth-Century America: Recent Interpretations* (1967); Manning Marable, *Race, Reform and Rebellion: The Second Reconstruction in Black America from 1945 to 1982* (1984); James R. Ralph, Jr., *Northern Protest: Martin*

Luther King, Jr., Chicago, and the Civil Rights Movement (1993); *Report of the National Advisory Commission on Civil Unrest* (1968); Cleveland Sellers with Robert Terrell, *The River of No Return: The Autobiography of a Black Militant and the Life and Death of SNCC* (1973); Harvard Sitkoff, *The Struggle for Black Equality, 1954–1992* (1992); William L. Van Deburg, *New Day in Babylon: The Black Power Movement and American Culture, 1965–1975* (1992); Milton Viorst, *Fire in the Streets: America in the 1960s* (1979).

The Rise of the New Left and the Counterculture

Edward Bacciocco, Jr., *The New Left in America* (1974); Wini Breines, *Community and Organization in the New Left* (1983); Peter Clecak, *Radical Paradoxes: Dilemmas of the American Left, 1945–1970* (1973); Morris Dickstein, *Gates of Eden: American Culture in the 1960s* (1977); Sara Evans, *Personal Politics: The Roots of Women's Liberation in the Civil Rights Movement and the New Left* (1979); Todd Gitlin, *The Sixties: Years of Hope, Days of Rage* (1987); Clinton Heylin, *Bob Dylan* (1991); Maurice Isserman, *If I Had a Hammer: The Death of the Old Left—and the Birth of the New Left* (1989); Kenneth Keniston, *Young Radicals: Notes on Committed Youth* (1968); Richard King, *The Party of Eros: Radical Social Thought and the Realm of Freedom* (1972); Cyril Levitt, *Children of Privilege: Student Revolt in the Sixties* (1984); James Miller, *"Democracy Is in the Streets": From Port Huron to the Siege of Chicago* (1987); Edward P. Morgan, *The 60s Experience: Hard Lessons About Modern America* (1991); R. David Myers, ed., *Toward a History of the New Left: Essays from Within the Movement* (1989); Philip Norman, *Shout! The Beatles in Their Generation* (1981); William Novak, *High Culture: Marijuana in the Lives of Americans* (1980); Tim Riley, *Tell Me Why: A Beatles Commentary* (1988); Theodore Roszak, *The Making of a Counterculture* (1969); Stanley Rothman and S. Robert Lichter, *Roots of Radicalism* (1982); Kirkpatrick Sale, *SDS* (1973); Anthony Scaduto, *Bob Dylan* (1971); William C. Seitz, *Art in the Age of Aquarius, 1955–1970* (1992); Bob Spitz, *Dylan: A Biography* (1986); Irwin Unger, *A History of the American New Left, 1959–1972* (1974); George R. Vickers, *The Formation of the New Left: The Early Years* (1975); Nicholas Von Hoffman, *We Are the People Our Parents Warned Us Against* (1968); Jon Wiener, *Come Together: John Lennon in His Time* (1984); Tom Wolfe, *The Electric Kool-Aid Acid Test* (1969).

Chapter Ten

OUT OF CONTROL: WAR IN VIETNAM, PROTEST AT HOME

They come by the hundreds, walking slowly down the gently sloping path and gazing silently at the black marble wall on which are inscribed the names of more than 57,000 young Americans. Some visitors weep quietly; others leave a flower or a message; still others seek out the name of a son, a brother, or a friend.

This is the Vietnam Veterans Memorial in Washington, D.C., an intensely moving monument in a city filled with statuary.* Other Washington monuments honor revered leaders or recall proud events; this one commemorates the nation's longest and most controversial war—a conflict that devastated the people whom it sought to save and that catalyzed wrenching divisions at home. Lacking victory or celebration, the war's conclusion left only relief that a long ordeal had ended at last. The Vietnam Veterans Memorial stands as a reminder not only of dead young soldiers but of strategies gone grievously awry, the collapse of two presidential administrations, human suffering on a horrendous scale, and an America torn by internal strife. In 1580 the words of English playwright John Lyly foreshadowed the Vietnam War's ultimate meaning for the United States: "The wound that bleedeth inward is most dangerous."

As we saw in Chapter 9, the inward wound of Vietnam festered in a body politic already feverish. The upheavals that tore U.S. society in the late 1960s had roots in ideological and cultural conflicts that predated LBJ's 1965 escalation of the Southeast Asian war. As the Vietnam struggle loomed ever larger, the mood turned angrier in the African-American community, and the New Left and the counterculture, already well entrenched, spearheaded a sharp challenge to the administration's war policies. The domestic turmoil that had first erupted in the mean streets of the nation's black ghettos now spread to the campuses of some of the nation's most prestigious universities.

Although the Vietnam conflict came to be called "Johnson's War," it was not

---

* The memorial design, by Yale art student Maya Ying Lin, incited sharp opposition from some veterans' organizations and others, including Texas tycoon Ross Perot, when it was unveiled in the early 1980s. Critics favored a more conventionally heroic and patriotic design.

entirely of his making. Its roots stretched back to decisions and actions taken by Dwight Eisenhower and John Kennedy, and indeed to a whole nexus of Cold War assumptions dating to the late 1940s. But Johnson's 1965 decision to commit U.S. power and prestige fully and almost irrevocably in an internecine war raging halfway around the world had reverberations that neither he nor anyone else anticipated. By 1968 not only the civil-rights cause and the liberal consensus, but the American social fabric itself, seemed about to unravel.

Vietnam 1963–1967:
The Years of Escalation

When Lyndon Johnson took office in November 1963, the United States had some sixteen thousand U.S. military personnel in Vietnam as advisors to the South Vietnamese army. The White House was firmly committed to maintaining a non-communist government in Saigon, where a coup had recently overthrown and assassinated Ngo Dinh Diem. Over the next four years, Johnson vastly expanded this investment; by the end of 1967, 485,000 U.S. troops were fighting in South Vietnam. U.S. bombers rained death across much of North and South Vietnam, and American forces grappled in full-scale combat in the south. But despite billions of dollars and a mighty military effort, the U.S. goal of a stable, popularly supported anticommunist government in South Vietnam stayed maddeningly out of reach.

The American commitment to a full-scale war in Vietnam had evolved gradually, through a series of decisions reflecting strategic calculations in Washington and actions by the North Vietnam government. A key set of decisions culminated in July 1965, when Johnson moved to stave off what seemed to be the imminent collapse of the Saigon regime. In March 1964, after much debate, North Vietnam had decided to escalate its military role in South Vietnam in order to unify the country under the rule of Hanoi and the Vietnamese Communist party. Ho Chi Minh, General Vo Nguyen Giap, and other top leaders, having defeated the French in 1954, bitterly resented the United States' snatching national unification from their grasp. To carry out the plan, North Vietnamese soldiers quietly slipped south to join the 23,000 Vietcong (VC) (the military arm of South Vietnam's communist-led National Liberation Front) already on the scene. In addition to the VC, fifty thousand local self-defense militia stood ready. Regular North Vietnamese army units moved south as well. Hanoi improved and extended the Ho Chi Minh trail, a vast network of roads and paths linking North and South Vietnam.

President Johnson, alerted to these moves by the U.S. ambassador in Saigon, Henry Cabot Lodge, fretted about becoming bogged down in the conflict. As he put it, he felt like a catfish that had swallowed "a big juicy worm with a right sharp hook in the middle of it." A coup by the South Vietnamese military in January 1964 brought to power yet another general, Nguyen Khanh, and underscored South Vietnam's political instability.

Despite Johnson's doubts, many factors drove him to up the ante in Vietnam. Key Kennedy advisers who now had Johnson's ear urged a strong U.S. military response to Hanoi's moves. Secretary of State Dean Rusk, Defense Secretary Robert

McNamara, national security adviser McGeorge Bundy, Walt Rostow of the State Department policy planning staff, and the Joint Chiefs of Staff all warned that without major U.S. intervention, South Vietnam would surely fall to the communists. This collapse, they somberly cautioned, could vastly expand China's power in Asia, particularly because Hanoi was siding with Beijing in the worsening Sino-Soviet dispute. Moreover, it could jeopardize Japan's security. Invoking President Eisenhower's domino theory, they predicted that if South Vietnam fell, Laos, Cambodia, Malaysia, Burma, and perhaps other nations of the region would topple into the communist camp as well. Because each of these nations had a common colonial past and ample reason to welcome indigenous radicals who championed the cause of independence, the domino theory seemed plausible. Moreover, Indonesia's unstable ruler, Sukarno, was granting increasing influence to the Indonesian Communist party. The rapid progress of Beijing's nuclear-weapons program, culminating in an atomic-bomb test in October 1964, deepened fears of China's future role.

Beyond the immediate geopolitics, these advisers believed that abandoning South Vietnam would stir doubts among America's allies about Washington's treaty commitments. If America allowed a communist takeover in South Vietnam, Dean Rusk asked rhetorically, how could the NATO allies trust Washington's pledge to defend West Berlin? More broadly, the situation in Vietnam appeared to fit the new Cold War paradigm that had evolved in the early 1960s. Initially the Cold War had focused on direct military confrontation with the Soviet Union, and both sides had amassed nuclear arsenals in pursuit of this rivalry. In the years 1960–1963, as we have seen, a more complex picture had emerged. Although an ultimate doomsday showdown with Moscow (or Beijing) remained a possibility, strategic calculations now focused more on the developing nations of Asia, Latin America, and Africa. Washington planners concluded that here, under the guise of anticolonial "wars of national liberation," the Cold War would be decided—not in a single Armageddon moment but in a series of local insurgencies. These uprisings, the administration surmised, would involve irregular forces and guerrilla bands inspired by Marxist ideology and equipped by Moscow or Beijing. The Sino-Soviet rivalry for the allegiance of the developing world; the strategic pronouncements of Mao Zedong and other Chinese leaders, with their emphasis on encouraging local insurgencies; and the success of Fidel Castro's revolution in Cuba lent credence to this analysis of the Cold War's evolving nature. Vietnam seemed the ideal opportunity to test America's ability to compete in the new arena.

This view of the Cold War derived ultimately from George Kennan's containment doctrine, with its picture of the Soviets' endlessly probing for weak spots in which to inject their power and influence. Yet Kennan had focused on Europe and other key geopolitical regions. By the early 1960s, "containment" implied a commitment to intervene in any region, especially in the developing world, that qualified as a cockpit of Cold War confrontation. In addition, although General Maxwell Taylor's flexible-response doctrine stressed America's counterinsurgency capability, Walt Rostow and others continued to portray the Cold War struggle as more than military. These strategists envisioned the use of economic aid and development programs to help Third World nations to evolve into modern, prosperous democracies. These enlightened states, the White House hoped, would pursue their own destinies immune to the lure of communism. But such reformist strategy required stable Third World governments, so the suppression of guerrilla uprisings and leftist insurgencies became the essential first step to achieving America's larger foreign-policy goals. Thus, economic development and democratic nation building, on the one hand, and counterinsurgency efforts on the other, were complementary features of the same strategic blueprint. Once again, Vietnam seemed the ideal place to showcase the new strategy.

As Johnson weighed his options in Vietnam, a dilemma arose in the Caribbean that underscored this enlarged view of the Cold War. In 1962, leftist Juan Bosch had won the presidency of the Dominican Republic in that island-nation's first free election since 1924, but a right-wing military coup soon overthrew him. When pro-Bosch forces rebelled against this military dictatorship in April 1965, President Johnson, fearing "another Cuba," sent in thirty-three thousand marines and army troops to squelch the uprising. Other member nations of the Organization of American States, pressured by Washington, supplied an additional two thousand men. Nine thousand U.S. troops stayed as late as 1966, when a presidential candidate acceptable to the Dominican army, and to Washington, defeated Bosch in a second election. LBJ avowed, "We don't intend to sit here in our rocking chair with our hands folded and let communists set up any governments in the Western Hemisphere." The successful Dominican intervention suggested that similar boldness in Vietnam could produce an equally satisfactory outcome.

To compound Cold War ideology, since the late nineteenth century America had viewed Asia as its special province. After the Spanish-American War of 1898, the United States had defeated a guerrilla army fighting for independence in the Philippines and had ruled the islands until 1946. During World War II, thousands of GIs had given their lives to free Asia from Japanese aggression. In the early 1950s, thanks to decisive action by President Truman, U.S. forces had prevented a takeover of South Korea by communist-led North Korea. This long history stirred in Johnson's mind as he pondered his course in Vietnam.

Domestic political calculations also dictated a strong stand in Southeast Asia. For years the Democrats had borne the onus of having "lost China," and Johnson, like Kennedy, vowed not to become the president who "lost Vietnam." The case for escalation involved psychological factors as well. With an election looming, Johnson was determined not to appear weaker than Kennedy, who had stood tall during the Berlin and Cuban crises. In addition, memories of the 1938 Munich Conference haunted the debate; the British and French had caved in to Hitler's territorial demands in Czechoslovakia and spurred the German dictator to further expansion. Would a failure to resist "communist aggression" in Vietnam similarly whet the appetite of Moscow and Beijing?

In retrospect, the flaws in the case for escalation seem all too evident. The poverty-stricken, peasant society of Vietnam had little strategic or economic significance for the United States. The domino theory ignored the complexity of the various societies supposedly lined up ready to fall. And as Kennan himself often complained, advocates of the containment doctrine who portrayed an aggressive Soviet Union or China muscling into every nook and cranny of the globe ignored the caution and prudence that usually guided both nations' foreign policy and blurred crucial distinctions between vital and peripheral regions. Nor did the Korean or Dominican precedents suggest much about the likely outcome of intervention in Vietnam; each situation was unique. As for China, the Vietnamese historically harbored intense suspicions toward their giant neighbor to the north, making it unlikely that Beijing would turn Vietnam into a puppet state. In general, then, Washington's Cold War strategists' thinking in broad-brush terms missed the nuances of specific situations. They tended to ignore, for example, the importance of nationalism for Hanoi's leaders and distorted it too, viewing it in Vietnam (and in other Third World nations) as a rhetorical fig leaf masking more sinister objectives orchestrated from abroad.

Naturally, all this analysis comes with the benefit of hindsight. The case against intervention was far less clear-cut in 1964–1965 than it would appear a generation later, after bitter defeat. Johnson's decisions about Vietnam, in short, were not bizarre aberrations; they arose from what appeared to be legitimate strategic calculations based on a virtual consensus among foreign-policy experts, the media, and the American public in the early and mid-1960s. The wonder is not that Johnson chose escalation but that he proceeded so cautiously, at least in public. Affirming America's commitment to a noncommunist South Vietnam, he nevertheless rejected calls for a major build-up. At the end of 1964, U.S. troop strength in Vietnam stood at 23,300; major expansion still lay ahead. Early that year, however, Johnson had approved a proposal for covert military action, including air raids against North Vietnamese and Pathet Lao (Laotian communist) bases in Laos and shelling of North Vietnamese installations by South Vietnamese gunboats. Johnson had plans for a full-scale war as well, and he laid the groundwork for the necessary escalation with the Gulf of Tonkin Resolution of August 1964.

On the night of August 1–2, 1964, North Vietnamese torpedo boats attacked the U.S. destroyer *Maddox* as it conducted espionage in the Gulf of Tonkin off North Vietnam. Earlier, South Vietnamese gunboats had shelled a North Vietnamese island, and the North Vietnamese no doubt held the *Maddox* responsible for that attack as well. The *Maddox* drove off the torpedo boats and, on Johnson's orders, continued its spying mission, joined by another destroyer, the *Turner Joy*. Two nights later, tossing on stormy seas and relying on radar and sonar rather than visual sightings, the two vessels reported another torpedo attack. Follow-up messages cast doubt on the first report, and no firm evidence of an attack ever surfaced. Johnson privately conceded that no one knew for sure what had happened ("For all I know the Navy was shooting at whales"), but he used the incident to justify a request to Congress for blanket authorization to respond as he chose to any future aggression.

The Gulf of Tonkin Resolution passed the House unanimously after a half-hour's discussion. The resolution stated:

> Congress . . . supports the determination of the President . . . to take all necessary measures to repel any armed attack against the armed forces of the United States and to prevent further aggression. . . . The United States is, therefore, prepared, as the President determines, to take all necessary steps, including the use of armed force, to assist any member or protocol state of the Southeast Asia Collective Defense treaty requesting assistance in defense of its freedom.

A few senators expressed reservations, but the more typical response was that of Senator Richard Russell of Georgia, who proclaimed, "Our national honor is at stake.

We cannot and will not shrink from defending it." The Senate passed the measure 88–2, with only Wayne Morse of Oregon and Alaska's Ernest Gruening in dissent. Later opponents of the war, George McGovern of South Dakota and Gaylord Nelson of Wisconsin, harbored doubts as well but voted for the resolution nevertheless. In public-opinion polls, Johnson's approval ratings jumped 30 points, to 72 percent.

Johnson deliberately opted for a resolution of this sort rather than a formal declaration of hostilities, which he feared might draw the Soviet Union or China directly into the conflict. Indeed, throughout the conflict, Congress never officially declared war. Furthermore, McGeorge Bundy advised him, a declaration of war would have "heavy domestic overtones." Adopting the useful fiction that South Vietnam was an independent nation, Bundy argued that the planned action was simply an effort to help an ally to defend itself against a domestic insurgency. Thus, Bundy reasoned, Washington's plan did not require an official declaration of war by Congress.

In short, the Gulf of Tonkin Resolution, together with later appropriations to pay for the conflict, provided the legislative foundation for the Vietnam War. The resolution, as Lyndon Johnson observed, was "like Grandma's nightshirt, it covers everything." When he requested this authorization, Johnson concealed the operations already under way and the detailed war plans waiting in the Pentagon. In the 1964 election campaign, Johnson had reassured voters made uneasy by Barry Goldwater's bellicose rhetoric. "We seek no wider war," LBJ soothingly promised. "We don't want our American boys to do the fighting for Asian boys," he declared in September. "We don't want to . . . get bogged down in a land war in Asia."

In 1965, however, the political instability in Saigon, combined with North Vietnam's stepped-up military campaign in the south, precipitated a series of decisions that moved the United States from a limited commitment in Vietnam to all-out war. In August 1964, Nguyen Khanh, South Vietnam's military ruler, had assumed near-dictatorial powers, sparking protests among Buddhists and other dissident groups in South Vietnam. In February 1965, as demonstrators took to the streets of Saigon, Khanh fled the country. "I'm sick and tired of this coup shit," exploded Johnson.

Johnson's top advisers had been urging him to launch an air war against North Vietnam; with the Saigon government unraveling, their exhortations grew more urgent. General Maxwell Taylor, the new ambassador to South Vietnam, cautioned, "To take no positive action now is to accept defeat in the fairly near future." On February 24, LBJ approved Operation Rolling Thunder, a large-scale bombing campaign drafted earlier by the Joint Chiefs of Staff. Soon U.S. bombers were conducting more than three thousand raids monthly north of the 17th parallel, the dividing line between the two Vietnams. To justify this dramatic move, Johnson cited recent Vietcong attacks on U.S. military installations, including one at Pleiku in Vietnam's central highlands that had killed nine Americans. Johnson again concealed from Congress and the public the full extent of his action and the larger plan underlying it. Instead, he presented his decision as merely a specific response to a particular incident. Thus, by "indirection and dissimulation," with no opportunity for full-scale debate, as historian George Herring has written, the nation edged closer to open war.

As Johnson took these fateful steps, we may pause to ask what would have constituted "victory" in Vietnam. The goal was not North Vietnam's surrender or even the overthrow of the Hanoi government. Instead, the United States strove to inflict enough damage through bombing (and later to kill enough Vietcong and North Vietnamese ground troops) to force Hanoi to stop trying to unify all Vietnam under the communist banner. Sufficiently heavy attrition, U.S. war planners believed, would compel Hanoi to accept America's fundamental war aim: an independent, noncommunist government in the south. This agenda rested on three assumptions: first, that a large show of force would persuade Hanoi to give up the struggle; second, that a Saigon regime could exercise effective leadership and create a viable noncommunist state; and third, that the American people would support the war long enough for the first two goals to be achieved. None of these premises proved sound.

One step up the escalation ladder led to the next. With the launching of the bombing campaign in 1965, General William C. Westmoreland, the U.S. military commander in Vietnam appointed by Johnson in 1964, requested U.S. combat forces to defend the airbase at Danang from VC attack. In early March, in a replay of legendary World War II Pacific island invasions, thirty-five hundred U.S. marines sloshed ashore near the base. Greeting them were bouquet-bearing young Vietnamese women and a large banner proclaiming, "Welcome to the Gallant Marines." By moving from an advisory to a ground-combat role, the United States had crossed a critical threshold.

From this initial small commitment, the numbers (and the casualties) rose steadily over the next three years. Upping the ante at a strategy session in Honolulu in late April, General Taylor and the Joint Chiefs asked that about forty thousand U.S. soldiers be assigned to Vietnam. The initial plan, to concentrate the troops around key U.S. installations, soon gave way to a more aggressive mission. In May, Congress approved Johnson's request for $700 million to pay for the expanded war. Johnson later claimed that this and similar funding votes, along with the Gulf of Tonkin Resolution, represented Congress's approval of the war. Critics responded that voting funds to support young Americans already in combat was no substitute for a declaration of war before hostilities were initiated, as required by the Constitution.

As the commitment of troops and dollars grew, the revolving door in Saigon continued to whirl. In June, a cabal of junior officers staged yet another coup. Air Vice Marshal Nguyen Cao Ky became premier. A swashbuckling French-trained pilot with a rakish mustache and a glamorous wife, Ky sported gold-rimmed sunglasses, black jumpsuits, and garish scarves. Once more, further escalation seemed the only answer to political chaos. Westmoreland, backed by the Joint Chiefs, requested another 150,000 troops. Only a major enlargement of the war, McNamara claimed, could bring Hanoi around and salvage a pro-U.S. government in Saigon. Walt Rostow, now very influential in Johnson's inner circle, enthusiastically supported the build-up. The president received the same advice from the "Wise Men," a group of senior counselors led by Dean Acheson whom he summoned on July 10.

Bucked up by this near unanimity, Johnson in mid-July 1965 ordered a vast expansion in both the air and ground war. In the initial phase of Operation Rolling Thunder, Johnson had sharply limited the choice of targets. "They can't even bomb an outhouse without my approval," he had boasted. Now he gave Westmoreland permission to expand the bombing in North Vietnam and to bomb suspected enemy concentrations in South Vietnam as well. Monthly B-52 sorties soon increased to nearly five thousand. Johnson also approved sending fifty thousand more GIs to South Vietnam immediately, with an additional fifty thousand soon to follow. Equally important, the president authorized a basic change in strategy. The combat troops sent to Vietnam earlier had served defensive duty, protecting the Danang airbase and other U.S. installations. This role was a variant of the enclave strategy advocated by James Gavin, a retired U.S. army general and later ambassador to France. Gavin urged that the United States commit itself only to defending Saigon and other major South Vietnam cities, not the whole country. Americans, he reasoned, would support a defensive mission with minimal casualties almost indefinitely—certainly long enough to force North Vietnam to the negotiating table.

But Westmoreland and the Joint Chiefs resisted what they saw as a weak, static strategy. "No one ever won a battle sitting on his ass," jeered General Earle Wheeler, chairman of the Joint Chiefs. Under intense pressure, Johnson agreed to a more aggressive plan. After July 1965, the U.S. combat role in Vietnam shifted from defense to a search-and-destroy mission aimed at seeking out and killing the maximum number of Vietcong and North Vietnamese forces. Surely this plan would force Hanoi to accept an independent, noncommunist South Vietnam, Johnson believed. Alone in the administration, Undersecretary of State George Ball continued to object. Ball warned Johnson, as he had Kennedy, of "an open-ended commitment of U.S. forces, mounting U.S. casualties, [and] no assurance of a satisfactory solution." "Once on the tiger's back," he added, "we cannot be sure of picking the place to dismount."

In his July 1965 decisions, Johnson chose options somewhat short of what his generals recommended. Although he enlarged the bombing, he confined it to the southern part of North Vietnam, and he granted Westmoreland 100,000 more troops rather than the requested 150,000. Nevertheless, even this middle way represented a massive escalation. By the end of 1965, 184,000 U.S. troops had amassed in South Vietnam. U.S. combat deaths had edged above six hundred, and the shift to a search-and-destroy strategy made heavier future losses inevitable. July 1965 was thus the pivotal point toward full-scale war. Yet Johnson, desperate to avoid congressional or public controversy that would jeopardize his Great Society programs, once more hid the full magnitude of the escalation.

In 1966 and 1967, the air and ground war grew exponentially. Washington planners especially favored air strikes, for here the Americans dominated overwhelmingly and suffered relatively light losses. Sorties against North Vietnam increased to more than a hundred thousand in 1967,* and the target range moved steadily north to the nation's rudimentary industrial and transportation facilities, including factories and oil tanks on the very outskirts of Hanoi and the port city of Haiphong. The civilian toll was heavy. All told, U.S. bombs killed an estimated one hundred thousand North Vietnamese civilians.

North Vietnam nevertheless remained grimly determined to drive the Americans from South Vietnam. General Westmoreland in an August 1966 report to Pres-

---

* The bombing was not constant throughout the year. It declined during Vietnam's rainy season (September to May) when visibility was poor, and it increased in other months.

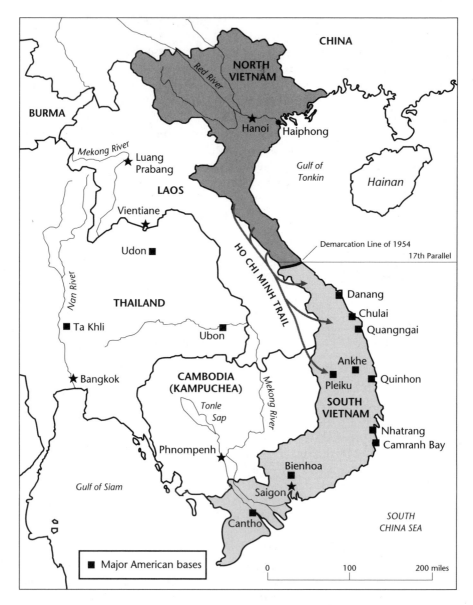

FIGURE 10.1
The Vietnam War to 1968

ident Johnson, saw "no indication that the resolve of the leadership in Hanoi has been reduced." Project Jason, a 1966 study ordered by Defense Secretary McNamara, confirmed that the air war in North Vietnam was having scant impact on either Hanoi or the guerrilla insurgency in the south. As Ton That Tung, a prominent Hanoi physician, told journalist Stanley Karnow after the war, "There was an extraordinary fervor then. The Americans thought that the more bombs they dropped, the quicker we would fall to our knees and surrender. But the bombs heightened rather than dampened our spirits."

The North Vietnamese moved factories underground, built a vast network of tunnels and shelters, and rebuilt roads and bridges with lightning speed. By 1967 some six thousand tons of supplies arriving daily from China and the Soviet Union diluted the effects of the bombing. Soviet aid increased sharply when Khrushchev's successor, Leonid Brezhnev, launched a drive to win Hanoi's allegiance.

Although the bombing campaign took a far smaller toll in American lives than did the ground war, it nevertheless exacted a high price. From 1965 to 1968, North Vietnam's deadly air defenses shot down nearly a thousand U.S. aircraft, valued at some $6 billion. Nearly six hundred captured pilots would serve the North Vietnamese as bargaining chips when peace talks finally began. The ground war in South Vietnam, too, grew in scope and intensity. A major battle in Ia Drang Valley in Pleiku Province in November 1965 proved a watershed. The battle pitted an outnumbered battalion of the U.S. Seventh Cavalry (the unit commanded by General George Armstrong Custer at the disastrous Battle of Little Big Horn in 1876) against a much larger North Vietnamese force. The bloody encounter left 230 American soldiers dead and 240 wounded. But the North Vietnamese toll of three thousand dead implied a favorable "kill ratio," confirming Westmoreland's judgment that a war of attrition eventually would break Hanoi's will.*

Pursuing the search-and-destroy strategy, Westmoreland requested ever more troops, and through 1966 Johnson complied. In June of that year, the president authorized 431,000 U.S. troops in Vietnam by the following summer. Nevertheless, the ground war continued to fare badly. Only a tiny fraction of search-and-destroy patrols led to engagement with communist forces. Operation Cedar Falls, a major search-and-destroy mission early in 1967 that sent thirty-five thousand troops north of Saigon to the Iron Triangle region, illustrates the pattern. The soldiers destroyed entire villages identified as VC hideouts. In Ben Suc, U.S. military forcibly removed people to a refugee camp and flattened their village with earth-moving equipment. During a similar operation in 1968 involving the Mekong Delta community of Ben Tre, a U.S. officer memorably commented, "It became necessary to destroy the town in order to save it." The number of VC killed during Operation Cedar Falls was claimed to be 720, but most enemy troops in the area simply withdrew into nearby Cambodia, and returned when the operation was over.

The ground war in South Vietnam was augmented by close air support, with bombers pouring explosives on suspected enemy centers. In free-fire zones covering most of South Vietnam, B-52s could bomb at will. Ironically, South Vietnam, America's ally, absorbed more than double the bomb tonnage dropped on North Vietnam, at a fearful cost in civilian lives. Gunships, including converted C-47 transport planes, rained deadly fire on VC forces. Helicopters of the First Air Cavalry Division provided rapid deployment of troops and evacuated the wounded. The use of napalm added to the toll. The gluelike flaming explosive, made of jellied petro-

---

* The story of the battle of Ia Drang, *We Were Soldiers Once . . . and Young* (1992), by Harold G. Moore, a battalion commander, and Joseph L. Galloway, a journalist who was present, powerfully conveys the reality of the Vietnam combat experience.

"It became necessary to destroy the town in order to save it." Quang Ngai province, 1967. Having evacuated the inhabitants, a U.S. Army team nicknamed the "Zippo squad" (after a brand of cigarette lighter) burned down this village to deny its use by the Vietcong. Here a G.I. rests following the operation's successful completion. (© *Philip Jones Griffith/Magnum Photos*)

leum and white phosphorus, adheres to whatever it touches, including human skin. Over the course of the war, U.S. bombers dropped an estimated 400 million pounds of the deadly substance.

An array of technological aids backed the ground war. IBM computers in Saigon identified likely points of VC attack. Infrared viewing devices pinpointed enemy hideouts. On Secretary of Defense McNamara's orders, the marines bulldozed and wired a twenty-five-mile-wide strip between North and South Vietnam to create an electronic barrier against infiltration. In Operation Ranchhand, the United States sprayed millions of gallons of herbicides and chemical defoliants such as Agent Orange over large areas of South Vietnam to deny the enemy concealment in the jungle. "Only you can prevent forests," sardonically joked the men who handled the stuff. In one of the war's many ironies, Johnson's policies brought environmental disaster to Vietnam while his wife preached beautification at home. The North Vietnamese commander General Giap ridiculed the U.S. reliance on technology and statistical measures of success. The Americans "question the computers . . . and then go into action," he jeered. "But arithmetical strategy doesn't work here . . . . When a whole people rises up, nothing can be done."

While strategists pored over their maps and computer printouts in Washington and Saigon, the ground war itself unfolded in the jungles, river deltas, and highlands of South Vietnam, with Vietnamese and American forces both paying a tremendous price. The troops at the front, nicknamed grunts, manned remote camps in hostile areas and conducted dangerous patrols to flush out the elusive foe.

For American soldiers in the field, a year-long tour of duty brought fatigue, psychological trauma, and the ever-present danger of sudden death or severe injury from a sniper or land mine. Moreover, the contrast between the grim conditions in the field and the tawdry amenities of Saigon and major bases like Danang only added a surreal dimension to the war. These centers boasted bowling alleys, movie theaters, and PXs loaded with reminders of home: the latest magazines, soft drinks, hamburgers, beer, and ice cream. Yet familiar treats offered only fleeting escape from the war's horrors. Plucked from city streets, farms, and small towns, often possessing only a high-school education and little experience of the world, these young men found themselves trapped in an utterly alien environment. They confronted a foe familiar with the land and its people and trained in guerrilla combat. There were few set-piece battles. Days of boredom might explode in murderous fire from an unseen sniper during a reconnaissance mission or in a stealthy VC attack on a base camp.

For the thousands of women who served in Vietnam on active, though noncombat, military duty or with private organizations, the war brought its own special traumas. According to the Veterans Administration, some eleven thousand women served in Vietnam as nurses or in other roles. The estimated total, including those employed by private organizations such as the Red Cross, varies from thirty-three thousand to fifty thousand. One army nurse recalled, "Our job was to look [wounded soldiers] in the eye and convince them that everything was all right. . . . [Y]ou finally built up a facade and could literally look at somebody dying and smile like Miss America or whatever we personified to them." Historian Marilyn Young has perceptively observed, "The war gave many women responsibilities and a sense of power usually denied them in civilian life. But this new status too was confusing and even distressing in that there was no way to extricate it from the death and dehumanization that were its occasion."*

Ultimately, remembered moments rather than mind-numbing statistics best convey the reality of Vietnam for those caught in its coils. Recounting the confusion of battle at Ia Drang in November 1965, one journalist recalled a seventeen-year-old's brush with death: "In the middle of all that, a kid wearing a white T-shirt stumbled out of the trees. . . . We all started yelling and waving to him to go back. . . . When he turned around we could see his back was shredded, the red blood startling against the white shirt." This youth survived, at least on that day; thousands perished. Another veteran remembered a single death among many. On a search-and-destroy patrol, a shot rang out of the jungle, hitting one of the men:

> The man . . . was writhing on the ground, his back arching up. He was gasping, hoarse, dragging air into his lungs. There was a perfect round hole about the size of a pencil, right in the middle of his sternum.
>
> Then he stopped moving. . . . I looked at him—blond, All-American, crewcut with these pale ice-blue eyes. I stood up and looked back into those eyes. Those eyes looked right through me, right through my skull and out the back of my head. I turned around and looked at the sky in the direction that his eyes were looking to see what he was staring at. I thought I was going to see something.
>
> It ran through my mind for a moment, "Did his mother feel something, did his father feel something, did anybody? Was she reaching for a can of peas in the supermarket and feel a tug or a jolt and not know what it was? Does anybody close to him know that he just died?"

The war took an especially heavy psychological toll on the combat forces, for many soldiers bitterly resented risking their lives in a conflict whose purpose seemed obscure and that was stirring bitter dissent at home. One veteran writing in 1985 angrily rejected the claim that the war could have been won if only Washington and

---

* Marilyn B. Young, *The Vietnam Wars, 1945–1990* (1991). In 1993 a statue honoring the army nurses of Vietnam was erected near the Vietnam Veterans Memorial in Washington, D.C.

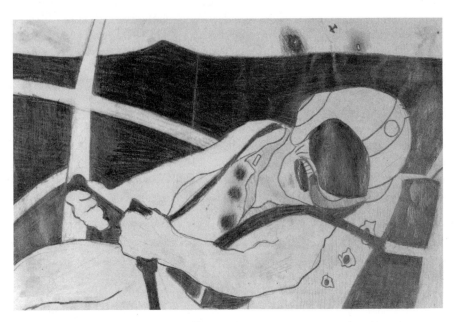

Some Vietnam veterans preserved their memories in paintings and drawings. Richard J. Olsen drew *Tay Ninh* in memory of a friend killed while piloting a helicopter. Wrote Olsen, "It's a hell of a way to die. I actually had tears in my eyes as I carved out this picture using a clumsy ebony pencil like a dagger." (Tay Ninh, *by Richard J. Olsen, 1967, pencil on rag paper*)

the American people had supported it long enough. "The bureaucrats didn't push us into a winnable war and then tie our hands," he charged. "What they did was actually far worse. They put us into a war that was as unwinnable as it was immoral. They put us into a war that even they could not explain, and so, young men died for old men's pride."

Although marked by moments of courage and heroism, the war also exacted a high price morally. In a struggle that blurred distinctions between civilian and soldier, friend and foe, some GIs came to despise all Vietnamese as "gooks," "slopes," or "slants." Napalmed bodies became "crispy critters." Ally and enemy looked identical, and soldiers struggled to distinguish them. Some broke under the pressure. One recalled an incident in which a few GIs, after twenty days in a free-fire zone, stopped a Vietnamese man and his daughter riding a motorbike. After ripping up the man's identification papers so that he could be classified as Vietcong, they killed him and raped his daughter "like an animal pack," then shot and mutilated her. Recounting this incident in graphic detail, the veteran continued:

> I got back to the World [the United States], but it wasn't the World that I had left. . . . I did not fit into the real world any more. . . . When my mom came to see me, she was a different person. I didn't hate her or nothing like that. But it was a different person. I couldn't communicate with her. I just looked at her. . . . I would just sit in the room in the hospital and my mind would flash back. I would have dreams about the Nam and action. I could see myself fighting, when I'm actually sitting in a VA hospital on the bed. I could see myself back in the Nam.

Of course, atrocities occurred on both sides. The VC and NLF forces killed wounded enemy troops, assassinated civilians who worked for or supported the Saigon government, devised fiendish ambushes that killed and maimed patrolling GIs, and held prisoners under terrible conditions. After the war, American suspicions that the North Vietnamese had taken far more GI prisoners than they officially acknowledged and that many soldiers reported as missing in action were still alive would roil American politics for decades and disrupt efforts to normalize relations with Vietnam. Furthermore, Ho Chi Minh, General Giap, and North Vietnam's other communist rulers proved ready to sacrifice hundreds of thousands of their followers' lives to achieve their goals. Nevertheless, it was the atrocities by U.S. forces, some of which gradually filtered out, that received heaviest attention from the American media, shaping home-front perceptions of the war.

The countless bombing raids and search-and-destroy missions served only to forestall the collapse of the Saigon regime, at enormous cost. The U.S. death toll reached 16,500 by the end of 1967—with almost 10,000 killed in that year alone. The monetary cost hit $21 billion in 1967. The Vietnamese paid the highest price in death, suffering, and disruption. From 1961 on, 451,000 South Vietnamese civilians died as a result of the war, with more than twice that number wounded. Some 6.5 million South Vietnamese were uprooted from their ancestral homes and turned into refugees. The U.S. Command sometimes portrayed the massive disruption of the civilian population as a strategic plus. As General Westmoreland responded when war correspondent Neil Sheehan asked him about the refugee problem, "It does deprive the enemy of the population, doesn't it."

Despite massive U.S. effort, the war failed in its central purpose: to force Hanoi to accept an independent, noncommunist South Vietnam. Ho Chi Minh matched the U.S. escalation step by step. Regardless of ghastly attrition rates, fresh waves of North Vietnamese troops arrived in the field as a younger generation came of age. By mid-1966, Hanoi could count on a force of more than 430,000 in South Vietnam, including North Vietnam regulars, VC, and local militia. When casualties reached prohibitive levels, the troops lay low awaiting reinforcements or regrouped in the North. Some withdrew to jungle bases in nearby Laos and Cambodia. Hanoi counted on outlasting the invaders, confident that America's tolerance for the bloodletting would eventually wear thin. As U.S. casualties mounted, predicted the astute General Giap, "their mothers will want to know why. The war will not long survive their questions."

Along with the bombing and the ground war, the United States also launched a pacification and nation-building program in South Vietnam designed to create a strong, democratic society loyal to the Saigon regime. Toward this end, Americans built schools and clinics in "pacified" areas. Saigon's New Life Hamlet Program, which replaced the Strategic Hamlet program described earlier, moved villagers to new settlements in regions supposedly under Saigon's control. (When this program grew unpopular, a variant was introduced called *Ap Doi Moi*, or "*Really* New Life Hamlet Program.") A related pacification effort, the Revolutionary Development Program, sent teams of South Vietnamese experts into villages for community building. But peasants conditioned to distrust officials remained leery of these emissaries from Saigon, and the VC or the North Vietnamese often assassinated the village leaders of the most successful efforts.

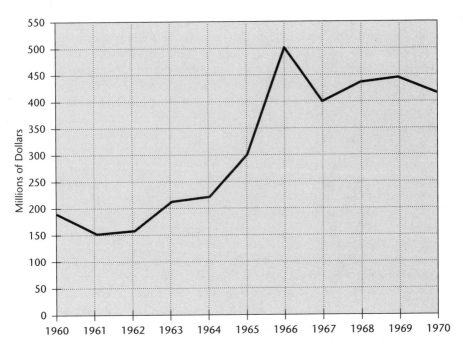

FIGURE 10.2

U.S. Government Grants and Credits to South Vietnam, 1960–1970

SOURCE: *Historical Statistics of the United States, Colonial Times to 1970* (1975).

Westmoreland's office gave priority to its military operations over the political goals of pacification and nation building, and the two programs bore little relation to each other. In May 1967, to resolve tensions between the military command and the pacification effort, Johnson placed the latter under Westmoreland's direct authority in a new program, Civil Operations and Revolutionary Development Support (CORDS). To head CORDS, Johnson chose an eager young National Security Council staffer, Robert Komer. Devising a computerized Hamlet Evaluation Survey, Komer proudly reported late in 1967 that 67 percent of South Vietnam's peasants supported the Saigon government. This statistical precision roused suspicions, particularly because Westmoreland's predecessor, General Paul Harkins, a commander notorious for his unflagging optimism, had reported precisely the same percentage in 1963. In fact, the military effort directly undermined the political goals. The continual bombing and search-and-destroy missions that shredded the fabric of life in this peasant society destroyed any hope of creating a viable nation on the U.S. model. One American official later bleakly observed, "It was as if we were trying to build a house with a bulldozer and wrecking crane."

The enormous U.S. intervention yielded other insidious effects as well. As Americans commandeered the war, they pushed the South Vietnamese aside and lost any prospect of a Vietnamese solution of the dispute. South Vietnam's forces stood at 800,000 by 1967 but were largely a paper army, with little taste for combat. High desertion rates further eroded the units' combat effectiveness. The American presence also catalyzed runaway inflation in South Vietnam, and the devastation in rural areas drove throngs of peasants into crowded urban shantytowns. Once-lovely Saigon became a teeming warren of bars, brothels, and black markets crowded with GIs. Even in remote villages, shacks made entirely of flattened beer cans cropped up—symbols of the American impact on Vietnamese society.

Saigon politics remained as muddled as ever. Prime Minister Ky, clinging to office longer than anyone expected, was lavishly feted by President Johnson at a meeting in Honolulu early in 1966. But Ky's graft-ridden regime exercised little real power and never won the trust of most South Vietnamese. In March 1966, Buddhists in Hué and Danang demonstrated against the Ky regime, prompting U.S. officials at conferences in Manila and Guam to urge Ky to modify his authoritarian rule. With much fanfare, the government adopted a constitution, complete with bill of rights. Distrusting the impulsive Ky, U.S. officials shifted their support to his more stable sidekick, General Nguyen Van Thieu. In a September 1967 election marked by irregularities worthy of LBJ's 1948 Senate campaign, Thieu won a weak plurality of the votes (35 percent) and became president. Ky settled for the vice-presidency, but intrigue and turmoil persisted unabated.

The U.S. military command, throughout these electoral machinations, remained firmly upbeat. Inflated enemy body counts ("If it's dead and Vietnamese, it's VC," was the rule in the field) ballooned still further as they passed through the chain of command. The flow of heartening but incorrect statistics not only lulled the U.S. public and official Washington but locked the military commanders themselves onto a doomed course. Military historians harshly criticize Westmoreland's obsession with quantitative yardsticks of kill ratios achieved, sorties run, tonnage dropped, acres defoliated, and villages pacified. As they see it, the preoccupation with statistics masked a failure of strategic vision and an appalling blindness to the war's social and political context. In Washington, the Joint Chiefs, far from the action and dependent on reports filed by officers in the field, mostly parroted Westmoreland's version of the war and rubber-stamped his calls for more troops. Up and down the chain of command, the military had a huge psychological and institutional investment in presenting the war in a favorable light.

But in this most heavily reported war in history, journalists filed stories and captured scenes on film that belied the optimistic official briefings. As early as May 1965, a *New York Herald Tribune* reporter coined the term *credibility gap* to describe the growing distrust of the government's version of the war. As relations between the military and the press soured, some officers accused reporters of disloyalty. Acid strands of doubt began to corrode official optimism.

Gnawing Doubts at High Levels

The war ground on, and Johnson's fundamental problems refused to disappear. The Saigon regime showed little long-term viability; nation building in South Vietnam had made meager progress. Hanoi, despite punishing losses, grimly pursued its efforts to drive out the Americans forcibly and to unite Vietnam. No one knew how long the American people would stand behind the war effort. To shore up support, President Johnson initiated several "peace offensives." As early as April 1965, speaking at the Johns Hopkins University, he offered Hanoi a regional development program for the Mekong River delta bigger than Franklin Roosevelt's TVA. A brief bombing halt accompanied this carrot, but to no avail. On Christmas Eve 1965, Johnson once more stopped bombing, largely for public-relations purposes. As Dean Rusk cabled Ambassador Lodge in Saigon: "The prospect of large-scale reinforcements in men and defense budget increases for the next eighteen-month period requires solid preparation of the American people. A crucial element will be a clear demonstration that we have explored fully every alternative but that the aggressor has left us no choice." Again no movement in the Hanoi government's position resulted, and the air strikes resumed on January 31, 1966.

Professing to have positive signals from Hanoi, Polish diplomat Janusz Lewandowski launched another plan for peace in June 1966. This effort collapsed, however, in part because Johnson, doubting Lewandowski's claim, refused even a temporary bombing halt. Indeed, in December, as low-level talks were about to begin in Warsaw, U.S. B-52s raided rail facilities on the edge of downtown Hanoi. Early in 1967, British prime minister Harold Wilson and Soviet leader Alexei Kosygin floated a British-Soviet initiative to bring the two sides to the negotiating table. This attempt failed as well, much to Wilson's annoyance. These initiatives collapsed because each side declined to modify its basic goals. Washington clung to the dream of an independent, noncommunist South Vietnam; with equal intransigence, Hanoi held to its demands: a bombing halt, complete U.S. withdrawal, and a government in Saigon that included the National Liberation Front.

As 1967 opened, General Westmoreland, as usual, reported progress on all fronts. Yet at a strategy session in Guam in March, he and the Joint Chiefs called for another big escalation: 200,000 more troops, mobilization of the reserves, expansion of the war to VC staging areas in Cambodia and Laos, heavier bombing in the North, and mining of the ports through which supplies reached North Vietnam. Hard-liners in Congress ("hawks" in the lingo of the day) such as senators John Stennis of Mississippi and Henry Jackson of Washington supported the call for escalation. A top aide to Westmoreland, General William Depuy, summed up the hard-line view: "The solution in Vietnam is more bombs, more shells, more napalm . . . till the other side cracks and gives up."

These demands finally set off warning bells in the White House. "When we add divisions, can't the enemy add divisions?" Johnson queried Westmoreland. "And, if so, where does it all end?" Key Johnson advisers harbored nagging suspicions that the military, in Vietnam and at home, had lost sight of political reality. George Ball, who had left the government, stepped up his criticism. President Johnson's press secretary, Bill Moyers, voiced skepticism and departed. Even Secretary of Defense Robert McNamara hesitated. So closely identified with the Vietnam escalation that antiwar activists derided "McNamara's War" and jeered him in his rare public appearances, McNamara grew disillusioned in 1966–1967. Using analytic and quantitative techniques, he found little evidence that the military effort was paying off. The 1966 Jason study of the air war's negligible effects deepened his doubts. In October 1966, on a fact-finding trip to Vietnam, McNamara told Johnson that he saw "no reasonable way to bring the war to an end soon." Furthermore, he had moral qualms about the devastation that mighty America was wreaking on a small Asian country. In a

May 1967 memo to Johnson, McNamara reflected, "The picture of the world's greatest superpower killing or seriously injuring 1,000 non-combatants a week, while trying to pound a tiny, backward nation into submission on an issue whose merits are hotly disputed, is not a pretty one."

McNamara's doubts came amid growing opposition to the war on college campuses and among a vocal minority of legislators, religious leaders, and editors. Picketers decried campus Reserve Officer Training Corps (ROTC) programs and harangued recruiters for the Dow Chemical Company, the maker of napalm. The Spring Mobilization Committee, a coalition of peace and civil-rights groups formed by long-time pacifist A. J. Muste, announced a New York City march for April 15, 1967. The event attracted from 125,000 to 400,000 demonstrators. (Crowd estimates for the antiwar rallies of the sixties vary wildly, depending on who was doing the estimating.) A San Francisco rally on the same day brought out some 75,000 marchers. Fighting back, the administration launched an illegal CIA domestic surveillance operation, code-named CHAOS, that compiled dossiers on antiwar organizations and leaders.

As 1967 dragged on, McNamara pressed for a scaling back of the war. Rather than plunging in deeper, he advised, the administration should seek a way out. To this end, he argued for a bombing halt or cutback, a cap on force levels in Vietnam, and a shift from search-and-destroy missions to protection of South Vietnam's major cities—General Gavin's enclave plan. McNamara also hinted that the United States might modify its rigid opposition to any National Liberation Front role in governing South Vietnam. In August, the defense secretary told the Senate Armed Services Committee, "Enemy operations in the south cannot, on the basis of any report I have seen, be stopped by air bombardment—short, that is, of the virtual annihilation of North Vietnam and its people." LBJ, personalizing the issue, convinced himself that McNamara's increasingly public doubts represented a political double-cross engineered by Robert Kennedy.

Full of self-pity, an exhausted Johnson pored over the dispatches and casualty reports from Vietnam. Endless White House meetings probed for a course that might hold promise. A bleary-eyed LBJ haunted the White House Situation Room at night, selecting targets for the next day's bombing raids. George Ball's 1964 warnings about the difficulties of dismounting the tiger now seemed prophetic. Clinging to a cause in which he had invested so much of the nation's blood and treasure—and so much of his own political capital—Johnson rejected the advice of McNamara, who resigned in November 1967. The wagons circled tighter. Dean Rusk and Walt Rostow, who had become national security adviser in 1966 when McGeorge Bundy left, still supported the war. So did McGeorge Bundy, now in private life, although he harbored reservations. "To stop the bombing today would give the communists something for nothing," Bundy advised in May 1967.

Johnson rejected McNamara's plan to scale back, yet he also found the military's call for further escalation dismaying. "Bomb, bomb, bomb, that's all they know," he complained of his generals. Another major build-up, the president feared, would require the reserves and a tax increase to pay the war's soaring costs and could tilt wavering U.S. public opinion decisively against the conflict. On the other hand, withdrawal might outrage the hawks and trigger the dreaded accusation that he had "lost" Vietnam.

On November 1, a despondent Johnson reconvened the "Wise Men." Far gloomier than in 1965, they saw no alternative but to stay the course, yet they warned LBJ of the political costs of escalation. The prolonged stalemate, they further cautioned, was eroding support for the war at home, a fact obvious to anyone who watched television or read newspapers. Appalled by this formula for more war and killing, George Ball exploded at the panel of aging statesmen and bankers: "I've been watching you across the table. You're like a flock of buzzards sitting on a fence, sending the young men off to be killed. You ought to be ashamed of yourselves."

Congressional opposition mounted as well. The handful of legislators who had opposed the Gulf of Tonkin Resolution in 1964 grew far larger by 1967. Senator J. William Fulbright of Arkansas, chair of the Senate Foreign Relations Committee, emerged as a powerful critic. As early as February 1966, Fulbright's committee held special hearings on the war. Dean Rusk and other administration leaders were grilled sharply, and James Gavin, George Kennan, and others criticized the war's underlying strategic assumptions. The hearings helped crystallize antiwar sentiment.

Although Johnson turned down the military's call for 200,000 more troops and a vastly expanded air and sea war, he approved 55,000 additional men and allowed the high rate of bombing to continue. As in 1965, Johnson again presented his decision as one that offered a middle way between two extremes. In fact, it translated into further substantial escalation. The United States had undertaken the 1965 escalation in the confident hope of forcing Hanoi to yield. The escalation of 1967 was the desperate action of a drained president and a defensive administration aware of their failure to achieve the war's goals but fearful of the backlash that open admission of this failure would trigger. The very fact of the war itself had become the major rationale for grimly slogging on.

Johnson mounted a propaganda offensive to flog waning home-front support. Under a White House mandate to report good news, the flow of impressive body counts continued. In April 1967 Johnson brought General Westmoreland home to address a joint session of Congress. Standing stiffly at attention, white hair gleaming and eyebrows beetling, the six-foot South Carolinian looked every inch the general as he smartly saluted the cheering legislators. But behind the facade of unanimity, the tense debate in the White House persisted. Even McGeorge Bundy, now one of the "Wise Men," advised LBJ that his generals' grasp on reality had slipped and that Johnson must find a way to quell the angry rumbles of domestic opposition. Geopolitical shifts in Asia as well stressed the need for a policy reassessment. In 1966 President Sukarno and the Indonesia Communist party had fallen from power in an army coup, rendering the more lurid forms of the domino theory less plausible. That same year, China turned inward in a drive for Marxist ideological purification known as the Great Cultural Revolution, and its already peripheral involvement with the war raging to the south dwindled.

"The Wound that Bleedeth Inward . . ."

Rising home-front opposition, fed by skeptical journalistic coverage from Vietnam, vastly complicated the president's efforts to sustain a consensus behind the war. The

Vietnam struggle did not give rise to the New Left or the counterculture—both had got well under way earlier—but after 1965, on a growing number of campuses, the conflict functioned as the white-hot focus of unrest and radical organizing. The discontents that had been building in American society for years now centered on a single issue, the Vietnam War.

SDS and the Black Power ideologues already had challenged the legitimacy of the established order in the early 1960s. As the administration plunged the nation into full-scale war in Vietnam, the crisis of legitimacy deepened. In the eyes of the war's opponents, the government became at first the object of suspicion, then of ridicule, and finally of scorn and hatred. For some on the radical fringe, America's political enemies became heroes, as the idealism and reformist mood of these years turned to sour alienation.

The antiwar movement—or "the movement," as it came to be called—began in March 1965 with a "teach-in" at the University of Michigan after Johnson announced the bombing war against North Vietnam. Adapting the term from the civil-rights sit-ins, the organizers conducted an all-night round of lectures and discussions about the war. Within days, teach-ins cropped up at the University of Wisconsin, Stanford, Harvard, and other schools. In April, SDS organized the first large demonstration against the war: a march on Washington that drew twenty thousand protesters. That spring and fall, local committees and groups from Berkeley to New York City initiated antiwar actions and marches. In January 1966, Johnson ended automatic draft deferments for college students, intensifying the emotional pitch of antiwar activity. From a small cadre of radical activists, SDS grew to a loosely knit national organization. Local chapters initiated protest actions, with the national office exerting minimal supervision. Indeed, the movement soon would expand beyond the control of any single organization.

For all its intensity, the movement initially had a comparatively narrow base. Its early leaders were often alumni of the test-ban movement and the early sixties' civil-rights marches, and most came from liberal, politically attuned families. In some cases, as we have seen, their parents had been socialists or communists in the 1930s. Antiwar leaders studying at the elite private or public institutions tended to major in the liberal arts, often history, sociology, or English. Generally from affluent backgrounds, they saw the college years as a time to explore ideas rather than to prepare for a vocation; protest proved a natural extension of this focus. Fewer activists came from the sciences, engineering, or the professional schools. Fraternity and sorority members, conservative students, and the politically passive generally remained aloof. As antiwar sentiment spread, however, more campuses and a broader spectrum of students would be drawn in.

Politically engaged writers also joined the cause. The poet Robert Lowell, invited to a White House cultural festival in 1965, wrote a public letter to President Johnson refusing to attend because of the war. At the event itself, John Hersey read from his book *Hiroshima*, and critic Dwight Macdonald circulated an antiwar petition. (Actor Charlton Heston huffed, "Are you really accustomed to signing petitions against your host in his own home?") When the festival finally ended, President Johnson sighed, "At least nobody pissed in the punchbowl."

Dramatist Barbara Garson, a veteran of the Berkeley Free Speech Movement,

FOCUS ON: *THE IMPERIAL PRESIDENCY*

The reaction against LBJ for waging war in Vietnam without explicit congressional approval—a reaction that culminated in the punitive War Powers Act of 1973—represented a particularly bitter phase in a debate that dates back to the founding of the nation. The framers of the Constitution, having repudiated the imperial claims of George III, feared that the presidency would evolve into a quasimonarchical institution. They surrounded the office with many constraints, balancing the president's prerogatives by giving at least equal authority to the legislative branch, especially the power of the purse. In principle, no president can spend a penny that has not been appropriated by the people's representatives in Congress.

Although the Whigs of the 1830s professed to find monarchical tendencies in "King Andrew" Jackson, the presidency remained weak through most of the nineteenth century. (The major exception was Abraham Lincoln's exercise of sweeping powers during the Civil War.) Theodore Roosevelt (1901–1909) and Woodrow Wilson (1913–1921) significantly enlarged the office. Roosevelt pursued an activist approach in conservation, business regulation, and foreign affairs ("I took Panama," he later boasted after wresting from Colombia the land on which the Panama Canal was built). The Wilson administration assumed broad economic and censorship powers during the war years of 1917–1918. Warren G. Harding and Calvin Coolidge in the 1920s, guided by their probusiness laissez-faire ideology, reverted to an earlier, narrower presidential role. Ironically, however, it was Coolidge who produced one of the more flowery characterizations of the presidency. The office, he mused, "does not yield to definition. Like the glory of the morning sunrise, it can only be experienced, it cannot be told."

With Franklin D. Roosevelt, the modern presidency took shape. Battling the Depression, FDR proliferated agencies, built a fanatically loyal personal following, and expanded the presidential office. Since his administration, presidents have been expected to set the national agenda and to introduce congressional programs that shape public discourse. Yet Roosevelt also stirred the old fears of a presidency slipping into dictatorship. When he tried to enlarge the anti–New Deal Supreme Court in 1937 to give it a more liberal coloration, albeit by constitutional means, Congress slapped him down. Roosevelt broke tradition by seeking, and winning, a third term in 1940 and a fourth in 1944, but Congress retaliated posthumously with the Twenty-second Amendment (ratified in 1951), which limits presidents to two terms.

The postwar presidency continued to grow in size and influence. In 1973 histo-

dashed off *MacBird!* a parody of Shakespeare's *Macbeth* featuring a thinly disguised Lyndon and Lady Bird Johnson as the murderous Scottish monarchs. Published in 1966, *MacBird!* quickly sold more than a hundred thousand copies. Critic Mary McCarthy visited Vietnam in 1967 and in a devastating series of essays on the air war in the *New York Review of Books* described B-52 Superfortresses flying over an already rian Arthur Schlesinger, Jr., published a cautionary study, *The Imperial Presidency*. (Schlesinger had earlier written admiring studies of two presidents—Andrew Jackson and Franklin Roosevelt—who had contributed to the expansionary process, and he had served as a speechwriter for a third, John F. Kennedy.) Richard Nixon's gross abuses of the office, culminating in his forced resignation, produced a temporary reaction against strong chief executives. Yet despite periodic shifts in the balance of power, the general trend toward a stronger presidency continued under Republicans and Democrats alike. Ronald Reagan repeatedly insisted on the need to trim the federal government, and the presidency in particular, yet during his two terms, total civilian employment in the executive branch increased from 2.8 million to 3 million. Moreover, for all Reagan's railings against government power, the Iran-contra affair, one of the more flagrant abuses of executive power in American history, unfolded during his watch.

Students of the presidency such as historian Henry F. Graff attribute its growth in the modern era not to individual ambition but rather to trends largely beyond control. The end of World War II left the United States as the world's colossus, and the advent of the Cold War gave the president the grandiose title "leader of the Free World." The president literally took on the power to launch a world-destroying holocaust. Simultaneously, as social problems grew more complex and more national in scope, the programs, administrative tasks, and regulatory functions assigned to the executive branch expanded exponentially. Television contributed to the "imperial presidency" as well, turning the occupant of the White House into a media celebrity and granting him instant access to millions worldwide.

As the Cold War waned, some analysts foresaw a diminished presidency. Columnist Leslie H. Gelb of the *New York Times* wrote in 1993:

> Success feeds power. And President Clinton has little prospect of a power-building success in foreign policy, one that would catapult him to new stature at home and abroad. . . . For 50 years, Presidents have defined themselves decisively and dramatically by their actions on the world stage. . . . Mr. Clinton is not likely to have such opportunities. . . . [He] faces mostly quicksand and mudholes.

Other observers, however, wonder whether decisive achievements on major domestic issues such as economic revitalization and health-care reform will serve as the functional equivalent of the bold foreign-policy initiatives by which earlier presidents enhanced their stature. If the long-term trends of nearly a century persist, the growth in presidential power seems likely to continue. Nevertheless, the checks and balances devised by the founders in 1787 remain effective. Confounding the dark warnings of Lyndon Johnson's antiwar critics in the sixties, the nightmare of a president so powerful and so megalomaniacal as to make a mockery of constitutional government has never materialized.

shattered land, seeking new targets: "The Air Force seems inescapable, like the eye of God, and soon, you imagine . . . , all will be razed, charred, defoliated by that terrible searching gaze."

With Bob Dylan's performance at the 1965 Newport folk festival and Barry Maguire's popular hit that year, "Eve of Destruction," the music of the counterculture also took on a sharp antiwar edge. Folksinger Pete Seeger, a link to an older generation of radical activism, evoked the Vietnam quagmire in "Waist Deep in the Big Muddy" (1967), which he performed on "The Smothers Brothers Comedy Hour," a popular television show.

The media, for its part, brought the movement into the living rooms of middle America. Just as film footage from Vietnam mocked the official version of the war, so TV images of the protests rocking Washington and some of the nation's campuses publicized, and at times magnified, the opposition. Learning from the civil-rights movement, protesters skillfully exploited television. As they reminded each other, "The whole world is watching." They displayed a vivid sense of theater: flaming draft cards, coffins, and rippling banners made for compelling television. Of course, how individuals interpreted the images that appeared in *Time* and *Newsweek* and on the nightly network news depended on their political orientation. Opponents of the war cheered, but scenes of mass protest dismayed conservatives. Already roused by the ghetto riots, they saw a society beset by disloyalty trembling on the brink of anarchy.

Political cartoonists expressed the rising tempo of home-front frustration with the Vietnam War. This bitter cartoon by Tom Engelhardt appeared in the *St. Louis Post-Dispatch* in July 1967. (*Engelhardt in the* St. Louis Post-Dispatch/*Reprinted with permission*)

'JUST GIVE US THE TOOLS AND WE'LL GET THE JOB DONE'

Responses to Vietnam: The Faces of Opposition and Support

Opposition to the war was not confined to writers, college students, or the New Left. Many other Americans of liberal leanings also argued against involvement in Vietnam. Church groups, too, already mobilized by the civil-rights campaign, passed antiwar resolutions and joined marches. As early as 1965, twenty-seven hundred ministers and rabbis, in a full-page *New York Times* ad, demanded, "Mr. President, In the name of God, stop it!" Indeed, the American people as a whole embraced a broad range of views about the war, and historians make sweeping generalizations at their peril. The differences among Hollywood celebrities epitomized the larger divisions within society. Whereas many stars such as Gregory Peck, Dustin Hoffman, Shirley MacLaine, and Jane Fonda vehemently opposed the war, other celebrities, including John Wayne, Bob Hope, Clint Eastwood, and Frank Sinatra, just as vigorously supported it.

Was social class an important determinant of attitudes toward the war? The evidence is mixed. George Meany, head of the AFL-CIO, firmly backed Johnson's war policies. An AFL-CIO poll of some thirty-five hundred labor leaders in 1967 found some 40 percent in support of the administration's prosecution of the war, nearly an equal number advocating further escalation, and only about 20 percent favoring deescalation or withdrawal from Vietnam. A few highly publicized incidents during which cursing construction workers physically assaulted peace marchers (see Chapter 11) buttressed the image of massive blue-collar support for the war. But some studies found the working class no more hawkish than other Americans, with patterns of support for and opposition to the war fairly consistent across class lines. Polls in 1964 and again in 1968 by the University of Michigan's Survey Research Center, for example, revealed nearly identical views about the war among the working class, the lower-middle class, and the upper-middle class.

The evidence for the role of religious belief in shaping attitudes toward the war is similarly ambiguous. Eminent Protestant figures, such as William Sloane Coffin, the chaplain of Yale University, and Reinhold Niebuhr of Union Theological Seminary, opposed the war, as did the leadership of the major liberal Protestant denominations. Naturally, pacifists like A. J. Muste and the historic peace churches—the Quakers, Mennonites, and Brethren—shared these views. Nevertheless, other Protestant spokespersons supported the war. Paul Ramsey, a professor of religion at Princeton, published a series of books and articles arguing that America's role in Vietnam met Christianity's classic just-war criteria.* Prowar sentiment flourished among fundamentalist and evangelical Protestants. Even in the liberal, social-activist denominations, the leadership often proved more outspoken in opposing the conflict than did the laity. Despite the antiwar activism of a few high-visibility Catholic pacifists such as the Berrigan brothers, Philip and Daniel, support for the war ran high among American Roman Catholics. Vigorously anticommunist and sympathetic with the plight of South Vietnam's many Catholics, U.S. Catholics consistently backed the war at a ratio from 6 to 10 percentage points higher than did Prot-

---

* See, for example, Paul Ramsey, *The Just War: Force and Political Responsibility* (1968).

estants. Jews were the first religious group to turn decisively against the war. As early as 1966, fully 63 percent of American Jews favored immediate withdrawal or a negotiated settlement in Vietnam, whereas only a minority of Protestants and Catholics embraced these dovish positions. Leading American rabbis strongly condemned Johnson's escalation on moral grounds.

The data on attitudes toward the U.S. intervention in Vietnam reveal gender as another significant variable. Opposition to the war among women at all educational and socioeconomic levels, and of all races and religions, consistently ran about 10 percentage points higher than opposition among the comparable male cohort. In 1966, for example, when 65 percent of white males supported the war, only 54 percent of white women agreed with them.

Opinion data also undermine the conventional wisdom about the role of age in determining attitudes toward the war. Young people, far from exhibiting exceptionally high levels of opposition to the war, supported the conflict more strongly than any other age cohort. In April 1965, for example, as Johnson's escalation unfolded, 76 percent of Americans under age thirty approved of the war, and a low 51 percent of those aged forty-nine or older backed it. Only a small fraction of eighteen to twenty-two year olds ever marched or demonstrated against the war. Indeed, a mere 10 percent of eighteen to twenty-two year olds, one study found, participated in any antiwar activity. Through 1967, a majority of this age cohort supported or acquiesced in Johnson's policy. Looking back on the sixties, political scientist John Mueller concluded in 1973, "No case can be made for the popular proposition that 'youth' was in revolt over the war. . . . The poll data argue that although *some* young people may have been deeply opposed to the war, 'youth' as a whole was generally more supportive of the war than older people."

Nor, without many qualifications, can one portray the antiwar movement as a matter of college students against the older generation. Not only did many older Americans resist the war, but many college students supported it. The nation's twenty-five hundred institutions of higher learning in the 1960s constituted a spectrum of schools, from large state universities to conservative church colleges. Students and faculty on many of these campuses generally backed the war, and fewer than half of the schools ever witnessed any organized antiwar activism. The stereotype of college students standing united in opposition to the war while superpatriotic blue-collar workers rabidly defended Johnson's escalation remains little more than a caricature, based on selective memories and distorted media images.

Nevertheless, the belief that all campuses were wracked by demonstrations and that college students uniformly opposed the war remains an article of faith in the mythology of the 1960s. This perception has several sources. First, opposition to the war did emerge quickly and strongly at some of the nation's best-known institutions of higher learning, including elite private universities such as Harvard and major public universities such as Michigan and Berkeley. These institutions' sterling reputations ensured the movement instant visibility. Second, for brief intervals, notably in the spring of 1970, campus protest spread very widely indeed, reinforcing the illusion that this phenomenon continued during the entire period of the war. Third, campus activists proved skillful at drawing TV attention. By conducting sit-ins, teach-ins, and marches, they created images of campus protest that pervaded the media from 1965 on. The erroneous perception that nearly all students on all campuses were engaging in antiwar activities widened rapidly. Finally, in a prime demonstration of the vocal-minority phenomenon, campus opponents of the war brought to their cause a passion and urgency generally lacking among those who supported Vietnam or felt ambivalent about it.

Of all sectors of U.S. society, none opposed the war more strongly or consistently than the African-American community. A few conservative black leaders—Roy Wilkins of the NAACP, Republican senator Edward Brooke of Massachusetts, U.N. diplomat Ralph Bunche—supported the war, or at least did not openly oppose it, but they constituted a tiny minority. The ghetto riots and the rising militance of young black activists unfolded against the background of a steadily escalating war that took a disproportionate toll among African-Americans* and that cut deeply into domestic social programs. In these circumstances, the black community, despite its overwhelming support for LBJ's domestic programs, turned quickly against his Vietnam policies. As early as March 1966, with some 60 percent of white Americans supporting the war, a majority of blacks already opposed the conflict. Of all groups surveyed, African-American women invariably showed the lowest levels of support for the war.

Opposition to the war linked prominent blacks who otherwise differed radically. The prizefighter Muhammed Ali, a Black Muslim, lost his heavyweight crown for refusing to register for the draft. The fiery orators of SNCC and CORE included the Vietnam War in their denunciations of white America, and Martin Luther King, Jr., attacked the war as early as 1965, breaking with Johnson and angering many Americans who still backed the president. In 1966–1967, King moved beyond a pacifist critique of Vietnam to highlight its negative impact on black America specifically. He pointed out the high proportion of young blacks in combat in Vietnam and deplored the war's devastating effect on social programs that benefited African-Americans. As long as Vietnam drained the nation's human and economic resources, he asserted in April 1967, the crisis in the inner cities would only worsen. He excoriated the government for sending young black men "to guarantee liberties in Southeast Asia which they had not found in Southwest Georgia and East Harlem." Having lauded Johnson for his civil-rights stand two years earlier, King now denounced the administration as "the greatest purveyor of violence in the world today."

Broad-brush data on the population as a whole make clear that despite the vocal opposition, the American public turned only slowly against the war, and never with anything approaching unanimity. A hefty 61 percent of Americans supported Johnson's escalation in 1965, with only 24 percent opposed. As late as the summer of 1967, Johnson's war policies still had the backing of a majority of citizens, with antiwar activists in a distinct minority. As peace marchers espoused their cause, hawks implored true patriots to rally 'round the flag. Senator Russell Long of Louisiana, launching a McCarthyite-like attack on activists "who encourage the Communists to prolong the war," orated, "I swell with pride when I see Old Glory flying from

---

* In the early stages of the war, blacks accounted for 23 percent of the U.S. fatalities. By 1969 the figure had dropped to 14 percent—still higher than blacks' 11 percent share of the population.

the Capitol. . . . My prayer is that there may never be a white flag of surrender up there."

Many Americans of all ages, education, and social class endorsed such sentiments. Ingrained habits of patriotism and loyalty to the government, especially in time of war, are not easily broken. With LBJ defining support for the war as a test of true citizenship, most Americans in this first stage of escalation gave the president and his policies the benefit of the doubt. Certainly the families and friends of the young men risking their lives in Vietnam did not look sympathetically on critics who attacked the war as immoral or unwinnable.

Hostility toward campus demonstrators further influenced many citizens' position on the war. Many working-class and middle-class Americans viewed the youthful protesters as spoiled, pampered offspring of a privileged elite. They had been reared in permissive families that had indulged their every whim, the litany typically went, and now they petulantly demanded their way in shaping national policy. The media's tendency to focus on moments of confrontation between demonstrators and the police or other authority figures heightened these stereotyped perceptions. This gut-level aversion to campus demonstrators and street marchers would crest in 1968–1970, but it had entered the equation from the beginning. For many conservatives, distaste for the war's opponents proved stronger than their distaste for the war itself.

As Vietnam and its domestic fallout increasingly dominated the news, numerous Americans tried to carry on as usual. The best-sellers in these years of escalating war and protest tellingly included such titles as *Happiness Is a Warm Puppy* (1963), Dan Greenberg's *How to Be a Jewish Mother* (1965), and Jacqueline Susann's steamy sex novel *Valley of the Dolls* (1966). Movies receiving Academy Awards for best picture included three lighthearted musicals: *My Fair Lady* (1964), *The Sound of Music* (1965), and *Oliver* (1968).

Yet even Americans who detested the protests could not see the light at the end of the tunnel in Vietnam that the administration professed to discern. As casualties mounted, victory receded ever further into the distance. Citizens trying to suppress growing doubts about the war found particularly dismaying its economic costs, which soared to $20.6 billion in fiscal 1967, a year that saw the sharpest rise in the defense budget since 1943. As early as December 1965, Gardner Ackley of the Council of Economic Advisers cautioned Johnson that "a significant tax increase will be needed to prevent an intolerable degree of inflationary pressure." Nevertheless, for two years, the president avoided such a step, trying desperately to provide both "guns and butter"—that is, to finance the war in Vietnam *and* his Great Society programs—without a tax hike.

Johnson's unwillingness to raise taxes led the administration to overly optimistic projections of the war's cost and probable duration. In 1965 Defense Secretary McNamara predicted that hostilities would cease by June 30, 1967—not for any clear military reason but because that was the end of the fiscal year. In 1967 a congressional committee estimated that the war's costs in that year alone would exceed the administration's projections by $5 billion to $6 billion. This juggling with figures and dates widened the credibility gap to a chasm.

Granted, the war fed the 1960s economic boom and stimulated employment. The jobless rate, which stood at 5.7 percent in 1963, fell steadily for the next six

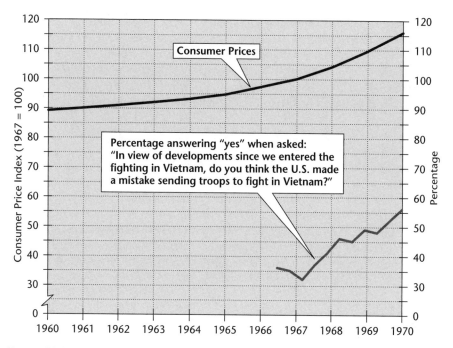

FIGURE 10.3

Inflation and Public Opinion on the Vietnam War, 1960–1970

SOURCE: *Historical Statistics of the United States, Colonial Times to 1970* (1975) and Gallup Poll data.

years to a low of 3.5 percent in 1969. But the conflict also increased federal deficits and fueled inflationary pressures. The 1966 inflation rate of 5 percent, although moderate by later standards, ranked as the highest since the Korean War and jolted a nation that had enjoyed price stability since the late 1950s. Inflation rose even more sharply thereafter, deepening Americans' uneasiness about the economic implications of the war.

At last in August 1967, Johnson proposed a 10 percent surcharge on individual and corporate taxes, which Congress passed the following June. Immediately after the president's tax-increase proposal, with no dramatic worsening in the news from Vietnam, a plurality of Americans for the first time turned against the war. Public-opinion polls in August 1967 reported that 46 percent of those polled now viewed the war as a "mistake," with 44 percent still in support. The negative tilt was almost imperceptible, but it had ominous implications for Lyndon Johnson. Rising inflation and the threat of higher taxes stirred grave questions about the war even among Americans who did not oppose it on ideological or moral grounds.

CONCLUSION

Faced with stalemate in Vietnam, shifting geopolitical realities in Southeast Asia, and protests and an eroding base at home, Johnson hesitantly agreed to a major review of the quagmire. Speaking in September 1967 in San Antonio, he modified the U.S. terms for peace talks and, like McNamara earlier, even hinted at a role for the National Liberation Front in ruling South Vietnam. Cautiously, the administration moved toward scaling down the U.S. commitment in Vietnam and turning over more of the fighting to South Vietnam, a strategy of "Vietnamization" that President Richard Nixon would implement fully in 1969 and the early 1970s.

Movement activists capitalized on the shifting mood. A. J. Muste's group, renamed the National Mobilization Against the War, joined other antiwar groups to call a march on Washington for October 16, 1967. Some hundred thousand participants rallied on the Mall. Thirty-five thousand of them, chanting "End the War" and "Hell No, We Won't Go," proceeded to the Pentagon, where they sat down at the entrance facing a line of armed guards. Soon the light from burning draft cards flickered in the darkness. Eventually military police cleared the demonstrators. Arresting 660 and clubbing many, they stirred memories of Birmingham, Montgomery, and other scenes of police violence against civil-rights activists. Lorraine Brill, a freshman at New York University, later recalled:

> We were out on the grass, chanting, "Peace now. Peace now." This went on for quite a long time, and then all of a sudden there was sort of a signal, and people were being hit by soldiers or MPs [military police]. . . . I remember people falling on me, and I remember seeing blood. It was all kind of chaos. One minute was peaceful and fun, and then all of a sudden they're hitting.

Those arrested included the Jesuit priest and activist Daniel Berrigan; famed pediatrician Benjamin Spock, a veteran of the nuclear-test-ban campaign; and novelist Norman Mailer, who described the march in a memorable piece of politically engaged journalism, *The Armies of the Night* (1968).

Johnson dragged Westmoreland home again in November for another round of optimistic speeches. "[Victory] lies within our grasp—the enemy's hopes are bankrupt," the general optimistically told the National Press Club. "With your support we will give you a success that will impact not only on South Vietnam but on every emerging nation in the world." But LBJ's edginess was apparent. "This is not Johnson's war," the president shouted angrily to reporters that fall. "This is America's war."

At the same time, a major battle appeared about to erupt around Khe Sanh, in northwest South Vietnam, where the North Vietnamese reportedly had massed forty thousand troops. As Westmoreland urgently reinforced the marine battalion stationed there, Johnson watched anxiously. Was this Dien Bien Phu all over again? Or would Khe Sanh at last provide the decisive victory that could turn the war around? In fact, Khe Sanh was a diversion. As 1968 opened, the enemy would strike a very different and unexpected blow, not at remote Khe Sanh but at the vital centers of American strength throughout South Vietnam. The Tet Offensive, a coordinated Vietcong and North Vietnamese attack in January, not only proved a pivotal point in the war but also became the overture to the bleakest, most divisive year in postwar American history.

SELECTED READINGS

The War in Vietnam

Christian G. Appy, *Working-Class War: American Combat Soldiers and Vietnam* (1983); Douglas S. Blaufarb, *The Counterinsurgency Era* (1977); C. D. B. Bryan, *Friendly Fire* (1976); William A. Buckingham, Jr., *Operation Ranch Hand: The United States Air Force and Herbicides in South East Asia, 1961–1971* (1982); Larry E. Cable, *Conflict of Myths: The Development of American Counterinsurgency Doctrine and the Vietnam War* (1986); Phillip Davidson, *Vietnam at War* (1991); Department of Defense, *Negro Participation in the Armed Forces and in Southeast Asia* (1971); George C. Herring, *America's Longest War: The United States and Vietnam* (rev. ed., 1985) and "Vietnam Remembered," *Journal of American History*, (June 1986) [essay review of seven books by Vietnam veterans]; Stanley Karnow, *Vietnam: A History* (1983); Raphael Littauer and Norman Uphoff, eds., *The Air War in Indochina* (1972); J. B. Neilands et al., *Harvest of Death: Chemical Warfare in Vietnam and Cambodia* (1972); James S. Olson and Randy Roberts, *Where the Domino Fell: America and Vietnam, 1945–1990* (1991); Bruce Palmer, Jr., *The 25-Year War: America's Military Role in Vietnam* (1984); Andrew J. Rotter, ed., *Light at the End of the Tunnel: A Vietnam War Anthology* (1991); Harrison E. Salisbury, ed., *Vietnam Reconsidered: Lessons from a War* (1985); Jonathan Schell, *The Village of Ben Suc* (1967) and *The Real War* (1987); Neil Sheehan, *The Bright and Shining Lie: John Paul Vann and America in Vietnam* (1988); Jack Shulimson and Maj. Charles M. Johnson, *The U.S. Marines in Vietnam: The Landing and the Buildup, 1965* (1978); Victor W. Sidel, "Napalm," *New England Journal of Medicine*, July 13, 1967; Wallace Terry, ed., *Bloods: An Oral History of the Vietnam War by Black Veterans* (1984); James Clay Thompson, *Rolling Thunder: Understanding Policy and Program Failure* (1980); William S. Turley, *The Second Indochina War: A Short Political and Military History, 1954–1975* (1986); Arthur H. Westing and E. W. Pfeiffer, "The Cratering of Indochina," *Scientific American* (May 1972); Marilyn B. Young, *The Vietnam Wars: 1945–1990* (1991).

Vietnam: The Strategic Planning Process

George W. Ball, *The Past Has Another Pattern: Memoirs* (1982); Loren Baritz, *Backfire: A History of How American Culture Led Us into Vietnam and Made Us Fight the Way We Did* (1985); Larry Berman, *Planning a Tragedy: The Americanization of the War in Vietnam* (1982) and *Lyndon Johnson's War: The Road to Stalemate in Vietnam* (1989); Vaughan Bornet, *The Presidency of Lyndon B. Johnson* (1983); Gloria Emerson, *Winners and Losers* (1976); John Galloway, *The Gulf of Tonkin Resolution* (1970); Leslie H. Gelb with Richard K. Betts, *The Irony of Vietnam: The System Worked* (1979); James William Gibson, *The Perfect War: The War We Couldn't Lose and How We Did* (1986); John Girling, *America and the Third World* (1980); Henry F. Graff, *The Tuesday Cabinet: Deliberation and Decision on Peace and War Under Lyndon B. Johnson* (1970); David Halberstam, *The Best and the Brightest* (1972); George C. Herring, "American Strategy in Vietnam: The Postwar Debate," *Military Affairs* (April 1982); Charles Roberts, *LBJ's Inner Circle* (1965); Walt W. Rostow, *The Diffusion of Power: An Essay in Recent History* (1972); Harry G. Summers, *On Strategy: The Vietnam War in Context* (1981); Kathleen J. Turner, *Lyndon Johnson's Dual War: Vietnam and the Press* (1981).

The Domestic Response to the War

Some of the titles already listed cover home-front responses to the war as well. See also Michael A. Anderegg, *Inventing Vietnam: The War in Film and Television* (1991); Michael J.

Arlen, *Living Room War* (1966); Balfour Brickner, "Vietnam and the Jewish Community," *Christian Century* 87 (1970), 531–534; Charles DeBenedetti, "On the Significance of Citizen Peace Activism: America, 1961–1975," *Peace and Change* (Summer 1983); Owen W. Gilman, *Vietnam and the Southern Imagination* (1992); Daniel C. Hallin, *The "Uncensored War": The Media and Vietnam* (1986); Alexander Kendrick, *The Wound Within: America in the Vietnam Years, 1945–1974* (1974); David W. Levy, *The Debate over Vietnam* (1990); Myra McPherson, *Long Time Passing: Vietnam and the Haunted Generation* (1984); Thomas Powers, *The War at Home: Vietnam and the American People* (1973) and *Vietnam, the War at Home: the Antiwar Movement, 1964–1968* (1984); Harold E. Quinley, "The Protestant Clergy and the War in Vietnam," *Public Opinion Quarterly* (Spring 1970); Jo Ann Robinson, *Abraham Went Out: A Biography of A. J. Muste* (1981); Timothy E. Scheurer, "Myth to Madness: America, Vietnam, and Popular Culture," *Journal of American Culture* (Summer 1981); Arthur M. Schlesinger, Jr., *The Bitter Heritage: Vietnam and American Democracy, 1941–1966* (1967); E. M. Schreiber, "Opposition to the Vietnam War Among American University Students and Faculty," *British Journal of Sociology* 24 (1973), 288–302; Melvin Small, "The Impact of the Antiwar Movement on Lyndon Johnson, 1965–1968," *Peace and Change* (Spring 1984); Peter W. Sperlich and William L. Lunch, "American Public Opinion and the War in Vietnam," *Western Political Quarterly* (March 1979); Robert M. Stevens, *Vain Hopes, Grim Realities: The Economic Consequences of the Vietnam War* (1976); Clyde Taylor, ed., *Vietnam and Black America: An Anthology of Protest and Resistance* (1973); Sidney Verba et al., "Public Opinion and the War in Vietnam," *American Political Science Review* (June 1967); James D. Wright, "The Working Class, Authoritarianism, and the War in Vietnam," *Social Problems* 20 (1972), 133–150; Nancy Zaroulis and Gerald Sullivan, *Who Spoke Up? American Protest Against the War in Vietnam, 1963–1975* (1984).

Chapter Eleven

1968 AND THE NIXON YEARS

On May 17, 1968, a band of nine antiwar activists entered a draft-board office in the Baltimore suburb of Catonsville, led by the brothers Philip and Daniel Berrigan, Catholic priests and radical opponents of the Vietnam War. As a secretary screamed, "Don't you take my files!" the nine loaded some three hundred file folders into baskets, carried them to the parking lot, and set fire to them. They used homemade napalm, manufactured according to a formula in the U.S. Army's *Special Forces Manual*. While the bonfire blazed, they encircled it, held hands, and recited the Lord's Prayer. Alerted beforehand, television crews crowded around, their cameras whirring.

Philip Berrigan, a World War II veteran who had played semiprofessional baseball before entering the priesthood, received six years in federal prison for the Catonsville burning. Looking back in the mid-1980s, he reflected, "My instinct is, if a person hotly objects to what his or her government is doing, then it's necessary to take a position against it—to resist it."

The Berrigans stood on the fringes of a rising swell of discontent with the Vietnam War. The Tet Offensive in January 1968 crystallized this deepening mood. After three years of mounting casualties and soaring costs, a majority of Americans finally turned against "Johnson's War." But frustration with the war did not translate into support for the New Left or the counterculture. On the contrary, continued campus unrest, two shocking assassinations early in 1968, and violence at the Democratic convention that summer sparked revulsion against radicalism and domestic turmoil. Richard Nixon's victory that November, reflecting this conservative shift, began an era of Republican dominance of the White House that, except for one four-year interlude, would continue until 1993.

Reversing course in Vietnam, Nixon and his national security adviser, Henry Kissinger, pursued negotiations and gradually cut U.S. troop levels; the last American combat units left South Vietnam in 1973. Within two years, the Saigon government collapsed, erasing Washington's twenty-year effort to maintain a noncommunist South Vietnam. Yet even amid peace talks, the war had persisted at a fierce pace, and when Nixon expanded the ground war to Cambodia early in 1970, new protests erupted. By that time, however, the New Left and the counterculture were on the wane, victims of internal divisions and the rightward shift of the larger political climate.

While withdrawing from Vietnam, Nixon and Kissinger reoriented U.S. foreign policy, crafting a strategy of détente—an easing of tensions—with China and the Soviet Union. The plan would stand as the major achievement of Nixon's truncated years in the White House. Domestically, the new president displayed the same innovativeness and opportunism that characterized his foreign policy. In grappling with welfare policy and economic issues, as with the communist powers, he willingly abandoned long-held Republican positions if it seemed politically expedient to do so. Shrewdly exploiting discontents and fears in grass-roots America, he focused on building a new Republican majority among the alienated voters whom he called "the silent majority."

1968: "The Center Cannot Hold"

Throughout the Vietnam War, the two sides had observed an informal cease-fire during Tet, the festive Vietnamese New Year—until 1968, when the National Liberation Front and the North Vietnamese chose Tet—January 31—to launch a sweeping, coordinated assault on cities, bases, and provincial capitals across South Vietnam. While the siege at Khe Sanh preoccupied the U.S. military command, 84,000 NLF and North Vietnamese troops stealthily maneuvered into position. NLF sympathizers in the cities joined in the attack. In a move that devastated American morale, nineteen NLF guerrillas penetrated the U.S. embassy compound in Saigon and held out for six hours before American soldiers finally gunned them down.

In Vietnam's ancient capital of Hué, the NLF held power for nearly four weeks, executing officials and others identified with the Saigon regime. As many as three thousand victims of the terror were buried in shallow graves on the city's outskirts. U.S. officials pointed to this massacre as proof of their contention that a communist victory in South Vietnam would mean a bloodbath. After U.S. bombing and shelling pounded Hué to ruins, marines wielding flamethrowers and tank cannons retook the city on February 25.

The Tet Offensive introduced a new stage of savagery in the war. Under the Phoenix Program, developed by the CIA, the Thieu government murdered some twenty thousand suspected opponents of the regime who had revealed themselves to be NLF supporters during Tet. Thousands more were jailed. The grim post-Tet phase also produced the single most notorious American atrocity of the war: the My Lai massacre. On March 16, 1968, a U.S. platoon commanded by Second Lieutenant William L. Calley, Jr., entered the village of My Lai in Quang Ngai province on a search-and-destroy mission. Finding no Vietcong, Calley's men, under intense pressure to maintain the weekly "body count," systematically shot more than three hundred peasants—women, children, and old men. In the spasm of violence, they raped and sodomized women, mutilated bodies, slaughtered every domestic animal, and burned the village to the ground. The story of My Lai broke in 1969 despite official efforts to suppress it. As other veterans and journalists spoke up, an even more chilling realiza-

A wounded GI evacuated from Hué, a scene of fierce fighting during the Tet Offensive. The military brass tried to put a positive spin on the outcome of Tet, but in the United States it sharply intensified opposition to the war. (*John Olson*/Life Magazine, © *Time-Warner*)

tion emerged: My Lai was unique only in its scale; the killing, rape, and torture of civilians occurred far more often than anyone had believed.*

Having beaten back the Tet invaders and regained precarious control of South Vietnam's cities, the high command in Saigon portrayed the Tet Offensive as a major U.S. victory. The desperate communists had gambled everything and had failed, they insisted. "The enemy is on the ropes," General Westmoreland crowed. For their part, the North Vietnamese found the military outcome of the Tet operation disappointing, but they steeled themselves once more to go on fighting. Whatever its military significance, Tet proved a propaganda disaster for the Johnson administration. Respected newsman Walter Cronkite asked, "What's going on here? I thought we were winning." If Tet was an NLF defeat, mused Senator George Aiken of Vermont, what would an NLF victory look like? Support for the war dropped to 41 percent, and Johnson's own approval rating sank to a pathetic 26 percent. Key periodicals, including *Time, Newsweek,* the *New York Times,* and the *Washington Post,* broke with the administration over Vietnam.

Another round of campus antiwar protests in the spring of 1968 compounded Johnson's woes. Demonstrations erupted on more than a hundred U.S. campuses, involving upwards of four hundred thousand young men and women and many faculty members. The movement spread even into high schools. Uprisings among the young in Paris and Berlin gave activists across the globe a sense of solidarity. Many schools canceled classes as students flocked instead to hastily organized teach-ins and gathered in dorm lounges for discussions of the war. At one such meeting at the University of Massachusetts, a young woman arose to speak. Was her brother's death in Vietnam meaningless? she tearfully asked. The question hung in the air, unanswerable.

---

* In the legal aftermath of the My Lai affair, a military court in 1971 convicted Lieutenant William Calley of premeditated murder of South Vietnamese civilians and sentenced him to life imprisonment. In fact, he went free in 1974 after serving thirty-five months, mostly under house arrest at Fort Benning, Georgia. Many felt that in singling out Calley, despite his proved complicity in the massacre, the army had failed to confront the larger pattern of atrocities against civilians in Vietnam.

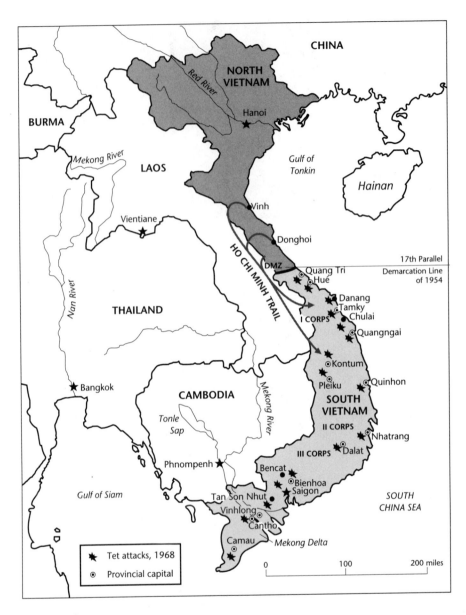

FIGURE 11.1
The Tet Offensive

At Columbia University in New York City, black militants and the local SDS chapter joined forces to protest Columbia's ROTC program, campus recruitment by the military and Dow Chemical, and Columbia's plan to build a gymnasium on university-owned property in nearby Harlem, a plan that would eliminate some black housing. The confrontation lasted for two months. Two mass sit-ins produced eight hundred arrests. For nearly a week, protesters occupied five campus buildings, including the office of the president, where they rifled files for evidence of university complicity in nefarious doings at home and abroad.

As the war dragged on, the movement took on a sharper edge and grew more confrontational. The speeches at protest rallies became more militant, the attacks on the Establishment more sweeping. Emulating the Berrigans, some activists moved from marches and speechmaking to acts of civil disobedience. More than sixty performers recorded Dylan's antiwar "Blowin' in the Wind." Folk singer Phil Ochs declared in one song:

> Call it "peace" or call it "treason,"
> Call it "love" or call it "reason,"
> But I ain't marchin' anymore.

The two sides eyed each other across a widening chasm of mistrust that poisoned the political climate. Hounded by protesters, Johnson abandoned domestic travel except to military bases. The only difference between himself and John Kennedy, he complained, was that his assassination was more drawn out. Revealing the administration's view of its critics as potential traitors, federal intelligence agencies stepped up their surveillance. Hundreds of paid informants supplied information on eighteen thousand antiwar leaders and organizations and even on elected officials who spoke out against the war.

Amid rising domestic discord, the high-level reassessment of the war triggered by Westmoreland's 1967 request for 206,000 more troops proceeded urgently. Westmoreland himself was removed from active command and became army chief of staff; General Creighton Abrams replaced him in Saigon. The new secretary of defense, Clark Clifford, the Democratic stalwart who had helped to craft Harry Truman's 1948 election strategy, urged Johnson to cut back the war. Even Dean Acheson, at a gloomy meeting of the "Wise Men" in March 1968, counseled ending the conflict.

On the political front, Johnson faced rebellion in his own party. In January, Senator Eugene McCarthy of Minnesota launched a campaign for the Democratic presidential nomination on an antiwar platform. A devout Catholic and a poet, the aloof McCarthy initially portrayed his candidacy as a moral gesture, but thousands of enthusiastic volunteers responded. The "Dump Johnson" movement even lured student activists back to party politics. In preparation for door-to-door canvassing, young men shaved beards and cut their hair; young women made similar bows to conventionality, to be "neat and clean for Gene."

In the New Hampshire primary on March 12, McCarthy scored a stunning moral victory, gaining 42.4 percent of the Democratic vote against the incumbent. Many disillusioned hawks joined the parade against Johnson, and hope buoyed the antiwar camp. The New Hampshire primary also set the stage for an even more formidable challenge to Johnson. Robert Kennedy, who had resigned as U.S. attorney general in 1964 and had won election to the U.S. Senate from New York, had carefully watched Johnson's ebbing fortunes. Four days after the New Hampshire vote, he threw his hat into the ring. Despite bitter complaints from the McCarthy camp, remnants of John Kennedy's old team, along with a wave of voters, rallied to the new Kennedy banner.

The third of four sons in a fiercely competitive family, Robert Kennedy had endured the nickname "the runt" for his small size. Perhaps in compensation, he had built a reputation for ruthlessness dating back to his days as an aide of Senator Joseph McCarthy. As attorney general, he had pursued Jimmy Hoffa of the corrupt Teamsters' Union and authorized wiretaps on Martin Luther King, Jr. By 1967–1968, however, he showed growing sensitivity to the alienated young and the poor. Some observers postulated a "bad Bobby" and a "good Bobby" warring for dominance in Kennedy's personality, but political calculation and the emotional impact of his brother's death doubtless shaped his development as well.

For a few weeks, the presidency seemed within his grasp. Lambasting LBJ for unleashing "the darker impulses of the American spirit" and linking the war to America's home-front crises, Kennedy pledged "to end the bloodshed in Vietnam and in our cities, . . . to close the gap . . . between black and white, between rich and poor, between young and old, in this country and around the world."

As Johnson watched his political base crumbling, he came to a decision. In a television address on March 31, 1968, LBJ announced yet another peace initiative. He would halt the bombing north of the 20th parallel, he promised, and thus spare North Vietnam's more populous and industrialized region. He called for negotiations as well.*

The shocker came at the end of Johnson's speech, as he tersely announced "I shall not seek, and I will not accept, the nomination of my party for another term as your President." He wanted to devote his remaining months in office to the search for peace, he said. Johnson's withdrawal threw the campaign wide open. While Mc-Carthy and Kennedy split the antiwar vote, Vice President Hubert Humphrey joined the race as well, hoping to rebuild the traditional Democratic coalition of farmers, blacks, union members, and big-city ethnics. Despite private doubts, Humphrey had publicly defended the war.

Governor George Wallace of Alabama also announced his candidacy for president on a third-party ticket, the American Independent party. Having "stood in the schoolhouse door" in 1963 to flaunt his opposition to integration, Wallace appealed to southerners and working-class whites resentful of blacks, campus agitators, and hippies. In rabble-rousing speeches, he denounced antiwar protesters and "pointy-headed intellectuals." Choosing as his running mate General Curtis LeMay, a super-hawkish former head of the Strategic Air Command, Wallace rose in the polls from 11 percent in February to 21 percent by September. The possibility of his playing a spoiler role in the election began to seem very real.

The ugly national mood reflected by the Wallace surge exploded in violence on April 4, 1968. As Martin Luther King, Jr., stood on the balcony of a Memphis motel room, an assassin gunned him down. White ex-convict James Earl Ray was arrested and found guilty of the murder. Although never conclusively proved, rumors circulated that Ray had hoped to collect a bounty for King's death posted by white su-

---

* Even in this speech, however, he clung to the deception that had often marked his Vietnam policies. Although reducing the range of the bombing, he increased the tonnage of bombs after March 31 and intensified the bombing of North Vietnamese bases in Laos. He spoke of a modest increase of 13,500 troops, yet in fact he had approved another 50,000. Some celebrated Johnson's address, thinking the war's end near. The United States would not actually withdraw finally for another five years.

premacist groups. In a sermon the night before his death, the thirty-nine-year-old King had described the threats on his life and had prophetically concluded:

> We've got some difficult days ahead. But it doesn't matter with me now. Because I've been to the mountaintop. . . . Like anybody, I would like to live a long life. . . . But I'm not concerned about that now. I just want to do God's will. And He's allowed me to go up to the mountain. . . . And I've seen the promised land. I may not get there with you. But I want you to know tonight, that we, as a people, will get to the promised land. And I'm happy tonight. . . . Mine eyes have seen the glory of the coming of the Lord.

James Earl Ray's gun silenced not only a towering moral leader but a voice that since 1965 had opposed the Vietnam War and championed the urban black poor. Despite the failure of his 1966 "Chicago Freedom Movement," aimed at widening opportunities for inner-city blacks, King had continued to stress economic issues. Indeed, he had come to Memphis to support a strike by the city's mostly black garbage collectors.

King's murder shocked the nation and unleashed a new round of inner-city violence. An outburst of rioting and arson venting black rage hit Chicago, Washington, D.C., and some 160 other cities, leaving forty-three dead. In Washington, arsonists and looters devastated parts of the area between the White House and the Capitol. In Chicago, Mayor Daley issued shoot-to-kill orders against arsonists and shoot-to-maim orders against looters.

And, the horror was not over yet. Two months after the King murder, another assassination shocked the nation. Robert Kennedy had swept the Indiana and Nebraska primaries, but McCarthy had triumphed in Oregon. The California primary on June 5 loomed as the crucial test. Kennedy won; then that night he, too, fell to an assassin's bullet at the Roosevelt Hotel in Los Angeles. The killer, Sirhan Sirhan, was a Palestinian who resented Kennedy's pro-Israel stand.

The King and Kennedy murders, against a backdrop of political turmoil and burning cities, sharpened the sense of a society unraveling and hastened the rightward shift of American politics. What political journalist Henry Fairlie had called "the politics of promise" that had begun with John Kennedy's election in 1960 had come to a dead end. From Left to Right, aspirants to elective office maneuvered for position on the heaving political terrain.

After Los Angeles, Eugene McCarthy persevered, though rather lethargically. At the Democrats' Chicago convention in August, Vice President Humphrey won a first-ballot nomination. In a wildly inappropriate speech, he buoyantly trumpeted his campaign theme: "the politics of joy." Humphrey boasted a strong liberal record, but he bore the stigma of "Johnson's War." He first drafted a platform plank pledging a bombing halt and renewed efforts for peace, but when Johnson angrily protested, Humphrey embraced the administration's position, further alienating antiwar Democrats. The New York delegation, filled with die-hard Kennedy loyalists, defiantly sang "We Shall Overcome" repeatedly on the convention floor.

The convention's most unforgettable moments occurred not in the hall but in Chicago's streets, thronged with five thousand antiwar activists. Principled protesters mingled with publicity seekers from the counterculture's fringe. Abbie Hoffman and Jerry Rubin, cofounders of a parody political movement, the Youth International (Yippie) party, presented a pig as their presidential nominee and titillated the media with fanciful threats to pour LSD into the city water supply and to seduce the wives and daughters of convention delegates. An unamused "Boss" Daley vowed to restore order. On August 28, the night of Humphrey's nomination, protesters jammed North Michigan Boulevard. Helmeted Chicago police waded into the throng, clubbing wildly. Many activists, as well as more than sixty television cameramen and journalists, suffered beatings, some severe. Tear gas drifted into the lobbies of nearby hotels. Images on news programs of rampaging police and bloody protesters reinforced the fearful impression of a society gone mad. An investigative panel harshly criticized the police. Although the officers were provoked, the panel concluded, they had ignored citizens' rights and unleashed a "police riot."

The beneficiary of this chaos was Richard Nixon. Since his defeat in the 1962 California gubernatorial race, Nixon had patiently rebuilt his Republican party credentials and had spoken at gatherings of the party faithful across the nation. In 1968 this doggedness paid off. Nixon easily outmaneuvered his rivals—governors Ronald Reagan of California, George Romney of Michigan, and Nelson Rockefeller of New York—to win the nomination. The carefully staged GOP convention in Miami seemed a model of tranquility in contrast to Chicago. Nixon's acceptance speech introduced his campaign theme. With a stalemated war abroad, chaos at home, and a president imprisoned in the White House, Nixon argued, the times demanded "new leadership in America."

Capitalizing on the public's revulsion against the war, Nixon assured voters that he had a peace plan for Vietnam, although he revealed no details. And amid rising dismay over domestic turmoil, he assured the "forgotten Americans"—the uneasy middle class—that he would toughen law enforcement and appoint hard-nosed jurists to the federal bench. "Law and order" became the code for cracking down on protesters, militants, and anyone else who challenged the status quo. Nixon's vice-presidential choice, jut-jawed Spiro Agnew, the governor of Maryland, echoed this theme. The Republican team battled Wallace for support in the South, where the lily-white Democratic party had fallen into disarray as the black electorate had grown. Shrewdly crafted GOP TV commercials juxtaposed images of war and disorder with Nixon's soothing voice pledging peace and tranquil times and subliminally linked Hubert Humphrey with violence and upheaval.*

Considering their initial liabilities, Humphrey and his running mate, Senator Edmund Muskie of Maine, ran a strong race. Starting sixteen points behind Nixon in the polls, Humphrey by the end turned the contest into a dead heat. Had the campaign gone on a week longer, some analysts believe, he would have won. In late September Humphrey finally broke with the administration, calling for a total bombing halt and a shift of the fighting from U.S. to South Vietnamese forces. The speech pushed his ratings still higher, although not enough to pull him to victory.

The breakthrough toward peace that could have put Humphrey over the top never came. After Johnson's March 31 address, the North Vietnamese had agreed to

---

* Journalist Joe McGinniss, having won the confidence of top Republican campaign strategists, later produced a devastating account of this media campaign, *The Selling of the President* (1969).

talks in Paris. Veteran diplomat W. Averell Harriman represented the United States, and Hanoi sent a former foreign minister, Xuan Thuy. The talks started in mid-May but quickly deadlocked. North Vietnam demanded a full bombing halt; the United States insisted on concessions in return. By October, Hanoi had agreed to stop sending North Vietnamese units south and shelling South Vietnamese cities, and Johnson announced the bombing halt. But President Thieu of South Vietnam boycotted the talks, and they remained mired in procedural details. In the campaign's final weeks, Nixon's manager, John Mitchell, discouraged Thieu from accepting a peace agreement until after the election and thus undermined Humphrey's chance for victory.

On election day, Nixon won six Deep South states and every state west of the Mississippi except Texas and Washington. He lost only eight states of the Upper South, Midwest, and Northeast to Humphrey. Wallace carried five Deep South states. Nixon got 43.4 percent to Humphrey's 42.7 percent and Wallace's 13.5 percent. In the closest electoral-college tally since 1916, Nixon received 301 votes, Humphrey 191, and Wallace 46. Had Humphrey carried California instead of narrowly losing it, Nixon would have fallen short of an electoral-college majority, and the election would have gone to the House of Representatives.

A kaleidoscope of forces—social unrest, the Vietnam stalemate, and middle-

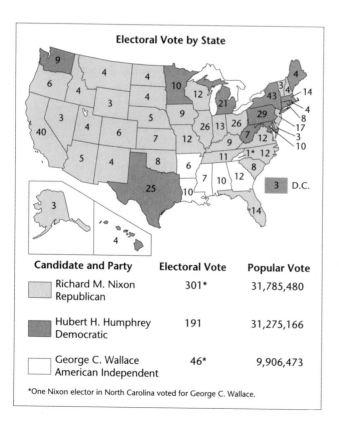

FIGURE 11.2

Presidential Election of 1968

Electoral Vote by State

Candidate and Party	Electoral Vote	Popular Vote
Richard M. Nixon Republican	301*	31,785,480
Hubert H. Humphrey Democratic	191	31,275,166
George C. Wallace American Independent	46*	9,906,473

*One Nixon elector in North Carolina voted for George C. Wallace.

class resentment of Johnson's antipoverty program—had fed into Nixon's win. The New Right movement also played a role, nurtured by conservative ideologues like William F. Buckley and by the 1964 Goldwater campaign. Although won by a slim margin, the 1968 election signaled a rightward shift that would characterize the American political landscape for years.

Wallace carried no states outside the South, yet he demonstrated surprising strength in the North. Indeed, Wallace in retrospect can be seen as a pivotal figure who mobilized resentments that in future years would drive mainstream politics. Populist politicians had once energized angry and alienated voters by directing their resentment against the rich and corporate elites. As Thomas B. Edsall and Mary D. Edsall have noted in an influential study, Wallace by contrast offered a new set of villains and targeted college students, intellectuals, the media, and Washington bureaucrats as a focus of working-class hostility.* The Alabama governor also blatantly exploited a growing white backlash against a decade of civil-rights activism and federal programs aimed at the inner-city poor.

The earliest and most decisive loser in 1968 was Lyndon Johnson. Johnson's consensus style of politics initially had served him well in the domestic realm, as he sought to grant everyone a slice of what one historian described as "the giant pizza in the sky he called the Great Society." But LBJ's preference for consensus over hard choices ultimately failed him even in the domestic sphere, and in Vietnam his efforts proved disastrous. His massive escalation of the war never achieved its objectives, and in 1968 he paid the price for his misjudgment.

Back on his Texas ranch, the ex-president let his graying hair grow long, conveying the odd impression of an aging hippie, and spoke wistfully of his Great Society. On the day after Nixon's inauguration for a second term, in January 1973, Lyndon Johnson would die of a heart attack at the age of sixty-four.

Nixon's War: Vietnam, 1969–1975

Vietnam had shattered Johnson's career and devastated him psychologically; now Richard Nixon seized the nettle. Fascinated by foreign policy, the new president welcomed the challenge. The cabinet could handle domestic affairs, he believed; the chief executive should concentrate on global issues. Nixon's national security adviser, Henry Kissinger, emphatically agreed. The stout, deep-voiced, owl-eyed Kissinger had lived in the United States since 1938 when, at the age of fifteen, his family had fled Nazi Germany. After serving in World War II and working with U.S. occupation forces in Germany, he graduated summa cum laude from Harvard and stayed on to earn a Ph.D. and to teach government. In his influential *Nuclear Weapons and Foreign Policy* (1957), Kissinger advocated the deployment of tactical nuclear weapons, in addition to intercontinental ballistic missiles, to advance U.S. strategic interests. A foreign-policy adviser in the 1950s to Nelson Rockefeller, who held various posts in Eisenhower's administration, Kissinger filled a series of various govern-

---

* Thomas B. Edsall with Mary D. Edsall, *Chain Reaction: The Impact of Race, Rights, and Taxes on American Politics* (1991).

ment positions in the 1960s and in 1968 had offered his services to both the Nixon and Humphrey camps. He thus was already a fixture in Washington when Nixon brought him to the White House in 1969.

The two men, although different in many ways, shared a love of power and a taste for broad-brush strategic thinking. Both were obsessively secretive, and tended to distrust the bureaucracy and even their own staff. Someone compared Kissinger's aides to mushrooms: "They're kept in the dark, get a lot of manure piled on them, and then get canned."* Nixon functioned as his own secretary of state, with Kissinger at his side. The man who actually held that title, William Rogers, a Wall Street lawyer largely ignorant of foreign affairs, posed no threat to the powerful pair. The president chose him for that reason. "No secretary of state is really important," Nixon believed. "The President makes foreign policy."

The new team's priority was the mess in Southeast Asia. When Nixon took office, the United States had 545,000 troops in Vietnam, and nearly 31,000 young Americans had already died there. Nixon's cryptically stated goal—"peace with honor"—was to withdraw U.S. ground forces so as to reduce the casualties that fueled home-front protest. Nixon also planned to turn the ground fighting over to U.S.-trained ARVN (Army of the Republic of Vietnam) forces while still seeking a settlement favorable to U.S. interests. Secretary of Defense Melvin Laird gave the policy a name: "Vietnamization." After assuring President Thieu of America's continued support, Nixon in June 1969 announced the withdrawal of 25,000 U.S. troops. By the end of 1970, American troop strength in Vietnam stood at 280,000; by December 1971, 140,000, only about half of them combat troops.

Reducing the U.S. combat role did not end American involvement in Vietnam, however. The ARVN forces still relied on U.S. training, weapons, vehicles, communications, and air support. Moreover, Nixon stepped up both the pacification program and the Phoenix Program, aimed at eradicating the VC infrastructure, and escalated the bombing of communist bases in Laos. In March 1969, amid a major North Vietnamese offensive, Nixon expanded the war's scope by ordering the secret bombing of North Vietnamese bases and supply trails in neighboring Cambodia. By April 1970, more than 3,600 B-52 sorties had dumped 110,000 tons of bombs on the tiny country.

When the *New York Times* reported the Cambodian bombing, Nixon and Kissinger became livid. Kissinger ordered the FBI to wiretap the telephones of National Security Council aide Morton Halperin and other suspected leakers. Soon the list of illegal wiretaps expanded to include journalists and White House aides. Indeed, the tangle of illegal activities that would drive Nixon from office in 1974 originated in this 1969 effort to conceal the Cambodian air war.

The object of Nixon's Vietnam policy was to pressure Hanoi to accept U.S. terms even as American troop strength declined. As Kissinger commented, "I refuse to believe that a little fourth-rate power like North Vietnam does not have a breaking point." Nixon put the matter in grander, Orwellian terms: "The true objective of this war is peace. It is a war for peace." The bombing also served to convince Hanoi

---

* A number of Kissinger's aides, including President Bill Clinton's national security adviser, Anthony Lake, did go on to distinguished careers in academia and government.

that Nixon was capable of any level of escalation. As he would later explain to his aide Robert Haldeman:

> I call it the madman theory, Bob. . . . I want the North Vietnamese to believe I've reached the point where I might do anything to stop the war. We'll just slip the word to them that, "For God sakes, you know Nixon is obsessed about Communists. We can't restrain him when he's angry—and he has his hand on the nuclear button"— and Ho Chi Minh himself will be in Paris in two days begging for peace.

In fact, the cease-fire talks remained stalemated. Like his predecessors, Nixon backed the Thieu regime and insisted that Hanoi withdraw its troops from South Vietnam. Hanoi, in turn, demanded the full withdrawal of U.S. troops and a government in Saigon that excluded Thieu. Kissinger met secretly in Paris with Xuan Thuy in August 1969 and in 1970 with Xuan's successor, Le Duc Tho, but to little effect. When Ho Chi Minh died in September 1969, Hanoi's new leaders vowed to carry on until "not a single aggressor" remained in their country.

As "Vietnamization" failed to end the war, youthful alienation deepened. The counterculture crested in August 1969 when four hundred thousand young people gathered on a farm near the village of Woodstock in upstate New York for a three-day festival featuring rock music, marijuana and other substances, and communal good feeling that triumphed over torrential rains. Except for some drug overdoses and the death of one youth when a tractor ran over his sleeping bag, the event proved remarkably trouble-free, and the counterculture acquired a new name: the Woodstock Nation. For decades after, participants would recall the festival as a de-

Woodstock, August 1969. This great counter-culture camp meeting, a heady mixture of marijuana, rock music, antiwar fervor, and celebratory sex, quickly became part of the folklore of the sixties. (*Bill Eppridge*/Life Magazine, © *Time-Warner*)

fining moment of their youth. Although more a cultural phenomenon than an explicitly political event, Woodstock in part became a vast antiwar rally. Antiwar themes and political alienation pervaded the music, most memorably in Jimi Hendrix's sardonic version of "The Star Spangled Banner."

The more overtly political antiwar movement, dormant since August 1968, also revived. Movement leaders designated October 15, 1969, as Vietnam Moratorium Day. Thousands of protesters left jobs and classes to rally in Boston, New York, and other cities and college towns across the country. Coretta Scott King, carrying on her slain husband's cause, led a candlelight parade of 30,000 in Washington, D.C. The weekend of November 13–15 saw another mass rally in Washington organized by an antiwar coalition called the New Mobilization. For forty-eight hours on Thursday and Friday, as a cold rain whipped the capital, 45,000 participants walked from Arlington National Cemetery to the Capitol, each carrying a candle and a placard bearing the name of a soldier killed in Vietnam. They called out the names as they passed the White House and at the Capitol deposited the placards in twelve wooden coffins. On Saturday, a throng variously estimated from 250,000 to 800,000 gathered on the Mall to decry the war. President Nixon let it be known that he had spent the day watching the Washington Redskins on television. At about the same time, the *New York Times*'s revelation of the gruesome My Lai massacre intensified revulsion against the war.

With Vietnamization, the morale of both U.S. and South Vietnamese troops who remained in the field plummeted. Units openly evaded combat; two infantry units flatly refused orders. Among GIs, drug use and racial tension soared. The army reported more than two thousand cases of "fragging"—attacks on officers by their own men—in 1970 alone. A Marine colonel warned in the *Armed Forces Journal* in June 1971, "Our army that now remains in Vietnam is in a state approaching collapse, with individual units avoiding or having refused combat, murdering their officers and noncommissioned officers, drug-ridden, and dispirited where not mutinous."

Still Nixon pressed on. On April 30, 1970, the president announced a joint U.S.–South Vietnamese ground attack on North Vietnamese bases in Cambodia. The goal, he asserted, was to eradicate the COSVN (Central Office for South Vietnam), the semimythic nerve center of Hanoi's war effort. Nixon and Kissinger had a larger, twofold aim, however. First, they sought to escalate pressure on North Vietnam to settle the war on America's terms. Second, they wished to support Cambodia's new pro-Western ruler, the right-wing military officer Lon Nol, who had overthrown the neutralist Prince Norodom Sihanouk a few weeks earlier. For years, Sihanouk had walked a tightrope to keep the worst of the war's ravages from Cambodia. After 1970, as a result of U.S. involvement, Cambodia increasingly sank into the maelstrom, with horrendous consequences for its people.

In announcing the Cambodian invasion, Nixon insisted that if America allowed communism to overrun Southeast Asia, the United States would become a "pitiful, helpless giant" respected by no one. If America failed in Vietnam, he cautioned, the world would know "that despite its overwhelming power the United States, when a real crisis comes, will be found wanting." Underscoring his law-and-order theme and linking his foreign and domestic policies, the president warned that radicals were undermining American institutions at home just as "small nations all over the world find themselves under attack from within and from without."

The Cambodian invasion revived the flagging antiwar cause. Congressional opponents of the war, quiescent since Nixon's election, aggressively challenged the administration. In a largely symbolic action, Congress terminated the 1964 Gulf of Tonkin Resolution under which Johnson had escalated the war.

The angry aftermath of Nixon's speech announcing the invasion saw classes canceled at over a third of the nation's colleges and universities. One campus caught up in this fresh wave of protest was Kent State University in Ohio, where radicals had recently burned the ROTC building. Ohio's Republican governor, James Rhodes, seeking his party's Senate nomination, took a hard line. Comparing antiwar protesters to Nazi stormtroopers, Rhodes ordered the Ohio National Guard to Kent State. On May 4, nervous guardsmen in gas masks—pharmacists, accountants, salesmen, and other nonmilitary men activated on a few days' notice—raked a crowd of students with M-1 rifle fire, killing two young men and two young women and injuring nine others.

A federal judge threw out a Justice Department indictment of the Ohio National Guard for conspiracy to violate the victims' civil rights. Apologists later claimed that the students had mortally threatened the troops, but insults and a few rocks thrown hardly justified the murderous fusillade. One guardsman later confessed that he had taken off his glasses to don his gas mask and could see only a blur as he fired into the crowd. Ten days later, amid campus protests over Vietnam and other issues at predominantly black Jackson State College in Mississippi, state troopers sprayed a dormitory with gunfire, killing two women and wounding nine.

The protests and campus killings of May 1970 marked the end of the major cycle of antiwar activism. Indeed, the movement's decline dates back to the discouragement and internal divisions that plagued its leaders after the November 1969 rally in Washington. They had poured enormous effort and emotional energy into this event, with little discernible result. Yet the demonstration may have thwarted a major escalation after all. Frustrated over the stalemate in Paris, Kissinger had ordered a National Security Council task force to devise plans for an offensive, possibly including tactical nuclear weapons, that would rain "savage, punishing blows" against North Vietnam. Massive home-front protests possibly persuaded Nixon to drop this plan in favor of accelerated troop withdrawals. Some historians also speculate that Nixon cut short the May 1970 Cambodian incursion because of unexpectedly fierce protests at home. In movement circles, however, a deep gloom had settled by the summer of 1970.

Why did a force that had roused such passion fade so quickly? Nixon's Vietnamization strategy and the decline in U.S. casualties clearly played a central role. The weekly toll of U.S. combat deaths fell from nearly two hundred in 1969 to thirty-five by early 1971. Nixon undercut the movement further by initiating changes in the draft law. In March 1969, Congress limited the draft to nineteen-year-olds, to be chosen by lottery on the basis of birth date. Males twenty and older no longer faced military duty. In January 1972, Congress ended the draft entirely. Although fear of the draft was hardly the sole source of antiwar activism—witness the central role of women students and older citizens—it had fueled protests.

A government propaganda campaign also helped to weaken and intimidate the movement. Nixon sneered at antiwar activists as "bums," and Vice President Agnew attacked them for sabotaging the president's quest for peace. Exploiting working-class resentment of college protesters, Agnew called the demonstrators an "effete corps of impudent snobs." The FBI, through its COINTELPRO program, spied on SDS and other antiwar (and civil-rights) groups by bugging their telephones, stealing their mail, paying informants, and planting rumors designed to discredit the leaders. In October 1968, the FBI warned its field offices that "the New Left with its anti-war and anti-draft entourage" would likely continue to disrupt campuses. These activists, the agency continued, even would try to stop military recruiting and interfere with the draft. Accordingly, the memo went on, each FBI office should give the COINTELPRO program full support "in order that no opportunity will be missed to destroy this insidious movement."

Nixon, his paranoid streak fed by class resentments rooted in childhood, the hostility of the liberal media, and the skullduggery that he believed had cost him the presidency in 1960, became obsessed with eradicating his enemies. To this end, he approved an elaborate—and patently illegal—plan by White House aide Tom Huston, a former Defense Department intelligence agent, for discrediting antiwar groups and leaders. Although not implemented because it overlapped with the FBI's ongoing program, the Huston plan reflected the White House's siege mentality.

Federal efforts to stifle the movement found parallels in state and local action against radicals, including the police riot at the 1968 Democratic National Convention and the 1970 Kent State killings. In May 1969, police fired on six thousand protesters in Berkeley, California, killing one and blinding another. The immediate issue was a police effort, under pressure from local business leaders, to clear a vacant lot owned by the university that had been taken over by the counterculture and designated People's Park. The National Guard, ordered in by Governor Ronald Reagan, occupied Berkeley for over two weeks. As tensions flared again in April 1970, Reagan snapped, "If it takes a bloodbath, let's get it over with. No more appeasement."

The FBI also targeted the militant Black Panthers, described in 1968 by J. Edgar Hoover as "the greatest threat to . . . internal security" facing America. Through informants, agents provocateurs, forged letters, and other means, COINTELPRO officials sought to destroy the party. In the predawn hours of December 4, 1969, Chicago police raided the headquarters of the Illinois Black Panthers. A hail of police gunfire cut down the party's charismatic state leader, Fred Hampton, and another local leader, Mark Clark, and wounded four others. A federal court later awarded the survivors, and the families of Hampton and Clark, $1.85 million in damages.

Incited by the government's inflammatory pronouncements and episodes of official repression, the public mood turned ugly. In opinion polls, most Americans rated campus unrest as a greater danger than the Vietnam War itself. A citizenry increasingly fearful of domestic turmoil generally sided with the authorities against "student rioters." Even as the war in Southeast Asia wound down, hostility toward "hippies," youthful radicals, and campus protesters remained intense, especially among older Americans. Yet this anger had a class as well as a generational dimension. Working-class Americans resented articulate, affluent college students who protested at home while poorer youth bore the brunt of combat in Vietnam. As the war's casualty toll fed doubts about the conflict, it also raised the emotional stakes, so that antiwar protests could be seen as somehow trivializing the sacrifice of the dead and wounded. Micheal Clodfelter's *The Pawns of Dishonor* (1976), the memoir of a Vietnam veteran, aptly captured the outlook of those who felt no enthusiasm for the war but who still recoiled from antiwar protesters:

> To so many of us the peace phalanx parading American streets were the spoiled, gutless middle class kids who cowered in college classrooms to escape the battlefield and who, to soothe their cowards' consciences and regain their lost self-respect and their girlfriends' admiration now campaigned with ball-less envy to destroy what honor and prestige we might earn through our courage and sacrifices in battle. The peaceniks might not be attacking the integrity of the American soldiers directly but they were proselytizing against the war as dishonorable and contemptible and we who were the participants in this conflict felt that, by implication, we too were being made contemptible. Few of us felt any loyalty to this war, but we did possess a great loyalty and kinship to each other, to our reputations as individuals and as units. We were like sons with little love left for our harsh and cruel mother, but fiercely determined to defend her name and honor against all slurs.

On May 8, 1970, four days after the Kent State shootings, construction workers at the New York World Trade Center, shouting "Kill the commie bastards," attacked a group of antiwar marchers, injuring seventy. They were particularly incensed by liberal Republican mayor John Lindsay's order to lower city flags to half-mast in honor of the college students killed in Ohio. A similar demonstration by "hard hats" erupted in St. Louis. Soon after, President Nixon proudly accepted a hard hat at a White House ceremony. On May 20, a hundred thousand New Yorkers, mostly construction workers and longshoremen, staged a prowar march, waving flags and singing "God Bless America." Nixon's "silent majority" had found its voice, and it was a howl of rage against college youth and others of the privileged classes. To these angry Americans, those opposing the war were heaping contempt on military service and patriotism, as well as scorning loyalty and duty.

But the movement also fell victim to internal erosion and conflicts. As frustration with the course of the war mounted, many despairing activists followed Timothy Leary's advice to drop out. SDS collapsed in bitter factional feuding between doctrinaire Maoists organized as the Progressive Labor party (PLP) and radical activists who called themselves the Weathermen.* At the 1969 SDS convention, the Weathermen, led by Bernardine Dohrn, a self-proclaimed revolutionary communist, walked out chanting "Ho, Ho, Ho Chi Minh." PLP inherited the remnants of the organization. SDS was finished; local branches soon fragmented and disappeared. By the end, lamented Todd Gitlin, a leader in its heady early days, SDS "had degenerated into a caricature of everything idealists find alienating about politics-as-usual: cynicism, sloganeering, manipulation." Far from articulating a bold vision of politi-

---

* The name came from a Bob Dylan line "You don't need a weatherman to know which way the wind blows." Shedding gender specificity, this faction later became known as the Weatherpeople or the Weather Underground.

cal renewal, the organization had become a swamp of soggy ideological disputes "that only the most dedicated—or masochistic—would bother to try slogging through."

Cut off from former friends and allies, a few hundred Weathermen went underground to "bring the war home" to America and to foment the revolution that their ideology assured them was imminent. They explained their dogma in tracts clogged with revolutionary rhetoric. One 1969 Weatherman manifesto declared:

> The main struggle going on in the world today is between US imperialism and the national liberation struggles against it. . . . US imperialism . . . has unified, allied with, and defended all of the reactionary forces of the whole world. . . . It is in this context that we must examine the revolutionary struggles in the United States. We are within the heartland of a world-wide monster. . . . The goal is the destruction of US imperialism and the achievement of a classless world: world communism.

The Weathermen and their sympathizers sought not U.S. withdrawal from Vietnam but U.S. *defeat* there. An NLF victory, they hoped, would hasten revolution at home and end American imperialism worldwide. The organization thus embraced the view of the war held by its most hawkish backers: A loss in Vietnam would destroy America's credibility worldwide.

In October 1969, several hundred Weathermen organized the "Days of Rage" in Chicago, smashing store windows and trashing parked cars. From September 1969 to May 1970, a handful of militants carried out some 250 bombings nationwide, including ROTC headquarters, draft boards, and other symbols of militarism or capitalism. One underground activist, arrested for bombing a Bank of America branch near Santa Barbara, explained, "It was the biggest capitalist thing around." On March 6, 1970, three Weathermen died when a blast rocked the Manhattan townhouse where they were making bombs. Several others escaped and went into hiding. (As late as 1981, a remnant of the Weather Underground would rob a Brink's truck in Rockland County, New York. The activists murdered a guard and two policemen; three of them received long prison sentences.) In August 1970, four radicals at the University of Wisconsin, calling themselves "the New Year's Gang," parked a truck loaded with explosives by a campus building housing the Army Mathematics Research Center. The explosives detonated in the middle of the night, shattering the building and killing a late-working student, himself an opponent of the war. The new militance influenced the mainstream antiwar movement as well. At the November 1969 rally in Washington, while most of the participants joined in the peaceful "March Against Death," several thousand descended on the Department of Justice shouting "Smash the state!" After ripping down and burning the U.S. flag, they raised an NLF flag in its place.

This extremist wing grew more visible as the antiwar movement weakened. On May 1, 1971, thirty thousand hard-core activists calling themselves the "May Day Tribe" arrived in Washington intent on "shutting the government down." Some lobbied members of Congress, but many adopted more confrontational strategies. As several of them blocked traffic, others broke windows and rampaged in the streets. A few days earlier, members of the recently formed Vietnam Veterans Against the War had publicly thrown away their medals and campaign ribbons in an angry ceremony at the Capitol. Yet neither street theater nor ventures in "smashing the state" had much apparent effect on the Nixon White House.

Unable to stop the war, some activists focused on exposing the process by which America had entered the conflict. Secretary of Defense McNamara, before leaving office, had asked his aides to compile a history of the war from Pentagon files. The documents that they assembled chronicled the stages by which the Kennedy and Johnson administrations had planned and prosecuted the war. In March 1971, one of these aides, Daniel Ellsberg, now an antiwar activist, gave the explosive documents to Neil Sheehan of the *New York Times*, which hastened to publish them. Nixon tried to halt publication, but the Supreme Court upheld the *Times*'s claim to First Amendment protection. The so-called *Pentagon Papers* revealed a pattern of official secrecy and deception of both Congress and the public and fed a growing suspicion of government that would deepen in the years ahead.

The publication of the *Pentagon Papers* exacerbated Nixon's and Kissinger's obsession with press leaks. On Nixon's orders, aides Robert Haldeman and John Ehrlichman assembled a secret team of former FBI and CIA operatives to trace leaks by using wiretaps and other means. Appropriately nicknamed the Plumbers, the group carried out operations that led directly to the scandal that would drive Nixon from office. In their first project, the Plumbers broke into the office of Daniel Ellsberg's psychiatrist, seeking evidence that would discredit Ellsberg and, indirectly, the entire antiwar movement.

Meanwhile, the Paris talks dragged on inconclusively. In May 1971, Kissinger abandoned the U.S. demand for a mutual troop withdrawal and instead offered to pull out within seven months of a cease-fire in exchange for the return of prisoners of war and Hanoi's pledge to stop sending troops to South Vietnam. When Hanoi and the NLF (now renamed the Provisional Revolutionary Government, or PRG) made a promising counteroffer, the peace talks took on new life. With South Vietnamese elections due in the fall of 1971, Le Duc Tho made the radical proposal that the process be honest, confident that Thieu would lose a fair election. Instead, Thieu excluded his two strongest rivals from the ballot and otherwise rigged the outcome to give himself an improbable 94.3 percent of the vote. The Paris talks sputtered.

Nixon and Kissinger were simultaneously pursuing improved relations with China and the Soviet Union (see p. 352), and they informed both superpowers that peace in Vietnam would further that goal. Both Moscow and Beijing discreetly advised Hanoi to reach a settlement, but the North Vietnamese decided to try again to achieve their ends on the battlefield. On March 30, 1972, hoping to overwhelm the Saigon government as U.S. troop strength dwindled, Hanoi resumed military operations in South Vietnam. As two hundred thousand North Vietnamese and PRG forces attacked, the ARVN forces fell back in panicked disarray. "The whole thing may well be lost," General Abrams cabled Washington.

Fearful that his policy of measured disengagement would turn into a humiliating rout, Nixon ordered new bombing around Hanoi and Haiphong, in an operation that he dubbed Linebacker. Lending credence to his "madman" conceit, he vowed grimly, "The bastards have never been bombed like they're going to be bombed this time." In April, seven hundred B-52 sorties pounded the environs of the two cities.

As the North Vietnamese advanced, taking Quang Tri City on May 1, Nixon stepped up the bombing of the north and of North Vietnamese strongholds in Quang Tri province and along the Cambodian border. Land already pockmarked by years of bombing again endured incessant B-52 raids. In the heaviest air strikes of the war, the United States dropped 112,000 tons of explosives on North Vietnam in June alone. Nixon also announced the mining of Haiphong harbor to disrupt the flow of supplies to North Vietnam, a step that the military had long urged.

A nation lulled by three years of Vietnamization suddenly confronted newly raging war. This time, however, U.S. casualties were low. Of ninety-five thousand GIs remaining in Vietnam, only six thousand were assigned to combat duty. Although U.S. bombers and weapons remained crucial to the conflict, the large-scale protests of the Johnson era had faded to intermittent outbursts. As Senator George McGovern of South Dakota observed, when the corpses changed color, American interest diminished.

In early October 1972, Hanoi made key concessions, agreeing to a cease-fire before a final political settlement and accepting Thieu's regime as one of two "administrative entities" in South Vietnam, the other being the PRG. A tripartite electoral commission made up of the PRG, the Thieu government, and neutralist elements, the negotiators agreed, would determine South Vietnam's political future. Kissinger, eager for a deal as the U.S. election neared, initialed a draft agreement on October 22. "Peace is at hand," he promised.

President Thieu denounced the draft, fearing for his political future and his very survival once the Americans withdrew. Nixon himself was incensed that Kissinger had negotiated an accord that all but abandoned the Saigon regime. Talks resumed, but Le Duc Tho rejected the sixty-nine changes that Thieu demanded in the draft agreement. Nixon, safely reelected, used the delay to transfer over $1 billion in military hardware to the Saigon government and promised Thieu "swift and severe" retaliation if Hanoi violated the agreement.

On December 18, with the Paris talks stalled, Nixon ordered renewed bombing around Hanoi and Haiphong and further mining of Haiphong harbor. The president left no doubt that he wanted to wreak maximum damage with these around-the-clock "Christmas bombings." In twelve days, thirty-six thousand tons of bombs fell, more than in the entire 1969–1971 period. Denunciations of Nixon's action poured in from around the world, and for a time it seemed that the embers of the antiwar movement might reignite. However, the Paris talks resumed, and on January 27, 1973, Kissinger and Le Duc Tho initialed a cease-fire accord, essentially the same one agreed to the previous October. Nixon renewed his pledge to Thieu to "respond with full force" if Hanoi violated the terms. Two months later, the last U.S. troops left South Vietnam. Nineteen years after the 1954 Geneva Accords and eight years after the 1965 escalation, America's longest and most inconclusive war ended, at least in terms of U.S. casualties. During "Nixon's War," 20,553 Americans had died, together with an estimated 107,000 ARVN forces and more than 500,000 North Vietnamese and PRG troops. The civilian toll ran into the hundreds of thousands.

Rooted in a Cold War mind-set that had evolved since World War II, the Vietnam War had exacted a high price in life and resources, battered America's reputation abroad, and raised profound questions about the nation's world role. For years,

Vietnam memories would fuel an intense aversion to any U.S. military involvement abroad. When President George Bush took the nation into another war in 1991, this time in the Persian Gulf, he did so in part, he asserted, to help Americans "kick the Vietnam syndrome once and for all."

The war also increased the power of the administrative branch of the federal government. In pursuing the conflict, Nixon and Kissinger, accelerating a trend already evident in the Kennedy and Johnson years, had vastly enlarged the role of the White House and the National Security Council in implementing foreign policy. In November 1973, over Nixon's veto, Congress passed the War Powers Act. This law requires the president to notify Congress "in every possible instance" before sending troops into combat or into situations where hostilities appear imminent. If advance notice is impossible, the president must give notice within forty-eight hours. Furthermore, troops must be withdrawn within six months unless Congress explicitly approves their further deployment. Had the law been in place in 1965, Lyndon Johnson would have found it difficult to take the nation into war without congressional and public debate. But the War Powers Act left unresolved the fundamental tension between the executive and the legislative branches over committing U.S. forces, and the issue remained under debate.

Vietnam stands as a watershed in postwar American history. Like the final proof of a complex algebraic equation, it underscored the logic behind twenty years of Cold War thinking. But it was also a definitive end point. In its aftermath, the nation turned to new concerns and set new priorities. Above all, the war raised troubling questions about the meaning of our national experience. After Vietnam, Americans could no longer unquestioningly accept certitudes about the nation's benign world role. Stanley Hoffmann, professor of government at Harvard, looked back on the ordeal in 1979. Focusing on the role of Nixon and Kissinger, he wrote, "At the root of this tree of evils one finds an extraordinary arrogance . . . , a self-intoxicating confidence in our capacity to manipulate other societies." Through the Vietnam experience, as a theologian might put it, America lost its innocence and learned the meaning of sin.

Realpolitik and Détente

For Nixon and Kissinger, trying to achieve "peace with honor" in Vietnam constituted only one move in the larger chess game of global politics that absorbed and fascinated them. Their overall goal was détente with the Soviet Union and China. Détente served many functions. Nixon and Kissinger used the lure of improved relations to persuade Beijing and Moscow to pressure Hanoi to reach a settlement in Vietnam. It had domestic advantages as well: Nixon the politician realized that easing Cold War hostilities could raise his stock with moderates and liberals in the 1972 election.

Yet at first glance, Nixon seems miscast in the role of either strategist or advocate of détente. His early worldview had reflected the simplistic polarities of the Cold War, and he had made his reputation by denouncing communism. But Nixon's thought had evolved. Shrewd, opportunistic, and highly intelligent, he adapted quickly to changed political realities. His 1967 article in *Foreign Affairs*, "Asia After Viet Nam," had won notice for its strategic analysis and its early recognition that the Vietnam trauma would reduce Americans' tolerance for military adventures. "Other nations must recognize that the role of the United States as world policeman is likely to be limited in the future," he predicted. With the Soviets achieving nuclear parity with the United States and the Chinese gaining significant nuclear strength, he had further noted, the world power balance was fundamentally shifting. Revealing his thinking on both global diplomacy and domestic politics, Nixon mused to journalist Garry Wills in 1968 that in coming years, "a man who knows the world will be able to forge a whole new set of alliances."

Nixon thus entered the White House holding a complex view of global geopolitical relations, not a simple bipolar outlook. He remained suspicious of both the Soviets and the Chinese, but he had concluded that normalizing relations with these Cold War adversaries would serve U.S. interests. His approach was more pragmatic and less ideologically driven than anyone familiar with his early career might have predicted.

Even more explicitly than Nixon, Henry Kissinger—national security adviser and, after 1973, secretary of state—held a *Realpolitik* view in which power calculations, not moral judgments, shaped foreign policy. On occasion Kissinger quoted Goethe: "If I had to choose between justice and disorder, on the one hand, and injustice and order on the other, I would always choose the latter." His first book had analyzed Metternich and Castlereagh, the conservative statesmen who had reconfigured Europe after the French Revolution and the Napoleonic wars. Fascinated by balance-of-power politics, Kissinger shared Nixon's view that America must outgrow dated Cold War slogans and reconceptualize international relations. Above all, the two men saw a historic opportunity to advance American interests by exploiting the split between the communist superpowers, China and the Soviet Union.

Both Nixon and Kissinger realized that the United States no longer dominated the world as it had after World War II. The Soviet Union had become a major nuclear power, China possessed the bomb, and Western Europe had emerged as a key player. On the economic front, the inflation that began in the mid-1960s had weakened the dollar on the global exchanges, and Germany and Japan were ascending as major trading competitors. From 1955 to 1968, America's share of the world's exports of manufactured goods fell from 28 percent to under 21 percent. By 1971, for the first time since 1894, the United States ran a trade deficit, as imports surpassed exports. For Nixon and Kissinger, strengthening America's world economic standing was crucial. In a 1971 speech in Kansas City, facing a projected trade deficit of $48 billion, Nixon presciently declared, "Economic power will be the key to other kinds of power . . . in the last third of this century."

In their quest for détente, Nixon and Kissinger focused first on China. Ever since the Chinese communists' victory in 1949, the United States had treated this vast nation as a pariah. Clinging to the fiction that Jiang Jieshi's Taiwan regime was China's true government, Washington had refused to have any dealings with "Red China," which the United States had also kept out of the UN. Now Nixon and Kissinger saw diplomatic and trade advantages in better relations with China. They believed that "playing the China card," for example, could help to extract concessions from the Soviet Union on arms control and other issues. The Chinese, worried about the 1 million Soviet troops amassed along their border, discreetly welcomed closer ties with the United States, despite the two nations' contrasting ideologies.

Nixon first signaled the shift in 1970 by speaking of "the People's Republic of China" rather than the usual "Red China" and by expressing curiosity about the distant land that no American president had ever visited while in office.* Beijing responded by inviting a touring U.S. table tennis team to visit China. Practicing "Ping-Pong diplomacy," the Chinese players—the world's best—politely lost to the visitors or took care not to beat them too badly. In June 1971, Henry Kissinger, indulging his taste for the clandestine and the dramatic, secretly flew to Beijing for meetings with Chinese leaders.

Kissinger's visit laid the groundwork for Nixon's historic February 1972 trip to China. At the airport, the president shook hands with Premier Zhou Enlai, erasing John Foster Dulles's insulting refusal to greet Zhou at the 1954 Geneva Conference. "Your handshake came over the vastest ocean in the world," said Zhou, "twenty-five years of no communication." Later, Nixon drank toasts with Zhou and Mao Zedong as an orchestra played "America the Beautiful." At the Great Wall of China, the president enthusiastically observed, "This truly is a great wall." He attended Beijing's current hit ballet, *The Red Detachment of Women*, choreographed by Mao's actress wife, Chiang Ching, who confided to Nixon that her favorite movie was *Gone with the Wind*. The visit ended with a joint communiqué calling for increased contacts between the two nations. Full diplomatic recognition would not come until 1979, but Nixon had greatly improved relations with a major Cold War adversary.

Next came détente with the Soviet Union. Nixon and Kissinger still embraced containment doctrine, and they maneuvered in many parts of the world to check Moscow's influence. But they also viewed the Soviet Union as simply another player in the global power game, not as an outlaw state. The Soviets—facing China to their east and NATO and a restive group of satellites to their west, spending vast sums on armaments, and grappling with weak agricultural output and other economic problems—welcomed Washington's overtures. In 1971, at Nixon's initiative, the United States and the Soviet Union, with the other wartime allies, signed an agreement ensuring western access to Berlin in return for West Germany's pledge not to absorb the city into the Federal Republic. The issue that had sparked so many Cold War crises was thus neutralized.

Hard bargaining with the Kremlin paved the way for another of Nixon's historic visits. In May 1972, fresh from Beijing, Nixon's entourage arrived in Moscow. The stepped-up fighting in Vietnam raised problems, but Nixon told the Soviet leaders, "There must be room in this world for two great nations with different systems to live together and work together." An Italian journalist who shouted "Viva Vietnam" at a gala performance of *Swan Lake* was quickly ejected. Nixon, a shrewd judge of people, summed up Brezhnev in a diary entry: "His Russian may not be as elegant, and his manner not as fine, as that of some of his sophisticated European and Asian colleagues, but . . . he has what it takes. . . . Brezhnev [is] like a big Irish labor boss, or

---

* President Ulysses S. Grant had stopped in China on a world tour after leaving the White House.

perhaps an analogy to Mayor Daley would be more in order, with no affront intended to either."

Improved trade relations remained a prime goal of détente, and in Moscow Nixon completed a deal whereby the Soviets agreed to buy $750 million in American wheat over the next three years. This arrangement eased the trade deficit and earned Nixon points in the farm belt. Yet missiles, not wheat, dominated Nixon's Moscow agenda. The years since the 1963 test-ban treaty had seen little arms-control progress. In the early 1960s, the Kennedy administration had vastly enlarged the U.S. nuclear arsenal, and the Soviets had kept pace. In 1969, however, the two sides began talks in Geneva on a strategic arms limitation treaty, known by the acronym SALT I. Nixon and Kissinger secretly completed the SALT negotiations with Soviet ambassador Anatoly Dobrynin in Washington. (Typically, they concealed the meetings from both the Geneva negotiators and the State Department.) The treaty, signed by Nixon and Brezhnev in Moscow, froze each side's arsenals of land-based and submarine-launched missiles for five years. However, SALT I did little to slow the nuclear-arms race, because it failed to address the latest technological advance: MIRV, or multiple independently targetable reentry vehicles. Through MIRVing, up to fourteen separately targeted warheads could be attached to a single missile. The United States was already MIRVing its missiles by 1972, giving it a two-to-one edge in warheads even though the Soviets had more missiles. The Soviets soon followed suit. MIRVed missiles were highly destabilizing, for they increased the odds of destroying most of the enemy's retaliatory missiles and thus encouraged a first strike. SALT I's failure to address this problem proved a fundamental defect in the treaty.

More important was the Anti-Ballistic Missile (ABM) Treaty, signed as part of the SALT accord. Over the years, nuclear strategists had insisted that deterrence theory—the premise that a nation vulnerable to a decisive counterattack would never initiate a nuclear assault—offered the best safeguard against nuclear war. But deterrence could work only if neither side possessed a defense against nuclear weapons. If one nation successfully deployed a full missile-defense system, that nation theoretically would be free to launch a nuclear attack, or to try nuclear blackmail, without fear of reprisal. Such calculations underlay the ABM Treaty, by which both sides pledged not to develop nationwide missile-defense systems. The ABM treaty institutionalized deterrence theory, and if SALT I failed to address the MIRV problem, it did cap the number of missiles for the first time. To this extent, the agreements somewhat lessened the threat of nuclear holocaust. On a 1973 visit to the United States by Leonid Brezhnev, the two sides agreed to pursue a more comprehensive arms-control treaty.

In a further move to expand America's foreign trade—one objective of the openings to China and the Soviet Union—Nixon in 1971 protested the barriers that other nations were erecting against U.S. manufactured goods. Suiting actions to words, he slapped a surtax on imports. The Japanese, the principal target of this warning, dubbed the move the "Nixon shock." The president's step revealed growing concern over the eroding competitiveness of the U.S. economy in global markets, a concern that would intensify in later decades.

As Nixon and Kissinger addressed superpower relations, they also maneuvered

FOCUS ON: *THE NUCLEAR THREAT*

The 1972 SALT I and ABM treaties brought a ray of hope to the long and often frustrating effort to restrain the nuclear-arms race. At every stage from 1945 through the 1980s, powerful forces shaped this effort, sometimes propelling it forward but more often dragging it down. These forces included Cold War suspicions, periodic upsurges of popular nuclear fear, and advances in the technology of destruction.

Nothing thwarted nuclear-arms control more often than the harsh realities of the Cold War. From the demise of the Acheson-Lilienthal plan in 1946 to President Carter's 1979 decision to withdraw from Senate consideration the SALT II treaty placing limits on each side's nuclear bombers and missiles (see p. 438), U.S.-Soviet hostility repeatedly sabotaged efforts to regulate missile competition. The Limited Nuclear Test Ban Treaty of 1963 did not include underground tests because the mutually suspicious superpowers could not agree on verification procedures.

Grass-roots fear of atomic war also influenced arms-control efforts, often in unexpected ways. As one example, after Hiroshima and Nagasaki, frightened U.S. scientists used terrifying descriptions of the bomb's effects to urge public demand for international control of atomic energy. In the long run, however, their campaign roused support not for disarmament but for keeping ahead of the Russians in nuclear competition. In the late fifties and early sixties, fear of radioactive fallout from nuclear tests led to strong popular support for a test-ban treaty. This grass-roots movement helped to produce the 1963 ban on atmospheric tests. Nevertheless, with protests focused on fallout rather than on the larger nuclear threat, the activist momentum faded after 1963, even though the nuclear-arms race continued unabated.

The ambiguous effects of nuclear fear and of antinuclear protest again became evident in 1981–1983, when a campaign to freeze the nuclear-arms race won broad backing. As in 1946, activists built support for their cause with graphic descriptions of thermonuclear annihilation. President Reagan, however, exploited the campaign for his own purposes. In a March 1983 TV address, Reagan professed his horror of nuclear war, but rather than suggest a freeze, he proposed a missile-defense system that he called the Strategic Defense Initiative (SDI). As Americans debated SDI, the freeze movement quietly expired.

Technological advances complicated arms control as well. Moscow's testing of an atomic bomb in 1949, for example, offered an opportunity for a renewed effort at international control. Instead, President Truman launched a race for the hydrogen bomb—a race that physicist Edward Teller assured him the United States could win. The Soviets quickly developed their own H-bomb, upping the nuclear ante still higher. Another breakthrough that frustrated arms-control efforts came in the 1970s, when U.S. technicians developed missiles that could carry multiple, independently targeted nuclear warheads or "reentry vehicles" (MIRVs). Although SALT I limited the number of missiles, it did not restrict the number of warheads that each missile could carry. Thus, thanks to MIRVing, the nuclear-arms race roared on despite the 1972 accord.

With the Cold War's end, the superpowers' nuclear competition faded at last. In 1992 George Bush and Mikhail Gorbachev signed a treaty imposing deep cuts on strategic missiles. In 1993, after soaking up $30 billion, the SDI program was ended by Defense Secretary Les Aspin. Americans sighed in relief as the threat of global holocaust receded. But a witches' brew of nuclear danger still simmered. The issue of either destroying or safely storing tons of radioactive waste from missiles, weapons factories, and nuclear-power plants posed problems of enormous complexity, both technologically and politically. Moreover, dismantling the former Soviet Union's nuclear arsenal proved a tricky business. Newly independent Ukraine, for example, resisted giving up the missiles on its soil, not out of any intention to use them but because of their value as economic bargaining chips.

Despite the easing of tension between the superpowers, the threat of proliferation persisted, a part of the nuclear dilemma from the beginning. The 1968 Nuclear Nonproliferation Treaty, signed by 153 states, had failed to halt the spread of nuclear weapons. As Iraq, North Korea, and other nations ruled by authoritarian regimes pursued weapons research, the specter of nuclear terrorism stalked humanity. In 1993 North Korea, after eight years as a signatory, withdrew from the Nonproliferation Treaty.

Another group for whom the nuclear threat remained all too real were the Americans exposed to radiation from weapons testing. In 1988 Congress permitted 62,000 veterans who had served as human guinea pigs in nuclear tests to file service-related disability claims if they developed one of thirteen types of cancer. The following year, 218 former civilian employees at the 1,350-square-mile Nevada test site sued the U.S. government for failing to adopt adequate safety procedures. Many of the 25,000 citizens exposed to windborne fallout in eastern Nevada and southern Utah lived in fear of developing cancer. In *American Ground Zero: The Secret Nuclear War* (1993), photojournalist Carole Gallagher offered a gripping visual and oral memoir of this bitter legacy. Ironically, the most devastating effects of a program designed to protect America had been wrought on the American people themselves. Post-Cold War revelations made clear that Soviet testing, too, had exposed thousands of troops and civilians to highly dangerous radiation levels in the 1950s.

More than twenty years after SALT I, in short, the nuclear menace lives on. Americans who had hailed the atomic bomb as the winning weapon of World War II could scarcely have guessed what lay ahead. Harry Truman's fateful decision to use the new weapon introduced a force that continues to drive global and domestic politics half a century later.

adroitly in the Middle East, a volatile region where the United States found itself walking a tightrope. As Israel's major patron, Washington supplied the military and economic aid that ensured the Jewish state's survival. Yet Americans depended on oil from the Arab states. Complicating the picture, the Mideast had become a crucible of Cold War rivalry, where the United States and the Soviet Union vied for allies. In the Six Day War of 1967, Israel had defeated its Arab foes and occupied the Golan Heights on its vulnerable northern border with Syria, the Egyptian-held Sinai peninsula and Gaza Strip, and the West Bank of the Jordan River and the Old City of Jerusalem, hitherto controlled by Jordan. In October 1973, backed by Soviet arms, Egypt and Syria launched a war against Israel to redress their grievances. The attack came on Yom Kippur, the holiest day of the Jewish year. Israel, aided by a rushed airlift of U.S. arms, fought off the attackers and pursued Egyptian troops across the Sinai. The war severely strained détente, as Brezhnev threatened to send troops to Egypt. The Pentagon went to DEFCON III, a high level of nuclear alert. To force Israel to halt its counterattack, the United States withheld military supplies. Clearly, in areas of regional conflict the Cold War remained very much alive.

The Yom Kippur War also illustrated the intricate links between foreign policy and the domestic economy. Angered by U.S. support for Israel, the oil-producing Arab states halted oil shipments to the United States. The embargo lasted from October 1973 to March 1974. Although the United States imported only 12 percent of its oil from the region, the American public felt the pinch. Fuel and gasoline shortages plagued the nation that winter, and in 1973–1974 gasoline prices soared from forty cents to fifty-five cents a gallon. Laughably low by later standards, these price hikes nevertheless spurred inflation and alarmed motorists accustomed to cheap fuel. Stock prices plummeted as the boycott's effects bit in. Hitting all sectors of the economy dependent on gasoline, including agriculture and trucking, the oil crisis contributed in 1974–1975 to the nation's worst recession since the 1930s.

The embargo focused attention on longer-term problems, too, including rising energy costs. Since OPEC's founding in 1960, oil prices had quadrupled. This increase was justified, according to the oil-producing nations, because their oil reserves were finite, and inflation forced them to pay higher prices for imported manufactured goods. As the shah of Iran candidly told Americans in 1973, "It's only fair that from now on, you should pay more for oil. Let's say . . . ten times more." The crisis also underscored America's disproportionate consumption of the world's natural resources. Home to only 6 percent of the population, the United States gobbled 40 percent of the earth's resources.

For both strategic and economic reasons, then, Nixon and Kissinger concluded that the United States must play a more assertive role in the Middle East and mend fences with the Arabs. During two years of "shuttle diplomacy" on a plane dubbed the "yo-yo express" because it took off and landed so often, Kissinger jetted to Middle East capitals negotiating disputes, currying favor with the Arab states, and countering Soviet influence. Although he failed to resolve the region's underlying animosities, he did achieve significant gains. As early as November 1973, he negotiated a cease-fire between Israel and Egypt and persuaded Israel to withdraw from Egyptian and Syrian land seized in the 1973 war. In return, the Arabs' oil boycott ended. Gasoline prices continued to rise, but the energy crisis eased for the moment. Escap-

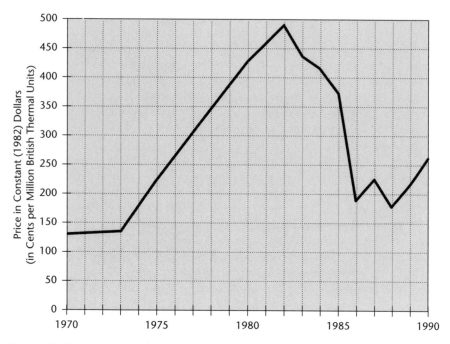

FIGURE 11.3

Crude Oil Prices, 1970–1990

SOURCE: U.S. Energy Information Administration, *Annual Energy Review.*

ing the Watergate crisis at home, President Nixon toured the region in June 1974. Egypt's new president, Anwar el-Sadat, having broken with the Soviets in 1972, now warmed to the United States.

Oriented toward power, the Nixon-Kissinger team readily supported authoritarian and even dictatorial regimes that served American strategic or economic interests. The administration granted millions of dollars in military assistance and foreign aid to the autocratic shah of Iran, the corrupt Ferdinand Marcos of the Philippines, South Africa's white-supremacist government, repressive regimes and military dictatorships in Argentina, South Korea, Brazil, Nigeria, and other nations. This *Realpolitik* approach exacted a high price. It ignored nations that did not at the moment fit into Washington's grand design but that might become crucial in the future, and it often allied the United States with rulers hated by their own people. When these despots fell, as they invariably did, the United States was reviled as well, making it difficult for Washington to build good relations with the new governments.

The administration's *Realpolitik* manifested itself most brutally in Chile. In a three-way 1970 presidential election, the Chileans gave Marxist Salvador Allende a 36.3 percent plurality. Major U.S. corporations such as International Telephone and Telegraph (ITT) had large investments in Chile, and the administration feared that Allende would jeopardize these interests. More important, like Lyndon Johnson and the Dominican Republic, Kissinger and Nixon defined Allende as a potential Castro who would transform Chile into a client state of Moscow. The administration maneuvered to get rid of him despite his victory in a democratic election. As Kissinger mused, "I don't see why we need to stand by and watch a country go communist due to the irresponsibility of its own people." Working through the CIA, Nixon plotted a military coup to prevent Allende from taking office. Failing that, the U.S. ambassador to Chile made American policy crystal clear in a conversation with a Chilean leader: "Once Allende comes to power, we shall do all within our power to condemn Chile and the Chileans to utmost deprivation and poverty, . . . to accelerate the hard features of a Communist society in Chile."

Nixon channeled $10 million to the CIA to disrupt Allende's government and to "make the [Chilean] economy scream." The president also cut off aid to the country and persuaded international monetary agencies to deny it development loans. All the while, Kissinger publicly insisted that the United States would never use clandestine means to upset the results of the Chilean election. When Allende tried to break up Chile's large landholdings and nationalized nearly $1 billion in U.S. corporate investments, the campaign against him grew more urgent. In September 1973, a military junta overthrew the government and murdered Allende. Nixon quickly recognized the new regime, and U.S. economic relations with Chile resumed. The CIA's role in the coup, if any, remains murky, but the administration clearly helped to create the conditions that led to it. When Chile's new rulers resorted to such brutalities that even the U.S. ambassador protested, Kissinger snapped icily, "Cut out the political science lecture."

Beyond the details, U.S. diplomacy in these years invites broader reflections, for Richard Nixon and Henry Kissinger reshaped the conceptual foundations of postwar U.S. foreign policy.* In the 1950s and 1960s, the architects of U.S. diplomacy tended to assume a bipolar world and to substitute crisis management and ideological formulas for long-range strategic analysis. Nixon and Kissinger, by contrast, envisioned a multipolar world in which power arose not only from military might but from economic and geopolitical realities. The emphasis on economic factors in diplomacy would prove especially important in laying the intellectual groundwork for the post–Cold War world of the 1990s.

Downplaying ideology, both men saw national interest and long-term strategic calculations as the key to nations' behavior, and they molded U.S. policy accordingly. As diplomatic historian John Lewis Gaddis writes, "It was the overall calculus of power that was important, not the defeats or victories that might take place in isolated theaters of competition." Concentrating on issues and areas that truly involved American interests, they moved away from a foreign policy driven by brushfire crises. Specifically, they disengaged from Vietnam, which Kissinger dismissed as "a small peninsula on a major continent." (Their determination to withdraw from that small peninsula on their own terms, however, took a heavy toll in life and suffering.) Instead, they opened the door to China, negotiated seriously with the Soviets, and pursued U.S. interests in the volatile Middle East. Their grand strategy echoed the realist approach to foreign policy enunciated by George Kennan in the late 1940s. Kennan, too, had stressed national interest. Downgrading ideology, he had focused

---

* Although Nixon's role ended with his resignation in August 1974, Kissinger would remain secretary of state until January 1977.

on major power relationships. After Kissinger became secretary of state, Kennan observed, "Henry understands my views better than anyone at State ever has."

The diplomacy of the Nixon-Kissinger years arose from long-term trends, notably the Sino-Soviet split, Moscow's rise to nuclear parity, and problems that plagued both the Soviet and the American economies. But although the times invited a rethinking of Cold War doctrine, personal factors played a role as well. Nixon and Kissinger—once described by Nixon as "the grocer's son from Whittier and the refugee from Hitler's Germany, the politician and the academic"—made an odd couple. Indeed, tension and jealousy plagued their partnership. Yet with a remarkable concordance of worldviews, objectives, and styles of operation, they left their stamp on American diplomacy.

The duo had detractors. Conservative Republicans such as Ronald Reagan and various "neoconservative" Democrats criticized them for supposedly weakening America's defenses through the SALT treaty and cuts in military spending.* More idealistic Democrats deplored the amorality and unconcern for human rights of their single-minded concentration on national interest and balance-of-power diplomacy. Unquestionably, their foreign policy had its brutal side. If their dealings with China, the Soviet Union, and the Middle East demonstrated the strengths of a pragmatic, self-interested diplomacy, their handling of Allende revealed its darker aspect.

Détente with Beijing and Moscow represents Nixon's greatest achievement. It did not end the Cold War, but it moved the conflict beyond the inflamed rhetoric and black-and-white worldview of earlier days. And the nation's premier Cold Warrior accomplished this turnaround. As historian Stephen Ambrose observes, Nixon's key asset in easing Cold War tensions was that he did not have to contend with Nixon: "Had anyone but Nixon tried to promote détente, Nixon . . . would have rallied the right wing to kill it." The president had this fact in mind when he told the Chinese, "In America, at least at this time, those on the right can do what those on the left can only talk about."

In pursuing their grand strategy, Nixon and Kissinger centralized the policymaking process and increasingly resorted to secrecy and deception. Both looked askance at popular movements, such as the antiwar protests, that aimed at influencing foreign policy. Diplomacy, they believed, should be left to the experts, a view that represented another link with the elitist Kennan. Both bypassed the foreign-policy bureaucracy and used shadowy back channels to negotiate with foreign leaders. "Without secrecy," Nixon insisted, "there would have been no opening to China, no SALT agreement with the Soviet Union, and no peace treaty ending the Vietnam War." But the deviousness took its toll by creating a climate laden with suspicion and fostering byzantine intrigues that ultimately would drag Nixon down.

Kissinger's reputation, too, fell grievously after he left office. He had no role in the new Republican ascendancy that began in 1981, and the breakup of the Soviet Union at the end of the eighties would render his balance-of-power strategies irrele-

---

* Although advocates of U.S. strategic superiority wanted the savings gained through withdrawal from Vietnam to be plowed into other areas of military spending, U.S. outlays for defense declined at a steady rate of 4.5 percent from 1970 to 1975. Defense Secretary Melvin Laird, who presided over this scaleback, became a central target of conservative attack.

vant. Kissinger's reputation for toadying to the powerful, his arrogance toward subordinates, and his contempt for the foreign-policy bureaucracy all hurt his reputation in the long run. His self-serving memoirs did little to salvage his image, and a massive biography published in 1992 denigrated him with grim single-mindedness.* But the reaction was as extreme as the earlier adulation, when cartoonists had portrayed him as a cape-wielding "Super-K." For all his flaws and the drawbacks of his worldview, Kissinger remains a towering figure. Emulating his heroes, the conservative statesmen of an earlier day, he set out to impose intellectual coherence on a foreign policy that had too often substituted rhetoric and bluster for broad-gauge thinking. To a great extent he succeeded—although in history's ever-shifting terrain, success is often written in the sand.

Domestic Policy: New Departures, Conservative Affirmations

Nixon would have preferred to concentrate on foreign affairs and turn over domestic issues to his cabinet, but in the shrinking modern world, the two were inextricably linked. As Lyndon Johnson had learned and as the 1973–1974 Arab oil embargo underscored, events abroad had immediate and often dramatic political and economic ramifications at home. Furthermore, Nixon's approach to foreign affairs and domestic issues was remarkably consistent. At home, as in the international arena, Nixon proved more open to innovation than his critics might have anticipated. The same opportunism and even cynicism that led him to pursue openings to the communist world after winning fame as an anticommunist zealot also gave him an adaptability and freedom from dogma in approaching domestic issues. The fact that he had won only 43 percent of the vote in 1968 and was the first incoming president since Zachary Taylor in 1848 to face opposition-party majorities in both the House and Senate no doubt encouraged this flexibility.

In his early years in office, Nixon adopted moderately progressive positions, adhering to the Eisenhower strategy of accepting reforms—the New Deal, the Fair Deal, and now the Great Society—while curbing their "excesses" and administering them more economically. Nixon signed Democratic bills raising social security benefits. He also increased federal funds for low-income public housing and even expanded the Job Corps. His first term saw steady increases in spending on mandated social-welfare programs, especially social security, Medicare, and Medicaid. Far from bucking this trend, Nixon in a January 1971 TV interview sketched a vision of post-Vietnam America reminiscent of Lyndon Johnson at his most expansive:

> If we can get this country thinking not of how to fight a war, but how to win a peace—if we can get this country thinking of clean air, clean water, open spaces, of a welfare reform program that will provide a floor under the income of every family with children in America, . . .—a new approach to government, reform of education, reform of health—if . . . people can think of these positive things . . . then we will have the lift of a driving dream.

---

* Walter Isaacson, *Kissinger: A Biography* (1992).

Such high-flown rhetoric alarmed conservatives. After the address, Nixon's pugnacious speechwriter Pat Buchanan fired off an angry seven-page memo accusing the boss of embracing "a liberal Democratic domestic program" and of relying too much on "pragmatic technicians" such as adviser John Ehrlichman rather than conservative ideologues like himself. True conservatives, groused Buchanan, were "the niggers of the Nixon administration." Nixon, as usual referring to himself in the third person, shot back, "What do [conservatives] think of Cambodia, etc.? You overlook RN's consistent hard line on foreign policy."

Nixon's most surprising departure from laissez-faire orthodoxy came with his 1969 proposal to provide a guaranteed minimum income to every U.S. family. The initial annual minimum, $1,600 for a family of four, plus food stamps to the value of $800 or more, represented nearly $9,000 in early-1990s buying power. This so-called Family Assistance Plan (FAP) was the brainchild of Nixon's urban-affairs adviser, Daniel Patrick Moynihan. Although a Democrat, a Harvard professor, and a former Kennedy administration official, the tall, chubby, rosy-cheeked Moynihan had ideas that appealed to Nixon, who appointed him head of the newly created Urban Affairs Council. Moynihan proposed to replace the nation's cumbersome social-welfare system, widely criticized for perpetuating a culture of dependence, with straight cash payments to bring society's poorest members up to an agreed-upon minimum. All this would be done, Moynihan hoped, without reducing the incentive of the needy to better themselves by working. In a television interview, Moynihan defended his plan: "The problem of the poor people is they don't have enough money. I would . . . put my faith in any effort that puts more resources into the hands of those that don't now have them. . . . Cold cash! It's a surprisingly good cure for a lot of social ills." Whereas Johnson's Great Society envisioned an array of federal programs to battle poverty, the FAP approach bypassed the welfare bureaucracy in favor of funneling money directly to the poor.

Winning approval in the House, the FAP failed in the Senate. Conservatives denounced it as socialistic, and liberals balked at the low level of payments. Although unsuccessful, the scheme reveals Nixon's capacity for domestic innovation. Many leftists and liberals not normally among Nixon's admirers cheered the FAP. Michael Harrington, the socialist whose *The Other America* had highlighted the problem of poverty a decade earlier, called it "the most radical idea since the New Deal."

Nixon's willingness to abandon traditional Republican shibboleths also emerged in his response to the nation's economic problems, although not at first. Johnson's "guns-and-butter" effort to finance both the Vietnam War and domestic social programs without raising taxes had ignited inflation and deepened the federal deficit. These problems worsened in Nixon's early years. In 1970, as the inflationary spiral continued, Congress authorized the president to freeze wages and prices. But Nixon demurred; not only did most economists oppose such controls, but Nixon as a young lawyer in the wartime Office of Price Administration had developed a strong aversion to elaborate federal regulation and bureaucratic red tape. "Price and wage controls simply do not fit the economic conditions which exist today," he asserted.

Instead, Nixon tried to curb inflation by cooling the economy. To this end, he trimmed government spending and prodded the Federal Reserve Board to tighten credit. The policy not only failed to halt inflation but contributed to a business downturn. With production falling and the jobless rate at a disturbing 5 percent, the nation stumbled into recession. The Dow-Jones index, in its biggest annual drop in three decades, lost one-third of its value and tumbled from 900 to 600. The economic by-products of Vietnamization—returning job-seeking veterans and canceled defense contracts—worsened the problem. Boeing, the Seattle aircraft giant, slashed its work force from 101,000 to 44,000. A strike at GM exacerbated economic woes. As the 1970 midterm election approached, the Democrats gleefully attacked "Nixonomics." Lawrence O'Brien, head of the Democratic National Committee, defined the term as "all the things that should go up—the stock market, corporate profits, real spendable income, productivity—go down, and all the things that should go down—unemployment, prices, interest rates—go up." As the economy sputtered, the Democrats gained twelve House seats in November, widening their already formidable majority.

In January 1971, unemployment rose to nearly 6 percent. Spending on the federal food-stamp program mushroomed from $250 million in 1969 to $2.2 billion in 1971. The 1971 federal deficit spurted to more than $23 billion, nearly matching Johnson's record 1968 deficit and mocking Nixon's predicted $1 billion surplus. To make matters worse, 1971 brought the first U.S. trade deficit since the 1890s. On the world's money markets, the dollar fell to its lowest point since 1949. In 1969 Americans had named Vietnam as the nation's most pressing problem; in 1971, inflation topped the list. Nixon would later describe early 1971 as "the lowest point" of his first term.

Demonstrating the same pragmatism that characterized his quest for détente, Nixon abruptly reversed course. On August 15, he called for "a new economic policy for the United States" and announced a program of federal economic intervention such as he had rejected only months earlier. In the first phase of his anti-inflation program, the president slapped a ninety-day freeze on prices, wages, and rents. Nixon took this action under powers granted the president by the Economic Stabilization Act, passed by the Democratic-led Congress in August 1970. At the time, Nixon had insisted he would never use these powers. In the second phase, launched in mid-November, he capped annual wage increases at 5.5 percent and price and rent increases at 2.5 percent. Stressing voluntary compliance, Nixon nevertheless set up the Cost of Living Council with authority to enforce these restraints. To stimulate the economy, he announced a 10 percent tax credit for corporate investment, a rollback of the 7 percent excise tax on automobiles, and other pump-priming steps.

To address the weak dollar and the growing trade deficit, Nixon imposed a 10 percent surcharge on imports. He also suspended the convertibility of the dollar into gold at the official price of $35 per ounce set by the 1944 Bretton Woods Conference. Bretton Woods had established the dollar as the standard to which all other currencies would be pegged, but as the dollar faltered, it could no longer serve this purpose. Furthermore, its artificially high valuation was hurting America's export business. Henceforth, the dollar would "float," finding its own value in relation to other currencies. The president, in effect, had devalued the dollar vis-à-vis other currencies. After August 1971, the dollar fell by about 10 percent in the official exchanges of the world capitals.* As the dollar became cheaper in relation to other currencies, Nixon hoped, U.S. products would attract more foreign buyers.

Proclaiming his conversion to Keynesian economics, with its advocacy of deficit spending as an economic stimulus, Nixon offered a "full employment" budget for 1972 that projected an $11.6 billion deficit. Fiscal conservatives protested, but the president defended his plan. As long as U.S. workers lacked jobs, he proclaimed in Rooseveltian phrases, deficits were justified. Like all other presidents, Nixon had shaped his economic program with one eye on the forthcoming electoral campaign.

For a time the medicine seemed to help. Inflation slowed, and the trade gap narrowed. The stock exchange broke 1000 for the first time late in 1971, a big psychological lift. But mandated welfare and health-care payments; rising imports, especially of fuel-efficient Japanese cars; and soaring energy costs stemming from the Arab oil boycott all worked against the president. The roller-coaster stock market dipped below 800 by the end of 1973, and the trade deficit widened. The administration continued to tinker with price controls, even briefly imposing a new freeze in mid-1973, but to no avail. Inflation spiraled upward, hitting 11 percent in 1974, with energy and food leading the way. Overall, consumer prices rose nearly 35 percent from 1969 to 1974. Unemployment reached 8.5 percent by 1975.

The picture looked bleak on all fronts. In constant dollars, median family income stagnated between 1970 and 1975. To compare, family earnings had risen steadily since World War II, growing by one-third in the 1960s alone. Similarly, U.S. productivity, having risen by more than 3 percent annually from 1947 to 1965, dropped to an anemic 1.4 percent in 1971–1975. The long cycle of economic expansion that had started after World War II began grinding to a halt, and the productivity that had kept the economy humming for more than two decades sputtered ominously. Americans sensed that the downturn involved more than just the usual pattern of a brief recession followed by a strong rebound. Severe structural problems had emerged.

Circumstances had led Nixon to impose the most drastic economic controls since World War II and to adopt stimulus strategies that were anathema to earlier Republicans. His actions revealed that the federal government's sense of obligation to foster prosperity—a legacy of the New Deal and the Employment Act of 1946— had become entrenched in the nation's polity, no matter which party held power. Ironically, Nixon's conversion to Keynesian theory had come as economists were growing skeptical of government's ability to fight recessions. Battling complex and long-term problems, neither Nixon nor his successors proved particularly adept at finding the ideal combination of measures to assure economic health.

In his role as party leader, Nixon continued to woo the middle-class and blue-

---

* At a Washington conference in December 1971, the world's ten leading industrialized nations adopted a new set of official exchange rates at which the value of the dollar was pegged at $38.00 for an ounce of gold, or about 10 percent weaker than the earlier $35.00 rate. In 1973, as the dollar continued to weaken, Nixon devalued it still further, setting a new rate of $42.22 for an ounce of gold. But even this figure wildly overstated the dollar's actual world value; on the free market, the price of gold at the time was $90.00 an ounce. By the summer of 1973, it had reached $127.00 an ounce. In the fall, the United States and the major nations of Western Europe abandoned the effort to set official rates for gold sales. By 1980, after years of worsening inflation in America, the free-market price of gold stood at $800.00 an ounce, but it fell sharply thereafter.

collar white vote so crucial to his 1968 victory. Kevin Phillips explained the strategy in *The Emerging Republican Majority* (1969). Republicans could gain dominance, Phillips argued, by enlarging their traditional conservative base to include "middle Americans." These voters had once gathered under the big tent erected by Franklin Roosevelt, but their Democratic loyalties had withered under antiwar demonstrations, black militancy, soaring welfare costs, and social turbulence. Political parties succeed, Phillips claimed, by understanding "who hates whom" and then exploiting those hatreds.

Nixon brought to the task of reshaping his party the same pragmatic willingness to form alliances of convenience that defined his approach to foreign affairs. Indeed, his style of party leadership mirrored his diplomatic style. As the Sino-Soviet bloc had broken up, Nixon and Kissinger had maneuvered to realign global power relationships to America's advantage. Similarly, as the New Deal coalition splintered, Nixon looked for opportunities to woo disaffected voting blocs.

To this end, the president counterbalanced heretical economic proposals such as FAP and deficit spending with a more predictably conservative stance on other issues. He vetoed more than twenty spending bills passed by the Democratic Congress. In the fall of 1971, he refused to sign a bill creating a comprehensive child-care system, including day-care centers for working mothers. Such "communal approaches" to child rearing, he charged, would "sovietize" America's children. Coming out squarely for "family values," he avowed, "Good public policy requires that we enhance rather than diminish . . . parental involvement with children."

The president also articulated middle-class frustration with the federal bureaucracy by calling for a reduction in Washington's role in American life. To this end, he proposed in his January 1972 budget message an annual rebate of $5 billion to the states, with the money to come from cuts in federal aid programs for minorities and the poor. In an obvious play for the votes of suburban homeowners, he predicted that his program would generate a 30 percent cut in local property taxes.

In October 1972, two weeks before the election, Congress passed Nixon's revenue-sharing bill, which provided for the distribution of more than $30 billion in federal revenues over a five-year period to state, county, and local governments, to use as they chose. At the same time, Congress placed a $2.5 billion annual cap on federal welfare spending. As Washington cut funding for social programs, the theory went, local governments would pick up the slack. But big cities, awash in poverty and social problems amid recession and high unemployment, complained that state legislatures used the federal-rebate windfall to cover their own chronic budget shortages and neglected urban needs.

Nixon's courting of the "hard hats" who demonstrated against antiwar marchers reflected a calculated campaign to win the hearts and minds of Americans disturbed by campus unrest and the alleged lack of patriotism of antiwar activists. Several high-visibility trials of radical leaders also served this purpose. The most notorious of these was the Justice Department's prosecution of the "Chicago Eight"—a group consisting partly of movement celebrities—on conspiracy charges arising from the demonstrations at the 1968 Democratic convention. The trial, held in Chicago from October 1969 to March 1970 before crusty, short-tempered Judge Julius Hoffman, turned into a media circus. The proceedings not only confirmed radicals' darkest beliefs about justice in what they had taken to calling "Amerika" but also conservatives' worst nightmares about radicals. The defendants, including Yippie showmen Abbie Hoffman and Jerry Rubin, Bobby Seale of the Black Panthers, and Tom Hayden and Rennie Davis of SDS, cheerfully took over an already politicized trial.* They openly ridiculed an increasingly apopleptic "Julie" Hoffman, laughed and shouted "bullshit" when paid informants testified, and otherwise disrupted the proceedings. Their "character witnesses" included Allen Ginsberg, Phil Ochs, Jesse Jackson, Norman Mailer, and former Johnson speechwriter Richard Goodwin. In a bizarre twist, Judge Hoffman ordered Seale bound and gagged. Beneath the farcical surface, a serious political psychodrama unfolded as the Nixon administration demonstrated that the forces of law and order, represented by the strong leader in the White House, could stand firm against anarchy.

Kevin Phillips's "emerging Republican majority" included blue-collar workers, as well as Catholic ethnics and upwardly mobile suburbanites. GOP strategists played on such groups' fears of urban violence and social disorder and charged that the Democrats were more interested in minorities and welfare clients than in the concerns of hard-working, patriotic citizens. The party of FDR, they told wavering Democrats, had been hijacked by antiwar protesters, New Left radicals, and entrenched bureaucrats out of touch with grass-roots America.

Nixon also avidly courted another prime Republican target group: white southerners. Although he made a few gestures toward blacks, such as appointing James Farmer an assistant secretary of the Department of Health, Education and Welfare (HEW), he devoted much more attention to extending his base in the white South. By April 1970 even Farmer complained that blacks felt "a growing spirit of hopelessness that the Administration is not on their side." With George Wallace planning another presidential run in 1972, Nixon stepped up his effort to attract white voters below the Mason-Dixon Line.

Nixon's friend and confidant John Mitchell, whom he appointed attorney general, helped to implement the president's southern strategy. The mournful-looking, pipe-puffing former partner in Nixon's New York law firm had managed Nixon's 1968 campaign. As attorney general, he opposed extension of the 1965 Voting Rights Act and thwarted enforcement of the 1968 Fair Housing Act. When he sued to delay school desegregation in Mississippi, even civil-rights attorneys in his own Justice Department protested. The Supreme Court slapped down this effort in *Alexander* v. *Holmes County* (1969), ordering that school desegregation proceed "at once."

When the Court in *Swann* v. *Charlotte-Mecklenburg Board of Education* (1971) approved school busing to achieve racial balance, Nixon found the kind of gut issue on which he thrived. On television he denounced the decision and demanded that Congress outlaw the policy. When HEW officials and Justice Department civil-rights lawyers drew up integration plans involving busing for several cities, the president fired off an angry memo to Ehrlichman: "*Knock off this Crap.* I hold [HEW and Justice Department officials] personally accountable to keep their left wingers in step with my express policy—Do what the law requires and not *one bit more.*"

---

* The other defendants were Dave Dellinger, a longtime pacifist and a leader of the coalition that organized the fall 1969 mobilization demonstration in Washington; John Froines, a radical activist professor; and Lee Weiner, a street organizer and midlevel movement activist.

Nixon's cultivation of southern white voters emerged most blatantly in his Supreme Court nominations. An unusual number of justices retired in 1969–1972, enabling him to make four appointments. When Chief Justice Earl Warren stepped down in 1969, Nixon nominated Warren Burger of Minnesota, a moderately conservative federal judge of the U.S. Court of Appeals of Washington, D.C. The Senate easily confirmed the choice. When another vacancy opened in 1969, Nixon offered a nomination clearly intended to further his southern strategy: Clement F. Haynsworth, chief judge of South Carolina's Fourth Circuit Court of Appeals. Haynsworth hailed from the home state of Senator Strom Thurmond, the 1948 Dixiecrat candidate for president who had later become a Republican and played a key role in helping Nixon to carry the South in 1968. A bitter opponent of the 1954 *Brown* decision and other examples of judicial activism, Thurmond favored jurists who believed in "strict construction" of the Constitution and avoided social issues such as racial integration.* Haynsworth filled the bill in this respect, but he also had a record of opposing labor unions and civil rights. Moreover, conflict-of-interest problems had arisen in cases that he had handled. The Senate rejected him, 55–45, with seventeen Republicans joining the Democrats in a stinging rebuke of Nixon. His eye on the South, the president denounced the attacks on Haynsworth as "vicious character assassination."

Nixon followed the Haynsworth nomination with a totally unqualified candidate, G. Harrold Carswell, a Florida appeals-court judge. The American Bar Association and legal scholars deplored Carswell's nomination. As a candidate for the Georgia legislature in 1948, the judge had declared, "Segregation of the races is proper and the only practical and correct way of life. . . . I have always so believed and I shall always so act." Carswell had renounced this statement, but he could not shake the charge of being professionally unfit for the high court. Nixon's key liaison man with Congress, Bryce Harlow, advised the president: "[Most senators] think Carswell's a boob, a dummy. And what counter is there to that? He is." One last-ditch Carswell supporter, Republican senator Roman Hruska of Nebraska, even tried to turn Carswell's mediocrity into an asset. Many Americans were mediocre, Hruska pointed out in a television interview; didn't they deserve Supreme Court representation as much as any other group? Despite Hruska's argument, the Senate in April 1970 turned back the Carswell nomination, 51–45. Extracting maximum political mileage from the episode, Nixon denounced the vote as an insult to the South. "I understand the bitter feeling of the millions of Americans who live in the South about the act of regional discrimination that took place in the Senate yesterday," he intoned. Among white southerners, accustomed to lost causes, Nixon's popularity soared.

Having made his gesture to the South, Nixon next nominated a moderate jurist, Harry Blackmun of Minnesota, who won easy confirmation in May 1970 and proved himself an essentially liberal justice. To fill the next two vacancies, which came in 1971, Nixon nominated Lewis Powell and William Rehnquist. Powell, a Virginian,

---

* Strict constructionists hold that in interpreting the Constitution, the courts should follow the precise meaning intended by the framers; the other view, broad construction, sees the Constitution as a flexible, growing document, adaptable to changed circumstances and conditions. The confrontation of the two approaches dates back to the time of Jefferson and Hamilton.

boasted a distinguished record, including the former presidency of the American Bar Association. Rehnquist was a classmate of John Ehrlichman at Stanford Law School and had been a Goldwater Republican in 1964. As an assistant attorney general under John Mitchell, he had shown himself to be a hard-nosed "law-and-order" advocate, supporting secret wiretaps, for example, when he was convinced that "national security" necessitated them. Both won confirmation, Powell by an overwhelming 89–1 vote, Rehnquist by a closer margin, 68–26.

Demonstrating the independence that justices often display when elevated to the Supreme Court, Burger, Blackmun, and Rehnquist all steered a moderate-to-liberal course. The new court took a tough stand on issues of obscenity and law enforcement but avoided reversing the liberal rulings of the Warren era. On some issues, such as affirmative action, school busing, and abortion, it moved in directions deplored by many conservatives. Justice Harry Blackmun, for example, wrote the majority decision in *Roe* v. *Wade*, the landmark 1973 decision upholding a woman's constitutional right to an abortion.

CONCLUSION

Richard Nixon's first term and the first year of his second brought striking initiatives and landmark achievements: disengagement from Vietnam, détente with the Soviet Union, the opening to China, and resourceful diplomacy in the Middle East. Domestically, he moved beyond traditional Republican positions in several key areas. A consummate politician, Nixon capitalized on the country's rightward turn and rallied his "silent majority" of suburbanites, blue-collar voters, white southerners, and others unsettled by recent events. More than anyone else, he set the terms of American political discourse for the coming decades.

But history's verdict on Nixon would prove far harsher than seemed possible in 1973. Behind the scenes, the president had engaged in and encouraged abuses and illegalities that would produce the gravest crisis in the history of the presidency. All occupants of the Oval Office wield vast power, but when Nixon overreached that power and put himself above the law, "the system" so criticized by radicals arose to force him out. As the nation grappled with broad-ranging social and cultural changes in the early 1970s, it also endured an ordeal that historians would sum up with a single word: Watergate.

SELECTED READINGS

1968 and the Vietnam War, from Tet to Cease-fire

Many of the works listed in the Selected Readings of Chapters 9 and 10 are relevant to the first two sections of Chapter 11 as well. In addition, see Jerry L. Avorn, *University in Revolt: A History of the Columbia Crisis* (1968); Michael Bilton and Kevin Sim, *Four Hours in My Lai* (1992); Bernard Brodie, "The Tet Offensive," in Noble Frankland and Christopher Dowling, eds., *Decisive Battles of the Twentieth Century* (1976); David Caute, *The Year of the Barricades:*

A Journey Through 1968 (1988); Lewis Chester et al., An American Melodrama: The Presidential Campaign of 1968 (1969); Todd Gitlin, The Whole World Is Watching: Mass Media in the Making and Unmaking of the New Left (1980) and The Sixties: Years of Hope, Days of Rage (1987); Joseph Goldstein, Burke Marshall, and Jack Schwartz, The My Lai Massacre and Its Cover-Up (1976); Francine du Plessix Gray, Divine Disobedience: Profiles in Catholic Radicalism (1970); Seymour M. Hersh, My Lai: A Report on the Massacre and Its Aftermath (1970); Peter Joseph, Good Times: An Oral History of America in the Nineteen Sixties (1974); Andrew Kopkind and James Ridgeway, eds., Decade of Crisis: America in the 60s (1972); Michael Mandelbaum, "Vietnam: The Television War," Daedalus (Fall 1982); Joan Morrison and Robert K. Morrison, From Camelot to Kent State: The Sixties Experience in the Words of Those Who Lived It (1987); Jack Newfield, Robert Kennedy: A Memoir (1970); Richard M. Nixon, RN: The Memoirs of Richard M. Nixon (1978); Keith W. Nolan, Battle for Hué: Tet, 1968 (1983); Don Oberdorfer, Tet: The Turning Point of the War (1983); The Pentagon Papers (1972); W. J. Rorabaugh, Berkeley at War: The 1960s (1989); Herbert Y. Schandler, The Unmaking of a President: Lyndon Johnson and Vietnam (1977); William Shawcross, Sideshow: Kissinger, Nixon and the Destruction of Cambodia (1979); Melvin Small, Johnson, Nixon, and the Doves (1988); Carl Solberg, Hubert Humphrey (1984); Ronald H. Spector, After Tet: The Bloodiest Year in Vietnam (1993); Irwin Unger and Debi Unger, Turning Point, 1968 (1988); Nigel Young, An Infantile Disorder? The Crisis and Decline of the New Left (1977).

Nixon-Kissinger Foreign Policy

The general histories of the Cold War cited in the Chapter 2 Selected Readings are relevant to the Nixon-Kissinger years as well. See also Stephen E. Ambrose, Nixon: Triumph of a Politician (1987); Coit D. Blacker, Reluctant Warriors: The United States, the Soviet Union, and Arms Control (1987); Henry Brandon, The Retreat of American Power (1973); Seyom Brown, The Crisis of Power (1979); McGeorge Bundy, Danger and Survival: Choices About the Bomb in the First Fifty Years (1988); Alan Dowty, Middle East Crisis (1984); Lawrence Freedman, The Evolution of Nuclear Strategy (1981); Raymond L. Garthoff, Détente and Confrontation: American-Soviet Relations from Nixon to Reagan (1985); John Girling, America and the Third World (1980); Seymour M. Hersh, The Price of Power: Kissinger in the Nixon White House (1983); Walter Isaacson, Kissinger: A Biography (1992); Henry Kissinger, White House Years (1979) and Years of Upheaval (1983); Walter LaFeber, Inevitable Revolutions: The United States in Central America (1985); Robert S. Litwack, Détente and the Nixon Doctrine: American Foreign Policy and the Pursuit of Stability (1984); Roger Morris, Uncertain Greatness: Henry Kissinger and American Foreign Policy (1977); John Newhouse, Cold Dawn: The Story of SALT (1973); Robert E. Osgood et al., Retreat from Empire? The First Nixon Administration (1973); Herbert Parmet, The World and Richard Nixon (1990); Gareth Porter, A Peace Denied: The United States, Vietnam, and the Paris Agreement (1975); Jonathan Schell, The Time of Illusion (1975); Gerard Smith, Doubletalk: The Story of the First Strategic Arms Limitation Talks (1980); Richard Smoke, National Security and the Nuclear Dilemma (1984); Lester A. Sobel, ed., Kissinger and Détente (1975); Steven J. Spiegel, The Other Arab-Israeli Conflict: Making America's Middle East Policy from Truman to Reagan (1985); C. L. Sulzberger, The World and Richard Nixon (1987); Tom Wicker, One of Us: Richard Nixon and the American Dream (1991); Daniel Yergin, The Prize: The Epic Quest for Oil, Money, and Power (1991).

Domestic Politics in the Early Nixon Years

Vincent Burke and Vee Burke, Nixon's Good Deed: Welfare Reform (1974); David Calleo, The Imperious Economy (1982); Jody Carlson, George Wallace and the Politics of Powerlessness

(1981); Thomas Byrne Edsall with Mary D. Edsall, *Chain Reaction: The Impact of Race, Rights, and Taxes on American Politics* (1991); Rowland Evans, Jr., and Robert D. Novak, *Nixon in the White House: The Frustration of Power* (1971); Richard Harris, *Decision* (1971) [Nixon's Supreme Court nominations]; Roger L. Miller, *The New Economics of Richard Nixon* (1972); Daniel Patrick Moynihan, *The Politics of a Guaranteed Income: The Nixon Administration and the Family Assistance Plan* (1973); R. P. Nathan, ed., *Monitoring Revenue Sharing* (1975); Leon E. Panetta and Peter Gall, *Bring Us Together—the Nixon Team and the Civil Rights Retreat* (1971); Herbert Parmet, *Richard Nixon and His America* (1990); Kevin B. Phillips, *The Emerging Republican Majority* (1969); A. James Reichley, *Conservatives in an Age of Change: The Nixon and Ford Administrations* (1981); William Safire, *Before the Fall: An Inside Look at the Pre-Watergate White House* (1975); Kirpatrick Sale, *Power Shift: The Rise of the Southern Rim and Its Challenge to the Eastern Establishment* (1976); Leonard Silk, *Nixonomics* (1972); Michael Tanzer, *The Energy Crisis* (1974); Garry Wills, *Nixon Agonistes: The Crisis of a Self-Made Man* (1970).

Chapter Twelve

Reform in the Nation, Crisis in Washington

On the afternoon of August 7, 1974, facing the supreme crisis of his life, President Richard Nixon gathered his family in the White House solarium: wife Pat, daughters Tricia and Julie with their husbands Edward Cox and David Eisenhower, grandson of the revered Dwight Eisenhower. In a quintessentially Nixonian touch, the president, over Pat's protests, summoned the White House photographer to record the moment "for history." In the photograph, Nixon's fists, so tightly clenched that the knuckles show white, belie his smiling face. A moment after the staged shot, the photographer captured a sobbing Julie embracing her father, his eyes screwed shut, as Tricia turns away weeping and Edward gamely smiles on. When the photographer at last departed, the family shared a grim, silent dinner. Nixon announced his resignation the following evening and left the White House by helicopter the next day. For the first and so far the only time, a U.S. president had involuntarily left office before the expiration of his term.

Nixon's efforts to conceal his role in a break-in at the Democratic party headquarters during the 1972 campaign had spawned further crimes and ultimately had unraveled. By the summer of 1974, he faced two choices: resign or be impeached. But the president's personal crisis paled in contrast to the nation's ordeal. Watergate stretched the fabric of constitutional government to the limit. Following in the wake of the distrust that had dogged LBJ's final White House years, the scandal further weakened the presidency, and Americans' trust in government fell to all-time lows.

Watergate dominates the seventies, making it difficult for historians to delineate the larger contours of this decade clearly. In contrast to both the sixties and the eighties, the seventies, with their eddying social, political, and cultural crosscurrents, remain curiously ill focused. In part, the period was marked by reaction and discouraged passivity after the traumas of the sixties. While Nixon rallied his "silent majority," some erstwhile activists and members of the counterculture bade farewell to social commitment, radicalism, and cultural protest. Some shifted their focus inward and cultivated personal well-being and material acquisition. But the sixties cast a long shadow, and the political and cultural trends of those years did not vanish as the new decade began. Despite the collapse of the New Left and the counterculture, the reformist spirit, radical energies, and drive for cultural innovation that had infused these movements persisted into the seventies. The context changed, but many activists turned to new causes, including environmental protection and feminism.

As in the sixties, this new wave of social activism stirred opposition, and deep political and cultural fissures continued to rend American society. As we shall see in this chapter and explore more fully in the next, movements that were perceived as threatening the status quo or that challenged strongly held values triggered a powerful conservative response. The political counterrevolution embodied in the Wallace movement and in Richard Nixon's election in 1968 continued through the 1970s, laying the groundwork for the apotheosis of conservatism that would come with the election of Ronald Reagan in 1980.

The nation may have longed for a breathing space as the sixties ended, but history offers no time-outs. The onset of the seventies brought fresh political crises, new movements and causes, and deepening social and cultural divisions. Janus-like, the decade faces both backward and forward; in some respects a continuation of the sixties, it also prefigured trends that would occupy the nation in the years that followed.

Escapism and Renewed Activism

The culture and politics of the seventies unfolded amid the wreckage of the antiwar movement and the apparent collapse of the counterculture. A combination of forces conspired to destroy or drastically alter these movements. The New Left faded as Nixon's policy of Vietnamization neutralized its most potent issue and as the political climate turned hostile to radical protest. Bitter ideological disputes finished off an already weakening movement. The counterculture also suffered from commercial exploitation, the devastation of drug abuse, and the actions of a few disturbed individuals attracted by its aura of nonjudgmental tolerance. A more insidious force silently eroded these movements as well: time. With each passing year, a new wave of activists and counterculture devotees started families, began and finished graduate school, entered the job market, or otherwise reached a truce with the society that they had reviled or ridiculed only a short time before.

As resourceful promoters coopted the counterculture's music and fashions,* the movement itself took a lurid turn and then collapsed. In December 1969, Charles Manson, a psychotic drug çultist, and his "family" of young followers recruited in San Francisco's Haight-Ashbury district ritually murdered pregnant actress Sharon Tate and four others in Tate's Beverly Hills home. A few underground publications on the counterculture's far outer fringe hailed Manson as a hero; to conservatives, the horror embodied everything that they feared in the movement. In 1970, the year in which the Beatles broke up, a rival British rock group, the Rolling Stones, set out to make a documentary movie on the model of the highly profitable film version of the

---

* *Hair*, a musical celebrating the "Age of Aquarius" (also the title of a popular counterculture song) and featuring eye-popping nudity, opened on Broadway in 1968.

Woodstock festival. The Stones staged a free concert at Altamont Raceway near San Francisco and, cultivating their outlaw image, hired the Hell's Angels motorcycle gang to provide security in return for $500 worth of beer. The event proved a disaster: Concertgoers molested physicians trying to treat drug-overdose victims; the Hell's Angels assaulted several people and fatally knifed a young black man as he approached the stage; three people died in drug-related accidents. The Manson murders, Altamont, and other evidences of antisocial, exploitive impulses tarnished the counterculture's avowals of peace and love.

In a post-Altamont article, "The End of the Age of Aquarius," Todd Gitlin excoriated the movement's failure to confront the havoc of drugs. "Why doesn't this contaminated culture, many of whose claims are based on the virtues of drugs, help its own brothers and sisters?" he lamented. "Why do the underground papers leave it to the media narcotizers to deplore the damaging possibilities of bad drugs?" Would the youth culture "leave anything behind but a market?" he mused bitterly. Years later, Gitlin—by then a Berkeley sociologist—reflected on the movement's sad end: "The revolutionary mood had been fueled by the blindingly bright illusion that human history was beginning afresh because a graced generation had willed it so. Now there wasn't enough life left to mobilize against all the death raining down." As the counterculture contingent of the baby-boom generation grew older, a few remained outside the mainstream and preserved the styles of the sixties in a kind of cultural time capsule. For most, however, their season of youthful rebellion survived only in memory.

As the counterculture disintegrated and the antiwar movement lost momentum, the cultural climate shifted markedly. Contrasted to what came before, the 1970s (again excepting Watergate) have gone down in history as passive and featureless and as lacking memorable highlights. Peter N. Carroll's 1982 analysis of the decade bears the tongue-in-cheek title *It Seemed Like Nothing Happened*. In some respects, this image is accurate. The decade was generally free of the riots, assassinations, campus turmoil, bitter confrontations, and superheated rhetoric that for many Americans defined the sixties. Indeed, Brandeis University, having opened a Center for the Study of Violence in 1966, closed it in 1973.

A nation shell-shocked by conflict and upheaval turned to benign icons of mass culture for reassurance. The antiwar, anti-Establishment, and drug-induced music of the late 1960s gave way to songs such as Don McLean's bittersweet and enigmatic 1971 hit "American Pie." John Denver's crooning "Rocky Mountain High" (1972) recommended unspoiled nature rather than LSD as a means of spiritual transcendence. Groups like Led Zeppelin and The Who carried on the hard-rock tradition but without the overt political content of late-sixties rock.

Television fed the escapist mood. The three major networks—CBS, ABC, and NBC—pushed their revenues from $1 billion to $3 billion in the 1970s. Their offerings typically featured situation comedies, 1950s nostalgia ("Happy Days," "Laverne and Shirley"), sexual titillation, and police dramas such as "Kojak" and "Hawaii FIVE-O." There were exceptions, of course. The long-running comedy-drama "M*A*S*H" premiered in 1972, marked by witty dialogue and the exploration of humane values in the unlikely setting of a Korean War medical unit. The show's implicit pacifist message captured the nation's post-Vietnam mood. For the most part, however, 1970s TV, driven by ratings and marketing demographics, lived down to the "vast wasteland" label that FCC chairman Newton Minow had applied to it in 1961. *New York Times* TV critic John O'Conner complained late in the decade that the medium was "dropping rapidly to kiddie levels."

Although television in the seventies reflected America's diversity more fully than it had in the 1950s, the effort proved fitful. The hugely successful ABC mini-series "Roots" (1976) offered a dramatic panorama of the African-American experience, but other series featuring blacks were less impressive. George Jefferson on "The Jeffersons" was a weak buffoon, and the prancing teenager J. J. on "Good Times" perpetuated the grinning, blackface minstrel stereotype dating to pre–Civil War days. Asians, Hispanics, and Native Americans appeared but rarely.

Hollywood shared in the infantilization of mass culture in the 1970s, despite a few gripping movies such as *The Deerhunter* (1978), a portrayal of the psychological effects of Vietnam service. Typical escapist fare included Sylvester Stallone's *Rocky* (1976), *Superman* (1978), and Steven Spielberg's and George Lucas's *Star Wars* (1977) with its simplistic mythic structure and computer-generated scenes of intergalactic warfare. These films retained the sixties' sense of powerful and insidious forces seeking global control but transferred this awareness from the arena of political activism to the realm of fantasy.

The so-called new ethnicity of the seventies similarly continued in depoliticized form a cultural trend rooted in the sixties. In the earlier decade, calls for black pride had arisen as part of the larger freedom struggle. In the seventies, the affirmation of African-American identity not only inspired the "Roots" phenomenon but stimulated the pride and self-awareness among white ethnic groups documented and applauded in Michael Novak's *The Rise of the Unmeltable Ethnics* (1973). For many blue-collar and middle-class ethnics, allegiance to the Democratic party had been a tradition since the 1930s. Now, as old party loyalties crumbled, an affirmation of one's specific ethnic identity, freed from political connotations, offered an alternative form of group identification.

The new ethnicity also gave many Americans a link to earlier times in an era of unsettling social change, but it was a link typically grounded in hazy memories of a semimythic past. Many first- or second-generation immigrants had broken painfully with their ethnic heritage in order to seize the opportunities that came with "Americanization." Now, with the separation successfully accomplished, the newly self-conscious ethnics of the 1970s could safely indulge in a sentimental journey into their past from the safety of their mainstream lives. But like most other generalizations about the 1970s, this one must be qualified. Despite its ambiguous meanings and its silly side (like buttons reading "Kiss Me, I'm Italian"), the new ethnicity also represented a healthy defiance of the white-bread blandness of the fifties and the corporate world's tendency to reduce Americans to blocs of consumers living in "media markets."

The heightened awareness of race, class, and ethnicity in American life underlay the most popular TV show of the seventies, "All in the Family." The series starred Carroll O'Connor as Archie Bunker, a bigoted longshoreman and part-time taxi driver who spouted venom against blacks, radicals, feminists, Jews, and other groups that he deemed threatening. Viewers gained little sense of the experiences that had shaped Archie's worldview. Only his wife Edith, brilliantly played by Jean Stapleton, offered occasional insights that went beyond caricature. "He'll never be more than what he is now," she says sadly in one show, "even though he had dreams once." The show's producer, liberal Democrat Norman Lear, clearly intended to satirize bigotry, but audience surveys revealed that many viewers applauded Archie's diatribes and his scornful attacks on "Meathead," his liberal son-in-law.

A more sensitive portrayal of working-class frustration emerged in the 1979 film *Breaking Away*, which explored the lives of blue-collar youth in the university town of Bloomington, Indiana. With humor, nuance, and regional authenticity, *Breaking Away* conveyed the shattered illusions and cultural splintering of post-Vietnam America, as well as the blend of envy, resentment, and aspiration with which its characters view the class structure of their community. Walking on the university campus, the hero's father, a displaced stonecutter reduced to selling used cars, recalls, "I cut the stone for this building. I was one fine stonecutter. I loved it. I was damned proud of my work." The hero, a recent high-school graduate who imagines himself an Italian bicycle racer, is devastated when a real-life, corporate-sponsored Italian racing team uses unfair tactics to prevent him from winning a race. "Everybody cheats," he surmises bitterly. "I just didn't know."

Novelists, too, examined ethnic sensibilities and tensions. Saul Bellow's *Mr. Sammler's Planet* (1970) and Bernard Malamud's *The Tenants* (1971) probed the uneasy relations between blacks and Jews. Toni Morrison's *The Bluest Eye* (1970), the debut novel of a major black writer, told of poverty-bound Pecola Breedlove, who dreams of having blue eyes like the characters in her Dick-and-Jane school reader. Torn by conflicting aspirations, Pecola descends into madness: "Elbows bent, hands on shoulders, she flailed her arms like a bird in an eternal, grotesquely futile effort to fly. Beating the air, a winged but grounded bird, intent on the blue void it could not reach—could not even see—but which filled the valleys of the wind."

Nineteen-sixties activists, meanwhile, moved in various directions. A few went underground or joined rural communes. Others, still suspicious of the Establishment's technocratic expertise, embraced mysticism and the occult. Zen Buddhism and teenage Indian gurus won many followers; interest in astrology, Native American religion, and techniques for heightening psychic insight and "self-actualization" soared. Former SDS president Paul Potter, writing in 1971, offered a snapshot of a radical in transit from public to private concerns:

> I am less involved in changing America. . . . This does not mean that I am less angry or upset or horrified by this country than before. If anything, I am more profoundly and intuitively aware, day to day, of what an ugly society this is and how desperately it needs change. But my information comes less and less from the papers—more and more from my own experience with it.

One-time radicals proclaimed their conversion to a "New Age" sensibility superior to old ways of thinking. Cultural critic Edwin Schur captured the trend in the title of a 1976 book: *The Awareness Trap: Self-Absorption Instead of Social Change.*

Other erstwhile activists, less mystically inclined, turned to physical fitness and material acquisitions. Many young, urban professionals (later dubbed Yuppies) whose acquisitive tastes would shape American life in the 1980s were veterans of the counterculture. In *The Greening of America* (1970), Charles Reich of Yale Law School, himself a late-blooming flower child, argued that America's transformation into a more peaceful and harmonious society would come effortlessly and spontaneously as the counterculture's values spread by a kind of osmosis. Some movement dropouts weary of political engagement welcomed Reich's message. Indeed, in 1976 journalist Tom Wolfe labeled the baby boomers the "Me Generation." The 1983 movie *The Big Chill* would offer a sad image of cynical ex-sixties radicals in avid pursuit of money, sex, and power.

Historian Christopher Lasch in *The Culture of Narcissism* (1979) analyzed the way in which the counterculture's dissident life-styles and the New Left's politics of confrontation, initially undertaken to expose and challenge suburban conformity and power-elite manipulation, had degenerated into "a politics . . . of style without substance." In treating political action primarily as "a mode of self-dramatization," charged Lasch, movement activists had contributed to the obsessive "navel gazing" of the 1970s. Citing psychiatrists' reports of patients driven by immediate self-gratification and incapable of setting long-term goals, Lasch argued that the turn toward narcissism also paralleled the nation's worsening economic problems:

> Having no hope of improving their lives in any of the ways that matter, people have convinced themselves that what matters is psychic self-improvement: getting in touch with their feelings, eating health food, taking lessons in ballet or belly dancing, immersing themelves in the wisdom of the East, jogging, learning how to "relate," overcoming the "fear of pleasure."

But it would be seriously misleading to suggest that all radicals sold out or that the political activism and counterculture energies of the sixties simply metamorphosed into careerism or narcissism in the 1970s. Much evidence, including some sociological studies, suggests that although the specific forms of protest and cultural alienation faded, a host of 1960s activists carried into the 1970s and beyond the commitment to social justice and the skeptical view of mainstream culture that they had acquired through involvement in civil-rights protests, antiwar marches, and the counterculture. As historians Maurice Isserman and Michael Kazin have written:

> The movements and events of the 1960s generated an attitudinal penumbra that glimmered long after SDS and SNCC had been eclipsed. Chastened by the collapse of "the movement," many pragmatic radicals entered the left wing of the Democratic party, helping transform its stance on foreign policy and producing at least a strong rhetorical commitment to equal rights for all disadvantaged groups. . . . [T]housands of others took up jobs and professions that did not represent a break with their earlier political aspirations. They became social workers, union and community organizers, public school teachers, Legal Services lawyers, or doctors involved in occupational or neighborhood health programs. . . . [M]any former radicals made careers in the "information industry," as academics, journalists, and media specialists.

Thus, although political reaction, cultural exhaustion, and mass-culture escapism compose part of the seventies picture, the decade cannot be so easily pigeonholed. In fact, the early seventies also gave rise to a series of highly significant cultural and social movements, all of them rooted in the sixties. Critic Morris Dickstein observed in *Gates of Eden*, a cultural study published in 1977, "The sixties are over, but they remain the watershed of our recent cultural history; they continue to affect the ambiance of our lives in innumerable ways."

The environmental movement, for example, which rose to prominence in the early seventies, drew strength from the distrust of the rational, technocratic order that had pervaded the New Left and the counterculture. Counterculture theorist Theodore Roszak wrote grandly in 1969, "[Our] primary project . . . is to proclaim a new heaven and a new earth so vast, so marvelous that the inordinate claims of technical expertise must of necessity withdraw to a subordinate and marginal status."

The responses to the moon landing of July 21, 1969, underscored Roszak's point and anticipated some of the environmental movement's central themes. On one level, this culmination of a project launched by John Kennedy stirred the nation's imagination. Television viewers thrilled as cameras recorded astronaut Neil Armstrong's boot touching the lunar surface and his prepared epigram: "That's one small step for [a] man, a giant leap for mankind." Yet the event stimulated less nationalistic jubilation than uneasy reflection on the implications of technoscientific advance. Many observers expressed fears that the achievement would add fuel to America's long infatuation with technology. Others warned that space missions would push the arms race into the heavens. Still others argued that such costly ventures ate up resources better directed to pressing social needs on earth.

Environmentalism and the related theme of energy conservation were not, however, simply extensions of the ideological preoccupations of the 1960s. A series of unsettling trends and events hastened their emergence as urgent public issues. Through World War II, America had produced more oil than it consumed. Yet as the long postwar boom got under way, oil use outran domestic supply, and Americans began to rely heavily on imports and offshore drilling in the Gulf of Mexico and along the Pacific Coast. A stark reminder of the hazards of these operations came in 1969 as leaking rigs in California's Santa Barbara channel turned seawater to oily scum. The accident blackened beaches and killed fish and shorebirds, and outraged

Environmental protest, January 1970. Led by an "Angel of Death" bearing the initials of the Pacific Gas and Electric Company, environmental activists demonstrate against PG&E's plans to run overhead power lines through a park near Oakland, California. (*Ralph Crane/ Life Magazine*, © *Time-Warner*)

the affluent community. TV images of napalmed children in Vietnam gave way to oil-soaked cormorants flapping helplessly on the beach.

A Santa Barbara citizens' group drafted the "Declaration of Environmental Rights" (1970), which became a manifesto of the new movement. Echoing Rachel Carson's *Silent Spring*, the document insisted that Americans accustomed to unlimited natural resources must begin to pay more attention to the environmental cost of their profligate life-style:

> We need an ecological consciousness that recognizes man as member, not master, of the community of living things sharing his environment. . . . We must find the courage to take upon ourselves as individuals responsibility for the welfare of the whole environment. . . . We must redefine "progress" toward an emphasis on long-term quality rather than immediate quantity.

On April 22, 1970, millions of Americans adopted an idea of Senator Gaylord Nelson of Wisconsin and observed the first Earth Day by marching, cleaning up beaches and vacant lots, and attending environmental teach-ins. The high-spirited mood of the day reflected the early naiveté and deceptive harmony of a cause that would prove both divisive and complex, but Earth Day symbolically placed the environment high on the public agenda for the seventies and beyond.

Two measures of 1970 expanded the growing body of environmental law. The Water Quality Improvement Act and the Clean Air Act aimed at purifying the nation's air and waterways after decades of neglect. The latter measure set emissions standards for auto exhausts. That year, President Nixon, attuned as always to issues worrying voters, signed bills creating the Environmental Protection Agency and the Occupational Safety and Health Administration with broad powers to enforce federal environmental and worker-safety regulations.

Nonetheless, the Nixon team viewed environmentalism with suspicion. Interior Secretary Walter Hickel chose Earth Day to approve an eight-hundred-mile Alaska oil pipeline opposed by environmentalists. John Ehrlichman avowed, "Conservation is not the Republican ethic," no doubt making Theodore Roosevelt spin in his grave. On a 1971 Ehrlichman memo lamenting the economic toll of pollution controls, Nixon scribbled, "I completely agree—We have gone overboard on the environment." Seeking a technological quick-fix to energy problems, Nixon pushed nuclear power. The head of the Atomic Energy Commission, Dixie Lee Ray, ridiculed those who questioned nuclear-reactor safety: "We can't live in a Garden of Eden and still have a technological society."

The environmental movement continued to grow, however, influenced not only by oil spills and boycotts but also by the more chronic problems of air and water pollution, shrinking wilderness areas, and the inexorable fact of declining natural resources amid a world population explosion. The media, having idealized a culture of consumption and endless growth in the 1950s, reflected the cultural shift and began to strike a different note. Calls for achieving a "sustainable economy," rather than heedlessly exploiting the world's resources, found a receptive audience. Once a specialized academic field, ecology become a fad. A cynical California politician called it "the political substitute for the word 'mother.'"

Shaped by a culture that had long worshipped technology and boundlessness,

Americans tentatively and uneasily began to envision limits and a less exploitive coexistence with the natural order. Dozens of books—including Barry Commoner's *The Closing Circle* (1971), Frances Lappe's *Diet for a Small Planet* (1971), Paul and Anne Ehrlich's *The End of Affluence* (1974), and E. F. Schumacher's *Small Is Beautiful: Economics as If People Mattered* (1973)—signaled the shift. The new consciousness also propelled the remarkable career of Ralph Nader, the young lawyer who in *Unsafe at Any Speed* (1965) had attacked the U.S. auto industry, especially GM's Chevrolet Corvair, for putting flashy design above safety. Nader's muckraking gave rise to the National Traffic and Motor Vehicle Safety Act of 1966. In the later 1960s and the 1970s, advocacy groups nicknamed "Nader's Raiders" lobbied against dangerous products, ranging from gas pipelines to insecticides and color television sets. In a general scold against corporate wrongdoing, Nader funded his operation in part with money that he won from General Motors in a legal battle.* Thanks to the ascetic, single-minded Nader, many young law-school graduates turned to the field of public advocacy in the 1970s.

While environmental advocates, exploiting the 1960s revulsion against technology, pitched their appeal to all Americans, irrespective of race, gender, or party affiliation, other groups drew inspiration from the civil-rights and Black Power movements in their more narrowly targeted struggles against oppression. Thus, the early seventies also saw a sharp rise in activism by specific groups pursuing their own particular agendas. If the "new ethnicity" phenomenon was largely apolitical, the rising self-consciousness of Native Americans, gays, and feminists found intensely political outlets.

In the late 1960s and early 1970s, a pantribal Native American organization, the American Indian Movement (AIM), took direct action. In 1969 eighty of its members claimed Alcatraz island in San Francisco Bay "by right of discovery." Demanding that Alcatraz become an Indian cultural center, they occupied the island until 1971. In 1972 AIM occupied the Bureau of Indian Affairs in Washington, D.C., charging the government with breaking its treaty obligations. A year later, AIM seized a trading post at Wounded Knee, South Dakota, a site with powerful symbolic resonance for Indians. Here, in 1890, the U.S. Army had massacred three hundred Teton Sioux. After a seventy-one-day siege, the occupation ended. Federal charges against the occupiers of Wounded Knee were dropped in 1974 after it was found that the government had withheld evidence and used illegal wiretaps in building its case.

Native American protests spurred a partial rectification of ancient wrongs. In 1970 the federal government restored forty-eight thousand acres to the Taos Pueblo of New Mexico, including the sacred Blue Lake region taken over by the U.S. Forest Service in 1906. The Alaska Native Land Claims Act (1971) restored 40 million acres to the Eskimos, Aleuts, and other native peoples of Alaska and granted over $960 million to tribal villages and associations in compensation for lands taken when Alaska became a state. In 1972 the federal government transferred to the Yakima Indians of Washington State some twenty-one thousand acres incorporated sixty-four years earlier into the Mount Rainier Forest Reserve. Eight years later, the

---

* GM had hired detectives to spy on him, and Nader had sued for invasion of privacy. GM settled out of court for $425,000.

Native American militancy, June 1971. Young AIM (American Indian Movement) activists remained defiant after federal marshals ended their occupation of Alcatraz Island in San Francisco Bay. (© *Ilka Hartmann/Jeroboam, Inc.*)

Supreme Court upheld a lower-court award of $107 million in damages to the Sioux of South Dakota and endorsed the Sioux claim that the Black Hills had been illegally seized from them during the 1870s gold rush. That same year, Congress granted $81.5 million to the Penobscot, Passamaquoddy, and other tribes of northern Maine in settlement of claims based on Maine's violation of a 1790 statute prohibiting the sale or disposal of Indian lands without the approval of Congress.

The Nixon administration also initiated an important change in the law governing relations between the federal government and the Native American population. In 1953, Congress had ended all federal benefits for Indians as a distinct category of citizens and had abolished the tribes' legal standing under federal law. When the tribes and Indian-advocacy groups protested in the 1960s, Washington modified the termination policy and made tribal governments eligible to participate in anti-poverty and Great Society programs. President Nixon in 1970 urged Congress to abandon the termination policy altogether. Criticizing government paternalism as well, Nixon supported the Indian Self-Determination Act (1974). This law restored the legal status of Indian tribes and granted them authority over federal programs on their reservations. Moreover, it gave tribes more autonomy than before in controlling reservation schools and colleges.

Homosexuals, another group historically subject to discrimination and hostility, had also grown more assertive amid the cultural ferment of the late 1960s. A symbolic turning point came on June 29, 1969, when police raided the Stonewall Inn, a gay bar in Manhattan's Greenwich Village. Homosexuals had tolerated such harassment in the past, but now the patrons resisted, pelting the bluecoats with bottles and stones. Having formerly found precarious security in secrecy and in a shadowy subculture, growing numbers of homosexual men and lesbians "came out of the closet" in the 1970s. Proudly embracing the "Gay Rights" banner, they proclaimed their sexual preference, formed organizations, founded newspapers, and protested legalized discrimination. The National Gay Task Force, founded in 1973, launched campaigns to include homosexuals as a protected class in civil-rights laws barring job or housing discrimination.* Dade County (Miami), Florida, was among the jurisdictions to pass such legislation. Responding to organized pressure, the American Psychiatric Association in 1973 removed homosexuality from the list of mental disorders in its diagnostic manual.

Of all the movements to arise in the wake of the political and cultural upheavals of the sixties, the most sweeping was the new feminism. After winning the vote in 1920, the women's movement had faded. In the 1950s, movies, TV shows, popular magazines, and baby books had all upheld strict gender distinctions: women in the home, men in the workplace; women as emotional and flighty, men as sober and rational; women as sexual prey, men as predators. The ideological demands of the Cold War and the desire to portray American society as harmonious, stable, and conflict free had reinforced these stereotypes. Yet even in the fifties, these polarities bore little resemblance to reality. The percentage of women in the workplace actually rose in the decade, for example, from 32 percent in 1950 to 36 percent in 1960. Instead, the stereotypes expressed the anxieties of a postwar decade seeking stability and traditional values in early marriage, close families, and suburban domesticity.

Betty Friedan's *The Feminine Mystique* (1963), which had sold 1.3 million copies by 1967, boldly challenged these images. A Smith College graduate who had dabbled in freelance writing while performing the expected duties of wife and mother, Friedan voiced the frustrations of many women of her generation as they confronted what she called "the problem that has no name." She wrote, "Each suburban wife struggled with it alone. As she made the beds, shopped for groceries, matched slip-cover material, ate peanut butter sandwiches with her children, chauffeured Cub Scouts and Brownies, lay beside her husband at night—she was afraid to ask of herself the silent question: 'Is this all?'" Friedan hit a nerve. Like a dam breaking, letters poured in releasing a vast reservoir of repressed anger. "I've seen too many women say they would 'do something' when the last children went to school,'" wrote one woman. "The something has usually been bridge, bowling or drinking." *The Feminine Mystique* welded isolated voices of discontent into a movement.

In the early twentieth century, feminists had focused on gaining the vote. Groups like the National League of Women Voters and the Women's International League for Peace and Freedom had concentrated less on women's issues than on social-justice and peace concerns in the 1920s. The new feminism of the 1960s and 1970s, by contrast, more closely resembled the original women's-rights movement of the antebellum era.† Its leaders launched a broad-gauge campaign to eliminate all barriers to full gender equality in American life. In time, the movement would divide

---

* In 1986 the name was changed to the National Gay and Lesbian Task Force.
† The goals of pre–Civil War women's rights advocates such as Elizabeth Cady Stanton included not only the vote but freer access to higher education and the professions, married women's property rights, more equitable divorce laws, and other reforms.

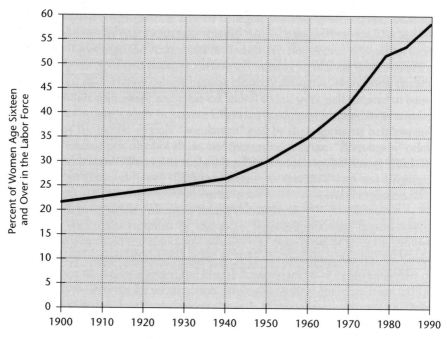

FIGURE 12.1

Women in the Labor Force, 1900–1990

into radical and moderate wings, but this initial phase was characterized by cohesiveness, unity, and confidence. In founding the National Organization for Women in 1966 (see p. 299), Friedan and others dedicated it to "equality of opportunity and freedom of choice" for all women and their "full participation in the mainstream of American society." On the new feminist agenda, NOW made clear, were not only politics but culture, including changes in the mass media's "false images of women" and in the domestic order: "A true partnership between the sexes demands a different concept of marriage, an equitable sharing of the responsibilities of home and children and of the economic burdens of their support." Female discontent, Friedan later wrote, had reached such "subterranean explosive urgency that it took only a few of us . . . to ignite the spark—and it spread like a nuclear chain reaction." By 1977 NOW had sixty-five thousand members. The Women's Political Caucus, founded in 1971, encouraged political activism and lobbied both parties on behalf of women's issues. Despite changes since the 1950s, women still faced massive wage discrimination in the workplace and remained underrepresented in politics, the media, higher education, most professions, and the managerial ranks of business.

The movement gained a sharper, more radical edge as recruits with experience from the civil-rights and antiwar campaigns of the 1960s rushed in. As young women protesting the exploitation of southern blacks or Vietnamese peasants had found themselves exploited by male leaders, their resentment had built. When women delegates at a 1968 radical conference in Chicago were jeered for demanding equal representation, they set out "to organize a movement for women's liberation." Such women soon moved into the vanguard of the reawakened feminist campaign. Challenging the older liberals of NOW (as Black Power advocates were challenging the mainstream civil-rights groups), younger feminists attacked the sexual status quo in new and radical ways. The broader sixties climate of protest and of skepticism toward the Establishment encouraged the questioning of gender roles as well. One antiwar-activist-turned-feminist wrote in 1971, "We have suddenly and shockingly perceived the basic disorder in what has been believed to be the natural order of things." If blacks could attack segregation and college students the military-industrial complex, could not women challenge the assumptions of a male-dominated social order? As Cold War certitudes crumbled in the era of détente, long-accepted assumptions about home-front social structures and hierarchies faced scrutiny as well.

The civil-rights and antiwar campaigns had provided tactics, a vocabulary, and a taste of activism for thousands of protofeminists. After the Mississippi Freedom Summer, one young woman wrote, "I learned a lot of respect for myself for having gone through all that." Movement experience also taught feminists how to attract media attention. They picketed the *Ladies Home Journal* offices just as antiwar protesters had picketed ROTC buildings. At Atlantic City in 1968, they paraded a sheep as Miss America, as the Yippies had nominated a pig for president. Emulating the Berrigans' burning of draft records, they immolated curlers, bras, and high-heeled shoes in "freedom trash cans." Students at Grinnell College in Iowa echoed the southern sit-ins and staged a "nude-in" when a *Playboy* representative visited campus.

Robin Morgan's *Sisterhood Is Powerful* (1970) and Gloria Steinem's *Ms.* magazine (1972) captured the exuberance of a burgeoning and diverse movement. Feminist writers explored issues ranging from wage inequities to media stereotypes to the merits of the clitoral orgasm. Journals such as *Signs* offered feminist explorations of literature, history, and social theory. Feminist theologian Mary Daly challenged patriarchal religion in *The Church and the Second Sex* (1968) and other works. *Our Bodies, Ourselves,* a women's health manual written by eleven women who a few years before had formed a discussion group on "women and their bodies," became a best-seller in 1973, appealing to women who felt infantilized and patronized by the male medical establishment. Rape-crisis centers, battered-women shelters, and feminist "consciousness-raising" groups proliferated.

Reviving a sexual revolution whose origins lay in the 1920s and even earlier in the pre–World War I bohemian culture of Greenwich Village, many young women claimed as their due the sexual freedom long considered an option only for men. Aided by a readily available array of contraceptive methods and access to abortion, they experimented with a variety of partners and postponed long-term commitments. As married women abandoned unsatisfying or constricting relationships, the divorce rate rose from 2.2 per 1,000 population in 1960 to 5.2 in 1980. The nation's lesbian community, emerging from furtive obscurity like its gay counterpart, grew more vocal. By 1976 even the conservative *Reader's Digest* acknowledged, "Women's Liberation has changed the lives of many Americans and thus the way they look at family, job, and sexual equality."

As the *Digest* article suggested, changes in the employment status of women, under way since the fifties, provided the economic context of the new feminist consciousness. Women, married and single, poured into the workplace in the seventies;

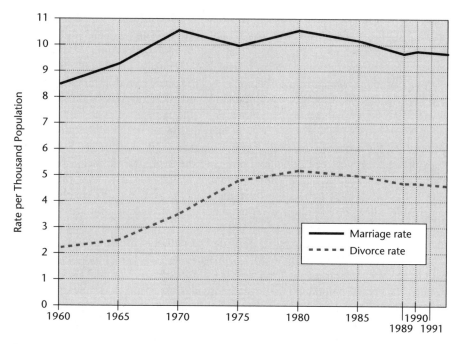

FIGURE 12.2

Marriage and Divorce Rates, 1960–1991

SOURCE: *National Center for Health Statistics.*

the percentage of women who were gainfully employed rose from 44 percent in 1970 to 51 percent by 1980. The reasons were often less ideological than economic. As inflation eroded families' income, many women went to work to make up the gap. The changing patterns of women's work, in turn, affected marriage and birth rates. Numerous young working women chose to remain single, opting instead for relationships of varying duration outside marriage. Many who were married delayed starting a family or chose to have only one or two children. The birthrate dropped steadily from the early sixties through the mid-seventies, when it leveled off. From a postwar peak of 25.3 births per 1,000 population in 1957, the rate fell to 18.4 in 1970 and 14.8 by 1975. Again economic calculations played a role; as the long postwar boom faltered, couples eager to sustain the high standard of living they had become accustomed to limited the number of their offspring.

For many women, these changes opened new possibilities for careers, higher education, and professional training. But the new openness could also stir confusion and uncertainty as marriage and domesticity became only one of many options. And millions of working-class women and those living in inner-city slums remained little affected by the demographic shifts and feminist ferment of these years.

On the political and judicial front, a series of victories for women, following on the Civil Rights Act of 1964, which had banned gender as well as racial discrimination in employment, came with deceptive ease. In 1972 Congress barred gender discrimination in higher education and sent to the states for ratification the equal rights amendment (ERA) to the Constitution outlawing all discrimination on the basis of sex. Within three years, thirty-two states had ratified the amendment, and final approval seemed certain. In 1973 the Equal Employment Opportunity Commission ordered the American Telephone and Telegraph Company to pay millions in back wages to women as well as minority employees to rectify past discrimination. That same year came *Roe* v. *Wade*, the Supreme Court's landmark decision upholding women's constitutional right to abortion.*

In the realm of gender relations, as in thinking about the environment and other issues, the decade of the 1970s became a fertile seedbed of change. Building on the pathbreaking work of Friedan and others in the 1960s, the women's movement challenged long-entrenched assumptions about sexual roles and masculine dominance. By the 1990s, a generation of women would catalyze social changes hardly imaginable in Dwight Eisenhower's America.

Despite the rapid alterations during the seventies, however, gender discrimination and stereotyping continued to pervade the nation's institutions and culture. Working women still found their male colleagues were promoted more rapidly and paid more for comparable jobs. One female insurance broker wrote, "I just had this notion that I could pull myself up by my bootstraps. And my bootstraps kept breaking." In the 1970s, the proportion of women attorneys rose from 3 percent to 13 percent and of women physicians from 7 to 10 percent, evidence of progress but also of the long road to full equality. Gloria Steinem lamented at mid-decade, "We are triumphantly galloping toward tokenism."

TV did portray a bright professional woman on "The Mary Tyler Moore Show," but even she reported to a male boss (played by Ed Asner) whom she invariably addressed as "Mr. Grant." But, this rare exception was more than matched by programs such as "Three's Company" and "Charlie's Angels" featuring sexual innuendo and young women in provocative costumes and situations. Fred Silverman, head of ABC, instructed the producers of "Three's Company" to make the show "the same kind of breakthrough in sexiness that 'All in the Family' was in bigotry." Originally planned to celebrate women professionals, "Charlie's Angels" with its three female detectives quickly degenerated into another exploitation show featuring skimpy outfits and wet T-shirts, inviting what historian James Baughman has aptly called "video voyeurism."

Moreover, recruits to the new women's movement remained overwhelmingly white, middle class, and college educated. While some black and Hispanic women responded, including talented novelists like Alice Walker and Toni Morrison, many remained skeptical or even openly critical and accused white feminists of diverting attention from the more pressing issue of racism. In 1971 the editor of *Essence*, a magazine for black women, called the new feminism "basically a family quarrel between white women and white men." Even this assessment overstated the case. Working-class white women tended to be unsympathetic or even hostile toward the effort. Catholic and evangelical Protestant women who opposed abortion or lesbian-

---

* "Jane Roe" (so-called to protect her privacy) was a Dallas woman who in 1970 brought suit against the district attorney of Dallas County, Texas, an official named Wade, challenging the constitutionality of a Texas statute making it a crime to perform an abortion except to save the life of the mother.

ism on religious or moral grounds bristled when the women's movement welcomed advocates of both into its ranks.

By mid-decade, as we shall see, a backlash against the new feminism would set in. Phyllis Schlafly, a campaigner for Barry Goldwater in 1964, who in the later seventies and eighties would emerge as a major conservative activist, formed a "Stop ERA" organization in 1972. Within the movement, conflict between moderate and radical wings and between lesbians and heterosexual women only worsened tensions. Male uneasiness about the new feminine assertiveness, expressed ironically in Woody Allen's nostalgic *Play It Again Sam* (1972), added fuel to the controversy. In Allen's movie, the Humphrey Bogart character rasps through gritted teeth, "Dames are simple. I never met one who didn't understand a slap in the mouth or a slug from a forty-five." As with the civil-rights movement on which it was patterned, the initial gains of the women's movement opened a hornet's nest of debate, with successes in the legislative and judicial arenas often undermined by rising opposition and resistance in the larger society.

In sum, the seventies, sometimes seen as a decade of reaction and quiescence, actually sustained the cultural revolution of the sixties and propelled it in new directions. The new feminism, the gay-rights movement, Native American activism, and the environmental cause all had their roots in the political and cultural ferment of the sixties. And as in the sixties, this reformist activism aroused hostility in parts of blue-collar and middle-class America. Just as Americans of the late sixties who had no enthusiasm for the Vietnam War still decried the antiwar movement, so citizens who recognized the importance of environmental protection often saw the more outspoken environmental activists as a troublesome fringe movement. Similarly, Americans who agreed in principle that gender discrimination was indefensible reacted with dismay to radical feminism, legalized abortion, and even the rising numbers of women in the workplace. The gay-rights movement stirred especially intense reactions among millions of Americans who found homosexuality personally threatening or offensive to their beliefs. Cumulatively, these movements threatened a familiar and known social order and raised troubling issues. The resulting anxieties often translated into Republican votes and contributed to the climate of reaction that formed part of the political culture of this volatile decade. For the poorer and less well educated, the tension triggered the same kind of class resentments that had surfaced in the late sixties against university-based antiwar activists.

The politics of race also remained central in the 1970s, although in complex and sometimes subtle ways. In contrast to the early civil-rights movement, when the struggle to stop segregation seemed clear and unambiguous and appealed to all people of goodwill, racial issues in the seventies tended to be divisive. The nation remained split between affluent, overwhelmingly white suburbs and poor, largely black and Hispanic inner-city slums, but no Martin Luther King, Jr., or Lyndon Johnson arose to prod the nation's conscience to a renewed crusade against the inequities of American life.

Instead, the nation viewed many of the social issues most worrisome to middle-class and blue-collar Americans—crime, drug abuse, decaying cities, rising rates of teenage pregnancy, soaring welfare costs—as racial in origin rather than as by-products of endemic poverty. Just as native-born Americans of the late nineteenth century had blamed the problems of an industrializing age on immigrant newcomers, so racial and ethnic minorities tended in the 1970s to be held responsible for conditions that were largely beyond their power to control. As we shall see, a racist backlash focused on such volatile issues as school busing gathered steam in parts of white America as the decade wore on. While environmentalists campaigned and educated white women organized, the problem of race festered, provoking fear and uneasiness but little positive action. Maurice Isserman's and Michael Kazin's characterization of the attitude of most middle-class white Americans on racial issues in the 1980s applies equally well to the 1970s: "They have, for the most part, fallen into a puzzled, if not indifferent, silence."

Superficially, a radical disjunction seems to divide the social trends of the seventies and the political history of the decade. With some exceptions, the social ferment of the period found only a feeble response in Washington. In fact, however, the two facets were closely linked. A profound failure of political leadership in these years exacerbated the unfocused and uncertain social mood and nurtured the backlash that would soon arise. Early in Nixon's second term, when the nation and its elected representatives might have begun seriously to address a broad range of domestic issues, America was instead distracted by a political crisis of unprecedented scope. Nixon had taken office promising healing; instead, he thrust the nation into the gravest constitutional crisis it had ever confronted.

Watergate: The Nation in Crisis

The term "Watergate," like "Teapot Dome" from the 1920s, encompasses a complex tangle of events. Although the scandal that forced Richard Nixon's resignation in August 1974 stemmed mainly from criminal activities carried out by the Nixon administration during the 1972 presidential campaign and the subsequent attempts to cover up those crimes, Watergate had far larger sources and implications. The specific actions that brought Nixon to the verge of impeachment in 1974 revealed the no-holds-barred style of politics that he had practiced for years and exposed fundamental flaws in his character. The crisis, in turn, raised questions about the growing power of the executive branch and its accountability, questions that went to the heart of the U.S. system of governance.

The scandal began, appropriately, under cover of darkness. In the early morning hours of June 17, 1972, Frank Wills, nightwatchman at the Watergate apartment complex in Washington, D.C., noticed a door lock taped open. Wills called the police, who arrested five burglars in the offices of the Democratic National Committee (DNC). One intruder was James W. McCord, Jr., a former CIA agent and chief of security for Nixon's campaign organization, the Committee to Reelect the President, headed by Attorney General John Mitchell. (The committee's preferred acronyn was CRP, but the press and public favored CREEP.) The others, Cuban exiles from Miami, had participated in the Bay of Pigs invasion.

The White House and other high administration officials denied any knowledge of what Nixon's press secretary Ron Ziegler pooh-poohed as "a third-rate burglary attempt." Most Americans at first agreed. The incident seemed trivial compared to

Nixon's momentous trips to China and the Soviet Union earlier that year. As the summer wore on, Nixon and his team clung to the story that Watergate was only a bungled "caper" by overzealous underlings, and a few weeks after the incident, John Mitchell, citing family problems, resigned as campaign manager. Mitchell's successor as attorney general, Richard Kleindienst, promised a full Justice Department investigation. Watergate was relegated to the back pages, and the campaign moved forward.

After the disastrous 1968 convention, the Democratic party had adopted sweeping reforms. As one result, the 1972 convention at Miami Beach included delegates from many groups hitherto underrepresented in party affairs: women, young people, blacks, Hispanics, radical activists. The party's traditional power brokers, such as big-city bosses like Mayor Daley, old-line politicians, and union officials, exerted less influence than in earlier conventions. As actress Shirley MacLaine quipped, convention visitors saw more hair and fewer cigars.

One potential candidate, Senator Edward M. Kennedy of Massachusetts, the surviving brother of the famous clan, had been tarred by a nasty scandal three years earlier. In July 1969, a car driven by Kennedy had plunged into Nantucket Sound off Chappaquiddick Island late one night, and Kennedy's young female passenger had drowned. Questions and rumors swirled around the tragedy and its aftermath and scuttled the senator's White House hopes. With Kennedy out of the running, Senator George McGovern of South Dakota, front-runner in the primaries, won a first-

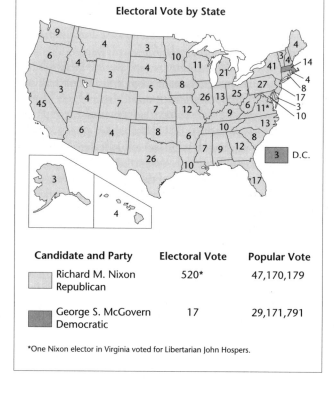

Electoral Vote by State

FIGURE 12.3

Presidential Election of 1972

Candidate and Party	Electoral Vote	Popular Vote
Richard M. Nixon Republican	520*	47,170,179
George S. McGovern Democratic	17	29,171,791

*One Nixon elector in Virginia voted for Libertarian John Hospers.

ballot nomination. A historian and former Methodist minister, McGovern favored immediate U.S. withdrawal from Vietnam, amnesty for Vietnam draft evaders, and broad domestic reforms. The first of McGovern's many problems arose with the revelation that his running mate, Senator Thomas Eagleton of Missouri, had on three occasions received electroshock therapy for depression. Eagleton withdrew, and McGovern, after several top Democrats turned him down, tapped Kennedy brother-in-law R. Sargent Shriver to complete the ticket.

The Republican convention, also in Miami Beach, renominated Nixon and Agnew by acclamation. The party platform opposed school busing and amnesty for draft evaders. Already the strong favorite, Nixon gained additional ground in May when Governor George Wallace, again running as a third-party candidate, was shot by a deranged man at a rally in Maryland and left paralyzed.

Nixon made few appearances and refused to debate McGovern, relying on television ads and on cabinet members and other surrogate speechmakers instead. Election day brought the president a landslide victory: 49 states and 520 electoral votes. McGovern, his support confined mainly to hard-core antiwar and liberal constituencies, carried only Massachusetts and Washington, D.C., for a paltry 17 electoral votes. Nixon garnered 49 million popular votes to McGovern's 29 million, but the president's coattails proved short. Although the Republicans gained thirteen House seats, they remained in the minority, and the Democrats actually picked up two Senate seats. In any showdown, Nixon would face a strongly Democratic Congress. The clash came soon.

Despite the administration's efforts, the Watergate break-in refused to vanish. An address book carried by one of the burglars and confiscated by the police had linked the operation to E. Howard Hunt, who worked for Nixon aide Charles Colson. Also implicated was G. Gordon Liddy, counsel of CREEP's finance committee, headed by former secretary of commerce Maurice Stans. Both Hunt and Liddy had taken part in earlier clandestine operations as members of the White House Plumbers (see p. 350). The FBI quickly traced money in the burglars' possession to CREEP, and bit by bit the sordid story emerged. Hunt and Liddy had planned the burglary, probably on the instructions of John Mitchell and deputy campaign director Jeb Stuart Magruder. In February 1972, Liddy had detailed the plan in a meeting with Mitchell, Magruder, and White House counsel John W. Dean III, who immediately had briefed the White House chief of staff, Bob Haldeman. Some investigators later would become convinced that Nixon had approved the plan in advance. As one surmised, "If Haldeman knew, the President knew."

In an earlier break-in at the DNC late in May, the burglars had photographed documents and tapped the telephones of Lawrence O'Brien, chairman of the DNC, and another Democratic campaign official. The second tap had worked well, and reports on the illegally recorded conversations went to Haldeman. But the O'Brien tap proved faulty, and the CREEP operatives had engineered the June 17 break-in to correct the problem.

Why did the Nixon campaign attempt such a high-risk crime? Some scholars link Watergate to the death of FBI director J. Edgar Hoover in early May 1972. With Nixon's normal channels of political intelligence (via Hoover) disrupted, they theorize, he was forced to improvise. Whatever the validity of this speculation, the immediate context of the break-in came from Nixon's urgent desire to learn how much O'Brien knew about contributions to the Republican campaign by large corporations in exchange for preferential treatment. The president especially feared that the Democrats knew of his shady financial dealings with billionaire Howard Hughes. More broadly, the operation continued a pattern of wiretaps and break-ins initiated by Nixon and Kissinger. As we have seen, John Ehrlichman had recruited the Plumbers in 1971 to track down leaks and to unearth damaging information on administration critics such as Daniel Ellsberg. Watergate, in short, was only part of a web of criminal activity spun in the Oval Office.

In mid-September 1972, a grand jury indicted the five burglars, together with Hunt and Liddy. The trial was scheduled for early 1973 before U.S. district court judge John Sirica. In late September, Bob Woodward and Carl Bernstein of the *Washington Post*, still pursuing the story, revealed that Mitchell, as attorney general, had managed a secret fund intended to gather damaging information on Nixon's political enemies and potential challengers. They also uncovered another fund targeted at sabotaging Democratic presidential hopefuls in the primaries by forging letters, planting spies, stealing campaign plans, and feeding false information to the media. According to the *Post*, Nixon's appointments secretary, Dwight Chapin, had a direct role in planning these illegal "dirty tricks."

The White House indignantly denied all the charges and accused Woodward and Bernstein of irresponsible journalism. Outside Washington, however, the Watergate break-in and the accusations appearing in the *Post* roused little interest. McGovern denounced the Nixon White House as "the most corrupt administration in history," but most voters dismissed the charge as campaign hyperbole. In November, Nixon won his smashing victory.

Despite Nixon's outward calm, the Watergate arrests had set off panic bells in the White House and triggered a massive effort by the president and his aides to conceal their complicity in the Hunt-Liddy operation and other crimes. John Dean, hinting vaguely that CIA security matters were involved, pressured L. Patrick Gray III, whom Nixon had appointed acting director of the FBI, to curb the FBI's Watergate investigation and to transfer FBI records in the case to Dean. Haldeman, drawing on a secret fund that he kept in his White House safe, gave $400,000 in cash to an intermediary for transfer to the seven Watergate defendants to ensure their silence about the role of CREEP and the White House in the break-in. Jeb Stuart Magruder perjured himself before the grand jury about his and Mitchell's links to the burglary. Other White House staffers lied to the FBI, to the grand jury, to Judge Sirica, and to the press.

In January 1973, the trial of the Watergate Seven began in Judge Sirica's court. A suspicious Sirica grilled witnesses sharply. Five defendants pleaded guilty; the two who asked for jury trials were convicted as well. Living up to his nickname "Maximum John," Sirica threatened the defendants with long prison terms unless they told what they knew. In late March, as Sirica sentenced the men, he read an explosive letter from James McCord revealing that the White House had paid him off and had promised him a pardon if he kept quiet. An outraged Sirica called for further investigation.

On another front, Patrick Gray, testifying in February before the Senate Judiciary Committee on his nomination as permanent FBI director, had revealed that John Dean had attended FBI interviews and had examined FBI files relating to Watergate. That month, the Senate also created the Special Committee on Presidential Campaign Activities to investigate the spreading scandal. Seventy-seven-year-old Sam Ervin, Democrat from North Carolina, chaired the committee. On March 21, John Dean warned Nixon, "We have a cancer—within, close to the Presidency, that's growing. It's growing daily. It's compounding, it grows geometrically."

Nixon counterattacked on April 30. Claiming that he had only just learned the full story of the burglary and the cover-up, he blamed everything on John Dean, whom he coldly dismissed. With lavish praise for his two top aides, he also announced the departure of chief of staff Haldeman and adviser John Ehrlichman. All earlier White House statements about Watergate, instructed press secretary Ziegler, were now "inoperative." Nixon then replaced Attorney General Kleindienst with Elliot Richardson, a Boston Brahmin of sterling reputation. On May 18, under instructions from the embattled Nixon, Richardson chose Archibald Cox, a law professor at Harvard, as a special prosecutor with broad powers to investigate the Watergate matter, to subpoena witnesses, and to bring charges. Two investigations were thus under way: the special prosecutor's, which could lead to criminal prosecution, and the Ervin Committee's, which could pave the way for impeachment.

On May 11, in still another twist, a California federal judge, W. Matthew Byrne, Jr., had dismissed all charges against Daniel Ellsberg in the Pentagon Papers case. In the course of this trial, Hunt's and Liddy's break-in at the office of Ellsberg's psychiatrist had come to the light. The press also reported that, during the trial, John Ehrlichman had dangled before Judge Byrne the prospect of the FBI directorship in what seemed like a bribe for an Ellsberg conviction.

The Ervin Committee began televised hearings on May 17. For six months, Americans watched fascinated as a parade of witnesses gradually uncovered the crimes and plots hatched in the Nixon White House. The craggy, beetle-browed Senator Ervin, who ingenuously referred to himself as a "simple country lawyer," possessed impressive constitutional expertise and a razor-sharp mind. Inexorably, the investigation circled closer to the Oval Office. Jeb Magruder now conceded that he and John Mitchell had helped to plan the break-in. Nixon lawyer Herbert Kalmbach admitted that he had raised $220,000 for the Watergate defendants and had managed a half-million-dollar fund earmarked for sabotage and espionage against Democrats. Mitchell, now in serious jeopardy himself, gave a fuller view of what he called the "White House horrors." Furious over Nixon's making him the fall guy, John Dean testified volubly against his former boss and White House colleagues. In key revelations late in June, Dean claimed that Nixon himself had directed the cover-up from the start. Dean's assertions, along with statements in the press, made clear that Watergate was only part of a pattern of illegal and unethical activities carried out at the president's initiative against politicians, journalists, and others on the president's "Enemies List." In an August 1971 memo to Ehrlichman on how the White House could use "the available federal machinery to screw our political enemies," Dean himself had outlined a campaign of wiretaps, tax audits, and other forms of harassment.

Charles Colson, another master of political chicanery, orchestrated the activities of E. Howard Hunt and the White House Plumbers. Hunt's tasks even included forging State Department cables to make it appear that President John Kennedy had ordered the murder of Ngo Dien Diem in 1963. The aim was to damage Senator Edward Kennedy, whom Nixon feared as a potential rival. Senator Ervin found especially heinous this assault on the memory of a man "sleeping in the tongueless silence of the dreamless dust for nine years."

The criminal goings-on, including the Watergate payoffs, together with legitimate campaign expenses, had been financed by a vast pool of cash raised from corporate contributors in return for promises or hints of special treatment. The International Telephone and Telegraph Corporation, for example, paid much of the cost of the 1972 Republican convention after Nixon apparently intervened to help ITT in a 1971 antitrust case. The dairy industry contributed hugely to the Nixon campaign after the president backed higher price supports for milk. In a similar case, John Mitchell and Maurice Stans were indicted on charges of soliciting a campaign gift of $200,000 from financier Robert Vesco in return for intervening on Vesco's behalf in a case pending before the Securities and Exchange Commission. (A jury acquitted Mitchell and Stans of this charge in April 1974.) The seamy record extended to Nixon's personal finances as well. Prodded by a report in the *Providence [R.I.] Journal*, a congressional tax committee found that Nixon owed some $475,000 in back taxes and interest for 1969–1972. The president's tax returns revealed a pattern of questionable deductions, including wildly inflated valuations placed on presidential papers contributed to the National Archives. Nixon would haggle with the government for years about his tax liability.

The Watergate scandal had broadened incredibly, but only Dean's testimony linked Nixon to criminal activity. Republican Senator Howard Baker of Tennessee asked the key question that became the leitmotiv of the Ervin hearings: "What did the President know, and when did he know it?" On July 16, 1973, Nixon aide Alexander Butterfield unexpectedly opened a way to answer Baker's fateful query. Nixon, testified Butterfield, had secretly tape-recorded all conversations held in the Oval Office. This testimony raised the possibility that direct evidence might tie Nixon to the cover-up.

The Ervin Committee and special prosecutor Cox demanded that Nixon release the relevant tapes, but the president refused, invoking national security and "executive privilege." Instead, he proposed a compromise: he would provide summaries of the requested tapes, and their accuracy would be verified by Senator John Stennis (D., Mississippi), seventy-two years old, deeply conservative, and partially deaf. Cox rejected this offer.

On Saturday, October 20, after Cox had secured a court order for the release of the tapes, Nixon instructed Attorney General Richardson to fire the prosecutor. Richardson refused, and resigned. Deputy Attorney General William Ruckelshaus also refused. He too was fired. Finally, the third-ranking Justice Department official, Solicitor General Robert Bork, signed the order dismissing Cox. With this action, Richardson later wrote, Nixon abused his power "more blatantly than at any other stage in the whole sordid history of Watergate. A government of laws was on the verge of becoming a government of one man."

The public reaction to Watergate had built slowly. Nixon's politics appealed to millions of Americans, he had compiled an impressive diplomatic record, and in November 1972 he had won an overwhelming mandate for a second term. But the erosion of his popular support was ominously steady. In this context, the "Saturday Night Massacre" precipitated an uproar. Impeachment demands mounted, and protest calls swamped the White House. Automobile horns blared around the White House, where picketers' signs urged, "Honk for Impeachment." On NBC-TV, John Chancellor declared solemnly, "The country tonight is in the midst of what may be the most serious constitutional crisis in its history." Under heavy pressure, the president appointed a new special prosecutor, Leon Jaworski. A Houston lawyer and former president of the American Bar Association, Jaworski was a friend of Lyndon Johnson and other prominent Texas Democrats, but he had supported Nixon in 1972.

Watergate now dominated the media. Woodward and Bernstein of the *Post* relied heavily on an unnamed informant whom they nicknamed "Deep Throat." One plausible theory holds that "Deep Throat" was an FBI official upset by Nixon's compromising of the Bureau's integrity.*

Compounding Nixon's troubles, Vice President Spiro Agnew resigned in October 1973 after a grand jury found that he had accepted bribes from construction companies while governor of Maryland and as vice president. In a negotiated settlement, Agnew pleaded *nolo contendere*—"I do not wish to contest," in effect a guilty plea—to a single tax-evasion charge. In exchange for the government's agreement not to prosecute, Agnew paid a $10,000 fine and received a three-year suspended sentence. As provided by the recently enacted Twenty-fifth Amendment, Nixon nominated as Agnew's successor House Minority Leader Gerald R. Ford, who won quick confirmation by the Senate and House.

Stories circulated of Nixon's heavy drinking. During the tense days of the October 1973 Yom Kippur War, Henry Kissinger took control. Even the decision to declare DEFCON III, the high state of nuclear alert, was made by Kissinger, Secretary of Defense James Schlesinger, and a handful of other officials at a midnight White House meeting as Nixon slept.

On November 12, 1973, a year after his stunning electoral victory, *Time* magazine called on Nixon to resign. Pressed at a gathering of newspaper editors to discuss his tax problems and other matters, the president finally exploded, "I am not a crook!" As Nixon's approval rating sank to 27 percent, the sharpest one-year drop for any other president since polling began in the 1930s, political columnist Elizabeth Drew described him as "running and maneuvering like a hunted man." In a defiant State of the Union address on January 30, he declared, "One year of Watergate is enough. . . . I have no intention . . . of ever walking away from the job that the people elected me to do."

Even as Nixon battled on, however, the House Judiciary Committee under chairman Peter Rodino (D., New Jersey) was gathering evidence of presidential wrongdoing—a first step toward impeachment. For the first time since 1868, the

---

* A twentieth-anniversary program on Watergate by the CBS-TV show "Sixty Minutes" in 1992 suggested that the FBI's L. Patrick Gray was probably Deep Throat. Alexander Haig, Nixon's chief of staff, has also been suggested.

Democracy in the streets. Clad in prison garb and sporting a Nixon mask, a demonstrator in Washington, D.C. made his views clear as the Watergate cover-up unraveled. (*AP/Wide World Photos*)

removal of a president by Congress seemed a real possibility.* In February 1974, by an ominous 410–4 vote, the House granted the Judiciary Committee full subpoena powers to pursue its investigations.

On March 1, a grand jury in Judge Sirica's court indicted Haldeman, Ehrlichman, Mitchell, four other former White House and CREEP staff members, and "other persons known and unknown" for conspiracy to obstruct justice. The charges included wiretapping, destroying documents, promising executive clemency, paying hush money, and lying to investigators. The indictments relied heavily on the testimony of John Dean, who had pleaded guilty to a single conspiracy charge and was cooperating with the grand jury. A few days later, Sirica turned over to the Judiciary Committee the grand jury's sealed report naming Nixon as an "unindicted co-conspirator" in the cover-up.

On a swing through the Midwest and South to shore up support, Nixon met mostly hostile crowds. Republican candidates in the upcoming midterm election distanced themselves from the president. A White House endorsement would be "the kiss of death," warned one. Even Vice President Ford told an audience of Republican faithful, "The political lesson of Watergate is this. Never again must America allow

---

* The impeachment powers of Congress, involving an initial finding by the House of Representatives and trial in the Senate, with removal from office by a two-thirds vote of the Senate, are grounded in Articles I and II of the Constitution, which set out the procedures for removing a president, vice president, or other civil officers "on Impeachment for, and Conviction of, Treason, Bribery, or other high Crimes and Misdemeanors."

an arrogant, elite guard of political adolescents like CREEP to bypass the regular party organization and dictate the terms of a national election."

On May 9, 1974, the Judiciary Committee began formal impeachment hearings. In mid-June, to divert attention from Watergate, Nixon toured the Middle East. A million people cheered him in a Cairo motorcade, but back home, Watergate, not the president's travels, dominated the headlines. A trip to Moscow at the end of June, which should have been a diplomatic triumph, now seemed a diversion from the domestic crisis. Kissinger found Nixon "preoccupied and withdrawn." Adding to the strain, Nixon suffered a flare-up of phlebitis: painful inflammation of veins in the legs which can lead to fatal blood clots. The release of the Ervin Committee's devastating final report in early July, a veritable catalog of presidential wrongdoing, brought impeachment yet another step closer.

Meanwhile, the tussle over the tapes had continued. In late November 1973, Nixon had turned over to special prosecutor Jaworski some recordings that convinced Jaworski of Nixon's complicity in criminal activities. The tape for June 20, 1972, three days after the break-in, contained a gap of eighteen and a half minutes. Nixon's secretary, Rose Mary Woods, loyally claimed to have erased this section inadvertently while answering the telephone. Alexander Haig, Haldeman's successor as White House chief of staff, blamed some "sinister force of energy." Most Watergate scholars hold Nixon himself responsible.

In April, Sirica ordered Nixon to give tapes of sixty-four post-Watergate conversations to Jaworski. Instead, Nixon released his own edited version of forty-two taped conversations, with many cuts and alterations. In one conversation, for example, he proposes "to get off the cover-up line." In the Judiciary Committee's later version of the same tape, the words are, "to get on with the cover-up plan." Nixon entirely edited out his order to John Mitchell on March 22, 1973: "I don't give a shit what happens. I want you to stonewall it, let them plead the Fifth Amendment, cover-up or anything else."

Even these doctored transcripts revealed the low tone of the Nixon White House, with participants spending long hours hatching plots against Nixon's many "enemies." The words "expletive deleted" recur repeatedly, adding another phrase to the lexicon of Watergate.* The collapse of Nixon's reputation, and with it the prestige of the presidency, wrought deep dismay. In a typical editorial, the Republican *Omaha World-Herald* deplored "the appallingly low level of political morality in the White House." Watergate, coupled with a 15 percent inflation rate, was devastating public morale.

On May 20, Judge Sirica again ordered Nixon to release the tapes subpoenaed by Jaworski. This time, Nixon's lawyers appealed Sirica's order to the Supreme Court. Still stonewalling, Nixon in June wrote to House Judiciary chairman Peter Rodino and U.S. district judge Gerhard Gesell that he alone would decide what

---

* Many of the expletives were mild words like "damn" and "hell," common in numerous people's everyday speech. As Nixon's biographer Stephen Ambrose points out, Nixon's private conversation was far freer of obscenity and vulgarity than Kennedy's, Johnson's, or even Eisenhower's. But the "expletive deleted" phrase allowed the public to imagine much worse.

evidence he would release, even under judicial or congressional subpoena.* The *New Yorker* wrote, "The President's two letters . . . are not just one more set of legal arguments. They are briefs against Constitutional government. They are a proposal for a new form of government, in which a President, once elected, is beyond restraint." On July 24, in *United States* v. *Nixon*, Chief Justice Warren Burger read the Supreme Court's unanimous ruling: Nixon must obey Sirica's subpoena and turn over the tapes. Although the Court noted Nixon's national-security claims, it held that the tapes contained vital evidence and must be released in the interests of "criminal justice." That same day, the House Judiciary Committee began six days of debate on the impeachment resolutions. Upwards of 35 million Americans followed the mesmerizing drama on TV or radio. Committee member Barbara Jordan, a black congresswoman from Texas, declared, "My faith in the Constitution is whole, it is complete, it is total, and I am not going to sit here and be an idle spectator to the diminution, the subversion, the destruction of the Constitution."

On July 27, the Judiciary Committee approved, 27–11, the first article of impeachment, charging Nixon with obstruction of justice in his attempt to delay and impede the Watergate investigation and to "cover up, conceal, and protect those responsible." In committing these deeds, the article concluded, Nixon had "acted in a manner contrary to his trust as President and subversive of constitutional government, to the great prejudice of the cause of law and justice and to the manifest injury of the people of the United States." All twenty-one Democrats and six of the seventeen Republicans voted for this article. Two further articles, approved a few days later, cited Nixon's use of the FBI, Internal Revenue Service, and CIA to abuse "the constitutional rights of citizens" and his defiance of a congressional subpoena to release the tapes. The committee voted down two additional articles of impeachment. One accused Nixon of violating Congress's warmaking powers with his secret bombing of Cambodia; the other accused him of demeaning the presidency by his handling of his personal finances, a reference to his massive underpayment of his federal income taxes.

Now came the final scene. On August 6, after a TV speech again justifying his withholding of the tapes, Nixon released them. Here at last was the "smoking gun": conclusive proof of Nixon's direct role in the criminal obstruction of justice. On the tape for June 23, 1972, Haldeman explains Dean's scheme to Nixon: the White House, citing "national security," will instruct the CIA to tell the FBI to halt its Watergate investigation. Nixon replies:

> All right. Fine. . . . You open that scab there's a hell of a lot of things and . . . we just feel that it would be very detrimental to have this thing go any further. . . . Play it tough. That's the way they [our enemies] play it and that's the way we are going to play it. . . . Don't lie to them to the extent to say there is no involvement, but just say this is sort of a comedy of errors, bizarre, without getting into it. . . . [The CIA] should call the FBI in and say that we wish for the country, don't go any further into this case, period!

---

* Gesell had ordered release of the tapes as evidence in a separate case involving the prosecution of John Ehrlichman and Charles Colson for their role in planning the break-in at the office of Daniel Ellsberg's psychiatrist.

The March 21, 1973, tape, in which Nixon approved paying more hush money to E. Howard Hunt in response to Hunt's blackmail threat, proved damaging as well, especially given that Hunt received $75,000 in cash a few hours later. In other tapes, Nixon urged his aides to lie to the grand jury—for example, "You can say I don't remember. You can say I can't recall. I can't give any answer to that that I can recall."

In early August, even before Nixon released the tapes, 66 percent of the American people had favored impeachment. With the tapes' release, public opinion against the president took a harsher turn. Even Nixon's last-ditch supporters now jumped ship. At a meeting of Republican senators on August 6, Senator Barry Goldwater growled, "There are only so many lies you can take and now there has been one too many. Nixon should get his ass out of the White House—today!" On August 7, GOP congressional leaders confirmed to Nixon that impeachment and removal from office appeared certain. In the White House solarium that evening, Nixon relayed his decision to his family.

On August 8, Nixon announced his resignation in a television address. Quitting was "abhorrent," he admitted, but having lost his "political base in the Congress," he had determined to step down. Obliquely apologizing for "any injuries that may have been done in the course of the events that led to this decision," he referred to Watergate only briefly and instead recited his foreign-policy triumphs. Defiant to the end, he conceded no wrongdoing and expressed no regret for damage done to the nation's constitutional fabric. The next day, after Nixon's emotional, and somewhat incoherent, farewell to his staff, he and Pat boarded a helicopter for the first leg of their flight to California. In his inaugural address, Gerald Ford declared, "Our long national nightmare is over."

CONCLUSION

Nixon's reputation fell into deep eclipse following his resignation, worsened rather than salvaged by President Ford's unconditional pardon of him a month later. But his amazing ability to bounce back remained intact. Slowly easing into the role of elder statesman, he revisited the scenes of his foreign triumphs and wrote extensively on global politics. His self-exculpatory memoirs appeared in 1978. By 1992, the twentieth anniversary of Watergate, Nixon would regain a degree of grudging public respect. His favorite bird, someone quipped, must be the phoenix.

Historians remain wary. Although they praise aspects of Nixon's record—détente, SALT I, certain domestic initiatives—they remind younger Americans who do not remember Watergate how brazenly he flouted the rule of law. Earlier presidential scandals, such as the Whiskey Ring of the 1870s and Teapot Dome of the 1920s, had involved the all-too-human motive of greed. Watergate entailed deliberate and far more sinister abuses, carried out over years, that revealed contempt for the U.S. Constitution and for citizens' most basic rights.

The political and constitutional crisis of 1972–1974—the gravest that the nation had faced since the Civil War—arose from the intersection of long-term trends and Nixon's own character. Since Franklin Roosevelt's day, if not Theodore

Roosevelt's, the executive branch had steadily expanded in size and power. The FBI wiretap on Martin Luther King, Jr., authorized by Robert Kennedy, the escalation of the Vietnam War secretly planned by Johnson and his advisers, the clandestine bombing of Cambodia by Nixon and Kissinger, and other abuses of presidential power all paved the way for Watergate. Nixon did point out accurately that every president since Franklin Roosevelt had authorized wiretaps. Lyndon Johnson, in fact, had approved a wiretap on Nixon's campaign plane in 1968.

But in the Nixon White House, isolated improprieties became commonplace. On the world stage, Nixon and Kissinger had operated at a rarefied level as they reshaped global alignments. Such power can breed a kind of megalomania, in which one feels exempt from the rules that govern others. In Nixon's case, the headiness of power combined in volatile ways with the paranoid streak in his character. Although he held the world's most important office, psychologically he remained the suspicious outsider, seeing shadowy enemies everywhere who had to be destroyed before they ruined him. This outlook elicited precisely the hostility that Nixon imagined. "Opponents are savage destroyers, haters," he reminded himself early in 1974. "[Their] whole purpose . . . is to discredit, destroy, harass everybody around the President." He reacted instinctively: "Time to use full power of the President to fight overwhelming forces arrayed against us."

From his early days in politics, Nixon had conducted underhanded campaigns. Moreover, he had attracted fanatically loyal aides who shared his suspicious nature and his compulsion not merely to defeat but to annihilate the opposition. This pattern led inexorably to the illegalities, abuses of power, and obstruction of justice that climaxed in Watergate. The post-Watergate conspiracy, which Nixon orchestrated "from day one," as a bitter Bob Haldeman later conceded, reflected Nixon's lifetime record. To him, Watergate was simply another eye-gouging, no-holds-barred vendetta of the kind that punctuated his entire political career. In superpower diplomacy, his ruthlessness and penchant for intrigue at times served him well; in the domestic arena, these traits proved fatal.

After Nixon resigned, editorial writers sighed in relief that "the system worked," and Americans rejoiced that the rule of law had prevailed. But the outcome was by no means certain. Congress had responded with much uncertainty and temporizing. Only amid bouts of indecision and paralysis did the legislative branch move ponderously toward impeachment. In the last analysis, it was Nixon's own engrained habits of distrust and deceit, symbolized by his secret taping of even his closest advisers, that undid him. As the conspirators turned on each other in panic, the whole skein of illegality unraveled. Historian Stanley Kutler writes, "Lies became the quicksand that engulfed Nixon, estranged him from his natural political allies, and eventually snapped the fragile bond of trust . . . that binds government and the people."

"The system worked," but Watergate revealed its vulnerability to those who will stop at nothing in their pursuit of power. Many observers at the time believed that Watergate had permanently crippled the presidency. "Make no mistake," warned a Judiciary Committee member as the hearings closed, ". . . our action here will . . . reduce the influence and power of the Office of the President." And, indeed, Nixon's immediate successors did inherit a much diminished office.

"The system worked," but Nixon's resignation offered no guarantee that it would survive another challenge by an even more ruthless successor. The Iran-contra scandal of the Reagan years (see Chapter 14) would offer a salutary reminder that no single crisis, even one as searing as Watergate, could grant permanent immunity against constitutional abuses by powerful officials operating out of the public eye.

"The system worked," but at a high price. For over a year, Watergate had obscured other urgent issues. In October 1973, ending a long journal entry about the Saturday Night Massacre, Elizabeth Drew noted, "It is announced on the radio that Saudi Arabia has cut off its oil supplies to the United States. Can't think about that now." In the long run, Watergate weakened the public's confidence in government further. Like Hiroshima, the Kennedy assassination, and the Vietnam War, Watergate haunts the nation with its legacy of unanswered questions—not only concerning its details but, more profoundly, about the vulnerability of a constitutional system too often taken for granted.

Watergate tainted scores of lives and derailed numerous careers. More than seventy persons were eventually convicted or pleaded guilty for their role in the scandal. Bob Haldeman, John Ehrlichman, and John Mitchell each served a year and a half in jail. White House aides Charles Colson, John Dean, and E. Howard Hunt; Nixon lawyer Herbert Kalmbach; Egil Krogh, Jr., of the White House Plumbers; and CREEP officials G. Gordon Liddy, James McCord, and Jeb Stuart Magruder also went to prison. Liddy served the longest term, from January 1973 to September 1977.

Henry Kissinger's judgment on his former comrade in détente was harsh: "In destroying himself, Nixon had wrecked the lives of almost all who had come into contact with him." Nixon's darker side brought out the worst in others. John Ehrlichman confessed to Judge Sirica, "I abdicated my moral judgments and turned them over to someone else." More serious than the personal toll was Nixon's assault on the fabric of American government. That the fabric endured—however precariously one can never be sure—testifies to the farsighted wisdom of an earlier and finer group of American statesmen.

SELECTED READINGS

Popular Culture and Reform in 1970s America

Lois Banner, *Women in Modern America* (1984); James L. Baughman, *The Republic of Mass Culture* (1992); Sally Bedell, *Up the Tube: Prime-Time TV and the Silverman Years* (1981); Mary Francis Berry, *Why the ERA Failed* (1986); Janet Boles, *The Politics of the Equal Rights Amendment* (1979); Peter N. Carroll, *It Seemed Like Nothing Happened: America in the 1970s* (1982); William H. Chafe, *Women and Equality: Changing Patterns in American Culture* (1977) and *The Paradox of Change: American Women in the 20th Century* (1991); Barbara Deckard, *The Women's Movement: Political, Socioeconomic, and Psychological Issues* (1983); Martin Duberman, *Stonewall* (1993); Alice Echols, *Daring to Be Bad: Radical Feminism in America, 1967–1975* (1989); Thomas Byrne Edsall with Mary D. Edsall, *Chain Reaction: The Impact of Race, Rights, and Taxes on American Politics* (1991); John D'Emilio, *Sexual Politics, Sexual Communities: The Making of a Homosexual Minority in the United States, 1940–1970* (1983) and, with Estelle B. Freedman, *Intimate Matters: A History of Sexuality in the United States* (1988); Sara Evans, *Personal Politics: The Roots of Women's Liberation in the Civil Rights Movement and* the New Left (1978); Jo Freeman, *The Politics of Women's Liberation* (1975); S. David Freeman, *Energy: The New Era* (1974); David J. Garrow, *Liberty and Sexuality: The Right to Privacy and the Making of Roe v. Wade* (1994); Todd Gitlin, *The Sixties: Years of Hope, Days of Rage* (1987) and *Inside Prime Time* (1985); Susan M. Hartmann, *From Margin to Mainstream: American Women and Politics Since 1960* (1989); Samuel Hays, *Beauty, Health, and Permanence: Environmental Politics in the United States, 1955–1985* (1987); Joan Hoff-Wilson, *Rites of Passage: The Past and Future of the ERA* (1986); Bell Hooks, *Ain't I a Woman? Black Women and Feminism* (1981); Maurice Isserman and Michael Kazin, "The Failure and Success of the New Radicalism," in Steve Fraser and Gary Gerstle, eds., *The Rise and Fall of the New Deal Order, 1930– 1980* (1989); Carolyn Johnson, *Sexual Power: Feminism and the Family in America* (1992); Jonathan Katz, *Gay American History: Lesbians and Gay Men in the U.S.A.: A Documentary History* (1992); Alice Kessler-Harris, *Out to Work: A History of Wage-Earning Women in the United States* (1982); Christopher Lasch, *The Culture of Narcissism* (1979); Kristin Luker, *Abortion and the Politics of Motherhood* (1984); Charles McCarry, *Citizen Nader* (1972); Eric Marcus, *Making History: The Struggle for Gay and Lesbian Equal Rights, 1945–1990* (1992); Donald G. Mathews and Jane S. De Hart, *Sex, Gender, and the Politics of ERA* (1990); Martin V. Melosi, *Coping with Abundance: Energy and Environment in Industrial America* (1985); Carolyn Merchant, *Major Problems in American Environmental History: Documents and Essays* (1993); Michael Novak, *The Rise of the Unmeltable Ethnics* (1972); Barbara Hill Rigney, *The Voices of Toni Morrison* (1991); Leigh W. Rutledge, *The Gay Decades: From Stonewall to the Present* (1992); Allan Schnaiberg, *The Environment: From Surplus to Scarcity* (1980); Peter Schrag, *The Decline of the WASP* (1971); Edwin Schur, *The Awareness Trap: Self-Absorption Instead of Social Change* (1976); Randy Shilts, *Conduct Unbecoming: Gays and Lesbians in the U.S. Military* (1993); Robert Sklar, *Prime-Time America: Life on and Behind the Television Screen* (1980); Melissa Walker, *Down from the Mountaintop: Black Women's Novels in the Wake of the Civil Rights Movement, 1966–1989* (1991); Winifred D. Wandersee, *On the Move: American Women in the 1970s* (1988); James D. Woods with Jay H. Lucas, *The Corporate Closet: The Professional Lives of Gay Men in America* (1993); Donald Worster, *The Wealth of Nature: Environmental History and the Ecological Imagination* (1993).

Watergate

Stephen E. Ambrose, *Nixon* (1987); Charles Colson, *Born Again* (1976); Congressional Quarterly, *Watergate: Chronology of a Crisis* (2 vols., 1973–1974); John W. Dean III, *Blind Ambition: The White House Years* (1976); James Doyle, *Not Above the Law: The Battles of Watergate Prosecutors Cox and Jaworski* (1977); John Ehrlichman, *Witness to Power* (1982); H. R. Haldeman, *The Ends of Power* (1978); Jim Houghan, *Secret Agenda: Watergate, Deep Throat, and the CIA* (1984); Leon Jaworski, *The Right and the Power: The Prosecution of Watergate* (1976); Stanley I. Kutler, *The Wars of Watergate: The Last Crisis of Richard Nixon* (1990); J. Anthony Lucas, *Nightmare: The Underside of the Nixon Years* (1976); Jeb Stuart Magruder, *An American Life: One Man's Road to Watergate* (1974); New York Times, *White House Transcripts* (1974); Richard Oudes, ed., *From the President: Richard Nixon's Secret Files* (1989); Jonathan Schell, *The Time of Illusion* (1975) and *Observing the Nixon Years* (1989); Arthur M. Schlesinger, Jr., *The Imperial Presidency* (1973); Peter Schrag, *Test of Loyalty: Daniel Ellsberg and the Rituals of Secret Government* (1974); John J. Sirica, *To Set the Record Straight* (1979); Fred D. Thompson, *At That Point in Time: The Inside Story of the Senate Watergate Committee* (1975); Bob Woodward and Carl Bernstein, *All the President's Men* (1974) and *The Final Days* (1976).

Part Four

UNCERTAIN TRIUMPH

The contemporary era of American history, from Watergate to the present, has seen profound social and economic changes and a radically altered international picture. These years have also witnessed a dramatic swing in the political pendulum, from conservatism to a cautious liberalism tempered by public suspicion of government. Richard Nixon's forced exit from the White House intensified this revulsion against Washington. However, the roots of the antigovernment mood lay deeper, in middle America's resentment of the Vietnam debacle, a costly welfare system, school busing, federal affirmative-action programs, and conflict over abortion and other issues. Inflation and other economic problems have only exacerbated middle-class anxieties and the reactionary spirit. The immediate beneficiary of these discontents, Washington outsider Jimmy Carter, rode the antiestablishment wave to the White House in 1976. But Carter's feat did not translate into a successful administration, and by 1980 his popularity would sink to its nadir. Carter's failure arose both from personal flaws and from factors largely beyond his control; in addition to runaway inflation and soaring energy costs, a humiliating hostage crisis in Iran plagued the unfortunate president.

Carter's ineffectual term accelerated the electorate's rightward shift. Ronald Reagan, former actor, ex-governor of California, and well-known champion of conservative causes, capitalized on the insurgent mood. Reagan's program, featuring laissez faire and Cold War militance, as well as a rollback of big government and the welfare state, won support from an electorate in full flight from New Deal/Fair Deal/Great Society–style liberalism. The "Reagan revolution" brought big tax cuts that especially benefited the wealthy, and deregulation of key sectors of the economy. Slashes in social programs and massive increases in military spending rounded out the new president's agenda. With inflation under control and the affluent profiting from favorable tax and regulatory policies, the decade saw a glow of prosperity. Giddy real-estate speculation and a wave of high-stakes corporate takeovers marked the Reagan years. Yet even as acquisitiveness and conspicuous consumption set the tone, festering economic and social problems warned of problems ahead.

The political coalition that elected Reagan in 1980 and 1984 survived long enough to send heir-apparent George Bush to the White House in 1988. But Bush had neither Reagan's charisma nor his clear-cut domestic agenda, and his administration drifted despite military exploits in the Persian Gulf that earned him a brief spurt of popularity. Amid a stubborn recession, the Reagan movement ultimately ran out of steam. Ironically, many of the obstacles that dogged the Bush presidency stemmed from the Reagan legacy. The recession, soaring federal deficits, the savings-and-loan crisis, and urban unrest that scourged America after 1988 all arose as unintended by-products of the Reagan revolution.

With the election of 1992, the baby boomers, now well into midlife, elevated one of their own—Bill Clinton—to the White House. Clinton shared the key ideological allegiances of many members of this generation, including feminism and environmentalism. Indeed, he appointed women to key posts, and he assigned his wife, Hillary Rodham Clinton, a central role in shaping health-care policy. His vice president, Senator Al Gore, had written a book much admired by environmentalists.

Reclaiming the White House for the Democrats after the Reagan-Bush ascendancy, Clinton focused on domestic issues. Although he had inherited the liberal tradition, postsixties conservatism remained strong, and he reflected the changed political climate. The new president spoke for a chastened party intent on winning back "Reagan Democrats." Mindful of the anti-incumbency mood and of worries about federal spending expressed in Ross Perot's third-party candidacy in 1992, Clinton focused initially on deficit reduction. He criticized the welfare system and urged federal spending cuts and reduction in the number of federal employees. Clinton further established his credentials as a "new Democrat" by calling for economic-growth measures that would stimulate the private sector, not supplant it, and by proposing a health-care plan that combined public and private components.

Clinton faced a number of economic and social challenges that seemed likely to dominate U.S. politics well into the twenty-first century: the gargantuan national debt, brutal trade competition, runaway health-care expenses, the rising cost of welfare and entitlement programs, and the social impact of post–Cold War cuts in military spending. The enormous task of uplifting an urban underclass trapped in welfare dependence remained urgent as well. Millions in the inner cities, along with blue-collar workers displaced by the industrial decline of these years, found themselves marginalized in an emerging high-tech economy that required fewer and more highly trained workers.

As the presidents of 1973–1992 came and went, the United States endured social and economic shifts that would shape U.S. history in the twenty-first century. American society grew increasingly multiracial and multiethnic, and gender roles, family structure, and even sexual identity seemed fluid and variable. The political system, the cultural arena, and social institutions all bent before the winds of such change. On the economic front, an agrarian society that had evolved into the world's industrial leader experienced an equally profound transformation. As the old industrial base eroded, a new economic order based on global markets, electronic data processing, the delivery of services, and the transmittal of knowledge and information began to emerge. Simultaneously, a new world of mass entertainment based on futuristic electronic technologies and vast corporate conglomerates loomed. While visionaries hailed these developments, others nervously pointed to the social and cultural tensions and economic hardship that seemed destined to mark the transition to the brave new world.

The closing decades of the twentieth century brought world changes that were no less dramatic. The Cold War, which had shadowed so much of American history since 1945, ended abruptly in the late 1980s as the Soviet empire collapsed, a victim of unremitting competition with the West and its own debilitating weaknesses. The United States now confronted a freshly complex globe in which the forces of consolidation and of disintegration warred for ascendancy. Islamic fundamentalism in the Middle East; ethnic conflicts in Eastern Europe; famine and feuding clans in East Africa; and the longer-term scourges of poverty, illiteracy, overpopulation, and environmental deterioration all clamored for attention. By the mid-1990s, a long cycle of American history that had begun with the victory celebrations of 1945 drew to a close. As the year 2000 approaches, the contours of a new era, one marked by urgent challenges both at home and abroad, are coming into focus.

Chapter Thirteen

PICKING UP THE PIECES:
POST-WATERGATE AMERICA

In 1976 the United States threw a year-long party to celebrate the two hundredth anniversary of the American Revolution. The American Revolution Bicentennial Commission sponsored a cornucopia of activities. Citizens in Albany, Georgia, performed a musical honoring the Constitution. The "American Freedom Train," laden with five hundred historic documents and funded by GM and other corporations, toured the nation. A VFW post in Ohio reenacted Washington's crossing of the Delaware. The Smithsonian Institution, with backing from General Foods, sponsored the "Festival of American Folklife." "The Bicentennial Wagon Train Pilgrimage," funded by Gulf Oil Company and supported by sixty thousand volunteers, lumbered across the nation from west to east and encamped at Valley Forge on July 4, 1976. That day, as President Ford delivered inspirational speeches, fireworks burst across the nation and the "tall ships"—a breathtaking flotilla of sailing vessels—entranced New Yorkers.

Despite the hoopla, however, the United States was still unsettled by the aftershocks of an era marked by assassinations, urban riots, and antiwar demonstrations. Watergate, history's worst presidential scandal, had left raw and angry scars. A grave mix of economic problems exacerbated the edgy mood. As energy prices soared, a combination of inflation and recession that journalists dubbed "stagflation" struck, and U.S. industry eroded. Gerald Ford, a Republican, and then Jimmy Carter, a Democrat, left the White House after brief presidencies that brought more frustration than achievement. Moreover, as the country moved sharply to the right both culturally and politically, a reactionary groundswell gained momentum. By 1980 it would startlingly alter the political landscape.

More than 150 years earlier, the German philosopher Georg Friedrich Hegel had written, "America is . . . the land of the future. . . . It is a land of desire for all those who are weary . . . of old Europe." As recently as 1941, the press tycoon Henry Luce had hailed "the American Century." By 1976 such soaring rhetoric was rare. Anxiety, not euphoria, marked the bicentennial year. Sociologist Daniel Bell found a "loss of faith in the nation's future" souring the American mood. The nation's third century, Bell speculated, could well provide "yet another illustration of the trajectory of human illusions." To many Americans, such gloom seemed fully warranted.

A Ford, Not a Lincoln

Watergate left the presidency diminished in prestige and political clout. Gerald Ford, after completing Nixon's second term, would fail to win election in his own right. Ford's Democratic vanquisher, Jimmy Carter, also would serve only one term. With mixed results, both leaders fought a hydra-headed array of economic problems that dominated the late seventies.

Gerald Ford's roots and deepest attachments lay in the "middle America" that Nixon had so avidly courted. His parents divorced when he was an infant, and he was later adopted by his mother's second husband, a Grand Rapids businessman whose name he took. The tall, athletic Ford played football at the University of Michigan, earned a law degree from Yale, and practiced in Grand Rapids. In 1948 he won election to Congress, and in 1965 he became minority leader. With his friendly smile and reputation for honesty, Ford enjoyed wide respect. His integrity and modesty ("I'm a Ford, not a Lincoln") provided refreshing contrast to the scheming Nixon of the Watergate tapes. Ford's wife, Betty, also won praise for her forthright stance in support of abortion rights and the equal rights amendment and for her candor in discussing personal crises such as her mastectomy and, later, her alcoholism.

But Ford's pardon of Richard Nixon in September 1974 "for all offenses against the United States which he . . . has committed or may have committed or taken part in" knocked his approval ratings from 72 to 49 percent. Ford denied that he had struck a bargain with Nixon and argued that an indictment and possible imprisonment of the ex-president would have prolonged the agony of Watergate. But suspicions of an unsavory deal—the executive office for Ford, pardon for Nixon—however unjustified, would shadow his presidency to the end.

Ford showed little of Nixon's openness to innovation in domestic policy. As a congressman he had opposed most of Johnson's Great Society program, and in his first year in office, he vetoed thirty-nine bills passed by the Democratic Congress, including one mandating increased regulation of strip mining. Espousing a 1920s-style laissez-faire ideology, he called for "maximum freedom for private enterprise." In 1974, Ford tellingly vetoed the Freedom of Information Act, which, reflecting the post-Watergate mood, granted citizens access to their government files. Congress promptly overrode his decision. Despite delays and various restrictions, the law ultimately opened the FBI and other agencies to public scrutiny and checked abuses of individual rights.

Ford encountered serious economic problems that had been temporarily eclipsed during Watergate. Inflation ranked first in urgency. Oil prices had risen 350 percent after the 1973 Yom Kippur War, and the 1973–1974 Arab oil boycott had pushed the inflation rate to a horrendous 11 percent in 1974. Taking office amid this price surge, Ford rejected Nixon's ineffective wage-and-price controls and chose a more ideologically congenial voluntarist approach. In the fall of 1974, Ford grandly announced his "Whip Inflation Now" (WIN) program to persuade businesses to re-strain prices voluntarily. When the effort fell flat, Ford himself conceded that it was "probably too gimmicky." With the oil boycott's end, inflation dropped to about 8 percent in 1975 and 5 percent in 1976 (it would spurt upward again in the late 1970s).

Compounding Ford's problems, the worst recession since the Great Depression struck in 1974–1975. As business stagnated, the unemployment rate hit 8.3 percent in 1975. To stimulate recovery, Congress cut taxes by some $23 billion in 1975. The economy rallied, but the tax cut worsened the budget deficit, which in 1976 surged to a new high of $60 billion. This increase, in turn, worsened inflationary pressures. The recession dealt a brutal blow to the nation's cities, already floundering as busi-nesses and middle-class taxpayers fled to the suburbs. By late 1975, New York City edged toward bankruptcy, barely able to meet its payroll or to pay the interest on its bonds. When New Yorkers in Congress proposed a federal bail-out, President Ford refused. "Ford to City: Drop Dead" headlined a Manhattan tabloid. Congress ap-proved emergency loan guarantees, averting the immediate crisis, but urban America's long-term problems would continue to fester.

Exploiting the economic mess, the Democrats devised the "Discomfort Index" by combining the inflation and unemployment rates. From 1972 to 1975, this mea-sure nearly doubled. In the 1974 midterm election, frustrated voters increased the Democratic majority in the House by forty-three seats and in the Senate by four seats. But GOP fiscal mismanagement was not wholly to blame for the recession. True, some of the administration's inflation-fighting measures—spending cuts, the Federal Reserve Board's tightening of credit—had contributed to the problem. How-ever, the downturn also had roots in economic changes (see pp. 420–423) beyond either party's control. Inflation, for example, stemmed mainly from the oil boycott and the resulting price hikes. The initial panic that produced long lines at service stations soon abated, but dismay over gas prices remained. Americans used to paying thirty-five cents for a gallon of gas stared in wide-eyed disbelief as prices edged to-ward seventy cents a gallon. Although gas remained far cheaper in the United States than in Western Europe, the increases shocked a public accustomed to cheap fuel. An added irritant, U.S. oil company profits more than doubled from 1972 to 1974 as domestic oil prices rose along with the cost of imported oil. The impact of soaring gasoline prices became apparent in the Energy Policy and Conservation Act of 1975, when Congress for the first time set fuel-efficiency standards for U.S. automobiles: an average of at least 27.5 miles per gallon by 1985. In a further fuel-saving measure, Congress set a national speed limit of 55 miles an hour, triggering more grumbling from drivers.

In international relations, Ford had a hard act to follow. Under the rubric "Vietnamization," Nixon and Kissinger had halted America's direct combat role in Vietnam. Pursuing détente, they had placed U.S. relations with the Soviet Union and China on a more amicable footing. Ford, after Nixon's abrupt departure, at least had the advantage of continuity in the foreign-policy arena: Henry Kissinger, ap-pointed secretary of state in 1973, remained in that post. But Ford's brief tenure offered few opportunities for major foreign-policy initiatives. In general, he pursued Nixon's policies and handled the consequences of Nixon's actions.

Under Ford, the final scenes of the Vietnam debacle unfolded. The end of overt U.S. military engagement in Southeast Asia had not stopped the fighting in the region. Indeed, the 1973 Paris agreement proved less a peace treaty than a license for the war to proceed without direct U.S. involvement. In fact, when Kissinger and Le Duc Tho jointly received the Nobel Peace Prize for 1973, Le Duc Tho pointed out that peace had not really been achieved, and he rejected his share of the award. America remained very much a player, however. U.S. naval and air power hovered nearby in the Gulf of Tonkin, in Thailand, and on Guam. Thieu's regime hired six thousand hastily discharged U.S. army officers as "civilian" advisers. And Nixon had continued to bomb Cambodia until August 15, 1973, when a congressional ban took effect. After the cease-fire ended U.S. bombing in Vietnam and Laos, Nixon had ordered a hundred additional B-52s to join the bombing raids on Cambodia, in a show of continued support for Thieu. "This was appalling," the secretary of the air force later wrote. "You couldn't even figure out where you were going to put them all. . . . How were you going to base them?"

During this interval, B-52s rained 250,000 tons of bombs on Cambodia's villages, fields, and jungles, ostensibly to destroy Khmer Rouge (Cambodian communist) strongholds. The consequent devastation created two million refugees in a population of seven million and, ironically, hastened the collapse of Lon Nol's U.S.-backed regime. The B-52s and the 1970 invasion had driven the North Vietnamese deeper into Cambodia and exacerbated the country's social and political chaos. In April 1975 the Hanoi-backed Khmer Rouge unseated Lon Nol and launched a reign of genocidal savagery. Before the Vietnamese overthrew the fanatical Khmer Rouge dictator Pol Pot in January 1979, his regime had slaughtered as many as two million people—25 percent of the population. Recounting these events in *Sideshow: Kissinger, Nixon, and the Destruction of Cambodia* (1979), British journalist William Shawcross reached a harsh conclusion about Washington's role: "Cambodia was not a mistake; it was a crime."

In South Vietnam, President Thieu, confident of U.S. support as pledged by Nixon, had refused to cooperate with the Provisional Revolutionary Government, and in 1974 he resumed the war. Without direct U.S. military power to back him, his cause was precarious. Soon after Nixon's resignation in August 1974, Congress rejected Kissinger's urgent request for $1.5 billion in military aid to South Vietnam. This denial crippled the South Vietnam military and ended whatever slim chance Thieu might have had to cling to power a bit longer.

North Vietnamese forces, advancing down the peninsula, built a highway and pipeline from the demilitarized zone to near Saigon and in January 1975 captured Phuoc Long province, north of Saigon. As Thieu abandoned the Central Highlands, Pleiku and Danang fell. The end now came with shocking suddenness. Hué yielded without a fight despite Thieu's order to hold it at all costs. The retreat turned into a rout, at a heavy cost in dead and wounded. In late April, after a three-hour speech on Saigon television denouncing the United States for failing to live up to its pledges, Thieu fled to Taiwan with fifteen tons of luggage.* The U.S. ambassador,

---

* Thieu eventually settled in Great Britain. His vice president, the flamboyant Nguyen Cao Ky, became a prosperous liquor-store operator in California.

Old beyond their years, Cambodian refugee children eye the camera. President Nixon's massive bombing of neutral Cambodia caused many civilian casualties, filled refugee camps, and worsened the nation's political instability. (© *Steve Weinrebe*)

Graham Martin, left Vietnam a few days later. Saigon fell on May 1 and was promptly renamed Ho Chi Minh City. In a final humiliating scene, South Vietnamese who had worked for American officials frantically scrambled aboard helicopters atop the U.S. embassy roof as North Vietnamese forces closed in.

Memories of the Vietnam quagmire would long haunt the American psyche and influence the nation's approach to global politics. On one hand, Americans desperately wished to avoid another Vietnam. On the other, they feared lest the world discount U.S. resolve. In this context, relatively minor incidents took on special significance. For example, in May 1975, when Cambodia's communist regime seized a U.S. merchant vessel, the *Mayaguez*, Ford spurned negotiations and ordered a military rescue by two thousand U.S. Marines based in Thailand. The thirty-nine *Mayaguez* crew members were "rescued"—at a cost of forty-one marines' lives. (In fact, unbeknown to Washington, the Cambodians had released the crewmen before the rescue operation began.) The symbolic value of Ford's macho display just weeks after the hasty evacuation from Saigon was clear. "It was wonderful," crowed hawkish senator Barry Goldwater. "It shows we've still got balls in this country." *Newsweek* hailed Ford's "daring show of nerve and steel." The families of the servicemen who died were left to count the cost of this fleeting boost to American self-esteem.

Yet Vietnam made Americans wary of engaging U.S. power. This reluctance underlay Congress's refusal to sanction U.S. intervention in the African nation of Angola, which became a cockpit of Cold War conflict after gaining its independence from Portugal in 1974. As civil war erupted among Angolan factions, the United States and China backed one group, Moscow another. When the Soviets flew in Cuban troops in 1975, Kissinger proposed clandestine but massive aid to the U.S.-

backed faction. Gripped by the "no more Vietnams" spirit, Congress refused. Kissinger disgustedly concluded that a nation traumatized by Vietnam was embracing isolationism. Other powers, he feared, would assume that Washington had "lost the will to counter adventurism or even to help others to do so." But Kissinger's own prescriptions struck many citizens as the very adventurism that had dragged the nation into the Vietnam quicksand.

Détente, another Nixon legacy, advanced haltingly in the post-Nixon era. At a 1974 meeting in Vladivostok, Siberia, Ford and Soviet leader Leonid Brezhnev made some progress on SALT II, an arms-control treaty intended to follow up the 1972 SALT I treaty. But final agreement eluded them; despite the rhetoric of détente, Cold War suspicions lingered on both sides. Nevertheless, the foreign-policy highlight of the Ford years came with a summit conference at Helsinki in August 1975. At this meeting, the nations of Europe, including the Soviet Union and its satellites, agreed to stabilize their national boundaries and the East-West power balance that had emerged after World War II. Equally important in the long run, they also adopted a set of accords on human rights and freedom of travel. These agreements strengthened the forces of political change behind the Iron Curtain and helped to create the conditions that would end the Cold War fifteen years later. At the time, however, U.S. Cold Warriors and many Americans of Eastern European origin denounced the Helsinki Accords for conceding Soviet hegemony in Eastern Europe.

A Sea of Troubles: The Carter Years

Domestic issues overshadowed foreign affairs in the Ford years, and as the recession dragged on, the 1976 Democratic presidential nomination began to look highly tempting to potential candidates. Aspirants included courtly Senator Lloyd Bentsen of Texas, who had close links to his state's oil industry; Senator Henry Jackson of Washington State (dubbed "the senator from Boeing" for his tireless support of the Seattle aerospace giant); California's maverick governor Jerry Brown, whose penchant for New Age mysticism led TV talk-show host Johnny Carson to dub him "Governor Moonbeam"; and James Earl (Jimmy) Carter, Jr., of Georgia, who had served a term as governor and then returned to the family's peanut business.

Like George McGovern in 1972, Carter benefited from the Democratic party reforms instituted after 1968, which increased the role of state primaries and grassroots activists in the selection of candidates. He also was helped by television, which allowed obscure candidates to win national visibility almost overnight. Supporters of Carter's better-known opponents jeered "Jimmy who?" but he won the Iowa and New Hampshire primaries and soon had the nomination sewn up. As his running mate, he chose Senator Walter Mondale of Minnesota, Hubert Humphrey's heir as leader of the Democratic party's northern liberal wing.

Exploiting post-Watergate suspicions, Carter offered a pledge of simple honesty ("I will never lie to you") that before Nixon would have sounded ridiculous. He struck a populist note as he accepted the nomination in New York's Madison Square Garden. Like Texas billionaire Ross Perot, who would seek the presidency in 1992, Carter announced, "It's time for the people to run the government." In his 1970 gubernatorial campaign, Carter had cultivated the common touch, ridiculing his well-dressed primary opponent, former governor Carl Sanders, as "Cufflinks Carl." A devout Baptist whose sister Ruth Carter Stapleton worked as a full-time evangelist and faith healer, Carter also proudly proclaimed himself a "born-again" Christian who strove to apply his faith in daily life. This open avowal of faith epitomized a larger religious trend that molded American life and politics in the 1970s (see pp. 430–431).

On the Republican side, President Ford withstood a strong challenge by former governor Ronald Reagan of California to win the nomination in his own right. On taking office, Ford had chosen as his vice president former governor Nelson Rockefeller of New York, a leader of the party's liberal eastern wing. For the 1976 campaign, however, the president sought to consolidate his conservative flank. Turning to the party's right wing, he named Senator Robert Dole of Kansas as his running mate.

Carter proved an inept campaigner, and his initial lead faded. In the end, he won a lukewarm 50.1 percent of the popular vote; Ford, 48 percent. The remainder went to minor-party candidates. The stricken economy and Watergate memories, exacerbated by the Nixon pardon, had cost Ford the victory. Both candidates, too, committed gaffes during the campaign. In a TV debate with Carter, Ford inexplicably claimed to see no evidence of Soviet domination of Poland. Carter revealed in

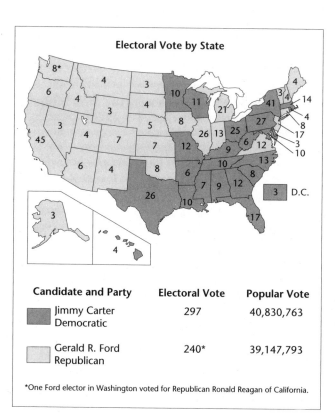

FIGURE 13.1

Presidential Election of 1976

Electoral Vote by State

Candidate and Party	Electoral Vote	Popular Vote
Jimmy Carter Democratic	297	40,830,763
Gerald R. Ford Republican	240*	39,147,793

*One Ford elector in Washington voted for Republican Ronald Reagan of California.

a *Playboy* interview that he had "lusted after women in my heart." As a pro-civil-rights southerner, Carter earned 94 percent of the black vote, providing the margin in thirteen states. The new president retrieved some—although by no means all—of the white working-class voters who had defected to Nixon or Wallace in 1968 and 1972.

The depth of voter alienation in the wake of the Nixon scandals emerged in a sobering statistic: Fewer than 55 percent of those eligible had bothered to cast a ballot. In other words, of the total electorate, a mere 27 percent had voted for Carter. Voter turnout had long been falling, but 1976 marked a low point. Apathy, it seemed, was the true winner in 1976, summed up in a cynical bumper sticker: DON'T VOTE, IT ONLY ENCOURAGES THEM.

On Inauguration Day, highlighting the contrast with Nixon's imperial presidency, a grinning and waving Carter walked in the January cold from the Capitol to the White House with his wife, Rosalynn, and daughter, Amy. Throughout his term, Carter would project a casual image, favoring blue denims and sports shirts and carrying his own garment bag aboard Air Force One. Fulfilling a campaign pledge, he immediately pardoned some ten thousand Vietnam War draft resisters. Veterans' organizations protested, but most Americans welcomed the gesture as a step toward healing the still-raw wounds of a divisive era.

On domestic issues, Carter built a far from negligible record. Honoring a platform promise to the teachers' union, a power in Democratic politics, he created the Department of Education in 1979. (The former Department of Health, Education and Welfare became the Department of Health and Human Services.) His civil-service reform bill, passed in 1978, introduced a merit-pay system and made it easier to fire incompetents, among other changes. At Carter's behest, Congress created a $1.6 billion environmental "Superfund" to clean up the nation's worst chemical pollution sites. The new president set aside over 100 million acres in Alaska, eyed by developers, as parkland, forest reserves, and wildlife areas. In addition, Carter appointed a record number of women and minorities to federal office, including three women cabinet members: Juanita Kreps as secretary of commerce; Patricia Roberts Harris, the former dean at Howard University Law School, as secretary of housing and urban development (and later of the new Department of Health and Human Services); and Judge Shirley Hufstedler as the first secretary of education. Civil-rights veteran Andrew Young became UN ambassador.

Carter's political skills proved deficient, however, and he failed to achieve such major domestic goals as welfare reform and improvement of the underfunded social security system. Additionally, revision of the labyrinthine federal tax code and creation of a national health-insurance system—a liberal objective since Truman's day—went unrealized. Despite Democratic majorities in both houses, his relations with Congress remained prickly. As early as 1977, TV journalist Eric Sevareid commented, "[Carter] has the mind of an engineer. . . . He's got a lot of little filing cabinets in his mind that he seems able to use as needed. But he doesn't seem to have much stylistic change of pace, and I fear he will become less and less stimulating." Happiest when analyzing issues and devising solutions on paper, the president lacked Lyndon Johnson's talent for political dealmaking. No one spoke in awe of any "Carter treatment." The outsider's role that had helped him to win the election also stymied his efforts to work with Congress, the quintessential "insider" institution. Finally, his personality caused problems; beneath the surface affability, he proved aloof and self-righteous. As his popularity fell, he withdrew still more, relying on a tight circle of advisers whom he had brought from Georgia.

Carter's liabilities emerged most starkly as he grappled with the economy. The same problems that had bedeviled Ford—inflation, recession, rising energy costs— haunted Carter as well. In October 1978, with inflation at 9 percent, Carter announced a program of voluntary wage-and-price restraints. But inflation kept spiraling, reaching 13.4 percent in 1979. By 1980 the dollar was worth only forty cents compared to 1967. Unemployment, having declined after 1975, crept up again, reaching 7 percent in 1980, and nearly double that number among black and Hispanic workers. The recession erased the gains of the War on Poverty. By 1978, 29 percent of black families and 23 percent of Hispanic families fell below the poverty line, more than three times the rate for whites.

In a maddening paradox, remedies for one part of the economic crisis worsened another. For example, to fight the recession, Congress, at Carter's request, cut taxes by $34 billion in 1977 and appropriated $4 billion for emergency public-works spending. But the stimulus came too late and only intensified inflationary pressure. Conversely, as the Federal Reserve Board tightened credit—the classic remedy to cool an overheated economy—interest rates soared as high as 20 percent, pushing home mortgages and business loans out of reach of most borrowers and deepening the recession. Carter never unraveled these dilemmas to devise a coherent and comprehensive economic plan.

The president's attempt to resolve energy issues, his top domestic priority, proved equally frustrating. A graduate of the U.S. Naval Academy, he applied his considerable analytic skills to the problem. In April 1977 a sweater-clad Carter sat by an open fire in the White House library and addressed the nation on energy. In a phrase coined by William James, he called the issue the "moral equivalent of war." Soon Congress created the new Department of Energy under the pipe-smoking James Schlesinger, a former secretary of defense, with a mandate to enforce energy legislation and to formulate national energy policy.

Carter sought to force Americans to conserve primarily by raising the cost of energy. Moreover, he aimed to reduce America's foreign oil imports, which grew from 35 percent of total consumption in 1973 to nearly 50 percent—some nine million barrels a day—in 1977. In an energy bill presented before a joint session of Congress two days after his address to the nation, Carter proposed phasing out the price controls that kept the cost of domestic oil and natural gas artificially low, while taxing domestic oil production to prevent windfall profits by oil and gas companies. He also called for stiffer federal taxes on gasoline, tax penalties on cars that violated federal mileage standards, tax credits for conservation measures, and increased use of America's most abundant energy source, coal, although under strict antipollution requirements.

The bill met strong opposition from oil and gas companies, which favored the end of price controls but opposed heavier taxes and federal regulation. Political ideology shaped the debate as well. Conservatives advocated a laissez-faire approach, arguing that easing environmental rules and lifting price controls on oil and natural gas, without corresponding windfall-profits taxes, would encourage drilling for new reserves. Liberals emphasized conservation measures, including higher gasoline taxes and even rationing. They also favored stricter vehicle gas-mileage standards and tax incentives to homeowners to reduce fuel consumption. The energy law that finally passed in October 1978 after long bargaining contained elements of both positions. It lifted price controls on natural gas in phased steps and penalized gas-guzzling cars. It also mandated coal use in new plants and provided tax credits for various energy-saving measures and equipment, including solar power and solar heating units. The law fell short of Carter's dream of a "national energy policy," but it was a step in this direction. The public remained skeptical, however, fearful of higher energy costs and unconvinced that the situation was as dire as Carter claimed.

The energy crisis took on stark new urgency in 1979–1980 when OPEC instituted a second round of hefty price increases. A revolution had unseated Iran's pro-U.S. government, and Iran's new regime, together with the other radical OPEC states of Iraq, Libya, and Algeria, pushed the cartel to raise prices sharply. Soon Saudi Arabian light crude, the industry benchmark, was selling for over thirty dollars a barrel, ten times the pre-1973 price. Long queues again formed at service stations, and gasoline prices broke the dollar-a-gallon barrier. Every home-heating bill and gas-station fill-up was a reminder that the days of cheap and unlimited energy had ended. Rising energy costs rippled through the entire economy, from producing and transporting consumer goods to college tuition and hospital fees. Americans paid over $16 billion in higher prices in these years, directly related to OPEC's price hikes. U.S. oil companies, by contrast, boomed as energy prices rose. The public growled when Exxon, Gulf, Mobil, and the other oil giants again announced soaring profits. Exxon's first-quarter profits in 1980, $1.9 billion, ranked the highest of any corporation in history.

The drive to conserve energy strengthened the environmental movement in some respects, but in other ways the two movements clashed. The nuclear-power industry, for example, promoted this panacea as the obvious way to conserve fossil fuels, cut pollution, and reduce U.S. reliance on imported oil. The industry had a case: utilizing water power, nuclear energy was renewable. Under normal operations, nuclear plants, unlike coal-burning generators, did not pollute. President Carter, who had served aboard nuclear submarines in the navy and often consulted Admiral Hyman Rickover ("the father of the nuclear submarine"), supported this option.

But environmentalists, already dubious about nuclear power because of its military connotations, warned of accidents and the hazards of radioactive-waste disposal. On February 22, 1974, Sam Lovejoy, an antinuclear activist in Montague, Massachusetts, loosened the bolts on a 500-foot tower marking the site of a planned nuclear-power plant. The tower crashed to the ground. Turning himself in, Lovejoy explained his gesture as an act of conscience against a project that he considered dangerous. As the antinuclear movement gathered momentum, led by such groups as New Hampshire's Clamshell Alliance and California's Abalone Alliance, the activist spirit of the 1960s and even the test-ban fervor of the 1950s revived. The 1970s campaign bridged the earlier protests and the nuclear-weapons freeze campaign of the early 1980s (see p. 453).

An accident at the Three Mile Island nuclear power plant near Harrisburg,

Pennsylvania, in March 1979 bore out the critics' warnings. Some 800,000 gallons of radioactive water burst from a cooling unit, threatening the lovely Susquehanna valley and its people with grave hazards. Tension mounted as the crisis unfolded. Jimmy Carter toured the plant, wearing safety gear, to reassure the public, but his toothy grin seemed forced. In a striking convergence of mass culture and reality, the 1979 movie *China Syndrome*, starring the 1960s antiwar activist Jane Fonda, dramatized the kind of accident that had actually occurred a few weeks earlier. Three Mile Island, its impact amplified by the coincidental release of *China Syndrome*, dealt the nuclear-energy industry a heavy blow. In 1979, 71 nuclear plants were operating in the United States, with more than 125 under construction or on order. In the wake of Three Mile Island, more than 30 planned plants were canceled, and new orders fell to zero.

President Carter doggedly pursued his battle for a comprehensive energy policy, targeting the federal price controls that kept domestic oil prices artificially low and that, he believed, encouraged profligate waste of a dwindling resource. Price controls were already scheduled to end in 1981, but in April 1979 Carter announced an immediate, phased decontrol of domestic oil prices. Again he called for a windfall-profits tax on the oil companies, with the revenue to go for public transportation, alternative-energy development, and heating-bill assistance for the poor. Simultaneously he proposed a freeze on imported oil and a multibillion-dollar government program to produce synthetic fuels from coal and shale. Congress took no action on these ideas, and in July the president geared up for yet another energy speech, his fifth.

The public's weariness with Carter's lectures on these complex issues deepened. As he wrote in his memoirs, "My repeated calls for action on energy had become aggravating, and were increasingly falling on deaf ears." Furthermore, his pollster Patrick Caddell convinced him that the basic problem was not public resistance to energy conservation but a more profound crisis of morale and loss of confidence in Carter himself. This conversation led to one of the more unusual episodes in the history of the presidency. Abruptly canceling his scheduled speech, Carter retreated to Camp David with Rosalynn and a few close advisers for ten days of brainstorming about his and the nation's problems. Some 130 men and women from various walks of life were shuttled in and out to conduct a kind of rolling seminar for one student: the president of the United States. As Carter and his wife scribbled notes, economists, preachers, journalists, and academics offered their opinions.

After the retreat, Carter gave his postponed speech, which he now used to explain his diagnosis of a national "malaise." Underlying America's inability to solve its energy problems, he insisted, was "a moral and spiritual crisis, . . . a loss of a unity of purpose." In phrases redolent of the pulpit, the president upbraided Americans for abandoning the old values:

> In a nation that was proud of hard work, strong families, close-knit communities, and our faith in God, too many of us now tend to worship self-indulgence and consumption. Human identity is no longer defined by what one does, but by what one owns. But we've discovered that owning things and consuming things does not satisfy our longing for meaning. We've learned that piling up material goods cannot fill the emptiness of lives which have no confidence or purpose.

Citing Vietnam, Watergate, inflation, and other reasons for this loss of civic spirit in the body politic, Carter conceded, "The gap between our citizens and our Government has never been so wide." Nevertheless, he ended on a cautiously hopeful note:

> There are two paths to choose. One is . . . the path that leads to fragmentation and self-interest. Down that road lies a mistaken idea of freedom, the right to grasp for ourselves some advantage over others. . . . All the traditions of our past, all the lessons of our heritage, all the promises of our future point to another path, the path of common purpose and the restoration of American values.

Many agreed that the nation suffered from a failure of nerve, often blamed on the psychic aftershock of Vietnam, which one observer compared to Great Britain's loss of empire. Opinion polls showed disturbing increases in feelings of alienation and powerlessness. Although Jimmy Carter was hardly the first chief executive to urge a renewal of national purpose, people had wearied of White House sermonizing. In fact, Americans castigated Carter himself for what they saw as a failure of leadership and a tendency to blame others for his own deficiencies. The president's firing of three cabinet members after his "malaise" speech and the resignation of two others highlighted this pattern of blame shifting. The fact that Energy Secretary Schlesinger and HEW Secretary Joseph Califano were among those dismissed underscored Carter's failure to resolve the problems to which he himself had given top priority.

Defining energy policy as the test of whether "we can seize control again of our national destiny," Carter sent to Congress a ten-year, $140-billion energy plan that encompassed research on synthetic fuels, higher oil and natural-gas taxes, and tougher automobile fuel-efficiency standards. Except for funding synthetic-fuel research and imposing a windfall-profits tax on oil companies, Congress once more took little action. Carter's four-year battle for a national energy policy had produced a few victories, much acrimony, and many frustrating setbacks.

By 1979 nearly 75 percent of the American people disapproved of Carter's performance. Even Nixon at his lowest point had escaped such abysmal ratings. At the *Boston Globe*, a joke title for an editorial on a Carter speech accidentally was printed: "More Mush from the Wimp." In August 1980, as domestic problems and the Iranian hostage crisis (see p. 439) battered the White House, journalist Hugh Sidey of *Time* magazine, while conceding that most Americans still admired Carter as a person, offered a harsh judgment of his performance as president:

> Carter is today a political cripple both at home and abroad because the larger issues have swamped him. . . . In his own inexperience and uncertainty, the President could not define a mission for his Government, a purpose for the country, [or] a means of getting there. . . . Carter's mind fixed on the small parts of the effort and not the whole.

No one doubted Carter's honesty, brilliance, or sense of duty, but he lacked key traits that make a successful president. Not blessed with the oratorical power of a Franklin Roosevelt, the charisma of a Jack Kennedy, the manipulative genius of a Johnson, or even the cynical opportunism of a Nixon, Carter gamely soldiered on in the face of deepening disapproval. After Johnson's and Nixon's involuntary departures and Ford's caretaker term, yet another failed presidency loomed.

But the tangle of economic problems confronting the nation in the late seventies could well have mastered even the ablest leader. No American president had the power, short of war, to stop OPEC's jacking up of world oil prices, the driving force behind the inflationary spiral. Adding to the economic conundrum, the baby-boom generation continued to flood the job market. In fact, the U.S. economy generated more than 26 million new jobs in the seventies, but the rising tide of job seekers only pushed unemployment rates upward. The combination of recession and inflation also made devising a coherent economic policy virtually impossible. The classic Keynesian solution to recession, adopted by both Democrats and Republicans in the postwar years, featured increased federal spending, tax cuts, and eased credit to stimulate recovery. As economists James Buchanan and Richard Wagner pointed out in *Democracy in Deficit* (1977), however, these measures made money and credit more plentiful and hence worsened inflation. Thus, the Carter administration vacillated between potential strategies.

Moreover, as always in politics, lobbying by different interest groups complicated decisionmaking. These pressures increased, ironically, in response to the campaign finance law of 1974. This post-Watergate reform measure provided for public financing of presidential campaigns through a check-off system on federal income-tax forms but permitted political-action committees (PACs) to contribute up to five thousand dollars to any one candidate. The law did not limit the number of PACs, and in the late 1970s they proliferated. By contributing to an array of PACs, a corporation or lobbying group could multiply its influence with a candidate. By 1980, the number of PACs approached three thousand, each a bulging political cash-cow promoting its particular legislative agenda. Union PACs, for example, blamed unemployment on imports and called for higher tariffs and trade restrictions. Business PACs, on the other hand, took advantage of the recession to launch a general assault on federal regulation of business. Carter reacted by deregulating the airline, barge, trucking, and railroad industries and persuading Congress to ease banking controls, thereby launching a wave of deregulation that President Reagan would pursue enthusiastically in the 1980s.

Conservative critics also blamed the nation's economic woes on the social-welfare system. Massive welfare spending, they charged, fed the federal deficits, which in turn worsened the recession. The critics had a point. Social-welfare spending, although proportionately modest when compared to that of Sweden and other Western democracies, did climb sharply in the 1970s. Adjusted for inflation, social-security payments rose by 131 percent during the decade. Public assistance, including welfare, jumped by 47 percent, the food-stamp program by 546 percent, Medicaid and other medical services by 186 percent, and on down the list. Overall, this sector of the federal budget, adjusted for inflation, more than doubled from 1970 to 1979, when it accounted for a whopping 61.7 percent of the total budget.

This trend placed enormous strains on the economy. As entitlement programs like social security and Medicare expanded and as welfare costs mounted with the deepening recession, the federal deficit ballooned. The government borrowed money to cover the shortfall and to service the public debt—the legacy of past deficits—and commercial interest rates multiplied under the resultant credit squeeze. Rising interest rates in turn inhibited home buying, consumer credit buying, and business borrowing for expansion. Only the boldest professed to have answers to the worsening dilemmas.

An Economy in Crisis

Beneath the inflation and unemployment that helped to torpedo Carter's presidency lay deeper, more ominous trends. The nation's industrial infrastructure, based in gritty midwestern cities such as Pittsburgh, Buffalo, Cleveland, Dayton, and Detroit, was crumbling. Cleveland made unwelcome history in 1978 by becoming the first U.S. city since the 1930s to default on its bonds. One by one, plagued by foreign competition, aging equipment, rising labor costs, and shifting consumer tastes, the mills and factories that had made America the world's industrial leader from the 1880s through World War II closed their gates. Journalists labeled the region the "Rust Belt." With the decline of basic industries, union membership fell. In 1970 about 28 percent of the nonagricultural labor force was unionized; by 1980 the figure had dropped to 23 percent. The erosion of organized labor in turn weakened a central prop of the Democratic party and contributed to the conservative drift of American politics in the 1970s.

The two core industries, automobiles and steel, typified the broader trend. In the 1950s and 1960s, U.S. automakers had ruled the domestic market. True, the Volkswagen "Beetle," an ungainly German import, had sold 4 million units by 1970, and other imports were edging into the market as well, but as late as 1970, the Big Three—General Motors, Ford, and Chrysler—still accounted for 89 percent of U.S. auto sales. All this changed in the seventies. With gasoline prices soaring and buying power eroded by inflation, car buyers welcomed affordable, more fuel-efficient im-

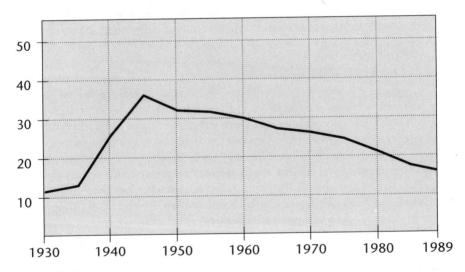

FIGURE 13.2

Percent of Labor Force Belonging to Unions, 1930–1989

SOURCE: Bureau of Labor Statistics.

ports like Japan's Toyota and Datsun. Ad campaigns stressing economy—summed up in the stark slogan "Datsun Saves"—challenged Detroit's traditional emphasis on glamor and style. Detroit, geared toward producing bulky six-passenger sedans, failed to convert in time, and its market drifted away. By 1980 imports had grabbed 34 percent of the U.S. auto market. The United States now imported 3.2 million foreign cars annually, about 60 percent of them from Japan. U.S. auto exports rose as well in the decade, but not enough to counterbalance the deluge of imports. Detroit's automotive giants, once America's pride, seemed to have become lumbering dinosaurs, stalked by wilier, hungrier, faster predators.

As the decade ended, conditions worsened. GM sank into the red in 1980 for the first time since 1921. Ford lost $1.2 billion that year. The weakest of the Big Three, Chrysler, hemorrhaging millions each month, slid toward bankruptcy. Only $1.5 billion in federal loan guarantees in 1980 saved Chrysler from immediate disaster.* The Chrysler bailout was orchestrated by the company's chairman, brash Lee Iacocca, whose campaign for federal aid illustrated how quickly laissez-faire ideology can fade when corporate survival is at stake. He later wrote, "[T]he last thing in the world I wanted to do was turn to the government. . . . I've always been a free enterpriser, a believer in survival of the fittest. Once the decision was made, however, I went at it with all flags flying."

Troubles in the auto industry aggravated the recession. GM, Ford, and Chrysler, employing 98 percent of U.S. autoworkers, laid off more than 225,000 workers in 1974 alone. Additional thousands faced lengthy "temporary leaves." Skilled workers in their peak earning years anticipating a comfortable retirement found themselves haunting employment offices instead. As the auto industry sickened, so, too, did an army of subsidiary suppliers of everything from steel bodies to tires, windows, and spark plugs. With 17 percent of the U.S. labor force directly linked to the auto industry, Detroit's problems rippled across the entire economy.

The steel industry, bedrock of America's industrial might since Andrew Carnegie's day, presented a similarly bleak picture. In earlier times, the great Bessemer converters and open-hearth mills of Pittsburgh, Youngstown, Wheeling, and other steel towns, using ore from Minnesota and abundant coal and coke, had provided jobs for millions of hard-working immigrants. As late as 1950, the annual output of U.S. steel mills stood at 97 million tons—nearly half the world's total. But change loomed. In 1959, with the steel industry plagued by a long strike involving a dispute over work rules, steel imports exceeded exports for the first time in the century. By 1980 U.S. steel output accounted for only 14 percent of total world production. In that year the Soviet Union, Japan, and the European Community (the twelve-nation consortium of nations forming in many respects a common economic bloc) all exceeded the United States in steel production, with Canada and even Brazil offering strong challenges as well. An industry dominated by the United States since the 1880s was faltering badly. In once-thriving steel centers, hulking mills stood dark and empty.

Although steel's decline had connections to the auto industry's troubles, the

---

* The controversial bailout worked. Chrysler returned to profitability in 1982 and the following year repaid the loans in full, including $23.4 million in interest to the federal government.

crisis went deeper, reflecting management's failure to adapt to new technologies. The 1950s had seen two key innovations in steelmaking. The first, the basic oxygen furnace, replaced the far less efficient open-hearth system. The second employed new technologies to produce steel in continuous sheets rather than in separate ingots. Foreign steelmakers such as Japan's giant Nippon Steel embraced these innovations at once, abandoning old mills and building new ones. The U.S. steel industry, by contrast, heavily invested in older mills, resisted the new technology. As late as 1963, not one of the six top U.S. steel companies possessed the more modern furnace. By 1980 Japan could make a ton of steel for one-third less than it cost U.S. producers. Even more telling, a congressional study that year found that Japanese steel companies plowed twice as much of their profits back into research and development as did U.S. companies.

The U.S. companies' behavior represented a departure from the boldness that had once characterized American steelmakers. Carnegie had never hesitated to adopt new equipment and more efficient methods. "Well, what shall we throw away this year?" he once demanded of his directors. Instead of emulating Carnegie and investing in technologies that might pay off years in the future, post–World War II steelmakers, answerable to dividend-hungry stockholders, maximized short-run profits. Buoyed by Cold War military spending, they counted on a ceaseless flow of Pentagon contracts. Furthermore, despite the myth of open competition, the U.S. steel industry was in fact a largely noncompetitive oligopoly of big companies, each with its established market share, charging uniform prices. This arrangement also discouraged innovation. American steel, once on the cutting edge of change, had grown fat and lethargic.

Although the faltering auto and steel industries told their own dramatic stories, statistics on overall U.S. productivity (that is, output per man- or woman-hour of work) proved revealing as well. During the long postwar boom from 1947 to the mid-1960s, the United States enjoyed average annual productivity increases of 3.2 percent. From 1965 to 1973, however, productivity growth averaged only 2.4 percent annually, a one-third drop from the earlier period. In the problem-plagued 1970s, the rate of increase slowed still more, and by 1978–1980, productivity was declining in absolute terms. At the same time, wage raises for unionized workers, often tied to inflation-driven cost-of-living increases, far outstripped productivity.

In explaining declining productivity, analysts reflected their ideological bias. Conservatives wrung their hands over government regulations, soaring worker-benefit packages, the eroding work ethic, and an indolent, overpaid unionized labor force. Liberals stressed management failures, short-term profit-taking, inadequate schools and job-training programs, and the lack of a governmental strategy for nurturing new technologies. But whatever their ideology, most analysts pinpointed anemic investment in research and development as a key problem. Not only the steel industry but many other corporations shied away from the costly long-term research investment essential to better productivity, instead pouring millions into advertising and stockholder dividends. Meanwhile, competitors abroad invested heavily in basic research and technological innovation.

As U.S. productivity flattened and even declined, that of the nation's trade competitors surged. This was especially the case in Japan and West Germany, the World War II foes whose economies, ironically, had rebounded with American aid.

In 1980 Toyota produced five times as many cars per worker as did Detroit auto-makers. As foreign-made products flooded in, U.S. imports far outran exports. The 1971 trade deficit, the first since 1888, amounted to $2.3 billion. By 1981 the figure had climbed to $28 billion; soon it would rise far higher. Not only cars but television sets, appliances, shoes, clothing, and countless other products now increasingly came from abroad, a shift that severely undercut U.S. manufacturers.

America's economic difficulties during the seventies must be kept in perspec-tive. Inflation and budget deficits, for example, plagued Western Europe as well. The U.S. economy remained the world's largest, and although unemployment persisted, the labor force grew by millions of workers in the 1970s. And while the trade gap widened with the surge of imports, U.S. exports more than doubled in the decade, from $158 billion to $343 billion—a hefty increase, even taking inflation into ac-count. For all its problems, America still enjoyed a standard of living that was the envy of the rest of the world.

Several analysts saw an economy not in decline but in transition. In any dy-namic economy, they pointed out, some sectors erode as others expand. They noted U.S. dominance in aerospace, electronics, information-processing, and other high-tech fields, and the success of companies such as Rochester's Xerox Corporation, a leader in the burgeoning photocopying industry. Other optimists singled out the computer field as a beacon of promise for the future. The earliest computers, called mainframes, were bulky and expensive, affordable only by the government and the largest corporations. IBM's 360 series, introduced in 1965 after a $5 billion develop-ment program, set the new standard for mainframes. Miniaturization came in the 1970s, transforming the industry. First, tiny, efficient transistors replaced bulky vac-uum tubes. Then sophisticated integrated circuitry made possible desktop computers as powerful as the behemoths of a decade earlier. By the mid-1970s, as computer sales edged upward, more and more people found employment in the growing industry, especially near Boston and San Francisco.

Personal-computer (PC) sales took off as the decade ended. In 1976 two college dropouts in Cupertino, California—Steven Jobs and Stephen Wozniak—built a pro-totype in the Jobs's family garage. (Like Henry Ford tinkering in his garage in the 1890s, the story would become the stuff of legend.) After selling early models to local hobbyists, Jobs and Wozniak founded Apple Computers in 1977. The company caught on at once; sales soared to $7.8 million in 1978 and $117.9 million by 1980. The "Cupertino comet" made *Fortune* magazine's list of the nation's top 500 corpo-rations faster than any other company in history. IBM introduced its first PC in 1981, and other companies rushed into the market. The computer revolution that would reshape American life in the eighties and beyond was under way.

Thus, while the Rust Belt languished, signs of renewal cropped up elsewhere. As the industrial work force fell, jobs in the service sector increased, attracting men as well as women flocking into the workplace. To a degree, of course, this shift simply continued a well-established trend. Each decade since 1900 had seen increases in the service-sector work force and corresponding declines in the percentage of farmers, manual laborers, factory operatives, and other blue-collar workers. But this long-term trend accelerated in the 1970s as basic industries declined. As economist Jona-than Hughes has observed, the United States of 1980 more closely resembled the middle-class consumer-and-service society portrayed in Edward Bellamy's 1888 utopian novel *Looking Backward* than it did Karl Marx's vision of a vast industrial proletariat mired in misery.

The service sector was broad, however, and those entering it did not necessarily rise in status. To be sure, this category included doctors, lawyers, executives, and other white-collar workers. But it also comprised the low-status, semiskilled jobs: janitorial labor, domestic service, car washing, supermarket check-out, restaurant and fast-food work, and so on. Such positions required little training and paid far less than unionized jobs in industry. Some laid-off factory workers found new jobs only by taking a sharp income cut in the lower ranks of the service sector. Economists, identifying an emerging long-term problem, spoke of the "de-skilling" of the work force. Other analysts warned of a bimodal labor force with highly paid white-collar professionals at one end, unskilled service workers (often minorities and recent immigrants) at the other, and little in between. For better or worse, the economic trends of the 1970s offered a preview of the future. Presidents Ford and Carter, unfortunately for them, were the first to confront the seismic changes transforming the economic landscape.

The economy thus presented a mixed picture, of bright spots amid disturbing trends, in the 1970s. While the southwestern oil belt, the necklace of high-tech industries encircling Boston, and California's "Silicon Valley"* boomed, the industrial heartland stagnated. Although the system absorbed many new workers, others remained jobless or underemployed. In the inner cities, minority youths seemed permanently frozen out of an economy that demanded not only a willingness to work but specialized skills and advanced education.

Hovering over the economy was the grim quartet of vultures that we have already met: recession, inflation, a growing trade gap, and a mushrooming federal deficit. With billions going for defense and for mandated entitlement programs at a time of depressed revenues, the deficit soared from $8.7 billion in 1970 to a whopping $72.7 billion in 1980. By the decade's end, the total federal debt approached $1 trillion. Carter's 1976 pledge to balance the federal budget by 1980 had become a bitter joke as his term ended. Worse lay ahead, but in the seventies the flood tide of federal red ink was already rising ominously.

To many, the nation's best years lay in the past, and the good times of the fifties seemed gone forever. Eighty years after historian Frederick Jackson Turner had explored the meaning of the closing of the geographic frontier, the end of the industrial frontier and the can-do spirit associated with it seemed at hand. Worry and resentments rooted in economic problems increasingly infiltrated the cultural and political climate as the seventies wore on.

Backlash: Culture and Politics in the Later Seventies

The 1970s was a paradoxical decade that defies easy categorization, for divergent and seemingly contradictory trends unfolded simultaneously. Self-absorbed narcissism,

---

* The nickname came from the silicon chip, a key component in the new integrated circuitry that made possible the miniaturized personal computer.

for example, coexisted alongside restlessly churning activist energies. Environmentalism, feminism, gay-rights protests, and other movements remained strong, even winning legislative and legal victories, yet the public as a whole turned steadily to the right. Amid the conflicting crosscurrents, one overall trend emerged with clarity: The liberalism that had peaked in 1964–1965 inexorably lost support, a development that laid the groundwork for a conservative triumph in the late seventies.

Tom Wolfe's "Me Generation" continued to be characterized by narcissistic self-absorption, which Christopher Lasch, writing in 1979, saw as the decade's key trend. "Americans have retreated to purely personal preoccupations," Lasch announced. Faced with Nixon's disgrace, intractable economic problems, and lackluster performances by Ford and Carter, many Americans gave up on politics and civic engagement. Like Candide at the end of Voltaire's novel, they cultivated their own gardens instead. The years following the Civil War, World War I, and World War II had all witnessed a turn from public to private concerns, and the aftermath of Vietnam brought a similar reaction.

The evidence for this shift was everywhere. Escapist novels like Erich Segal's *Love Story* (1970) and Peter Benchley's *Jaws* (1974) spawned hit movies. Baby boomers "gentrified" decaying urban neighborhoods, creating islands of trendy sophistication amid inner-city blight. A jogging fad swept the middle class, inspiring a 1978 *Newsweek* story that began with the Whitmanesque line, "I hear America puffing." James Fixx's *The Complete Book of Running* sold 800,000 copies. (Sales fell after Fixx died of a heart attack while jogging.) The fitness vogue also heightened interest in natural foods and healthy diets. Beef sales fell; fish and chicken consumption rose. Low-calorie "lite" foods and beverages crowded the supermarket shelves. The loosening of sexual taboos that in the 1960s had been linked to radical protest now proceeded on its own, unencumbered by ideology. The lavishly illustrated *Joy of Sex* by the aptly named Alex Comfort became a 1970s best-seller.

As two-career households proliferated, often because of economic necessity, couples postponed having children or placed their offspring in day-care facilities. In 1977, the first year for which data are available, 35 percent of all children under age five spent their days with a nonrelative or in a child-care center. Semimythic stories circulated of middle-class parents' scrambling to place their darlings in prestigious nursery schools that would enhance the little ones' chances of gaining admission to an Ivy League college.

But narcissism and self-absorption composed only part of the cultural ambiance of the 1970s. Millions of Americans became deeply engaged with public issues, most typically by protesting what they viewed as deplorable cultural trends and social movements. The activist energies of the 1970s generally found conservative, even reactionary, outlets, as the national mood tacked sharply to the right. This conservative impulse took many forms and found numerous targets. Some former leftists adopted a neoconservative stance. Politically engaged intellectuals such as magazine editor Irving Kristol, art critic Hilton Kramer, and cultural commentator Michael Novak, repelled by the excesses of the 1960s and dismayed by liberalism's collapse under the radicals' onslaught, moved rightward. Warning against the lure of left-wing utopian ideologies and invoking traditional moral and spiritual values, the neoconservatives praised the free-enterprise system and preached a vehement anti-communism.

The rightward shift manifested itself outside the political arena as well. Indeed, one reason for the fragmented nature of conservative protest in the 1970s is that Nixon's forced resignation stymied the movement's political expression and momentarily derailed the Republican party's emergence as the New Right's political voice. As Thomas Byrne Edsall and Mary D. Edsall wrote, "Watergate . . . effectively choked off the growth of conservatism from 1973 through 1976, but the suppression meant that instead of finding an outlet within the political system, rightward pressure built throughout the decade to explosive levels. . . . Watergate resulted in a political system out of sync with larger trends." The resentments first exploited by George Wallace and Richard Nixon in the 1960s intensified in the midseventies, but lacking an effective political outlet, they flowed into other channels.

This disjunction between the political process and the national mood produced striking anomalies. For example, while the Supreme Court issued rulings protecting the rights of arrested persons and convicts, and even for a time abolished the death penalty, many Americans, alarmed by rising crime rates—according to FBI statistics, the number of reported violent crimes (murder, robbery, assault, and rape) rose from 738,000 in 1970 to 1,345,000 in 1980—demanded a crackdown on criminals. Similarly, as the Office of Federal Contract Compliance, the Equal Employment Opportunity Commission, the Civil Rights Division of the Justice Department, and other federal agencies promoted minority rights and developed affirmative-action programs to rectify the cumulative injustices of the past, many whites turned against what they labeled "reverse discrimination."

The conservative winds that lashed the cultural landscape in the 1970s also had ties to economic trends. Oil shocks, recessions, inflation, and industrial decline dealt a direct, dramatic blow to individual families. In 1973, for the first time since World War II, the median income of the average U.S. family, adjusted for inflation, actually fell. In constant (1985) dollars, median family income in 1960 had stood at $20,415. By 1973 it had risen to $29,172 but then began a protracted decline, dropping by $927 in 1974 and another $824 in 1975. Various factors worsened the economic pinch. Congress regularly increased social security taxes in these years, thereby reducing workers' take-home pay. Millions of Americans also experienced "bracket creep." As cost-of-living clauses in union contracts pushed their wages up (with no increase in buying power), they found themselves in a higher tax bracket, forking over a larger share of their earnings to Uncle Sam.

The most direct expression of nagging economic worries was a grass-roots tax revolt. In 1978 California voters by a two-to-one margin passed Proposition 13. The brainchild of an elderly Californian named Howard Jarvis, the law slashed real-estate taxes, creating havoc for the state's education and welfare systems. Similar referenda soon appeared on ballots across the nation. Carter pollster Pat Caddell declared in awe, "This isn't just a tax revolt. It's a revolution against government." Conservative congressman Jack Kemp of New York exulted, "We've changed the focus of politics in America from their ground to our ground. . . . They're now arguing on our turf."

But working-class and middle-class economic anxieties also fueled a broader reaction against Johnson-style liberalism with its emphasis on expanding the rights and improving the status of disadvantaged or marginalized social groups. In a time of economic well-being, the majority had supported such programs. But as middle

America saw its own status eroding, sympathy for such reforms vanished. In its place, hostility against welfare recipients and a broad spectrum of groups demanding special attention and more equitable treatment intensified.

The women's movement became a prime target of this backlash. As the economy weakened, the flow of women into the workplace stirred resentment among men fearful of losing their own jobs. Conservatives of both sexes attacked "radical feminism" as proabortion and antifamily and tainted by lesbianism and as a general threat to traditional values. Working-class women sensed that the feminist movement mainly addressed the concerns of college-educated and professional women, and turned against it, illustrating the power of class over gender. Marabel Morgan's *The Total Woman* (1975) appealed to such resentments, urging women to eschew agitation and discover new meaning in traditional roles. "A total woman caters to her man's special needs," she wrote, "whether it be in salads, sex or sports." Formulaic romance novels set in distant times and exotic locales featured panting women ravished by domineering males. These "bodice rippers" sold 20 million copies in the 1970s, mostly to women readers. As 1950s-style gender roles blurred, the romance novels conjured up a fantasy world in which "men were men and women were women."

In 1978 twenty thousand feminists gathered in Houston for the National Women's Conference. The rhetoric sizzled as delegates enjoyed what journalist Gail Sheehy called "a giant self-esteem bath." But in a counterrally, eight thousand conservative women cheered Phyllis Schlafly, who proclaimed, "The American people do not want the ERA, and they do not want government-funded abortion, lesbian privileges, or [federally funded] . . . universal child care." Schlafly's fifty-thousand-strong Eagle Forum fought the equal rights amendment as the entering wedge of a radical assault on morality and tradition.

In the end, the ERA would fall victim to the antifeminist backlash. Although the amendment needed only three more states for ratification as the 1979 deadline neared and 60 percent of the public told pollsters that they backed it, the process bogged down despite Congress's granting a three-year extension for ratification. ERA would force women into combat, opponents charged, and even require unisex toilets. The amendment so terrified one Missouri housewife that she baked and sold 450 coconut cakes and sent the proceeds to Schlafly. The Watergate investigation's elderly hero Sam Ervin, retired from the Senate, denounced the ERA and expressed gratitude that "when the good Lord created the earth, he didn't have the advice of [feminists] Bella Abzug and Gloria Steinem."

The battle over abortion proved even more bitter and emotion laden. *Roe v. Wade*, the 1973 Supreme Court decision establishing women's right to terminate pregnancy, called forth the highly vocal Right to Life movement. As the number of legal abortions rose from 18,000 in 1968 to 1.3 million in 1977—more than three for every ten live births—opinion polls showed a nation deeply divided by the issue. An uncertain middle group, although hesitant to criminalize the procedure, harbored doubts about its ethics. This ambivalence opened the way for a well-organized assault on *Roe v. Wade* led by the Roman Catholic church, Protestant evangelical groups, and Orthodox Jews.

In 1976, at the instigation of Representative Henry Hyde of Illinois, Congress barred the use of Medicare funds to finance abortions. To the dismay of prochoice forces, the Supreme Court upheld the Hyde amendment in 1977. In 1978 Congress extended the ban on federally funded abortions to military personnel and their families and to Peace Corps volunteers. By 1980, abortion would become a defining issue in American political culture.

As the homosexual-rights movement expanded, it, too, drew hostile attention. Thousands of gays and lesbians "came out," marching in "Gay Pride" parades and protesting discrimination. Beginning around 1973, under pressure from the Gay and Lesbian Alliance, states and municipalities adopted gay-rights ordinances barring discrimination on the basis of sexual orientation. But reaction soon set in. Conservative religious leaders denounced homosexuality as immoral and a sign of national degeneracy. Right-wing politicians deplored the movement as an example of 1960s-style liberalism run amok. When Miami adopted a gay-rights statute in 1977, pop singer Anita Bryant, best known for her TV commercials praising Florida orange juice, mounted a protest campaign. "If homosexuality were the normal way, God would have created Adam and Bruce," she pointed out. In a referendum, Miamians repealed the statute by a two-to-one margin. Voters rejected similar measures in St. Paul, Minnesota; Wichita, Kansas; and Eugene, Oregon.

Above all, the conservative backlash focused on issues of race. In the 1950s and early 1960s, a consensus had supported civil rights and antipoverty programs aimed at uplifting inner-city minorities. In the altered economic and social climate of the 1970s, that consensus collapsed. Goodwill gave way to resentment, and cities torn by

San Francisco, 1978. Buoyed by the black freedom struggle and the women's movement, homosexuals, too, began to protest discrimination and to assert pride in their identity. (© *Rose Skytta/Jeroboam, Inc.*)

racial violence in the sixties elected get-tough "law-and-order" candidates in the seventies. As the struggle against racial discrimination shifted northward, it sparked complex reactions involving not only race but social class. Two issues catalyzed the tensions: school busing to achieve racial balance and affirmative-action plans to compensate for past discrimination.

Busing plans ignited angry white protest in Louisville and other cities, as the "neighborhood school" became the rallying cry of busing opponents. Critics denounced busing as federal meddling with a local issue in the interests of an abstract social ideal. The fact that the officials who mandated the school busing schemes often lived in affluent suburbs unaffected by the plans added a class dimension to the resentment. The most heated dispute erupted in Boston. There, local black leaders had pressed for a school-integration plan, but the city's school committee under Louise Day Hicks had refused. In 1974 federal judge W. Arthur Garrity, finding "systematic . . . segregation" in Boston's schools, ordered the school committee to develop a desegregation plan that included busing. Irish-American and other ethnic neighborhoods of South Boston and Charlestown—insular, conservative, and economically hard-pressed—exploded at the meddling of affluent "limousine liberals" like Garrity. That fall, white students boycotted South Boston High School, and their supporters stoned black students arriving by bus from nearby Roxbury. When a white youth was stabbed, a mob trapped 135 black students in the school for four hours. Eerily echoing Little Rock in 1957, white parents marched under banners such as ROAR (Restore Our Alienated Rights). Young white thugs, one of them wielding a flagpole bearing the stars and stripes as a weapon, beat a young black lawyer outside Boston City Hall. President Ford, following Nixon's script, fueled the protests by denouncing forced busing.

The seventies also saw bitter fighting over plans—especially quota systems—to increase blacks' access to skilled jobs, education, and the professions. The issue reached the courts when Allan Bakke, a white, sued the medical school of the University of California at Davis, charging that his rejected application was stronger than that of others who had been admitted under a racial quota system. In 1978 the Supreme Court, by a 5–4 vote upheld Bakke's claim and ordered the school to enroll him. Ruling that admissions offices might consider race as one factor in their decisions but not set specific quotas for minorities, the majority held, "The purpose of helping certain groups . . . perceived as victims of 'societal discrimination' does not justify . . . [imposing] disadvantages upon persons like [Bakke], who bear no responsibility for whatever harm the beneficiaries of the special admissions programs are thought to have suffered." Justice Thurgood Marshall, veteran black civil-rights activist who as an NAACP attorney had argued the *Brown* v. *Board of Education* case in 1954, angrily dissented, citing the nation's history of discrimination. Affirmative-action programs, even quotas, he declared, were an appropriate minimal response by white America to centuries of racial injustice.

Memories of the 1963 March on Washington, when all Americans of goodwill had seemed to agree on a civil-rights agenda, faded as race-related issues spawned acrimony. Jimmy Carter, who owed his election to African-American voters, appointed a number of blacks to office but did not place race high on his agenda. Distracted by economic worries, white America from the White House on down had wearied of demands for racial justice. Moreover, issues that had seemed clear-cut in the sixties now appeared riddled with ambiguity. Even some black leaders criticized busing to achieve integration, for example, urging more attention to upgrading black schools. In *The Declining Significance of Race* (1978), William Julius Wilson, a black sociologist at the University of Chicago, argued that the central division in modern America was no longer between the races but between middle-class, upwardly mobile Americans—white and black—and the inner-city underclass cut off from jobs, education, and hope.

The backlash hit other minorities as well, including the more than 12 million Hispanics, 60 percent of them Chicanos of Mexican origin. Not only did the Hispanic jobless rate exceed the national average, but the wages of male Hispanic workers averaged only 70 percent of white male earnings. One and a half million job-seeking Hispanics entered the United States legally in the 1970s, including 637,000 from Mexico, 760,000 from the Caribbean, and 132,000 from Central America. Many more came clandestinely, mostly from Mexico. Yet in this anxious decade, the Hispanic poor were less an object of solicitude than a target of resentment, viewed as competitors in a constricting labor market.

The nation's Asian population also rose sharply in the 1970s as 1.8 million immigrants arrived from the Philippines, Korea, China, Vietnam, India, and other Pacific Rim nations. Fueled by immigration, the ranks of Asian-Americans grew to 3.7 million by 1980, contributing to the rich diversity of the American demographic palette. Again, however, economic stress produced an edge of hostility toward these newcomers, who were viewed as rivals for scarce jobs. This response, too, contributed to the decade's broader conservative tendency.

The reactionary mood reflected middle America's fears of society's splintering into self-seeking groups. Channeled positively, such concern can lead to a quest for new sources of community, as in the rise in ethnic awareness and interest in family roots. But fear of social fragmentation also expressed itself as hostility to all those— blacks, gays, feminists, abortion-rights advocates, job-hungry immigrants, welfare recipients, even prisoners—who seemed to demand special attention and privileges in difficult times. Other groups demonized under various labels—"liberals," "the mass media," "secular humanists"—were seen as threats to "traditional values," a catch-all term for the mythical moral and cultural unity of earlier, simpler days.

Both the search for community and the new conservatism found an outlet in religion. A fifteen-year trend of declining church attendance reversed in the mid-1970s, owing in large part to an upsurge in evangelicalism. In the 1950s, despite the popularity of revivalist Billy Graham, the mainstream liberal denominations had set the tone of American Protestantism. Many observers of religious trends, particularly liberals, had long believed that Protestantism's theologically conservative wing, known as evangelicalism, and its even stricter variant, fundamentalism, had been fatally discredited by the 1925 Scopes case, in which a Tennessee high-school teacher, John T. Scopes, was tried for violating a state law barring the teaching of evolution in the public schools. During the famous trial, the free-thinking Chicago lawyer Clarence Darrow had bested fundamentalist William Jennings Bryan.

Yet evangelicalism not only survived but flourished, sustained by a grass-roots network of local congregations, church colleges, publishing houses, and influential regional leaders. In the 1970s, the liberal denominations lost membership, but groups like the evangelical Assemblies of God church burgeoned. A powerful faction within the giant Southern Baptist Convention insisted on biblical literalism as a test of fellowship. As the larger culture became more conservative, evangelical churches, with their biblical emphasis and clear-cut moral codes, were well situated to benefit. The decade also saw a surge in private Christian academies founded by evangelicals dismayed by the public schools' "secularism" and by their apparent helplessness in the face of teenage sex, alcohol abuse, and increasing drug use. "Born-again" celebrities included Nixon's Watergate accomplice Charles Colson and former Black Panther Eldridge Cleaver. Jimmy Carter saturated his speeches with the language of evangelicalism, promising a government as "good and honest and compassionate and as filled with love" as the American people themselves.

Many Americans troubled by the social fragmentation and impersonality of modern life welcomed the emotional warmth and close sense of community offered by the typical evangelical congregation. In *Why Conservative Churches Are Growing* (1972), Dean M. Kelley accused the liberal denominations of neglecting their own members in their fervor for social action, while evangelical churches more fully met parishioners' spiritual and psychological needs. Evangelical bastions like Dallas's First Baptist Church, with fifteen thousand members, seemed to confirm Kelley's analysis.

In a 1978 survey, 22 percent of Americans identified themselves as evangelicals; other polls put the total as high as one-third. Although strongest in the rural South, with its high concentration of Protestants, and among the less well educated, evangelicalism flourished in all regions and at all socioeconomic levels. With good reason, the journal *Christianity Today* proclaimed 1976 the Year of the Evangelical. Reinforced by conservative Catholics, Mormons, and Jews, Protestant evangelicals wielded potent influence in 1970s America.

Evangelicals had long used the latest technology, from high-speed printing presses to radio and films, to spread the gospel. Now they exploited the paperback revolution. Thousands of Christian bookstores marketed evangelical paperbacks that racked up massive sales. One popular genre used Bible prophecy to explain world events. The nonfiction best-seller of the 1970s, Hal Lindsey's *The Late Great Planet Earth* (1970), found the Cold War, the nuclear-arms race, Russia's destruction, and the emerging global economy all foretold in the Bible. In the last days, he predicted, the Antichrist, a demonic figure portended in the Bible, will win a universal following and control all commerce by means of giant computers and orbiting TV satellites.

But if television posed dangers, it also served evangelicals well. Indeed, TV preachers led the evangelical resurgence. Oral Roberts built a vast TV ministry based on evangelical preaching and divine healing. By the 1970s, Roberts's complex in Tulsa included a state-of-the-art media center, Oral Roberts University, Oral Roberts Medical School, and a planned 777-bed "City of Faith" hospital. Jimmy Swaggart of Louisiana, Jack Van Impe of Michigan, Jim and Tammy Bakker of South Carolina, and many others reached worldwide audiences via satellite. Pat Robertson's Christian Broadcasting Network (CBN) aired many of these programs. Robertson's

FOCUS ON: *THAT OLD-TIME RELIGION*

The election of a born-again Christian, Jimmy Carter, as president in 1976 focused attention on the contours of postwar American religion, particularly on the continued vitality of evangelical Protestantism, a surprise to many who long ago had written its obituary.

In nineteenth-century America, evangelicalism was a powerful force. From the Second Great Awakening that climaxed on the Kentucky frontier in 1801 to a long series of urban revivals led by Charles Finney, Dwight L. Moody, and others, evangelical piety pervaded American life. While missions, Sunday schools, and tract societies spread the faith in the cities, Methodist circuit riders and intrepid missionaries carried the Word to isolated interior settlements. Evangelicals led many nineteenth-century reforms; Harriet Beecher Stowe, author of the antislavery best-seller *Uncle Tom's Cabin* (1852), was the daughter of a prominent evangelical minister Lyman Beecher.

By the end of the century, however, evangelicalism seemed on the wane. From the 1890s through the 1920s, the liberal Social Gospel dominated mainstream Protestantism. Evangelicals fought back, battling "modernism" and codifying the fundamentals of their faith, including the verbatim inspiration of the Bible and the resurrection and Second Coming of Jesus Christ. In the interwar years, regional leaders such as Aimee Semple McPherson of Los Angeles attracted large congregations and employed the new medium of radio to spread the message.

The faith continued to make steady gains after World War II, thanks to evangelists like Billy Graham and organizations such as Youth for Christ. The Assemblies of God church and other charismatic or "pentecostal" groups that featured divine healing and highly emotional worship grew rapidly. In the 1970s and 1980s, with mainstream Protestantism in decline, evangelicalism attracted waves of new adherents. Evangelical paperbacks sold by the millions; "Bible-believing" independent churches proliferated across the land; TV preachers entered countless homes via cable and satellite; and evangelical missionaries made dramatic inroads among the Catholic populations of Latin America. By the year 2000, predicted Jeffrey Haddan and Anson Shupe in *Televangelism* (1988), conservative Christianity could be "the single most powerful force in the United States."

Long ignored, evangelicalism drew increasing scholarly notice. In *American Evangelicalism: Conservative Religion and the Quandary of Modernity* (1983), sociologist James Davison Hunter examined evangelicals' highly adaptive response to modernity. According to Hunter, evangelicals found ways both to resist and accommodate contemporary trends in a process that he called "cognitive bargaining." For example, evangelical authors published many self-help books offering techniques for achieving personal happiness and emotional well-being—popular themes in the general culture—but written from a specifically evangelical theological perspective. Returning to the theme in *Culture Wars: The Struggle to Define America* (1991), Hunter portrayed religious conservatives as key players in a battle for the nation's soul. "America," he wrote, " is in the midst of a culture war that [reverberates]

. . . not only within public policy but within the lives of ordinary Americans every-where."

What were the political implications of this struggle? Some believers repudiated the wicked world and withdrew into their own spiritual realm. At its most extreme, this separatist impulse produced phenomena such as David Koresh's Branch Davidian sect, whose members barricaded themselves in a heavily armed compound near Waco, Texas, to await—indeed to help precipitate—the end. In April 1993, after a long standoff with the FBI, Koresh and most of his followers perished in a fiery holocaust that tragically fulfilled their prophecies of a final Armageddon-like confrontation.

More typically, however, religious conservatives turned to politics to realize their moral vision. In the 1980s, the Moral Majority led by televangelist Jerry Falwell enthusiastically supported the Reagan movement. In the 1990s, Pat Robertson's Christian Coalition mobilized conservative activists who ran for school board, city council, and other local offices, building a righteous nation at the grass-roots level. Founded in 1989, the Christian Coalition boasted 350,000 members in 750 chapters by 1993. In many states and communities, well-organized religious conservatives maneuvered for control of the Republican party.

Scholars observing this trend saw a decline in traditional denominational loyalties and a rise in special-agenda groups—the Christian Action Council, the Christian Heritage Center, the National Pro-Family Coalition, the American Coalition for Traditional Values, and scores of others—that pursued specific agendas while sharing a common goal. Nineteenth-century evangelicals had formed single-issue organizations such as the Anti-Saloon League (1895) but had lacked the sophisticated computer-based direct-mail techniques available to their modern-day successors. Mobilizing around what they saw as defining moral issues, politically active religious conservatives embraced symbolic causes such as creationism, school prayer, and "family values," and battled abortion, pornography, homosexuality, radical feminism, sexual permissiveness in the media, sex education in the schools, government support for "obscene" art, and the worldview that they denounced as "secular humanism." The latter term, though widely used in conservative religious circles, proved difficult to define. One skeptic called it "a label used by the Far Right to attack virtually everything that they disagree with about the schools and society at large."

Mark Twain once dismissed reports of his death as "greatly exaggerated," and the same might be said of evangelical religion in modern America. Amid turbulent world events and unsettling social changes at home, millions of American men and women still find meaning and reassurance in religious beliefs and folkways. As they enter the public arena to apply their religious vision to public policy, they demonstrate once again evangelicalism's central role in U.S. history and life.

own "700 Club" featured talk-show-style interviews with evangelical leaders. The "pope" of the electronic church, Jerry Falwell of Lynchburg, Virginia, broadcast his weekly "Old Time Gospel Hour" on 325 TV stations and 300 radio stations. Televangelists reached millions each week and raked in massive contributions from what they fondly called their "television family." By the decade's end, they had become a major force not only in religion but also in politics.

Energized by the TV preachers, newly confident evangelicals boldly engaged political and cultural issues. Via TV, magazines, paperbacks, and local pulpits, they deplored the nation's moral breakdown. Pat Robertson, who regularly denounced "the humanistic/atheistic/hedonistic influence" eating away at America, was one of many highly political televangelists. The Reverend Tim LaHaye, writing in 1980, cited an array of trends, from divorce, abortion, and gay rights to "militant feminism" and "leniency towards pornography, prostitution, and crime," that made America a modern Sodom and Gomorrah. In *Listen, America* (1980), Jerry Falwell attacked feminism for eroding family values and denigrating women's proper role:

> Most of the women who are leaders in the feminist movement promote an immoral life style. In a drastic departure from the home, more than half of the women in our country are currently employed. Our nation is in serious danger when motherhood is considered a task that is "unrewarding, unfulfilling, and boring." . . . [T]o be a wife and mother is the highest calling in the world.

The political mobilization of the Christian Right, initially directed against federal efforts to deny tax-exempt status to Christian schools, quickly gained momentum and broadened in focus. The Moral Majority, for example, an organization founded by Falwell in 1979 to spearhead America's spiritual regeneration at the ballot box, attracted numerous adherents and intense media attention. But politicized evangelicals took aim at many targets. On the mass-media front, they decried sex magazines like *Playboy*, offensive movies, TV shows, and rock music. In Tupelo, Mississippi, hitherto best known as Elvis Presley's birthplace, the Reverend Don Wildmon's National Federation for Decency organized boycotts of advertisers that sponsored sexually suggestive TV shows. Turning to education, evangelicals prescribed prayer in the schools and eradication of "secular humanism" from textbooks. Strongly patriotic, they urged morality in government, denounced the Soviet Union, and called for increased military spending to fight "godless communism."

The popularity of the TV evangelists underscored the urgent longing for connectedness and moral clarity spawned by the later 1970s cultural disarray, economic troubles, and political failures. Indeed, the alienation and political frustration of these years became almost palpable. In Robert Altman's unsettling 1975 movie *Nashville*, lonely, unfulfilled people hover like moths around Nashville's glamorous country-music stars while a sound truck for a mysterious, unseen presidential candidate blares endlessly in the city's streets. Nostalgia for a sense of community lost somewhere in the past surfaced in cultural products as diverse as the bicentennial projects of 1976, the 1977 "Roots" miniseries, and Woody Allen's poignant chronicling of a failed relationship in *Annie Hall* (1977). It emerged, too, in the pop-culture mythologizing of America's past offered in John Jakes's *Kent Family Chronicles*, which sold 30 million copies between 1974 and 1980.

Right-wing political movements exploited this volatile stew of economic worries and white backlash, evangelical moralism and traditionalist longings. Conservative think tanks such as Washington's Heritage Foundation (1973), financed by Colorado beer baron Joseph Coors, funded New Right intellectuals. William F. Buckley's venerable *National Review* flourished, although some New Right firebrands found the patrician Buckley insufficiently aggressive in his conservatism. In addition, a network of interlocking organizations channeled the New Right's amorphous energies. Mass-mail specialist Richard Viguerie, a Louisiana-born Roman Catholic, marshaled computerized lists of names to raise funds for conservative causes and candidates. Viguerie's single-issue appeals focused on emotion-laden themes: gun control, abortion, gay rights, the death penalty, and school prayer. John Dolan's National Conservative Political Action Committee assembled a war chest of more than $4 million to defeat liberal candidates. The American Conservative Union in 1978 boasted 300,000 members and contributions of $3 million.

In *Thunder on the Right* (1980), Alan Crawford, an old-style conservative made uneasy as the New Right coalesced politically, explored the many manifestations of "the politics of resentment" that had sprung up in the 1970s. Crawford concluded:

> These leaders and others are building a political movement that has already reshaped . . . the face of Congress, stalled legislation in its tracks, and pushed through initiatives and referenda. It has its eye on the presidency . . . , vowing, as one New Right leader told me, "to take control of the culture." Unlike right-wing zealots of the recent past, the New Right has built the organizational structure to make good that promise.

Jerry Falwell succinctly put it this way: "We have enough votes to run the country. And when the people say, 'We've had enough,' we are going to take over."

As the Watergate trauma faded, the New Right found its political legs. In 1976 candidate Jimmy Carter moved to the right, downplaying his party's traditional championing of the underdog and emphasizing instead such themes as fiscal restraint, governmental efficiency, and tax-code revision. Even so, working-class whites abandoned the Democratic ticket in ominous numbers that year. In 1960, 61 percent of lower-status whites had voted for John F. Kennedy; in 1976, only 53 percent of the voters in this category cast their ballots for Carter.

By the 1978 midterm election, the political realignment was fully under way. Much of the $17.3 million spent by PACS that year came from conservative sources. Right-wing PACs targeted key liberal legislators for defeat and key conservatives for support, using computerized mailing lists to reach receptive voters in the targeted states and districts. With an overall voter turnout of under 38 percent, such motivational tactics proved effective: liberals like Senator Dick Clark of Iowa and Floyd Haskell of Colorado fell, while New Right favorites such as Jesse Helms, seeking a second term in North Carolina, sailed to victory. Antiabortion candidates backed by the National Right-to-Life Committee won elections across the nation, Proposition

13 passed in California, and Republicans enjoyed a net gain of nearly three hundred seats in state legislatures across the nation.

The nation's rightward drift affected both parties—conservative Democrats such as mayors Sam Yorty of Los Angeles and Frank Rizzo of Philadelphia capitalized on the white backlash—but the main beneficiary was the GOP. Arising from the ashes of Watergate, the Republicans gradually remade themselves. Historically the party of economic privilege, the GOP now redefined itself as the vehicle of grassroots resentments and fears. The successes of 1978 portended a far more dramatic triumph that would come two years later. With inflation raging, unemployment rising, and family income continuing to sag in 1978–1980, the anger surging throughout middle America intensified.

Fierce political forces thus ripped at America as the Carter years ended. In the 1960s, liberalism had come under attack from the Left; now it faced a far stronger assault from the Right. Political conservatism had once been the domain of corporate America and the monied class, who had denounced high taxes, big government, and federal regulation. These issues remained alive, but the New Right democratized conservatism, reaching out to the grass roots not only with political and economic appeals but with cultural and moral themes lamenting the alleged breakdown of values and tradition in American life.

The New Right showed a genius for mobilizing free-floating grievances; whether it had the capacity to govern remained to be seen. One last crisis, centered in distant Iran, drove the final nail into Jimmy Carter's political coffin and buoyed conservative Republican hopes as the 1980 election neared.

Carter Diplomacy and the Middle East Hostage Crisis

As in the Ford years, Richard Nixon's agenda continued to shape U.S. foreign policy during Carter's term. In 1979, for example, Carter formalized full diplomatic relations with the People's Republic of China, completing the process that Nixon and Kissinger had initiated a decade earlier. Carter also set out to apply his problem-solving skills to foreign policy no less than to domestic issues, but forces beyond his control ultimately thwarted his ambitions abroad, just as they did at home.

In assembling his foreign-policy team, Carter drew on his contacts as a member of the Trilateral Commission, a private organization started in 1972 by David Rockefeller, head of Chase Manhattan Bank, and Zbigniew Brzezinski, professor of international relations at Columbia University. The commission brought together political, economic, and strategic leaders of the United States, Western Europe, and Japan to address issues of global concern. As secretary of state, Carter named Cyrus Vance, a New York lawyer, seasoned diplomat, and pillar of the foreign-policy establishment. As national-security adviser, he chose Brzezinski. The son of a pre–World War II Polish diplomat, Brzezinski, like Kissinger, had emigrated to America as a youth. A confirmed Cold Warrior, he deeply distrusted Moscow. U.S.

foreign policy in the late 1970s reflected the personalities and ideology of these three men.

Like Woodrow Wilson, Jimmy Carter believed that morality had an important role in foreign policy. "Fairness, not force," he counseled, "should lie at the heart of our dealings with the nations of the world." Avowing an "absolute" commitment to human rights around the world, he implicitly rejected Kissinger's Realpolitik approach, which largely ignored the internal policies of nations friendly to U.S. interests. Cyrus Vance found Carter's goals congenial. Using U.S. influence, along with threats to cut off foreign aid, he prodded Chile, Argentina, Ethiopia, South Africa, and other nations to improve their human-rights record. Carter and Vance focused more on Africa and Latin America than had Nixon and Kissinger, who had viewed these regions simply as arenas for pursuing the superpower game.

Carter particularly hoped to make Latin America a showcase of his human-rights policy, yet when leftists rebelled against Nicaragua's right-wing dictator, Anastasio Somoza, in 1977, Carter showed more concern about the spread of communism than about Somoza's brutal suppression of the insurgency. When the rebel Sandinistas (named for an earlier revolutionary hero, Augusto Sandino) overthrew Somoza in 1979, Carter recognized the new regime but gave it little attention. In El Salvador, terrorist "death squads" supported by the ruling junta assassinated many thousands, including the archbishop of El Salvador and four American Roman Catholic missionaries in 1980. Washington's protests proved ineffectual. When Carter's term ended, he left festering problems in both countries to his successor.

In Panama, by contrast, Carter's moralism and U.S. strategic interests converged. In the 1960s, alarmed by anti-American demonstrations in that small Central American nation, President Johnson had begun talks to renegotiate the one-sided 1903 treaty by which the United States owned and operated the Panama Canal. Under Carter, the two nations at last reached agreement on a pair of treaties. The first accord restored Panamanian sovereignty to the Canal Zone; the second pledged the United States to transfer operations of the canal to Panama by 1999. The Senate approved the treaties 68–32—the bare two-thirds necessary. Although the agreements safeguarded U.S. security interests, the New Right seized upon them as another symbol of the failure of American will. A conservative mass mailing denouncing the Panama treaties contained two small flags: one a stars and stripes; the other, a white flag of surrender.

Extending another Nixon initiative, Carter at first pursued détente with Moscow. Meeting in Vienna in June 1979, Carter and Leonid Brezhnev initialed the SALT II Treaty limiting each nation to 2,250 missile launchers. As required by the Constitution, Carter submitted the treaty to the Senate for ratification. There, it met a storm of protest, with conservatives denouncing it for conceding too much to the Soviets and accepting the principle of nuclear parity instead of U.S. superiority. Hawkish neoconservative Democrats formed a lobbying group, the Committee on the Present Danger, to fight the treaty. To reassure his hard-line critics and in response to pressure from Brzezinski to hang tough against the Soviets, Carter approved a new nuclear missile system, the MX, to replace the older Minuteman ICBMs. He also sanctioned a giant new missile-launching submarine, the Trident, ratcheting up the nuclear-arms race even as he tried to push SALT II through the Senate.

Prospects for the ratification of SALT II, already dubious, collapsed in December 1979 when the Soviets invaded Afghanistan, on their southern border. The Soviet Union was trying to squelch a militant Islamic fundamentalist movement that jeopardized the pro-Soviet regime in Kabul and threatened to spread to Islamic regions of the Soviet Union itself. Whatever its rationale, the invasion poisoned U.S.-Soviet relations. Many Americans, convinced of Moscow's desire to rule the world, saw the action as proof of their worst fears. National security adviser Brzezinski, already suspicious of détente, pushed Carter toward a tough anti-Soviet stance. Under his influence, Carter's human-rights policy, initially applied worldwide, became mainly a club for bludgeoning Moscow. Amid rising anti-Soviet sentiment, Carter withdrew SALT II from the Senate. Pronouncing the Afghan invasion "the most serious threat to world peace since World War II," he canceled various trade agreements with the Soviets and even pulled the United States out of the 1980 Moscow Olympics.

On January 23, 1980, in a belligerent address before a joint session of Congress, the president proclaimed the Carter Doctrine. The Soviet invasion of Afghanistan, he warned, had brought them within three hundred miles of the Persian Gulf and menaced the flow of oil to the West. Echoing the 1947 Truman Doctrine, Carter proclaimed that any "attempt by an outside force to gain control of the Persian Gulf" would be deemed a threat to the vital interests of the United States. Détente lay in shambles. The harshly anti-Soviet tone that characterized the early Reagan years was set by Jimmy Carter in 1980.

Carter's greatest foreign-policy achievement and his costliest failure both centered on the Middle East. In the Nixon-Ford years, Henry Kissinger had worked tirelessly but in vain for a comprehensive peace settlement in this conflict-ridden region. President Carter avidly pursued this goal, impelled by more than strategic considerations. His evangelical beliefs placed an aura of special meaning around Israel, God's chosen nation, and its history. Carter's peacemaking impulse gained a boost in November 1977 when Egyptian leader Anwar el-Sadat, in a surprise visit to Jerusalem, initiated talks with the Israelis aimed toward ending the state of war between the two nations.

The talks stalled, however, and in September 1978 Carter invited Sadat and Israeli prime minister Menachem Begin to Camp David for further negotiations. For thirteen days, with Carter as mediator, the bargaining progressed. On September 18, announcing that a "framework" of peace had been agreed on, Carter asserted, "Today we are privileged to see the chance for one of the bright moments in human history. . . . [T]hese two brave leaders found within themselves the willingness to work together to seek a lasting peace." Begin returned the praise. Carter had "won the day," he declared, "and peace now celebrates a great victory." On March 26, 1979, Sadat and Begin signed a peace treaty at the White House. Egypt recognized Israel, and Israel agreed to return the Sinai peninsula to Egypt by 1982. True peace in the Middle East remained a distant vision, but Carter served as midwife to an important first step. Amid mounting frustrations on the domestic front, the Egyptian-Israeli accord scored a rare success for an embattled president.

But events in the Middle East also brought Carter's administration to its nadir. Since 1953, Iran had been ruled by Shah Reza Pahlavi, whose army defended U.S. interests in the Persian Gulf. Having crushed his domestic opponents with CIA help in 1953 (see p. 119), the shah had loyally backed U.S. policy and brutally repressed his internal foes. Yet he proved no match for the fundamentalist energies roiling the Islamic world. In January 1979, the shah fled Iran in the face of a revolutionary uprising led by the Ayatollah Ruhollah Khomeini, a leader of Islam's intensely orthodox Shiite sect that fanatically hated the shah's secular, Westernizing regime.

When Carter admitted the shah to the United States for cancer treatment a few weeks later, Iran's Shiites exploded. With the blessings of Khomeini, who regularly denounced the United States as "the Great Satan," Shiite militants occupied the U.S. embassy compound in Tehran and seized seventy-six American hostages. Six escaped unseen and took refuge in the Canadian embassy, and the kidnappers soon released thirteen lower-level embassy employees, all of them blacks or women. Washington expelled Iranian students and froze Iranian assets in the United States but seemed powerless to break the impasse.

The "hostage crisis," reported daily in stark newspaper headlines and on TV news shows, dominated the rest of Carter's term. The Khomeini regime took full advantage of America's obsession with the prisoners. Television brought into American living rooms scenes of blindfolded hostages paraded by their captors and of kidnappers using American flags to carry out garbage. The more the U.S. media focused on the hostages, the greater their propaganda value became for Iran.

In April 1980, an attempted U.S. rescue operation failed before the would-be rescuers even reached Tehran. Three helicopters broke down in dust storms in the Iranian desert, forcing the military to abort the botched mission. During the evacuation, a helicopter and a C-130 transport collided and burned, killing eight Americans. The catastrophe heaped additional humiliation on the United States. Secretary of State Vance, who had opposed the operation, resigned, to be replaced by Senator Edmund Muskie of Maine. Carter's approval ratings, already feeble, sank even further. The ordeal consumed him. Recalling the protracted crisis in his memoirs, Carter admitted, "The release of the American hostages had become almost an obsession with me."

CONCLUSION

Few other presidents have entered an electoral campaign more weakened than Jimmy Carter did in 1980. The continuing inflation-recession cycle further undermined his standing. Responding to critics on the Right, Carter called for cuts in federal welfare spending, an approach that cost him the support of liberal Democrats without winning back the angry, alienated white working class.

Late in 1979, Senator Edward Kennedy, heir to the Camelot legend as the last surviving Kennedy brother, challenged Carter for the 1980 Democratic nomination. The president fended off the threat, in part because Chappaquiddick still clouded Kennedy's reputation, but Carter would ultimately lose the general election. Returning to private life, he founded the Carter Presidential Center at Atlanta's Emory

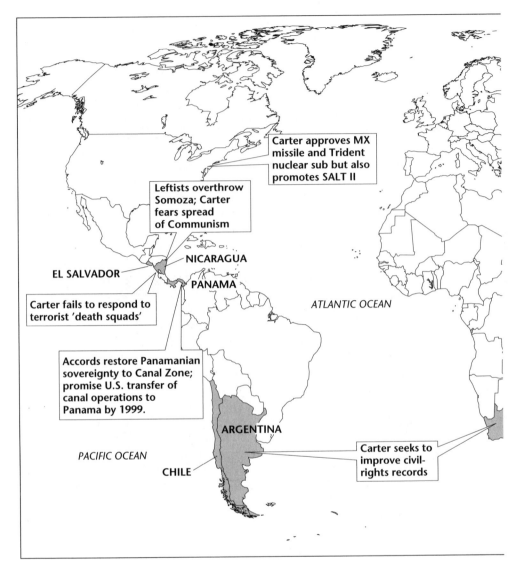

Figure 13.3

Carter Diplomacy

University, where he organized seminars and conferences aimed at the peaceful resolution of regional conflicts. He also worked with Habitat for Humanity, a volunteer group that rehabilitated slum housing. Although his reputation, like Nixon's, would later revive, few Americans in 1981 regretted seeing him leave the White House that he had entered so exuberantly four years earlier.

With America awash in problems at home and abroad, the decade that had begun with the invasion of Cambodia and the killings at Kent State at last dragged to a close. Few argued with the judgment passed by *Time* magazine: "Nobody is apt

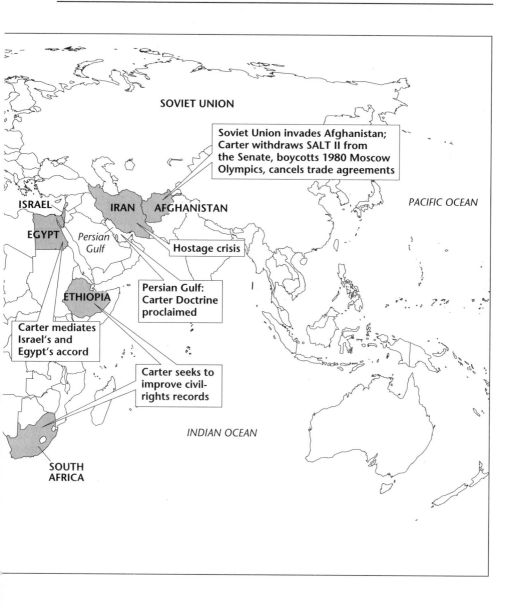

to look back on the 1970s as the good old days." After the turmoil that began in the mid-1960s, it is small wonder that Americans in the 1970s seemed drained by psychic fatigue. Giving up on the public sphere and the quest for a common vision, they fragmented into diverse interest groups, pursued purely private goals, or embraced allegiances that often seemed based more on suspicion and fear than on positive values. Jimmy Carter correctly identified a national "malaise" in his much-maligned speech of 1979; the problem was that he proved unable to lead the United States out of its collective funk. By 1980 the nation clearly craved ideological direction and new sources of political energy. Eager to provide that direction and energy, the New Right delivered its movie-star hero: Ronald Reagan.

SELECTED READINGS

Politics and the Economy
in the Ford and Carter Years

Carl Abbott, *The New Urban America: Growth and Politics in the Sunbelt Cities* (1981); Ken Auletta, *The Underclass* (1981); Barry Bluestone and Bennett Harrison, *The Deindustrialization of America* (1982); James Buchanan and Richard Wagner, *Democracy in Deficit* (1977); James Cannon, *Time and Chance: Gerald Ford's Appointment with History: 1913–1974* (1993); Jimmy Carter, *Keeping Faith* (1982); Thomas Byrne Edsall with Mary D. Edsall, *Chain Reaction: The Impact of Race, Rights, and Taxes on American Politics* (1991); Gerald R. Ford, *A Time to Heal* (1979); Betty Glad, *Jimmy Carter* (1980); David Halberstam, *The Reckoning* (1986) [decline of the U.S. auto industry]; Robert T. Hartmann, *Palace Politics: An Inside Account of the Ford Years* (1980); John P. Hoerr, *And the Wolf Finally Came: The Decline of the American Steel Industry* (1988); Steven B. Hunt, *The Energy Crisis* (1978); Burton I. Kaufman, *The Presidency of James Earl Carter, Jr.* (1993); David P. McCaffrey, *The Politics of Nuclear Power* (1991); Peter R. Odell, *Oil and World Power* (5th ed., 1979); Richard Reeves, *A Ford and Not a Lincoln* (1975); A. James Riechley, *Conservatives in an Age of Change* (1980); J. Harvey Wilkerson, *From Brown to Bakke* (1979); William Julius Wilson, *The Truly Disadvantaged: The Inner City, the Underclass, and Public Policy* (1987); Jules Witcover, *Marathon* (1977) [1976 election]; Daniel Yergin, *The Prize* (1991) [U.S. and world petroleum industry].

Social and Cultural Trends
in the Seventies

Mary Berry, *Why the ERA Failed* (1986); Paul Boyer, *When Time Shall Be No More: Prophecy Belief in Modern American Culture* (1992); Peter Carroll, *It Seemed Like Nothing Happened* (1983); Alan Crawford, *Thunder on the Right* (1980); John Crewden, *The Tarnished Door: The New Immigrants and the Transformation of America* (1983); Donald W. Dayton and Robert K. Johnston, eds., *The Variety of American Evangelicalism* (1991); Barbara Epstein, *Political Protest and Cultural Revolution: Nonviolent Direct Action in the 1970s and 1980s* (1991); Ethics and Public Policy Center, *No Longer Exiles: The Religious New Right in American Politics* (1993); Jo Freeman, *The Politics of Women's Liberation* (1979); James William Gibson, *Warrior Dreams: Paramilitary Culture in Post-Vietnam America* (1994); Douglas Glasgow, *The Black Underclass* (1980); Nathan Glazer, *Affirmative Discrimination* (1975); Dean M. Kelley, *Why Conservative Churches Are Growing* (1972); Christopher Lasch, *The Culture of Narcissism* (1978); Michael Lienesch, *Redeeming America: Piety and Politics in the New Christian Right* (1993); Kristen Luker, *Abortion and the Politics of Motherhood* (1984); George M. Marsden, *Understanding Fundamentalism and Evangelicalism* (1991); Michael Moritz, *The Little Kingdom: The Private Story of Apple Computer* (1984); Maureen Muldoon, *The Abortion Debate in the United States and Canada: A Source Book* (1991); George H. Nash, *The Conservative Intellectual Movement in America Since 1945* (1976); Timothy J. O'Neill, *Bakke and the Politics of Equality* (1985); Jerome Price, *The Antinuclear Movement* (1982); Quentin J. Schultze, *Televangelism and American Culture* (1991); Edwin Schur, *The Awareness Trap: Self-Absorption Instead of Social Change* (1976); Carol B. Stack, *All Our Kin: Strategies for Survival in a Black Community* (1975); Suzanne

Staggenborg, *The Pro-Choice Movement* (1991); Melvin Urofsky, *The Continuity of Change: The Supreme Court and Individual Liberties, 1953–1986* (1991); Winnifrid D. Wandersee, *On the Move: American Women in the 1970s* (1988); William J. Wilson, *The Declining Significance of Race* (1978); Mark Royden Winchell, *Neoconservative Criticism* (1991); John Woodridge, *The Evangelicals* (1975); Robert Wuthnow, *The Restructuring of American Religion: Society and Faith Since World War II* (1988); Daniel Yankelovich, *New Rules: Search for Self-Fulfillment in a World Turned Upside Down* (1981); Jeffrey S. Young, *Steve Jobs: The Journey Is the Reward* (1988).

America and the World in the Seventies

James Bill, *The Eagle and the Lion: The Tragedy of American-Iranian Relations* (1987); Zbigniew Brzezinski, *Power and Principle* (1983); Alan Dawson, *55 Days: The Fall of South Vietnam* (1977); Raymond L. Garthoff, *Détente and Confrontation: American-Soviet Relations from Nixon to Reagan* (1987); Arnold R. Isaacs, *Without Honor: Defeat in Vietnam and Cambodia* (1983); William E. LeGro, *Vietnam from Ceasefire to Capitulation* (1981); George D. Moffett, III, *The Limits of Victory: The Ratification of the Panama Canal Treaties* (1983); William B. Quandt, *Decade of Decisions* (1977) and *Camp David* (1987); Barry Rubin, *Paved with Good Intentions* (1983) [U.S.-Iranian relations]; David Schoenbaum, *The United States and the State of Israel* (1993); Lars Schoultz, *Human Rights and U.S. Policy Toward Latin America* (1981); William Shawcross, *Sideshow: Kissinger, Nixon, and the Destruction of Cambodia* (1979); Gary Sick, *All Fall Down: America's Tragic Encounter with Iran* (1986); Gaddis Smith, *Morality, Reason and Power: American Diplomacy in the Carter Years* (1986); Strobe Talbott, *Endgame* (1979) [SALT II]; Cyrus Vance, *Hard Choices* (1983).

Chapter Fourteen

Prime-Time Politics: The Reagan Years

Jimmy Carter paced the White House halls all night on January 19, 1981, awaiting word that Iran had released the U.S. hostages. As his final presidential act, Carter hoped to announce the good news and write *finis* to a crisis that had absorbed countless hours of his time. Hope had stirred in September 1980, when the aged Ayatollah Khomeini had signaled a readiness to bargain. With the Algerian government as go-between, Washington and Tehran had begun formal negotiations on November 2, two days before the presidential election. On January 8, 1981, both sides agreed on terms, including the transfer to Tehran of frozen Iranian assets held by U.S. banks. Even as he rode to Ronald Reagan's inaugural on January 20, his eyes puffy from lack of sleep, Carter was on the phone, seeking word of the hostages' release. But this final balm eluded him. Not until a few minutes after Ronald Reagan took the oath of office did Iran, after 444 days, at last free the Americans.

Taking office under these auspicious circumstances, Reagan set about achieving the political agenda of the New Right, whose advocates had gained ground steadily in the 1970s. At the time, his policies won broad support. In retrospect, however, Reagan's two terms saw grave economic problems ignored or worsened. The federal deficit and trade gap widened, and the industrial infrastructure crumbled even further. And as piratical corporate behavior intensified, the nation's inner cities decayed.

Aggressively pursuing the Cold War, Reagan sharply accelerated the military-spending increases and rhetorical assaults on Moscow that had begun at the end of Carter's administration. He also turned his attention to battling communism in Africa and Latin America. Indeed, the latter campaign would spawn the worst scandal of his presidency, the Iran-contra affair. Yet by the end of his watch, sweeping changes within the Soviet Union heralded nothing less than the Cold War's end. The thaw in U.S.-Soviet relations ultimately led to Reagan's final, incongruous public display: a warm embrace of the world's top communist in Moscow's Red Square.

The Reagan revolution gave political voice to the mood of reaction and backlash that had gripped middle America in the troubled 1970s. The individualistic, acquisitive, and socially conservative outlook that Reagan personified influenced American culture no less than American politics, and the 1980s remains indelibly the Reagan era. Indeed, during his two terms, Reagan enjoyed great personal popularity. Only after his departure did the nation begin to grasp the grave consequences of his policies. Nevertheless, the public never seemed to hold Reagan responsible. Envious Democrats would dub him the "Teflon president."

The New Right Takes Charge: 1980–1984

In resorting to Richard Nixon in 1968, frustrated voters had rejected radicalism, redistributive liberalism, and affirmative action in favor of conservatism and the status quo. The process had continued in the 1970s, fed by economic worries and white blacklash, as well as unsettling social changes. New Right activism crested in the 1980 presidential campaign; as in 1896, 1912, and 1932, the election that year proved a watershed in American political history.

On the Democratic side, Senator Edward Kennedy tried for the nomination, hoping to exploit the lingering aura of Camelot and to attract liberals who had soured on Carter. Yet Kennedy, still dogged by that 1969 summer night on Chappaquiddick, proved a weak campaigner, and President Carter trounced him in twenty-four state primaries. Kennedy's convention speech evoking the party's reformist tradition won a nostalgic ovation, but in the end the divided and dispirited Democrats renominated Carter.

The confident Republicans turned to Ronald Reagan, who had nearly snatched the prize from Gerald Ford in 1976. Reagan had bested five challengers easily in the Republican primaries. The most liberal of the five, Congressman John Anderson of Illinois, later ran in the general election as an independent. Reagan chose as his running mate one of his erstwhile rivals, George Bush, a party stalwart who had held a variety of posts under Republican presidents, most recently as director of the CIA.

The GOP platform attacked abortion and the equal rights amendment, two emotional issues inherited from the 1970s. Exuding Cold War militance, it criticized SALT II and demanded increased military spending. On the economy, the platform embraced two seemingly contradictory goals: major tax cuts and a balanced budget. Reagan's acceptance speech, a preview of his campaign, stressed lower taxes, less government regulation, and a beefed-up national defense. Praising "family values" and the free-enterprise system, he ended with a paean to "this . . . beloved and blessed land."

Reagan's acting skills shone in a televised debate with Carter. His rhetorical query, "Are you better off today than you were four years ago?" resonated with voters battered by inflation. When Carter warned of the dire consequences of Reagan's policies, Reagan merely smiled benevolently and sighed, "There you go again." On voting day, the former California governor won a narrow 51 percent of the popular vote. Carter trailed with 41 percent, and Anderson picked up 7 percent. In the electoral count, Reagan carried a hefty 44 states, with 489 electoral votes. Only Georgia and Minnesota (the home states of Carter and Mondale), Hawaii, Maryland, Rhode Island, West Virginia, and Washington, D.C., withstood his appeal. The Republi-

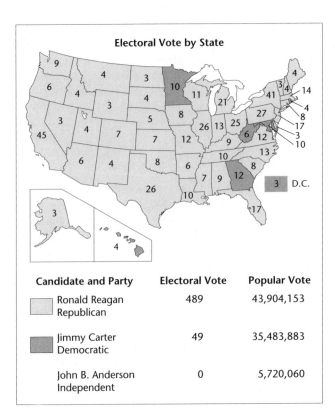

FIGURE 14.1

Presidential Election of 1980

Electoral Vote by State

Candidate and Party	Electoral Vote	Popular Vote
Ronald Reagan Republican	489	43,904,153
Jimmy Carter Democratic	49	35,483,883
John B. Anderson Independent	0	5,720,060

cans won control of the Senate for the first time since losing it in 1954 and cut the Democrats' majority in the House from 119 to 50. The vote revealed an anti-Carter, anti-inflation protest as well as an affirmation of the New Right agenda, but Reagan confidently claimed a clear public mandate for his program, and the new Congress largely went along.

Ronald Wilson Reagan, the oldest president ever elected, was just short of his seventieth birthday when he took office. Yet aided by his Hollywood training and his skillfully dyed hair, he projected a sprightly image. Of Irish immigrant stock (the name was originally O'Regan), he grew up in Dixon, Illinois, where his alcoholic father held various jobs and supported the family during the Depression as a local New Deal relief administrator.

Reagan graduated from Eureka College in Illinois and worked as a radio sports announcer in Des Moines. In 1937, after taking a screen test arranged by a friend, he signed a contract with Warner Brothers. He appeared in supporting roles in a series of movies that ended with *The Killers* (1964), in which he played his only part as a villain. His best-known role, as the dying football player George Gipp in *Knute Rockne—All American* (1940), featured the famous line addressed to Pat O'Brien as Rockne: "Ask the boys to go in there and win just one for the Gipper."

Reagan voted for Roosevelt in 1932, but as a postwar president of the Screen Actors Guild amid investigation of communist influence in Hollywood, he had turned to the right. In 1954 he began hosting TV's "General Electric Theatre" and became GE's corporate voice. A ceaseless round of speechmaking in these years fixed his palette of political ideas. Reagan's second marriage in 1952, to actress Nancy Davis, a staunch conservative (Barry Goldwater was a family friend), deepened his right-wing political bent. A Reagan TV speech glorifying Goldwater in 1964 won national attention.

Elected governor of California in 1966 with financing from wealthy business friends and momentum from a backlash against campus turmoil at Berkeley, Reagan served until 1975. In that capacity he denounced campus antiwar protests and in 1970 stood firm against student demonstrators protesting the Cambodian invasion. He resumed his speechmaking to conservative audiences after leaving the governorship and soon gained a national following.

The Reagan who won the presidency in 1980, a seasoned politician and well-known conservative, was above all a creature of the media. Beneath the scripted TV speeches and staged appearances, the man himself proved remarkably elusive. Reagan watchers marveled at the chasm between the media image and the person behind the image. The former was charismatic, eloquent, and deeply thoughtful about politics and the human condition. The latter, while capable of charm, was detached and rather vague, bored by details, remote even from his children, and fairly inarticulate except when telling a joke or recounting an anecdote that supported his conservative ideology. A surge of nostalgic affection for Harry Truman in the 1980s perhaps reflected Americans' awareness of the contrast between the down-to-earth, plain-spoken Truman and the media-savvy Reagan.

Exuding optimism in his inaugural address, Reagan insisted that the key to renewal lay in unleashing private initiative. "Government is not the solution to our problem," he announced in a well-worn line. "Government *is* the problem." The inaugural became a festival of privilege, as private jets shuttled in Hollywood stars and the Reagans' rich friends. TV's Johnny Carson joked, "This is the first administration to have a premiere." As the rented limousines ferried partygoers around Washington, a Utah Republican gushed, "They give you a feeling of pride and accomplishment . . . [and] enthusiasm for your leaders." At Washington's elegant Union Station, scene of one inaugural party, street people mingled with invited guests to filch hors d'oeuvres from the groaning tables.

The new administration nearly ended tragically ten weeks after it began when, on March 30, 1981, a deranged young man fired six bullets at Reagan as he emerged from a Washington hotel. One bullet hit presidential press secretary James Brady, paralyzing him and inflicting brain damage. Brady and his wife would later champion the cause of gun control.* Another bullet punctured Reagan's lung. He survived after surgery, although in graver condition than the public realized. Borrowing a movie line, he quipped, "I forgot to duck." His already high approval ratings soared.

Another defining moment early in Reagan's term came in August 1981 when the 11,600-member Professional Air Traffic Controllers Organization (PATCO)

---

* The Bradys' long campaign gained a partial victory on November 30, 1993 when Congress passed the so-called Brady Bill requiring a five-day waiting period for the purchase of a handgun, to allow for a background check of the prospective purchaser.

called an illegal strike. Although PATCO had endorsed Reagan, the president fired the strikers when they defied a back-to-work order. Some found his action needlessly harsh, but many Americans, judging PATCO workers arrogant and overpaid, applauded his tough stance. The failed PATCO strike symbolized the weakened clout of organized labor. Indeed, by 1987 only 17 percent of American workers belonged to unions, down from 23 percent in 1980.

Reagan's domestic program, a pastiche of New Right themes, featured four key elements: tax cuts, reduced federal regulation, increased military spending, and—somewhat improbably—a balanced budget in three years. As a further, unstated goal, the administration hoped to reduce the government's commitment to affirmative action for minorities and vigorous enforcement of the civil-rights laws.

Reduced taxes, Reagan claimed, citing the ideas of California economist Arthur Laffer, would jump-start the economy as consumers spent their windfall and as businesses invested in new plants and new technology. The resulting boom would increase tax revenues even at lower rates. Laffer summed up this theory, known as supply-side economics, in the "Laffer curve," a chart that he had first sketched on a restaurant napkin in 1974. His analysis showed economic activity rising as tax rates fell. Most economists had severe doubts about Laffer's simplistic theory, viewing it as wishful thinking. George Bush, during his own try for the Republican nomination in 1980, had called it "voodoo economics." Once on the ticket, Bush quickly reversed himself, an early example of the kind of behavior that would gain him a reputation for opportunism. Yet the *Wall Street Journal* and other influential voices endorsed Laffer's ideas, and Ronald Reagan, long convinced that high taxes served as socialism's entering wedge, had proved an easy convert.

Reagan's tax-cutting, probusiness ideology won a boost also from George Gilder, a conservative polemicist who argued in *Wealth and Poverty* (1981) that of all possible economic systems, capitalism most fully expressed humankind's highest spiritual aspirations. The capitalist, he declaimed, must have "faith in man, faith in the future, . . . faith in the mutual benefits of trade, [and] faith in the providence of God." In these years of rising evangelical fervor, the line between social policy and religious dogma thus often blurred.

Reagan's youthful budget director, David Stockman, shared his boss's tax-cutting fervor. Stockman had joined SDS in the sixties, but by 1976 he was off to Congress as a Republican. For him, as he revealed in a candid *Atlantic Monthly* interview in December 1981, tax cuts were part of a larger project: to move toward a "minimalist" government and to dismantle the welfare state. Supply-side economics, he conceded, was simply the old "trickle-down" theory: if the rich get richer, the benefits will find their way to the rest of society. As budget director, he proposed an incredible 30 percent tax cut over three years. Only slightly modifying this request, Congress in May 1981 approved a 25 percent cut: 5 percent in 1981 and 10 percent in each of the next two years.

Many congressional Republicans, joined by conservative southern Democrats called "boll weevils," supported the call for spending cuts. The list of social programs that felt the budget-cutters' knife grew long and included food stamps, child nutrition, job training, and Aid to Families with Dependent Children. Ironically, despite cuts of $45 billion in specific programs, total federal spending on social welfare, including entitlement programs, such as social security and Medicare, rose from $313 billion in 1980 to $533 billion by 1988. Even determined Reaganites could do no more than chip away at the welfare state. Yet the slashes in social spending were significant, reflecting both a budget-balancing impulse and middle-class fears of growing welfare dependency. Charles Murray, a former social worker, expressed this rising frustration in *Losing Ground: American Social Policy, 1950–1980* (1984). Social programs intended "to provide more for the poor," Murray charged, had merely "produced more poor instead."

Viewed in simplest terms, Reagan's tax cuts and the reduced social spending of the early 1980s redistributed income from the poor to the wealthy. In 1980 the poorest 20 percent of U.S. households received 4.9 percent of total after-tax income. By 1985 this figure had fallen to 4.6 percent. In the same period, the after-tax income share of the top 20 percent of households rose from 40.6 percent to 42.6 percent, the highest since World War II. In actual dollar terms, the inflation-adjusted annual income of the poorest 10 percent of American families fell by 10.5 percent over 1980–1985. The very richest Americans, the top 1 percent, saw their taxable income from investments, adjusted for inflation, jump by 112 percent between 1980 and 1990, and income from salaries grew by 81 percent.

These changes did not derive entirely from the tax cut. The rise in taxable income at the upper levels, for example, stemmed in part from the more favorable tax climate, which led the wealthy to shift capital from tax shelters to taxable investments. Among the poor, the loss of factory jobs contributed to the income decline. Immigration influenced income statistics as well. The Hispanic population, fed by a steady flow of newcomers from Mexico and the Caribbean nations, grew by 53 percent in the 1980s. As immigrants continued to flood in from the Philippines, China, Korea, and Vietnam, the Asian-American population doubled. Whereas some of the new arrivals, particularly those from Asia, were well educated and moved quickly into good-paying jobs, most began their life in America at the lowest rungs. Changes in income patterns had complex sources in the 1980s, but Reagan's tax policies played a central role.

Although the administration insisted that a "safety net" protected the truly needy, cuts in social spending made life harder for the poor. The number of homeless grew markedly. A policy of deinstitutionalizing the chronically mentally ill, implemented in these years, added to the ranks of street people. In 1987 one of five American children lived in poverty, up by 24 percent from 1979. A few activists still championed the cause of the poor, but to unreceptive ears. Marian Wright Edelman of the Children's Defense Fund calculated that the money spent annually on operating a private dining room for the secretary of defense would restore morning snacks for 1 million low-income school children, one of many Reagan-era budget cuts. In *Rachel and Her Children: Homeless Families in America* (1988), Jonathan Kozol described life in a New York City welfare hotel:

> There are families in this building [who] . . . , like refugees . . . in the midst of war, cling to each other and establish a small zone of safety. [But] most people here do not have resources to create a zone of safety. Terrorized already on arrival, they are quickly caught up in a vortex of accelerating threats and are tossed about like bits of wood and broken furniture and shattered houses in an Arkansas tornado. Chaos and

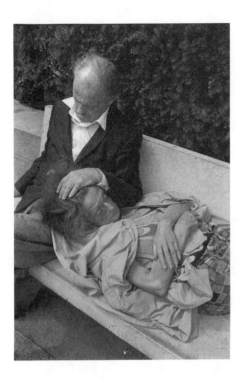

Beneath the booming prosperity of the Reagan years, severe social problems festered. A homeless man and woman, wearily resting on a park bench in Philadelphia, were witnessed by a photographer in 1986. (© *James Conroy*)

disorder alternate with lethargy and nearly absolute bewilderment in face of regulations they cannot observe or do not understand.

Reaganomics struck even at Americans who had jobs. In 1988, *U.S. News and World Report* found that some 9 million working adults earned incomes below the poverty level, including "people like Glen Witbeck, a short-order cook whose $8,000 annual salary doesn't stretch to cover his two little girls' medical bills. Or like Charlie Scott, a construction worker whose money woes forced him and his wife into a shelter and then, most recently, provoked a separation. Or Pamela Kelley, a one-time airline-passenger screener who shifted to canned food at home because pot roast was too expensive for her and her two-year-old daughter." An advanced degree offered no guarantee of upward mobility in the spotty Reagan economy. In 1988 the Ambassador Cab Company of Cambridge, Massachusetts, reported six Ph.D.s among its drivers.

Not even the middle class particularly benefited from the tax cuts. State taxes rose to cover new costs caused by drops in federal spending, and other charges and fees went up as well. In 1983 Congress raised social security taxes, further diluting the effects of the income-tax cut for low- and middle-income families. Overall, the average family's total tax burden remained about the same or increased slightly in these years. And although Reagan justifiably boasted of 20 million new jobs created in the 1980s, these were often service-sector positions with low pay, few benefits, and little prospect of advancement. As in the 1970s, many skilled workers in declining industries found their wages cut as they left the factory for unskilled work in the lower ranks of the service sector.

On the credit side of the ledger, Reagan's first term saw the end of the raging inflation of the 1970s. Owing to the Federal Reserve's continued tight-money policy and a drop in world oil prices, the inflation rate fell from 13.5 percent in 1980 to 6.2 percent by 1982 and to 1.9 percent by 1986. On the other hand, the remaining component of the 1970s economic crisis, the recession, worsened as the Fed's credit policies, designed to starve inflation, impeded business recovery. The "Reagan recession" of 1981–1982 produced painfully high jobless rates. With some 10 million Americans out of work in 1982–1983, the unemployment rate for both years remained stuck at 9.5 percent, the highest since 1941. Bank failures and business bankruptcies soared. The recession gradually bottomed out, however, and in November 1982 the stock market began a five-year rise. The later Reagan years would bring better times.

Just as the Fed's credit policies had both positive and negative effects, so, too, did other measures of the early 1980s. For example, the 1983 hike in social security taxes that diluted the economic stimulus intended by the income-tax cut was part of a much-needed overhaul of the entire social security system. In the long run, the reforms shored up a program hard hit by expanding benefits and ballooning Medicare costs, not to mention a tide of retirees. The 1983 reform taxed the benefits of well-to-do retirees and restricted automatic cost-of-living benefit increases while offering incentives to workers to delay retirement.

Implementing a New Right goal backed by many economists and by Jimmy Carter, the administration also set out to deregulate the economy. Indeed, many Reagan appointees scorned the entire concept of federal regulation, and the 1970s antigovernment mood burgeoned in Washington. Secretary of the Interior James Watt of Colorado, a leader of the "Sagebrush Rebellion" promoting private development of public lands, did his best to reduce federal control and to open these lands to exploitation. Watt's religious beliefs reinforced his laissez-faire ideology. Asked at his confirmation hearing whether he wished to protect the environment for future generations, he responded that he did not know how many generations remained before the Second Coming. Watt's bigotry (he characterized one advisory panel as "a black, a woman, two Jews, and a cripple") soon made him a liability, and Reagan dumped him in 1983. Nevertheless, the antiregulatory ideology that he personified lived on. The budget of the Environmental Protection Agency was slashed, for example. The head of EPA, Anne Gorsuch Burford, in charge of the $1.4 billion Superfund to clean up hazardous sites, showed favoritism toward polluters, with whom she had close links. A Burford aide indicted for lying to Congress served three months in jail. The head of the Securities and Exchange Commission (SEC), John Shad, a Wall Street insider and true believer in deregulation, radically reduced the SEC's oversight of the stock market. In 1984, when Shad became worried by the orgy of "insider" stock trading,* corporate takeovers, and dubious investment practices that resulted, laissez-faire ideologues in the SEC pressured him to maintain a hands-off policy.

The deregulation spirit pervaded the Federal Home Loan Bank Board, too, an

---

* "Insider trading" means profiting on the stock market from illegally acquired advance information on planned mergers or other corporate moves likely to cause a stock to rise in price.

agency charged with overseeing the savings and loan (S&L) industry. The subsequent wave of risky speculation and outright fraud would leave many S&Ls in ruins by the end of the 1980s (see p. 469). A multibillion-dollar federal program to salvage failed S&Ls and to reimburse depositors became part of the price of the deregulation mania.

Reagan's choice to head the Federal Communications Commission, Mark Fowler, was another disciple of deregulation. Fowler ridiculed the notion that TV had a public-service role. "Television is just another appliance," he insisted. "It's just a toaster with pictures. . . . [It is] time to move away from thinking about broadcasters as trustees, [and to] treat them the way almost everyone else in society does—that is, as business." Under Fowler, the FCC increased the amount of time that television stations could air commercials and dropped the rule that some programming time must be devoted to public-service broadcasts.

During Reagan's tenure, the Federal Trade Commission, the Occupational Safety and Health Administration, the Department of Transportation, the Justice Department's antitrust division, and other agencies sabotaged the regulatory laws that they existed to uphold. In his inaugural address, Reagan had joked, "It's not my intention to do away with government," yet zealots in his administration often seemed determined to do just that. Indeed, the agency monitoring consumer-product safety faced a 17 percent budget cut.

Along with tax cuts and deregulation, a beefed-up military ranked high on the Reagan agenda. The 1980 GOP platform had warned of an alarming post-Vietnam decline in U.S. armed might and called for a massive build-up. Once in office, Reagan launched the largest military expansion in peacetime history. Excluding veterans' affairs, the defense budget surged from $157 billion in 1981 to $273 billion in 1986. Corrected for inflation, the increases voted by Congress averaged nearly 7 percent a year in this period. The administration's enthusiasm for reactivating battleships illustrated the symbolic component of the military build-up. These dinosaurs had little utility in an era of missiles, nuclear submarines, and communications satellites that could easily track them; nevertheless, Reaganites' nostalgia for the glory days of World War II when U.S. battleships had symbolized American power ignored such arguments.

Secretary of Defense Caspar Weinberger presided over this build-up. As President Nixon's budget director, Weinberger had won the nickname "Cap the Knife" for his tightfistedness. Now at the Pentagon, he opened the tap wide. In his annual reports to Congress, Weinberger warned apocalyptically about America's "dangerous slide" in military preparedness and defended his huge budget requests as essential to U.S. security.

Reagan's admirers would later argue that the frantic military spending forced Moscow into a foolhardy effort to keep pace and thereby drove the Soviet economy and the entire system into crisis. The U.S. build-up may have been a factor, but political and economic conditions within the Soviet sphere itself probably explain the U.S.S.R.'s collapse more accurately. Whatever its global impact, Reagan's military expansion exerted profound political and economic effects at home. It benefited defense contractors and buttressed their political clout, and it generated thousands of jobs, especially in the Sun Belt. Glamorous high-tech weapons systems proliferated on the drawing boards. But ballooning defense budgets also enlarged the federal deficit, worrying even conservatives. "The United States can't afford everything the Pentagon wants," cautioned *Business Week* in a 1987 article, "Defense Spending: The Wild Blue Yonder."

Many Americans, including the conservative, patriotic, blue-collar and middle-class citizens who made up Richard Nixon's "silent majority," cheered Reagan's martial emphasis. Smarting over the Vietnam defeat, taught to expect the worst of the Soviet Union, and angered by OPEC rulers and Middle Eastern sheiks who seemed to tweak Uncle Sam's nose with impunity, they welcomed the boost to morale that came from pouring billions into military hardware. In liberal churches, on college and university campuses, and among peace advocates and antinuclear activists, however, the arms expansion met opposition. The Federal Emergency Management Agency (FEMA), with its plans to disperse city dwellers to rural areas if nuclear war threatened, helped to revive nuclear anxiety. So did the views of Undersecretary of Defense T. K. Jones, who argued that backyard fallout shelters would make nuclear war tolerable. "If there are enough shovels to go around," Jones promised cheerily, "everybody's going to make it." President Reagan contributed to the growing uneasiness by taking no arms-control initiatives in his first two years.

Events in Europe fed nuclear worries. Seeking parity with Soviet missiles in Eastern Europe, NATO and the Carter administration had agreed to deploy 572 U.S. cruise and Pershing II missiles in Great Britain and West Germany in 1979. NATO also affirmed its "first-use" policy on nuclear weapons: a Soviet thrust into Western Europe could trigger a nuclear response. Reagan's first secretary of state, Alexander Haig, vigorously championed this policy and described the utility of "nuclear warning shots" in conventional war situations.

As the planned deployment proceeded, protests spread across Europe. With TV newscasts showing antinuclear marchers in Great Britain, Germany, and elsewhere, U.S. activists also mobilized. The antinuclear power movement of the 1970s now targeted nuclear weapons. Protests reached levels not seen in America since the test-ban campaign of a quarter century before. Organizations such as SANE, the National Committee for a Sane Nuclear Policy, dusted off their mailing lists.

The movement coalesced around the "nuclear freeze" idea of Randall Forsberg, a Massachusetts arms-control specialist. Her plan was simple: while pursuing arms-reduction talks, the nuclear powers should declare a mutual freeze on building, testing, and deploying nuclear weapons. In the winter of 1981–1982, town meetings in New England passed freeze resolutions. *Time* magazine reported on the movement in a March 1982 cover story featuring a mushroom cloud. In June, 800,000 nuclear protesters—the largest political rally in U.S. history—gathered in New York's Central Park. That fall, voters in nine states, including California and Wisconsin, approved nuclear-freeze referenda.

Liberal church bodies endorsed the movement. *The Challenge of Peace*, a 1983 statement by the nation's Catholic bishops, raised grave doubts about U.S. nuclear policies. College students, writers, artists, and film makers joined the campaign. In the 1983 movie *War Games*, an out-of-control Defense Department computer nearly obliterates the world. Jonathan Schell's *The Fate of the Earth* (1984) pondered the meaning of a nuclear holocaust that could leave a planet devoid of all memory that

"The Day After." This 1984 ABC-TV special, which graphically portrayed the effects of a thermonuclear attack on Kansas City, both reflected and heightened the nuclear jitters of the early Reagan years. (*Copyright © 1985, ABC-TV/Capital Cities, Inc.*)

human beings had ever existed. "The Day After," a 1984 ABC-TV special, portrayed the effects of nuclear war on Kansas. Tim O'Brien's 1985 novel, *Nuclear Age*, explored the hero's memories of growing up with the bomb. Scientist Carl Sagan and others warned that the atmospheric effects of thermonuclear war could lower average temperatures over vast regions and bring on a permanent "nuclear winter."

Meanwhile, however, Reagan had struck back in a TV speech on March 23, 1983. Conceding the horror of nuclear war, the president offered his remedy: not a nuclear freeze but the Strategic Defense Initiative (SDI), a space-based defensive shield with computerized laser beams and other high-tech weaponry to destroy incoming missiles. Reagan's proposal, a surprise to the Pentagon, was the brainchild of physicist Edward Teller, "the father of the H-bomb," whom Reagan much admired.

Nicknamed "Star Wars" by the media, SDI drew criticism from scientists who derided its futuristic technology, including fantastically complex computer systems that could never be fully tested except under actual attack conditions. Arms-control specialists warned that SDI would violate the 1972 Anti-Ballistic Missile Treaty, which had outlawed missile-defense systems that might tempt a nation to deliver a first strike. Nonetheless, legislators were unwilling to invite accusations of neglecting the nation's defense, and they voted funds for SDI research that eventually totaled $30 billion. The program would stumble on until 1992, when the Bush administration quietly shelved it. In 1993 the *New York Times* revealed that key SDI tests had been rigged, not only to deceive the Soviets but also to ensure continued funding. However impractical, SDI had served Reagan's immediate political purpose: He had seized the initiative from the antinuclear activists, and by 1984 the freeze movement was fading fast.

Increased defense spending coupled with tax cuts mocked President Reagan's budget-balancing pledges. In fact, the annual federal deficit zoomed from $74 billion in 1981 to $185 billion in 1984. During Reagan's first term, the total federal debt rose from $994 billion to a gargantuan $1.8 trillion. This result did not surprise the administration. David Stockman in his 1981 *Atlantic Monthly* interview admitted that tax cuts coupled with increased defense spending would yield huge budget deficits. In fact, he had gambled that Congress, faced with a choice between massive deficits and radical cuts in domestic spending, would choose the latter. In making this choice, the legislature would thereby sever what Stockman called "the umbilical cords of dependency that ran from Washington to every nook and cranny of the nation." In short, the administration deliberately induced budget deficits to starve domestic social spending.

Attuned to the nation's conservative mood, Reagan also sympathized with the white backlash that had fueled the New Right. He had opposed the civil-rights acts of 1964 and 1965 and in private told stories of a mythic "welfare queen" who had amassed a fortune by defrauding the welfare system. As president, he emulated the Nixon-Ford strategy of foot-dragging on civil rights. The White House encouraged local school boards to resist mandatory busing orders and slashed the budgets of the Equal Employment Opportunity Commission and the Office of Federal Contract Compliance. As head of the Justice Department's civil-rights division, Reagan named William Bradford Reynolds, a corporate lawyer who had no background in civil rights. In a telling illustration of the decade's mood, Reynolds openly proclaimed his goal of reversing the division's vigorous support for affirmative-action programs.

New Militance: Reagan and Foreign Policy

If Reagan's domestic policy reversed the activism of discredited liberals, his foreign policy was highly activist and reflected the New Right's intense hostility to communism. The administration moved aggressively to fight communism and leftism in the Third World, especially in Latin America, and adopted a highly belligerent stance toward the Soviet Union. Reagan continued and amplified the anti-Soviet tone of Jimmy Carter's final year in office. But the White House also faced foreign challenges that did not lend themselves readily to the stark polarities of Cold War ideology, especially in the Middle East. Despite the Israeli-Egyptian treaty, peace proved elusive. White House attention initially centered on Lebanon, an unstable nation prey to its powerful neighbors Syria and Israel. The Palestine Liberation Organization (PLO) had its headquarters in the Lebanon capital of Beirut, and in southern Lebanon thousands of displaced Palestinians eked out lives in squalid refugee camps.

In June 1982, countering terrorism committed by an extremist faction within the PLO, Israel attacked PLO strongholds and established an Israeli-controlled "security zone" in southern Lebanon. The invasion led inadvertently to a massacre of Palestinian refugees by Lebanese Christian militia linked to Israel. Conflict among the various groups vying for power in that troubled nation intensified. The PLO high command, expelled from Lebanon, shifted to Tunisia. President Reagan, as part of an international force overseeing the PLO withdrawal and trying to mediate among warring factions, ordered two thousand U.S. Marines to Lebanon. Because of America's close ties to Israel, radical Shiite Muslim groups reviled the marines. In October 1983 a Shiite terrorist drove a truck loaded with explosives into the lightly guarded U.S. barracks near the Beirut airport. The shattering blast killed 239 marines. Fifty French troops died in a related attack. Reagan withdrew the remaining U.S. forces.

At the same time, Secretary of State George Shultz, who replaced Alexander Haig in 1982, tried in vain to revive the stalled Middle East peace process. Deeming the Palestinians and their political representatives a key to long-term stability in the region, Shultz sought to bring PLO leader Yasir Arafat and Jordan's King Hussein into the negotiations. Yet Israeli security fears, Syria's opposition to negotiations, and PLO suspicions of Hussein all conspired to scuttle Shultz's efforts. So, too, did growing Jewish settlements in the West Bank territories seized by Israel from Jordan in the 1967 war.

Closer to home, the Reagan administration fought radical insurgencies in Latin America. Plagued by explosive population growth and vast disparities of wealth and poverty, this region had long suffered military coups and guerrilla violence. Reagan, ever the Cold Warrior, saw in all these complexities the sinister hand of Moscow. Here was an opportunity to resume the anticommunist struggle that Lyndon Johnson had pursued in Vietnam, but this time with success. In El Salvador, the White House helped to fund a right-wing military regime fighting a guerrilla insurgency backed by Nicaragua and Castro's Cuba. But aware that a less repressive regime was more likely to win popular support, the State Department backed the moderate José Napoleon Duarte in a 1984 presidential election. Duarte's victory did not end the efforts of El Salvador's ruling elite to stamp out its opposition by brutal means, however. Death squads linked to the army continued to murder civilians, from poor farmers to professionals such as teachers and physicians suspected of opposing the regime.

In Nicaragua, as we saw in Chapter 13, President Carter had recognized the Marxist-led Sandinistas who overthrew dictator Anastasio Somoza in 1979. Reagan, accusing the Sandinistas of aiding the rebels in El Salvador, not only reversed Carter's policy but committed the United States to the Sandinistas' overthrow. The Soviet Union, he charged, wanted to turn Nicaragua into another communist enclave like Cuba. Under director William Casey, the CIA in 1982 organized, trained, and financed the contras, a ten-thousand-strong anti-Sandinista guerrilla army based in Honduras and Costa Rica. Some top contra leaders had close links to the discredited Somoza regime. Infiltrating Nicaragua, the contras conducted raids, carried out sabotage, and used a CIA manual that explained how to "neutralize" local Sandinista officials. Civilians suffered heavily in the shadowy war, but the contras won President Reagan's praise as "the moral equivalent of our Founding Fathers."

Home-front opposition to the CIA-run contra war soon flared. Members of Congress as well as ordinary citizens accused the administration of perpetuating the old practice of backing Latin American elites against the masses and of deceiving the American people in the process. Others feared another inconclusive, Vietnam-style conflict in Latin America. In December 1982, Congress halted military aid to the contras for one year. Matters came to a head in 1984. That April, the *Wall Street Journal* reported, CIA agents, with the written approval of President Reagan, had mined Nicaragua's harbors, running the risk of sinking Soviet or other foreign vessels. Members of the Senate Select Committee on Intelligence, charged with overseeing the CIA, seethed, for CIA head William Casey had concealed the operation from them. Senator Barry Goldwater, chairman of the committee, wrote angrily to Casey, "It gets down to one little, simple phrase. I am pissed off!" In October 1984 the House passed an amendment introduced by Representative Edward Boland of Massachusetts imposing a two-year ban on contra aid.

Amid the controversy, the contra insurgency itself faltered. In 1988 the Sandinistas and the contras would reach a truce arranged by President Oscar Arias Sánchez of Costa Rica and by other Central American leaders. To the end of his term, however, Reagan continued to hope for a contra victory.

On another Latin American front, two thousand U.S. Marines in October 1983 invaded the tiny West Indian island nation of Grenada, where Cuban-backed radicals had seized power. The United States ostensibly aimed to rescue U.S. students attending a Grenada medical college, yet the White House proclaimed a larger purpose: to prevent the emergence of another outpost of Cuban-Soviet power and to show America's post-Vietnam willingness to protect its interests. Expelling Cuban workers building an airfield, the Marines installed a pro-U.S. government in Grenada.

With Soviet troops still in Afghanistan and Reagan accusing Moscow of fomenting trouble in Latin America, relations with Moscow sank to their lowest point in years. In a March 1983 address to a gathering of evangelical leaders, Reagan lambasted the Soviet Union as an "evil empire" and "the focus of evil in the modern world." Relations further deteriorated that September when a Soviet SU-15 fighter shot down a Korean airliner that had flown far into Soviet air space. All 269 passengers, including 61 Americans, died, and the circumstances of the tragedy remained unclear. Rejecting Moscow's charge that the plane had been conducting espionage, the White House and right-wing political groups used the disaster to step up their denunciations of Soviet monstrousness and perfidy.* Détente, floundering at the end of Carter's term, now seemed moribund.

Apart from the Middle East, U.S. foreign policy during Reagan's first term saw a sharpening of Cold War hostility, evidenced by increased military spending and the neglect of arms control. Belligerent speeches and pronouncements and vigorous resistance to Soviet expansion, real or imagined, in Latin America completed the picture. These measures won applause from the New Right, as proof that America's post-Vietnam funk had lifted. Although a tonic at home, Reagan's ideologically

---

* In 1992, with the Cold War over, Moscow would admit that the intrusion had come about because of navigational error.

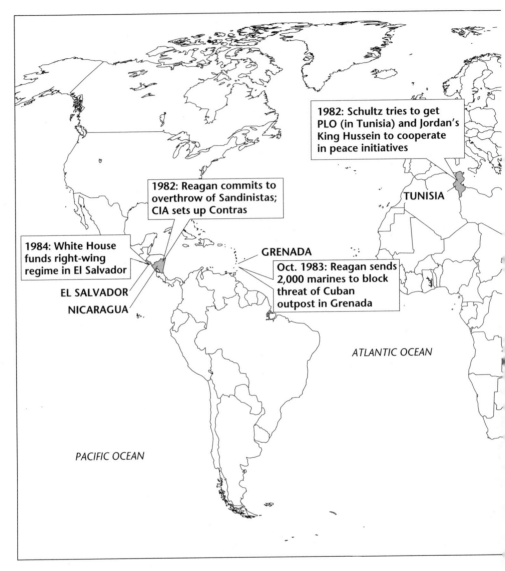

FIGURE 14.2
Reagan and the World, 1980–1984

driven diplomacy failed to sustain Nixon's important détente initiative, or to take into account the indigenous sources of the conflicts raging in the poverty-wracked nations south of the U.S. border.

Buoyed by the new militance in foreign affairs, Reaganism reached its apogee in the 1984 election year. Belying the carping of a dwindling cadre of liberal critics, most Americans rated Reagan's first term a success. He had chalked up some achievements, and even the setbacks did not hurt his standing. Reagan's unabashed patriotism stirred a powerful response, and sports fans waving the stars and stripes

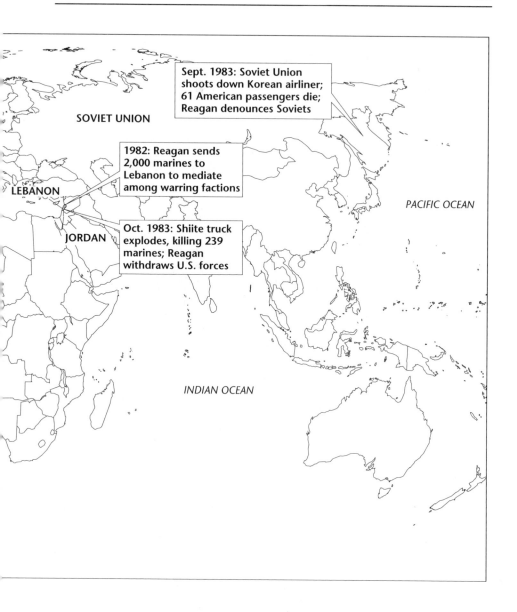

Sept. 1983: Soviet Union shoots down Korean airliner; 61 American passengers die; Reagan denounces Soviets

SOVIET UNION

1982: Reagan sends 2,000 marines to Lebanon to mediate among warring factions

LEBANON

Oct. 1983: Shiite truck explodes, killing 239 marines; Reagan withdraws U.S. forces

JORDAN

PACIFIC OCEAN

INDIAN OCEAN

and chanting "We're Number One" at the 1984 Summer Olympics in Los Angeles summed up the expansive mood. Despite encouraging results in the 1982 midterm election, in which the Democrats had gained twenty-six seats in the House, Reagan's popularity posed a serious hurdle for Democratic presidential hopefuls. Walter Mondale of Minnesota, Carter's vice president and a prominent liberal, won the party nomination, although not without a fight. Senator Gary Hart of Colorado beat him in the New Hampshire primary. Chicago's Jesse Jackson, a former aide of Martin Luther King, Jr., enjoyed the allegiance of many African-Americans. In the end, though, Mondale, backed by the party leadership, lined up the labor and teacher unions, women's organizations, and other interest groups, and earned the nomination. Criticizing Reagan's military build-up and belligerent rhetoric, he also ridiculed SDI as unworkable. Mondale pleased union backers by calling for import quotas and other barriers on manufactured products from abroad.

The high point of Mondale's campaign came at the Democratic convention, when he named Congresswoman Geraldine Ferraro of New York as his running mate, the first woman to appear on a major party presidential ticket. But his prospects faded when he announced in his acceptance speech that as president he would raise taxes. Mondale hoped that this admission would win him points for candor, but to many voters it simply confirmed GOP charges that Democrats were the "tax-and-spend" party. The Mondale campaign also lost momentum in its early weeks owing to a controversy over the tangled real-estate dealings of Ferraro's husband.

Despite soaring deficits, Reagan again promised to balance the budget and blamed free-spending Democrats in Congress for sabotaging this goal. In a TV debate, the seventy-four-year-old president jokingly pledged not to make a campaign issue of his fifty-six-year-old opponent's "youth and inexperience." The Reagan-Bush ticket triumphed in a landslide. Without a third-party challenge as in 1980 to siphon off support, Reagan garnered 59 percent of the popular vote to Mondale's 41 percent. Mondale collected a mere thirteen electoral votes: his home state of Minnesota and the District of Columbia. Even with Ferraro on the ticket, he failed to carry New York or to win a majority of women voters. Blacks and Hispanics (except for pro-Reagan Cuban exiles in Florida) voted heavily Democratic but could not stem the Reagan tide. Portraying Mondale as a captive of "special interests," Reagan ran well in white working-class neighborhoods, where the Democratic vote dropped by 15 percent from the 1980 totals.

The 1984 election revealed the scope of the post-1960 shift in U.S. politics. In place of the liberal consensus stood a new coalition of disaffected "middle Americans" forged in the reactionary social climate and economic stresses of the 1970s. The New Right comprised an unstable but potent alliance of wealthy Americans, corporate leaders, evangelicals, Catholic ethnics, and white blue-collar workers. Whatever their differences otherwise, these groups shared an antipathy to intrusive federal regulations and cultural trends that threatened "traditional values." With one voice, they decried public policies that favored minorities, welfare recipients, feminists, homosexuals, and others who seemed to seek preferential treatment from the government.

The election outcome also reflected the demographic shifts of these years, as Rust Belt workers sought greener pastures. Whereas the Northeast and Midwest grew only slightly in 1970–1990, the South's population exploded from 63 million to 87 million; the Pacific states, from 27 million to 39 million. California, having already passed New York as the most populous state in the 1960s, blossomed by another 20 percent in the 1980s, from 24 million to 30 million. These changes contributed to the 1984 Reagan landslide as the South and West, enjoying the lion's share of Reagan-era military spending, voted solidly Republican. In the onetime Democratic bastion of Texas, for example, 64 percent of the voters chose Reagan. Across the Sun Belt, a similar story unfolded, as ideology and demography converged.

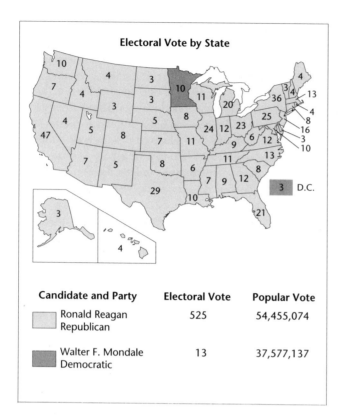

FIGURE 14.3

Presidential Election of 1984

Electoral Vote by State

Candidate and Party		Electoral Vote	Popular Vote
	Ronald Reagan Republican	525	54,455,074
	Walter F. Mondale Democratic	13	37,577,137

Scandal and Surprises: Reagan's Second Term

Reagan's second inaugural address, delivered inside the Capitol rotunda because of bitingly cold weather, again struck a note of soaring optimism and love of country. The president evoked an American past of praying generals, singing pioneers, and other sturdy individualists. But Reagan's mellow rhetoric obscured the sink-or-swim ideology and cuts in social programs that underlay his message. For all its inspiration, Reagan's limning of a society made safe for acquisitiveness and competition offered no unifying vision other than a rather jingoistic patriotism. Moreover, a rising cycle of Middle East terrorism and the Iran-contra affair marred Reagan's foreign policy of 1984–1988. The latter scandal, a tangle of high-level illegalities, would dominate national attention and for a time threaten to cripple another presidency. In retrospect, however, the most momentous developments of Reagan's second term would unfold not in Washington but in Moscow, where a dramatic series of events portended nothing less than the collapse of the Soviet Union and the Cold War.

Equally important, three Supreme Court retirements, two during his second term, enabled Reagan to place his stamp on the judicial branch. In 1981 he had appointed Sandra Day O'Connor of Arizona, the first woman to serve on the high court. When Chief Justice Warren Burger retired in 1986, Reagan elevated William

Rehnquist, a Nixon appointee, to the chief justiceship and named to the vacancy the conservative Antonin Scalia, a federal judge who had taught at the University of Chicago Law School. Scalia soon emerged as a rigid advocate of presidential power. The third opening, in 1987, sparked a fight. The Senate rejected Reagan's first nominee, Robert Bork. Opinionated, sarcastic, and harshly critical of judicial activism, Bork struck many as unsuited both by temperament and by judicial philosophy for a seat on the Court. Reagan's next choice, Judge Douglas Ginsburg, withdrew after revelations that he had smoked marijuana while a Harvard Law School professor. Reagan finally turned to Anthony M. Kennedy of San Francisco, who gained easy confirmation. Although chosen for their conservative credentials, O'Connor and Kennedy would emerge in the 1990s as centrists in contrast to the Court's more doctrinaire right wingers.

On the economic front, Reagan in his second term achieved one goal that had eluded Jimmy Carter. The tax-reform law of 1986 plugged some loopholes and exempted millions of poor Americans from paying taxes altogether. But it also extended the regressive feature of Reaganomics, cutting tax rates for the wealthiest Americans to a maximum of 28 percent. On the other hand, inflation remained low, and unemployment declined in the later 1980s. Yet in Washington the red ink gushed on. After soaring to $238 billion in 1986, the federal deficit dropped somewhat but still stood at $206 billion in 1989, the year that Reagan left office. The ever-rising national debt hovered near $3 trillion by 1989. Washington borrowed billions each year merely to pay interest on the debt, straining the credit market and threatening to push up interest rates and bring back recession. Only heavy purchases of U.S. government securities by investors in Japan and Western Europe staved off this disaster. Liberal economist Stanley Weintraub satirically crowned Reagan "king of the deficit makers and undisputed master of the national debt mountain." Princeton economist Uwe Reinhardt warned in 1987 of prosperity achieved at the expense of future generations who would have to pay the bills.

As the deficit grew, Congress at last trimmed the Pentagon's budget. The rate of increase in defense spending, in constant dollars, fell from 8.8 percent in 1985 to under 1 percent in 1988. Budget worries also led to the Gramm-Rudman-Hollings Act of 1985, which aimed to achieve a balanced budget by the early 1990s by mandating specific deficit-reduction targets. Both Congress and the administration showed great creativity in evading the law, however, and in 1986 the Supreme Court ruled that one of its key enforcement provisions violated the constitutional principle of separation of powers.

The United States' international economic position weakened in Reagan's second term as the trade gap widened. In 1984 Americans imported $112 billion more than they exported; by 1987 the gap reached $160 billion, with imports from Japan and other Asian nations accounting for nearly 80 percent of the total. Alarmed, the administration pressured Japan to open its insular domestic market to more U.S. imports and to stop "dumping," or selling exports below cost to maintain market dominance. In 1987, Reagan retaliated for Japan's dumping of microchips and imposed duties on Japanese electronics. The White House rejected calls for more protectionism from sectors of the economy hurt by imports, however, and in 1988 signed a free-trade pact with Canada to eliminate most trade barriers between the two nations by 1999.

While the defense industry, the service sector, and certain high-tech businesses prospered in the eighties, other elements of the economy continued to languish. Joblessness among inner-city minorities remained a chronic problem. As Americans caught the acquisitive spirit, total consumer debt exploded from $302 billion in 1980 to $671 billion by 1988. All of these problems—the deficit, the trade gap, the spotty economic picture, the upsurge in credit buying—fostered uneasiness. On October 19, 1987, the five-year stock-market boom crash-landed with a shocking 500-point plunge. In the worst one-day drop ever, the value of the nation's stocks shrank by 20 percent. The market slowly recovered, but the 1987 collapse exposed the nagging doubts gripping the nation after six years of Reaganomics.

Despite such economic woes, world events and their domestic fallout dominated Reagan's second term. In 1988, during a Palestinian uprising against Israeli's occupation of Gaza and the West Bank, George Shultz launched a final Middle East peace effort. He based his approach on a "land for peace" formula: Israel would give up the occupied territories in return for security guarantees by the PLO and the Arab nations. Under U.S. pressure, PLO head Yasir Arafat renounced terrorism and conceded Israel's right to exist. But Israel's government, now headed by Yitzhak Shamir of the right-wing Likud party, who favored continued Jewish settlements on the West Bank, rejected Shultz's efforts. Within five years, Israel and the PLO would sign a peace accord, but that dramatic breakthrough seemed remote in 1988.

Terrorism, not peace hopes, more typically preoccupied the White House in these years. The 1983 bombing of the U.S. Marine barracks in Beirut heralded a larger campaign of fear launched by shadowy groups linked to the PLO, to Iran's Hezbollah (Party of God), and to Libya's ruler, Muammar el-Qaddafi. Terrorists demanding the release of Israeli-held Palestinians hijacked airplanes and attacked airports across Europe. In June 1985, 135 passengers aboard TWA flight 847 hijacked over Greece endured seventeen nightmarish days of captivity. That October, PLO agents seized an Italian cruise ship, the *Achille Lauro*, and murdered a wheelchair-bound Jewish-American passenger. In April 1986, terrorists linked to Libya bombed a Berlin discotheque popular with GIs. An irate Reagan ordered a raid by F-111 bombers on military sites around Tripoli. The cycle of terrorism escalated. In December 1988, a Pan Am jet en route from London to New York crashed near Lockerbie, Scotland, killing all 259 aboard, including numerous Americans. Investigators found evidence of a bomb hidden in the baggage section. In 1991 the U.S. and British governments, blaming Libya for the bombing, demanded the extradition of two Libyan officials for trial. Qaddafi refused, and the stand-off continued.

A wave of political kidnappings also hit Beirut, a hotbed of radical Palestinian and Shiite ferment. Carter's obsession with the Iranian hostages had shown the potency of this technique, and from 1982 to 1985 terrorists seized nine Americans. One, William Buckley, head of the CIA bureau in Beirut, died in captivity on June 3, 1985, probably under torture. Hostages from Britain and various European nations were taken as well. Although Reagan agonized less publicly over the hostages than had Carter, he was equally preoccupied with winning their freedom.

Two administration goals—release of the Beirut hostages and support for the contras—led to the web of misdeeds known as the Iran-contra affair. In August 1985, unbeknown to Congress or the public, President Reagan had approved the sale of 504-TOW antitank missiles to Iran, then at war with Iraq. National security adviser Robert McFarlane had directed the deal. In return, officials hoped that Tehran would use its influence to secure the release of the U.S. hostages in Beirut, especially the CIA's William Buckley, who was thought to be alive. Israel shipped the arms, with a former member of the shah's secret police, Manucher Ghorbanifar, acting as middleman. In all, the U.S. sold 2,004 TOWs and 18 HAWK antiaircraft missiles to Iran. The effort bore little fruit; one hostage went free in September 1985, and two more late in 1986, but three more were seized, and Iran remained stridently anti-American. The deal contradicted Reagan's repeated pledges never to negotiate with terrorists and mocked his pressure on other nations to boycott Iran. It also violated the Arms Control Export Act and an arms embargo against Iran imposed by Congress in 1979.

On November 3, 1986, a Beirut newspaper broke the story of these arms shipments and added startling details. In May 1986, the paper said, Robert McFarlane (having resigned as national security adviser the previous December) had flown with a shipment of HAWK parts to Tehran, bearing a Bible autographed by President Reagan for presentation to the Ayatollah Khomeini. McFarlane called the story "a piece of pure fiction," and Reagan denounced it as "utterly false," but confirming

Though political cartoonists compared Watergate and the Iran-contra scandal, the latter left President Reagan nearly unscathed. (© *Bill Day*/Detroit Free Press)

evidence soon leaked out. Shocked Americans learned that their government had sold arms and curried favor with the same U.S.-hating regime that had perpetrated the hostage ordeal of 1979–1981.

Later in November came still more explosive news: Funds from the Iranian arms sales had been secretly diverted to the contras, at a time when Congress had explicitly forbidden such aid. Lieutenant Colonel Oliver North of the U.S. Marine Corps, a National Security Council aide, had directed the operation from his White House office. Using various middlemen, including a retired air force general, North had funneled millions of dollars to the contras. North had also raised some $37 million for the contras from Saudi Arabia and other governments, as well as from wealthy U.S. conservatives, and thus had further circumvented the Boland amendment. North's operation had its own airplanes, pilots, ship, and communications system. The deal unfolded in deep secrecy, with no accountability to Congress or to the public.

When this story broke, North and his secretary shredded key documents and erased computer files in his office just before FBI investigators arrived. Some files remained on back-up disks, however, and provided crucial evidence of North's activities. On November 25, President Reagan praised North as "a national hero"—but dismissed him nevertheless. Rear Admiral John Poindexter, McFarlane's successor as national security adviser, resigned.

In December, Reagan named an investigative panel headed by ex-senator John Tower of Texas. Its March 1987 report criticized Reagan's lax management style but blamed the Iran-contra debacle mainly on White House aides, especially Chief of Staff Donald Regan, who also resigned. On TV, President Reagan denied knowing of any illegalities but admitted "mistakes." "What began as a strategic opening to Iran," he claimed, "deteriorated into trading arms for hostages."

In May–July 1987, a joint House-Senate committee conducted hearings on the scandal. Under two Democratic cochairmen, Senator Daniel Inouye of Hawaii and Congressman Lee Hamilton of Indiana, the committee heard 250 hours of testimony, much of it televised to a fascinated nation. Oliver North, a decorated Vietnam veteran, sat ramrod straight in full-dress uniform during his six days of riveting testimony. He admitted lying under oath, destroying documents, and falsifying records to conceal the White House role in the arms-for-hostages and contra-diversion schemes, but he insisted that love of country had motivated his every action. He claimed that he had kept his superiors informed and that he had worked closely with CIA director William Casey (who died in May 1987) to develop a covert-operations network beyond the reach of Congress. Many people thought North mawkish and self-serving, but others found his patriotism inspiring. A wave of "Olliemania" swept the country, and North remained a hero to the political Right for years after.

Pipe-smoking John Poindexter admitted that he had approved North's plan to divert funds to the contras but loyally insisted that he had not told Reagan, in order to give the president "plausible deniability." Poindexter also revealed that he had destroyed Reagan's written approval of the initial arms sale to Iran, to spare him future political embarrassment.

In its report, the joint committee cited a litany of illegal acts, including failure to notify Congress of the arms sales, destroying and altering official documents, and diverting funds to the contras despite Congress's ban. The committee also noted a pervasive contempt for the law and for Congress by North and others. The committee found no evidence of Reagan's direct knowledge of criminal activity but echoed the Tower Commission's criticism of lax White House procedures: "The President created or at least tolerated an environment where those who did know of the diversion believed with certainty that they were carrying out the president's policies." The scandal, the report concluded, had not only strained relations between the White House and Congress but also gravely compromised the credibility of the presidency—and, indeed, of the United States.

Attorney General Edwin Meese in the meantime, much criticized for his casual initial investigation of the scandal, had appointed special prosecutor Lawrence Walsh to handle the criminal aspects of the case. In March 1988, a federal grand jury indicted North, Poindexter, and two of North's intermediaries, Richard Secord and Albert Hakim, on various charges. Robert McFarlane, having survived a suicide attempt, pleaded guilty to misleading Congress (a misdemeanor) and cooperated with the prosecution. In May 1989, North was convicted of destroying evidence and other offenses. Federal judge Gerhard Gesell, pointedly calling him "a low-ranking subordinate" in the scheme, fined North $150,000 and ordered him to perform twelve hundred hours of community service. (By this time North was earning up to $200,000 a month on the lecture circuit.) In June 1990, a jury found John Poindexter guilty on five felony charges; he received a six-month jail term. A federal appeals court reversed both convictions in 1991, ruling that they had rested in part on congressional testimony given under grants of immunity against self-incrimination.*

In contrast to Richard Nixon's fate, the Iran-contra scandal left Reagan relatively unscathed. Not only did the president enjoy a deeper reserve of public goodwill, but no "smoking gun" comparable to the Nixon tapes linked him directly to illegal activities. Many Americans, too, agreed that the operation, however misguided, arose from motives of patriotism. Yet the affair again underscored the vulnerability of constitutional government to executive abuse. When North's secretary, Fawn Hall, justified her shredding of documents (and smuggling of others out of the White House in her underclothes) by asserting that "sometimes you have to go above the written law," the arrogance of power became apparent. In an exchange with John Poindexter, Lee Hamilton flatly rejected Poindexter's claim that the ends justified the means, even in a good cause: "[If] we subvert our democratic process to bring about a desired end, no matter how strongly we may believe in that end, we've weakened our country."

As the Iran-contra affair receded, events on the main Cold War stage seized the limelight. Under President Mikhail Gorbachev, who came to power in 1985, the Soviet Union experienced profound transformation. Decades of control by Communist party officials in Moscow had stifled the Soviet economy and had led to massive

---

* The felony charges against Secord and Hakim were dropped, and they received two years' probation on the remaining charges. In 1992, six years after the scandal broke, Walsh would secure an indictment against former secretary of defense Caspar Weinberger, citing evidence that he had known more about the operation than he later testified. President George Bush granted Weinberger a full pardon, however, and Walsh dropped the indictment.

shortages in food and consumer goods. In addition, unrest simmered in Soviet-dominated Eastern Europe and in the Soviet republics, including Latvia, Estonia, and Lithuania, swallowed up by Moscow in 1940. To foster *glasnost* (openness) and *perestroika* (restructuring), the twin banners of his reform program, Gorbachev urgently sought improved relations with the West.

A hint of the new order came during arms-control talks between Reagan and Gorbachev at Geneva in 1985 and Reykjavik, Iceland, in 1986. Although differences over inspection procedures and SDI derailed the Reykjavik summit, momentum on arms control had revived. In 1987 the two nations agreed on the INF (Intermediate Nuclear Forces) Treaty, providing for the withdrawal of some twenty-five hundred missiles from Europe. Whereas the 1972 SALT I Treaty had simply capped future missile levels, the INF Treaty for the first time eliminated an entire category of weapons. A big breakthrough, it allowed for on-site inspections to verify compliance. In December a smiling Gorbachev traveled to Washington to sign the treaty. The Soviet leader also announced a unilateral reduction in Soviet military forces and troop withdrawals from Eastern Europe and Afghanistan.

Change swept the Soviet Union and Eastern Europe, and Americans contemplated the unthinkable: the end of the Cold War. Ronald Reagan, despite his years of anti-Soviet rhetoric, responded imaginatively to the altered realities. In May 1988, the Senate having consented to the INF Treaty, the president flew to Moscow for the final signing. Talks also continued on a strategic-arms reduction (START) treaty. For several days the two leaders conversed, wined and dined one another, and strolled through Red Square.

Reagan's defection from anti-Soviet orthodoxy dismayed the Far Right. In New Hampshire, the reactionary *Manchester Union Leader* called his Moscow trip "a sad week for the free world." But most Americans sighed in relief as the Cold War, dominant in U.S. politics and culture for more than forty years, crumbled. Diplomatic historian John Lewis Gaddis wrote early in 1989, "[D]uring his eight years as president, Ronald Reagan has presided over the most dramatic improvement in U.S.-Soviet relations—and the most solid progress in arms control—since the Cold War began. History has often produced unexpected results, but this one surely sets some kind of record."

A Decade of Greed

Reagan's contempt for government, coupled with his glorification of self-interest, provided fertile soil for a series of Washington scandals in which officials placed personal gain above the public interest. The so-called Wedtech affair is typical. For years, the Welbilt Corporation in the South Bronx, a machine shop founded by the son of Puerto Rican immigrants, had tried with little success to win government contracts set aside for minority-owned companies. Its fortunes rose dramatically when it hired lawyer E. Bob Wallach, a close friend of Attorney General Edwin Meese, and retained the Washington public-relations firm headed by Lynn Nofziger, Reagan's former political director, who had left the White House in January 1982. With these patrons, the renamed Wedtech Corporation won $250 million in no-bid minority Pentagon contracts for engines and pontoons. The insiders who aided Wedtech's rise profited as well. In 1986, shortly before the Small Business Administration cut Wedtech from its minority-business program, a group of investors including Nofziger sold their stock for $10 million. Clouded in scandal, Wedtech soon went bankrupt. Wallach and others were indicted on fraud, conspiracy, bribery, and racketeering charges. Wallach was charged with taking payments of more than half a million dollars from Wedtech for influence peddling.

Other Pentagon-procurement abuses proliferated as runaway military spending and slack regulation invited fraud. Defense contractors freely indulged in what Haynes Johnson of the *Washington Post* called "plunder in the name of patriotism." Arkansas senator David Pryor spoke of "an eight-year feeding frenzy at the Department of Defense." Cheating took many forms: deceptive pricing, inflated labor costs, substitution of cheaper materials for contracted ones. By 1985 nearly fifty of the Pentagon's largest contractors had come under investigation.

The most unsavory of all federal agencies in the Reagan years was the Department of Housing and Urban Development (HUD), set up in 1965 to provide housing for the poor. As the White House cut HUD's staff and budget, employee morale plummeted. Meanwhile, the department's top brass funneled millions in federal contracts to contractors and consultants with political connections. James Watt, for example, back in the private sector after his brief tenure as secretary of the interior, earned $420,000 by making a few telephone calls to HUD for friends. Other insiders profited handsomely for their role in securing HUD contracts. HUD secretary Samuel Pierce, a Reagan appointee, proved a weak administrator who left day-to-day operations to his executive assistant, the daughter of an influential Republican family whose prior work experience consisted of tending bar during her college years. As the HUD scandals unfolded, even Reaganites held their noses. Conservative columnist James J. Kilpatrick wrote, "The more one hears of this rotten affair, the worse it gets."

Dedicated public servants still worked in Washington, but a climate of opportunism and greed hung over the capital. By 1989, 138 administration officials had been convicted or indicted or otherwise had run afoul of the law. Among Reagan's inner circle, deputy chief of staff Michael Deaver received a three-year suspended sentence for perjury related to influence-peddling charges. Lynn Nofziger's conviction under the 1978 Ethics in Government Act was later overturned on appeal. Edwin Meese underwent a fourteen-month criminal investigation by a special prosecutor and grand jury on charges including bribe taking, filing a false income-tax return, and conflict of interest in his actions as attorney general. In 1988 Meese's two top aides resigned, disgusted by his official conduct. In the end, Meese escaped indictment. The special prosecutor found insufficient evidence to sustain the bribery charge and lack of proof that Meese's other alleged misdeeds had been motivated by a desire for personal gain.

The laissez-faire individualism and shriveled social vision of the Reagan presidency both reflected and shaped the larger culture of the 1980s. As in the Gilded Age and the 1920s, amassing wealth became a national obsession. President Reagan declared in June 1983, "What I want to see above all is that this remains a country where someone can get rich." The 1960s had honored John Kennedy and Martin

Luther King as heroes; the eighties idolized entrepreneurs who flaunted their wealth and power. Donald Trump, a pudgy New York real-estate tycoon, became a celebrity for his flamboyant life-style; Americans snapped up his best-selling *Trump: The Art of the Deal* (1987). Chrysler head Lee Iacocca revealed his success formulas in *Iacocca* (1985). Some pushed him for president. Leona Helmsley, wife of another New York real-estate baron, posed as the regal "Queen" in ads for one of her husband's hotels, the Helmsley Palace.

In the decade's go-go economic climate, high-flying dealmakers ruled Wall Street. As early as 1984 a frenzy of business takeovers had grown so intense that even SEC head John Shad, in a speech entitled "The Leveraging of America," warned, "In today's corporate world, Darwin's survival of the fittest has become 'Acquire or be acquired.'" The years 1985–1987 saw twenty-one corporate mergers involving stock transfers of over $1 billion each. The torrent of mergers eventually totaled more than twenty-five thousand, many of them hostile takeovers by raiders seeking a quick killing. T. Boone Pickens, Ivan Boesky, Carl Icahn, and other raiders became household names. Having acquired a company, they wrote off weaker divisions as tax losses and sold the remaining units at huge profits. They ignored the impact of their maneuverings on workers or local communities.

Speculators in junk bonds, high-risk stocks offered to speculators attracted by possible vast profits, financed this wave of corporate takeovers, and young Michael Milken reigned as their king. Employed by the Wall Street investment firm Drexel Firestone, Milken displayed a genius for complex takeover deals. From his office in Beverly Hills, he directed the junk-bond division of the renamed Drexel Burnham Lambert firm. His business style evoked that of the legendary Gilded Age tycoons. Using the telephone like a bodily appendage, he worked around the clock to set up intricate deals. His 1987 income, including profits on his own stock holdings, exceeded $1 billion. Milken's annual High Yield Bond Conference in Los Angeles earned a revealing nickname: the Predators' Ball.

The turbulent history of the savings-and-loan (S&L) industry exemplified the economic climate of the eighties. S&Ls had traditionally given small investors a modest but secure return on home-mortgage loans. The high interest rates of the late 1970s, however, had impelled S&Ls to raise *their* rates to attract deposits, even though much of their capital was tied up in long-term mortgages at low rates. In the deregulatory climate of the 1980s, many S&Ls resorted to risky investments and high-pressure marketing tactics to generate high returns and to lure new depositors, some of whom invested their life savings. Congress increased federal insurance on S&L deposits from $20,000 to $100,000, attracting still more funds. Flush with money, many S&Ls, especially in the Southwest, made large loans on high-risk commercial ventures: malls, apartment complexes, office towers, and so on. As S&L interest rates soared, full-page newspaper ads promised fantastic returns and generated an infusion of deposits that the S&Ls sank into ever more shaky real-estate projects.

As we shall see in Chapter 15, the giddy economic carnival of the Reagan years would soon shudder to a halt. As the economy turned sour, hundreds of S&Ls went bankrupt, and some S&L officials faced criminal indictments. The era of endless corporate takeovers, highly leveraged buyouts, and junk-bond millionaires faded. Ivan Boesky, Michael Milken, Leona Helmsley, and others went to jail for various white-collar crimes. Jerry Sterner's 1989 play, *Other People's Money*, dissected the get-rich-quick mania of the Reagan years and chronicled the destruction of a venerable firm, "New England Wire and Cable," by corporate raiders. Commented Sterner:

> There hasn't been a more selfish generation in the United States since this country was founded. This is the only generation that has deliberately made it worse for their kids. It took us 200 years to build up to a trillion dollar deficit . . . and in one decade we upped it to three trillion. We suffer from a disease. . . . It's called instant gratification. We expect it from our politicians, our investments, . . . even our wars. We've come from an era of "What can I do for my country?" to "What's in it for me?" to "What's in it for me TODAY?"

Other writers, too, captured the decade's mood. In *Rabbit Is Rich* (1981), John Updike chronicled the success of his fictional hero Rabbit Angstrom as a sleek and prosperous Toyota dealer. Mystery writer Sara Paretsky examined the sleazy world of Yuppie lawyers and white-collar lawbreakers in 1980s Chicago in *Guardian Angel* (1992). And Tom Wolfe's *Bonfire of the Vanities* (1987) did for the eighties what F. Scott Fitzgerald had done for the twenties in *The Great Gatsby*. The novel offered a panorama of New York City life, from stockbrokers' Park Avenue penthouses to the harsh streets of Brooklyn and the South Bronx.

Reflecting the prevailing economic climate, the mass media became more consolidated as conglomerates swallowed up one company after another. By 1990 one such conglomerate, controlled by S. I. Newhouse, owned twenty-seven newspapers; the upscale magazines *Vanity Fair*, *Vogue*, *House and Garden*, and the *New Yorker*; and the publishing behemoth Random House with its many imprints, including Knopf, Pantheon, Ballantine Books, and Vintage. A vast infusion of foreign capital transformed the once-staid world of book publishing in the 1980s. The German corporation Bertelsmann, the Australian-born tycoon Rupert Murdoch, and the British press lord Robert Maxwell all acquired major U.S. publishing firms in the 1980s.

The consolidating process extended to the newspaper world as well. By 1986 twelve newspaper chains accounted for nearly half of total U.S. daily circulation. The ultimate generic newspaper, *USA Today*, had appeared in 1978. With its splashy color graphics and simple, human-interest stories, *USA Today* lacked regional flavor or editorial distinctiveness. This concentration of media ownership muffled the intellectual diversity and clash of opinion on which a healthy democracy and vibrant culture depend.

The movie industry, too, reeled under a wave of corporate takeovers. Sprawling Gulf + Western Corporation acquired Paramount Studios. Time Inc. bought Warner Communications, already an entertainment octopus, for $13 billion in 1989. At the same time, the movie studios entered TV production and made millions by selling their film libraries to TV networks or to independents like Ted Turner, whose successful Atlanta superstation broadcast nationwide via satellite. The Disney Corporation not only made movies but produced TV series, owned a record company, and ran theme parks in Florida and California. By the late eighties, the mass-culture industry had become so interconnected that the tangled relationships nearly defied sorting out.

As with the print media, foreign capital poured into the entertainment industry in the 1980s, as the dollars paid for foreign imports returned in the form of investment. Japan's SONY Corporation acquired Columbia Pictures for $3.4 billion in 1989. Not to be outdone, the Matsushita Corporation, a leader in consumer electronics, snapped up MCA-Universal, another U.S. media conglomerate, for $7 billion. Bertelsmann bought RCA Records, and Rupert Murdoch gained control of 20th-Century Fox. By 1990 four of the five top U.S. record companies were foreign owned. Sustained by multinational corporate investment and multibillion-dollar deals, U.S. mass culture in the 1980s extended its reach to every realm of national life. The nation's inner cities might be decaying, the schools in crisis, and class divisions widening, but the vast machinery of commercial amusement hummed on.

Early in the twentieth century, John Dewey, Walter Lippmann, and other intellectuals had noted the paradox of economic consolidation at a time when society seemed to be fragmenting in other ways. A similar phenomenon happened in the 1970s and 1980s. As society splintered and individualist ideologies reigned supreme, corporate consolidation proceeded rapidly. The United States seemed able to achieve in the economic arena the cohesion that eluded it in the civic realm. Underscoring the paradox, an increasingly consolidated mass media targeted a more and more segmented market. As a result, the common culture eroded further, and the outlets for civic discourse diminished. While thoughtful periodicals such as *Harper's* and the *Atlantic Monthly* limped along, special-interest periodicals sprang up, each seeking a narrow market niche. Magazine publishers targeted readers interested in photography, golf, the Civil War, antiques, travel, computers, fitness, specific cities and regions, and countless other topics. Even sex magazines specialized, offering titillation for women as well as men, gays and lesbians as well as heterosexuals.

Radio grew more segmented as well. In earlier days, nearly all Americans had listened to the same shows. By the 1980s, stations targeted particular audiences. Some featured news; others offered nonstop call-in programs; still others catered to musical tastes ranging from "Top 40" and "Easy Listening" to country, religious, and rock. Stations for black and Hispanic listeners proliferated. National Public Radio (NPR) had begun in 1971 with funding from the federal government and listener contributions. By the eighties, some three hundred noncommercial public-radio stations appealed to more affluent and highly educated listeners with classical music, jazz, and in-depth news analysis.

Technology promoted both the segmentation and the privatization of popular culture. As one example, the rise of cable TV gave subscribers access to a dizzying array of channels and splintered the viewing audience. By 1989 the three major networks' audience share had shrunk to 61 percent. Many viewers now watched channels specializing in religion, business, black interests, sports, and so on. Direct-marketing channels hawked everything from jewelry and cosmetics to fashions and kitchenware. Viewers could catch first-run movies on Home Box Office, continual news on CNN, explicit sex on the Playboy Channel, and even gavel-to-gavel coverage of Congress on C-Span. Another new technology promoting privatized leisure, the videocassette recorder (VCR), enabled people to record TV shows for later viewing and to watch rented movies at home. Introduced in the 1960s, VCRs enjoyed explosive growth in the 1980s. By mid-decade, 70 percent of American homes had VCRs, and the nation boasted more videocassette rental stores than movie theaters.

In his futuristic 1953 novel *Fahrenheit 451*, Ray Bradbury had imagined a citizenry for whom the fantasy world of the media was the only reality; by the 1980s, some found Bradbury's nightmare disturbingly at hand. The Walkman—a radio and tape cassette unit worn on the head, muting the sounds of the outside world—symbolized a larger mass-culture trend toward privatized pleasure and away from social engagement. Nineteen-fifties social critics had vaguely feared a blandly homogeneous, standardized culture. By the 1980s, the question had sharpened: Could a highly segmented populace caught up in socially isolating patterns of consumption and mass-media diversion sustain a common public discourse or a sense of shared social obligation?

As consolidation and new technologies transformed the mass-culture industry, one trend remained glaringly obvious: television's dominance. Average daily viewing time crept to nearly seven hours by 1990, up from about six hours in 1970. In a 1976 survey, 51 percent of Americans had rated television their "most believable" news source; only 22 percent described newspapers in this way. Ironically, the big magazine success of the postwar era was *TV Guide*, founded in 1952. With rare exceptions such as some offerings on public television or the subtle police drama "Hill Street Blues," the masters of this ubiquitous medium continued to aim abysmally low in the 1980s. Escapism, violence, and sexual innuendo filled the screen. The popular "A-Team" featured cartoon cut-out crime fighters. The successful "Miami Vice" offered music videos and fashion statements in the guise of limp police drama.

The FCC's lax regulation under Reagan made television more than ever a vehicle for commerce. By 1990 annual TV ad revenues surpassed $26 billion. Enormous technical expertise and "creative talent" went into producing commercials for cars, antacid pills, breakfast cereals, pet food, toilet paper, breath fresheners, and hemorrhoid remedies. A parade of Saturday morning children's cartoons with formulaic plots and simulated violence peddled plastic toys and sugared breakfast cereals. Even public TV's award-winning educational program "Sesame Street" sparked criticism for mimicking commercial TV. "Commercials" for "the letter R" or "the number 7," for example, whatever their pedagogical value, further acculturated children to actual TV ads and the consumerist ethos that lay behind them.

The symbiotic link between television and professional sports also tightened in the 1980s. A thirty-second commercial during the Super Bowl could cost as much as $675,000. By 1990 the Super Bowl accounted for eight of the ten largest audiences in TV history. Contract negotiations between the professional sports leagues and the networks became major corporate events. Details of superstars' multimillion-dollar contracts and product endorsements filled the sports pages. Because the big-money professional sports were mostly male dominated, television sharpened the disparity in the attention given to men's and women's sports at the high school and college levels and aroused feminists' ire.

Other critics deplored television's effects on politics. In *Amusing Ourselves to Death* (1985), Neil Postman contrasted the infantile level of TV campaigning to the more elevated public discourse of the nineteenth century, as exemplified by the Lincoln-Douglas debates of 1858. Indeed, from 1968 to 1988, the average TV "sound bite" in reporting presidential campaigns shrank from 42 to 10 seconds.* Without question, TV's role in the electoral process, already great by the 1960s, increased in the 1980s. Haynes Johnson of the *Washington Post* perceptively wrote, "Ronald Reagan and television fitted into American society like a plug into a socket. . . . He was the Sun King, presiding over the new national celebration from the White House. Under his reign, all lines blurred; news and entertainment, politics and advertising." In one sobering example of the power of visual images, Leslie Stahl of ABC News showed a film segment of Reagan's visit to the Special Olympics (an event for physically impaired competitors) during the 1984 campaign. As the segment played, Stahl read a report documenting the administration's spending cuts on programs for the handicapped. To Stahl's surprise, a Reagan media adviser called to thank her for the wonderful story. When she reminded him of her negative commentary, he taunted her, "Nobody heard what you said. They just saw the five minutes of beautiful pictures of Ronald Reagan. They saw the balloons, they saw the flags, they saw the red, white, and blue. Haven't you people figured out yet that the picture always overrides what you say?"

The Reagan-era ethos found its TV apotheosis in the prime-time soap opera "Dallas," which chronicled the business deals and torrid sex life of oilman J. R. Ewing. Another popular show explored "Lifestyles of the Rich and Famous." Fantasy and reality blurred when Reagan's first wife, Jane Wyman, starred in "Falcon Crest," still another TV drama of intrigues among the wealthy. By contrast, America's minorities, migrant workers, rural poor, and others left behind in the glitzy 1980s only rarely appeared on TV. The occasional "Special Report" on such groups attracted minuscule audiences. In "Sanford and Son," the veteran black comedian Redd Foxx played a salty old junk dealer who meets adversity with a quip. The popular "Cosby Show," a throwback to 1950s domestic sitcoms, portrayed the family of an affluent black professional couple but ignored the far larger portion of the black population: the inner-city poor.

The differences over Vietnam that in the 1960s had raged in the streets erupted again in the 1980s, this time on the cultural front. While films such as *The Deer Hunter* (1978), *Platoon* (1986), and *Born on the Fourth of July* (1989) explored the experience of combat and the war's psychological toll, Sylvester Stallone's *Rambo* (1985) offered a comic-strip version of the war in which America triumphs, as the national mythology held that it should. Even Maya Ying Lin's design for the Vietnam Veterans Memorial raised angry disputes. Some found the listing of the dead on a black marble wall somber and defeatist and demanded a traditional monument emphasizing military valor instead. Texas billionaire and political gadfly Ross Perot was among those who campaigned for a more conventionally patriotic memorial. In the end, a group statue was erected near the memorial wall, but its three young soldiers look more fatigued and uncomprehending than heroic.

Hollywood offered mixed fare in the 1980s, as always, but the most successful movies provided fantasy and diversion. Stephen Spielberg's fairy tale *E.T.* (1982), for example, recounted the friendship between a small boy and a lost wanderer from

---

* A sound bite is a brief comment or catchy phrase uttered by a politician in hopes that it will be shown on later TV news shows.

outer space. *E.T.* fans praised it as a parable of cross-cultural understanding, but a wave of escapist movies with little apparent social significance soon followed. *Porky's* (1982) offered a steamy adolescent fantasy of life and sex among Florida teenagers in the 1950s. In the series of cartoon-like *Rocky* movies, Sylvester Stallone played a prizefighter who prevails over various fearsome opponents. Apart from the better Vietnam films, the real world rarely impinged, even in fictional form, on such fare. In one notable exception, the 1987 hit *Wall Street*, Michael Douglas played an Ivan Boesky–like corporate buccaneer who gets his comeuppance. Douglas also co-starred in *Fatal Attraction* (1987), in which a psychotic career woman (Glenn Close) nearly destroys his marriage after a weekend sexual fling. To some critics, the movie tapped into a rising level of hostility toward the growing ranks of professional women.

Pop music increasingly involved the high-tech marketing of images. On MTV, a pop-music channel, rock groups and singers lip-synched their hits in minidramas called music videos. Michael Jackson, a global superstar, became a reclusive eccentric whose androgynous and racially ambiguous image heightened his mystique. Madonna blatantly flaunted her sexuality as she branched out from popular music to movies, TV videos, concert tours, and a 1992 book of verbal and photographic erotica entitled, with admirable economy of language, *Sex.*

Music-reproduction technology, having progressed from 78-RPM records to long-playing 33-1/3-RPM disks to cassette tapes, evolved further with the advent of the compact disc (CD) in 1982. The CD, in which laser beams "read" dots molded into concentric circles on a metallic disk, provided remarkably high fidelity, although some found the sound, like the decade, a bit sterile. On Broadway, the 1980s saw the rise of extravagant sound-and-light shows whose flashy production outshone the music or the story. The most successful of these high-tech musicals, the garish and ostentatious *Les Misérables*, derived, ironically, from Victor Hugo's tale of the poor of Paris.

Personal computers, the hot new data-processing technology of the 1970s, also proliferated in the 1980s. In 1981 some 2 million Americans owned PCs; by 1988 the total stood at 45 million. Students now took PCs rather than typewriters to college. Even small businesses did their recordkeeping by computer. Writers loved the new technology; a few keystrokes made possible revisions that formerly would have required hours of retyping or cutting and pasting. Library research speeded up enormously as continually updated electronic data bases replaced card catalogs and bulky multivolume indexes. The number of public schools using PCs in instruction rose from 1,035 in 1985 to 2,355 four years later. Some visionaries foresaw a day when computer instruction would render human teachers largely superfluous.

Many trends—political, cultural, technological—contributed to the privatization of life in the eighties and furthered the turning away from the public sphere that had begun in the late sixties. Critics worried that the new technologies of entertainment and communication would produce a generation that experienced life vicariously as computer bytes, TV images, or aural messages emanating from a CD player. In a media-dominated world, they feared, both the capacity to distinguish and respond to direct experience and the sense of social connectedness would atrophy.

As in earlier decades, TV roused criticism for allegedly reducing all reality to a common level. TV was producing a nation of "couch potatoes," critics charged, who passively absorbed an endless stream of programming in the hermetic isolation of their living rooms. A car-bomb explosion in Beirut, starving children in Ethiopia, upheavals in Eastern Europe, a drive-by shooting, a fashion show at a suburban mall, reports of the dreadful new disease AIDS, commercials for perfumes and weight-loss products—all flickered by on the tube, creating a mishmash of dissonant and unconnected sensory impressions. One critic described Americans as "metaphorically chained to their TV screen and, like Plato's cave dwellers, blind to the real world behind them, unable to differentiate between shadow and substance." Such judgments overstated the passivity of mass-culture consumers and understated the degree to which Americans remained linked to actual social networks and the real world through family, church, neighborhood, and work. Nevertheless, the media's dominance raised legitimate concerns.

Mass culture remained America's hottest export and helped to reduce the trade deficit. The *Economist* of London summed matters up in 1989: "America is to entertainment what South Africa is to gold and Saudi Arabia is to oil." By the late 1980s, the U.S. entertainment industry earned $5.5 billion annually in foreign exchange; annual broadcasts of U.S. TV programs in Europe alone earned some $600 million; and the U.S. music industry, mainly rock and other pop genres, garnered 70 percent of its revenues from overseas sales. One show-business executive commented, "Hollywood, unlike Detroit, has found a product that the Japanese can't improve on."

The world's image of America increasingly derived from mass-culture exports. A Jamaican journalist bitterly noted, "Because of what they see on television, everyone in Jamaica thinks . . . that everything in America is wonderful. Shows like 'Dallas' make it look like the land of milk and honey. It makes people think that money and material wealth are the only ways to be rich in this world." Certainly American democracy continued to inspire other peoples in the 1980s, particularly in regions breaking free of communism. But the United States as an exemplar of political freedom increasingly gave way to another image: a society of self-seeking individuals absorbed in the pursuit of money, amusement, and material possessions.

Amid rampant individualism, the sense of community waned. In *Habits of the Heart: Individualism and Commitment in American Life* (1985), the University of California sociologist Robert Bellah and four other scholars examined contemporary U.S. society and found it wanting. The title echoed Alexis de Tocqueville's warning in *Democracy in America* (1835) of an individualism so powerful that each citizen would be "shut up in the solitude of his own heart." Probing the historic roots of the American obsession with the self, the authors speculated that in modern America this extreme individualism, severed from a balancing social vision, "may have grown cancerous." Their interviews with more than two hundred middle-class men and women revealed a pervasive longing for stronger communal bonds and implied inadequacies in Reagan's laissez-faire ideology. The search for "a moral language that will transcend . . . radical individualism," they suggested, could lead back to religion and to republican political thought, with its stress on the common good and its sense of shared duties and obligations. "Our problems today," they concluded, "are not just political. They are moral and have to do with the meaning of life. . . . We are beginning to understand that our common life requires more than an exclusive concern for material accumulation."

Habits of the Heart portrayed troubled, atomistic citizens caught up in individualistic pursuits, driven by acquisitive pressures, and lacking much sense of common purpose. Critics questioned its sermonlike tone and its assumption that a recovered religious or even "republican" tradition could give rise to a new sense of community. Yet Bellah's picture of middle-class America at the high noon of Reaganism was disturbing.

And what of democratic self-government and the general welfare in such a society? The decade's media-dominated politics and socially barren ideology added immediacy to these perennial questions. Benjamin Barber, commenting in *Harper's* magazine on the individualistic theme of Reagan's second inaugural address, offered a sharply critical assessment:

> [T]he great American dream has always been a *public* dream. . . . Entrepreneurs may make money, but only citizens can make justice. The struggle for common goods—clean air, justice, peace—is a common struggle in which democratic government is our only ally. President Reagan asks much of individuals but nothing of citizens; he burdens the market with demands for progress and prosperity, but of the community and the government that is the community's instrument he asks nothing.

CONCLUSION

Ronald Reagan's farewell address, delivered on January 11, 1989, proved a vintage performance. After highlighting his achievements and gliding over failures, he concluded with a lump-in-the-throat call for a rebirth of patriotism. As Reagan returned to California, the nation assessed the man who had occupied the White House for eight years.

Reagan's popularity had remained high throughout his two terms, enhanced by the sudden outbreak of peace and by the glow of prosperity at home. Insiders, however, still depicted a remote, uninvolved figure. In part, these traits reflected the infirmities of age; Reagan wore hearing aids in both ears after 1985. But the issue went deeper. More than any other president in memory, Reagan was a performer—the "Great Communicator"—smiling on cue and reading speeches with consummate acting skill. Journalist Lou Cannon wrote in *President Reagan: The Role of a Lifetime* (1991), "Acting took early hold of him, and never let him go." Unconcerned with the nitty-gritty of politics and most at ease in front of the camera, Reagan seemed more a master of ceremonies than a president. Tom Shales of the *Washington Post* commented, "Historians can decide if Ronald Reagan was a great president, but any TV viewer can see he has been a great leading man." Indeed, during White House briefings, Reagan displayed shocking ignorance of basic issues and relied instead on shop-worn anecdotes. Supporters contended that he preferred to sketch broad goals while leaving details to others. Yet his tendency to reduce complex issues to formulaic bromides represented a triumph of ideology over pragmatism rare in U.S. politics.

The most damaging picture of the Reagan presidency came from insiders. David Stockman revealed not only the cynicism of the Reagan economic plan but also the intellectual vacuity of the White House inner circle. Donald Regan, forced out during the Iran-contra scandal, got his revenge in *For the Record* (1988), in which he portrayed his boss as a marionette controlled by his handlers: "He listened, acquiesced, played his role, and waited for the next act to be written." A daily schedule leaked to the press in 1988 showed that Reagan's every public word was scripted, down to the most trivial small talk. *For the Record* also described the behind-the-scenes power of Nancy Reagan, who sometimes planned her husband's trips on the basis of astrological advice. Mrs. Reagan epitomized the materialism of the era as well, spending more than $1 million on redecorating the White House and wearing high-fashion gowns on loan from New York couturiers delighted by the free advertising.

To his admirers, Reagan had restored American patriotism, rebuilt an eroded military, ended inflation, stimulated the economy, and reaffirmed the old verities of individualism and self-reliance. One of his fans, Great Britain's conservative prime minister Margaret Thatcher, affirmed, "He has left America stronger, prouder, greater than ever before, and we thank him for it." But skeptics saw him as substituting right-wing rhetoric for serious policy analysis and, with his repeated ridicule of "the government," contributing to a corrosive cynicism about politics. Certainly Reagan was likeable, with a self-deprecating manner and impulsive warmth when confronted with individual suffering or need. Nevertheless, the ideology that he so artfully championed revealed an impoverished social vision.

Reagan's critics are left to account for his phenomenal popularity, certified by two sweeping electoral victories to which millions of "Reagan Democrats" contributed. Of the old New Deal coalition, only black Americans resisted the lure of Reaganism; the white working class defected in droves. Journalist Garry Wills in *Reagan's America* (1987) saw Reagan's serene confidence as one key to his appeal: "Self-assurance reassures others, and that has not been the least of Reagan's gifts to us, at a time when the nation needed some reassuring." Deeper still, Wills saw in Reagan the embodiment of the American dream: perennial optimism, infinite renewal. The *Albuquerque Journal*, in assessing Reagan's farewell address, acknowledged the thinness of his "Don't worry, be happy" message but concluded that what had been true in 1981 remained true in 1989: "America really likes Ronald Reagan."

Ultimately, however, the issue is not Reagan as a person but his policies. The "Reagan revolution" cut social services and ratcheted up the arms race while emasculating federal regulatory agencies and shifting income and resources away from the neediest Americans. Celebrators of the top-down prosperity of the mid- and later 1980s typically ignored profound problems such as the trade gap, the growing federal debt, the S&L crisis, and major abuses in the world of investment banking. They also overlooked the plight of millions of lower-income Americans and urban minorities, as well as displaced industrial workers and even struggling members of the middle class.

In retrospect, the eighties seem years of drift, with rhetoric supplanting substance and short-term private gain often substituting for long-term public advance. Reagan did not single-handedly cause the materialism, selfishness, and preening vulgarity of the 1980s, but his endless mantras in praise of unrestrained individualism served to valorize some of the era's less appealing features. Urgent national issues—from inner-city joblessness, troubled schools, and drug abuse to environmental threats, the AIDS epidemic, and health care—suffered neglect as persons intent on accumulating as much as possible as quickly as possible set the political and cultural tone. Despite Reagan's personal decency and kindly manner, the decade to which he gave his name offered little by way of inspiration or guidance to the future. Instead, Reagan primarily bequeathed to his successors an array of festering problems.

SELECTED READINGS

Ronald Reagan and Reagan-Era Politics

Frank Ackerman, *Reaganomics* (1982); Sidney Blumenthal, *The Rise of the Counter-Establishment: From Conservative Ideology to Political Power* (1988); Sidney Blumenthal and Thomas Byrne Edsall, eds., *The Reagan Legacy* (1988); Paul Boyer, ed., *Reagan as President: Contemporary Views of the Man, His Politics, and His Policies* (1990); William J. Broad, *The Star Warriors* (1985) and *Teller's War: The Top-Secret Story Behind the Star Wars Deception* (1992); Lou Cannon, *President Reagan* (1991); John F. Cogan, *Federal Budget Deficits: What's Wrong with the Congressional Budget Process* (1992); Robert Dallek, *Ronald Reagan: The Politics of Symbolism* (1984); Thomas Byrne Edsall with Mary D. Edsall, *Chain Reaction: The Impact of Race, Rights, and Taxes on American Politics* (1991); Rowland Evans and Robert Novak, *The Reagan Revolution* (1981); Jack W. Germond and Jules Witcover, *Blue Smoke and Mirrors* (1981) [1980 election]; Haynes Johnson, *Sleepwalking Through History: America in the Reagan Years* (1991); Jonathan Lash, *A Season of Spoils: The Story of the Reagan Administration's Attack on the Environment* (1984); Sar A. Levitan and Clifford M. Johnson, *Beyond the Safety Net* (1984); Edward T. Linenthal, *Symbolic Defense: The Cultural Significance of the Strategic Defense Initiative* (1989); Charles Murray, *Losing Ground: American Social Policy, 1950–1980* (1984); Peggy Noonan, *What I Saw at the Revolution: A Political Life in the Reagan Era* (1990); Kevin Phillips, *Post-Conservative America* (1982) and *The Politics of Rich and Poor* (1990); Frances Fox Piven and Richard A. Cloward, *The New Class War: Reagan's Attack on the Welfare State and Its Consequences* (1982); Michael Rogin, *Ronald Reagan: The Movie* (1987); Kirkpatrick Sale, *Power Shift: The Rise of the Southern Rim and Its Challenge to the Eastern Establishment* (1975); Bob Schieffer and Gary Paul Gates, *The Acting President* (1989); Herman Schwartz, *Packing the Courts* (1988); C. Brant Short, *Ronald Reagan and the Public Lands: America's Conservation Debate, 1979–1984* (1989); David A. Stockman, *The Triumph of Politics: How the Reagan Revolution Failed* (1986); Theodore White, *America in Search of Itself* (1982) [1980 campaign]; Garry Wills, *Reagan's America* (1987).

U.S. Foreign Policy, 1981–1988

Michael R. Beschloss and Strobe Talbott, *At the Highest Levels: The Inside Story of the End of the Cold War* (1994); Seweryn Bialer and Michael Mandelbaum, eds., *Gorbachev's Russia and American Foreign Policy* (1988); Raymond Bonner, *Weakness and Deceit: U.S. Policy and El Salvador* (1984); Thomas Crothers, *In the Name of Democracy: U.S. Foreign Policy Toward Latin America in the Reagan Years* (1991); Theodore Draper, *A Very Thin Line: The Iran-Contra Affairs* (1991); Thomas L. Friedman, *From Beirut to Jerusalem* (1989); John Lewis Gaddis, *The United States and the End of the Cold War* (1992); Patrick Glynn, *Closing Pandora's Box: Arms Races, Arms Control, and the History of the Cold War* (1992); Roy Gutman, *Banana Diplomacy* (1988); David E. Kyvig, ed., *Reagan and the World* (1990); Michael Mandelbaum and Strobe Talbott, *Reagan and Gorbachev* (1987); Constantine Menges, *Inside the National Security Coun-*

cil (1988); Kenneth Oye et al., *Eagle Defiant: U.S. Foreign Policy in the 1980s* (1983) and *Eagle Resurgent? The Reagan Era in American Foreign Policy* (1987); Eric F. Petersen, "The End of the Cold War: A Review of Recent Literature," *History Teacher* (August 1993); David Schoenbaum, *The United States and the State of Israel* (1993); Charles D. Smith, *Palestine and the Arab-Israeli Conflict*, (2d ed., 1992); Strobe Talbott, *Deadly Gambits: The Reagan Administration and the Stalemate in Nuclear Arms Control* (1984).

Economic Trends, Protest, and Social Thought in the Eighties

Carl Abbott, *The New Urban America: Growth and Politics in the Sunbelt Cities* (1981); Robert Bellah et al., *Habits of the Heart* (1985) and *The Good Society* (1991); Connie Bruck, *The Predators' Ball: The Inside Story of Drexel Burnham and the Rise of the Junk Bond Raiders* (1989); Fox Butterfield, "Anatomy of the Nuclear Protest," *New York Times Magazine*, July 11, 1982; Paul S. Dempsey, *The Social and Economic Consequences of Deregulation* (1988); Barbara Ehrenreich, *Fear of Falling: The Inner Life of the Middle Class* (1989) and *The Worst Years of Our Lives* (1990); Barbara Epstein, *Political Protest and Cultural Revolution: Nonviolent Direct Action in the 1970s and 1980s* (1991); Benjamin Friedman, *Day of Reckoning: The Consequences of American Economic Policy Under Reagan and After* (1988); Larry N. Gerston et al., *The Deregulated Society* (1988); J. David Hoeveler, *Watch on the Right: Conservative Intellectuals in the Reagan Era* (1991); Harry Hurt, *The Lost Tycoon: The Many Lives of Donald J. Trump* (1993); J. Anthony Lukas, *Common Ground: A Turbulent Decade in the Lives of Three American Families* (1986); Frances Fox Piven and Richard A. Cloward, *The New Class War: Reagan's Attack on the Welfare State and Its Consequences* (1982); Clyde V. Prestowitz, Jr., *Trading Places: How We Allowed Japan to Take the Lead* (1988); Jerome Price, *The Antinuclear Movement* (1982); Patricia Cayo Sexton, *The War on Labor and the Left: Understanding America's Unique Conservatism* (1991); James B. Stewart, *Den of Thieves* (1991) [Wall Street trading scandals]; Sidney Weintraub and Marvin Goodstein, eds., *Reaganomics in the Stagflation Economy* (1983); William J. Wilson, *The Truly Disadvantaged: The Inner City, the Underclass and Public Policy* (1987).

Popular Culture in the Eighties

"America's Hottest Export: Pop Culture," *Fortune*, December 31, 1990; Michael A. Anderegg, *Inventing Vietnam: The War in Film and Television* (1991); Bob Carroll et al., *The Hidden Game of Football* (1988); Richard M. Clurman, *To the End of Time: The Seduction and Conquest of a Media Empire* (1992) [merger of Time, Inc. and Warner Communications]; Richard O. Davis, *America's Obsession with Sports and Society Since 1945* (1994); Stuart Ewen and Elizabeth Ewen, *Channels of Desire: Mass Images and the Shaping of American Consciousness* (2d ed., 1992); "Fancy Free: A Survey of the [U.S.] Entertainment Industry," *Economist* London, December 23, 1989; Todd Gitlin, *Inside Prime Time* (1985) and *Watching Television* (1986); Ron Grover, *The Disney Touch* (1991); Daniel Ichbiah, *The Making of Microsoft* (1991); Donald Lazere, ed., *American Media and Mass Culture: Left Perspectives* (1987); Steven Levy, *Insanely Great: The Life and Times of Macintosh, the Computer That Changed Everything* (1993); Nicholas Mills, ed., *Culture in an Age of Money* (1991); Edward Palmer, *Television and America's Children: A Crisis of Neglect* (1988); Neil Postman, *Amusing Ourselves to Death* (1985); Randy Roberts and James S. Olson, *Winning Is the Only Thing: Sports in America Since 1945* (1989); Michael Sorkin, ed., *Variations on a Theme Park: The New American City and the End of Public Space* (1993); Michael Winship, *Television* (1988).

Chapter Fifteen

THE SEARCH FOR NEW DIRECTIONS
AT CENTURY'S END

Unrest rumbled across East Germany in the summer of 1989, as demonstrators boldly protested the oppressive regime headed by the aging hard-line communist Erich Honecker. With Honecker's forced resignation in October, his successor, Egon Krenz, nervously promised reforms. But few anticipated what would come next. On the evening of November 9, in a move that would have been unthinkable only a short time before, Krenz opened the Berlin Wall. As the news spread, jubilant Berliners flocked to the squat gray barrier that had long bisected their city. Their celebration continued far into the night. At the historic Brandenburg Gate, near what had once been Hitler's Reichstag, young people danced atop the wall. Others used hammers and chisels to chip off souvenir bits of cement.

The next day, East Berliners by the tens of thousands poured through once heavily guarded checkpoints for their first view of life beyond the wall. One woman, overwhelmed by the shops along West Berlin's glittering and elegant Kurfürstendamm, murmured, "There is so much color, so much light. It's incredible." A blind man came with his seeing-eye dog. "I just wanted to smell the air of a free Berlin," he explained. Another East Berliner returned several books to a West Berlin library that he had borrowed twenty-eight years earlier, the day before the wall went up in 1961. "Berlin Is Berlin Again!" shouted the city's newspapers. Soon after, Leonard Bernstein conducted a gala performance of Beethoven's stirring Ninth Symphony in the reunited metropolis, restoring *Freiheit* ("Freedom") for *Freude* ("Joy") in the choral movement.

The opening of the Berlin Wall, for all its compelling symbolism, was only one of many events that stunned the world as the 1990s began—events that cumulatively spelled the end of the Cold War. The dramatic collapse of Soviet power and the emergence of fragile noncommunist governments in the former Soviet sphere eased global tensions but also posed challenges for the United States internationally. Even as Americans contemplated the new global scene, they confronted problems seething within American society in the early 1990s and worsened by another recession. Changing demographics; inner-city joblessness and despair; and concerns over education, the environment, and the nation's long-range economic prospects all fed uneasiness about the future. By 1992, with the economy stagnant, a frustrated electorate vented its discontent at the polls. After twelve years of Republican rule, voters ushered Democrat Bill Clinton into the White House. With high energy, the Clinton team set about crafting a new version of liberalism that would reflect the altered political climate. World trends continued to flow America's way, but the task of devising a post–Cold War political and economic order proved maddeningly complex.

Campaign '88

In 1988, Vice President George Bush claimed his chance at the top spot. As Bush won a string of primaries, challengers including televangelist Pat Robertson, former secretary of state Alexander Haig, and Kansas senator Bob Dole fell by the wayside, and the nomination was his. Bush's acceptance speech, crafted by speechwriter Peggy Noonan, evoked a psychological mood rather than proposing a program as he called for "a kinder, and gentler nation." He also pledged, "Read my lips: No new taxes." To general surprise, Bush tapped Indiana senator Dan Quayle, son of a conservative newspaper publisher, as his running mate. Few discerned presidential qualities in Quayle, and doubts about him deepened with revelations that during the Vietnam War, which his family's newspapers had supported, he had pulled strings to get into the Indiana National Guard and thereby avoid the draft.

Several Democrats also grabbed for the brass ring. Jesse Jackson, again the favorite among African-Americans, bettered his 1984 showing with white voters in several state primaries. But the field quickly thinned. Senator Gary Hart of Colorado withdrew after the *Miami Herald* revealed his affair with a Florida model. The ultimate victor was Governor Michael Dukakis of Massachusetts, a Greek-American whose state had prospered in the 1980s, in part because the military build-up had showered contracts on the electronics and computer industries around Boston. Touting the "Massachusetts miracle," Dukakis clinched the New York and California primaries and soon had the nomination in hand. As his running mate, he chose Senator Lloyd Bentsen of Texas. Dukakis delivered a rousing acceptance speech and surged to a wide lead in the polls. Democrats saw Bush, with his penchant for malapropisms, as an easy target. "Poor George," gibed Texas Democratic leader Anne Richards, "he was born with a silver foot in his mouth."

But Dukakis's lead soon evaporated. An inept campaigner, he bored even fellow Democrats. He refused to challenge the Reagan-Bush ideology and instead stressed his administrative competence, a claim that many in Massachusetts disputed. By contrast, Bush pointed to the new jobs, reduced world tensions, and low inflation of the 1980s. Naturally, he ignored the budget deficit and Iran-contra scandal, as well as other embarrassments. The Bush forces further damaged Dukakis with insidious TV commercials. The most notorious of these featured Willie Horton, a black convict who had committed rape and murder while on a weekend pass under a Massachusetts prisoner-furlough program. Implying that Dukakis was soft on crime, the commercial also subtly exploited racial stereotypes. Both sides pandered to the

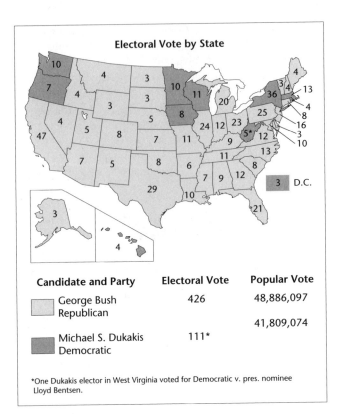

FIGURE 15.1

Presidential Election of 1988

Electoral Vote by State

Candidate and Party	Electoral Vote	Popular Vote
George Bush Republican	426	48,886,097
		41,809,074
Michael S. Dukakis Democratic	111*	

*One Dukakis elector in West Virginia voted for Democratic v. pres. nominee Lloyd Bentsen.

ubiquitous television cameras: Bush visited flag factories; Dukakis posed in an army tank. With the candidates marketed as if they were deodorants, serious debate rarely interrupted the sound bites and photo opportunities.

Aided by prosperity and Dukakis's ineffective campaign, Bush grabbed 54 percent of the popular vote. Carrying forty states, including vital California and Texas, he dominated the electoral tally 426–112. Dukakis claimed only ten states plus the District of Columbia. Except for West Virginia, he lost every southern and border state. Yet despite Bush's triumph, voters returned Democratic majorities to Congress. This outcome reflected the advantage of incumbency in good times, reinforced by heavy PAC contributions. The White House thus was controlled by one party and Congress by the other, with neither inclined to cooperate. The resulting impasse contributed to four years of what by 1992 would come to be called "gridlock."

Marking Time: The Bush Interlude

George Herbert Walker Bush, the son of a Connecticut senator, epitomized New England's WASP elite. An Episcopalian and avid sportsman, he attended a private academy and then Yale College. During his college years, he led the baseball team and gained admission to the venerable secret society Skull and Bones. In World War

II, Bush flew fifty-nine missions in his Grumman Avenger, was shot down, and won the Distinguished Flying Cross. After the war he married Barbara Pierce, daughter of a prominent magazine publisher, and moved to Texas, where he used family contacts to enter the oil business. He turned to politics, winning election to Congress in 1966, but lost to Lloyd Bentsen in a 1970 Senate race. Out of his Texas years came a close friendship (tempered by a well-concealed rivalry) with James Baker III, an astute alter ego whom Bush would appoint as secretary of state.

In the 1970s Bush held various appointive posts, including CIA director and chief of the U.S. liaison office in Beijing. As vice president, he avoided entanglement in the Iran-contra affair but also gained a reputation for opportunism. On the abortion issue, for example, he abandoned a long-held prochoice position and courted the antiabortion vote in his race for president. "I will do anything to win," Bush once candidly told an interviewer. His vaguely uplifting inaugural address called on Americans to ignite "a thousand points of light" and to view the future as "a door you can walk right through into a room called tomorrow."

Like Nixon, Bush savored the role of world leader, but although he served in stirring times, he did little to put his personal imprint on U.S. foreign policy. The upheavals in the Soviet Union and Eastern Europe that had begun in the mid-1980s accelerated early in Bush's term. In 1989, as communist regimes long propped up by Soviet power collapsed, Lech Walesa of Poland's independent labor movement Solidarity and Václav Havel, a Czech playwright and former political prisoner, were elected presidents of their nations. In Rumania, the dictatorship of Nicolai Ceausescu and his wife ended as the pair was hunted down and shot. A new government headed by ex-communists took power. In Germany, the opening of the Berlin Wall in 1989 proved the prelude to the collapse of East Germany's communist regime itself. The division of Germany, a legacy of World War II, ended in October 1990 as the Bonn government assumed power over all Germany.

Soon the Soviet Union itself fragmented. In 1989–1990, Estonia, Latvia, and Lithuania moved toward independence. Moscow feebly resisted, but in 1991 the three Baltic republics gained their freedom. Mikhail Gorbachev had hoped to introduce democratic socialism while preserving the Soviet Union and heading a reformed Communist party. But in 1991 the forces that he had unleashed overwhelmed him. As the party's grip weakened, the Soviet economy faltered and nationalism reawakened in the Soviet republics. In August, Soviet military officers alarmed by the pace of change staged a coup and briefly held Gorbachev captive. President Boris Yeltsin of the Russian Republic, backed by a mass outpouring of Muscovites, defied the coup leaders' tanks and restored Gorbachev to freedom. But Yeltsin himself, riding a tide of Russian nationalism and revulsion against communist rule, soon muscled Gorbachev aside. Later in 1991, the fifteen republics of the Soviet Union formally split up, replacing the former polity with the amorphous Commonwealth of Independent States. The Communist party collapsed, and Gorbachev, at the pinnacle of power for six years, suddenly found himself a private citizen. Europe's last great empire had dissolved into a jumble of new nations torn by ethnic turmoil, border disputes, and economic problems, united only in their repudiation of bolshevism. Statues of communist leaders toppled; Leningrad resumed its ancient name of St. Petersburg. In May 1992, speaking at Westminster College in

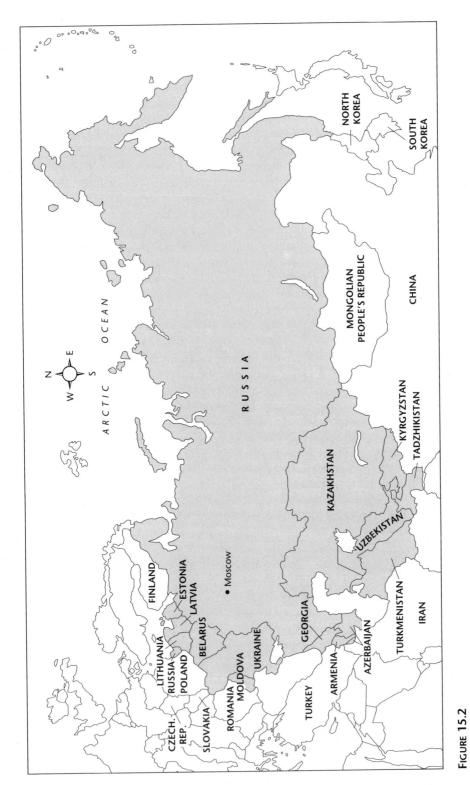

FIGURE 15.2
The Former Soviet Union

Missouri, the scene of Churchill's famous "Iron Curtain" address of 1946, Gorbachev declared the Cold War over.

The end of the long conflict had redrawn the map of Europe, affected world power relationships, and forced a reassessment of the premises underlying U.S. foreign policy. For Americans reared on "the Soviet threat," the change proved difficult to absorb. Relief, disorientation, and residual mistrust vied for dominance. As John Updike's Harry Angstrom reflected in *Rabbit at Rest* (1990), "It's like nobody's in charge of the other side any more. I miss it, the cold war. It gave you a reason to get up in the morning." For Russia and the other former Soviet republics, the transition from a state-run economy to a free-market system on the Western model—but without commercial banks, investment capital, and a free-enterprise tradition—proved monumentally difficult. As Russia's economy foundered and production fell, Yeltsin urgently sought Western help. Washington dragged its feet, but early in 1992, prodded by Richard Nixon, Bush proposed a $35 billion aid package. Russian leaders, as well as some Western economists, urged a far more ambitious program lest Russia revert to despotic rule.

The Cold War's end dramatically advanced the arms-control process. In August 1991, shortly before Gorbachev's fall, President Bush flew to Moscow to sign the START treaty cutting the two nations' nuclear arsenals by one-quarter. In June 1992, Boris Yeltsin, in Washington seeking action on Bush's aid package, accepted still deeper cuts in ICBMs. Tacitly conceding the altered balance of power, Yeltsin agreed to give up all of Russia's land-based MIRV missiles, whereas the United States would cut its submarine missile force only by half. The Russian president also pledged to deactivate all missiles targeted on the United States.

In a move that further rearranged the Cold War landscape, NATO and the Soviet-sponsored Warsaw Pact signed a nonaggression agreement late in 1990. With the Warsaw Pact's collapse soon after, NATO announced a 50 percent troop reduction. For decades, the existence of a common foe had cemented the Western alliance. With the Soviet threat gone and with Western Europeans forging a single economic bloc, the question of America's future relationship with Western Europe gained urgency. Indeed, the end of the Cold War disoriented U.S. foreign policy, which for decades had resonated to the single theme of anticommunism. From Truman to Reagan, containment of the U.S.S.R. had given coherence to American diplomacy. Suddenly the old formulas seemed irrelevant. Unlike the Nixon-Kissinger team, Bush had no grand strategy; he simply reacted to events as they occurred.

The new era rattled the Pentagon too. Bush's secretary of defense, former Wyoming congressman Dick Cheney, proposed a 4 percent annual reduction in military spending and a 25 percent cut in the military over five years. Democrat Les Aspin, chair of the House Armed Services Committee, advocated doubling Cheney's proposed cuts. Whatever the levels, job losses were inevitable. President Eisenhower in 1961 had warned of the dangers of a militarized economy, and events now dramatized Ike's point. At the peak of the Reagan build-up, annual military spending had neared $375 billion, and 1.4 million Americans had worked in military-related jobs. By 1992 military spending had fallen below $300 billion, and defense jobs declined by some 200,000.

Bush won plaudits for his performance during the Persian Gulf War of 1990–1991, but the long-term results proved ambiguous. On August 2, 1990, Iraq invaded its neighbor, the tiny but oil-rich emirate of Kuwait, with which it had a long-running dispute over control of the vast Rumaila oil field. Iraqi dictator Saddam Hussein, eager to gain access to the Persian Gulf, claimed that historically Iraq had ruled Kuwait. Even before the attack, Saddam had roused fears with his anti-Israel threats, his hostility to other Arab states, and his nuclear- and chemical-weapons research. Nevertheless, during Iraq's war with Iran (1980–1988), Washington had given Saddam weapons and satellite intelligence, as well as agricultural credits to aid his battle against Tehran's anti-American Shiites. Using Italy's Banca Nazionale del Lavoro as a front, the Reagan White House and the CIA had secretly funneled weapons, electronics, and computers to Saddam while concealing the fact from Congress. The flow of aid and military hardware had increased under George Bush, even though the Iran-Iraq war had ended and Iran had softened its anti-American tone after Ayatollah Khomeini's death in 1989.*

With Saddam's invasion of Kuwait, President Bush suddenly shifted gears. Comparing the Iraqi strongman to Hitler, Bush denounced the attack on Kuwait as a threat to regional stability and a violation of international law. Perhaps most important, Saddam's action jeopardized two major oil producers with close ties to the West, not only Kuwait but also neighboring Saudi Arabia.

A unanimous UN Security Council slapped trade sanctions on Iraq, ordered its withdrawal from Kuwait by January 15, 1991, and authorized member states to use "all means necessary" to achieve this end. The Pentagon rushed U.S. air and sea power to the Persian Gulf and deployed 400,000 ground forces in Saudi Arabia. Bush assembled a coalition of nations led by the Saudis, Great Britain, Egypt, and France. Avoiding LBJ's mistake in Vietnam, he cultivated home-front backing by defining the issues starkly: resisting aggression and protecting U.S. strategic interests. He then spelled out his goal: Iraq's withdrawal from Kuwait.

On January 12, 1991, over the opposition of Democrats who argued for more time to allow the sanctions to take effect, both houses of Congress authorized Bush to take military action.† Four days later, the Allies launched Operation Desert Storm under U.S. commander General H. Norman Schwarzkopf. For a week, 2,000 Allied warplanes rained 88,000 tons of bombs on Iraqi forces in Kuwait, military targets in Iraq, and strategic sites in Baghdad itself. On February 23, after U.S. Marines feinted an amphibious assault, 200,000 ground forces moved across the desert into Kuwait. Despite fears of fierce resistance, what Saddam called "the mother of all battles" proved pitiably one-sided. U.S. forces destroyed 3,700 Iraqi tanks, for example, while losing only 3. The United States counted 467 wounded and 148 dead, 35 of whom were killed accidentally by U.S. fire. An estimated 100,000 Iraqis died, both soldiers and civilians. The war's most dramatic moments came when Iraq, trying to provoke another Arab-Israeli war, fired Soviet-made Scud missiles against Tel Aviv and

---

* In 1991–1992, as these secret operations became known, the Bush administration would engage in a systematic effort to keep the relevant documents from Congress and the public. See Alan Friedman, *Spider's Web: The Secret History of How the White House Illegally Armed Iraq* (1993).
† The vote was 52–47 in the Senate and 250–183 in the House. Of the Senate Democrats, 10 voted for the resolution authorizing military action and 45 against.

other targets in Israel. Saddam also launched Scuds at U.S. staging areas in Saudi Arabia. U.S. Patriot missiles destroyed most incoming Scuds or threw them off course by exploding in their general vicinity. Americans watched fascinated as CNN broadcast scenes of the aerial fireworks live.

Indeed, the whole war played well on TV. Unlike the harrowing scenes from Vietnam, death or close-up destruction rarely intruded on the images of surrendering Iraqis and abandoned Iraqi equipment. This was no accident; having learned the lesson of Vietnam, the Pentagon restricted press access to the war. The skillfully edited shots of bombs exploding on distant targets, some filmed through the bomb-sights of U.S. aircraft, resembled the video games found in countless shopping-mall arcades.

The media-enhanced victory boosted the morale of a nation still scarred by Vietnam. Bush gloated, "By God, we've licked the Vietnam syndrome once and for all." Before a wildly cheering Congress, Bush underscored the war's lessons: "We hear so often about our young people in turmoil; how our children fall short; how our schools fail us; how American products and American workers are second-class. Well, don't you believe it. The America we saw in Desert Storm was first-class talent." Bush's approval rating spurted to 89 percent; Schwarzkopf enjoyed a hero's welcome. In contrast to the Vietnam era, citizens hailed the returning troops in parades across the nation. The untelevised war, including the heavy loss of Iraqi lives, hardly impinged on the American consciousness.

Kuwait, 1991. In a scene from the Persian Gulf War that did not appear on prime-time television, three GIs impassively consider the body of an Iraqi soldier incinerated by American firepower. (© 1991 *Peter Turnley/Black Star*)

Euphoria soon gave way to second thoughts, however. Iraq had left Kuwait, but Saddam remained in power, crushing uprisings by Kurds in the north and Shiites in the south. The cease-fire provided for the UN-supervised ending of Baghdad's nuclear- and chemical-weapons programs, but Saddam raised many roadblocks. Revelations about Washington's earlier aid to Saddam further diluted the sweet tang of victory. The political bonus to Bush of the Desert Storm triumph would soon dissipate.

President Bush also confronted disturbing events in China, where an aging communist oligarchy clung to power while edging toward a freer economy and pursuing détente and trade with the West. In 1989, when Chinese students calling for democracy occupied Beijing's Tiananmen Square, the government at first tolerated the protest but then ordered a tank assault that left hundreds dead. A systematic crackdown on dissidents followed, including arrests and public executions. Bush condemned China's authoritarian turn and proposed economic sanctions, but he resisted congressional demands that he sever trade and diplomatic relations with Beijing.

Bush's essentially reactive foreign policy manifested itself as well in South Africa. In 1986, overriding a Reagan veto, Congress had barred all U.S. trade or corporate investment in South Africa with its all-white government and its system of apartheid. These economic sanctions and other countries' efforts induced South Africa to moderate its racial stance. A major breakthrough came in 1990 when President F. W. de Klerk released Nelson Mandela, leader of the African National Congress (ANC), the major political organization of black South Africans, after twenty-seven years of detention. In 1991, as de Klerk dismantled apartheid, President Bush lifted U.S. sanctions. In a dramatic moment in September 1993, with South Africa's first universal election scheduled for early 1994, Mandela appeared before the UN to call for an end to all economic sanctions against his nation. As with the former Soviet Union, specialists on the region called for major loans and investments by the international community to aid South Africa's transition to multiracial democracy.

Elsewhere in Africa, a severe drought in 1992 threatened 40 million people with famine, especially in war-torn Somalia with its 6.7 million people. Relief agencies stepped in, and the United States, under UN auspices, supplied emergency food shipments. When warring factions diverted relief shipments to the black market, President Bush in December 1992 ordered in thirty thousand U.S. troops to protect food deliveries. His action reflected less a strategic decision than a response to TV images of famished Somalis. The U.S. role in Somalia would soon generate controversy, but at the time the nation supported Bush's action. As one citizen told a reporter, "You see these starving kids on T.V., and you think how could we not do this?"

In Latin America, the Soviet collapse reoriented U.S. policy. Bush and Baker reversed Reagan's failed contra policy in Nicaragua, and backed efforts to reintegrate the contras into the country's life and politics. A 1990 election brought an anti-Sandinista coalition to power. In neighboring El Salvador, U.S.-promoted peace talks finally bore fruit in 1992. The guerrillas and Alfredo Cristiani's right-wing government signed an agreement inaugurating various reforms, and the costly twelve-year civil war ended. Foreign policy and domestic concerns intersected in December 1989 when U.S. forces invaded Panama. The objective was to capture strongman Manuel Noriega, accused of aiding the flow of cocaine from Colombia and Peru to U.S. cities. The action cost five hundred Panamanian and twenty-three U.S. lives, but it won applause in America and from many Panamanians relieved to be rid of Noriega. In 1992, convicted of drug trafficking by a federal court in Miami, Noriega went to prison. As with U.S.-Iraqi relations, however, the story proved complex. Noriega had long been on the CIA payroll, and only after his involvement in the drug traffic became too blatant to ignore did Washington resort to military action to overthrow him.

If the Cold War's end eased some regional conflicts, it worsened others. In the former Soviet Union and Eastern Europe, long-smoldering ethnic and religious hatreds burst into flame, perplexing U.S. diplomats accustomed to dealing with the Soviet bloc as a single entity. Territorial disputes between Armenians and Azerbaijanis cost hundreds of lives. In 1992 the Czechs and Slovaks went their separate ways, as Czechoslovakia split into the Czech Republic and Slovakia. Ancient animosities turned especially murderous in the Balkans when Yugoslavia's communist state splintered in 1991. The region was historically unstable as a result of tensions and territorial disputes between Catholic Croatians, Orthodox Serbs, and a small minority of Muslims. As Yugoslavia's western provinces of Slovenia, Croatia, and Bosnia-Herzegovina proclaimed their independence, the Serb-dominated federal government in Belgrade launched military operations first in Croatia and then in Bosnia aimed at Croats and Muslims living in areas dominated by ethnic Serbs. Well-armed Serbian guerrillas besieged Sarajevo and other Bosnian cities, killing residents, cutting off food and medicine, and leaving hundreds of thousands homeless. Troops loyal to Serbian president Slobodan Miloslovic murdered, raped, imprisoned, and deported Muslims and other non-Serbs in a heartless campaign of "ethnic cleansing" reminiscent of the Nazis. (In World War II, the tables had been turned. Then, Croatian fascists allied with Hitler had brutalized the Serbs.) The crisis highlighted the limited capacity of outsiders to halt local conflicts in the post–Cold War era. UN-imposed sanctions against Serbia had little effect, and proposals for military intervention won scant support. President Bush, wary of engaging American forces in such a complex situation, confined the U.S. role to assistance in safeguarding UN food and relief convoys sent to Sarajevo and other besieged centers in Bosnia.

The administration's most substantial diplomatic achievement, significantly, came on the economic front and underscored Washington's shifting post–Cold War priorities. In August 1992, U.S. trade representative Carla Hills and her counterparts from Canada and Mexico completed the North American Free Trade Agreement (NAFTA). Under the treaty, the three nations created a single trading bloc containing more people and more production than the European Community. Bush would pass to his successor the delicate task of persuading Congress to ratify NAFTA, but he defined its larger meaning: "The Cold War is over. The principal challenge now facing the United States is to compete in a rapidly changing, expanding global marketplace."

In sum, the Bush administration compiled a mixed diplomatic record, highlighted by the NAFTA accord and coordination of the international response to Iraqi aggression. Beyond these partial successes, the shapers of U.S. foreign policy groped uncertainly toward what Bush hopefully called a "new world order." As historian Stephen Graubard observed, "Like many Americans of his generation, Bush had become so habituated to living with the Cold War, was so much formed by its values, that he lacked any moral or political compass to guide him when he wished to turn away from its simple and brutal verities." Graubard noted that Bush was hardly alone in this uncertainty and loss of direction.

The Fabric Strained: Inequities and Tensions in Contemporary American Society

As Americans slowly adapted to the changing world, they also struggled to absorb demographic and social trends that would mold U.S. life in the years ahead. The country's population of some 260 million in 1994 comprised a mosaic of Native Americans, blacks, Hispanics, Asians, and whites. Each of these groups, in turn, included an array of subgroups differentiated by geography, ethnicity, religion, and economic status. Five million immigrants in 1985–1990—the highest rate in eight decades—produced a population that was nearly 8 percent foreign born, up from 4.7 percent in 1970. In the 1950s, the media had portrayed America as blandly homogeneous. Unrealistic even then, the stereotype collapsed a generation later as diversity, not uniformity, characterized U.S. society. By 1990, more than a fifth of all Californians were foreign born.

For Native Americans, these years brought a quickening of ethnic pride. More than 1.7 million persons identified themselves as American Indians in the 1990 census, over twice the 1970 total. These figures reflected not only natural increase but also the growing numbers of Indians eager to affirm their ethnic roots. A network of some thirty tribal colleges provided educational opportunities and cultural sustenance. Under a 1961 law permitting tribes to buy or develop land for commercial purposes, Indians pursued business ventures ranging from vacation resorts to gambling casinos. The latter generated revenue but also led to intratribal disputes and conflicts with opponents of commercialized gambling. Yet Indians remained among the nation's poorest citizens. Both on the reservations and in the cities, joblessness, alcoholism, and inadequate health care inexorably took their toll.

The Asian-American population continued to expand as well, fed by immigration from the Philippines, Korea, and Vietnam and by well-established Chinese-American and Japanese-American communities. In 1990 Los Angeles was more than 9 percent Asian, up from 5 percent a decade earlier. With their strong family culture and emphasis on academics, Asian-Americans showed high rates of college attendance and upward mobility. As in most other immigrant groups, however, generational tensions plagued these communities as young people wavered between traditional ways and the lure of the mass culture.

The African-American population remained divided along economic lines. At one end of the spectrum, the black professional and upper-middle class enjoyed good incomes, stable families, and college degrees. In 1990, 12 percent of college students were black, more than double the 1965 rate and close to the ratio of the general population. From 1967 to 1990, the proportion of black workers earning more than $50,000 (in constant 1990 dollars) rose from 7 percent to 15 percent. In 1990 some 46 percent of African-Americans in the labor force held white-collar jobs. Communities like Cranwood in Cleveland, Chicago's Auburn Park, and Baldwin Hills in Los Angeles featured the attractive homes and well-tended lawns of this black professional and middle class. A growing number of blacks held public office. In 1989 New York City elected its first black mayor, David Dinkins, and Virginia the nation's first black governor, L. Douglas Wilder. African-Americans prominent in the Bush administration included Dr. Louis Sullivan, secretary of the Department of Health and Human Services, and General Colin Powell, chairman of the Joint Chiefs of Staff.

At the other end of the scale were the impoverished inner-city blacks, perhaps a third of all African-Americans. From this battered group, whose education often ended well before high-school graduation, came the blacks who accounted for 55 percent of all murder arrests and 69 percent of all arrests for robbery. Although strong families, thriving churches, and vigorous social institutions existed in the inner city, the social pathologies were powerful. Among black youngsters aged fifteen to nineteen, the death rate by homicide stood at nearly ten times the rate for white youths. In a trend for which analysts offered various explanations, pregnancy rates among black teenagers spiked upward. In 1989, 66 percent of all black births were to single women, in contrast to 18 percent in 1950. Scarcely beyond childhood themselves, these new mothers often had no means of support. As a result, more than two-thirds of all black children had been on welfare by their eighteenth birthday.

As the factory jobs once open to urban workers disappeared, inner-city unemployment soared as high as 60 percent. Lacking the training for skilled jobs that in any event were often located in distant suburbs, youths faced life on the streets or marginal service-sector jobs in car washes or fast-food establishments. Inner-city crime, welfare dependency, and teenage pregnancy were inseparable from the problem of joblessness. For the unskilled, one economist observed, the America of the 1990s had become "a harder, rougher place."

Illegal drug use, although found at all income levels and among all races, reached epidemic proportions in inner-city minority neighborhoods plagued by poverty. In some two hundred urban areas, drug gangs waged lethal struggles over the lucrative cocaine and heroin trade. In many communities, children as young as eight or nine, lured by drug dealers' gold jewelry and flashy cars, acted as lookouts or made deliveries. The drug of choice in the inner cities was crack, an extra-potent form of cocaine. Public-health officials estimated that from thirty thousand to fifty thousand "crack babies" came into the world annually, addicted at birth.

Caught in the coils of joblessness, welfare dependence, and destructive behavior, millions in the inner cities seemed at risk of becoming a permanent undercaste. Books such as Alex Kotlowitz's *There Are No Children Here* (1991) and movies like John Singleton's *Boyz 'N the Hood* (1991), with its portrayal of young Los Angeles blacks devastated by drugs and gang warfare, evoked the individual human tragedies behind the aggregate statistics. Most discouraging of all, the twenty-fifth anniversary of the Kerner Commission found the United States nearly as segregated as ever. Sociologist Douglas Massey, in a study of ten metropolitan areas, reported a pervasive

FOCUS ON: *THE MULTICULTURALISM DEBATE*

"E pluribus unum," the nation's motto proclaims: "Out of many, one." Yet in the post-1960 decades, the ideal of a common national culture proved elusive. As U.S. society grew more fragmented, with an array of groups clamoring for cultural as well as political equality, debate raged over how literature and history should be taught.

The so-called multiculturalism controversy took many forms. Advocates for women, African-Americans, Native Americans, Hispanics, Asian-Americans, gays and lesbians, and other groups protested the way in which traditional pedagogy had ignored or marginalized them. Even evangelical Christians, once the dominant cultural group, complained that the academic world ignored and devalued their beliefs. In English departments, academics argued over whether to reconstruct a canon dominated by works of "dead white European males." Instructors devised new courses that privileged works by women, persons of color, and Third World writers. History textbook writers and publishers scrambled to give more space to nonelites.

Some observers, however, saw in these efforts an erosion of any sense of common American identity: the *pluribus* seemed triumphant, the *unum* in retreat. In *Cultural Literacy: What Every American Needs to Know* (1987), E. D. Hirsch, Jr., cautioned that American culture was becoming a "tower of Babel." Yet many judged Hirsch's own effort to define a common culture traditionalistic and exclusionary. The University of Chicago classicist Alan Bloom, an unabashed elitist, defined culture more narrowly still. In his best-selling polemic, *The Closing of the American Mind* (1987), Bloom lamented the erosion of standards and called for an intellectual elite that would disdain the ephemera of politics, social conflict, and mass culture to ponder the great themes of Western civilization. Historian Arthur Schlesinger, Jr., in *The Disuniting of America* (1991) urged a renewed effort to define a common core of American citizenship and culture. Finally, historians warned lest the impulse to enhance the self-esteem of minority groups encourage shoddy history.

The dispute spilled over into politics. Cities such as Miami with large Hispanic populations debated resolutions making English the official language. President Reagan's choice to head the National Endowment for the Humanities, Lynn Cheney, (spouse of Defense Secretary Dick Cheney), battled multiculturalism and lauded the classical tradition. Pat Buchanan, the conservative columnist who briefly ran for president in 1992, rallied the forces of the Right at the Republican convention, stridently summoning cheering supporters to take back "our cities, our culture, and our country." These critics often idealized the past's cultural unity and intellectual harmony in contrast to today's fragmentation and raucous conflicts. In fact, a close look at history from ancient Greece onward shows not harmony but conflict and disputatiousness remarkably similar to our own era.

It is not surprising that the "multicultural" demand eventually became so vehement. Up to the very recent era, courses in history and literature did focus on the exploits and writings of white male elites of European origin. In U.S. history courses, Indians appeared solely as a quickly vanquished foe, blacks mainly as victims of slavery, and Hispanics and Asian-Americans hardly at all. Absent, too, was working-class culture, of whatever ethnic character. A few women merited notice, but the historical experience of women as a whole—half the population—was ignored. As these groups asserted themselves politically, the corresponding demand to rectify decades of cultural distortion soon followed.

Some proponents of "multiculturalism" and "politically correct" speech dismissed their critics as expressing the bigotry and xenophobia that have always existed in America. Indeed, as early as the 1740s, Benjamin Franklin warned of the German immigrants who were "polluting" Pennsylvania's Anglo society with their alien ways and language. Throughout American history, prejudice against newcomers and minorities has led to periodic demands for exclusion and control.

Yet the contemporary debate involves more than just covert prejudice and has unfolded in a unique cultural setting. In the past, minorities were either powerless or had far less power than the dominant elite. In modern America, advocates for the underdog occupy powerful positions in government, the media, and academia. When demands for the redress of minority grievances in the cultural realm come from such quarters, they can be accompanied by credible threats to impose sanctions that will enforce acceptable standards of conduct and expression. This potential for abuse raises legitimate concerns about "Big Brother" and the repression of individual freedom. It also can encourage a culture of victimization, in which individuals and groups demand legal redress for insensitive behavior or speech that, however deplorable, may be the price of a free society. Conflicts once fought out in private now land in the courts. Furthermore, the obsession with "political correctness" can stifle discussion in the classroom and elsewhere, as people become so fearful of giving offense that they choose to remain silent rather than express potentially unpopular views. Thus, the debate over multiculturalism and "political correctness" can inhibit the vigorous give-and-take on which democracy thrives.

Some observers have tried to move the controversy off dead center. In *Beyond the Culture Wars* (1992), Gerald Graff of the University of Chicago viewed the debate as evidence not of disintegration but of cultural renewal. Passivity over issues of cultural meaning is far more to be feared than discord, Graff contended. He urged teachers to incorporate the cultural debate into the curriculum as a way of bringing texts alive for students. Despite occasional excesses, the multiculturalism debate has in fact pumped new energy into education. Textbooks and course syllabi now more closely reflect the ethnic and gender realities of the larger society. Students vigorously debate issues of gender, race, and social class in canonical works that they once accepted without question.

One champion of multiculturalism, the Japanese-American historian Ronald Takaki, insists that only by recognizing the reality of cultural diversity can the "E pluribus unum" dream ever be realized. Hopes for a genuinely inclusive culture, Takaki wrote in *A Different Mirror* (1993), lie in "'unlearning' much of what we have been told about America's past and substituting a more inclusive and accurate history of all the peoples of America." Takaki's point is well taken, but the risks remain: Intolerance in pursuit of multiculturalist or "politically correct" goals can lead to new forms of intolerance, pressures toward a sterile conformity, and the prospect of a backlash damaging to all concerned. Clearly this complex debate is far from resolved as the end of the century approaches.

pattern of de facto segregation that isolated most African-Americans from mainstream U.S. society.

Inner-city tensions exploded into violence in Los Angeles in 1992 amid black outrage over the Rodney King case. On March 3, 1991, L.A. police had arrested King, a twenty-five-year-old black man, after a high-speed chase on the freeway. Though unarmed, the intoxicated King showed signs of resisting arrest. After zapping him with a 50,000-volt stun gun, the police forced King to the ground, and four officers took turns kicking and clubbing him with heavy truncheons. Eleven other policemen stood by and watched. The vicious burst of violence left King with eleven skull fractures, a shattered cheekbone, a broken ankle, chest burns from the stun gun, and brain damage. Unknown to the police, a nearby resident had captured the mayhem on videotape. Soon TV viewers worldwide were watching the horrifying display of brutality. Four policemen faced trial, but despite the videotape, a jury acquitted them in April 1992. As word of the verdict spread, violence erupted in South Central Los Angeles, a black and Hispanic district. For thirty-six hours, gangs roamed the streets, burning and looting. Black youths viciously beat a white truck driver. Rioters especially targeted the shops of Korean merchants that dotted the district. In scenes unhappily reminiscent of the 1960s, entire blocks went up in flames. "Can't we all get along," pleaded Rodney King in a televised call for calm. When an uneasy quiet returned, Los Angeles counted 44 dead, nearly 1,800 injured, 6,345 arrests, and $500 million in property damage. One young woman who was shot gave birth a few hours later; the baby survived, but with a bullet lodged in its tiny body. In the next two weeks, Californians bought 20,578 guns. The "Rodney King riots" starkly underscored the pressure-cooker environment of inner cities mired in poverty and joblessness.

The politics of race continued, as the notorious Willy Horton TV ads of 1988 illustrated. While Democratic candidates racked up large black majorities, Republicans used taxes, crime, and welfare abuses as race-linked issues to attract white voters. As Thomas Edsall wrote in 1992, "Direct appeals to racial prejudice may no longer be acceptable in American politics, but race, in an indirect and sometimes subliminal way, remains a strong undercurrent in presidential politics." Tellingly, many black officeholders in the 1980s and 1990s served in cities that were economically stagnant and losing their political clout as the middle class dwindled.

In 1990 the nation's 20 million Hispanics—more than double the 1970 total—composed America's fastest-growing minority. Indeed, demographers predict that by the year 2000, Hispanics will supplant blacks as the nation's largest minority. This population included 14 million Mexican-Americans centered in the Southwest; Cuban Americans living in Florida; and immigrants from the Caribbean and Central America residing along the East Coast. Puerto Ricans, who are U.S. citizens, arrived in great numbers as well. Like earlier immigrants, Hispanics came to America seeking a better life, especially as falling oil prices rocked the Mexican economy. Between 1980 and 1985, the Hispanic population of California and Florida grew by some 30 percent; Texas's, by 23 percent. By 1990 both Miami and Los Angeles were one-third Hispanic.

Despite the 1986 immigration law that tightened border controls and imposed tougher restrictions on hiring undocumented aliens, as many as 12 million Hispanics lived in the United States illegally in the early 1990s. With few health benefits or other protections, they worked long hours for low wages as domestics, garment work-ers, and migrant farm laborers. Hispanic family, church, and cultural institutions pro-vided support, but life in America was harsh. In 1990 nearly a fifth of Mexican-Americans and 30 percent of Puerto Ricans lived below the poverty line, scourged by drugs, crime, school dropout, and teenage pregnancy.

The crisis in the inner cities got little federal attention in the Bush years. Jack Kemp, the former professional football player who headed the Department of Hous-ing and Urban Development, urged tax incentives to encourage inner-city job cre-ation by private capital, but the White House showed scant interest. After the Rod-ney King riots, Bush and Congress agreed on a $5 billion urban aid package, but Washington's attention soon waned. Cornel West, director of Afro-American stud-ies at Princeton University, drew a larger lesson from the riots. He wrote, "What we witnessed in Los Angeles was the consequence of a lethal linkage of economic de-cline, cultural decay, and political lethargy in American life. Race was the visible catalyst, not the underlying cause."

White America tended to ignore inner-city minorities except when riots erupted, yet two elements of the urban crisis—drug abuse and welfare dependency—generated much self-interested concern. Middle America linked drugs to rising crime rates and soaring welfare costs to high taxes. Addressing the nation's $50 bil-lion illegal drug traffic, Bush urged a doubling of the federal antidrug budget and named William Bennett, a former secretary of education, as "drug czar." Bennett adopted a get-tough policy that included jailing drug dealers, but although drug-related arrests rose to a million each year, he had little to show for his efforts and soon departed in frustration. The 1992 comment of a St. Louis crack dealer provided a key to the problem: "They could lock up a thousand brothers, even 10,000 broth-ers. There's always going to be someone new out here selling [drugs]. . . . [T]here's nothing else to do: No type of recreation, no work, nothing." One answer, experts advised, lay in treating drug abuse less as a crime and more as a public-health prob-lem and barometer of other social issues.

On the welfare front, the number of women and children receiving AFDC (Aid to Families with Dependent Children) benefits had mushroomed from 8 million in 1970 to 13.5 million in 1992. Social observers spoke of the feminization of poverty. Some 56 percent of aid recipients were black or Hispanic. As taxpayer anger over rising welfare costs intensified, some states considered cutting payments while others experimented with "workfare" programs to get aid recipients into the labor force. Reform strategies reflected political ideology. In *Declaring War on Welfare* (1992), the liberal Mickey Kaus proposed replacing welfare with a vast New Deal–style fed-eral jobs program. Conservatives favored the Jack Kemp approach of luring private-sector employers back to the inner cities with tax breaks and other incentives. Drug addiction and welfare dependency were serious issues, but both reflected deeper problems rooted in economic changes whose full implications America had only begun to grasp.

While conditions in the inner cities elicited alarm, the changing status of Amer-ican women was generally hailed as a major social advance, although in some quar-ters it roused uneasiness and even hostility. The statistics were impressive. Women writers, artists, and scholars energized the cultural and intellectual scene, and women's history emerged as a lively field. In the realm of black literature, once largely a male domain, women such as Alice Walker, Maya Angelou, and Toni Morrison now held sway. Morrison won the Pulitzer Prize in 1987 for her novel *Beloved* and the Nobel Prize for literature in 1993. Moreover, the proportion of women in the work force rose from 42 percent in 1970 to 57 percent by 1991. Even Rabbit Angstrom's long-suffering wife, Janice, became a realtor. Women found employment at all levels, from domestic service and the building trades to white-collar jobs. Their share of executive and managerial positions grew from 32 percent in 1983 to 41 percent in 1991. Although only about 20 percent of physicians and lawyers were female in 1991, the figures grew each year. In the fall of 1993 at the University of Wisconsin–Madison, 45 percent of the entering medical students and 43 percent of the entering law students were women. Nevertheless, many women still confronted wage inequities and workplace discrimination. The top ranks of business and the professions remained male bastions as employed women clustered in the lower ranks of the labor force, held down by entrenched patterns of gender discrimination that became known as the "glass ceiling."

Shifting marital and family patterns shaped women's lives as well. With births to unmarried women climbing and nearly half of all marriages ending in divorce, single-parent families, usually headed by a female, grew steadily. The proportion of children living in traditional, two-parent families fell from 85 percent in 1970 to 72 percent in 1991. (For white children, the figure was 80 percent; for black children, 42 percent.) The birthrate remained low, with couples opting for one or two children or none at all. All these trends directly influenced women's life choices. As the journal *Public Interest* noted in 1993, "In a long-life-expectancy, low-birth-rate society, there really is no serious alternative to major lifelong working careers for most women. The career of full-time wife, mother and homemaker has simply ceased to be an adequate life project."

Amid these profound changes, feminism came under assault from conservatives who deplored its emphasis on autonomy and careers as antifamily and a threat to "traditional values." In *Backlash: The Undeclared War Against American Women* (1991), Susan Faludi saw a systematic drive in politics, fashion, and advertising to reassert old stereotypes of women as subordinate, deferential sex objects. Feminists themselves questioned some of their own earlier assumptions. As early as 1981, in *The Second Stage*, Betty Friedan criticized feminists who focused on career issues and women's rights and who left family-related issues to conservatives.

With greater autonomy came a heightened awareness of all forms of exploitation, including rape and sexual harassment. Susan Brownmiller's *Against Our Will: Men, Women, and Rape* (1975) had placed this issue on the feminist agenda, and it remained there in the eighties and nineties. Businesses and educational institutions adopted tough sexual-harassment codes. But this issue, too, stirred controversy. Some critics claimed that the statistics on rape and sexual harassment were being inflated, and that they encouraged young women to think of themselves as in constant mortal danger from brutish males. In *The Morning After: Sex, Fear, and Feminism on Campus* (1993), Katie Roiphe argued that the broadening of "rape" to include a wide range of ambiguous sexual encounters represented a resurgence of Victorian prudery in a more politically correct guise. Conservative writer Charles

Sykes in *A Nation of Victims* (1993) attacked what he called the "sexual nightmare" of some feminists who were peddling "the politics of victimization."

Abortion, too, continued to rouse strong emotions. While the abortion rate held steady at about 1.4 million annually, the debate raged on. Books such as *Life Itself: Abortion in the American Mind* (1992) by journalist Roger Rosenblatt and *Life's Dominion* (1993) by law professor Ronald Dworkin sought grounds for compromise, but such efforts failed to sway the committed partisans of either camp. These authors underestimated the moral passion of both the prochoice and antiabortion groups. While the former defended unrestricted access to abortion as a right, the latter, mostly Catholics and evangelical Protestants, denounced the procedure as deeply immoral. Abortion foes portrayed their cause as part of a larger crusade to affirm the sanctity of all life. Prochoice advocates linked their battle to the larger campaign for gender equality; the war against abortion rights, they insisted, was part of a broader drive to subordinate women. Interestingly, some prominent feminists expressed reservations about abortion, and opinion polls generally showed greater opposition to abortion among women than among men.

Civil disobedience, once the province of antiwar and civil-rights activists, now became a technique of antiabortion groups like Operation Rescue, whose members courted arrest in their demonstrations against clinics and even against individual physicians. From 1978 to 1993, extremists bombed or set fire to more than a hundred clinics. In March 1993, an antiabortion activist in Pensacola, Florida, shot and killed a physician whose photograph had earlier appeared on a "Wanted" poster circulated by Operation Rescue. Nearly all "prolife" leaders condemned violence, but these acts revealed the passions that the issue had catalyzed.

When two Supreme Court justices retired during Bush's term, the abortion question inevitably became entangled in the succession process. The first nomination, in 1990, went to Judge David Souter of New Hampshire. Despite his scant record on major issues, Souter proved thoughtful and open in his confirmation hearings, and he won easy confirmation. Together with Sandra Day O'Connor and Anthony Kennedy, Souter emerged as a centrist on abortion and other highly charged legal matters.

Bush's 1991 choice of Clarence Thomas to replace Thurgood Marshall proved more divisive. Both men were black but otherwise very different. Marshall, an NAACP attorney before joining the high court, had long upheld liberal and civil-rights causes. Thomas, a Roman Catholic and an ideological conservative, had risen from a poor and disrupted Georgia boyhood to attend Holy Cross College and Yale Law School. Head of the Equal Employment Opportunity Commission (EEOC) under President Reagan, he had been appointed a federal appeals-court judge only in 1990.

Mindful of the fate of the loquacious Robert Bork, Thomas concealed his legal views in his confirmation hearings. He had never discussed *Roe v. Wade*, he told a skeptical Judiciary Committee, and had no fixed opinion on abortion. The hearings took a startling turn when a former associate at EEOC, Anita Hill, accused Thomas of sexual harassment. Thomas angrily denied the charges, and Republican committee members harshly grilled Professor Hill. In the end, Thomas narrowly won Senate confirmation, 52–48. Once on the bench, he consistently took the most conservative position. Judges must try to discern the "original intent" of every law, he held, including the Constitution and the Bill of Rights, and not twist them to "address all [the] ills of our society."

In 1992 the Supreme Court upheld parts of a Pennsylvania law limiting abortion rights by a 5–4 vote. Justice Thomas took the occasion to call for a reversal of *Roe*, but Justice Souter outraged abortion foes by joining the majority in coupling a partial endorsement of the Pennsylvania law with a strong defense of *Roe* itself. The majority ruled that "an entire generation has come of age free to assume *Roe*'s concept of liberty in defining the capacity of women . . . to make reproductive decisions. . . . To overrule *Roe* . . . [would cause] profound and unnecessary damage to the Court's legitimacy, and to the Nation's commitment to the rule of law." Indeed, the bitterness of the controversy obscured the fact that a broad national consensus supported the Supreme Court's position. This consensus approved the availability of abortion in the first trimester of pregnancy but also endorsed the right of states to impose restrictions such as waiting periods and parental notification (or even parental consent) for minors.

As the abortion argument ground on, the environmental cause gained momentum and incited controversy. Environmental concerns had sharpened in March 1989 when the giant oil tanker *Exxon Valdez* ran aground in Prince William Sound, Alaska. The ship dumped 10.8 million gallons of crude oil that blackened miles of coastline; killed hundreds of sea otters, bald eagles, and shorebirds; and endangered Alaska's fisheries. George Bush deplored the disaster but insisted that oil drilling in Alaska was necessary to meet America's energy needs. Similar clashes between conflicting interests proliferated. In the Pacific Northwest, for example, the campaign to preserve the last old-growth forests and their delicate ecosystem, including the northern spotted owl, angered loggers and timber companies worried about jobs and profits.

As it had earlier with the appearance of Rachel Carson's *Silent Spring*, the environmental movement took on fresh urgency as new health threats emerged. Scientists warned of acid rain, a product of atmospheric pollution that kills plant and animal life in lakes and forests. They also pointed to the thinning of the Earth's ozone layer caused by chlorofluorocarbon gases from spray cans and other sources. Ozone filters out carcinogenic ultraviolet radiation. In addition, scientists grew alarmed by the threat of global warming as atmospheric pollution prevented the Earth's heat from escaping. Such reports built support for the Clean Air Act of 1990, a bipartisan measure intended to reduce smog, acid rain, and industrial pollution. At the local level, cities urgently established recycling programs to avoid choking on their own refuse, estimated to reach 216 million tons per year by 2000.

In *Earth in the Balance* (1992), Senator Al Gore of Tennessee spotlighted the environmental crisis. The industrialized world continued to deplete dwindling natural resources and energy supplies, while in poor nations such as Egypt and India, the drive for economic development often overrode environmental concerns. In South America and parts of Asia, rain forests rich in biological diversity and ecologically vital to the entire world faced destruction. Recognizing the global dimensions of the issue, the UN in 1992 convened Earth Summit, an environmental conference in Rio de Janeiro that drew thirty-five thousand participants. The delegates signed treaties related to biodiversity and global warming and endorsed "Agenda 21," a sweeping, although nonbinding, manifesto. Nevertheless, the event mainly served to focus attention on the need for international cooperation to save the human habitat.

The AIDS quilt was comprised of thousands of individual panels, each honoring someone who died of the disease. This meticulously stitched panel commemorates a young Wisconsin man who fell victim to AIDS five days before his twenty-eighth birthday. (© *1987 Matt Herron*)

President Bush won scant praise from environmentalists. He signed the Clean Air Act, but he also appointed officials who undercut the rules that they were pledged to enforce. These appointees advocated expanded logging on public lands, more oil exploration in Alaska, and the commercial development of protected wetlands. The Competitiveness Council, an agency headed by Vice President Quayle, attacked environmental regulations for supposedly stifling business growth. Bush's petulant, defensive speech at the Rio Earth Summit boasting of his environmental record and attacking his critics further alienated environmental activists.

Health matters also took center stage in the 1990s. With medical costs rising twice as fast as the consumer-price index, the federal budget felt the strain (see p. 455). The medical and social needs of a burgeoning elderly population also loomed large. Feminist pioneer Betty Friedan, now seventy-two years old, addressed this issue in *The Fountain of Age* (1993). The health issue that attracted the most attention was AIDS (acquired immunodeficiency syndrome), the fatal disease, first identified in 1981, that had claimed 204,000 American lives by September 1993. More than 130,000 people suffered from the illness, and an estimated one million more carried the human immunodeficiency (HIV) virus, precursor of AIDS. The disease posed an even grimmer threat in sub-Saharan Africa and parts of Asia. The World Health Organization in 1991 projected 10–20 million new cases by 2000, mostly in the developing world.

AIDS spreads by the direct transmission of bodily fluids. The most vulnerable populations are homosexuals or bisexuals, persons having unprotected sex with infected individuals, and drug users sharing needles. Early in the epidemic, blood transfusions also spread the virus. With no cure in sight, public-health agencies urgently advised protective measures, including the use of condoms. Actor Rock Hudson, who had hidden his homosexuality during his movie career, died of AIDS in 1985. Basketball superstar Earvin "Magic" Johnson and tennis pro Arthur Ashe announced in 1991–1992 that they were HIV positive. Ashe, who had become infected from a blood transfusion, died in 1993.

The onset of the AIDS epidemic shook American society. While some viewed the disease as God's "punishment" of homosexuals, gay-rights and AIDS activists protested the ostracizing of sufferers and called for expanded research budgets and quicker testing of promising drugs. The radical group ACT UP disrupted politicians' speeches and used other direct-action techniques to publicize their cause. Hospice organizations and support networks helped people with the disease, and a giant AIDS quilt made of panels crafted by victims' friends and relatives toured the nation. In novels and in plays such as Larry Kramer's *The Normal Heart* (1985) and Tony

The AIDS quilt. "America does not have a person to waste," President Bill Clinton vowed to AIDS marchers in Washington, D.C., in 1993 as he proposed strengthening funding for AIDS research. (*Gregory Zabilski*)

Kushner's two-part epic *Angels in America* (1993), writers explored the devastation of AIDS and the courage that it could call forth. The AIDS crisis added urgency to the larger debate over the allocation of medical-research funds, the availability of promising but untested drugs, and other complex issues.

Economic Stagnation and Middle-Class Anxieties

A tangle of economic problems further vexed these years. The annual trade deficit hovered at around $40 billion in the early nineties. In 1992 President Bush converted a planned visit to Asia into a trade mission. The heads of GM, Ford, and Chrysler, invited along by the president, ham-handedly pressured the Japanese to buy more U.S. cars. When a flu attack caused Bush to collapse and vomit on Japan's prime minister at a state dinner, the mishap seemed symbolic of America's foreign-trade woes.

The federal deficit also continued to rise as the impact of the tax cuts and increased military spending of the 1980s, together with the cost of ever-growing entitlement programs, became painfully evident. In 1990 Congress and the president, after acrimonious bargaining, agreed on a five-year deficit-reduction package. The plan cut spending and, breaking Bush's "read my lips" pledge, increased a variety of taxes. Yet the deficit still soared, reaching $290 billion in 1992, with $331 billion forecast for 1993. The costs of entitlement programs, the S&L bailout,* and coming baby-boom retirements all promised to increase the flow of red ink in future years. So did interest payments on the $4 trillion national debt, which by 1992 was eating up $200 billion annually, 15 percent of all federal spending.

If the trade and budget deficits remained abstract to many citizens, the recession that hit in 1990 proved all too real. Unemployment rose; sales, housing starts, and business investment plummeted. By mid-1992, despite some hopeful trends, consumer confidence remained depressed, and the jobless rate stood at 7.8 percent. The Federal Reserve Board slashed interest rates to thirty-year lows, but the economy responded only fitfully. Burned by the credit binge of the 1980s, banks held back on loans, and consumers and businesses hesitated to borrow, even at bargain rates. The GNP, which had grown 14 percent during Reagan's two terms, increased but an anemic 2.2 percent in the recession-battered Bush years. The problem had several sources, including reduced defense spending and a collapse of the commercial real-estate market after overexpansion in the 1980s. A further cause lay in the boom of the eighties, when Americans had plunged heavily into debt, not to finance long-term investment but to sustain high levels of consumption. The bill came due in the early 1990s, and the economy reacted by contracting sharply.

The structural ills that had stalled economic growth in the 1970s hung on. The shift of jobs from the industrial to the service sector continued, with many of the latter positions low-paying and unskilled. In December 1991, after a bleak sales year, GM announced plans to close twenty-one plants and to slash its labor force by seventy thousand. The revelation that top management at the Big Three automakers had received fat raises and stock benefits as their firms lost billions and laid off workers stirred bitter resentment. IBM lost $4.97 billion in 1992 and, in a difficult step for a company proud of never having laid off employees, revealed plans to shed twenty-five thousand workers. IBM stock plunged to half its value.

Groping for solutions, some economists urged a federal "industrial policy," a research and development (R&D) program to promote new technologies. In Japan and Western Europe, they pointed out, governments actively fostered industrial growth. In 1989, while 0.2 percent of the U.S. federal research budget went for industrial research, the figures for Japan and Germany were 8 percent and 19 percent, respectively. Industrial-policy advocates also cited the success of the Airbus, an advanced aircraft produced by a four-nation European consortium with $20 billion in government subsidies. In sales, the Airbus clipped the wings of its U.S. competitors, McDonnell-Douglas and Boeing. Economist Lester Thurow of MIT made the case for industrial policy in *Head to Head: The Coming Economic Battle Among Japan, Europe, and America* (1992). Noting the Pentagon's role in shaping U.S. industrial policy during the Cold War, Thurow urged the government to play a similar role in promoting post–Cold War economic growth.

---

* In 1989, Washington set up procedures for bailing out the nation's insolvent S&Ls, whose depositors were federally insured up to $100,000. Budget experts estimated the cost at $195 billion through 1998. In the most notorious case, Charles Keating, chairman of California's Lincoln Savings & Loan, was convicted in December 1991 of securities fraud for inducing seventeen thousand investors to buy $250 million worth of uninsured bonds.

Not everyone embraced the industrial-policy idea. Laissez-faire conservatives deemed it needless government meddling. Some economists argued that while Washington could foster a climate favorable to new technologies through job training programs, tax credits for research, and so forth, the market, not politicians, should determine the flow of research funds. The *New York Times* sarcastically asked whether "the people who brought the world $300 billion annual deficits could summon the vision to decide whether gallium arsenide chips or liquid crystal displays were the technologies to bet on." When Japan's economy weakened in 1992 and some of its industrial-policy decisions soured, enthusiasm for taking Japan as a model cooled.

Yet the economy continued to show strengths along with weak spots. The productivity rate improved in 1991–1992, for example, and U.S. automakers' market share, under 70 percent in 1991, edged up in 1992 to around 72 percent. The Ford Taurus, GM Saturn, and Plymouth Reliant won high marks for quality and efficiency. Such diverse high-tech industries as desktop computers, software, telecommunications, and high-definition TV showed encouraging progress. IBM stumbled, but smaller, nimbler U.S. computer companies expanded. Despite the overall trade deficit, America's trade surplus in advanced technology grew from $16 billion in 1986 to more than $35 billion in 1991.

But even the good news came with caveats. Ironically, one of the most advanced new factories of the early 1990s was foreign owned: Toyota's state-of-the-art auto plant in Georgetown, Kentucky. And the success of high-tech industries did not necessarily benefit U.S. workers, for their assembly plants often lay in other countries. Eighty percent of the employees of the Conner Company, a big computer disk-drive manufacturer, for example, worked in foreign factories.

While economists ruminated, ordinary Americans grappled with the effects of a stalled economy. As usual, the recession hit the poor most severely, but it also brought bad news for the middle class and exacerbated a long-term economic erosion. From 1989 to 1991, median household income (adjusted for inflation) fell from $31,750 to $31,125. High-school and college graduates faced the worst job market in memory in 1992. Of recent college graduates who were employed, 20 percent held jobs not requiring a degree, leading one economist to observe that four years of college was no longer "a risk-free investment." In *Boiling Point: Republicans, Democrats and the Decline of Middle Class Prosperity* (1993), Kevin Phillips documented that the real income of the middle class had been falling since 1973, worsened by the tax cuts of the 1980s that had redistributed income from the lower and middle ranks to the wealthy. The baby-boom generation born between 1946 and 1964, noted anthropologist Katherine Newman in *Declining Fortunes: The Withering of the American Dream* (1993), was "the first . . . since the Great Depression that can expect to have a *lower* standard of living than its parents." The anxieties gnawing at the middle class would profoundly influence the politics of 1992.

Campaign '92

George Bush had made extravagant promises in 1988. In addition to the "Read My Lips: No New Taxes" pledge, broken in 1990, he had spoken glibly of 30 million new jobs, vowed an end to illegal drugs, and proclaimed himself the "education" president and the "environmental" president. His call for a "kinder, gentler America" had suggested concern for those left behind in the 1980s. In fact, Bush disdained what he called "the vision thing" and largely ignored domestic issues. Not until 1991 did he unveil an education agenda. The plan included national student testing, competency exams for teachers, and a system by which students could attend private or church-run schools at public expense. While private-school administrators praised the "school choice" idea, the Carnegie Foundation for the Advancement of Teaching and others criticized it as doing little to help a public-school system battered by recession and neglect.

Apart from a law barring discrimination against persons with disabilities, even Bush's admirers had trouble identifying domestic achievements. Bush boasted of ending the Cold War and standing up to Iraq, but his flip-flop on taxes and his neglect of economic issues amid a recession severely weakened him. The depth of voter discontent emerged in a special election held in November 1991 to fill the seat of Senator John Heinz, a Pennsylvania Republican killed in a plane crash. Richard Thornburgh, who resigned as attorney general to run, opposed Democrat Harris Wofford, a civil-rights aide in the Kennedy White House. Voicing middle-class worries about the economy and health-care issues, Wofford won handily. By the summer of 1992, Bush's approval rating had sagged to 34 percent, and fewer than 20 percent of Americans approved his handling of the economy.

Bush's post–Persian Gulf popularity had led top Democrats like New York governor Mario Cuomo to opt out of the 1992 presidential race. Into the vacuum stepped former senator Paul Tsongas of Massachusetts, ex-governor of California Jerry Brown, senators Tom Harkin of Iowa and Bob Kerrey of Nebraska, and Governor Bill Clinton of Arkansas. Each had liabilities: Tsongas had left the Senate after cancer treatment, and doubts about his health lingered. Brown's "Governor Moonbeam" reputation for eccentricity still dogged him. Harkin's traditional liberalism had limited appeal, and Kerrey proved a bore. Clinton battled rumors of extramarital affairs, charges that he had avoided the Vietnam War draft, and insinuations of "character flaws" summed up in the epithet "Slick Willy."

Public cynicism about politics-as-usual emerged on many fronts in 1992. *JFK*, a movie postulating a bizarre conspiracy theory to explain Kennedy's assassination, scored big at the box office. At the same time, a congressional banking scandal hit the newspapers. Congress had long operated a bank in which members' paychecks could be deposited. In 1992 the press revealed that many members had overdrawn their accounts, some by thousands of dollars. Although no public funds were involved, the revelations intensified the anti-incumbency mood. So did the PAC money that showered down on Washington. In 1992 Speaker of the House Tom Foley received $401,000 in PAC contributions, and majority leader Richard Gephardt raked in a whopping $1.2 million.

The insurgent mood inspired the third-party candidacy of Ross Perot, a Texan whose EDS Corporation, a data-processing firm, had made him a billionaire. Perot's politics remained obscure apart from a deficit-cutting obsession, but he enjoyed a reputation for can-do activism. Above all, he was an outsider, untainted by old-style politics. Bypassing the primaries, he revealed his White House aspirations on a TV call-in show and then confined himself mainly to such forums, which he enlivened with salty one-liners. Millions flocked to Perot's banner, stirring fears that the election, for the first time since 1824, might be thrown into the House of Representatives.* But the mercurial Perot, angered by media scrutiny and tripped up by his own off-the-cuff style, withdrew from the race in July. He reentered to participate in the televised presidential debates but never regained his momentum.

Bill Clinton easily won the Democratic nomination. Born in 1946, he grew up in a household dominated by an abusive stepfather. Young Clinton adored Elvis Presley and briefly contemplated a career as a saxophonist, but instead he attended Georgetown University, Oxford University as a Rhodes scholar, and Yale Law School. In 1978, at age thirty-two, he won election in Arkansas as the nation's youngest governor.

Clinton's acceptance speech focused on health care, education, jobs, and economic growth and earned him a spurt in the polls. So did his choice of Senator Al Gore as running mate. The two at once set off on a midwestern bus tour reminiscent of Harry Truman's 1948 whistle-stop campaign. To attract younger voters, Clinton appeared on MTV and the popular Arsenio Hall talk show, sporting sunglasses and saxophone. Hillary Clinton, also a Yale Law graduate and a high-powered lawyer, had initially put off many voters who considered her too aggressive, but she softened her public image—challenging Barbara Bush to a cookie recipe contest, for example—and emerged as an asset to her husband's cause.

Both Clinton and Gore belonged to the Democratic Leadership Council (DLC), a moderate group intent on wooing back Reagan Democrats. To this end, the DLC combated the Democrats' reputation as a "tax-and-spend" party beholden to minorities and special interests. Clinton thus distanced himself from Jesse Jackson and from union leaders. His acceptance speech praised "the hard-working Americans who make up our middle class" and included tough talk on welfare. The party platform echoed the theme, describing welfare as "a second chance, not a way of life." Clinton called for a two-year limit on welfare payments, coupled with education, job training, and child-care programs to help recipients to find work. He demanded tough laws to compel delinquent fathers, or "deadbeat dads," to support their offspring. A sign at Clinton headquarters summed up the campaign's key theme: "The Economy, Stupid." Clinton hammered at the sluggish economy and pledged to make it his top priority. Advised by fellow Rhodes scholar Robert Reich, a lecturer at Harvard who would be appointed secretary of labor, Clinton called for government programs to promote economic growth through education and job training.

A faltering Bush never offered a coherent second-term agenda, and Vice President Quayle added little to the ticket. Already a butt of humor, Quayle drew more ridicule when he misspelled *potato* while presiding over a school spelling bee. Yet the

---

* If no presidential candidate receives an electoral-college majority, Article II, section 3 of the Constitution places the decision in the hands of the House of Representatives, each state delegation casting a single ballot.

Republicans faced deeper problems than Quayle's spelling. The coalition that had elected Nixon in 1968 and 1972 and Reagan in 1980 and 1984 was inherently unstable. It comprised an uneasy alliance of laissez-faire ideologues who hated "big government," and corporate executives and wealthy citizens who favored lower taxes but often took a liberal stand on social issues. The coalition also accommodated millions of white blue-collar and middle-class Americans, frequently Protestant evangelicals or Catholic ethnics, who concerned themselves with such issues as abortion, pornography, homosexuality, school prayer, "family values," and alleged favoritism to minorities. Through the 1980s, the Soviet threat and the prevailing aura of prosperity, together with Reagan's charisma, had held the coalition together. But by 1992 the Cold War had ended, the economy was in recession, and Reagan had been replaced by the lackluster Bush.

As the GOP splintered, the party's well-organized right wing flexed its muscle. Bush's post–Persian Gulf complacency provided a further opening for critics within his own party. In several early primaries, Bush suffered the embarrassment of a strong challenge by conservative columnist Pat Buchanan. The party platform embodied the New Right's cultural agenda. The convention celebrated Barbara Bush and Marilyn Quayle for devoting themselves to their husbands' careers and attacked Hillary Clinton as a "radical feminist." Delegates representing Pat Robertson's Christian Coalition cheered a slashing speech by Pat Buchanan in which he vowed all-out ideological war on a variety of cultural and moral issues.

To revive his fortunes, Bush brought James Baker from the State Department as campaign strategist in August. Baker sketched a high-minded theme: President Bush, having devoted his first term to global issues, would work to solve domestic problems in his second term. Yet the campaign quickly sank to the low level that seemed the new political norm. Issues were reduced to sound bites, and innuendo and stereotypes substituted for thoughtful discussion. Clinton blamed Bush for chronic economic problems that could hardly be charged entirely to the White House. When Bush, on the other hand, denounced the Democratic platform for omitting "three simple letters, G-O-D," even jaded political observers groaned.

Election day 1992 thrilled victory-starved Democrats. Although Perot denied him a majority, Clinton triumphed solidly, with 43 percent of the vote to Bush's 38 percent and an electoral margin of 370–168. Riding a tide of economic discontent, Clinton won back Reagan Democrats and cut deeply into Republican strongholds in the southern and mountain states. More than 75 percent of African-American voters pulled the Democratic lever. With Democratic majorities returned to both houses of Congress, the legislative and executive branches were controlled by the same party for the first time in twelve years. Still, the outcomes also sent a cautionary signal to Bill Clinton: 19 percent of voters had opted for Ross Perot, the best third-party showing since Theodore Roosevelt's in 1912. As for George Bush, the *New York Times* summed up a prevailing view in a postelection editorial entitled "The Half-Way Man." The *Times* conceded Bush's foreign-policy achievements but observed that on domestic policy he "created the disquieting and ultimately fatal impression that he didn't know what to do, and worse, didn't much care."

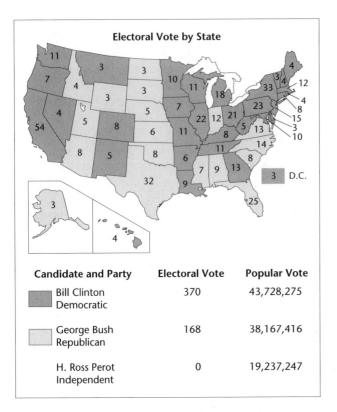

Electoral Vote by State

FIGURE 15.3

Presidential Election of 1992

Candidate and Party	Electoral Vote	Popular Vote
Bill Clinton Democratic	370	43,728,275
George Bush Republican	168	38,167,416
H. Ross Perot Independent	0	19,237,247

A Chastened Liberalism: Clinton at the Helm

As in 1960, the 1992 election brought both a change of party and a generational shift. George Bush would be the last president to have fought in World War II and to have lived through the entire Cold War as an adult. With Clinton and Gore, and 110 new members of Congress, the baby boomers emerged as the nation's leaders. This generation's formative memories were not of Munich, Pearl Harbor, Stalin, and Bing Crosby, but of the Peace Corps, civil-rights marches, antiwar protests, John Kennedy, Woodstock, and the Beatles. The Clintons' daughter, Chelsea, was even named for a popular sixties' ballad, Joni Mitchell's "Chelsea Morning."

The election dramatized the emergence of women in American public life. Voters sent six women to the Senate and forty-eight to the House of Representatives. California became the first state to elect two women senators—Barbara Boxer and Dianne Feinstein—and Illinois the first to send an African-American woman, Carol Moseley Braun, to the upper chamber. Women still remained a small minority in Congress, but the men's club atmosphere was fading.

Clinton's appointments further highlighted the new gender dynamics of U.S. politics. He chose women to head the Environmental Protection Agency and the Council of Economic Advisers and named a woman as U.S. representative to the United Nations. Breaking precedent further, he appointed the first woman attorney general, Janet Reno, a Florida prosecutor. Donna Shalala, chancellor of the University of Wisconsin—Madison, became secretary of health and human services; Hazel O'Leary, a lawyer and executive vice president of Northern States Power Company of Minneapolis, was appointed secretary of energy. When Byron White retired from the Supreme Court in 1993, Clinton chose a woman, Ruth Bader Ginsberg. A federal appeals court judge, Ginsberg had taught at Rutgers Law School. The president also made clear that Hillary Rodham Clinton would be more than a ceremonial First Lady. He gave her an office in the White House West Wing—the official side—and named her to head the Task Force on National Health-Care Reform.

Fulfilling a campaign call for "a government that looks like America," Clinton chose Ron Brown, African-American chairperson of the Democratic National Committee, as secretary of commerce, and two Hispanics, Henry Cisneros, the mayor of San Antonio, and Federico Peña, to head HUD and the Department of Transportation, respectively. The new Congress reflected greater variety as well, with not only more women but also thirty-eight African-Americans (up from twenty-five), seventeen Hispanics (up from ten), the first Korean-American congressman, and the first American Indian senator, Ben Nighthorse Campbell of Colorado, who rode an appaloosa in the inaugural parade in full Cheyenne regalia.

After an inaugural address on the theme of "American renewal," a poem by Maya Angelou, and a round of parties at which the First Saxophone was again heard, Clinton buckled down to the task of governing. The early weeks brought some hard lessons in Washington politics. Fulfilling a campaign pledge, Clinton called for an end to the exclusion of homosexuals from military service. The move roused fierce controversy, and in the end the president submitted the issue to a study commission. Clinton's first two choices as attorney general, a Connecticut corporation lawyer and

January 1993: New Democrats in power. All smiles, President Bill Clinton and Vice President Al Gore exchange greetings after taking their oaths of office. (*AP/Wide World Photos*)

a New York judge, both withdrew after allegations that they had hired illegal aliens for child-care services or had failed to pay social security taxes for domestic employees. The media feasted on "Nanny-gate."

Shaping his administration's domestic themes, Clinton addressed three key issues: economic renewal, deficit reduction, and health care. (Welfare reform and campaign-financing reform, heavily emphasized in the campaign, were relegated to the back burner.) In defining these issues, Clinton offered a chastened, scaled-down version of liberalism adapted to the cautious and conservative political climate of the nineties.

Clinton came to office pledged to focus "like a laser beam" on the economy. His economic team included the venerable Lloyd Bentsen as secretary of the treasury, Robert Reich as secretary of labor, and Berkeley economist Laura Tyson as head of the Council of Economic Advisers. As budget director and deputy director, Clinton named Congressman Leon Panetta and Alice Rivlin, a former director of the Congressional Budget Office. In pursuing the dual goals of economic revitalization and deficit reduction, Clinton got conflicting advice. Moderate Democrats of the DLC variety and budget hawks like Panetta and Rivlin wanted to prove that Democrats could be fiscally responsible. They thus gave highest priority to deficit reduction. Others saw economic stimulus as fundamental; Tyson championed industrial-policy strategies. And social-activist Democrats such as Marian Wright Edelman of the Children's Defense Fund, in which Hillary Clinton and Donna Shalala were active, wanted substantial spending on a wide range of social programs.

In late February 1993, Clinton offered his economic plan. An amalgam of the different viewpoints, the strategy combined an array of spending cuts and tax increases aimed at a net deficit reduction of $325 billion over four years. Cuts included a further tightening of military outlays, a one-year freeze on federal salaries, and elimination of a hundred thousand federal jobs through attrition. The plan capped Medicare and Medicaid payments to doctors and hospitals and reduced funding for such big-ticket projects as the space station and the superconducting supercollider. Clinton's proposed tax hikes hit the richest Americans with the stiffest increases, went much easier on the middle class, and spared families earning under $30,000 a year.

Clinton's new spending proposals, totaling $169 billion in economic "stimulus and investment" over four years, aimed at job creation and economic growth. Along with increases in Head Start and worker-training programs, the president called for tax credits for small-business investment and more funds for mass transit, as well as creation of a national fiber-optic data network. Finally, he recommended a national service corps by which college students could pay off federal education loans through community work. Despite rhetoric about the need to keep the economy "on the cutting edge of change," Clinton's spending package emphasized traditional liberal approaches such as block grants to mayors and summer-job programs while requesting 75 percent less for basic R&D than he had proposed in the campaign. To avoid the familiar Republican charge that the Democrats favored "big government," Clinton insisted that the chief impetus for economic growth must come from the private sector. Echoing Ross Perot and Ronald Reagan, he declared, "The time has come to show the American people that we can limit [government programs], that we can not only start things but we can actually stop things."

Mixed economic signals complicated the debate over the need for a stimulus. The GNP, adjusted for inflation, rose by 2.1 percent in 1992, after a decline in 1991, with a weak 1.6 percent growth predicted for 1993. But this modest recovery did not lead to a surge in jobs. Unemployment still stood at around 7 percent through 1993, with the number of long-term jobless stuck at about 2 million. In parts of the country, notably California, the jobless rate remained as high as 10 percent. Thirty-six million Americans struggled below the poverty line, and the number of Americans receiving food stamps reached the highest point since the program began in 1964. Large-scale layoffs by GM, IBM, Sears, aerospace companies, and other top corporations further weakened the job market. Many displaced skilled workers took positions in the service sector at steep cuts in wages. A 1993 study of two thousand workers fired by RJR-Nabisco Corporation, for example, revealed that those who found employment elsewhere on average earned less than half their former pay.

Cutbacks in Pentagon contracts and consequent layoffs in defense industries also clouded the economic picture. Boeing prepared to trim its work force by fifty thousand; McDonnell-Douglas, by ten thousand. By 1995, the Pentagon estimated, nine hundred thousand defense workers would lose their jobs. In March 1993, Secretary of Defense Les Aspin announced the closing of thirty-one military bases and cutbacks at other installations. President Clinton proposed a program to retrain displaced workers, to aid communities hit by base closings, and to help defense industries convert to civilian production, but the cutbacks in military spending inevitably jolted an already weak economy.

Although Clinton called for tax increases unmatched since World War II, 79 percent of Americans—including Ross Perot—initially backed his plan. Congressional Democrats generally proved supportive, but Republicans (and some Democrats) grumbled that the tax increases would come before the spending cuts. They demanded deeper and faster cuts to prove the government's seriousness about deficit reduction. Clinton, well aware that the nub of the deficit problem lay in popular entitlement programs such as Medicare and social security, invited his critics to submit specific proposals for further cuts.

In early August, after long debate, Congress by razor-thin margins enacted a five-year economic plan quite different from Clinton's original proposal. The president's requested tax increase, projected to raise $240 billion, survived more or less intact. The bill raised the top tax rate from 31 to 36 percent while further easing the tax burden of the poor. To this extent, the measure partially reversed the retrogressive features of the Reagan-era tax cuts. But the measure appropriated only about 38 percent of what Clinton had sought for education, retraining, and apprenticeship programs aimed at upgrading the U.S. work force. Furthermore, the bill's deficit-cutting potential was limited, both because the tax increase remained modest and because the spending cuts spared the mushrooming entitlement programs. At best it would produce annual deficits of around $200 billion as the 1990s wore on, in contrast to some $300 billion in 1993.

The passage of even a modified economic plan spared Clinton a major embarrassment early in his term, but the act was not a solution to the deficit crisis or the nation's long-term economic problems. Ominously, the bill passed without a single Republican vote, and with many Democratic defections. Polls showed the American people deeply divided over the issue, favoring deficit cuts in principle but leery of the bitter medicine that serious deficit reduction would demand.

Clinton's hopes for economic renewal included the North American Free Trade Agreement (NAFTA). Negotiated by the Bush administration, the plan incorporated Mexico into the free-trade zone already created by the United States and Canada. NAFTA roused both strong support and harsh criticism. Union leaders and their political friends, including House majority leader Richard Gephardt, warned of job losses to Mexico. Supporters of NAFTA, including most economists and the irrepressible Lee Iacocca, conceded that about 150,000 low-wage jobs in labor-intensive industries might be lost. However, they insisted that NAFTA would create more high-wage jobs by opening the Mexican market to U.S. machinery and other products.

The treaty posed tricky political challenges for Clinton. It threatened to alienate the blue-collar workers whom the Democrats hoped to win back, and it invited charges of insensitivity to ordinary Americans. As NAFTA became a symbol of larger economic worries, Ross Perot mounted a demagogic attack on the agreement. But the public was wearying of Perot's negativism and his slippery use of facts, and Vice President Gore roundly defeated him in a televised debate on NAFTA. After a classic display of White House dealmaking with wavering legislators, the House of Representatives in November passed NAFTA by a comfortable 234–200 margin, handing Clinton another political victory. The administration followed up the NAFTA success with a campaign for expanded U.S. trade opportunities in Asia. In addition, it completed a complex multilateral agreement to lower trade barriers among the members of the General Agreement on Tariffs and Trade (GATT), the umbrella organization of the world's trading nations established in 1948.

Next on Clinton's agenda came health-care reform, a goal of liberals since the 1930s. The problem had two elements: coverage and cost. Some 37 million Americans, most of them poor, lacked medical insurance. Millions more, including many middle-class citizens, feared losing coverage in an uncertain economy. And costs continued to soar as patients demanded access to the latest treatments and technologies and as physicians prescribed batteries of expensive tests and procedures to forestall possible malpractice suits. From 1980 to 1992, Medicare and Medicaid payments ballooned from $48 billion to $196 billion and expanded from 8 percent to 14 percent of the federal budget.

Besieged by lobbyists for physicians, hospitals, drugmakers, business groups, and the insurance industry, Hillary Clinton's health-care task force set out to devise a program to control runaway costs and to extend coverage to those who lacked it. In October 1993, the administration unveiled a plan that called for a restructured system by which all Americans would be guaranteed medical and dental coverage and an array of preventive services. The plan proposed to contain costs by limiting Medicare and Medicare reimbursements, capping health-insurance premiums, fostering competition among providers, and curbing the inefficiency and paperwork of the present system. By means of financial incentives, the new system would enroll all Americans into large regional purchasing groups, called health alliances, set up by the states. These alliances would monitor costs and negotiate with health-care providers. Individuals could join either a fee-for-service plan, enabling them to choose their own physicians, or a less expensive health maintenance organization (HMO), whereby they would be limited to the physicians belonging to that HMO. A seven-member national health board chosen by the president would oversee the nation's overall health budget. Under Clinton's plan, employers would pay 80 percent of workers' insurance costs. The self-employed would buy their own (tax-deductible) insurance, and Medicaid would continue to protect the poor. To cover the plan's estimated $100 billion in added initial costs, Clinton proposed stiff new taxes on tobacco. With tobacco-related illnesses killing 418,000 Americans annually, adding massively to health-care costs, this proposal won general support.

The president took the plan to the people, describing it in broad-brush outline and stressing his central theme: the security of guaranteed health coverage. Hillary Clinton, meanwhile, showed an impressive mastery of detail in congressional testimony. Critics warned of government meddling, bloated bureaucracies, and a decline in health-care quality and ease of access. Several experts questioned whether the plan would produce the savings that Clinton envisioned. The 290,000-member American Medical Association, long a foe of "socialized medicine" and armed with a $7 million lobbying budget, attacked key parts of the plan. Former drug czar William Bennett, a potential Republican challenger in 1996, blasted it as "a monumental assault . . . on individual liberty." But the initiative remained with Clinton. In pushing his health-care plan, the president consciously emulated Franklin Roosevelt's 1935 campaign for social security. Indeed, his proposed "health security card" was modeled on the social security card that had reassured Depression-era Americans.

But although Clinton drew on New Deal symbolism, the liberalism that he espoused differed markedly from the past. He recognized the nation's rightward shift and the collapse of the older liberal consensus. Whereas at times he echoed FDR's confidence in governmental answers to society's ills and LBJ's calls for compassion to the poor, Clinton more typically stressed such classic conservative themes as individual responsibility, the merits of free enterprise, and the dangers of expecting the government to solve all problems. His health plan, for example, rejected Canada's centralized, government-run system in favor of a decentralized plan of "managed competition" that mixed private enterprise and public oversight. Clinton's liberalism still embodied notions of entitlement—such as the right of all Americans to health care—but he also stressed fiscal restraint, managerial efficiency, and the importance of drawing on the private sector. Although not ignoring inner-city minorities, Clintonian liberalism focused on the economic anxieties of the vast American middle class.

The new president's approach reflected the electorate's rejection of 1960s-style liberalism, as well as the pervasive voter cynicism about government itself that Perot had exploited. In contrast to Lyndon Johnson's soaring rhetoric and ambitious reform agenda, Clinton's tone was restrained and his initiatives cautious. Tellingly, while Clinton pushed health-care reform, Vice President Gore led a task force that developed proposals for "reinventing government" by cutting wasteful paperwork, trimming bureaucratic fat, and tightening management controls. The Clinton administration, in short, offered liberalism for skeptics, a bargain-basement vision of government's role in social change that was tempered by harsh economic and political realities. Nevertheless, the president skillfully used his office—which Theodore Roosevelt once called a "bully pulpit"—to shape the nation's domestic agenda and to revive, however cautiously, the liberal tradition of vigorous governmental engagement with social issues.

As Clinton's first term unfolded, the public verdict on the new liberalism remained tentative. The conservative coalition that had arisen in the 1970s and captured the White House in 1980, although under strain, remained a force. The economic, racial, and cultural concerns that had spawned the post-1960s reaction persisted. Pat Robertson's Christian Coalition, having shown its muscle at the 1992 GOP convention, patiently elected candidates to local school boards and town councils. Robertson's organization rallied the Christian Right not only on such social themes as school prayer and pornography but also on political issues such as the budget deficit and health care. Neoconservative intellectual William Kristol, Dan Quayle's former chief of staff, derided Clinton's program as the product of a decayed liberalism that had "lost its force, its real conviction, and its real confidence in itself." Republican hopefuls waited in the wings in case Clinton faltered, among them former Reagan-Bush cabinet secretaries Dick Cheney, William Bennett, and Jack Kemp; senators Phil Gramm of Texas and minority leader Bob Dole of Kansas; and the combative Georgia conservative, Congressman Newt Gingrich. But with no obvious spokesperson on the horizon, the GOP faced a tough challenge.

Reversing Bush's priorities and placing domestic issues above world affairs, Clinton met with serious problems in setting his administration's foreign-policy goals and priorities. The United States remained a great power, yet Clinton's diplomacy seemed unfocused. His vacillation on Somalia and Bosnia illustrated the pattern. Clinton endorsed Bush's decision to send U.S. troops to Somalia to protect food intended for famine victims. But this humanitarian mission soon gave way to an effort to restore order in Somalia's anarchic capital, Mogadishu, and specifically to capture elusive warlord Mohammed Farah Aidid. The U.S. force was part of a larger UN peacekeeping army, and UN secretary general Boutros Boutros-Ghali had played a central role in redirecting the Americans' mission. As U.S. casualties mounted, so did home-front calls for U.S. withdrawal. Cartoonists drew Somalia in the shape of Vietnam. TV scenes of starving Somali children gave way to images of dead GIs. In October 1993 Clinton announced full withdrawal in six months and emphasized that in the interim he, not Boutros-Ghali, would decide the U.S. role. But he also increased the U.S. force in Somalia to ten thousand, and suspicions that Washington had lost its way continued. In December 1993, Secretary of Defense Les Aspin became the first member of Clinton's cabinet to be forced out, in part because he was perceived as indecisive on a variety of military issues, including the Somalia operation.

Somalia illustrated a larger problem in redefining America's global role. During the Cold War, U.S. policy in the Third World, for better or worse, had been shaped by strategic calculations. Somalia's ports, for example, had been prized as a key to control of the Indian Ocean. The Cold War's end reduced the Third World's strategic importance at the same time that it unleashed a Pandora's box of ethnic and religious hatreds. This confluence of forces left American foreign policy rudderless, prey to passing gusts of media-influenced public opinion. The administration seemed unable to clarify the extent to which it wished to commit U.S. power and prestige in situations that did not involve vital American national interests.

The same dilemma hamstrung U.S. policy toward the ongoing conflict in Bosnia and Herzegovina, where fighting among Serbs, Bosnians, and Croatians had left 100,000 dead by early 1993, created 3.6 million refugees, and wrought untold suffering. Clinton ordered the U.S. Air Force to drop food and relief supplies to besieged Bosnian Muslims, but like Bush he refrained from a deeper military engagement. Unfortunately for the Bosnians, their country, unlike Kuwait, had no oil. Clinton did endorse a plan negotiated by former secretary of state Cyrus Vance and Lord Owen of Great Britain on behalf of the European Community, a plan that divided Bosnia and Herzegovina into a patchwork of ethnic regions, but he left unclear the U.S. role should the plan go into effect. In any event, the warring factions showed little interest. The murderous fighting raged on into 1994 and underscored the impotence of outside parties, including the United States, to effect a solution.

Meanwhile, conditions in Russia and elsewhere in the former Soviet sphere remained volatile. In 1993, as falling productivity and hyperinflation battered the Russian economy, right-wing nationalists and former Communist *apparatchiks* in the parliament moved to strip President Boris Yeltsin of his power. Visions of a Russia awash in anarchy and civil war, or even of a return to dictatorship and renewed Cold War tensions, haunted Washington. The crisis peaked in October, as Yeltsin's hardline opponents, nostalgic for the days of empire and one-party rule, made a last stand in the parliament building. After several tense days, Yeltsin crushed the resistance. Clinton and other Western leaders endorsed Yeltsin but mainly watched from the sidelines. In Russian parliamentary elections later that year, disgruntled voters backed a constitution proposed by Yeltsin but gave surprising support to the party of Vladimir Zhirinovsky, a rabid Russian nationalist, antisemite, and neofascist who openly admired Adolf Hitler. Again Washington responded with renewed expression of support for Yeltsin, but little else.

Those who followed the administration's waffling policy in Somalia, Bosnia, and Russia for clues to America's post–Cold War role found scant reason to cheer in Clinton's first year. In international-trade issues, where foreign policy and domestic economic concerns overlapped, the administration displayed considerable skill and focused energy. But on larger issues of global politics and international relations, Washington's attention span seemed short and largely driven by short-term considerations. The *Economist* of London, commenting in October 1993 on Clinton's attempt to define his global vision in a UN speech, expressed deep skepticism: "[S]omehow the fire is not in Mr. Clinton's belly when he speaks on foreign policy. It will probably be events, not speeches, that define American foreign policy more clearly."

On another front, the hijackings and other terrorist acts that had tormented Carter and Reagan abated in the early 1990s. But in February 1993, horror struck in the United States itself when terrorists planted a massive bomb in a parking garage under the twin towers of New York's World Trade Center, a vast 110-story complex housing 50,000 workers and 350 companies. The blast killed five people and left scores of victims of smoke inhalation and other injuries. Thousands of office workers and tourists had to grope their way down smoke-filled stairs. The FBI arrested two Shiite fundamentalists, followers of a militant sheik earlier implicated in the assassination of Egypt's Anwar el-Sadat, and charged them with complicity in the bombing and in plots against the Lincoln Tunnel, the United Nations, and other targets. The tragedy offered a sobering reminder of the dangers that still stalked the world despite the easing of superpower tensions.

By contrast, U.S. efforts for peace in the Middle East at last bore fruit early in Clinton's term. While the end of the Cold War unleashed conflicts in the former Soviet realm, in the Middle East as in Latin America it eased tensions. Cut adrift by their former patron Moscow, hard-line Arab leaders like Syria's Hafez-al Assad grew more flexible. Secretary of State James Baker had seized the moment and nudged the Arabs toward talks with Israel while simultaneously pressuring Israel to stop building Jewish settlements on the occupied West Bank. President Bush had added to the pressure by withholding $10 billion in loan guarantees urgently sought by Israel to settle 360,000 Jewish immigrants who had poured in from the former Soviet Union. Talks had begun in Madrid in November 1991. Premier Yitzhak Shamir of Israel's right-wing Likud party showed little interest, but Shamir's successor, Yitzhak Rabin of the Labour party, who came to power in 1992, proved more receptive. When Rabin curbed Jewish settlements in the West Bank and proposed limited Palestinian self-government in the territories, Bush approved the loan guarantees. While President Clinton's secretary of state, Warren Christopher, pursued the Baker initiative, Rabin initiated secret talks with Yasir Arafat's Palestine Liberation Organization. September 1993 brought a startling breakthrough. Israel and the PLO announced an accord granting the Palestinians limited autonomy in the Gaza Strip and in the West Bank city of Jerico. In return, Arafat renounced terrorism and recognized Israel as a nation. On September 13, flanking a smiling Bill Clinton, the two leaders signed the accord at the White House. Encouraged by Washington, Israeli peace talks with Jordan and Syria moved forward. The process would take time and patience, but prospects looked brighter than ever before.

Late in 1993 and early in 1994, after a year of ad hoc coping with crises and criticism, the administration sought to burnish its foreign-policy image. In January 1994, Secretary of State Christopher conceded that the diplomatic issues of the post–Cold War era were too complex to be summed up in a single term such as *containment*, the lodestar of American diplomacy for more than forty years. Implicitly confessing a lack of clarity in the administration's initial approach to international affairs, he pledged to focus tightly on issues and regions where U.S. national interests were clearly engaged. That same month, Clinton undertook a ten-day transatlantic mission to reassure nervous Western European leaders of America's continued interest in their region's well-being. Clinton also hoped to encourage the fragile new democracies of Eastern Europe, and to confer with Boris Yeltsin and his embattled Russian government.

While the end of the Cold War forced a radical reorientation of U.S. foreign policy, it also had profound domestic effects. As we have seen, the sharp drop in defense spending rattled the U.S. economy. Moreover, the easing of Cold War alarms encouraged voters in 1992 to opt for a presidential candidate whose strengths and interests clearly lay in the domestic-policy arena, not in foreign affairs. Indeed, American politics focused on domestic issues in the early Clinton years to a degree unheard of since the mid-1960s. The changed international climate also allowed a reassessment of the Cold War's often negative effects on American life. Late in 1993, for example, the press revealed secret radiological experiments conducted on unwitting human subjects in the late 1940s, the 1950s, and even later by the Atomic Energy Commission and other federal agencies. The test subjects often comprised the weakest and most vulnerable members of society: prisoners, the very ill, institutionalized retarded persons, and newborn infants of poor parents, particularly African-Americans. Simultaneously, journalists reported the government's long efforts to suppress information about these ethically dubious tests. As the press further explained, the White House had fought lawsuits by veterans, southwestern ranchers, and workers in nuclear-weapons factories who claimed to have contracted illnesses from exposure to radiation in their work or from atmospheric nuclear tests. Energy Secretary Hazel O'Leary called for a policy of maximum disclosure and for compensation of victims. Although several of these matters had partially come to light earlier, only with the waning of the Soviet threat did they emerge fully.

CONCLUSION

The American people and their government faced a formidable task in the nineties, as they charted a new course in a still dangerous world while grappling with complex domestic issues. At home, a series of large-scale social movements, coupled with vast technological, economic, and demographic changes, had almost literally spawned a new society and tested the political system's capacity to adapt. Clearly, the United States would not adjust to these radical shifts overnight, or even in one decade; uncertainty and false starts were inevitable. The *New Yorker* commented wryly in 1993, "The nineties just don't seem to be coming together in the focused and vigorous way one likes to see in a decade." Yet creative responses began to pop up, and the years since 1945 gave Americans reason to hope. The political crises, social conflicts, and structural changes that the United States had undergone in these five decades might have swamped a less resilient society. That the nation endured and even showed signs of renewed civic vitality offered encouragement as Americans girded for fresh challenges. These challenges, while markedly different from earlier ones, could scarcely be more demanding than those that the nation had met and mastered in the half-century since World War II. With every passing year, that now-distant event receded deeper into the shadowy recesses of the nation's collective memory.

SELECTED READINGS

For contemporary trends and issues, the *New York Times*, *Los Angeles Times*, *Boston Globe*, *Washington Post*, and other major newspapers can provide valuable background and perspective. So, too, can the leading news magazines, journals of opinion, and special-topic periodicals. See, for example, *Atlantic*, *Business Week*, *Christian Century*, *Christianity Today*, *Economist* (London), *Foreign Affairs*, *Fortune*, *Harper's*, *Ms.*, *Nation*, *National Review*, *New Republic*, *New York Review of Books*, *New York Times Magazine*, *Newsweek*, *Progressive*, *Public Interest*, *Science*, *Time*, *Variety*, and *U.S. News and World Report*.

Politics and Public Policy
in the Bush and Clinton Years

Charles F. Allen, *The Comeback Kid: The Life and Career of Bill Clinton* (1992); Michael Duffy, *Marching in Place: The Status Quo Presidency of George Bush* (1992); Thomas Byrne Edsall, "Clinton So Far," *New York Review of Books*, October 7, 1993; Jack W. Germond and Jules Witcover, *Whose Broad Stripes and Bright Stars: The Trivial Pursuit of the Presidency, 1988* (1989) and *Mad as Hell: Revolt at the Ballot Box, 1992* (1993); Ken Gross, *Ross Perot: The Man Behind the Myth* (1992); Nicholas King, *George Bush: A Biography* (1980); Robert S. Mc-Elvaine, *The End of the Conservative Era: Liberalism After Reagan* (1987); Kevin P. Phillips, *The Politics of Rich and Poor: Wealth and the American Electorate in the Reagan Aftermath* (1990) and *Boiling Point: Republicans, Democrats, and the Decline of Middle Class Prosperity* (1993); John Podhoretz, *Hell of a Ride: Backstage at the White House Follies, 1989–1993* (1993); *The President's Health Security Plan* (1993); Richard Rose, *The Post-Modern President: George Bush Meets the World* (1991); Tom Rosenstiel, *Strange Bedfellows: How Television and the Presidential Candidates Changed American Politics, 1992* (1993); James L. Sundquist, ed., *Beyond Gridlock: The Prospects for Governance in the Clinton Years—and After* (1993).

America and the Rest of the World
in the Post–Cold War Era

Rick Atkinson, *Crusade: The Untold Story of the Persian Gulf War* (1993); Michael R. Beschloss and Strobe Talbott, *At the Highest Levels: The Inside Story of the End of the Cold War* (1994); Zbigniew Brzezinski, "The Cold War and Its Aftermath," *Foreign Affairs* (Fall 1992); John Lewis Gaddis, *The United States and the End of the Cold War* (1992); Stephen R. Graubard, *Mr. Bush's War: Adventures in the Politics of Illusion* (1992); Richard Hallion, *Storm over Iraq: Air Power and the Gulf War* (1992); Roger Hilsman, *George Bush vs. Saddam Hussein* (1992); Kim R. Holmes and Burton Yale Pines, *George Bush's New World Order* (1991); Robert D. Kaplan, *Balkan Ghosts: A Journey Through History* (1993); Gale Stokes, *The Walls Came Tumbling Down: The Collapse of Communism in Eastern Europe* (1993); U.S. News and World Report, *Triumph Without Victory: The Unreported History of the Persian Gulf War* (1992).

Economic, Social, and Cultural
Trends in the Nineties

Peter Arno, *Against the Odds* (1992) [AIDS research and politics]; Michael A. Bernstein and David E. Adler, eds., *Understanding America's Economic Decline* (1993); Michael Binstein and Charles Bowden, *Trust Me: Charles Keating and the Missing Billions* (1993); Dallas A. Blanchard, *The Anti-Abortion Movement* (1994); Paul Carroll, *Big Blues: The Unmaking of IBM* (1993); Stephen L. Carter, *The Culture of Disbelief: How American Law and Politics Trivialize Religious Devotion* (1993); Ellis Cose, *The Rage of a Privileged Class: Why Are Middle-Class Blacks Angry?* (1993); Susan Faludi, *Backlash: The Undeclared War Against American Women* (1991); Elizabeth Fee and Daniel M. Fox, eds., *AIDS: The Burdens of History* (1988) and *AIDS: The Making of a Chronic Disease* (1992); Henry Louis Gates, Jr., *Loose Canons: Notes on the Culture Wars* (1993); Al Gore, *Earth in the Balance: Ecology and the Human Spirit* (1992); Allen D. Hertzke, *Echoes of Discontent: Jesse Jackson, Pat Robertson, and the Resurgence of Populism* (1992); Sylvia Ann Hewlett, *When the Bough Breaks: The Cost of Neglecting Our Children* (1991); Denis Lynn Daly Heyck, ed., *Barrios and Borderlands: Cultures of Latinos and Latinas in the United States* (1993); Bill Ong Hing, *Making and Remaking Asian America Through Immigration Policy, 1850–1990* (1993); Arlie Hochschild, *Second Shift: Working Parents and the Revolu-*

tion at Home (1989); Robert Hughes, Culture of Complaint: The Fraying of America (1993); James Davison Hunter, Culture Wars: The Struggle to Define America (1991); Jong-deuk Jung, A Study of Korean Immigrants in America (1991); Alex Kotlowitz, There Are No Children Here: The Story of Two Boys Growing Up in the Other America (1991); Paul Light, Baby Boomers (1988); Martin Lowy, High Rollers: Inside the Savings and Loan Debacle (1991); National Institute on Drug Abuse, Trends in Drug Use . . . (1991); Christopher Pierson, Beyond the Welfare State? The New Political Economy of Welfare (1991); Roger Rosenblatt, Life Itself: Abortion in the American Mind (1992); Kirpatrick Sale, The Green Revolution: The American Environmental Movement, 1962–1992 (1993); Arthur M. Schlesinger, Jr., The Disuniting of America (1991); Philip Shabecoff, A Fierce Green Fire: The American Environmental Movement (1994); Randy Shilts, And the Band Played On: Politics, People, and the AIDS Epidemic (1987); Peter Skerry, Mexican Americans: The Ambivalent Minority (1993); Arlene S. Skolnick, Embattled Paradise: The American Family in an Age of Uncertainty (1991); Suzanne Staggenborg, The Pro-Choice Movement (1991); William Wei, The Asian American Movement (1993).

Looking to the Future

Henry Brandon, ed., U.S.-European Relations (1992); McGeorge Bundy, William J. Crowe, Jr., and Sidney D. Drell, Reducing Nuclear Danger (1993); Gerald Graff, Beyond the Culture Wars (1992); Patricia Albjerg Graham, S.O.S.: Sustain Our Schools (1992); William W. Grimes, Refocusing U.S. Technology Policy (1993); David Halberstam, The Next Century (1991); Paul Kennedy, The Rise and Fall of the Great Powers (1987) and Preparing for the Twenty-First Century (1993); Edward N. Luttwak, The Endangered American Dream (1993); Joseph S. Nye, Bound to Lead: The Changing Nature of American Power (1990); John Rawls, Political Liberalism (1993); Robert Reich, The Work of Nations: Preparing Ourselves for 21st Century Capitalism (1991); Lisbeth B. Schorr with Daniel Schorr, Within Our Reach: Breaking the Cycle of Disadvantage (1988); Thomas Toch, In the Name of Excellence: The Struggle to Reform the Nation's Schools (1991); Robert W. Tucker and David C. Hendrickson, The Imperial Temptation: The New World Order and America's Purposes (1992); Daniel Yergin and Thane Gustafson, Russia 2010 (1993).

Epilogue

AMERICA POISED BETWEEN TWO ERAS

In August 1945, Americans greeted the return of peace with ecstatic celebrations and high hopes. Four months earlier, when leaders of the victorious Allied powers had gathered at San Francisco to launch the United Nations, journalists and statesmen had spoken grandly of a new world order. But the triumphant mood proved fleeting, and the high hopes soon withered. The wartime alliance splintered, deep divisions fractured the postwar world, and the Cold War began. At home, the early postwar years brought social tensions and charges of domestic subversion. On the economic front, pent-up consumer demand and then Cold War military spending prevented the return of the depression that many feared, but amid unprecedented abundance, millions still staggered under the burden of poverty. The later 1950s brought a wave of anxiety that automation would eliminate millions of jobs. Indeed, the manual labor and factory work that had provided an escalator of mobility for millions of immigrants seemed to be drying up.

In some ways, the United States in the 1990s seems strikingly similar. Americans once more feel the euphoria of victory, this time in the Cold War struggle that lasted four decades. But again victory has failed to provide a lasting reprieve from history's inexorable pressures. Social and economic woes of the gravest kind loom at home, and the post–Cold War world reveals potential for menace as well as promise.

Domestically, the "jobless recovery" from the recession of 1990–1991 suggests profound structural changes in the economy. As economist John Judis argued in 1993, the early 1990s presented the puzzling phenomenon of continued high unemployment amid increased productivity and revived prosperity. In an era of automated production and high-tech industries, it seems, the economy can thrive with fewer and fewer workers. Under fierce price pressure from foreign competitors, domestic manufacturers have cut costs and trimmed payrolls. From 1979 to 1992, the manufacturing work force declined by 15 percent, yet industrial output rose by more than a third. Defense spending and a growing service sector cushioned the impact of these trends for a time, but now that cushion is deflating. Military spending has fallen with the end of the Cold War, and even in the service sector, automation and the urgency to economize have reduced the demand for new workers.

In his 1992 economic manifesto, *A Vision of Change for America*, Bill Clinton insisted that the key to job creation lay in "modernizing factories and equipment, developing skills and accelerating the advance of technology." Yet the early 1990s seemed to teach that technological progress might no longer possess the magical job-producing powers of the past. High-tech growth might actually worsen the job crisis.

As the twentieth century draws to a close, one long cycle of American economic history, in which nearly anyone willing to work could find a job, is ending. A new economy needing fewer but more highly skilled workers seems to have arisen in its place. "What Ever Happened to the Great American Job?" inquired *Time* in a November 1993 cover story on the gathering crisis. The "automation" scare of the 1950s had anticipated this development—indeed, fear of technological obsolescence is as old as the early-nineteenth-century Luddites—but in the 1990s its contours have come into sharper focus. In the trend toward "simultaneous growth and unemployment," John Judis wrote, one can discern "the fundamental metamorphosis of American capitalism from an economy whose growth depends on the expansion of its labor force to an economy whose growth depends, paradoxically, on its contraction."

If this analysis is correct, the long-term technological unemployment identified by John Maynard Keynes as early as 1930 looms as the dominant problem of the future. The phenomenon is familiar in American agriculture, where for decades productivity rose while the number of farmers dwindled. Now the same pattern has spread to the economy as a whole. Displaced farmers entered the industrial and service sectors. Where will displaced industrial and service workers go?

In 1968 the Kerner Commission warned of the emergence of two nations, divided along racial lines. Although this danger has remained, a related economic bifurcation threatens as well. American society seems to have split into a managerial or professional elite and comparatively small, highly trained labor force on the one hand, and a vast underclass of men and women either jobless or toiling at mind-numbing, dead-end tasks on the other. The problem has many faces: the jobless inner-city youths dealing drugs on the street corner, the displaced industrial worker sinking into despair, the eager college graduate facing bleak prospects, the unemployed and perhaps unemployable millions swelling the welfare rolls. Even highly skilled workers and white-collar corporate managers find themselves suddenly without jobs in the rapidly evolving economy. These realities will test to the limit the abilities of whichever party holds power in Washington in the years ahead. The economy of the future, reflecting new production technologies, new patterns of global trade, and new communications systems, stirs the imagination of visionaries. Yet it also rouses apprehension over the social disruptions that seem inevitable as the very meaning of *work* and *labor* undergo radical redefinition.

Along with these staggering economic changes, an increasingly diverse and heterogeneous American society has emerged. With traditional gender roles dissolving and old racial and ethnic hierarchies fading, the social and cultural contours of the United States of the future promise to differ markedly from the past. Some react with disgruntled apprehension as familiar cultural patterns and status hierarchies come under challenge. Others, however, thrill to the prospect of bubbling cultural ferment and a varied and diverse population. Americans have long paid lip-service to change and novelty as fundamental elements of the national experience; in the twenty-first century, society's actual tolerance for change will likely be tested to the limit.

Internationally, the early 1990s have brought a fundamental transition amid the welter of confusing news reports of crises and conflicts. Yale historian Paul Kennedy wrote in 1993, "As we move toward the 21st century there is a compelling need for politicians and nations alike to raise their eyes from day-to-day issues, however pressing and tragic, and devote time to considering our global condition as a whole." From this perspective, one can see both the hazy outlines of George Bush's "new world order" and the difficulties in achieving it. A planet no longer held in thrall to superpower conflict or a nuclear-arms race now has a chance to craft a stable global system. World leaders face the challenge of reversing the assault on their common environment and ameliorating the poverty, disease, illiteracy, and overcrowding that afflicts much of the world. If present fertility trends continue, the UN reported in 1992, the planet's human population will reach 28 billion by the year 2050. The explosion in numbers has widened the chasm between a relatively well-off northern hemisphere and a destitute southern hemisphere, a chasm that represents a chronic source of instability and unrest.

As humanity grapples with these colossal problems, it seems suspended precariously between the tendencies fostering international cooperation and those inclining toward disintegration and anarchy. In many regions, fragmentation appears in the ascendancy. For all the glib talk of a new order, wrote historian John Lukacs in 1993, "nationalism and tribalism remain the strongest element holding masses of people together." Even President Clinton, belying the hopefulness of his inaugural address, described a world torn by "ancient hatreds and new plagues."

The United Nations illustrates the conflict. In the early nineties, the blue-and-white UN flag flew over peacekeeping forces and humanitarian teams from Bosnia to Somalia to Cambodia. UN-sponsored conferences and treaties attracted world attention. This much-maligned organization, so long a pawn of the Cold War, at last seemed poised to play the role envisioned for it in 1945 and still earlier by Woodrow Wilson. It would, world leaders hoped, serve as a vehicle for peace and human betterment, and lead the way in easing regional conflict and addressing environmental, nutritional, public-health, and population issues of universal human concern.

But the UN is no panacea, and it often grows paralyzed in the face of mounting demands for its good offices. As Somalia has revealed, tensions between the UN and its constituent members, including the United States, can easily stymie its usefulness. The world organization holds great promise, yet it is only as strong as the collective will and commitment of its members, especially the wealthy and powerful nations. Whether the UN and the internationalist ideal that it represents can move from the periphery to the vital center of policymaking in the capitals of the world poses a stark question for the new century.

At this pivotal point in both domestic and global policy, our nation must pause to assess our recent history and to seek new direction. Will we prove equal to the tasks of addressing America's domestic problems and of redefining our role in a world vastly different from that of 1955 or even 1985? In 1992, reflecting on the kind of leadership needed in the coming decades, Stephen Graubard wrote:

Only an American able to mobilize the nation to address its internal problems, . . . to understand why their resolution is imperative, can be relied on to . . . lead the nation out of its present lethargy. No greater opportunity has existed since 1945; none, perhaps, in this century. The Cold War is indeed over, . . . a new age is opening, likely to be revolutionary, chaotic, and dangerous. In these circumstances, the society must again be involved, believing in its future, able to imagine it beyond the year 2000. Self-serving myth and fable are useless in a situation that calls for candor and intelligence, for giving new dignity to vision and moral concern.

As Graubard made clear, to call for a higher quality of leadership is simply another way of summoning the American people themselves to a new level of commitment to the public good. The patrician historian Henry Adams once cynically concluded that politics is nothing more than organized hatred. The challenge of the 1990s is to prove Adams wrong: to show that a sense of shared purpose and a capacity to resolve differences in a civil manner can animate the political process. Amid sound bites, media distractions, and rampant commercialism, will the body politic achieve the clarity of analysis and the will to act that the times demand?

Despite the signs of political renewal that many observers discerned in the 1992 election, the trend in recent decades has suggested a pervasive erosion of trust in America's political institutions. At a time when fledgling democracies around the world look to the United States for inspiration, many in the American electorate have grown jaded or apathetic. Opinion surveys reveal unprecedented distrust of political leaders' ability to resolve or even to understand ordinary citizens' concerns. Some pollsters suggest that the remoteness of governmental institutions and the complexity of public-policy issues have overwhelmed Americans and rendered them impotent. The Ross Perot phenomenon and the sour anti-incumbency mood of 1992 all underscored the depth of voter alienation.

To concede the magnitude of the problems that we confront, however, and to advise caution in thinking of the years ahead is not to surrender to hand-wringing pessimism. As always, the future invites hope as well as apprehension. In his 1990 book, *Peril and Promise: A Commentary on America*, journalist John Chancellor looked forward to the year 2000:

> In ten years the country may be on the steep slope of national decline, accelerating so quickly that the slide may be irreversible. It need not happen. The United States remains, incomparably, the richest and most productive country on the planet, with the world's most durable political system, abounding in energy and creativity. The U.S.A. has stumbled in recent years, but it hasn't fallen. And the power to keep it from falling is in the hands of the American people.

Taken separately, neither visionary pronouncements nor passionless analytic studies can cure America's ills or create a more just and humane social order. In synergistic combination, however, intelligence infused with social vision and a will to action could mold a society of which Americans of the year 2050, looking back on the preceding half century as we look back on the years since 1945, may have reason to be proud.

INDEX